D1570931

A BIBLICAL
THEOLOGY
OF THE
OLD TESTAMENT

A BIBLICAL
THEOLOGY

OF THE

OLD TESTAMENT

ROY B. ZUCK
EDITOR

EUGENE H. MERRILL

CONSULTING EDITOR

MOODY PRESS
CHICAGO

© 1991 by
THE MOODY BIBLE INSTITUTE
OF CHICAGO

Library of Congress Cataloging in Publication Data

Biblical theology of the Old Testament / edited by Roy B. Zuck.
      p.   cm.
    Includes bibliographical references.
    ISBN 0-8024-0738-2
    1. Bible. O.T.—Theology.   I. Zuck, Roy B.
BS1192.5.B523   1991
230--dc20   91-8550
                                                      CIP

2 3 4 5 Printing / AK / Year 97

Printed in the United States of America

Dedicated to
Dr. Donald K. Campbell,
president of Dallas Theological Seminary, 1986–,
and faculty member since 1954,
on the occasion of his 65th birthday,
July 6, 1991

Roy B. Zuck (A.B., Biola University; Th.M., Th.D., Dallas Theological Seminary), general editor, is Senior Professor Emeritus of Bible Exposition at Dallas Theological Seminary. He is editor of *Bibliotheca Sacra* and coeditor of *The Bible Knowledge Commentary.* He is also the author of *Open Letter to a Jehovah's Witness* and the Everyman's Bible Commentary on Job.

Eugene H. Merrill (M.A., New York University; M.Phil, Ph.D., Columbia University), consulting editor, Old Testament, has served fifteen years at Dallas Theological Seminary and is now professor of Old Testament studies. He is the author of *Kingdom of Priests, A History of Old Testament Israel,* and the Wycliffe Exegetical Commentary *Haggai, Zechariah, Malachi.*

CONTENTS

FOREWORD

This volume on Old Testament biblical theology is the best book I have read in a long while—if for no other reason than because it made me think, and because it delves deeply into one of my favorite fields of study, biblical theology. This kind of theology builds directly on biblical exegesis and leads—or should lead—to systematic theology.

What this ultimately means is that the church must be prepared to modify its traditions, creeds, and confessions if such biblically based exegesis and theology clearly dictate it should. Such modification should not be needed in the case of universally acknowledged doctrines of the historic Christian faith, but it could happen from time to time with the church's understanding of other doctrines and certain passages of Scripture. If this means that systematic theology must to some extent always be in a state of flux, so be it. In the final analysis, Scripture itself, when interpreted properly through the process of biblical exegesis and when synthesized legitimately through the process of biblical theology, must stand in judgment on all our humanly devised systems of theology. All of us need to be more careful in biblical interpretation lest we become unduly influenced by the preunderstandings we bring to the text from a philosophically based systematic theology (as opposed to a biblically based theology).

I am in essential agreement with the authors' stated center of biblical theology—basically the kingdom principle of Genesis 1:26-28. Most statements of a theological center are too limited (e.g., promise or covenant), too broad (e.g., God), or too man-centered (e.g., redemption or salvation-history). It seems clear that, although there are several great theological themes in Scripture, the central focus of biblical theology is the rule of God, the kingdom of God, or the interlocking concepts of kingdom and covenant (but not covenant alone). This theocratic kingdom is realized and consummated primarily through the mediatorial work of God's (and David's) messianic Son. Significantly, Ephesians 1:9-10 appears to indicate that God's ultimate purpose in creation was to establish His Son—the "Christ"—as the supreme Ruler of the universe.

For many years I have longed for a revival of solid biblical exegesis and sound biblical theology, particularly among evangelical scholars. Moody Press's 55-volume *Wycliffe Exegetical Commentary* series is a giant leap forward in biblical exegesis, and now this volume is a significant step forward in biblical theology. For such substantial ventures Moody is to be congratulated and thanked.

One does not need to agree with all points of interpretation in this book to profit from it and to recommend it to others (I myself do not agree with all views expressed). But such differences of opinion about difficult passages are mere trifles compared with the overriding excellence of this work as a whole. Indeed, in my estimation it is the best evangelical volume to appear on the subject of biblical theology in my lifetime, and I hope it will be widely welcomed and used, as it deserves to be.

KENNETH L. BARKER

PREFACE

The Old Testament is rich in a variety of ways—in its several kinds of literature (narrative, law, poetry, prophecy), in its historical span (from creation to the restoration of Israel from the Exile), in its prophetic details regarding the first and second comings of Christ, and in its multifaceted subject matter. Anyone reading the Old Testament is struck with the range of subjects, which include, broadly speaking, God; man; sin; God's convenantal, redemptive relationship to man; and the future messianic rule of God's Son, the Messiah. How various segments of Scripture relate to these themes is the concern of biblical theology: what the *Bible* teaches *theologically*.

This volume takes the reader progressively through the Old Testament from the Pentateuch to prophecy, from hymns of praise to words for wise living, and examines the books for their theological content and emphases. One cannot help but be impressed with the consistency of Scripture in its doctrinal teachings.

Through its varied literary genre and in its sweeping historical content, a handful of subjects consistently thread their way through the Old Testament. God created man to be blessed and to have dominion over creation; man fell into sin, thereby forfeiting those blessings; God chose Abraham to be the progenitor of a nation through whom He would mediate His kingdom rule; and God's Son, a descendant of Abraham, will rule over mankind and the universe. The downward path of man's rebellion against God is met at times with mercy (God is merciful to sinners) and other times with judgment (God judges sin). Individuals are wise to the extent that they accept God's forgiving grace, follow the path of righteous living, stand in praise of their loving Redeemer and awesome Sovereign, and anticipate with eagerness the coming establishment of the Sovereign's rule over the earth.

The authors of this volume, colleagues of mine in the ministry of Dallas Theological Seminary, have taught the Old Testament for many years. With unusual insight into the theological content of the Old Testament Scriptures, they have enunciated these great themes clearly and cogently. My hope is that this volume will assist many readers in acquiring a better and deeper understanding of what the Old Testament is all about, and how its great theological truths impinge on their relationship to God.

INTRODUCTION

The terms *biblical* and *theology* by themselves conjure up a host of connotations and associations. What, then, may be said of the combination *biblical theology*? Is not their use together tautological? Is it not self-evident that *biblical* and *theological* are virtually synonymous and that, in any case, theology is inconceivable apart from the Bible?

These and similar questions have surfaced since Old Testament times and throughout the course of church history and have demanded fresh responses in each generation. Never has this been more true than now, in the last decade of the twentieth century, for never have the twin disciplines of theology and biblical scholarship been in such disarray, and seldom has the church been less sure about their interrelationships.[1]

ITS DISTINCTIONS FROM SYSTEMATIC THEOLOGY

The traditional understanding of biblical theology manifests itself in one of two forms: (1) it is the body of truth contained in the Bible, whether systematized at some point or not; or (2) it is truth that originates in the Bible, but which finds expression in logical and philosophical categories.[2] The latter form, more properly defined as systematic theology, is essentially deductive in its method and articulation, whereas the first form, biblical theology in the narrow and technical sense, is inductive. In other words, biblical theology seeks to find its theological categories and emphases within the Bible itself and not from rational or classical patterns derived from without and imposed upon Scripture.

Another difference between biblical theology and systematic theology is in terms of development and dynamicism on the one hand and completion and stati-

---

1. James Barr, "The Theological Case against Biblical Theology," in *Canon, Theology, and Old Testament Interpretation,* ed. Gene M. Tucker, David L. Petersen, and Robert R. Wilson (Philadelphia: Fortress, 1988), pp. 3-19.
2. Gerhard Ebeling, "The Meaning of 'Biblical Theology,'" *Journal of Theological Studies* 6 (1955): 210.

1

cism on the other. To put it theologically, one is diachronic in outlook and the other synchronic.[3] Systematic theology is concerned to view and articulate biblical truth in terms of the complete canonical witness without particular concern for the developmental process at work to create its final shape. It is the more synthetic of the disciplines and aims at a unified result. Biblical theology is concerned to discern, trace, and describe the progress of divine revelation throughout the canon from its earliest to its latest expression. It logically precedes systematics and is the bridge between exegesis and systematics.

These two approaches to theology, if understood and defined correctly, are by no means mutually exclusive. A genuinely Christian systematic theology will find its doctrine in Scripture alone and will be concerned to limit its organizational categories to those inherent in Scripture. However, it still employs an essentially synthetic method in assessing the theological raw material with which it works. For example, its soteriology, sensitive as it is to Old Testament and New Testament differences, will search the Scriptures from beginning to end for data that together compose the doctrines of salvation. A Christian biblical theology, on the other hand, will trace the history of salvation a step at a time throughout the Bible, allowing the history to take whatever form appropriate at any given stage of revelation, recognizing how the doctrine developed as revelation progressed. Then and only then will biblical theology seek to organize and synthesize the results of its inquiry.

In an effort to distinguish between biblical and systematic theology, it is fallacious to pit the one against the other as though they were at odds, with one or the other being superior. They are simply two ways of viewing and expressing the same body of revelation. Yet much harm has been done by an inability to perceive their respective natures, priorities, and relationships. Those who practice only biblical theology sometimes fail to understand the proper integration of the strands of truth they discover in their longitudinal quest. They see the development of divine revelation but come short of understanding the fullness to which the process leads. They frequently end up with parallel strands of truth that are never systematized into a coherent pattern. Systematic theologians, however, are sometimes guilty of bringing epistemological frameworks to the biblical revelation that are either alien or extraneous to that revelation. They then force the material into conformity with their philosophical gridwork without considering the possibility that God's truth is intractable and must therefore yield its own categories.[4]

Good theologians of both approaches will recognize their indebtedness to each other. The systematician understands that the material with which he works must be mined by the exegete and biblical theologian, and the biblical theologian knows

---

3. Gerhard Hasel. *Old Testament Theology: Basic Issues in the Current Debate,* 3d ed. (Grand Rapids: Eerdmans, 1982), pp. 42-43, 69-70.

4. For an early but still important treatise on this matter of the relationship of biblical and systematic theology, see the Altdorf Address of Johann Gabler in J. Sandys-Wunsch and L. Eldredge, "J. P. Gabler and the Distinction between Biblical and Dogmatic Theology: Translation, Commentary, and Discussion of His Originality," *Scottish Journal of Theology* 33 (1980): 133-58.

that his work is not complete if he has merely located and traced the major theological themes of given portions of the Bible. Those themes must be integrated and woven together in such a way as to produce a self-consistent, harmonious, and balanced arrangement of divine revelation. This task, he concedes, is that of the systematic theologian.

Logically and methodologically, then, there must be a cooperative enterprise in doing God-honoring theology. The biblical theologian must work his way through the biblical test, inductively and progressively discovering its theological truth. In the process he may or may not discern patterns and paradigms, but he must make the effort to extract principles that provide the hard data for synthesis. That is, he must be diachronic, sensitive to the gradual but progressive revelation of God's self-disclosure. The systematic theologian must provide the capstone of the theological enterprise. He ideally refuses to read into any given text what is not there, builds off the principles by which the biblical theologian works (if not his product), and refuses to manufacture a philosophical strait jacket into which the data derived inductively must be squeezed.

ITS APPLICATION IN THESE VOLUMES

The contributions to these volumes[5] are deliberately and self-consciously limited to biblical theology in the sense in which it has just been described. They are an effort to survey the Bible as a whole from an analytical and inductive stance and to extract from it those themes and emphases that are inherent to it and that recur with such regularity and in such evident patterns as to generate their own theological rubrics. There is no pretense here, then, to a fully integrated and comprehensive systemization of biblical doctrine. That is the task of the systematic theologican who, it is hoped, will use these and similar studies in undertaking his own work. Nor is there total uniformity of viewpoint within these chapters, for each student of Scripture comes to it with certain biases and usually reads these biases into and out of the text. The best efforts at objectivity are often not successful. Moreover, Scripture itself is not uniform in its presentation of the revelation of God. That is, in the very nature of progressive revelation and the multiformity of the literature and literary genres, there are bound to be different themes and emphases. The major theological concepts of Joshua, for example, are not likely to be those of Romans. Therefore, the biblical theology that emerges from these respective books is bound to be different in both content and expression.

At the same time, one would expect ideally that these different aspects and phases are harmonious and complementary to one another (certainly not contradictory). Furthermore, they should have the potential at least to contribute to a common theological core or center that is sufficiently narrow to serve as a single statement of divine intention and sufficiently broad to encompass the great variety

5. *Biblical Theology of the New Testament* is projected as the second of two volumes in this series.

of its expression in Scripture. If the Bible in its totality is God's Word, a reflection of His mind and purpose, it is only reasonable to expect that it is organized around a central core no matter how elusive that truth might be in certain parts of Scripture and how variegated it might be in other parts.[6] The following essays have been written with this conviction in view, and it is quite evident that a broad consensus has emerged despite the lack of any attempt at theological editorship. What this core is and how it is manifest throughout the canon will be clear to the careful reader of these volumes.

ITS DEVELOPMENT IN RECENT CENTURIES

Though the distinctions between biblical theology and systematic theology should be clear by now, it is important to remember that this distinction is of rather recent vintage.[7] Until about two hundred years ago theology was theology, namely, the study of God, His attributes, and His ways in the world. The adjective *biblical* was considered superfluous, for theology obviously derived from the Bible and had biblical contents as the proper object of study. In earliest times, including the era of the New Testament writings, theology was not even systematized. It consisted only of the appropriation of Old Testament truth as foundation and support for God's revelation in Jesus Christ. In a real sense it was true to the concept and principles of biblical theology because no effort was made either by Judaism or primitive Christianity to create logical and mutually exclusive rubrics according to which biblical (i.e., Old Testament) revelation was to be understood. On the other hand, such theological endeavor was not truly biblical theology in the modern sense, for neither the New Testament nor other early Jewish and Christian writings undertook the kind of analytical and synthetic investigation of the biblical record as these volumes are attempting. Thus theology, as the term is understood in the twentieth century, was a foreign notion in earliest times.

The rise of systematic theology, sometimes known as dogmatic theology, accompanied the rise of neoclassical studies in the Western church, especially the study of Platonic and Aristotelian philosophy. This came about in two ways: (1) as a response to and polemic against the paganism associated with such philosophical thought and (2) by the appropriation of the metaphysical and epistemological arguments employed by those philosophers themselves. There were thus both negative and positive aspects of the Christian use of classical philosophy.

Unfortunately it was not long before the formal nature of philosophical analysis and reconstruction became confused with its material nature. That is, theology, in an attempt at systemization, began to imbibe not only philosophical categories of organization but extrabiblical and even antibiblical content derived from

6. Though Hasel rejects the possibility of such a center, his discussion of various ideas and options is illuminating. See his "The Problem of the Center in the OT Theology Debate," *Zeitschrift für die Alttestamentliche Wissenschaft* 86 (1974): 65-82.
7. For a history of the earlier biblical theology movement, see John H. Hayes and F. C. Prussner, *Old Testament Theology: Its History and Development* (Atlanta: John Knox, 1985), pp. 1-142.

philosophical rationalism. The result was the imposition of extrabiblical structures and thought on the theological data of the Bible. It was in reaction to this that the modern biblical theology movement of the mid-eighteenth century was born. The cry became "back to the Bible" for both the substance of theology and the methodology to be employed in ascertaining that substance. So strong was the reaction that the very concepts of systematic or dogmatic theology were in jeopardy until it was at last realized that the two, far from being inherently antithetical, could be complementary and that both disciplines were necessary. Biblical theology took its rightful place as the storehouse from which systematic theology drew its resources and systematic theology recognized that it could speak with biblical authority only as it drew both its categories and its substance from Scripture mediated through biblical theology.

The foregoing analysis primarily reflects the work and attitude of traditional, orthodox theologians, but with the dawning of modern higher criticism, approximately contemporary with this new distinction between biblical and systematic theology, there developed a skeptical rationalism toward the Bible that often eviscerated it of scientific, historical, and even theological authority. The result was that Old Testament biblical theology became nothing more or less than the history of Israel's religion while systematic theology became an objective and no longer normative attempt to organize the content of a discredited Scripture. The shift from the Bible as the ground and focus of theology resulted in such new approaches as philosophical theology or the history of doctrine.

The devastating implications of this for the life and even survival of the church became clear to many Christian thinkers both inside and outside the evangelical community. There thus came to be the initial stirrings of the "new biblical theology" movement immediately after World War I, a movement that stressed the centrality of the Bible for theological resource apart from or even in spite of its deficiencies as defined by historical criticism. This was an effort undertaken primarily by scholars committed to modern critical method. Those of an orthodox persuasion had never abandoned either a proper biblical or systematic theology, though the former was sadly neglected as a method in favor of the latter.

The "new biblical theology" movement has now become old, but there is no sign of any flagging interest in the enterprise. Protestant, Roman Catholic, and even Jewish scholars are busily engaged in a variety of approaches to the matter, approaches that range from theology as a statement of the unfolding revelation of God in a timeless and inerrant Bible to theology as a prism through which one can understand ancient Israel as a religious and sociological phenomenon. Whether the momentum of the movement, with all its novel and creative features, can be sustained much longer is impossible to foresee.[8]

The present volumes attest to the significance of biblical theology in the per-

8. For the state of contemporary Old Testament theology and projections as to its future, see Gerhard Hasel, "Old Testament Theology from 1978-1987," *Andrews University Seminary Studies* 26 (1988): 133-57; and Marvin E. Tate, "Promising Paths toward Biblical Theology," *Review and Expositor* 78 (1981): 169-85.

ception of most of the evangelical community. Some excellent individual works have been done in the past half century[9] but this is perhaps the first of this kind, a collaborative effort by a team committed to a high view of the authority of the Bible and to the proposition that sound systematic theology must find its roots and substance in a properly undertaken biblical theology. The contributors are the first to recognize the tentativeness of what they have done but they are convinced that such a step, preliminary as it might be, is necessary if evangelicalism is to have any credible input into contemporary theology.

EUGENE H. MERRILL

9. See, for example, Geerhardus Vos, *Biblical Theology* (Grand Rapids: Eerdmans, 1954); J. Barton Payne, *The Theology of the Older Testament* (Grand Rapids: Zondervan, 1962); C. K. Lehman, *Biblical Theology*, 2 vols. (Scottdale, Pa.: Herald, 1971-72); Walter C. Kaiser, *Toward an Old Testament Theology* (Grand Rapids: Zondervan, 1978); William Dyrness, *Themes in Old Testament Theology* (Downers Grove, Ill.: InterVarsity, 1979); Walter C. Kaiser, *Toward an Exegetical Theology* (Grand Rapids: Baker, 1981); Elmer Martens, *God's Design* (Grand Rapids: Baker, 1981); W. J. Dumbrell, *Covenant and Creation* (Nashville: Thomas Nelson, 1984); Thomas McComiskey, *The Covenants of Promise* (Grand Rapids: Baker, 1985); Willem Van Gemeren, *The Progress of Redemption* (Grand Rapids: Zondervan, 1988); L. D. Hurst, "New Testament Theological Analysis," in *Introducing New Testament Interpretation,* ed. Scot McKnight (Grand Rapids: Baker, 1989): 133-61.

1

A THEOLOGY OF THE PENTATEUCH

EUGENE H. MERRILL

INTRODUCTION

A theology of the Bible, or of any of its parts, must give careful consideration to the setting of the original composition—time, place, situation, and author—and to the matter of final canonical form and function.[1] This is especially true of a theology of the Pentateuch, for it is universally regarded by both the Jewish and Christian traditions as being foundational to whatever else the Old and New Testaments say theologically. Attention to the background of the Pentateuch, in which such elements of setting are addressed, is of utmost importance.

The position of the Pentateuch at the beginning of every known arrangement of the biblical canon is in itself a confirmation of the premise that these five books

---

1. For a careful argumentation connecting the genesis, transmission, and creative synthesis of the biblical texts and the theological relevance of each of these stages, see Gerhard Hasel, *Old Testament Theology: Basic Issues in the Current Debate,* 3d ed. (Grand Rapids: Eerdmans, 1982), pp. 169-83.

EUGENE H. MERRILL, M.A., M.Phil., Ph.D., is professor of Old Testament studies at Dallas Theological Seminary.

are the fountainhead of theological inquiry.[2] The very order of the books—Genesis, Exodus, Leviticus, Numbers, Deuteronomy—is, according to every tradition, intrinsic to original Mosaic composition as well as final canonical shape.

A theology of the Pentateuch must, then, take cognizance of the historical circumstances in which it was created and, more important, the theological concerns that motivated both its divine and human origination, and its precise form and function. Until such prolegomena are understood, it is impossible to understand and correctly articulate the theological message of the writing of Moses.

HISTORICAL BACKGROUND

The Bible affirms (e.g., Ex. 17:14; 24:4; Num. 33:1-2; Deut. 31:9; Josh. 1:8; 2 Kings 21:8) that the Pentateuch was the creation of Moses, the great Exodus liberator, who communicated to his fellow Israelites the revelation of God concerning Himself and His purposes for His recently redeemed people. This took place on the plains of Moab, forty years after the Exodus, on the eve of Israel's conquest of Canaan and establishment as a national entity in fulfillment of the promises to the patriarchal ancestors.[3] Though there no doubt had been an unbroken oral (and perhaps written) tradition about their origins, history, and purpose, it was not until Moses gathered these traditions and integrated them into the corpus now known as the Torah that a comprehensive and authoritative synthesis emerged. The significance of the Exodus and of the Sinaitic Covenant in light of the ancient patriarchal promises became clear. Beyond this, the role of Israel against the backdrop of creation and the whole world of nations took on meaning. In short, the setting of the Pentateuch was theological as much as it was geographical and historical. It became the written expression of God's will for Israel in terms of His larger purposes in creation and redemption.

THE PENTATEUCH AS LITERATURE

The name *Pentateuch* reflects the size of the composition—it consists of five scrolls. A more accurate and informative term is used in the Jewish tradition itself, namely the *Torah,* which means "instruction." This name suggests that the purpose of the Mosaic writings was to educate Israel regarding the general meaning of creation and history and regarding its specific function within that cosmic framework.[4] Where did the people originate? Why were they called by Yahweh? What was the meaning of the covenant? What were God's requirements for His redeemed people in civil, moral, and cultic regulations? What were (and are) His purposes for

---

2. Roger Beckwith, *The Old Testament Canon of the New Testament Church* (Grand Rapids: Eerdmans, 1985), pp. 128, 359.

3. For detailed support of this milieu, see Eugene H. Merrill, *Kingdom of Priests: A History of Old Testament Israel* (Grand Rapids: Baker, 1987), pp. 21-25.

4. Michael Fishbane, "Torah and Tradition," in *Tradition and Theology in the Old Testament,* ed. Douglas A. Knight (Philadelphia: Fortress, 1977), pp. 275-76.

them in the future as related to the nations of the earth?

The unfortunate translation of "law" for *tôrāh* gives the impression that the Mosaic writings are essentially legal texts. Such texts in the corpus are well recognized, but they by no means predominate. Genesis is narrative and genealogical for the most part. Exodus 1-19 is mainly narrative, with the remainder divided between "legal" prescription and its implementation. Leviticus is basically cultic instruction, legal in the sense of prescribing regulations for worship. Numbers is of mixed genre, most of it clearly narrative with only a few chapters devoted to law. Deuteronomy is cast in the form of major Mosaic addresses delivered to Israel as a farewell speech just before Moses' death and Israel's conquest of Canaan. Form-critically Deuteronomy has come to be seen as a long covenant text including parenetic comments on various elements of its constituent documents.[5] The "law" in Deuteronomy is, then, the stipulation section of a treaty text that regulates the behavior of the vassal Israel toward Yahweh the Sovereign.

Thus the Pentateuch is a collection of diverse writings. But this does not vitiate the traditional understanding of the collection as Torah, or instruction. By story, poem, genealogy, narrative, prescription, and exhortation the theological message is communicated with one single objective: that Israel might be instructed as to her meaning and purpose. Literary form, as helpful as it might be in specific instances, has little to say about the fundamental character of the Pentateuch as theological literature.

ASSUMPTIONS IN A THEOLOGY OF THE PENTATEUCH

Though one might wish for a totally objective, unpredetermined approach to biblical theology, this is an impossibility, as all theologians freely confess.[6] One can never come to his task with no preconceptions as to the shape and conclusions of his endeavor. Yet the goal is to engage in an inductive study of the literature so that it may yield its own categories and results. Even granting this as an indispensable methodological principle one still must make certain assumptions about the raw material under his purview and the stance from which he will examine it. The following assumptions undergird the present approach to the theology of the Pentateuch.

Assumptions about God. God exists and is unified, self-consistent, and ordered. It is clearly impossible to do anything other than a "history of Israel's religion," or "descriptive theology," unless one concedes the existence of God. One must also concede that God's purposes are noncontradictory and comprehensible at some level of human understanding.

God has revealed Himself in Scripture. This revelation is unified, consistent

5. J. A. Thompson, *Deuteronomy: An Introduction and Commentary* (Downers Grove, Ill.: InterVarsity, 1974), pp. 17-21.
6. John Goldingay, "The Study of Old Testament Theology: Its Aims and Purpose," *Tyndale Bulletin* 26 (1975): 37-39.

with Himself, and systematic. If theology is to be done, it must be done with data revealed by God for it to claim any authenticity and authority. God's self-revelation, moreover, was given in human terms, that is, it was communicated in such a way as to conform to human thought processes and verbal formulations.

God has a purpose for all He does and that purpose, granting its divine origination, must be noncontradictory, self-consistent, systematic, and knowable. This is not to say that all God's purposes are intelligible to human beings or even are communicated to them but that those purposes incumbent on them must be so.[7]

Assumptions about revelation. The purpose of revelation is to reveal God and His purposes. The need or desire to communicate obviously presupposes the mechanism for communicating as far as God's objectives are concerned. It is unthinkable that God has requirements for His creation that He would not reveal in meaningful terms.

Revelation must express the purpose of God propositionally. If all that is in view is the noun (i.e., God), it may be that one could glean something by general revelation alone, for "the heavens declare the glory of God; the skies proclaim the work of his hands" (Ps. 19:1; Rom. 1:18-23). If, however, verbs (i.e., God's purposes) are to be revealed, they must be clarified in verbal statements, for mere isolated acts and events—or even patterns of events in a historical continuum—are at worst meaningless and at best ambiguous. "Event" must be accompanied and interpreted by "word" if it is to be revelatory.[8]

The revelation of purpose may be derived either inductively from the text (by abstraction of a principle or a theme) or deductively (from a purpose statement) or both. In fact, the two are mutually informing and must continually be held in tension. A purpose statement that cannot be sustained in light of the total biblical witness is of course an invalid theological starting point.

Assumptions about purpose. Creation must from the outset be conceded as integral to the purposes of God, for though He could have existed forever independently and yet with purpose, creation has taken place and with it an implied purpose. If purpose, then, is bound up with creation (or vice versa), the statement(s) of creation's purpose should be in chronological and canonical proximity to the creation event itself. This naturally leads to the Pentateuch and specifically to the earliest portion of Genesis.

The statement(s) of purpose should be such that it can be validated by subsequent revelation as a whole, is adequate to accommodate the variety of biblical revelation, and is specific or restricted enough to make a meaningful statement

7. This is what Brueggemann means by a theology of "coherence and rationality" (Walter Brueggemann, "A Shape for Old Testament Theology, I: Structure Legitimation," *Catholic Biblical Quarterly* 47 [1985]: 41).
8. John Goldingay, *Approaches to Old Testament Interpretation* (Downers Grove, Ill.: InterVarsity, 1981). pp. 74-77; James Barr, "Revelation through History in the Old Testament and in Modern Theology," *Interpretation* 17 (1963): 197.

about God (subject) and His purposes (predicate).

The statement(s) of purpose must suit the canonical structure of the entire Bible. Regardless of one's view of inspiration and revelation, the present canonical shape of the Bible clearly reflects the theological stance of the communities that received and molded it under the direction of the Spirit of God.[9] Again, therefore, because it stands at the head and source of the canonical tradition, one would expect Genesis to yield the fundamental statements of purpose.

Assumptions about theological method. Within the present canon, whose arrangement reflects broad theological method and concerns (namely, the Torah, the Prophets, the Writings, and the New Testament), one must attempt to discover chronological order so that the progress of revelation might be discerned and brought to the service of more narrow theological interests. In the case of the Pentateuch this is an easy matter because universal tradition attests to the priority of the Pentateuch and the canonical form places Genesis first.

Once the purpose statement (also now to be construed as the center) has been determined, one must read the biblical revelation in that light, a reading based on proper attention to (1) well-established principles of hermeneutics, (2) literary/rhetorical criticism, (3) form criticism, (4) historical/cultural background, and (5) detailed exegesis.

The purpose statement must then be reevaluated to see if it still meets the criteria listed in the above purpose section.

Proper method for the Christian requires that the New Testament be viewed in continuity with the Old Testament and that both Testaments be seen as mutually informing. This does not mean that one can read the New Testament back into the Old, but that one must recognize that the two Testaments are indivisibly parts of the same revelation of the one God and that nothing in the Old Testament can in any way contradict the revelation of the New.[10]

THE SEARCH FOR A CENTER

The foregoing discussion suggests that the revelation of Scripture is a unified, purposeful, self-consistent phenomenon reflecting the purposes of a self-consistent God who wishes to disclose His intentions to His creation. It has been argued that these intentions can be reduced to a statement to be expected at the beginning of the historical and canonical process. Unfortunately it is impossible here to trace that statement and its implications throughout the entire Bible because this chapter is concerned with the theology of the Pentateuch alone. But it is precisely in the

9. Brevard S. Childs, *Old Testament Theology in a Canonical Context* (Philadelphia: Fortress, 1985), pp. 15-16.

10. See the excellent discussions by T. C. Vriezen, *An Outline of Old Testament Theology* (Oxford: Basil Blackwell, 1958), pp. 79-93; A. A. Anderson, "Old Testament Theology and Its Methods," in *Promise and Fulfillment,* ed. F. F. Bruce (Edinburgh: T. & T. Clark, 1963), pp. 12-13.

Pentateuch that such a statement must first appear if the foregoing set of assumptions is to have any validity at all.

Though there may be an overarching, comprehensive statement of divine purpose (hereafter, center), there may be minor, secondary statements that are essential to the achieving of the one grand objective.[11] The very occasion of the composition of the Pentateuch is a case in point. Clearly Moses prepared the written Torah as instruction on the origin, purpose, and destiny of the people Israel. The Exodus and the covenant relationship certified at Sinai were sufficient to prove beyond any doubt that whatever purposes God had for creation and all the peoples of the earth, these purposes somehow were to be served by the election of Israel to a position of special responsibility.

Exodus 19 and the theological center. The Sinai Covenant, made possible historically and practically by the miracle of the Exodus, is of central concern to the Old Testament. The text of that covenant is introduced in Exodus 20:1 and continues through 23:33, but its purpose is outlined in 19:4-6, a passage that is crucial to the understanding of the function of Israel and of the Sinaitic Covenant in biblical theology. It is so important that it could well be considered the central purpose statement concerning God's election and redemption of Israel.[12]

After rehearsing His chastening of Egypt (Ex. 19:4*a*), His mighty act of Exodus deliverance (v. 4*b*), and His bringing of His people to Himself in covenant fellowship (v. 4*c*), Yahweh challenged them to be obedient to His covenant requirements so they could be His own special possession (v. 5), a kingdom of priests (v. 6). The redemptive prerequisite to covenant relationship is unconditional—God delivered them and brought them to Himself at His own initiative. What was conditional was their success in achieving His purpose for them, that they be a priestly kingdom, a holy nation.

Many theologians view this complex of events itself as the primary focus of Old Testament theology.[13] Because the bulk of the Old Testament revelation is concerned with Israel and with Yahweh's relationship with Israel, it is argued that that must be the central concern of God's revelation. But theological significance cannot be measured by lines of text alone. There must be careful attention to exegesis, to literary and theological context. Granting that Exodus 19:4-6 is a fundamental statement about the divine plan for Israel, is there anything in this passage to suggest that God's purposes are limited to Israel? Or is there any suggestion as to the role Israel was to play, a role that in itself would lead to a far more comprehensive understanding of God's objectives?

The answer is to be found in the very nature of priesthood. Whatever else might be said of the office, the fundamental notion that comes to mind in consid-

11. For various approaches to the search for a center, see Hasel, *Old Testament Theology,* pp. 117-43.
12. W. J. Dumbrell, *Covenant and Creation* (Nashville: Thomas Nelson, 1984), pp. 80-81, 90.
13. Jakob Jocz, *The Covenant* (Grand Rapids: Eerdmans, 1968), pp. 31-32.

ering the ministry of the priest is that of mediation and intercession. A priest stands between God and a person (or persons) who is in need of making contact with God. So Israel must be viewed as bearing a mediatorial responsibility, of serving as an intercessor between a holy God and all the peoples of the earth. But this suggests that Israel itself and its covenant relationship to Yahweh cannot be the focal point of biblical theology. Israel's role is not an ultimate objective but merely a means of facilitating that objective—that God and the peoples of earth might have unbroken communion. Israel's importance, then, is functional. For just as the priest did not serve for his own sake but only as a means of bridging the gap between the worshiper and the worshiped, so Israel was made a priestly nation to achieve communion between man and God. As will be emphasized later, even the form of the Sinaitic Covenant—a sovereign-vassal treaty—points to this functional meaning of Israel's existence.

If Exodus 19 is not a statement of *ultimate* theological purpose but only one outlining the *role* of Israel, is there a statement elsewhere that would satisfactorily explain the reason for the election and covenant responsibility of Israel in the first place? In line with the previous discussion of chronological and canonical indicators, it is proposed that the search for such a statement of center must begin precisely at the beginning—in the earliest parts of Genesis.

Genesis 1:26-28 as the theological center. Unquestionably the underlying purposes of God for man are bound up in His creation of the heavens and the earth, which provide the arena of His activity.[14] One would naturally expect the Bible, as a historical and theological treatise, to commence its story with creation, the earliest possible event. If, however, there were theological concerns that transcended creation and its purposes, one could have every right to expect the inspired record to begin with these because the canonical shape is not always exclusively sensitive to chronological concerns. Therefore, the very priority of creation *both historiographically and canonically* should point to its theological centrality.

There are two complementary accounts of creation; Genesis 1, which is cosmic and universal in its scope; and Genesis 2, which is decidedly anthropocentric. This canonical structure alone suggests the climactic way the creation of man is viewed. He is the crowning glory of the creative process. This is clearly seen even in Genesis 1, for man is created last, on the sixth day of creation.

A mere description of the divine creative activity is not sufficient, however, to communicate the theological message involved, for there must be statements of motive to give the act intelligent and intelligible meaning. The fundamental question that must be asked of the creation accounts is, "So what?" Answers to this question are not long in coming. Following the creation of light, God said that it was good (Gen. 1:4). Similarly He endorsed the appearance of the dry land (v. 10), the

---

14. Eugene H. Merrill, "Covenant and the Kingdom: Genesis 1-3 as Foundation for Biblical Theology," *Criswell Theological Review* 1 (1987): 295-308.

emergence of plant life (v. 12), the placement of the heavenly bodies (v. 18), and the creation of marine and aerial life (v. 21) and of earthbound creatures (v. 25). The whole is summarized in verse 31: "God saw all that he had made, and it was very good."

The judgment that all these things were "good" is of course a statement of purpose. It suggests that creation serves aesthetic ends at least.[15] But aesthetics alone is an insufficient basis on which to build the eternal, divine objective. To see that objective in more concrete and specific terms one must ascertain the particular purposes attached to the creation of man, because it is man who is the image of God and for whom the rest of creation provides a setting.

This leads to Genesis 1:26-28, the first and foundational text to articulate the functional aspect of the creation of man. The formal, anthropological aspect is found in Genesis 2.

The first part of the statement of purpose is that man is made in the image and likeness of God (1:26a), a purpose reiterated as having been accomplished with the added nuance of gender distinction (v. 27). In line with recent scholarship, it is argued here that the translation of *bᵉṣalmēnū* ("in our image") and *kidmūtēnū* ("according to our likeness") ought to be "as our image" and "according to our likeness" respectively.[16] That is, man is not *in* the image of God, he *is* the image of God. The text speaks not of what man is like but of what he is to be and do. It is a functional statement and not one of essence.[17] Just as images or statues represented deities and kings in the ancient Near East, so much so that they were virtually interchangeable,[18] so man as the image of God was created to represent God Himself as the sovereign over all creation.

This bold metaphor is spelled out beyond question in Genesis 1:26b, which explains what it means for man to be the image of God: "Let them rule over the fish of the sea and the birds of the air, over the livestock, over all the earth, and over all creatures that move along the ground." The mandate to accomplish this follows in verse 28: "Be fruitful and increase in number; fill the earth and subdue it. Rule over the fish of the sea and the birds of the air and over every living creature that moves on the ground."

The key words in this statement of purpose are the verbs "rule" (1:26, 28) and "subdue" (v. 28). The first verb appears in the jussive ("let them rule") and imper-

---

15. Von Rad suggests that the word "good" contains "less an aesthetic judgment than the designation of purpose, correspondence" (Gerhard von Rad, *Genesis: A Commentary* [London: SCM, 1961], p. 50).

16. Ibid., p. 56.

17. Only Christ is the image of God in an ontological sense. Man is such representationally or functionally. See Peter T. O'Brien, *Colossians, Philemon,* Word Biblical Commentary, vol. 44 (Waco, Tex.: Word, 1982), pp. 43-44.

18. For a full discussion of this view (which he does not accept), see Claus Westermann, *Genesis 1-11: A Commentary* (Minneapolis: Augsburg, 1984), pp. 151-54.

ative ("rule ye") of the Hebrew *rādāh* ("have dominion, rule, dominate").[19] The second occurs also in the imperative plural, the Hebrew verb being *kābaš* ("subdue, bring into bondage").[20] Both verbs carry the idea of dominion. Both may be traced back to the verbal root meaning "to tread down." Hence, man is created to reign in a manner that demonstrates his lordship, his domination (by force if necessary) over all creation.

Two principal passages in the Old Testament provide glimpses of what human domination under God entails. The first is Genesis 2:15 (cf. v. 5), 19-20, and the second is Psalm 8.

As noted earlier, Genesis 2 gives the account of the creation of man in which he appears as the climax of the creative process, almost its raison d'être. In this account, described in highly anthropomorphic terms, the Lord formed man from the dust of the ground and breathed into his nostrils the breath of life, making him a living being (v. 7). He then placed man in the garden "to work it and take care of it" (v. 15). This must be seen in light of verse 5, which points out that before the creation of man no shrub or plant had sprung up because there was as yet no rain and, more significantly, no man to "work the ground." Clearly, then, a major purpose for the creation of man was that he should "work the ground."[21] Work by itself was not a curse; indeed it was the very essence of what it meant to be the image of God. To work the ground is one definition of what it means to have dominion.

A second definition may be found in Genesis 2:19-20, which states that man was given the responsibility of naming the animals. As is now well known, in the ancient Near East to name could be tantamount to exercising dominion.[22] When Yahweh brought the animals to Adam "to see what he would name them," He was in effect transferring from Himself to Adam the dominion for which man was created. This of course is perfectly in line with the objects of human dominion listed in the pivotal text of Genesis 1:26: fish, birds, livestock, and "all the creatures that move along the ground."

The second major Old Testament passage that clarifies the meaning of man's function as sovereign is Psalm 8. The entire hymn deserves detailed discussion but only two points can be made here. First, a clear reference to the *imago dei* is conveyed by verse 5: "You made Him a little lower than the heavenly beings and crowned Him with glory and honor." As the NIV suggests in the footnote, "heavenly beings" may be translated "God" (Heb. *'ĕlōhîm*). This in fact is the better

19. Francis Brown, S. R. Driver, and Charles A. Briggs, *A Hebrew and English Lexicon of the Old Testament* (Oxford: Clarendon, 1962), p. 921.

20. Ibid., p. 461.

21. Manfred Hutter, "Adam als Gärtner und König," *Biblische Zeitschrift* 30 (1986): 258-62.

22. Von Rad, *Genesis*, p. 81. For a careful nuancing of this, however, see George W. Ramsey, "Is Name-Giving an Act of Domination in Genesis 2:23 and Elsewhere?" *Catholic Biblical Quarterly* 50 (1988): 24-35.

translation in view of the well-established fact that this psalm is a commentary of Genesis 1:26-28. As God's image and viceroy, man himself is a king crowned with glory and honor.

What that kingship means is clear from Psalm 8:6-7, where man has been appointed ruler (causative of *māšal*) over all creation, with everything "under his feet." This image is reminiscent of the fundamental meaning of "have dominion" (*rādāh*) and "subdue" (*kābaš*) in Genesis 1:28, namely, to tread upon. The objects of the dominion are exactly the same (though in different order) as those of the Genesis mandate: flocks and herds, beasts of the field, birds of the air, and fish of the sea (Ps. 8:7).

A THEOLOGY OF GENESIS

THE COVENANT MANDATE AND ESCHATOLOGY

If the purposes of God are bound up in His act of creation and dominion, one would expect these twin themes to prevail throughout the biblical revelation, and indeed they do. The devastating interdiction of sin necessitated adjustment of the implementation of those purposes, however, so that the ability of man to fulfill the terms of the mandate was seriously impaired and required modification. But what became submerged in the course of human history will reemerge in the eschaton when man's full covenant-keeping capacity will be restored. This is crystal clear from an examination of several passages in the prophets.

Nowhere is the restoration to the pristine conditions of the original covenant statement more brilliantly unfolded than in Isaiah. In Isaiah 11:6-9, a messianic passage especially oriented to the millennial age, the prophet predicts the following:

> The wolf will live with the lamb,
> > the leopard will lie down with the goat,
> The calf and the lion and the yearling together;
> > and a little child will lead them.
> The cow will feed with the bear,
> > their young will lie down together,
> > and the lion will eat straw like the ox.
> The infant will play near the hole of the cobra,
> > and the young child put his hand into the viper's nest.
> They will neither harm nor destroy
> > on all my holy mountain,
> For the earth will be full of the knowledge of the Lord
> > as the waters cover the sea.

The docility of the animals, particularly their noncarnivorous nature, clearly speaks of the paradisaical conditions before man's Fall (cf. Gen. 9:2-3). Moreover, the verb used to describe the leading of animals by a child in Isaiah 11:6 (*nāhag*) is one that speaks of leadership or headship,[23] a most appropriate synonym for dominion.

Another remarkable passage is Hosea 2:18. There the prophet speaks of a day when Yahweh "will make a covenant for them [i.e., Israel] with the beasts of the field and the birds of the air and the creatures that move along the ground." There is an unmistakable allusion here to the covenant mandate of Genesis 1:26-28 although, to be sure, it is Israel specifically that will be involved in its implementation.[24]

THE COVENANT MANDATE AND THE LIFE OF JESUS

The apostle Paul described Jesus as the Second Adam, an epithet associated with His salvific and redemptive work and with His role as the "first Man" of a regenerate community. "For as in Adam all die, so in Christ all will be made alive" (1 Cor. 15:22; cf. 15:45; Rom. 5:12-17). Although this redemptive aspect of Jesus as the Second Adam cannot be emphasized too much, it may be instructive also to view the *life* of Jesus as the life of the Second Adam, and to note that Jesus came not only to die but also to live. And the life He lived demonstrated by its power and perfection all that God created Adam and all men to be. In other words, Jesus fulfilled in His life the potentialities of unfallen Adam just as by His death He restored all mankind to those potentialities.

A few examples from the gospels must suffice. On one occasion Jesus and His disciples were crossing the Sea of Galilee when a furious storm overtook the boat and threatened to swamp it. Jesus, awakened by the disciples, rebuked the winds and waves, and so startling were the results that His friends asked, "What kind of man is this? Even the winds and the waves obey him!" (Matt. 8:23-27). Although one could easily argue that Jesus worked this miracle because of His deity, that does not seem to be the conclusion of those who witnessed the event. Of particular interest in the account (see also Mark 4:36-41; Luke 8:22-25) is the disciples' sense of Jesus' sovereignty over creation. Jesus spoke to the elements as their lord and they obeyed Him. Is this not akin to the dominion to which Adam was appointed?

A similar incident may suggest even closer affinities to the domination over creation enjoined by the Adamic Covenant. Matthew 14:22-23 (cf. Mark 6:45-51; John 6:16-21) relates the story of the disciples who again were in the grip of the angry sea when suddenly they saw Jesus walking on the water. Emboldened by this, Peter asked Jesus to allow him to walk on the waves as well. Successful at first, Peter lost his confidence and began to sink and only the strong arm of the Lord preserved him.

Certain features stand out and give evidence of theological themes and antecedents that provide a rationale for the event. First, there is the concept of the chaotic waters that must be dominated, a concept seen in the narrative of Matthew

---

23. Brown, Driver, and Briggs, p. 694.
24. Hans Walter Wolff, *Hosea* (Philadelphia: Fortress, 1974), p. 51.

8 was well. Here, however, Jesus did not speak to the waves; instead he trod them underfoot. This is in keeping with the fundamental idea of *rādāh* and *kābaš* in Genesis 1:28, namely, to tread or trample on. Second, Peter himself apparently saw in the mastery of the elements by Jesus a warrant for his own mastery. For him to imagine that he could emulate Jesus as God would be nothing short of blasphemy. To emulate Him as the Second Adam would, however, be only what God intended him and all men to do.

A third example of Jesus' lordship over creation is that of the extraction of the Temple tax from the mouth of a fish (Matt. 17:27). When Peter inquired as to how the penniless disciples were to pay their tax, Jesus instructed him to catch a fish and in its mouth would be the exact amount needed. Though again one might plead miracle here, it could equally as well be explained as the natural consequence of the sinless Man invoking the privilege of the original creation covenant in which He was to have dominion over "the fish of the sea."

A fourth incident is that of Jesus riding into Jerusalem triumphantly on the first day of Passion week (Matt. 21:1-11; Mark 11:1-10; Luke 19:29-38). What must be noted here is that He did so on an animal—as Mark and Luke were careful to point out—"upon which no one has ever ridden" (Mark 11:2). This comment is generally overlooked, but in the context of the triumph of the Lord, which was being celebrated by the throngs, it is particularly significant that that triumph is specifically focused on His dominion of the animal world, in this case the unbroken colt. Jesus entered Jerusalem as King, a role He fulfilled not only as the Lord God but also as the Second Adam and the Son of David.

SIN AND THE INTERRUPTION OF COVENANT PURPOSE

The origin of sin is a mystery that remains undisclosed in biblical revelation. What is clear is that sin is a reality and that it followed hard on the creation of man and his covenant between God and man, and between them and all other creatures. The remainder of the biblical story is the plan of God whereby that alienation can be overcome and His original purposes for man—that he have dominion over all things—can be reestablished.

The God-man relationship was of a sovereign-vassal nature. God had created man for the express purpose of conveying to him the status and function of image, that is, man was to represent God in his dominion over all creation. Such a privilege entailed also responsibility, chief of which was unqualified loyalty and obedience. In a sinless world it is impossible for obedience to be tested and authenticated, for a sinless world is one with no options. This perhaps explains the existence of Satan, who appears as the antagonist and accuser, the one who gives man a choice of sovereigns and courses of action.[25] His role as alternative lord is already presupposed by the limitation placed on the man in the garden. "You are free to eat

---

25. Gustave F. Oehler, *Theology of the Old Testament* (1883; reprint, Grand Rapids: Zondervan, n.d.), pp. 158-59, 448-51.

from any tree in the garden; but you must not eat from the tree of the knowledge of good and evil, for when you eat of it you will surely die" (Gen. 2:17).

This prohibition is the reverse side of the statement of covenant purpose. Positively man was to "be fruitful and increase in number; fill the earth and subdue it" (Gen. 1:28). Negatively he was to refrain from one part of that creation, the tree of the knowledge of good and evil. Whatever that tree might convey by its fruit, it symbolized the principle that in covenant-keeping there are "shall nots" as well as "shalls." To have dominion over all things is not a blanket endorsement for man to do as he will. Human dominion must be exercised within the framework of the permissions and prohibitions of the King of whom man is only the image.

The tree serves, therefore, as the testing point of man's covenant fidelity. To partake of it is to demonstrate false dominion, a hubris in which man has become in some mysterious sense like God. "The man," God says, "has now become like one of us, knowing good and evil" (Gen. 3:22). By attempting to reverse roles and assert his independence of limitations, man became a marred and defective image, one who no longer could represent his sovereign in an unhampered and perfect way. Sin had introduced an alienation that affected not only the God-man relationship but also made the man a dying creature who could never hope to fulfill the covenant mandate as long as he remained in that condition.

The alienation extended also in a horizontal direction: man became alienated from woman and vice versa. The covenant statement had said, "So God created man in his own image, in the image of God he created him; male and female he created them" (Gen. 1:27). Man is male and female and both genders are the image of God. Both men and women, therefore, represent God on the earth and are the agents through whom He exercises dominion.[26]

This statement of covenant purpose is qualified by the account of covenant function in Genesis 2, which delineates further the male-female relationship. The Lord Himself observed that "it is not good for the man to be alone," so He determined to "make a helper suitable to him" (v. 18). This is followed by the "making" of a woman from man's side and the pun to the effect that she is woman (*'iššāh*) because she was taken out of man (*'îš*) (v.23).

No idea of superiority/inferiority with respect to the sexes can be found here. That woman was taken from man no more implies the inferiority of woman to man than the taking of man from the ground (*'ādām from 'ǎdāmāh*) implies the inferiority of man to the ground. Nor does the term "helper" connote subordination. This is clear from the context in which the need is for man, like the animals, to have a mate, a partner who would complement or correspond to him. Man as male is only half of what God wants him to be as the image of God. It is, moreover, important to note that the Hebrew term for "helper," *'ezer*, is frequently used of the

---

26. Walther Eichrodt, *Theology of the Old Testament* (Philadelphia: Westminister, 1967), 2:126-27.

Lord Himself as man's Helper (Deut. 33:7; Pss. 33:20; 115:9-11; 146:5; Hos. 13:9). A helper then is not necessarily dominant or subordinate but one who meets a need in the life and experience of someone else.[27]

Sin, however, radically altered the man-woman relationship just as it did that between God and His creation. The woman, having been tempted by Satan, yielded and encouraged her husband to join her in her violation of covenant prohibition. As a result, Satan, the woman, and the man fell under divine condemnation and became subject to a covenant that now incorporated stipulations appropriate to a universe no longer in willing compliance to its Sovereign. The old demand to "be fruitful and increase in number; fill the earth and subdue it" was still in effect, but it could hereafter be carried out only partially by unredeemed humanity and imperfectly even by those God would restore to Himself in saving grace. Sin and history must run their course before the perfect conditions of covenant fulfillment can come to pass.

Meanwhile, it is important to explore the man-woman relationship and God-man relationship in their functional aspects as a result of the alienation caused by sin. The covenant statement relative to these matters is preceded by the glorious redemptive promise that though the offspring of Satan would strike the heel of the Descendant of the woman that Descendant would in turn crush the head of the evil line (Gen. 3:15). The messianic character of this promise is almost universally recognized, though, of course, the specificity of the woman's offspring cannot be established in this text alone.

More immediately relevant to the question of male-female relationship within the context of covenant fulfillment in a fallen world is Genesis 3:16. There the woman is assigned the curse of painful child-bearing, and there it is said that "your desire will be for your husband, and he will rule over you." The setting of this statement is human society in a fallen world. Whatever the curse might involve, it is not relevant to the original status of man and woman nor indigenous to their creation as coregents of the dominions of the Lord. Nor will it endure beyond the confines of history, for the eschaton ultimately is a restoration of all things as they were and as they were intended.

The problematic phrase is that in which the man is said to move beyond the role of coregent with his wife to that of lord over her. That this is not merely predictive of what the future would hold but prescriptive of the man-woman functional relationship from that time forward is clear from apostolic teaching on the matter. To cite one or two texts only, Paul forbade women to speak in the churches because they "must be in submission, as the Law says" (1 Cor. 14:34). To the same church he pointed out that "the head of every man is Christ, and the head of the woman is man, and the head of Christ is God" (1 Cor. 11:3; cf. Eph. 5:23-24; Titus 2:5; 1 Pet. 3:1; etc.). One would not, of course, gather from this that God (the Father) is superior in essence to Christ, but only in function. Likewise all that is being

---

27. Westermann, *Genesis,* p. 227.

avowed by the apostle is that man is superior to woman in a functional sense, in man's role in the hierarchical structure of kingdom domination.[28]

More difficult still is the phrase "your desire will be for your husband" (Gen. 3:16). The Hebrew construction of the verse reflects poetic parallelism in which the first line of the couplet carries the same meaning as the second. The second ("and he will rule over you") requires that the "desire" of the woman for her husband also convey the idea of domination. The word translated "desire" (*těšûqāh*) occurs also in Genesis 4:7, which says that sin "desired to have you [Cain], but you must master it." Interestingly the same Hebrew verb translated "master" (*māšal*) here was translated "rule" in Genesis 3:16. This suggests that the woman will turn to the man for her dominion and that his rule over her will come to pass.[29] As a rule, then, the headship of the man will be the pattern as long as the fallen world of history remains.

The alienation brought about by sin not only affected the God-man and the man-woman relationship; it also disrupted the harmony between man and creation. These three relationships may be described as the vertical-above, the horizontal, and the vertical-below, respectively. Man was created subordinate to God, coordinate to the woman, and dominant over all other creatures. He had been charged with the task of "working" the ground (Gen. 2:15), bringing it and all other things into his service and under his dominion as the vice-regent of God.

Now, however, sin has intruded, and fallen man has forfeited his untrammeled mastery of his environment. He had listened to his wife, thereby submitting to her authority, so now the ground he was created to work would be resistant to his husbandry. His toil now would be painful, the earth would produce worthless and annoying brambles and weeds, and the ground from which he was taken and over which he had been set would conquer him as he was laid beneath its soil in death (Gen. 3:19).

The immediate repercussion was the permanent exile of the man and the woman from the garden, an exile that symbolized their fallenness and exclusion from the privileges of the covenant stipulations for which they had been created. Life outside the garden spoke of life apart from the intimacy of relationship with God, with one another, and with the created order. Such an exile was a repudiation of all the purposes of God for creation, however, so a means of undoing the curse of sin and ultimately its very existence must be set in motion.

COVENANT PURPOSE AND SOTERIOLOGY

The curse of alienation requires an act of reconciliation, and it is this act, both as event and process, that is the definition of biblical salvation.[30] Soteriology,

---

28. So, for example, F. L. Godet, *Commentary on First Corinthians* (1899; reprint, Grand Rapids: Kregel, 1977), p. 539.

29. Walter C. Kaiser, Jr., *Toward Old Testament Ethics* (Grand Rapids: Zondervan, 1983), pp. 204-6.

30. Claus Westermann, *Elements of Old Testament Theology* (Atlanta: John Knox, 1982), p. 45.

then, is obviously a major theme of biblical theology, though it clearly is not *the* central motif. This is evident in that salvation implies deliverance *from* something *to* something and is thus a functional rather than a teleological concept. In other words, salvation leads to a purpose that has been frustrated or interrupted and is not a purpose in itself.

Many scholars' attempts to see salvation as a central theme even in the creation account are not convincing because such attempts draw most of their support from pagan mythology in which creation occurs as a result of the subjugation of primeval chaotic waters by the gods.[31] There is no hint of such a thing in the Old Testament except in passages where such mythic themes may be used as poetic illustration of Yahweh's victory over His enemies, who are at times likened to chaotic and destructive floods.

The earliest reference to salvation is obviously identified with its earliest need, namely, in response to the disruption of covenant purpose occasioned by man's sinful rebellion against his God. Genesis 3:15 describes the ultimate conquest of evil by the seed of woman. Also relevant, as has been noted throughout the history of interpretation, is the clothing of man and woman with animal skins provided graciously by the Lord. Although one must be cautious about unwarranted theological conclusions based on such a laconic text, there can be no question that the covering of nakedness, first perceived after man's sin, cannot be achieved by the fig leaves on his own making (3:7) but requires divine initiative (3:21).[32]

The need for salvation is a persistent theme of biblical history, for that history is one of continuing and increasing spiritual and moral defection. For every act of divine grace there is a human counteract of sin. Following every expression of God's covenant purposes there is a human word and deed of rebellion against it. Created to be the image of God and thus to manifest the sovereignty of God in all areas of life, man has become a marred and misshapen vestige of the image who, without the intervention of redemptive and reconciling grace, is unable to serve the purposes for which he was created.

This is seen in such examples as the murder of Abel by his brother Cain (Gen. 4:1-15), an act of brutality followed by the vengeful boast of Lamech, the descendant of Cain, that whoever attempted to avenge Cain would himself be avenged many times over (vv. 23-24). This narrative shows not only the continuing horizontal alienation of man from man but a proud assertion by Lamech that the preservation of Cain by the Lord (v. 15) is inadequate and its perceived inadequacy must be remedied by human intervention.

Similarly the intermarriage of the sons of God and the daughters of men was indicative of a waywardness that prompted the Lord to comment that man's wicked-

---

31. See, for example, Gerhard von Rad, "The Theological Problem of the Old Testament Doctrine of Creation," in *The Problem of the Hexateuch and Other Essays* (London: SCM, 1984), esp. pp. 142-43.

32. Franz Delitzsch, *The Pentateuch,* Commentary on the Old Testament, vol. 1 (Grand Rapids: Eerdmans, n.d.), p. 106.

ness was great and that "every inclination of the thoughts of his heart was only evil all the time" (Gen. 6:5). Contextually it seems that intermarriage speaks of an intercourse between angelic and human beings, an illegitimate bridging of divinely segregated orders of creation that produced the monstrous "Nephilim," the "heroes of old, men of renown" (v. 4).[33] Again man, the image of God who was commissioned to rule over all things, placed himself in subjection to demonic powers over which he should have been master.

NOAH AS A "SECOND ADAM"

Man's sin in Noah's day was grievous and painful to the Lord, who regretted He had created man in the first place. He therefore determined to bury man beneath the waters of the sea just as He had buried Adam beneath the surface of the ground. The chaotic waters that had yielded submissively to the hand of the Creator so that dry land appeared would be unleashed now by the Creator as an instrument of His vindictive wrath. But even so the original creative purposes would not be stymied and curtailed because God would begin again with another Adam, another image who would maintain the mandate of sovereignty. This "Adam" of course was none other than Noah.

Noah, though righteous and blameless, was nonetheless chosen not because of his upright condition but as an object of the elective grace of God (Gen. 6:8). That election clearly had salvific overtones—he was saved from the Flood—but beyond that and most fundamentally it was election to the covenant arrangement for which Adam had been created. Noah was to be the beginner of a new undertaking of covenant commitment, a new vice-regent through whom the sovereign purposes of God could find fruition.

Beyond question, this is the meaning of Genesis 6:18: "But I will establish my covenant with you." "My covenant" can refer only to something antecedent and the only possible antecedent is that covenant implied by Genesis 1:26-28.[34] The old Adamic Covenant would be established (*hēqîm*) with Noah, and all that the Lord had entrusted to and required of Adam would devolve on Noah and his descendants.

When at last the watery judgment was over, Yahweh articulated the significance and specifications of the covenant terms. This was prefaced by the solemn promise that never again would Yahweh "curse the ground" because of man nor would He destroy all living creatures so long as human history ran its course (Gen. 8:21-22). The Bible goes on, however, to attest to an ultimate destruction and renewal of the earth by fire, a destruction that will mark the end of time and the commencement of the eternal and uncursed kingdom of God (2 Pet. 3:3-7).

The covenant text itself is spelled out in Genesis 9:1-7, a unit bracketed by the

---

33. Willem A. Van Gemeren, "The Sons of God in Genesis 6:1-4," *Westminster Theological Journal* 43 (1981): 343.
34. Dumbrell, p. 26.

familiar Adamic Covenant statement "Be fruitful and increase in number and fill the earth" (vv. 1, 7). The next part of the command to Adam—"subdue it [the earth]" and "rule over the fish," and so forth—is, however, radically different in its Noahic form because now the earth was cursed and alienation had fractured the harmonious structures of sovereignty that attended the pre-Fall creation. "Subdue" and "rule" now have come to be expressed as follows: "The fear and dread of you will fall upon all the beasts of the earth and all the birds of the air, upon every creature that moves along the ground, and upon all the fish of the sea" (v. 2). The domination by Adam (exemplified by Jesus) that was effected by the spoken word alone must now be enforced by man's superior intellectual and rational powers. Voluntary subservience in the animal world has been replaced by coercion, and man and animal live in uneasy coexistence. So violent is the bifurcation and so drastic the effects of the Fall that animals not only must submit by force to the dominion of man but they may be slain by him to provide his nourishment (v. 3).[35]

The line must be drawn again at the horizontal level, however, for man cannot take the life of his fellow any more now under Noah than he could before under Adam. The reason is clearly stated: "for in the image of God has God made man" (9:6). That fundamental fact has never changed, the sin of the Fall notwithstanding. To attack and to destroy man is tantamount to attacking and attempting to destroy the sovereign Himself, of whom even fallen man is the image.

The text of the Noahic Covenant is followed by the promise of the Lord that the earth will never again be destroyed by a flood (Gen. 9:9-11) and by the pledge of that promise, the rainbow. The rainbow, in fact, became the sign of the covenant itself, a sign that far transcends in its significance the promise of preservation from flood and that speaks of the intactness of the dominion mandate given to mankind from the beginning.[36] He who sees the rainbow can rest assured that the purposes of God from creation are in full effect and will some day reach their predestined, perfect accomplishment.

The history of the covenant transmission following Noah may be traced in the Genesis genealogies; in fact, the very purpose of the genealogies is to disclose the ever-narrowing focus of covenant development that finally finds its center in Abraham and his descendants.[37] Like Adam, Noah had three sons, only one of whom was the agent of covenant descent. Seth, the third son of Adam, was progenitor of Noah, a "second Adam." Shem, the third son of Noah, was likewise chosen to be the heir of the covenant promise. His genealogy (Gen. 10:21-31; 11:10-26) included Eber, the patronymic of the Hebrew people, and Peleg, in whose days the earth was divided (10:25), and culminated in Abram, the youngest of the three sons of Terah.

35. Geerhardus Vos, *Biblical Theology* (Grand Rapids: Eerdmans, 1954), p. 64.
36. Dumbrell, p. 29.
37. Gerhard F. Hasel, "The Meaning of the Chronogenealogies of Genesis 5 and 11," *Origins* 7 (1981): 69.

THE TOWER OF BABEL

The importance of the Tower of Babel lies in its interruption of the implementation of the covenant mandate, a feature it shares in common with the account of the intermarriage of angels and men in Genesis 6:1-4. That act of rebellion resulted in the catastrophe of the Flood, following which the offspring of Noah "were scattered over the earth" (Gen. 8:16). Similarly, as a result of the Lord's preempting the tower construction, He "scattered them over the face of the whole earth" (11:9). The language is too formulaic and precise to be considered coincidental. The two stories themselves must be addressing common themes and interests in addition to the general idea of disobedience of the Adamic Covenant.[38]

What is fundamentally at work in the story of the angels and men is the demonic attempt to frustrate the purpose of God that man should "be fruitful and increase in number" (Gen. 1:28), for the narrative begins by observing that the intermarriage commenced precisely "when man began to increase in number" (6:1). Whatever else the "sons of God" and "daughters of men" might mean, their illicit relationship resulted in the crippling of that aspect of the mandate. Perhaps they had begun to produce a race of monsters genetically incapable of reproduction, thus leading to an end of humanity.

The Tower of Babel story reveals unmistakably that the tower builders had one objective in mind: "that we may make a name for ourselves and not be scattered over the face of the whole earth" (Gen. 11:4). That is, they refused to obey the second element of the Adamic mandate, to "fill the earth and subdue it" (1:28). The two episodes then combined to present a full portrayal of covenant disobedience.

Not without importance, because it is common to both stories, is the reference to the "heroes of old, men of renown" (Gen. 6:4) and to Nimrod, "a mighty warrior on the earth" (10:8). The connection between Nimrod and the Tower of Babel is evident from the chronological priority of Genesis 11 to Genesis 10 and the fact that one of the centers of Nimrod's kingdom was Babylon (i.e., Babel). Quite likely Nimrod himself was one of the tower builders. In any event his description as a "mighty warrior" is based on the Hebrew *gibbôr,* the very word translated "heroes" in 6:4. Moreover, these heroes were "men of renown" or, literally, "men of the name." It is surely worthy of note that one of the desires of the Babel tower builders was that they might "make a name" for themselves.

Clearly then these two stories of covenant violation point to the same root problem. Man, charged as the image of God to be His vice-regent on the earth, was dissatisfied with that high and holy calling and rebelled against his sovereign with the end in view of supplanting His lordship and assuming it for himself. He want-

---

38. D. J. A. Clines demonstrates clear thematic strands in Genesis 1-11 (a theme he describes as "creation–uncreation–re-creation") in his "Theme in Genesis 1-11," *Catholic Biblical Quarterly* 38 (1976): 499-502.

ed to be like God or, to put it in the biblical language itself, "the man has now become like one of Us" (Gen. 3:22) and "nothing they plan to do will be impossible for them" (11:6).

The divine response to this insubordination took the form of judgment (the Flood and the dispersion) and covenant renewal (with Noah and with Abraham).

THE ABRAHAMIC COVENANT

The tenor of the biblical narrative suggests that the call of Abram to covenant service was as much an act of divine elective grace as was the creation of Adam and the choice of Noah, his two most illustrious covenant forebears. He was told to leave Ur, his homeland, and go to a land that God would show him. Obedience to this call would result in his being made a partner with Yahweh in the process of blessing the world and bringing it back in line with its Creator's intentions.

Though Abram's opportunity to participate in the covenant privileges was obviously conditioned on his leaving Ur and going to Canaan, the subsequent covenant itself was unconditional. As most scholars now recognize, the covenant and its circumstances were in the form of a royal (land) grant, a legal arrangement well attested in the ancient Near East.[39] This type of organ was initiated by a benefactor such as a king who, for whatever reason, wished to confer a blessing on a subject. It was often construed as a reward for some service rendered by the subject, but many times there was no expressed rationale. The grant was a boon explicable by nothing other than the sovereign pleasure of the benefactor. And just as its bestowal was unconditional so was its maintenance. The covenant could stand, regardless of the behavior of its recipient. All that could be affected positively or negatively by the response of the grantee was the enjoyment of the benefits of the grant and their continuation.

Thus the Abrahamic Covenant, along with its Adamic and Noahic predecessors, must be viewed as an unconditional grant made by Yahweh to His servant Abram, a grant that was to serve a specific and irrevocable function. Much more expansive and variegated than the other two statements, the Abrahamic, nevertheless, is built squarely on them in all its essential elements. Yet there is a dimension that goes beyond the earlier covenant mandate, for the Abrahamic Covenant not only reiterates in its own way the Genesis injunction to "be fruitful and increase in number; fill the earth and subdue it," but it also incorporates the strategy by which that purpose might be achieved.

This is immediately apparent in Genesis 12:1-3, the initial and programmatic statement of the covenant. Abram was told that he would be made into a great nation that would be the means by which Yahweh would bless all peoples on earth. God's concern was still clearly universalistic, but the *means* of addressing that concern was very specific—the nation of Abram.

Subsequently Abram learned that the land in and from which the reconciling people would minister to the world was Canaan itself (Gen. 12:7; 13:14-17). Then, in a second expression of the covenant promise, Abram learned that the promise of descendants is valid even though he had no children (15:2-5), and the land would be his even though it was then populated by others (15:7-21). Abram trusted Yahweh in all this, so Yahweh considered him to be in perfect covenant compliance (15:6).

When after the passing of many years the promise of seed had not yet been fulfilled, Yahweh appeared once more to Abram with a remarkable exposition and amplification of the original promise. He was to become the father not only of a nation but of many nations (hence the name change to Abraham) and kings (Gen. 17:4-6). The covenant, once more affirmed as eternal, would be certified by the sign of circumcision, a physical token of the special status of the covenant people.

Careful attention to the major themes of these various expressions of the covenant with Abraham reveals that they affirm in every respect the covenant mandate of Genesis 1:26-28, with the special proviso that Abraham and his descendants were to serve as models of, as well as witnesses to, the implementation on the earth. That is, the Abrahamic nation would become a microcosm of the kingdom of God and would function in that capacity as an agency by which God would reconcile the whole creation to Himself.

The first part of this promise—that Abraham's offspring would become a great nation (Gen. 12:2; 15:5; 17:4-5)—is a reflection of the command to mankind in 1:28, "Be fruitful and increase in number." The sovereignty aspect is clearly seen in references to the kings who were to emerge in the line of Abraham (17:6, 16). These kings would exercise dominion over that nation (and others) that God would raise up as a model of His creation purposes. Thus a direct connection to 1:28 again must be admitted: "fill the earth and subdue it [and] rule."

The second part of the promise finds no antecedent in the Genesis 1 mandate but is nonetheless to be understood in reference to it. This is the role the Abrahamic nation was to play as the touchstone in reference to which the peoples of the earth are to be blessed or cursed: "I will bless those who bless you, and whoever curses you I will curse; and all peoples on earth will be blessed through you"[40] (Gen. 12:3; 18:18; cf. Gal. 3:8). This suggests a mediatorial function for this chosen nation, a responsibility to stand between the sovereign God of heaven and earth and His fallen creation and to minister His salvific grace.

This dual aspect of the Abrahamic Covenant must be kept carefully in view if the centrality of the creation mandate to biblical theology is to find consistent validation throughout the biblical revelation. To understand the covenant as only a continuation of the Adamic-Noahic is to deny Israel its crucially important place as a servant people. However, to understand it only as a preparation for the Sinaitic

---

40. For justification of this passive rendering of the verb "to bless," see O. T. Allis, "The Blessing of Abraham," *Princeton Theological Review* 25 (1927): 263-98.

Covenant is to deny the transhistorical, universalistic concerns that transcend the narrow confines of a chosen people. This duality will continue to inform this discussion and will properly locate Israel in the theological as well as historical purposes of God.

Transmission of the Abrahamic Covenant continued as it had begun, by divine elective grace. Isaac, son of Abraham and Sarah's old age, was chosen rather than Ishmael (Gen. 17:18-19). To him was given almost verbatim the same promises and privileges enjoyed by his father (26:3-4, 24). And to him also would be given a son who would inherit the covenant responsibility.

This son was Jacob, younger son of Isaac and Rebekah. And so Jacob too, like Isaac, was chosen in contradiction to the norms of filial succession. Before his birth it was said of Jacob that he would rule his older brother (Gen. 25:23), a promise that eventually came to pass with Israel's domination over Edom. The central covenant text, however, is Genesis 27:27-29, which recounts to Jacob the blessing of his dying father. There Isaac prayed that Jacob may exercise regnal power over nations and even over his own brothers. He then asserted in the style of blessing that those who curse Jacob will be cursed and those who bless him will be blessed (v. 29). On subsequent occasions the covenant pledge was confirmed by Isaac (28:3-4) and by Yahweh Himself (28:13-14; 35:9-15; 46:2-4). The unbroken thread throughout is the promise of nationhood, kings, land, and most important, the ministry of Jacob (=Israel) as the means of blessing all the earth.

Tokens of the nature and function of the Abrahamic Covenant, the full expression of which came to pass only after the Exodus deliverance and Sinaitic Covenant, may be found throughout the patriarchal narratives of Genesis and indeed may be the principal thrust of those narratives. Attention first may be addressed to the significance of land.

Land is essential to any meaningful definition of dominion and nationhood. The very creation of the heavens and the earth, in fact, was to provide a locus in which the reigning purposes of God for mankind would be carried out. The Garden of Eden then became the microcosmic expression of kingdom territory, the place where God dwelt on earth in a unique way and where He had fellowship with His image, His vice-regent. This is surely the background against which the eschatological descriptions of the eternal kingdom as a paradisal garden find their source.

The violent disruption and alienation occasioned by sin resulted in man's expulsion from the garden, but it did not terminate either the Adamic mandate or its need for a geographical arena in which to function. Adam had been told that though the center of his covenant activity was the garden, he was to move beyond that narrow base and fill the earth with his descendants. The garden, then, was the hub but not the exclusive realm of man's existence. It bespoke the divine intention to inhabit certain places that by His very presence would then be holy, but it did not suggest that He was limited by them.

With this in mind, it becomes easier to understand the importance of the land promises attached to the Abrahamic Covenant. The patriarch was told to "go to the land I will show you" (Gen. 12:1). Having arrived in Canaan he heard further, "To your offspring I will give his land" (12:7). The definition of the land, "from the river of Egypt to the great river, the Euphrates" (15:18), further specifies both its historical and geographical reality and its extent.

Canaan thus became the focus of God's redemptive and reigning activity on the earth. This explains why the patriarchs and their Israelite descendants hallowed the land and valued it as a theological sine qua non.[41] Testimony to this is the erection of altars at significant sites, places that Yahweh particularly invested with His presence (Gen. 12:7; 13:18; 26:25; 33:20; 35:1, 7). The patriarchal desire (still alive in pious Judaism today) to be buried in the Holy Land also attests to its special association with the dwelling place of Yahweh. The biblical witness is that Israel is inconceivable without land, whether in historical or eschatological times.

The promise of multiplication of descendants also is part and parcel of the Abrahamic Covenant and is in fulfillment of the original command to "be fruitful and increase in number." Just as the patriarchal seed was to be as numerous as the stars (Gen. 15:5), the dust (13:16), and the sand of the seashore (22:17; 32:12), so the whole earth would be overspread by humanity in accord with the purpose of God.

Evidence of the twin problems (and blessings) of land and population is seen early on in the struggle between Abraham and Lot over grazing lands. "The land could not support them while they stayed together, for their possessions were . . . great" (Gen. 13:6). As a result they separated and Abraham was assigned "the length and breadth of the land" (13:17). Later Abraham bought a burial spot at Machpelah (23:18-20) where his wife (23:19), he himself (25:9), his son Isaac (49:31), and his grandson Jacob (49:29-30) were buried. The blessing of great population came to pass, however, not in Canaan but in Egypt. The seventy of Israel who descended there grew to a mighty host so numerous as to threaten the security of mighty Egypt itself (Ex. 1:1-7, 9, 12, 20, etc.). All through preexilic times Israel enjoyed the benefit of land and people, and only when it became apparent that she had forfeited her covenant privileges were both so violently and irretrievably taken from her.

The third element of the patriarchal covenant—that Abraham's seed would be the occasion of blessing or cursing of the nations—also may be traced in the historical account. As noted, this functional aspect of the covenant corresponds to the mandate to "fill the earth and subdue it" and to rule over all things. Israel as the seed, then, served as the reigning agent of Almighty God in the sense at least of dispensing His blessing on the one hand or judgment on the other.

Patriarchal dominion and intercessory ministry are clear from Genesis 12. Pharaoh "treated Abram well for [Sarah's] sake" (12:16), and yet Yahweh inflicted Pharaoh with all kinds of maladies for Sarah's sake (v. 17). In the account of the

---

41. Though Brueggemann surely exaggerates when he says that "land is a central, if not *the central theme* of biblical faith" (italics his), it clearly is a dominant Old Testament theological motif (Walter Brueggemann, *The Land* [Philadelphia: Fortress, 1977], p. 3).

kings of the east, Abraham prevailed (14:13-16) because of divine intervention (v. 20). In his encounter with Yahweh at Mamre, Abraham interceded on behalf of Sodom and Gomorrah (18:16-21), a plea that God heard because He would not hide from His chosen one what He planned to do (v. 17).

The Philistine Abimelech also came to know the alternation of cursing and blessing from his contact with Abraham (Gen. 20:3, 7, 17). He recognized that God was with Abraham (21:22), and he benefited from the friendship the two of them solemnized by covenant (21:27-34). Later on Abimelech came to know Isaac and envied him for his success and prosperity (26:12-17). Wherever Isaac dug wells he found water, the refreshment of which was enjoyed also by the Philistines.

The Jacob stories are rich in allusion to the blessing that was possible through friendly association with the patriarch. Laban, devious to the end, had to confess that Yahweh had blessed him on account of Jacob (Gen. 30:27). Jacob himself enriched his brother, Esau, for Yahweh had blessed him beyond measure (33:11). Jacob's son Joseph clearly was the source of blessing for Egypt in time of catastrophic famine. Even before his elevation to great power, Joseph was perceived by Potiphar to be the explanation for his remarkable success. "The Lord blessed the household of the Egyptian because of Joseph" (39:5).

GENESIS IN THEOLOGICAL RETROSPECT

The book of Genesis, written presumably on the eve of Israel's conquest of Canaan, serves at least two clear canonical and theological purposes. First, it satisfies Israel's immediate need to know of her origins, her purpose, her prospects, and her destiny. These questions are explicitly or implicitly addressed in such a way as to leave Israel in no doubt that she came into existence in fulfillment of divine purpose and promise. But that purpose and promise are hinged to a more ultimate design, an overarching plan of which Israel is not the object but the means: namely, the creation and domination of the earth and all other things by God through His image, the human race. Israel thus came to see herself as important to the purposes of God but not coextensive to those purposes. Man, having sinned and so having forfeited his privileges as regent, was brought back to fellowship with God by sovereign grace so that he could resume his privileges as spelled out in the Adamic mandate. In that condition, with its liabilities and imperfections, the believing remnant community would model before the world the meaning of dominion and would proclaim and mediate the saving blessings of the Lord to it. The patriarchal seed, Israel herself, was that remnant, a nation that would exist as a microcosm of the kingdom of God and the vehicle through which the messianic king would come to reign over all creation (Gen. 49:10).

A THEOLOGY OF EXODUS

THE EXODUS AS ROYAL ELECTION

The choice of Israel as a servant people was already implicit in the patriarchal covenant statements (Gen. 12:1-3; 15:13-21; 18:18; 22:18; 26:3-4; etc.), but not until the Exodus deliverance did the nation as such come into historical existence. The Exodus, therefore, is of utmost theological importance as an act of God marking out a decisive moment in Israel's history, an event marking her transition from a people to a nation. But it transcends even this in significance, for, properly understood, the Exodus also is precisely the event and the moment that coincides with the historical expression of God's election of Israel. The choice of Israel as the special people of Yahweh occurred not at Sinai but in the land of Goshen. The Exodus was the elective event; Sinai was its covenant formalization.

That this is the intent of the canonical structure may be seen in a careful perusal of the early chapters of Exodus, which are replete with allusions to this very order of events. The Hebrew people, until the Red Sea deliverance, were seen as heirs of the patriarchal covenant promises to be sure, but their election to servanthood as a historical and even theological event took decisive form only in the redemptive act itself.

While Moses was in Midianite exile, the king of Egypt died, thus providing opportunity for Moses to return. More important, however, was the prompting of the Lord, who "remembered his covenant with Abraham, with Isaac and with Jacob" (Ex. 2:24). This statement clearly connects the ancient promises with the imminent act of salvation. Then in formulaic covenant language the Lord appeared to Moses in the burning bush and identified Himself as "the God of your father, the God of Abraham, the God of Isaac and the God of Jacob" (3:6). He came, He said, to deliver "My people" and to bring them to the land of promise (3:8). When Moses asked by what name God was pleased to reveal Himself to the people, he was told that it was Yahweh, "the God of your fathers" (3:15). Once more the thread binding the patriarchs to their Hebrew descendants is strongly affirmed, and yet the moment of choice grounded in a decisive event remained unfulfilled.

On the eve of Moses' departure for Egypt, Yahweh appeared again and instructed Moses to tell Pharaoh that "Israel is my firstborn son" and that His son must be set free of Egyptian dominion or Pharaoh himself would suffer the loss of his own eldest son (Ex. 5:22-23). This bold language of kinship hints at an elective, adoptive relationship that goes beyond the promise of patriarchal seed, as glorious as that was.[42] Israel then is not only a nation among nations, set apart by virtue of her descent from Abraham, but also a nation distinct and apart from others because she is the very firstborn of God. Adoption is still only a term of relationship and not of function. Israel is the child of God as heir of the elective grace extended to Abraham, but her servanthood—her functional task—is not thereby apparent.

Further evidence of this bifurcation between sonship and servanthood appears in the second grand revelation to Moses—the one of God as Yahweh, in Exodus 6:29. Here the Lord repeated the names of the patriarchs. He said that to them He was preeminently El Shaddai but now was known as Yahweh. He was the ground of the redemptive promise—the Almighty One; but now as Yahweh He was its

---

42. Shalom M. Paul, "Adoption Formulae: A Study of Cuneiform and Biblical Legal Clauses," *MAARAV* 2 (1979-80): 178.

effecter. The need now was not for a promise of deliverance but for the act itself.

Thus, the Lord said, "I have remembered My covenant," and as Yahweh He said, "I will bring you out," "I will free you from being slaves [and] will redeem you," and, "I will take you as my own people, and I will be your God" (Ex. 6:5-7). Of crucial importance is the language of redemption that would make of Israel "my own" people, for Israel had already been identified as the child of God and national heir of the patriarchal seed promises. What is new here is the role Israel was to play, her function as the servant people. Complete vindication of this understanding must now be undertaken.

EXODUS 19:4-6 AND COVENANT SERVANTHOOD

Without doubt Exodus 19:4-6 is the most theologically significant text in the book of Exodus, for it is the linchpin between the patriarchal promises of the sonship of Israel and the Sinaitic Covenant whereby Israel became the servant nation of Yahweh.[43] It embraces the Exodus event, which marked the election of Israel, and offers to the elected people opportunity for the privileged role of mediation between the sovereign Lord and the whole realm of creation. It is important therefore that attention be focused here in more than usual detail.

The passage begins with a review of the historical process by which Israel was brought to the present moment of decision. Yahweh affirmed that He had vanquished Egypt, the former sovereign of Israel, and on eagles' wings had brought the people to Himself. This supports the contention already proposed that it was the Exodus miracle itself that effected the covenant relationship, at least from the divine viewpoint, and not the negotiations at Sinai. And it further distinguishes between the sonship of Israel, which existed by virtue of Israel's descent from Abraham, and Israel's status as servant people. Her sonship had already been affirmed, for it was Israel as son who was being redeemed. Therefore, when Yahweh now said, "I . . . brought you to myself" (19:4), it must be in reference to another relationship, one spelled out in this very passage.

Before that is addressed, however, it is important to note briefly (for now) the instrument by which the new relationship will be effected, namely, the so-called Sinaitic (or Mosaic) Covenant. Yahweh revealed to Moses and the people that "if you obey me fully and keep my covenant then out of all nations you will be my treasured possession" (19:5). This is a remarkably striking avowal for many reasons. First, it is clear that the covenant in view was conditional or had at least some conditional elements. This stands in stark contrast both to the Genesis covenants, which were generically and theologically unconditional grants, and to the establishment of Israel as the people of Yahweh by virtue of the Exodus redemption, itself an unconditional act of sovereign grace. That Israel was (and still is) the people of God is a matter of unqualified divine initiative; that Israel was to function in a special way as the people of God would now rest in Israel's free choice.

43. Dumbrell, pp. 80-81.

Second, Israel, having submitted to the covenant terms, would be above all nations the "treasured possession" of the Lord. This term, *sĕgullāh* in Hebrew, refers to personal property.[44] Yahweh is the sovereign of all nations, but He holds Israel among His choice possessions, one that serves a special purpose in His grand design.

That purpose emerges in Exodus 19:6: "you will be for me a kingdom of priests and a holy nation." As many scholars have noted, there is a poetic balance in the passage[45] in which "out of all nations you will be my treasured possession" (*sĕgullāh mikkol-hâ'ammîm*), "a kingdom of priests" (*mamleket kōhănîm*), and a "holy nation" (*gôy qādôš*) are virtually synonymous and mutually interpretive. That is, Israel's value as God's possession lay precisely in her function as a holy kingdom of priests.

THE SINAI COVENANT TEST

The conditional nature of the covenant offered by Yahweh (Ex. 19:4-6) and accepted by the people (19:8) is evident beyond any doubt by the form of the covenant text itself. This document, consisting of Exodus 20:1–23:33, has for many years now been identified as a sovereign-vassal treaty text analogous to political instruments attested to all over the ancient Near East from Old Akkadian to Neo-Assyrian times.[46] Most particularly the Sinaitic form resembles that of documents recovered from the New Kingdom Hittite capital city of Hattushash. Those documents regulated affairs between the various great kings of the Hittites and their subordinate, dependent allies. Like the Hittite documents, the Exodus text and its related material (especially Exodus 24) contains six indispensable elements that make possible the identification of its literary form.

Standard in these treaties was an initial preamble statement identifying the parties involved in the covenant arrangement and, in the Hittite versions, doing so in grandiloquent and exaggerated terms in reference to the king. The preamble in the biblical text is Exodus 20:2a, a statement incomparably sublime in its simplicity. All that is said is, "[I] am the Lord your God." There is no need here for the heaping up of platitudes and honorifics, for the majesty and infinite power of the great King is inherent in the covenant name itself and in His elective, redeeming work on Israel's behalf.

This leads to the second element of the covenant form, the historical prologue. This generally consisted of a lengthy discourse concerning the relationship between the Hittite sovereign and his ancestors and the vassal ruler and his ancestors. It presented the former as a beneficent protector who acted unselfishly on behalf of his weaker friend. It frequently emphasized that the protector's grace

44. Brown, Driver, and Briggs, p. 688.
45. So, for example, John I. Durham, *Exodus,* Word Biblical Commentary, vol. 3 (Waco, Tex.: Word, 1987), pp. 261-62.
46. George E. Mendenhall, "Covenant Forms in Israelite Tradition," *Biblical Archaeologist* 17 (1954): 50-76.

was extended despite the waywardness and disloyalty of the vassal. The prologue was designed to establish the historical basis and framework on and within which the covenant relationship could be successfully undertaken.

The biblical account is again startlingly concise and to the point: "I . . . brought you out of Egypt, out of the land of slavery" (Ex. 20:2*b*). In contrast to the boring, self-serving litany of the Hittite kings stands the majestic affirmation of Yahweh's claim to covenant initiation and fidelity—He is the one who rescued His people from their helpless and hopeless bondage to Egyptian despotism. Such a king was surely qualified to be and to do all His servant people required.

The third section of a sovereign-vassal treaty was the stipulation section, which on occasion was subdivided between a general set of requirements and one that outlined specific and detailed requirements. Frequently the latter would be tantamount to amendments to or explanations of the principles embodied in the general stipulations.

This is the case in the Sinaitic model, for Exodus 20:3-17 (the "Ten Commandments") contains the general stipulation clauses, whereas 20:22–23:33 (the "Book of the Covenant") corresponds to the detailed exposition or specific stipulation section. This distinction is clear from the interruption of the document itself between 20:17 and 20:23 and also from the technical terms used later on to describe the respective parts. Exodus 24:3 points out that Moses told the people "all the Lord's words and laws." "Words" is a translation of the Hebrew *dĕbārîm,* a term used elsewhere to describe the Ten Commandments, whereas "laws" renders *mišpātîm,* regularly used to speak of specific statutes. The relationship of these two stipulation sections will be explored in detail later on.

The fourth division, provision for the deposit of the document and for its periodic public reading, lies outside the Exodus covenant text per se. In fact, only the deposit of the text is mentioned here, though the Deuteronomy version includes also a requirement for public reading (Deut. 6:4-9). The importance of the placing of the covenant document within the Tabernacle (and later the Temple), the earthly residence of Yahweh, may be seen, however, in the Ark of the Covenant's being the first article of "furniture" listed in the instructions for Tabernacle construction (Ex. 25:10-22). It was a chest of acacia wood that served as both a receptacle for the Sinaitic Covenant text and a symbolic throne on which Yahweh the Sovereign could sit in regal splendor among His people.

Virtually every sovereign-vassal treaty incorporated a list of deities before whom the solemn oaths of mutual fidelity were sworn. These "witnesses" could not, of course, be invoked in the case of the biblical covenants, for there were no gods but Yahweh and no higher powers to whom appeal could be made in the event of covenant violation. The counterpart of this is not lacking, however, for the ceremony of covenant-making described in Exodus 24 clearly includes "witnesses" to the transaction. These are in the form of the altar, which represented Yahweh, and the twelve pillars, which represented the twelve tribes. Although there is no explicit word to the effect that these objects were witnesses as well as representations, the use of inanimate objects in that capacity elsewhere certainly allows for that possibility here.[47]

The sixth and last sine qua non of vassal treaty form was the recitation of curses and blessings that would attend the vassal's disobedience and obedience respectively. Again these are lacking in the Sinaitic document itself and even in its literary proximity. Such a list does occur, however, in Leviticus 26 where, in clearly covenantal language, blessing is promised to the nation for obedience to the "decrees" (*ḥăqqîm*) and "commands" (*miṣwôt*) (v. 3) and curse is threatened for disobedience. The "blessing section" (vv. 2-13) is predicated on the covenant formula of Exodus 20:2: "I am the Lord your God, who brought you out of Egypt so that you would no longer be slaves to the Egyptians" (Lev. 26:13). Its central thrust, however, ties into the ancient Abrahamic Covenant: "I will look on you with favor and make you fruitful and increase your numbers, and I will keep my covenant with you" (26:9). The blessing for covenant obedience, then, is the fulfillment of the Abrahamic Covenant expectations for Israel, the seed of Abraham.

The "curse section" (Lev. 26:14-39) associates curse with covenant violation (v. 15), an act of rebellion that reverses the promises of fertility, prosperity, and security in the land. Continuing unrepentance would at last bring deportation of the people and desolation of the land, a reverse of the Exodus event itself by which the servant people of Yahweh became slaves of another lord.

That the curses and blessings of Leviticus 26 are part and parcel of the Sinaitic treaty text, which in the strict sense is limited to Exodus 20-23, is established by the last verse of the chapter. As a summary statement that includes not only Exodus 20-23 but also the remainder of Exodus and Leviticus 1-26, the observation is made that "these are the decrees (*ḥuqqîm*), the laws (*mišpăṭîm*) and the regulations (*tôrôt*) that the Lord established on Mount Sinai between Himself and the Israelites through Moses" (Lev. 26:46).

By its very form as well as language the Sinai Covenant is a compact in the mold of a sovereign-vassal treaty. It thus differs from the Adamic-Noahic-Abrahamic Covenant(s) in that respect, though it functions in continuity with and fulfillment of them. It is the vehicle by which Israel, the chosen seed of Abraham, obligated herself to be Yahweh's servant people in mediating the salvific grace of God to His fallen and alienated creation. The election of Israel to be the people of Yahweh by promise and redemption was unconditional, but her function and capacity as a holy nation and priestly kingdom depended on her faithful adherence to the covenant made through Moses. This will become more clear in the subsequent investigation of Deuteronomy, the fullest expression of the vassal treaty that bound Israel to her God.

ISRAEL AND COVENANT RESPONSIBILITY

How Israel was to live out her national life in light of her commitment is spelled out in the Sinaitic (and later Deuteronomic) Covenant, specifically in the great

47. Deuteronomy 4:26; 30:19; 31:28. See Meredith Kline, *Treaty of the Great King* (Grand Rapids: Eerdmans, 1963), p. 15.

stipulation sections of that covenant text. It has been customary in biblical scholarship to refer to the Ten Commandments and the following Book of the Covenant as *law* in the sense of ordinary jurisprudence. Even though this is not a totally erroneous notion,[48] the more recent recognition that these sections are nothing less than the stipulation clauses in a treaty document has had the salutary effect of locating them more precisely within their historical, literary, and theological milieu.[49] These stipulations are designed not to regulate human behavior at large, though the principles they embody are heuristic and timeless, but they find their setting in a contract whose purpose is to provide legal, moral, and religious guidelines for a special people chosen for a special task. And even for these people the regulations were not a means whereby salvation could be obtained—that was symbolized by the Passover and the Exodus—but an instruction manual by which the covenant people were to order their national life in their mission as a priestly, mediatorial people. The stipulations were *tôrāh* in the sense of instruction.

Having established the nature of Israel's law as covenant stipulation, it is still important to remember that the great stipulation section of the treaty is itself divided into two parts, as already noted. The first, the Ten Commandments, is completely different in form and function from the second section, the Book of the Covenant. As many scholars have shown, the Commandments are couched in the structure of apodictic law.[50] This refers to their general, unconditional, principial nature expressed in almost every instance by a "Thou shalt not." The Book of the Covenant, on the other hand, is cast in the form of casuistic law. Its regulations address specific instances or classes of incidents and usually consist of protasis-apodosis statements, that is, "If a person does thus and so, then here is the penalty."[51]

A further observation is that the shorter, general stipulation section is akin to a "constitution" to which the longer set of stipulations relates as a body of amendments or, better, examples of specific application. So each of the Ten Commandments finds elaboration in the ensuing Book of the Covenant, with the result that the principles are fleshed out with precise reference to practical, everyday life.

THE COVENANT AND THE TEN COMMANDMENTS

It is impossible here to undertake detailed exegesis of the verses that make up the Decalogue (Ex. 20:3-17), nor is that necessary because their fullest meaning

---

48. Though he has to excise the Decalogue from its covenant setting, Phillips still makes a case for the Decalogue as fulfilling a civil and legal function as well as a covenant function (Anthony Phillips, "The Decalogue—Ancient Israel's Criminal Law," *Journal of Semitic Studies* 34 [1983]: 1-20).

49. Erhard Gerstenberger, "Covenant and Commandment," *Journal of Biblical Literature* 84 (1965): 43; Walther Eichrodt, "Covenant and Law," *Interpretation* 20 (1966): 309-11.

50. The fundamental study is Albrecht Alt, "The Origins of Israelite Law," in *Essays on Old Testament History and Religion* (Garden City, N.Y.: Doubleday, 1968), pp. 101-71.

51. For an excellent discussion of the form-critical analyses involved, see Harry W. Gilmer, *The If–You Form in Israelite Law* (Missoula, Mont.: Scholars Press, 1975), pp. 1-26.

derives from their canonical situation as covenant stipulation. It is with that setting in mind that the following observations are made.

The first commandment. This first commandment directly addresses the heart of the relationship presupposed by the sovereign vassal treaty. Yahweh, by virtue of His election and saving deliverance of His people from another lord (Egypt), commands them to undertake and maintain an attitude of undivided loyalty to Him. "You shall have no other gods before me" (v. 3) is a categorical affirmation of Yahweh's exclusive claims to lordship and worship. To violate this commandment is to repudiate the entire covenant relationship, for it is nothing short of high treason.

The second commandment. This precept (vv. 4-6) prohibits the representation of Yahweh by any kind of idol or likeness, for to do so is to limit the transcendent and ineffable God and to confuse the Creator with His creation. To bow down and to worship (lit. "to serve") such an image constitutes failure to recognize and respond properly to the sovereignty of the Lord. The motive for obedience of this requirement is twofold and is expressed in the form of an abbreviated curse-and-blessing formula. Those who practice idolatry are the "haters" of Yahweh (v. 5) whereas those who do not are His "lovers" (v. 6). In covenant context these verbs are most instructive, for "to hate" means to reject and "to love" means to choose.[52] Idolators, by their very act of idolatry, reject the true God as He has chosen to disclose Himself and choose instead a figment of their own imagination. On the other hand, those who love (choose) Him, that is, who obey Him (v. 6), become the recipients of His reciprocal love, His *ḥesed.* Loyalty to Yahweh on the part of His servant people will bring the response of loyal and unfailing commitment to them.

The third commandment. The third commandment connects the name of Yahweh—an extension of His very being—with Yahweh Himself. The "misuse" of the divine name (v. 7) is tantamount to sacrilege, for in the ancient Near East and in Israel names not only described the attributes, character, and destinies of the individuals named but became at times synonymous with the person. This is certainly true with reference to God as the entire biblical witness attests (Ex. 23:20-21; 1 Kings 8:33; Pss. 54:3; 86:9; 118:26; 148:5; Phil. 2:9-10; etc.). To misuse His name or to use it without purpose (*laššāw'*) or in an unseemly manner is to attempt to manipulate God to human ends and purposes. It is an arrogant effort by the vassal to gain advantage for himself by prostituting that holy name and Person, thus reversing the role for which he was brought into covenant fellowship.

The fourth commandment. This one shifts the focus from proper recognition of and respect for the Person of Yahweh as the Lord of Israel to a regulation of the exercise of man's dominion over the earth. He is to "remember the Sabbath

---

52. W. L. Moran, "The Ancient Near Eastern Background of the Love of God in Deuteronomy," *Catholic Biblical Quarterly* 25 (1963): 77-87.

day by keeping it holy" (Ex. 20:8). This is achieved by the interruption of ordinary labor on the seventh day by the Israelite family, its servants, and even its beasts of burden. The theological significance of this prohibition must be gathered from the motive clauses (v. 11*a*, 11*b*), which suggest that the reasons for setting the day apart are (1) that Yahweh made all things in six days and rested on the seventh and (2) that He celebrated that cessation of creative work by setting aside the rest day for a memorial. Creation establishes the uniquely sovereign claims of Yahweh and, as a most profound historical event, it must be remembered by man so that man will all the more remain loyal to His covenant commitment.[53] The credentials of Yahweh as Covenant-maker are remembered and recited. He is Lord over both space and time. Man as God's vice-regent and image must also cease his labor in anticipation of a "day of rest" of both historical and eschatological dimensions. In terms of the Sinaitic Covenant, the Sabbath was to remind Israel of her own role as servant people and of the fulfillment of that role in the ultimate day of rest.

The fifth commandment. The transition introduced by the fourth commandment continues in the fifth, "Honor your father and your mother" (20:12). The reference to labor in the fourth is now connected to that of land in the fifth, for obedience with respect to the proper estimation of parents will result in long life in the land. More important is the reminder of order and structure within the governmental framework of Yahweh's dominion. In the total covenant relationship there are spheres of responsibility and function. The vassal, though ultimately responsible only to the Great King, must, in keeping with the hierarchical structure of his society, honor those placed over him. The covenant of Yahweh with Israel is later expressed in familial terms, such as husband and wife (Hos. 2:2-8) and father and child (11:1-4), so it is appropriate that human parents be honored as the very representatives of Yahweh to whom the utmost deference and honor must be paid. To honor the parents is to honor Yahweh and to dishonor them is nothing short of covenant violation and disloyalty. The fifth commandment, then, pertains to vertical dimensions of human relationship. There are levels of authority (the parent-child being only one example) that must be scrupulously respected and maintained, inasmuch as they reflect the essence of what it means to have dominion under God.

The sixth commandment. "You shall not murder" (Ex. 20:13), is an apodictic way of restating the ancient *lex talionis* of the Noahic Covenant: "Whoever sheds the blood of man, by man shall his blood be shed; for in the image of God has God made man" (Gen. 9:6). Of particular significance here is the motive clause because it clarifies the profound heinousness of the terse form of the command in the Decalogue. A man must not murder his fellow man, for such a murder is in effect a lethal attack against God Himself. Because life is sacred to God generally (hence, blood must not be spilled on the ground carelessly or eaten) and that of

53. Matitiahu Tsevat, "The Basic Meaning of the Biblical Sabbath," *Zeitschrift für die Alttestamentliche Wissenschaft* 84 (1972): 495.

man especially (in that he is the image of God), the violation of man to the point of death is an affront to the sovereignty of God, an assault on His earthly representative. Only this theological rationale can adequately explain the severity of the punishment for murder, which is a capital offense, and account for the trans-Israelite, universal condemnation and redressing of the act. The covenant violation implied by a vassal taking the life of a vassal (at least within the context of the Sinaitic Covenant) is obvious.

The seventh commandment. A similar infringement of covenant expectation occurs with disobedience to the next commandment, "You shall not commit adultery" (Ex. 20:14). Adultery on the human level is unfaithfulness, indeed, covenant violation, and so it is an apt analogue to covenant infidelity on a higher plane, the divine-human. The biblical revelation is pervasive with phrases such as "whoring after other gods," imagery that speaks of Israel's abandoning the redeeming Sovereign in favor of another who has no covenant claim or legitimacy (Ex. 34:15-16; Lev. 17:7; 20:5; Deut. 31:16; Judg. 2:17; Ps. 73:27; Ezek. 6:9; etc.). Adultery then is the mixing of the true and the false, the holy and the profane, the pure and the corrupt. It is an overstepping of the lines that circumscribe the trusting relationship between partners who have made mutual pledge of loyal commitment. It is covenant rupture of the most serious kind.

The eighth commandment. This command concerns an essential for vassalage: possessions and their proper management and disposition. "You shall not steal" (Ex. 20:15) takes on its proper and fullest meaning only as one recognizes that all people (and especially Israel) are vassals of the Creator-Redeemer God who has gifted them and who expects reasonable stewardship of them. The King has not only allocated realms of authority and responsibility but has also given each vassal the means by which to achieve on the earth what He has in view for each. To steal, therefore, is to commit at least three sins against the King: (1) to take from another what he has been given and needs in order to exercise his stewardship; (2) to fail to fulfill one's own assignment on the basis of what God has given; and (3) to undermine the wise purposes of God who gives to each according to his role and ability. All things, material and immaterial, belong to God and must be dispensed by His gracious pleasure.

The ninth commandment. Correct relationships between vassals in the network of covenant affiliation are summed up by the injunction "You shall not give false testimony against your neighbor" (Ex. 20:16). Though "neighbor" (*rēaʿ*) does frequently designate the stranger (*gēr*) or even the foreigner (11:2), in the framework of a covenant document it clearly refers to a fellow Israelite.[54] The language is that of technical, legal terminology, and in a most immediate and practical sense of commandment teaches that in a court of law one must not offer perjured testimony concerning an accused party (cf. Ex. 23:1, 7; Deut. 19:15-19). The word for

54. Durham, p. 296.

testimony (*'ēd*) is cognate to the standard term (*'ēdût*) employed for the statutes of a covenant document in Israel and the ancient Near East.[55] Therefore, this commandment suggests at least the impropriety of any relationship between covenant brothers outside the covenant itself; irrelevant standards must not be brought to bear in governing relationships within the covenant community. In the fellowship of common covenant commitment, negotiations between an Israelite and his fellow must be as reliable and trustworthy as that between a vassal and his lord. To bear false witness is to stir up strife within the community and to disrupt the smooth and orderly functioning of the kingdom.

The tenth commandment. The "last" commandment, that prohibiting covetousness (Ex. 20:17), is, as has been noted by virtually all scholars, in the realm of the subjective or internal.[56] The other commandments inevitably manifest themselves in an outward expression to some degree or other, but covetousness can theoretically exist only in the mind and heart and never betray itself in external act. The moment it does so it is no longer covetousness. For that reason it is an apt climax to the stipulation section of the covenant document. It raises the covenant requirement to a higher, more spiritual dimension and properly locates the motive for human action, good or bad, in the volitional side of man. Improper desire is a more "spiritual" level of theft, adultery, and the like and is forbidden for that reason.

Even if covetousness never finds fruition in overt behavior, it is still a serious breach of covenant regulation because the Lord who knows the heart is offended by it. It is an expression of dissatisfaction with one's possessions and with his general lot if life. It violates (if only in spirit) the sanctity of personal property and relationships and tends to disrupt the balanced and equitable jurisdiction assigned by the Sovereign of the kingdom. In effect, covetousness impugns the wisdom and goodness of God by questioning His bestowal of life's blessings in accord with His omniscient plan.

In conclusion, the formal and theological function of the Decalogue becomes clear when viewed in the context of the redemptive act of the Exodus and the elective purposes of God for Israel as a vassal people brought into covenant fellowship with Him in order to serve as a kingdom of priests. The Abrahamic promise certified that the patriarch would be blessed with innumerable seed, that that seed would inherit a land, and that the land would provide a geographic base from which the elect nation could become a means by which God would bless the world. The Exodus had freed that nation from its bondage to another lord so that it might begin to discharge its responsibilities under Yahweh. The covenant text, and most particularly the Ten Commandments, provides the guidelines within which that privileged people was to order itself if it was indeed to be a holy nation capable of both exhibiting the kingdom of God and mediating its saving benefits and promises to the larger world of alienated humanity.

55. K. A. Kitchen, *Ancient Orient and Old Testament* (London: Tyndale, 1966), pp. 106-8.
56. Brevard S. Childs, *The Book of Exodus: A Critical, Theological Commentary* (Philadelphia: Westminster, 1974), pp. 425-28.

THE BOOK OF THE COVENANT

The Ten Commandments, as argued above, are formally the general stipulation section of the Sinaitic Covenant document recorded in Exodus 20:1–23:33. The so-called special stipulation section that follows the Decalogue consists of a number of statutes cast in the form of case (or casuistic) law, which together are designated "the Book of the Covenant." It is clear that these statutes are not exhaustive in scope but are illustrative of the manner in which the principles of covenant stipulation are to be applied in individual cases. They also amplify and clarify the intent of those stipulations and even go beyond them, particularly in areas of cultic principle and practice.[57]

It is impossible here to deal with all the individual examples of legislation in the Book of the Covenant, but it will be helpful to survey the collection at least and to draw appropriate theological conclusions.[58]

The Book of the Covenant begins technically with Exodus 20:22, having been separated from the Decalogue by a brief narrative (vv. 18-21) describing the people's response to the phenomena accompanying Moses' encounter with Yahweh on Sinai (cf. 19:16-25). The technical term "ordinances" (*mišpāṭîm*), which describes the specific stipulations of the covenant, does not occur until 21:1, so 20:22-26 serves as an introduction to the stipulation section. This introduction underlines Yahweh's exclusivity, His self-revelation to His people, and His demand to be worshiped wherever He localizes His name and in association with appropriate altars.

The Book of the Covenant is concluded in precisely the same way. Its stipulations end with 23:13[59] and there follows a section (vv. 14-33) in which Yahweh commanded a thrice annual appearance of the community before Him (vv. 14-17) to present sacrifices offered in the appropriate manner (vv. 18-19). He then promised to go with them to the land of promise and to drive out their adversaries provided they maintain their covenant commitment to Him by destroying the images of alien gods and refusing to make alliance with them (vv. 20-33).

The casuistic covenant stipulations. It is worth noting that the stipulations are enfolded within matching frames that stress the exclusivity of Yahweh (Ex. 20:22-23; cf. 23:24-25, 32-33), His presence in specified places (20:24; cf. 23:14-17, 20, 28-31), and a proper protocol and ritual by which He may be approached by His servant people (20:24-26; cf. 23:18-19). It is within the context of a vertical covenant relationship, then, that the horizontal, societal, and interpersonal relationships of the Book of the Covenant take on their ultimate meaning.

Appropriately the first stipulation concerns bondage (21:2-6) because the

---

57. Ibid., p. 459.
58. For suggestions as to the arrangement of the stipulations in the Code, see C. M. Carmichael, "A Singular Method of Codification of Law in the Mishpatim," *Zeitschrift für die Alttestamentliche Wissenschaft* 84 (1972): 19-24.
59. For support of the analysis, see Durham, p. 332.

essence of the covenant was the deliverance of Israel by Yahweh from bondage to Egyptian domination. Hebrews who found themselves indentured to other Hebrews were allowed to go free in the seventh year, a fact that clearly relates the significance of redemption to creation. The universe was created by Yahweh in six days and on the seventh it entered into the rest of His sovereignty, a rest in which man shared the freedom of lordship. But the other side of the matter was the freedom of the slave to decide to remain with his master. This shifts the focus from that of deliverance from an evil master to commitment to a gracious one. The slave, given the opportunity to disrupt the relationship with his lord, declared his covenant loyalty by asserting that he loved his master (v. 5).[60] He followed this declaration by submitting to the slave mark (v. 6), thus bearing witness to the world of his voluntary vassalage and of his intention to serve his master forever. The analogy to Israel as a vassal people to Yahweh is obvious.

The second stipulation (21:7-11) is not a case of slavery in the strict sense but a marriage arrangement by a father in financial need. There was no automatic manumission as in the preceding case. This was certainly an accommodation to the prevailing custom of Israel's cultural world,[61] but the theological truth to be seen is the tempering of divine mercy in the recognition of the girl as something other than mere chattel. If the husband to whom she was "sold" did not live up to the obligations expected of him, she could return to her father and her husband relinquished financial claims. Thus the rights of the helpless maiden were protected and the institution of marriage, which itself is a covenant arrangement modeled after that of God with His people, was preserved and safeguarded.

The third stipulation (21:12-17) concerns homicide, assault on parents, kidnapping, and the cursing of parents—all of which were capital offenses. They all take on profound consequences because they impinge on man as God's image. In the first case, because murder is an act of assault on God, an insubordination of indescribable proportions, the perpetrator must die (v. 12). Accidental homicide was not a capital crime, of course, and had its own special provisions for adjudication (v. 13; cf. Num. 35:22-23; Deut. 19:4-5). Any exception to capital punishment for murder lay in the grace of God as, for example, in the case of David's murder of Uriah (2 Sam. 12:13).

In the event of physical attack on parents (Ex. 21:15) the punishment again was death, for parents as God's representatives in the hierarchy of the covenant community commanded such reverence that injury to them was insubordination to the Sovereign Himself (cf. 20:12-13).[62] Even injury by word, that is, by cursing one's parent (21:17), was worthy of death for it was the same attitude of disrespect and covenant disloyalty.

60. For the "quasi-juridical" use of this term in extrabiblical texts, see Shalom Paul, *Studies in the Book of the Covenant in the Light of Cuneiform and Biblical Law* (Leiden: Brill, 1970), p. 49, n. 2.
61. Ibid., pp. 52-61.
62. Ibid., p. 64.

That kidnapping should warrant execution is also to be explained by the sacredness of man and his dignity as God's image. To steal or to buy and sell a human being is to regard him as something less than what he truly is in the eyes of the Lord, who is over all men in common.

The fourth stipulation refers to laws of physical assault (21:18-27). What they hold in common is the lack of premeditation, but in each case this did not absolve the guilty party of responsibility and consequence. In the event of altercation in which injury ensued, financial compensation had to be made to the aggrieved party (vv. 18-19). This was to preclude rash, intemperate behavior and to emphasize again the dignity of human beings under God. Likewise, even the injury or death of a slave had to be recompensed (vv. 20-21), for even he was the image of God and not just property. If the mistreatment was abusive and not merely disciplinary (as vv. 20-21 seem to suggest), the slave had to be set free (vv. 26-27), for the image of God, in whatever societal form it appeared, was at stake. If a third party was injured in a fight between two men, specifically a pregnant woman and/or her fetus (vv. 22-25), *lex talionis* had to be invoked.[63] That is, if there was no harm done, a monetary fine was sufficient, but if there was injury up to and including death, the guilty party was required to suffer in kind.

The next stipulation shares in common the relationship between man and beast insofar as injury and loss is concerned. If one owned an ox, for example, and that animal caused death or harm to another human being, it had to be slaughtered and its owner punished according to the status of the victim and the owner's previous knowledge of the animal's temperament (21:28-32). The fate of the ox gives clear evidence of the theological principle of the subordination of the animal world to human sovereignty. That the fatal goring of one ox by another required only compensation shows the relative insignificance of the animal-to-animal relationship (vv. 35-36).

If, however, an animal died from falling into a covered pit (21:33-34) or was stolen by a thief and then killed or sold (22:1-4), its owner in the first case could demand fair compensation (since it was an accident) and in the second case could require fourfold or fivefold restitution. Furthermore if the thief was slain by the homeowner while in the act of breaking and entering in the night, the homicide was justifiable. In no other kind of theft was such harsh penalty applied, so it is clear that the bond between an animal and its owner (i.e., its master) is of a different kind from that of a man and his inanimate possessions.[64]

Exodus 22:5-17 pertains to what might loosely be called laws of property. The

---

63. Meredith G. Kline, *"Lex Talionis* and the Human Fetus," *Journal of the Evangelical Theological Society* 20 (1977); 193-201; H. Wayne House, "Miscarriage or Premature Birth: Additional Thoughts on Exodus 21:22-25," *Westminster Theological Journal* 41 (1978): 108-23. For talionic justice as a principle, see Paul, pp. 75-77.

64. Most scholars view Exodus 22:2-3 as a parenthesis explaining the fate of thieves in general. There is no reason, however, not to see the passage as a vital part of the context of the theft of animals in particular.

first case (v. 5) concerns crop damage suffered through the grazing of an unpenned animal, a violation that required even restitution. The second (v. 6) speaks to the same kind of loss, only through fire, and demanded the same penalty. The third case (vv. 7-15) involved the safekeeping of entrusted property. If it was stolen or (in the case of an animal) injured or killed, the trustee had to swear before the judges that he was innocent. If he was, he went free. If, however, he was party to the loss, he was required to pay double indemnity. The teaching in all this is that property, though not of ultimate value, nevertheless represents part of what an individual is. A man is not only who he is but what he possesses and to defraud him of those things for which he is responsible is to infringe on his own lordship. For one to borrow from his friend something that became damaged or lost in his absence was to require just compensation, unless he had paid a fee for its use in advance (vv. 14-15).

The stipulation concerning the seduction of a virgin (vv. 16-17) appears here perhaps as an extension of the previous requirements concerning laws of "property," for in this context the ensuing negotiation was between the seducer and the father of the maiden. In a sense she was his "property," a possession that had been violated and with respect to which a *mōhar* payment had to be made whether or not she became the wife of the perpetrator. The reason payment had to be given even if the girl did not became the wife of the seducer was that her virginity had been lost and she no longer could command a bride price. The father, then, had lost a valuable source of income, a loss that demanded compensation.[65]

The apodictic covenant stipulations. As many scholars recognize, the second half of the Book of the Covenant begins at Exodus 22:18 and the stipulations undergo a change in content to match what is clearly a change in form. The first half (Ex. 20:22–22:17) is fundamentally casuistic, whereas the latter half is not.[66] That is, the stipulations now are expressed as prescriptions or prohibitions with little or no reference to the penalty attached to violation in each case.

The unifying theme of the first stipulation of this section is that of covenant fidelity, first with reference to the Lord (22:18-20) and then with reference to fellow covenanters (22:21–23:9). A sorceress had to be killed because she was an envoy of false gods and a false religious system and therefore was treasonous (22:18). Bestiality is an abomination (v. 19) because man is a unique creature made to be the image of God and to rule over all things including animals. To place himself on a level with the brute beast is to surrender the sovereignty with which man was endowed and is thus an affront to God Himself. Sacrifice to false gods (v. 20) is so obviously an act of rebellion that its penalty could be nothing less than obliteration by *ḥērem* or the ban.

Loyalty to the covenant brother had to extend first to the sojourner (22:21), because the Israelites themselves were strangers in Egypt and suffered cruelty at

65. Ronald de Vaux, *Ancient Israel* (New York: McGraw-Hill, 1961), 1:26-27.
66. Childs, *Exodus,* p. 477.

despotic hands. Even more defenseless were the widows and orphans so they, the weakest members of the community, had to be protected and nurtured (vv. 22-24). The poor of the land also had to receive mercy and special material consideration, for the Lord, who is gracious, expects nothing less of those who represent Him on the earth. This concern finds expression here with respect to loans made to a poor brother (v. 25). Though interest could be charged to outsiders (Deut. 23:20-21), it could not to an Israelite, for to do so was to profit from his misfortune. If the poor man's garment was taken as surety for the loan, it had to be returned to him every evening so he would not suffer from the cold. The motive is clear: God is gracious, so those who serve Him must exhibit grace to the vulnerable around them (Ex. 22:26-27).

The reverse side of consideration of the poor and defenseless is proper respect for God and human rulers (22:28). To demonstrate the practical application of this attitude, the Israelite, in line with his role as the submissive vassal of Yahweh the Great King, was required to bear his tribute in the form of harvest of produce and firstborn of animal and of his own male progeny. That the firstborn were surrendered on the eighth day (v. 30) established the linkage with the Abrahamic Covenant (cf. Gen. 17:12) because the circumcision of the infant male was a hallmark of his identification as a member of the covenant community.

In conclusion of this section, the Lord urged holiness on His people, for to serve Him was tantamount to separation to Him and from all other masters (Ex. 22:31). This fundamental idea of holiness and separation carries with it moral and ethical overtones. Separation as a principle, then, must work itself out in patterns of practice and behavior. This was at the very heart of Israelite worship, as will be seen later. Meanwhile, and as an example only, the stipulation declared that any animal not ritually slaughtered could not be eaten. Besides ensuring the complete draining of the blood, the slaughter of animals for meat according to strict ritual requirements raised the act to the level of worship and set it within the context of covenant relationship.

The code next addresses the matter of justice (23:1-9). In line with the commandment about bearing false witness (20:16), the covenanter was not to be induced by social pressures to perjure himself or slander the innocent. Though the tendency could be to victimize the poor, one was also to take care that his compassion for the poor not alleviate him of the penalty of the law when it was due. In other words, justice must be evenhanded.

This was so much the case that even one's enemies had to be his beneficiaries. If the enemy's ox or donkey were lost it had to be returned, and if it lay fallen beneath a burden it, with its burden, had to be raised up and otherwise attended (23:4-5). The poor, the innocent, the foreigner—all had to receive protection of the law. This meant there could be no miscarriage of justice, whether through bias, bribery, or prejudice. The model is God Himself for He does not justify the wicked (v. 7); and the motive, especially with regard to the alien, is clear. Israel of all people ought to have known how to deal with the stranger with fairness and compassion, for she was a foreigner herself in the land of Egypt (v. 9).

In line with these principles of justice, particularly as they related to the poor and the alien, are instructions as to the welfare of those disadvantaged. God Himself had blessed His people with land. Now the bounty of that land was to be shared with the landless. The seventh year therefore had to be a sabbath year in which the land lay fallow, yielding only what grew up of its own accord (23:11-19). The poor in a sense became the owners of the land in that sabbath year, harvesting the fields and vineyards at will and, if anything remained, allowing the animals to forage unimpeded. Thus the dispensing of grace, which originates in the loving heart of God Himself, results in the blessing of the brute beast of the field.

This blessing of the sabbath year in which the earth itself could rest was matched by the sabbath day, which demanded that man and animal rest (23:12), a point articulated in the Decalogue with great emphasis (20:8-11). In summation of all the ordinances up to this point (i.e., from Ex. 21:2–23:12), the Lord enjoins on His people absolute compliance that centers once more on His uniqueness and exclusiveness (23:13).

Covenant pilgrimage and tribute. As argued previously, the stipulation section of the Book of the Covenant ends with the summation in Exodus 23:13. The next section (23:14-17) consists of the protocol of tribute that Israel the vassal was to follow in approaching Yahweh the King at stated times. The first of these was the presentation of unleavened bread (or *maṣṣôt*) at the time of the harvest of barley. This agricultural festival was, of course, linked to the historical event of the Exodus and the Passover (cf. 12:15-20). This therefore required, in addition, the presentation of the firstborn of both man and animal for redemption or sacrifice (34:18-20). How fitting that Israel, whose firstborn sons were delivered from death as well as from Egypt, should present her sons as living sacrifices to Yahweh in an act of tribute at the beginning of every religious year.

The second pilgrimage to the presence of the Lord (Ex. 23:16*a*) occurred fifty days later. This feast of harvest (*qaṣîr* or *šᵉbûôt*) celebrated the ripening of the wheat (34:22) fifty days after Passover (hence "Pentecost" or fifty days). Its purpose was to recognize the Lord as the source of all life and bounty and to present the first of the wheat, the staff of life, to the Great King who had made possible its maturation as an act of His grace.

The third and final appearance before the Lord (Ex. 23:16*b*) occurred in the seventh month of the religious year or the first month of the civil year. Described here as the "Feast of Ingathering" (*'asîp*), otherwise "Feast of Tabernacles" (or *sūkkôt*), it marked the harvest of crops at year's end, especially the grains and grapes (Deut. 16:13). Beyond this it commemorated the miraculous provision of Yahweh for His people in the desert of their forty-year wandering (cf. Lev. 23:39-44).

Then, in excess of what was required of vassals in the ancient Near East, Israel, represented by her males, expressed her ongoing covenant commitment by making the trek not once but three times annually to the earthly dwelling place of her God. In pre-Conquest times this place, of course, was wherever the Tabernacle was erected. Later it was at Gilgal, Shechem, Shiloh, and eventually Jerusalem. By this act the nation presented not only the best of its produce and the firstborn of its sons, but it reaffirmed its understanding of and commitment to its role as the servant people of Yahweh.

As might be expected, even this act of devotion was to follow prescribed conventions. The animal sacrifices were not to be offered with leavened bread (which symbolized corruption) and the portions to be eaten were to be consumed in that very day of festival (cf. Ex. 12:10). The very best of the harvest of field crops was to be offered and a kid was not to be boiled in its mother's milk (23:19). This apparently disconnected prescription is in fact a most appropriate way to conclude the section on pilgrimage and festival because, by contrasting the abominable practices of the Canaanites among whom Israel would shortly come to live (cf. Deut. 14:21)[67] it encapsulizes the essence of what it meant to be the holy people of Yahweh. The very ritual of God's people must be antithetical to that of their neighbors so that their incomparable beauty and truth might be highlighted all the more.

INSTRUCTIONS FOR THE JOURNEY

Following the text of the covenant code Yahweh assures His people of His ongoing commitment.[68] He had not brought them out of Egypt and made covenant with them only to forget them in the wilderness. He had promised to give them land, so now He speaks of the process by which they would enter the land and the circumstances they would face there (Ex. 23:20-33).

The way to Canaan would be led by the Angel of Yahweh,[69] that same angel who had appeared to Moses in the burning bush as Yahweh Himself (Ex. 3:2). It was He who had appeared long before to Abraham (Gen. 18) and who had already led the Israelites from Egypt to Sinai in the theophany of cloud and fire (Ex. 4:19; cf. 13:21-22). It was He moreover in whom God had placed His own name (23:21*b*; cf. 3:14; 6:3). If Israel obeyed that divine angel, she could rest assured of victory over all her foes because he would fight for her in holy war (23:22-23).

A corollary to holy war was the destruction of all the trappings of alien, pagan worship and unreserved devotion to Yahweh (Ex. 23:24). This would result in prosperity, health, and long life and the eventual evacuation of all hostile forces from the land. At last the fullness of the land promises to the fathers would become a reality—Israel would extend from the Gulf of Aqaba to the Mediterranean Sea and from the Negev to the mighty Euphrates River (v. 31). Covenant violation (i.e.,

---

67. See U. Cassuto, *The Goddess Anath* (Jerusalem: Magnes, 1971), pp. 50-51.
68. This kind of commitment is typical of the sovereign-vassal treaty. See F. Charles Fensham, "Clauses of Protection in Hittite Vassal-Treaties and the Old Testament," *Vetus Testamentum* 13 (1963): 141.
69. For a good review of the doctrine of the "Angel of Yahweh," see Vos, pp. 122-23.

submission to other gods) would, of course, threaten the benefits achievable through holy war and would invite the displeasure and punishment of Yahweh, their Sovereign (vv. 32-33).

COVENANT CEREMONY

Having outlined the general (Ex. 20:1-17) and specific (20:22–23:19) stipulations of the covenant, Yahweh, in accord with standard procedures of covenant-making, met with Israel in a ceremony of ratification and celebration (24:1-18).[70]

Moses, Aaron, Aaron's two sons, and seventy elders represented the entire nation on this holy occasion, though Moses alone was invited to encounter Yahweh on the mountaintop (Ex. 24:1-2). Before he did so he rehearsed with the assembly of Israel all the *d^{e}bārîm* (the Ten Commandments or general stipulations) and the *mišpātîm* (the Book of the Covenant or specific stipulations), and as they had done when first challenged with the prospect of entering into covenant with Yahweh (cf. 19:8), the people accepted the covenant terms and pledged to uphold them (24:3).

With this pledge Moses constructed an altar to symbolize the presence of Yahweh and twelve pillars to represent the tribes. He then offered burnt offerings and peace offerings—in themselves testimonies to covenant solidarity—and sprinkled their blood on the altar and pillars, dramatizing thereby the union of the contracting parties. Once more he read the text of the covenant document and once more the people asserted their fealty (Ex. 24:7). This done, Moses made his way up the mountain where he, along with Aaron, Nadab, Abihu, and the seventy encountered the awesome presence of Yahweh seated in regal splendor on His throne. Then and there Yahweh accepted the covenant response of His people with favor as is seen in His restraint toward them and their celebration by a covenant meal in His very presence (v. 11).

Once more Moses alone ascended to the gates of glory (cf. Ex. 24:1-2) to receive the stone tablets bearing the *tôrāh* (Ten Commandments) and the *miṣwāh* (Book of the Covenant) in order that they might be preserved in the archives of Israel for all time. For six days he remained there, shrouded in the glory of Yahweh, until finally on the seventh day Yahweh, resplendent and terrifying in His garments of glory, broke His silence. Then for forty days and forty nights Yahweh elaborated on the cultic implications of the covenant, particularly as they centered on the Tabernacle and the priesthood.

AN APPROACH TO THE HOLY

The establishment of a covenant relationship necessitated a means whereby the vassal party could regularly appear before the Great King to render his account-

---

70. E. W. Nicholson, "The Covenant Ritual in Exodus 24, 3-8," *Vetus Testamentum* 32 (1982): 83-84.

ability. In normal historical relationships of this kind between mere men, some sort of intercession was frequently mandatory and, in any case, a strict protocol had to be adhered to.[71] How much more must this be required in the case of a sinful people such as Israel, who must, notwithstanding, communicate with and give account to an infinitely transcendent and holy God.

The meeting place. Yahweh had already promised to condescend to His people by localizing His presence among them so that they might meet with Him (Ex. 23:17). Now on the mountain He outlined to Moses in detail the form that that meeting place must take (chaps. 25-27; 30-31) and the priestly apparatus that must be in place to afford intercession between the Holy One and His people (chaps. 28-29).

The sanctuary could not be the product of Moses' or Israel's own imagination, for its every part and furnishing had to typify some aspect of the Person and purposes of Yahweh. Therefore it had to follow the pattern and specifications revealed by Yahweh Himself (Ex. 25:9), a structure on earth modeled after a heavenly prototype (cf. 1 Chron. 28:12, 19; Acts 7:44; Heb. 8:2, 5).

The Ark of the Covenant (Ex. 25:10-22), the solitary object in the Most Holy Place, was to function both as the repository of the covenant text (vv. 9, 21) and the throne on which Yahweh sat invisibly among His people (v. 22). The Tabernacle therefore was the palace of the King, and the Most Holy Place was His throne room.

In the Holy Place were the table of the bread of the Presence (Ex. 25:23-30) and the six-branched lampstand (vv. 31-40). The former was to receive the regular donations of unleavened bread as tribute to the beneficence of the Lord who provided each day's necessities, while the latter, the lampstand, represented the illumination of His revelation and guidance (cf. 27:20-21). The Tabernacle itself, with its curtains (26:1-14), boards (vv. 15-25), bars (vv. 26-30), veil (vv. 31-35), and screen (vv. 36-37), had to be erected in strict conformity to the pattern of divine revelation (v. 30), for its materials and measurements served the higher purpose of typological and theological instruction.

In addition to the Tabernacle, the principal object inside the outer court (27:9-19) was the great altar of bronze (27:1-8) on which the atoning and fellowship offerings of Israel were to be presented to her Lord (cf. 29:38-46). Its function in the context of covenant will be addressed presently.

The priesthood. The place of meeting having thus been described, the Lord addressed the matter of intercession, a matter that presupposed and gave rise to the order of the priesthood. The approach to the Holy One, both within the biblical tradition and outside it, has always included some kind of mediatorial ministry, for it is inherent in any kind of "high religion" that an otherwise unbridgeable

---

71. For Hittite practice, for example, see O. R. Gurney, *The Hittites* (Baltimore: Penguin, 1964), pp. 74-75.

chasm exists between ineffable deity and finite mankind.

In earliest times, of course, Yahweh met directly with His creation, which in turn communicated with Him in word and act. With the passing of time and the rise of patriarchal familial and clan structures, the father of the household functioned also as its priest, the minister who stood between the family and its God. Finally—and even before the covenant at Sinai—there had developed some kind of order of priests, as Exodus 19:22 expressly declares. How that ministry originated and how it functioned cannot be determined, but it seems clearly to have come about coincident with the transition of Israel from a partriarchal clan to the thousands who multiplied and prospered in the land of Goshen. The desire of Yahweh that His people be freed to hold festival and to worship Him in the wilderness also testifies to a cultic apparatus that would of necessity require some kind of priestly officiants (cf. 3:18; 5:1, 3, 8; 7:16; 8:25-29).

A significant turning point was reached, however, with the consolidation of the Israelite people into a corporate body in covenant with Yahweh. No longer could private, or even familial, worship suffice to express the theological meaning of the new relationship. A corporate people needed, as a people, a means of access to the Lord of the covenant, a means that found spatial focus in the Tabernacle but that also required a level of intercession appropriate to the changed character of the people as a solidarity who as one entity must appear before her God.

Perhaps solely by virtue of his being the brother of Moses—who had been already designated as covenant mediator—Aaron and his sons were selected to found the priestly order (Ex. 28:1). They had already participated as such in a preliminary way when they, and seventy of the elders, had accompanied Moses part way up Sinai in the act of meeting Yahweh in covenant ceremony (24:1, 9). This encounter in itself defined what it meant to be a priest, namely, to represent the people before their God.

Surprisingly, perhaps, the first requirement after the selection of Aaron and his sons was the manufacture of appropriate vestments in which they would minister, each part of which was significant. They consisted first of an ephod (Ex. 28:6-14) made of the same materials as the curtains of the Tabernacle (26:1). The principal purpose of this apronlike garment was to provide, on its shoulder straps, settings for two precious stones on which were engraved the names of the twelve tribes of Israel, six on each stone. The meaning of all this is clear: the high priest must bear before Yahweh all the peoples of all the tribes so that He would "remember" them with favor (28:12).

A breastplate (or pouch) was affixed to the front of the ephod (Ex. 28:15-30), and in this were set twelve precious stones in rows of three. Each of these would also be inscribed with the name of a tribe, and because the breastplate was worn over the heart (v. 29) it spoke of the compassionate intercession undertaken by the priest as he entered into the presence of Yahweh on each tribe's behalf. An important aspect of this mediatorial role was the communication of the will of God to the people, especially before the rise of the formal prophetic movement. Thus, the breastplate also contained the Urim and Thummim, two objects by which the priest could discern the yes-and-no responses of the Lord to questions addressed in an appropriate manner.

Another part of the priestly attire was the blue robe, all of one piece (Ex. 28:31-35). This he wore in the Holy Place in his work of intercession. Similarly he was adorned with a mitre on which was a gold plate inscribed with the words "Holy to Yahweh" (v. 36). This symbolized the holy attitude God's people were to exhibit as they made their offerings of tribute to Him. Aaron, as a "holy man," consecrated himself so that in him as her representative the nation might appear blameless before God.

Finally, reference is made to linen undergarments, the purpose of which was to protect the modesty of the priests (Ex. 28:42-43). This reminder of the shame of nakedness associated with the Fall was in striking contrast to the demeanor of pagan priests who often performed their duties naked. Indeed, all the garments of the priests of Israel were designed to communicate two of the attributes of God Himself—glory and beauty (29:2, 40). They spoke simultaneously, then, of His remoteness and yet of His approachability.

The ceremony of consecration, which required the preparation of the holy garments just described, follows next (Ex. 29:1-37). It consisted first of the presentation of animals and grain, a ceremonial washing of the candidates, their adornment with the priestly regalia, and their anointing with oil. Next was the slaughter of a bull on which Aaron and his sons had placed their hands, thus transferring their guilt to the innocent animal (v. 14). A ram was then sacrificed as a whole burnt offering to be "consumed" by Yahweh in line with covenant protocol (vv. 15-18). A second ram was slain and its blood was applied to the ear, thumb, and big toe of the priests. The purpose clearly was to consecrate these to the service of Yahweh so that the priests might hear and do the will of God and walk faithful to their calling. Next followed the offering of the choice parts of the beast to Yahweh and the consumption by Aaron and his sons of the parts designated for them. This fellowship offering spoke of the attainment of a covenant status between Yahweh and the priestly order, a sort of covenant within a covenant. To Israel had been granted the privilege of being a special people; to Aaron and his sons was granted now the privilege of being a special mediating instrument between that people and Yahweh, their Lord. A covenant meal was always part of such an arrangement (cf. 24:11; 32:6), and that is precisely what is implied in the sharing of the ram of consecration by Yahweh and the priests.

The tribute. The consecration of the priests, which featured appropriate sacrifice, leads naturally to the function of sacrifice in the cultus, a subject exhaustively described in the book of Leviticus. But here in Exodus 29:28-46 the linkage between priest and Tabernacle is first suggested. Yahweh indicated that He, the Great King, would meet with His covenant people in a special, unique way in the portable shrine of the Tabernacle. Moreover, He would do so via the mediating ministry of the priests. Now the visible expression of the means whereby the approach of the people to their God can become possible must be articulated.

Fundamentally, acceptable approach to and standing before God is the essence of religious sacrifice, or perhaps its purpose. That is, the worshiper dare not come before deity empty-handed, for some kind of vicarious offering must establish his right to do so and some kind of gesture of devotion must signify his recognition of his status. In covenant terms (and this was what governs all Israel's relationships to Yahweh), sacrifice was synonymous with tribute, a point made crystal clear in the passage in view.

The twice-daily burnt offerings of lambs had to be made at the door of the Tabernacle where, Yahweh says, "I will meet with you to speak to you" (Ex. 29:42). It was in the Tabernacle that Yahweh would dwell and where He would manifest His sovereignty among and over His people (v. 45). All this is predicated historically on His redemptive act of Exodus deliverance. He brought them out of Egypt so that He might dwell among them and exercise His kingly prerogatives (v. 46). Their recognition of both His lordship and His residence among them would be expressed by Israel, His people, by their devoted presentation of offering, of tribute, to Him.

The requirement of sacrifice at the Tabernacle and the role of the priests in carrying out its regular presentation demanded a holiness of priest and people alike in order for it to be efficacious. Though the covenant faith was expressed corporately and by priestly intercession, the people nonetheless had access to the Lord as individuals and in personal communion. Thus, provision was made for atonement and prayer.

Immediately in front of the veil that partitioned off the Most Holy Place stood the altar of incense, the function of which was to burn the spices symbolizing the sweetness of the prayers of the covenant people as they ascended up to His throne in glory (Ex. 30:1-9; cf. Rev. 5:8; 8:3). Clearly there was sacrifice of prayer as well as of property.

Part of the ritual of annual atonement was the purification of this altar (Ex. 30:10) and hence of the people themselves. All the adults were to pay equal tribute of a half shekel annually to sustain this ministry and to signify in their giving the real essence of atonement—that a ransom had been made for their lives (vv. 11-16). Moreover, Moses was to create concoctions of perfumes and oils with which he would anoint the Tabernacle with all its appurtenances as well as Aaron and his sons, a tradition to be followed in all the generations to come. Again, the purpose was to designate these as holy, separated to Yahweh for His own use and glory (vv. 29, 32). These ingredients, as well as the incense for the gold altar of incense, must be manufactured according to a strict and unique prescription for they spoke of the unique holiness and worthiness of Israel's God (vv. 32, 38).

Israel's approach to Yahweh, her Great King, was clearly multisensory. The people saw His glory in the fire and cloud, heard Him in the thunder and quaking, and in the fragrance of the perfumes they smelled something of His sweetness.

The God beyond sensory perception nonetheless revealed Himself metaphorically in ways that sentient human beings could understand.

The approach to the Holy One is summarized in Exodus 31. All the physical apparatus necessary to its accomplishment—the Tabernacle with its furnishings and equipments—is listed (vv. 7-11), and workmen, qualified by their selection by Yahweh and their enduement with the very Spirit of God, are set aside (vv. 1-6). The whole section concludes with a reaffirmation to Moses by Yahweh of the covenant, the heart of which is engraved in the tables of stone (v. 18). But if these tablets testify to God's faithfulness and commitment, Israel's response was to take shape in her devotion to the sign of the Sinaitic Covenant, scrupulous observance of the Sabbath (vv. 12-17). The steadfastness of Yahweh's redemptive work in history and in promise rested in His mighty work in creation. It was fitting indeed that the celebration of the completion of that creative work on the seventh day be translated into celebration of the new creative work by which Yahweh made Israel His own people in redemption and covenant.

COVENANT VIOLATION AND RENEWAL

Even before Moses could descend the mountain to share the wondrous secrets of the approach to the Holy with his countrymen, they engaged in attitude and action that nullified the possibility of that kind of fellowship. The Creator who, by virtue of His sovereign power had brought the nation into covenant with Himself, was replaced by a god created by the same people. Whether the golden calf was a representation of Yahweh or merely a pedestal on which He stood invisibly is immaterial. The point is that the first two commandments had been egregiously and openly violated and in their violation the very basis of covenant arrangement was undermined.

That the sin of Aaron and the people was tantamount to covenant repudiation is clear from the account of the making of the calf. The calf was hailed as "the god . . . who brought you up out of Egypt" (Ex. 32:4), the exact language of the historical prologue of the Sinaitic Covenant in which Yahweh described the basis of His authority to be Israel's God (20:2). Moreover, Aaron built an altar for the purpose of covenant affirmation and ceremony (v. 5), precisely as Moses had done previously on the people's commitment to the covenant arrangement (24:4). Aaron's proclamation concerning a festival and its implementation on the following day (32:5-6) was again identical to the celebration that attended the mutual acceptance of the covenant terms under Moses (24:11).

With Israel's repudiation of the covenant came a statement of response from Yahweh: He too would break off His commitment and would begin with a new nation sired by Moses himself (Ex. 32:10). But Moses reminded Yahweh of the unconditional nature of the covenant promises to the patriarchs (v. 13). For Yahweh to break His sworn word to them would vitiate His own integrity and thus reveal that He somehow was less than God.

The covenant with the fathers thus remained intact, but its expression in Israel as the seed and, more particularly, as the means by which the whole earth would be blessed was seriously jeopardized. To impress on His people the heinousness of their covenant infidelity Moses shattered the tablets containing the basic stipulations of the covenant. This demonstrated visually the rupture of the alliance that had bound Yahweh and His people together. He then destroyed the golden calf, an act not so much of violent rage as one by which the new, illicit covenant relationship was shattered and indeed annihilated.

That God's covenant faithfulness remained unimpaired is affirmed by His call to Moses to undertake the journey to the land He had promised to the fathers (Ex. 33:1-3). But until Israel herself recognized the unwavering reliability of Yahweh and responded to Him in repentance and covenant reaffirmation, the promise could never find fulfillment. In this manner the tension between the patriarchal covenants as unqualified promise and the Sinaitic as conditional reappeared. The nation of Israel remained in covenant linkage with Yahweh on the basis of His own irrefragable promise, but the experience of blessing in that covenant depended on the degree to which Israel responded in faith and obedience.

Though the people repented of this act of covenant violation (Ex. 33:4-5), Moses requested that he might have some sign, some tangible evidence that all was well between the Lord and Israel (vv. 12-16). To satisfy this understandable need, Yahweh promised to reveal Himself to Moses in theophany, to show him His glory (vv. 17-23).

This same kind of theophanic encounter between Yahweh and Moses, the covenant mediator, had taken place at the time of the initial act of covenant-making at Sinai (Ex. 19:9-25). God had come amid thunder, lightning, and thick cloud, warning the people to avoid the scene of such awesome glory lest they perish (v. 21). Moses, Aaron, Aaron's sons, and the seventy elders could ascend part way together (v. 24; cf. 24:1), but only Moses could approach the very presence of Yahweh (24:2, 15-18). There, garbed in the cloud and fire of glory, Yahweh declared to Moses His covenant word.

The manifestation of this same glory following Israel's apostasy was in turn followed by the reestablishment of the covenant (Ex. 34:1-9). Moses was to prepare two more tablets, ascend solitarily to the summit of Sinai, and receive the promise of forgiveness and of renewed relationship. It was the *hesed*-faithfulness of Yahweh that guaranteed its continuation despite Israel's waywardness (vv. 6-7).

Renewal of covenant demanded the same response as had the original statement of covenant obligation. And it was based on the same commitment of Yahweh, a pledge to demonstrate His sovereignty over Israel and among the nations by His mighty works in nature and history (Ex. 34:10). This would most particularly be apparent in reference to the conquest and occupation of Canaan for it was there that the role of Israel as covenant people would be played out.

Yahweh, as Lord of the whole earth and the One who divided it and allocated its parts to the nations, would drive out Canaan's inhabitants and thereby set the stage. Israel, therefore, had to refrain from making covenant with these nations and their gods for this would contradict the purpose of Yahweh in declaring His uniqueness and the uniqueness of His covenant design for His redeemed people (Ex. 34:10b, 14-16). This meant, then, that the gods of Canaan were to be absolutely repudiated (v. 14) and the physical structures of their ritual worship were to be eradicated from the earth (vv. 13, 17).

Exodus 34:10-17 constitutes an elaboration of the first two commandments, the prohibition against the worship of other gods and the making of images to represent them (or even Him). This was necessary because it was in respect to these two that Israel's apostasy under Aaron had taken place. The golden calf was a rejection of the uniqueness of Yahweh as liberator and a violation of the aniconic principle that God the Creator cannot be represented by a creation of human hands.

The remainder of the restatement of covenant regulation (Ex. 34:18-26) is clearly connected to the great underlying principles of the first two commandments just elaborated. The recognition of Yahweh as Great King carries with it appropriate acts of response, acts to be undertaken at stated times and places. Thus, the center of attention is the festivals and holy days, for these provided the occasion whereby Israel the vassal could render homage to her Sovereign, whose incomparability had already been addressed.

The first of these—the Feast of Unleavened Bread (and its concomitant, the Passover)—draws attention to Yahweh's redemptive act in saving His son Israel from cruel and hopeless bondage (Ex. 34:18-20). This calls for the offering of all Israel's firstborn to Him in either sacrifice or redemption.

The second is the Sabbath, here commanded without a motive clause but in anticipation of the agricultural life of Canaan, where plowing and harvesting would be regular employment (Ex. 34:21). Even in those busy times the seventh day must be made free for the worship of Yahweh.

The third and fourth festivals, those of the Firstfruits and of Tabernacles respectively, must also be set aside to permit pilgrimage to the courts of Yahweh, God of Israel (Ex. 34:22-24). Again the purpose is clear: The God who had chosen Israel as His own possession and who has redeemed her with mighty power must receive of her hand the tribute commensurate with His majesty and appropriate to her life in the land. In this way the covenant that binds them can find tangible expression.

The material of the tribute, though not elaborated here, has its own significance (Ex. 34:25-26). Positively, it had to follow proper prescription as part of an indigenous rite of Israel as covenant partner (vv. 25-26a), but negatively it had to avoid anything that smacked of Canaanite paganism (v. 26b). Israel as a unique people worshiping an incomparable God had to adhere strictly to a cultus that emphasized and derived meaning from that special relationship.

Having received the Ten Commandments once more, Moses descended Sinai to share the divine communication with his people (Ex. 34:27-28). The afterglow of the radiance of God's glory, a luminescence suggested also in His previous encounter with the Lord (24:17), so intensely shone on Moses' face that he was forced to wear a veil when he stood before the people. The physical nature of this phenomenon must remain a mystery, but its theological meaning is crystal clear. Moses, as covenant mediator, was authenticated as such by his resemblance to the God of glory whom he represented. It is precisely for this reason that Moses and Elijah shared the radiance of the transfigured Jesus (Luke 9:31-32).

THE BUILDING AND OCCUPATION OF THE TABERNACLE

The renewal of covenant made possible the erection of the place of meeting, the tent-shrine whose design and specifications had already been revealed (Ex. 25:1–26:21; 30:1-38). What was required foremost were willing and wise hearts to prompt the people to give to the project and to undertake its accomplishment (35:5, 10, 21, 22, 25, 29; 36:1). These men and women, together with their Spirit-filled leaders Bezalel and Oholiab, would express by their sacrifice and labor the essence of servanthood. They would build a place of residence from which their Sovereign could exercise His kingship among them.

Obedient in every respect, the workmen toiled with unrelenting diligence, and in the exquisite beauty of their efforts they rendered covenant homage to their God. Thus, the narrator wrote that they did all their work "just as the Lord had commanded Moses," and when Moses inspected it he "saw that they had done it just as the Lord had commanded" (39:42-43).

When the completed parts had been assembled and the Tabernacle stood ready, Yahweh, as it were, "moved in" and took occupancy of His earthly dwelling place. This move took the form of the covering cloud and its permeation of every nook and cranny of the Tabernacle (Ex. 40:34). So intense was the heavenly presence that even Moses could not enter, at least on this occasion of Yahweh's claim of ownership and occupation. Subsequently the glory, though not disconnected from the Tabernacle entirely, functioned by cloud and fire as a beacon to lead the people on their trek to the land of promise (vv. 36-38). Yahweh, with them, had become for the time a nomad—but a nomad whose face was set toward the land of permanent habitation in accord with the promises made to the patriarchs centuries before.

A THEOLOGY OF LEVITICUS:
FELLOWSHIP WITH THE HOLY

Though the covenant arrangement up to this point clearly specified the need for Israel, the vassal, to appear before her Lord on stated occasions and singled out first Moses and then the priesthood as mediators in this encounter, there yet remained the need to describe the nature of the tribute to be presented, the precise meaning and function of the priesthood, the definition of holiness and unholiness, and a more strict clarification of the places and times of pilgrimage to the dwelling place of the great King. This is the purpose of the book of Leviticus.

The very heart of the covenant relationship—fellowship between Yahweh and His people—and the means of its achievement are spelled out in the opening statement of Leviticus where, with respect to the burnt offering, Yahweh says, "He must present it at the entrance to the Tent of Meeting so that He will be acceptable to the Lord" (Lev. 1:3). The servant, therefore, had to approach his Sovereign at His dwelling place by presenting an appropriate token of his obedient submission.

In ordinary political terms it was inevitable that a vassal prince would at least occasionally offend his overlord and thus need to make appropriate overtures to sue for peace and normalization of relationships. Even if this were not the case, it was incumbent on him to appear regularly at the palace to reaffirm his loyalty and friendship, a reaffirmation that must find expression in his voluntary offering of tribute in addition to the mandatory assessment inherent in his vassalship.

The fact that the covenant between Yahweh and Israel was modeled after those of the ancient Near East in both form and function allows one to understand the myriad of cultic detail in the Pentateuch with unusual clarity. The sacrifices and offerings were designed to demonstrate the subservience of Israel, to atone for her offenses against her Sovereign, Yahweh, and to reflect the harmoniousness and peaceableness of the relationship thus established or reestablished.[72]

The burnt and cereal offering (Lev. 1-2) served to identify the offerer as a servant of the king, one who dared not come before him emptyhanded. The sin and trespass offerings (chaps. 4-5) served to restore a relationship that had become disrupted because of the servant's disobedience. They were his recompense to an offended lord. The peace (or fellowship) offerings (chap. 3) constituted an expression of thanksgiving by the vassal for a state of fellowship that currently existed. They were freewill, nonobligatory testimonies to a heart filled with thanksgiving and praise for the goodness of the Lord.

The role of the priest in mediating these offerings is also significant. He too was a vassal and had to follow proper protocol in his ministry on behalf of the people. Thus, he carried out the ritual relative to the various offerings of the nation just described (Lev. 6-7), and, as special servant of Yahweh, he enjoyed a portion of the tribute for himself (7:28-30).

As a special servant the priest was to be appointed and consecrated (chap. 8), to be instructed in the appropriate means of sacrificial intercession (9:1–10:7), and to understand that his privileged office and ministry required unique canons of integrity and conduct (10:8-15). In other words, the priest was a holy man serving a holy God on behalf of a holy people.

The essence of the priestly ministry is articulated in Leviticus 10:10-11: "You must distinguish between the holy and the profane, between the unclean and the clean, and you must teach the Israelites all the decrees the Lord has given them though Moses." Israel, then, was a people separated to Yahweh from among all

---

72. Gordon J. Wenham, *The Book of Leviticus,* The New International Commentary on the Old Testament (Grand Rapids: Eerdmans, 1979), pp. 25-26.

the nations of the earth. Her lifestyle and, indeed, her very character must advertise to all peoples the meaning of that identity and mission.

This explains the elaborate restrictions and prescriptions concerning certain things: the offering and eating of animals (Lev. 11:1-23); the impurity of carcasses (vv. 24-28); the pollution of vessels and articles contaminated by unclean creatures (vv. 29-46); the impurity suggested by menstruation (12:1-8), leprosy (chaps. 13-14), and the issuance of bodily fluids (chap. 15). In most cases these were not considered unclean because of any inherent corruption but were identified as such by Yahweh Himself to provide pedagogical reference points. A people (such as Israel) is holy because of Yahweh's elective and saving decrees. All else is holy or unholy by virtue of divine deliberation and mandate. It is not so by nature but becomes so by the will of God.[73]

The holy people had to maintain that state in conduct as well as in decree, so provision for the nation as a whole to restore it regularly to a position of purity was essential. This was done by means of the corporate act of repentance and forgiveness expressed in the ritual of the Day of Atonement (Lev. 16). But this annual event of repristinating the purity of covenant relationship must be lived out every day in the framework of a code of national and individual behavior. Thus, most scholars describe Leviticus 17-26 as "the Holiness Code."[74]

The underlying theme of this great treatise on holiness is summed up in the phrase "I am Yahweh" (e.g. 18:2, 5-6, 21, 30; 19:2-4, 10, 12, 14, 16, 18, 26, 28, 30-31).[75] Human character and behavior (that of Israel particularly in this context) must, if it is to be called "holy," reflect the character and behavior of God Himself. He is the standard of holiness by which all else must be measured, and He is at the same time the motive and motivator for human achievement of holiness. Fundamentally God is holy because He is unique and incomparable. Those whom He calls to servanthood must therefore understand their holiness not primarily as some king of "spirituality" but as their uniqueness and separateness as the elect and called of God. But holiness must also find expression in life by adhering to ethical principles and practices that demonstrate godlikeness. This is the underlying meaning of being the "image of God."

The call to holiness involved regulations concerning the sanctity of blood (Lev. 17); prohibition of incest (18:1-18) and other sexual perversions (18:19-23); the keeping of the Decalogue (19:1-18) and related laws (19:19–20:27); and proper behavior of the priests in private and public life (chaps. 21-22).

The people of Israel, as a holy nation, also had to understand that holiness required strict adherence to holy days, to stated times of convocation before the Lord. These included the weekly Sabbath (Lev. 23:3), the Passover and Unleavened

---

73. For a full and excellent discussion of criteria of cleanness and uncleanness, see ibid., pp. 166-71.

74. So Martin Noth, *Leviticus: A Commentary* (Philadelphia: Westminster, 1977), pp. 127-28.

75. For this phrase in the "Holiness Code" and elsewhere in the Old Testament, see Walther Zimmerli, *I Am Yahweh* (Atlanta: John Knox, 1982), esp. pp. 2-5.

Bread festival (23:4-8), the feast of Firstfruits (23:9-14), the feast of Weeks (23:15-22), the feast of Trumpets (23:23-25), the Day of Atonement (23:26-32), the feast of Tabernacles (23:33-44), the sabbatical year (25:1-7), and the year of Jubilee (25:8-55). The purpose of these occasions was manifold, but in the framework of holiness it was to remind God's people that not only are persons, places, and actions holy, but times are also holy. There must be days set apart from the calendar of "secular," self-serving activity so that the servant people might ponder the meaning of their existence and of the holy task to which they had been called. The special days and seasons put them in touch in a unique way with the person and purposes of the God of eternity who transcends life on a cyclical, calendrical level and who calls His people again and anew to their servanthood in the earth.

That this is the underlying meaning of holiness and the holiness code is clear from the covenant language with which the section closes.[76] In terms reminiscent of the inauguration of the covenant at Sinai (Ex. 21:1-4), Yahweh speaks of His uniqueness and exclusivity (Lev. 26:1), a fact that demanded unquestioning loyalty (26:2).

Obedience to the Sovereign who broke the bonds of Egyptian slavery in the redemptive act of the Exodus (Lev. 26:13) would result in Israel's material prosperity (vv. 4-5), military success (vv. 6-8), and the guarantee of His continued presence and covenant commitment (vv. 9-12). Disobedience, however, would result in defeat (vv. 14-17), impoverishment (vv. 18-20), plague (vv. 21-26), and even banishment from the land (vv. 27-33).

Even in exile there would be hope, however, for though covenant blessing depended on obedience the covenant itself would remain intact for it was based on the unconditional promises of God, which antedated the making of the covenant at Sinai.[77] Indeed, it found its roots in the pledges made to the patriarchal fathers of the nation hundreds of years before the nation itself existed (Lev. 26:42). The restoration would be in response to the repentance of God's people, but even that spirit of confession would be something initiated by God's own gracious favor (vv. 40, 44-45).

Fellowship with the Holy One demands a holiness of disposition and behavior on the part of God's people, the very structures of which He dictates. Adherence to those standards ensures the continuation of fellowship and favor but disobedience brings inexorable judgment. The nature of the covenant commitment is such, however, that the purposes of the Lord must prevail and His people must, sooner or later, fulfill the purposes for which He elected and redeemed them.

A THEOLOGY OF NUMBERS: PILGRIMAGE TO POSSESSION

A major component of the covenant promise to the fathers and to Israel the nation was, as noted repeatedly, the inheritance and occupation of a land. This

76. Wenham, pp. 327-28.
77. Ibid., pp. 31-32.

land was representative of the whole earth. As man was placed in the Garden of Eden to keep and rule it, so Israel would be placed in Canaan to keep and rule it as a fiefdom from the Great King. At last, when the saving purposes of the Lord will have been accomplished, all the earth—indeed all creation—will fall under the rule of mankind, who will "have dominion over all things."

Israel's occupation of Canaan, then, is to be seen as a stage in this process of claiming all creation for the Creator. Canaan is a microcosm of the earth, a *pars pro toto* that lay under the control of wicked, anti-god forces that must be overcome before Israel could enter into her rest. Thus the act of election and redemption by which Yahweh brought His people out of Egypt and the encounter at Sinai by which they became His priestly servants required, for their fulfillment, a geographical framework in which they could exhibit the meaning of their covenant status and from which they could engage the nations of the world in their ministry of reconciliation. Like the Tabernacle, Canaan would be the focal point of Yahweh's residence among men, the place where His sovereignty would find historical expression through His specially chosen people.

Entrance into the land required pilgrimage and conquest, however. Between covenant promise and covenant possession lay a process of rigorous journey through hostile opposition of terrain and terror. Israel had to understand that occupation of the land could be achieved only through much travail, for Canaan, like creation itself, was under alien dominion and it had to be wrested away by force, by the strong arm of Yahweh, who would fight on behalf of His people.

The theology of pilgrimage and conquest finds expression in the narratives of Numbers.[78] In clearly military terms, Moses recorded the census of the tribes (Num. 1) and the arrangement of their encampment (Num. 2) in anticipation of their departure from Sinai en route to Canaan. The Levites, the keepers of Yahweh's dwelling place, were to surround the Tabernacle. They were particularly close, both in location and function, because they represented the firstborn of Israel whom Yahweh spared in the Exodus (3:12-13, 44-45; 8:5-26). It was their responsibility to attend to the sanctuary (chap. 4) for it is ever the ministry of the eldest son to serve his father and protect his interests. Their needs, as well as those of the priests, would be met by the offerings of the community on whose behalf they undertook their mediatorial role (chap. 18).

Pilgrimage does not imply cessation of cultic obligation or of social regulation. Indeed, the peculiar circumstances of nomadic transit in the wilderness demanded restatement of principles and practices already articulated. Hence there were special stipulations concerning leprosy (Num. 5:1-4), accusations of adultery (5:11-31), the Nazirite vow (6:1-21), the Passover (9:1-14), offerings (15:1-31, 37-41; 28:1-29; chap. 40), purification (chap. 19), vows (30:1-16), and inheritance (36:1-12). Rooted in the original covenant declaration, they nonetheless reflect amendment and

78. Brevard S. Childs, *Introduction to the Old Testament as Scripture* (Philadelphia: Fortress, 1979), pp. 197-99.

modification essential to the pilgrim people who anticipated passage from a lifestyle of wandering, with all its impermanence, to one of sedentary settlement in a land that would be their home forever.

The journey itself is of theological significance for it serves paradigmatically as the experience of every pilgrim who makes his way from promise to possession. On the eve of its commencement—just after the Tabernacle had been assembled and invested with the fullness of God's glory—the leaders of Israel's tribes brought enormous loads of tribute to be used in the service of the Tabernacle (Num. 7:1-2, 5). In this manner they asserted their commitment, as leaders of their respective tribes, to support the ongoing ministry of the priests and Levites. The journey was about to begin, a move sanctioned by and attested to by the generous response of the covenant people. They were headed to the land of promise where they would experience the good things of which the Lord had spoken (10:29).

Though the Lord had commanded the march and went before His people as a mighty, conquering warrior (Num. 10:33-36; 14:8-9), they failed over and over again to trust Him to see them safely through. They murmured against the Lord (chap. 11; 20:1-13), rebelled against the leadership of Moses (chaps. 12-14; 16-17), and engaged in outright apostasy and covenant repudiation (chap. 25).

Despite all this, the Lord remained true to His covenant pledge. He provided relief for His servant Moses by supplying Spirit-filled leaders (Num. 11:16-30; 13:30; 14:24), by meeting physical needs (11:31-35; 21:4-10), and by defeating enemies that rose up against them on every hand (21:1-3, 21-32, 33-35; 22-24; 31:1-11). Constantly He reaffirmed His commitment to them (11:23; 14:20; 15:41), even through the medium of the false prophet Balaam (23:19-24; 24:3-9, 15-24). Israel might (and did) prove unfaithful, but God could not deny Himself. He who had elected and redeemed, who had made covenant and had come to live among His people, would guarantee their successful pilgrimage to the land of rest.

As an earnest of this promise, God commanded Moses to spy out the land (Num. 13) so that the people could learn firsthand of its beauty and bounty (13:27). Though their rejection of the minority report of Caleb and Joshua resulted in postponement of the land's enjoyment by all Israel, some of the tribes—Reuben, Gad, and part of Manasseh—had a foretaste in the form of the Transjordanian territories occupied by the Amorites. To them the Lord granted these areas which, though outside the limits of the land of promise as described to the patriarchs, became for a time at least a portion of Israel's allotment.

As for the remainder of the land, that of Canaan proper, Moses designated its allocation even before it had become Israel's by conquest. The principle is clear: the promises of God often are already available for the appropriation. But until the appropriation is actually accomplished the promise remains in potential only. So the Lord commanded that the inhabitants of Canaan be driven out, that their idols be demolished, and their lands possessed by His own chosen people (Num. 33:50-56). This would make possible the division of the land by tribe and the assignment within it of cities for the Levites (35:1-8), cities of refuge

(35:9-28), and other allotment (36:1-12).

Thus, the stage was set for conquest and occupation of the land God had promised to the patriarchs and reaffirmed to Moses and Israel. Historically and geographically the covenant people had arrived at the threshold of fulfillment of this crucial element of covenant relationship. It remained only to move across the Jordan, conquer and occupy the land, and dominate it as the expression of divine rule in the earth. But that step was to be taken by a new generation who must work out the covenant requirements in a new and changed environment, that of permanent existence in an urbanized setting. That required a modified covenant statement to be affirmed by the successors of the original covenant people.

A THEOLOGY OF DEUTERONOMY

COVENANT RENEWAL

Fundamental to any serious study of Deuteronomy in the present day is the recognition that it is in form a covenant document, a point that has been put beyond debate by a number of scholars across the theological spectrum.[79] In light of this form—specifically that of the suzerain-vassal treaty, well attested in Hittite sources—the content therefore, according to expectation, reflects covenant language and concerns. In fact it is not an overstatement to propose that covenant is the theological center of Deuteronomy.

That being the case, one must recognize that God is the covenant initiator, the Great King; Israel is the covenant recipient, the vassal; and the book itself, complete with the essential elements of standard treaty documents, is the organ of covenant. Moreover, any attempt to deal with Deuteronomy theologically must do so with complete and appropriate attention to its form and its dominant covenant theme. This means that God's revelation of Himself and of other matters must be understood within a covenant context because it is His purpose in the document to represent Himself in a particularized role—Sovereign, Redeemer, covenant-maker, and benefactor.

To employ the standard rubrics and classifications, then, without investing them with covenant content, is to abuse the book of Deuteronomy theologically and hermeneutically. But to understand Yahweh in this specialized covenant sense one must see how He reveals and describes Himself in Deuteronomy. That is, one must determine the means of divine self-disclosure and its content. The self-disclosure may be subsumed under acts, theophany, and word, and the content under His names and epithets, person, attributes and character, and function. All this, again, must be informed by the covenantal framework in which it deliberately operates.

---

79. Peter C. Craigie, *The Book of Deuteronomy,* The New International Commentary on the Old Testament (Grand Rapids: Eerdmans, 1976), pp. 24-28.

THE DIVINE REVELATION: ITS MEANS

One of the principal means by which God has revealed Himself is in historical event, that is, by acts the community of faith could recognize as divine.[80] To Israel on the plains of Moab, these acts made up the constellation of mighty deeds Yahweh had displayed before them and on their behalf from the days of the patriarchs to their present hour. It was on the basis of such historical interventions, in fact, that Yahweh's claim as Sovereign could be made.

Elsewhere in the Old Testament the foundational act of God is creation itself, but here the matter is less cosmic; the focus of Deuteronomy is not on God's universal concerns but on His special purposes for His people. This means that the first act involved the selection and call of the patriarchal ancestors, a call that established Yahweh in the role of selector (Deut. 26:5-9; 10:22; 32:15-18).

The election of a people, accompanied by promises as to its successful implementation, found expression centuries later in the mighty Exodus event, which, along with the ensuing wilderness experience, established Yahweh as Redeemer of His people (Deut. 3:24; 4:3, 20, 34-39; 5:6; 6:12, 21-23, and elsewhere).[81] He who had called them by elective grace endorsed that call historically by an act of deliverance from an oppressive overlord so that His people might understand IIis faithfulness and His incomparable power.

That power was particularly evident to Israel as Yahweh bared His arm on their behalf as warrior. He had defeated Sihon and Og (Deut. 1:4) and had humiliated the Pharaoh (1:30). He would continue to achieve victory over His foes in days to come (7:1-2, 20-24; 9:3-5; 20:4, 13; 21:10, 23:14; 31:4) and thus prove to all that He indeed is worthy of obedience and praise. The transhistorical struggle with the dominions of evil and darkness found, and would find, historical expression in Israel's success on the field of battle.

Yahweh's interventions on behalf of Israel showed Him to be a benefactor, a protector whose care was evident in the bestowal of His grace in multiplying their numbers (Deut. 1:10; 10:22) and in granting them physical and material prosperity (32:15-18). To be called and delivered by Yahweh is to enter into a life of blessing. Vassalship demands commitment, but it also carries with it a security and prosperity that only a beneficent and inexhaustibly wealthy Lord can provide.

Moreover, the promises of God were not terminated with the present experience of redemption, for a glorious prospect lay ahead. He would take His people into a land of milk and honey, where they would partake of blessing no nation had ever before experienced (Deut. 7:12-16; 11:13-15; 12:20, 29; 19:1, 8; 28:1-14; 30:3-9; 31:3; 33:2-29). On the other hand, disobedience to His covenant mandates

---

80. G. Ernest Wright and Reginald H. Fuller, *The Book of the Acts of God* (Garden City, N.Y.: Doubleday, 1960), pp. 9-10.

81. Brevard S. Childs, "Deuteronomic Formulae of the Exodus Traditions," *Hebraische Wortforschung,* ed. Walter Baumgartner (Leiden: Brill, 1967), pp. 30-39.

would vitiate these blessings and invite the chastisement of the Lord. He who had been Savior and Benefactor would become Judge (4:27: 28:15-68; 31:17; 32:19-43).

In addition to His self-disclosure in event, in history, Yahweh revealed Himself as sovereign in theophany. In this manner the glorious splendor of the King contributes to His aura of majesty and power and is thereby persuasive of His dignity and authority. Almost without exception the theophanic revelation was in the form of fire and its opposite, darkness (Deut. 1:33; 4:11-12, 33, 36; 5:4, 22-26; 9:10, 15; 10:4; 33:2; cf. Pss. 50:2; 80:2; 94:1). Yahweh is *Deus absconditus,* He who continually retreats in His self-disclosure. The darkness speaks of His transcendence, His *mysterium,* His inaccessibility. On the other hand, the fire represented His immanence, the possibility of His being known even if in only a limited way (cf. Ezek. 1:4, 27-28; Dan. 7:9; Rev. 1:14).[82] The covenant relationship implied the real existence of both parties to the arrangement, both Yahweh and Israel. But Yahweh was unlike any human king no matter how remote and majestic the latter might be. Yahweh is God and as God must always be ineffable and unreachable. As covenant partner, however, that chasm between Him and His people had to be bridged if the relationship was to have any kind of epistemological and ontological reality. Theophany was the means of addressing this need in Old Testament times, a means that was itself excelled only in the New Testament incarnation of deity in man, the God-man Christ Jesus.

The third means of divine self-disclosure in the context of the Deuteronomic covenant was by word. It is important to note, however, that in the ancient Near East and in the Old Testament there is no essential distinction between act and word, for the act is produced by the word and the word is never without effective purpose. It is dynamic, entelic, purposeful, creative, powerful (cf. Gen. 1:3, etc.). It does not exist (as in Greek philosophy, for example) as a theoretical or neutral abstraction. In terms of revelation, and especially in Deuteronomy, it is necessary to see the powerful word as a covenant instrument; the word of the Sovereign commands and communicates, but it also effects, empowers, and creates. This will be elaborated later under the discussion of Deuteronomy as a covenant text.

THE DIVINE REVELATION: ITS CONTENT

The will and purposes of Yahweh are clearly revealed in His acts, theophany, and word, but His nature as sovereign Lord must be understood in ways beyond these, in a more immediate and specific self-disclosure. Moses and the people of Israel did indeed hear, see, and experience Yahweh, but in ways unknown to man today (cf. Deut. 34:10-12). He communicated more fully and clearly the wonder of His Person and plan. These characteristics emerge as they are unfolded in the revelation of Deuteronomy, a revelation not limited to Israel of that day but made available to all who read its pages.

Again, what is read must be seen and interpreted in the light of the role

82. Samuel Terrien, *The Elusive Presence* (New York: Harper & Row, 1978), pp. 109-12.

Yahweh assumed in the document—that of the Great King who entered into covenant with His humble and undeserving servant. For convenience's sake the content of self-revelation will be summarized under Yahweh's names and epithets, His Person, His attributes and character, and His function.

Yahweh's names. Yahweh. The name *Yahweh,* that name most expressive of God's covenant role, occurs without qualification more than 220 times in Deuteronomy. It appears 35 times in the prologue (chaps. 1-4), 119 times in the stipulation section (chaps. 5-26), 51 times in the sanctions section (chaps. 27-31), and 16 times in the poetry (chaps. 32-33). As Adonai Yahweh it appears twice, once in the prologue and once in the stipulations. "Yahweh, God of the fathers," occurs 7 times, 3 in the prologue, 3 in the stipulations, and once in the sanctions. "Yahweh, your God" occurs about 300 times—46 in the prologue, 207 in the stipulations, and 46 in the sanctions. Several theological observations may be made based on the distribution of the divine name Yahweh in Deuteronomy.

(1) Almost exclusively this is the name used in the so-called narrative and parenetic sections. This clearly denotes the covenant character of Deuteronomy: the covenant name of God both testifies to the covenant content of the document and derives from its covenant form.

(2) The predominant use of Yahweh as the name of God in the historical prologue (85 out of 94 occurrences of divine names there) reveals Yahweh to be the God of history, particularly in reference to the history of Israel.

(3) The predominant use of the epithet "Yahweh your God" among the occurrences of Yahweh in the historical prologue (46 out of 85) emphasizes the covenant relation—He is *their* God.

(4) The predominant use of Yahweh or one of its combinations in the stipulation sections (144 out of 162 divine names in chaps. 5-11 and 186 out of 200 in chaps 12-26) reinforces the idea of Israel's obligation to the covenant God who is none other than Yahweh.

(5) The predominant use of Yahweh or one of its combinations in the sanctions (98 out of 116 divine names) supports the concept of the Sovereign who bestows blessing and inflicts judgment as the Covenant-maker.

Elohim. The second major name for God in Deuteronomy, *Elohim,* with its related forms, occurs 38 times. It appears alone 23 times (5 in the prologue, 6 in the stipulations, 8 in the sanctions, and 4 in poetry). *El* occurs 12 times (3 in the prologue, 4 in stipulations, 5 in poetry), *Elyon* once (in poetry), and *Eloah* twice (both in poetry). In addition, 'ĕlōhîm as a generic for "gods" is attested 37 times (once in the prologue, 22 times in the stipulations, 10 times in the sanctions, and 4 times in the poetry). At least four observations can be made from these data:

(1) There is a lack of creation/cosmic revelation, a revelation usually attached to the divine name El/Elohim, except in the theophany sections where transcendence is to be expected and emphasized.

(2) Rare forms (El, Elyon, Eloah) are found mainly in poetry (8 out of 15

uses); the only exception is El and this appears outside poetry only in chaps. 1-11.

(3) Reference to the heathen gods is primarily in the stipulations and sanctions (32 out of 37 occurrences), where Yahweh is compared and contrasted to alternative gods.

(4) The equal distribution of Elohim and Yahweh (12 and 16 uses, respectively) in poetry is because of the more transcendent quality of poetry and its attention to transcovenantal, universalistic themes.

Yahweh's Person. God's self-revelation is also expressed in statements pertaining to His Person, that is, His essence and being. Since the biblical witness everywhere attests to His radical difference and distance from all other things, His self-disclosure must take anthropomorphic and anthropopathic forms. Thus, Deuteronomy refers to God's hand (2:15; 3:24; 4:34; 7:19; 11:2; 26:8; 33:11; 34:12) and arm (4:34; 5:15; 7:19; 11:2; 26:8) as expressions of His power. His eyes (11:12; 12:28; 13:18; 32:10) represent His omniscience and constant attention, while His face (5:4; 31:18; 33:20; 34:10) and mouth suggest His communication of His glory and word. In fact the "mouth" of Yahweh is a metonymy for His word as propositional revelation (1:26, 43; 8:3; 9:23; 17:6, 10-11; 19:15; 21:17; 34:4).

In startlingly human terms Yahweh is said to write (10:4), to walk (23:14), and to ride (33:26). No other nation has a god so near (4:7, 39; 31:8), one who dialogues with Moses and Israel (9:12-24) and moves about in Israel's camp (23:14), and yet who is so utterly transcendent (4:12, 35-36, 39; 5:4, 22-26; 7:21; 10:17; 28:58) that He cannot and must not be represented iconically (4:12, 15) but only by His name (12:5, 12, 21; 14:23, 25; 16:2, 6, 11; 26:2). He is the *only* God, the incomparable One (3:24; 4:35, 39; 5:7; 6:4, 15; 32:39; 33:26), who is sovereign (10:17-18; 32:8-9) and eternal (30:20; 32:40; 33:27). In the warmest human terms Yahweh is a Father to His people (14:1; 32:5-6).

Yahweh's attributes and character. The divine self-disclosure manifests itself first in the full panoply of Yahweh's attributes and character. He is a gracious God, one who has made unconditional promises to the fathers and to Israel (Deut. 1:8, 11; 3:18, 20-21; 4:31; 6:10; 7:8; 9:5, 27-28; 10:15; 11:9, 21; 28:9; 29:13) and who continues to offer blessings to His people in the present and the future (1:10, 20-21, 25, 35; 2:7; 7:13-16; 8:10, 18; 10:22; 11:14-17; 12:1, 21, 14:24, 29). Particularly noteworthy are the occurrences of *hesed* in this respect, for this distinctive covenant term certifies the covenant dependability of the Lord who has graciously obligated Himself to His chosen ones (5:10; 7:9, 12; 33:8).[83]

Another of the attributes of God particularly relevant to Deuteronomy as a covenant text is that of His love. This is demonstrated in His fatherly affection for Israel (1:31), but most especially it is used as a *terminus technicus* to describe the Lord as Covenant-maker (4:37; 7:7-8, 13; 13:18; 23:5; 30:5; 33:12).[84] In fact His love

83. Nelson Glueck, *ḤESED in the Bible* (New York: Hebrew Union College Press, 1967).

84. Moran, pp. 77-87.

for and election of Israel are one and the same. He chose this people to be His own special possession, not because they were great or mighty—for they were anything but that—but because He loved them (7:7-8). That is, the choosing and the loving are mutually defining, and they result in salvation and covenant.

As the covenant initiator, God is faithful to His commitment (Deut. 7:9, 12; 31:6, 8; 32:4), powerful in defending it and His people (4:34, 37; 5:15; 6:21-22; 7:19), and absolutely holy (5:11), glorious (5:24-26; 28:58), and upright in all His ways (32:4). He is righteous and just (4:8; 10:17-18; 32:4) in His dealings with Israel, but He is also a jealous God, one who cannot and will not tolerate competing allegiances (4:24; 5:9; 6:15; 13:2-10; 29:20; 33:16, 21). If His people walk in disobedience and go after other gods or otherwise violate the covenant mandates of Yahweh, they can expect to be visited by His anger and judgment (1:37; 3:26; 4:21, 25; 6:15; 7:4; 9:18-20, 22; 11:17; 13:17; 29:20, 23, 25, 27-28; 31:29; 32:21-22). Their repentance will, however, be met by His unqualified mercy (4:31; 13:17; 30:3).

Yahweh's function. The second and perhaps more clearly perceived and understood mode of God's self-revelation in Deuteronomy is His historical and even suprahistorical activity. In light of the covenant structure and content of Deuteronomy the dominant (and perhaps all-inclusive) function of Yahweh is that of sovereign Lord of the universe who has elected to make covenant with Israel so that she might carry out His plan for the world. Given this assumption, an assumption that an analytical theological approach sustains, it is appropriate methodologically that one see specific divine activity and relationships in Deuteronomy as constituting elements of the exercise of God's suzerainty.

The revelation of Yahweh as seen in the manner of its expression in previous discussion and in terms of His names and epithets, person, and attributes must, of necessity, impinge on and even coincide with that revelation clarified by His role as overlord. But the approach that follows will heighten the covenant theme of Deuteronomy and indeed the entire Pentateuch and will hopefully contribute to an understanding of God's revelation of Himself in the proper hermeneutical context of covenant relationship.

Creator. Fundamental to God's acts in history is, of course, His work as Creator. Though this is a major biblical motif elsewhere, only Deuteronomy 4:32 addresses it clearly in all the corpus of covenant text under review here. Even here it is almost incidental, for the point that is being made is that there was no historical precedent since creation for God's having spoken to and redeemed a people as He did with Israel. Clearly then the emphasis is not on the universal covenant with all mankind whereby God has mandated them to assume dominion over all things created. Rather, the emphasis in Deuteronomy is on the covenant with Israel by which she was called from among the existing nations to bear witness to the Creator God whose work as Creator is presupposed. The call to Israel is not to fill the created earth but to occupy a land. The role of the Lord here, then, is not that of Creator but of Redeemer and initiator of covenant.[85]

Redeemer. His function as Redeemer is made clear from a number of passages (Deut. 5:6, 15; 6:12, 21-23; 7:8; 8:14; 9:26, 29; 13:5, 10; 15:15; 16:1; 24:18; 26:8). On the basis of His love alone He defeated the Egyptian slavemaster, delivered His son Israel against impossible odds, and brought His people to the point where they could confront His covenant invitation with all its promises and expectations. These were mighty acts that occurred in history, acts so momentous and humanly inexplicable that the whole world must see in them that the God of Israel was indeed without peer. The work of redemption was an array of events that testified to the sovereignty of Yahweh over all creation and to His gracious purposes in calling a people who themselves would be a channel for His ongoing work of redemption on a universal scale.

The immediate objective of the redemptive act was to bring the redeemed people into covenant fellowship with Yahweh. Yahweh, therefore, is the covenant God, the one who initiated this special relationship and who brought it to pass in a concrete, historical event. And it was not an afterthought, merely a logical succession to the Exodus, for Yahweh had promised the fathers of Israel that He would call their seed apart, save them in mighty power, and bring them to Himself as a special possession. In fact Deuteronomy everywhere predicates the Sinaitic and Deuteronomic Covenant and its benefits precisely on the promises to the patriarchs (1:8, 11, 21, 35; 6:3, 10, 19; 7:8, 12; 8:18; 9:5, 27; 11:9; 19:8; 26:3; 29:13; 30:20; 34:4).

From his historical and geographical vantage point in the plains of Moab, Moses looked back thirty-eight years to the actual moment when Yahweh had effected the covenant that they now were being charged to reaffirm. At the encounter at Sinai He had given them the Ten Commandments as the vital heart of the covenant relationship (Deut. 4:13), a relationship founded on His redemptive grace (4:20, 34) and election (7:6-8; 10:15; 32:9-13).

In the context of covenant renewal, which is the essence of the Deuteronomic message, the most obvious benefit of the covenant to the assembly at Shittim was the conquest, occupation, and settlement of the land across the Jordan, the land of Canaan. Though there were many other promises attached to the covenant, both in patriarchal promise and Sinaitic affirmation, nothing looms larger in Deuteronomy than land.[86] For more than 400 years the Israelites had been strangers in hostile Egypt and ever since the Exodus had been rootless nomads in the Sinai wilderness. No wonder the anticipation of permanent settlement in their very own land was so dominant a theme in Moses' farewell address to Israel. Having been constituted as a nation with law and cultic worship, all they lacked was a territory in which they could live out before all nations the purpose for which they had been called and

---

85. Bernhard W. Anderson, *Creation versus Chaos* (Philadelphia: Fortress, 1987), pp. 59-60.

86. Dumbrell, *Covenant and Creation,* pp. 116-23; Patrick D. Miller, "The Gift of God: The Deuteronomic Theology of the Land," *Interpretation* 23 (1969): 451-65.

commissioned. That land now lay before them as the final piece in the mosaic of God's covenant purposes (Deut. 1:8, 20-21, 39; 2:24, 29, 31; 3:18, 20; 11:24-25, 31; 12:1, 10; 13:12; 15:7; 17:14; 18:9; 19:2-3, 7, 10; 20:16; 21:23; 24:4; 25:15, 19; 32:49, 52).

The land of promise would be gained only by conquest, however, for the kingdoms of Canaan, like all the kingdoms of the earth, were antithetical to the purposes of Yahweh, and in their fallenness they refused to acknowledge His sovereignty over them. Their hostility to Yahweh would obviously extend to Israel, His servant people, so that Israel's appropriation of the land of promise—the very land those foes occupied as illegitimate squatters—could come about only by struggle and war, a conflict that Israel was ill-equipped to undertake.

The land of the promise was not, after all, Israel's land but Yahweh's. As noted before, Canaan epitomized in a microcosmic way all the earth God had created as the realm of His dominion in and through mankind. Man's failure to be the image of God had resulted in His forfeiture of earthly and historical regency, a disbarment from authority that will continue until the kingdoms of this world finally "become the kingdom of our Lord and of His Christ" (Rev. 11:15). Israel was elected, however, to demonstrate historically what the rule of God on the earth should be, and the land of Canaan was chosen as the arena in which the world could glimpse that sovereignty in action. Its conquest and occupation would serve, therefore, as a prototype of universal conquest and occupation that is so much a theme of the eschatological message of the prophets.

If Canaan was really "God's land," then no one other than God could dispossess its unlawful occupiers and enable His own servant people to put down their roots in its soil. This gives rise to the view that the war of conquest was not Israel's war but God's.[87] It was not Moses or Joshua or any human leader who would make success possible but only Yahweh, for He is the warrior who goes forth to battle to accomplish exploits on behalf of His people, exploits that result in victory and dominion. Deuteronomy is replete with references to Yahweh as warrior and conqueror, He who fights Israel's battles on her behalf (1:4, 30, 42; 2:15, 21-22, 33, 36; 3:2-3, 21-22; 4:3; 5:15; 7:1-2, 16, 18, 22-24; 9:3-5; 11:23; 12:29; 18:12; 19:1; 20:4, 13; 28:7; 31:3-6, 8).

Warrior. Yahweh's role of divine warrior leads to a consideration of other ways in which He declared and demonstrated His gracious beneficence on behalf of His people Israel. The promise of and conquest of the land was indeed a major constituent of the covenant and its blessings, but it was not by any means all that God intended. He would provide continued bounty in the land (Deut. 6:10-11; 7:13-15; 8:7-10; 11:14-15; 14:29; 15:4, 6; 16:15; 28:3-6, 11-12; 29:5-6; 33:24) just as He had in the past (2:7; 8:3-4). This would include plentiful harvests, abundant rain, good

---

87. P. D. Miller, "God the Warrior: A Problem in Biblical Interpretation and Apologetics," *Interpretation* 19 (1965): 39-46; idem, *The Divine Warrior in Early Israel* (Cambridge: Harvard U., 1973).

health, and long life. More important, Israel would see the promise continued through an unending line of posterity (1:11; 7:13-14; 10:22; 28:4).

Though this latter promise clearly spoke in physical terms, the greater blessings of the Lord would be in the spiritual realm. He would show His *ḥesed,* His covenant commitment, to generations yet unborn (Deut. 5:9). Their own days would be immeasurably blessed in the land as the people of Israel reciprocated in obedience (5:16, 33; 6:2-3; 11:26-27). They would, in fact, be set above all the other nations on the earth (28:1-2, 13). Even if they proved to be disobedient and unworthy of His favor, Yahweh would forgive and restore them to a place of covenant responsibility (30:3-10; 32:43).

Prosecutor and Judge. The reverse side of Yahweh's function as Redeemer and warrior on Israel's behalf, however, is that of prosecutor and judge. As just intimated, Israel could (and would) depart from her covenant privileges and for this must be disciplined and punished. The covenant fellowship offered incalculable opportunity and privilege to Israel but it also demanded compliance to its mandates. To be the vassal of Yahweh was an awesome prospect for it entailed the highest reward or the most serious condemnation.

Yahweh therefore revealed Himself as a judge (Deut. 1:17) who had already shown His displeasure in the Israelites' past (9:14, 19-20, 25-26; 11:2-6) and who would punish rebellion in days to come (5:9; 6:15; 7:4, 10; 8:19-20; 11:17). This would be particularly manifest in His uprooting them from the land of promise and scattering them to the ends of the earth (4:27; 28:20-68; 29:20-28; 32:23-26). This would not be for the purpose of destroying them, however, but it would have the salutary purpose of disciplining them until they should return repentantly to serve the Lord once more as the people whom He chose in unconditional grace.

THE REVELATION OF MAN

Because the Old Testament consistently describes man as the crowning glory of God's creative and redemptive activity and because Israel is seen from the Abrahamic Covenant onward as the special "possession-people" whom God has elected to serve Him and the world redemptively, no further justification is needed to consider the revelation of man as a fundamental Old Testament theological theme. In light of the obvious covenant structure and content of Deuteronomy, it is manifest that the divine covenant-maker, Yahweh Himself, must be in covenant with someone. This someone is, of course, Israel, but because Israel's election is telic and serves a higher end—that of proclaiming the Sovereign's redemptive purposes— consideration needs to be given to mankind in both a larger and a more specified sense than Israel alone. The discussion then may logically and theologically proceed from a consideration of Deuteronomy's revelation concerning mankind, the nations, Israel, and the individual.

The revelation concerning mankind. Deuteronomy includes only four occurrences of *'ādām,* the normal word for the human race (4:28, 32; 8:3; 32:8). The first of these refers to the idols as the work of men's hands, while the next two speak of God's creation of man and His distribution of them on the earth. In 32:8 *'ādām* is parallel to *gōyîm*, a word that usually signifies political and territorial categories.[88] Other uses of *'ādām* in Deuteronomy appear to indicate something other than gentilic mankind (5:21; 20:19), probably the individual. Deuteronomy 8:3 teaches that mankind must live by more than food—he must also have the divine Word. With this, however, there is little attention to the human race as such.

The revelation concerning the nations. Deuteronomy describes the nations by the terms *gôy* and *'am* in addition to their proper names. *Gôy* first appears in 4:6-8 where Israel is distinguished from the nations by having a superior revelation and law. Deuteronomy 4:34 describes her as a "nation from the midst of a nation" (Egypt), emphasizing again the elective, separative character of God's people (cf. 26:5, 19). In the curse section, a punishing nation (Assyria) is predicted, one that will carry Israel off and show her no mercy (4:27; 28:36, 49-50, 65; cf. 30:1; 32:21). Moses is told that Yahweh will destroy Israel and make of Moses another nation (9:14).

The Canaanite nations must be driven out of the land because of their wickedness and so that Israel might inhabit it (Deut. 4:38; 7:1, 17, 22; 9:1, 4-5; 11:23; 12:2, 29-30; 19:1; 20:15; 31:5). Israel also will go on to rule over these and other nations (15:6, 28) and be a source of blessing to them (28:12). In the eschatological age they will rejoice with Israel in God's salvation (32:43). The nations must not be emulated in their idolatry (12:29-30; 18:19, 14) nor in their political structures (17:14), for Yahweh is Israel's Sovereign. If Israel sinned she would be punished even as Yahweh punishes the nations (8:20).

The second major term, *'am*, is frequently parallel to *gôy* in Deuteronomy (as elsewhere), but it has more the technical meaning of ethnicity. Where it is parallel to *gôy* or juxtaposed in such away as to suggest synonymity, further comment is unnecessary. Striking examples of the ethnic content of *'am* are the Anakim, who are a giant race (9:2), and the invading hordes whom Yahweh will allow to overrun the land as a punishment of Israel (28:33).

The revelation concerning Israel. That Israel's identity was more than political is stressed in her election as a people (Deut. 4:20; 7:6; 14:2, 21; 26:18-19; 33:29) and in her innate characteristics of stubbornness (9:6, 13) and foolishness (32:6). Her nonpolitical nature is commonly seen in the addresses of Yahweh and Moses to and about "the people" (2:4, 16; 3:28; 4:10; 5:25; 9:13, 27; 10:11, passim). Very significant is the statement that "today you have become the *'am* of Yahweh your God" (27:9). One might expect *gôy* here, but the ethnic content of the concept "Israel" is as important as the national. In fact, this passage may well teach (contra Noth[89] et al.) that there was more to Israel than a federation of originally unrelated tribes. Israel was and always had been "twelve sons of one father," that is, an eth-

88. *Theological Dictionary of the Old Testament* (1975), s.v.i *goy*, 2:426-433.
89. Martin Noth, *The History of Israel* (New York: Harper & Row, 1960), pp. 85-97.

nic, eponymous people (cf. 29:13). The covenant character of the people is seen in their description as the people of Yahweh (9:26, 29; 21:8; 26:15; 32:9, 36, 43) and, in irony, Yahweh spoke of them angrily as the people of Moses (9:12).

The revelation concerning the individual. Old Testament anthropology finds its pentateuchal roots in Genesis (as already seen), but the remainder of the Torah is little concerned with the doctrine of the individual. The reason should be obvious: beginning with Abraham the historical and theological focus is on the nation Israel and its character and role and not mankind in general or the individual human being in particular. Even the individual Israelite was important only as he related to the covenant nation.

In Deuteronomy, as well as in the rest of the Old Testament, the word '*îš* is the usual one to denote the individual person as opposed to mankind (generic) or people(s). Synonyms of '*îš* are *'ĕnōs, geber, zākār,* and *ba'al,* all used in Deuteronomy in specialized ways or with particular nuance. All these terms, including '*îš,* have no theological meaning in Deuteronomy but are used invariably merely to point out the individual or to distinguish the male from the female (22:5; 4:16).

The usual psychosomatic terms occur in Deuteronomy and with their usual meanings. *Nepheš* most frequently is a designation for the person himself (4:9; 10:22; 13:7; 24:6-7; 27:25), but sometimes it indicates, idiomatically, the vital personality, that is, the essential being (6:5, 12:28; 19:6; 19:11, 21; 22:26; 30:6); the emotional element (24:15; 28:65); emphatically, the entire person (4:29; 10:12; 26:16; 30:2, 10); or the will or desire (12:15, 20-21; 14:26; 18:6; 23:25).

The term *lēb* ("heart") describes more particularly the intellectual/mental aspect of man (Deut. 4:39; 6:6; 8:5; 29:3, 18; 30:11; 32:46), though often it is parallel to *nepheš* or collocated with it and other similar terms so as to yield the meaning "person" (4:9, 29; 6:5; 10:12; 26:16; 28:65; 30:2, 6, 10). There is clearly an emotional quality as well (15:7, 9-10; 19:6; 20:3, 8). Finally, *lēb* is a synonym, like *nepheš,* for the person *qua* person, the individual (2:30; 7:17; 8:17; 9:4; 10:16; 18:21).

Rûah as an anthropological concept occurs only once in Deuteronomy (2:30) and than parallel to *lēb. Lēb* is "hardened" by Yahweh, suggesting that it speaks of a man's inner disposition, his essential psyche.

In conclusion, as stated earlier, there is no distinctive anthropology in Deuteronomy because in this covenant text the individual is of relatively little significance. It is Israel, the vassal, that is highlighted in the book whose purpose is to show the Sovereign's redemptive, covenantal claims on and relationship to a people through whom He would manifest His saving will.

THE REVELATION OF COVENANT

Now that the covenant-maker (Yahweh) and the covenant recipient (man, especially Israel) have been considered, it is necessary to give attention to that apparatus that bound them together in their peculiar relationship—the covenant itself. To do this, one must recognize both the formal and the substantial aspects of the relationship, that is, the framework and the content.

The form of the Deuteronomic Covenant. In the wake of the work of scholars like Korošec, Mendenhall, Kline, and Baltzer,[90] it has become generally recognized that Old Testament covenant form and pattern resemble those of Late Bronze Age Hittite vassal treaties. Despite disclaimers from McCarthy, Frankena, Weinfeld,[91] and others, this recognition appears to be increasingly prevalent in Old Testament form-critical and theological circles.

Deuteronomy has especially commended itself to this analysis. The essential features of Hittite unilateral treaties are found by most scholars in Deuteronomy and in the traditional order. The following outline is typical:

I. Preamble (1:1-5).
II. Historical Prologue (1:6-4:40)
III. (Introduction to Stipulations) (4:41-49)
IV. The Basic Commandments (chaps. 5-11)
V. The Specific Legislation (12:1–26:15)
VI. (Exhortation and Narrative Interlude) (26:16–27:10)
VII. Curses and Blessings (27:11–28:68)
VIII. (A Concluding Charge) (chaps. 29-30)
IX. Covenant Deposition and Continuity (chap. 31)
X. Covenant Witnesses (chap. 32)
XI. (The Blessing of Moses) (chap. 33)
XII. (Narrative Epilogue) (chap. 34)

All the necessary or usual ingredients of the secular treaty patterns are included in Deuteronomy and in the normal order. The correctness of these comparisons will become self-evident in the following detailed theological analysis.

The content of the Deuteronomic Covenant. To achieve a certain objectivity it is necessary to proceed inductively to determine the actual teaching of Deuteronomy on the covenant relationship between God and Israel. This will yield results compatible with the structure just suggested.

Geographically the setting of Deuteronomy was the land of Moab (Deut.

90. V. Korošec, *Hethitische Staatsverträge* (Leipzig: T. Weicher, 1931); George Mendenhall, *Law and Covenant in Israel and the Ancient Near East* (Pittsburgh: Biblical Colloquium, 1955); Kline, *Treaty of the Great King;* Klaus Baltzer, *The Covenant Formulary in Old Testament, Jewish, and Early Christian Writings* (Philadelphia: Fortress, 1970).

91. D. J. McCarthy, *Treaty and Covenant: A Study in Form in the Ancient Oriental Documents and the Old Testament* (Rome: Pontifical Institute, 1963); idem, *Old Testament Covenant* (Atlanta: John Knox, 1972); R. Frankena, "The Vassal Treaties of Esarhaddon and the Dating of Deuteronomy," *Old Testament Studies* 14 (1965); 122-54; Moshe Weinfeld, *Deuteronomy and the Deuteronomic School* (Oxford: Clarendon, 1972).

1:5), just opposite Jericho. Forty years had passed since the Exodus and Israel's redemption and thirty-eight years since the making of the covenant at Sinai. The old generation of the Sinaitic Covenant had passed from the scene, and Moses, about to die, stood before the assembled host of the new generation to rehearse to them the gracious ways of Yahweh in the past and to urge on them His promises of blessing and success to come.

Fundamental to an understanding of Deuteronomy is the recognition that it is not so much a covenant document as a covenant-renewal text. The covenant itself had been made and recorded at Horeb/Sinai (1:6; 4:1-2, 5, 10, 15, 23, 33-40, etc.), but it must now be restated and reaffirmed because a new generation had been born that had not personally made its commitment to Yahweh. Moreover, new historical and sociopolitical forces were at work. The nomadic life of post-Sinaitic times was about to be replaced by sedentary occupation of the land of promise, a transition that obviously required tremendous adjustments in those areas of the covenant text having to do with civil, social, and economic life (5:12-15 [cf. Ex. 20:8-11]; 7:1-5 [cf. Ex. 23:32-33]; 12:5 [cf. Ex. 29:24]; 15:12-18 [cf. Ex. 21:2-6]).

That this is a sovereign-vassal arrangement is clear, as already seen in the analysis of the Sinai Covenant (Ex. 19:4-6). Yahweh had taken the initiative and Israel had accepted the responsibility to participate and be obedient. Throughout there is a free use of the technical terms and ideas of this kind of treaty. There is reference to the past (19:4); injunctions to obey; use of *berîth* and *segullāh*, both of which are precise covenant terms; and the conditional form "if . . . then" (19:5-6), a clear hallmark of the sovereign-vassal language.

It is at this point that covenant form and covenant content coincide and become mutually informing. That is, the postulate that Deuteronomy is a sovereign-vassal text now finds confirmation in the analysis of its content, for only that kind of form allows the content to become meaningful in its fullest sense.

The Preamble. The covenant setting becomes, in the first place, the initial element in the Hittite treaty model, the preamble. It refers to the "words [cf. Akk. *am/watu,* a technical covenant term][92] of Moses," the covenant mediator who stood in a particular place and time to remind Israel of the original statement and act of covenant at Horeb (Deut. 1:2). The preamble thus forms the bridge between the original covenant and its renewal to the new generation.

The Historical Prologue. The historical prologue, the second element in standard treaty forms, is in effect a detailed résumé and itinerary of God's dealings with Israel from Horeb to the plains of Moab (Deut. 1:6–4:40). It harks back to the past (1:6–3:29) and addresses the present as well (4:1-40).

Moses rehearsed the events at Horeb (Deut. 1:6-18) where Yahweh had reminded the people of the promise to the fathers and had commanded them to move out and take the land of promise (v. 8). Moses next had appointed theocrat-

---

92. *Chicago Assyrian Dictionary,* ed. M. Civil et al. (Chicago: Oriental Institute, 1968), II/1:34-35.

ic leaders to assist him but reminded them and all Israel that it was Yahweh who possessed ultimate authority, not they (v. 17).

At Kadesh Barnea (Deut. 1:19-46) Moses had urged the people to go at once to occupy the land of Canaan, a request they failed to honor even though Yahweh was the mighty warrior who would fight for them (v. 30). The result was the rejection of that evil generation and the transmission of covenant responsibility and blessing to the next generation (v. 39). This is a most important development, for it provides at least part of the rationale for the covenant renewal document itself. A generation of Israel might fail, but the promise was intact. God would over and over again affirm His promises, for He cannot deny Himself.

The third significant stage of the immediate past was the encounter with Edom, a brother nation that must be left in peace (Deut. 2:1-7). It is noteworthy that the land of Edom was sacrosanct and inviolable precisely because Yahweh had given it to Esau just as He had given Canaan to Jacob (2:5). Thus, the sovereignty of Yahweh, though especially focused on Israel in the Old Testament, is seen to extend to other nations as well, particularly to those that also trace their ancestry to Abraham.

The same principle applied to Moab and Ammon, descendants of Lot and his daughters (Deut. 2:8-25). They had been set in their own land of promise and not even Israel could uproot them without challenging the kingship of the Lord who determined the allocation of the whole earth in accord with His wisdom and grace.

At Heshbon, however, the situation was quite different, for the Amorites were not a brother-people but were bitter foes of Yahweh and Israel who must be placed under *ḥērem,* the edict of annihilation (Deut. 2:26-37). In one of the most crucial texts of the Old Testament relative to the decrees of the Lord, Moses pointed out that though Israel could have treated a compliant Amorite people exactly as she had treated Edom, Moab, and Ammon, Yahweh had other plans. He alone knew the difference between the Amorites and these other nations, and for purposes that lay solely in His own sovereign prerogatives He hardened the heart of Sihon, the Amorite king, so that the Amorites might provoke Israel to destroy them (v. 30). The immediate cause was that the land occupied by the Amorites was not theirs by divine allotment but was territory to be occupied by Israel as a part of the promise (v. 31).

Bashan similarly was under *ḥērem,* and its land came under the dominion of Yahweh and His vassal nation Israel (Deut. 3:1-11). When all this was accomplished the Transjordanian lands were divided among Reuben, Gad, and Manasseh as their allotment (3:18), and the other tribes received the pledge that they too would prevail over the Canaanites to the west, for Yahweh would fight for them (v. 22).

The final episode of the past was the denial to Moses of his own personal access to the Promised Land (Deut. 3:23-29). The covenant mediator, the most privileged of all the people of the Lord, had failed to set the high example incumbent on him by virtue of his office (cf. Num. 20:12) and so was unable to participate in conquest and enter into rest. As the Lord Jesus Himself later said, "From everyone who has been given much, much will be demanded" (Luke 12:48).

The second part of the historical prologue consists of the exhortation delivered by Moses to his own contemporary recipients of the covenant (Deut. 4:1-40). This parenetic section shows that the covenant terms and its blessings and/or curses were being urged on the vassal by the spokesman of Yahweh, the great King. The following points are noteworthy, particularly in view of the covenant nature of the material:

1. There is an appeal to obedience as the condition of covenant blessing (4:1, 6, 40).
2. There is the recognition that the document is inviolable; one must not add to or subtract from it (4:2; cf. 12:32).
3. There is a recognition of the equity and rightness of the document and its terms (4:8).
4. There is expression of the need for the covenant obligations to be rehearsed to generations to come (4:9-10, 40).
5. There is witness to the authoritative role of the covenant communicator, Moses (4:14).
6. The splendor and glory of Yahweh the Sovereign are clearly articulated (4:11-12, 15, 33, 36, 38).
7. The Sovereign's uniqueness, exclusiveness, and incomparability are emphasized (4:16-20, 23-24, 34-35, 39).
8. There is an appeal to covenant witnesses, particularly to the heavens and the earth (4:26; cf. 30:19-20; 31:28; 32:1; Isa. 1:2).
9. There is warning about covenant disobedience (4:26-28) and promise of restoration on the basis of confession and repentance (4:29-31).

Taken all together, these elements beyond question locate the material about to follow squarely within a covenant context.

The historical prologue ends with Deuteronomy 4:40,[93] which urges the audience to "keep his [Yahweh's] decrees and commands which I am giving you today, so that it may go well with you and your children after you and that you may live long in the land the Lord your God gives you for all time." This great summary statement brings to an end the recounting of the past and the exhortation of the present and paves the way for the delineation of the principles of covenant that would guide the chosen people for the ages to come.

Before these are delivered, there is a brief narrative interlude (Deut. 4:41-43) describing the selection of the cities of refuge in the Transjordan, a matter that is addressed also later (19:2-13; cf. Ex. 21:13; Num. 35:6; Josh. 20:7-9).

The so-called stipulation section of the covenant text embraces Deuteronomy

---

93. As Craigie points out, Deuteronomy 4:41-43 is not a part of the historical prologue but a section inserted between the prologue and stipulations, which are introduced in 4:44-49 (p. 145).

4:44–26:19, but this long section is in turn subdivided, primarily between the basic stipulations, or principles of covenant (chaps. 5-11), and the specific stipulations, or application of the principle (12:1–26:15). This kind of bifurcation between principle and practice is well attested from secular covenant models.[94] Failure to understand the proper relationship of the two parts will result in an inability to account for a certain degree of overlapping and repetition between them and, more important, will not allow for the fundamental theological premise that God's specific requirements are always grounded in some expression of His Person, nature, and eternal objectives. They are never purely arbitrary or disconnected from a pattern of covenant expectation.

The Basic Stipulations. The basic stipulations are introduced (Deut. 4:44-49) by a brief statement of historical recapitulation that once more locates the covenant in the act of Exodus and Sinai and traces it to this moment of restatement and reaffirmation. The basic technical terms of covenant stipulation—'ēdôth ("testimonies"), ḥuqqîm ("statutes"), mišpātîm ("judgments')—are all here (v. 45), forming part of the definition of tôrāh itself (v. 44).

A second element of introduction to the basic stipulations is Moses' opening exhortation to observe covenant renewal (Deut. 5:1-5). His harking back to Horeb (v. 2) shows once more that Deuteronomy is a covenant-renewal document whose purpose is to bring the original compact up to date in light of the changed conditions of the present and those anticipated in the immediate and distant future. One implication is that the normal structure of prologue, stipulation, and so forth is punctuated and interrupted by allusions to the original covenant and its subsequent course and by frequent parenesis exhorting obedience from now on in contrast to past patterns of disloyalty. Besides here, Horeb appears in 5:22-33; 9:8-21; 10:1-5. Past disloyalty is documented in 6:16; 8:2-5; 9:7, 22-24. Exhortation (usually with šᵉma', "hear") occurs elsewhere in 6:3-25; 9:1-5; 11:18-21. The difference between parenesis and covenant requirement in the strict sense is often difficult to detect, for Moses' exhortations may be construed as stipulation and vice versa.[95] Further form-critical study is needed at this point.

The basis for and heart of the covenant stipulation as a whole lies in the Ten Words (cf. Deut. 10:4), or Ten Commandments, discussed in detail previously in connection with the Sinai Covenant. Its form is frozen, though of course it contains variations in wording from the Horeb statement, because it is now embedded in a renewal document. With the exception of the blessings and curses (which, however, Beyerlin[96] and others argue are implicit in apodictic law), the essential covenant clauses are found in both this recension and that of Horeb (cf. Ex. 19:4-6; 20:2-17).

---

94. Thompson, p. 160.
95. A. D. H. Mayes, *Deuteronomy,* The New Century Bible Commentary (Grand Rapids: Eerdmans, 1981), pp. 48-49.
96. W. Beyerlin, *Origins and History of the Oldest Sinaitic Traditions* (Oxford: Oxford U., 1965), p. 54.

Deuteronomy 5:22–11:32 in turn consists of an elaboration of the basic principles of the Ten Words, namely, loyalty to Yahweh and love within the human relationship.

This second statement of the Ten Words is followed by another narrative interlude relating the Horeb revelation and Israel's response to it (5:22-33). This also has parenetic overtones in that it includes a statement of Yahweh Himself in which He urges obedience (vv. 23-31).

The principles that flow out from the Ten Words are defined as *miṣwāh, huqqîm,* and *mišpāṭîm* (Deut. 6:1). Perhaps the *miṣwāh,* the "command," is amplified in Deuteronomy 6-11, the general stipulation section, while the *huqqîm* and mišpāṭîm the "statutes" and "judgments," are spelled out in chapters 12-26.[97] If the Ten Words are the heart of the stipulations as a whole, the principle of the Words is encapsulated in the so-called Shema (6:4-5), which defines who the Sovereign is and reduces the obligation to Him to one of exclusive love and obedience.[98] As both Jesus (Matt. 22:36-38) and the rabbis taught, this is at the very center of what God requires of men, so much so that all other biblical revelation is actually a commentary on it.

But mere intellectual understanding of the principles of covenant requirement is not enough. They must be perpetuated in personal application and made the subject of ongoing catechetical instruction (Deut. 6:6-25). They again are described as "these words" (6:6; cf. 5:22), that is, the Ten Words. They and their adumbration, the Shema, must be observed as the fundamental duty of the vassal, a duty expressed by giving Yahweh exclusive recognition and worship (6:10-15) and obedience (vv. 16-19).

The content of the principles is revealed in Deuteronomy 7-11. They deal first with the dispossession of nonvassals from the land of promise (chap. 7). They had to be destroyed, that is, placed under *hērem,* because otherwise they would cause Israel to become disloyal (7:1-5). Moreover, Israel is the exclusive vassal of Yahweh, and only she is entitled to the land (vv. 6-11). Dispossession will result in God's abundant blessing (vv. 12-16) and will be possible because Yahweh is her warrior (vv. 17-26).

The second great area of concern has to do with Yahweh as the source of blessing and life in the land (chap. 8). His supply of manna in the wilderness is historical proof of this (8:1-5) and should prompt Israel to obedience, submission, and recognition of the ongoing and heightened blessing of the Lord of the land (vv. 6-10). Failure in these obligations will bring about the Sovereign's displeasure (vv. 11-20).

Third is the principle that Yahweh's past and future blessings are a product purely of His grace (9:1–10:11). Israel's possession of the land is not because of her just claim to it but because of Yahweh's ancient promises and His sovereign plea-

---

97. Thompson, p. 120.
98. E. W. Nicholson, *Deuteronomy and Tradition* (Philadelphia: Fortress, 1967), p. 46.

sure (9:1-5). And this is in spite of Israel's sins at Horeb (vv. 6-21) and elsewhere (vv. 22-24). The unique and effective mediatorial role of Moses stayed the wrath of Yahweh (vv. 25-29; cf. Ex. 34:9-10) so that the covenant was not abrogated but concluded and its tablets properly restored and deposited (Deut. 10:1-11).

The fourth major emphasis in this stipulation section is a love for Yahweh that must also be expressed in love for man (10:12-22). This summary and recapitulative passage (10:12; cf. 4:37; 6:5; 10:15) prescribes behavior among vassals (10:18-19; cf. 5:16-21) as well as loyal obedience to Yahweh (10:20-22).

Finally, the principle is set forth that blessings and curses (11:26-32) will follow according to Israel's attitude toward (1) the past dealings of Yahweh (vv. 1-7), (2) His promise to her of a good land (vv. 8-17), and (3) her obedience to and instruction of the covenant requirements (vv. 18-25).

The basic stipulation of covenant, then, (1) lays a foundation for the specific stipulations, a foundation that consists of a recognition of Yahweh's election of Israel by love and grace, (2) forms a recapitulation of and commentary on that fundamental principle of covenant as seen in the Ten Words and the Shema, the latter in turn being an adumbration of the former, and (3) urges (as seen in the historical review and hortatory sections) compliance with the covenant mandate of the Ten Words and with the specific stipulations that follow.

The Specific Stipulations. The specific stipulations occupy most of the remainder of Deuteronomy (12:1–26:15). Their purposes clearly are to elucidate further the basic covenant principle of chapters 5-11 and to define precisely the terms of the covenant relative to cultic, moral, and social/interpersonal/interethnic relationships. The rationale for the present canonical arrangement of the material is elusive,[99] but the following seems to honor the literary and theological requirements reasonably well.

(1) The exclusiveness of Yahweh and His worship (12:1–16:17). The set of regulations embodied in this section begins with attention to a central sanctuary (12:1-14), a place set apart in opposition to rival shrines, which not only had to be avoided but destroyed for they represented the alleged ownership of the land by competing sovereigns (vv. 4-5, 13-14).

In connection with the sanctuary is its offerings and sacrifices. Particularly significant is the blood (vv. 15-28), the sacredness of which stands in radical contrast to pagan notions of life, its source, and its sustenance. Life is common to men and animals; therefore its medium—blood—is common to all. It is a gift from God Himself in each and every case (cf. Gen. 9:4-7; Lev. 17:10-14).

The pagan gods (whether truly existent or only imaginary) were an abomination (Deut. 12:29-31), for they constituted a rival claim to the sovereignty of Yahweh. Their prophets likewise were evil (13:1-19). They professed to hear communication from other gods and therefore had to be slain as aiding and abetting sedition and treason.

---

99. See, however, Stephen A. Kaufman, "The Structure of the Deuteronomic Law," *MAARAV* 1/2 (1978-79): 105-58.

The Great King Yahweh demands homage and tribute of His people. This could not be willy-nilly, however, but had to be rendered in accord with profound and binding principle. In the first place, animals that were offered in sacrifice had to be clean (14:1-21). This was predicated not so much on hygienic principles but on the fact that "you are the children of the Lord your God" (v. 1) and a holy people and treasured possession (v. 2; cf. Ex. 19:5-6). That is, the arbitrary distinction among animals testifies to God's arbitrary election of Israel from among all the nations of the earth.[100]

Another important aspect of tribute is the tithe (Deut. 14:22-29), the purpose of which was to attest to the fact that Yahweh was the Lord of the land and that His kingdom servants, particularly the Levites, had to be sustained by its bounty. Other kingdom citizens also had to be protected and provided for. Thus is commanded the septennial release of bondservants (15:1-18). This took several forms: forgiveness of a brother's debt (vv. 1-6), an illustration of Yahweh's own forgiving grace and compassion for the poor (v. 2); constant regard for the poor even between years of release (vv. 7-11), for poverty among Yahweh's vassals was a disgrace; and the granting of freedom to an indentured servant, if he wished release (vv. 12-18), a release reminiscent of Yahweh's gracious Exodus deliverance (v. 15).

The dedication of firstborn male animals was also an act of tribute to Yahweh (15:19-23). If they were suitable, they had to be sacrificed and eaten before Yahweh as *š ᵉlāmîm*, or fellowship offerings (cf. Lev. 7:15-18). Otherwise they could be slain and eaten by the offerer at his own home. This separation of the firstborn was a token of Yahweh's deliverance of Israel's firstborn in the tenth plague in Egypt (Ex. 13:2, 11-16).

The principal times of presentation of tribute were those of the thrice annual festival pilgrimages to the central sanctuary where Yahweh held court (Deut. 16:1-17). The first of these, the Passover/Unleavened Bread complex (vv. 1-8), was to celebrate God's redemptive grace in delivering His people from their oppressive bondage. The feast of Weeks (vv. 9-12) served to remind Israel of her burdensome labor in Egypt (v. 12). The feast of Huts (vv. 13-17) commemorated the blessing of God on the land Israel was about to possess. Its original significance with respect to the marvelous provision of shelter in the wilderness where Israel dwelt in booths was to be replaced by a harvest festival attesting to the abundance of a settled life in Canaan.[101]

(2) The identification and role of kingdom officials (16:18–18:22). With the regency of Yahweh and the proper protocol by which He had to be approached having been established, the covenant text then addresses the human leaders who serve Him and exercise authority over the nation at large.[102]

The first of these, the judges and *šôṭᵉrîm* ("officials"), above all had to be fair

100. Thompson, p. 177.
101. This, of course, is opposite to the view of critical scholarship, which views the allegedly late Deuteronomic legislation as positing an original harvest festival as the basis for the festival of booths or huts. See de Vaux, *Ancient Israel,* 2:501.
102. For the setting and literary connection of the passage, see Mayes, p. 262.

and impartial in accord with the character of the Sovereign Himself (Deut. 16:18-20). The basis and authority of their judgment was the covenant text, and right and wrong were determined by the degree to which there was fidelity to the covenant principles (16:21–17:1). In easily resolved matters the judges did not need to be involved; the citizens themselves could handle such matters in the local village courts (17:2-7). In complicated cases that exceeded local jurisdiction, appeal had to be made to the supreme court where the priest (God's attorney?) and judge (man's attorney?) would adjudicate according to the *tôrāh* and *mišpāt* they decided (v. 11; cf. 2 Chron. 19:5-11).

As for the kings (Deut. 17:14-20), they had to be Israelites chosen by Yahweh. The king was never to rely on human resources but always had to observe the Torah (vv. 18-20), for he was only a viceregent of the King of kings and therefore had to implement the policies of his own Sovereign (cf. 2 Kings 11:12).

Religious leadership was to be in the hands of the priest-Levites (Deut. 18:1-8), the entire tribe of which would be sustained by the offerings of the people both in their local villages and in the central sanctuary. As selected servants of the King, they were entitled to the support of public largess.

The final office, that of the prophet, was to emerge in the future, but guidelines for its nature and function are given in the covenant text in anticipation of the soon-expected encounter with the false prophets of Canaan (18:9-22). Because the pagans employed manipulative techniques to determine the will of their gods, such methods were taboo to Israel. The true prophet and prophetic succession would speak with divine authority ("in My name") and their message could be tested by their resemblance to Moses and by the fulfillment of their predictive word.

(3) The establishment of civil law (19:1–22:4). Basic to any society, theocratic or otherwise, is a system of law by which its members govern and protect themselves. This might be said to be law on the horizontal dimension as opposed to cultic law, which regulated the vertical relationship (that between God and man).

The first category of civil law in the Deuteronomic code concerns that most heinous of human crimes, the taking of human life (19:1-13). Because manslaughter of any kind results in the death of a fellow vassal (particularly if he was an Israelite), it calls for proper punishment and yet proper protection of the accused. Unpremeditated cases permitted protection from the clan avenger and eventual exoneration of charges of murder (cf. Num. 35:9-34). Premeditation required the execution of the murderer by the avenger with the permission of the local elders (Deut. 19:12-13).

The law pertaining to the removal of boundary stones (19:14) was more important than it might seem at first glance, for it protected against the violation of territory allocation established by the great King Himself.[103] He who assigned all of

103. Kaufman goes so far as to say that "Deut. 19:14 is the axis, as it were, around which the rest of the Deuteronomic Law revolves" (p. 137). Although this may be an exaggeration, it does draw attention to the disrespect of one man for another as the root of much more serious covenant breach, including murder.

Canaan to Israel assigned its each and every part to clans and families who must occupy it forever in His name.

Accusation of wrongdoing in any case had to provide safeguards for the accused so he would not be the victim of mere vindictiveness or caprice (Deut. 19:15-21). The accused had to have been observed in his act by at least two witnesses, he was not to be condemned without proper legal procedure, and he had to be punished fairly, if and when culpability had been established.

War, a necessary evil in the defense of the Sovereign's interests, had its own set of regulations (20:1-20).[104] Because Yahweh was God not only of Israel but also of all the earth, these interests extended far beyond Israel's narrow concerns. He was, however, Israel's God in a special way, and as such He would lead His people in battle as the divine warrior (20:4). The local affairs of the people, such as property, family responsibilities, and even timidity had to be respected when the summons to war rang out. The "ordinary" enemy had to be permitted, for humane reasons, to surrender and become tributary. Failing this overture, the men thereof would be put to death. The people of inheritance lands (i.e., Canaan) all had to be placed under *ḥērem,* however, for they were hopelessly unrepentant in kingdom terms and represented potential subversion.

Death by murder, manslaughter, and war obviously do not exhaust the possibilities. On occasion there would be violent human death by unknown cause (Deut. 21:1-9). In such an event the populace of the village nearest the scene of the crime was required to slaughter a heifer in recompense. In this manner it, as a corporate entity, would be absolved of responsibility.

Finally, civil law had to deal with miscellaneous interpersonal relationships: the taking of wives from among prisoners of war (21:10-14); the protection of "secondary" wives from discrimination, particularly in terms of their sons' inheritance rights (vv. 15-17); the treatment of incorrigible and rebellious children (vv. 18-21); the proper disposition of the corpse of an individual who had been executed and publicly displayed (vv. 22-23; cf. Josh. 8:29; 10:26-27; John 19:31); and the care of a brother's lost or disabled property (Deut. 22:1-4).

(4) The establishment of cultic law (22:5–23:18).[105] As suggested above, the covenant relationship between Yahweh and Israel presupposed a law on a vertical plane, a set of guidelines to regulate precisely the form and manner of man's access to a holy God. The arena in which this takes place formally is worship, but because there was no ultimate distinction between sacred and profane in Israel, all actions of the community and its citizens had to be couched in terms of purity and righteousness. All that can be done here is to list the examples that illustrate what law in the realm of the God-Israel relationship entailed.

---

104. For the ethical and theological issues involved, see Kaiser, pp. 172-80.

105. Kaufman attempts (with limited success) to integrate Deuteronomy 22:5-8 around the principle of avoidance of manslaughter and to connect 22:9–23:19 to the prohibition of adultery (pp. 135-39).

The laws of purity (22:5–23:18) dealt directly or indirectly with forms of separation and care for safety and the helpless (though some are difficult to integrate), and they testify to the need for Israel to maintain its covenant purity and separation: the prohibition of the wearing of mixed clothing (v. 5); the protection of mother birds (vv. 6-7); safety rails on roofs (v. 8); the use of mixed seed, animals, and cloth (vv. 9-11); the requirement to wear fringes on garments by which to remember Torah (v. 12; cf. Num. 15:37-41); harlotrous daughters (Deut. 22:13-21); adultery (v. 22); unfaithfulness to one's betrothed (vv. 23-24); rape (vv. 25-29); incest (23:1); sexual deficiency (v. 2); the denial to illegitimate children of community rights (v. 3); the denial to Ammonites and Moabites of access to the assembly (vv. 8-9); impurity of bodily emissions and excrements (vv. 10-15); refuge for escaped slaves (vv. 16-17); and the prohibition of sacred prostitution (vv. 18-19).

(5) The establishment of laws of interpersonal relationships (23:30–25:19). This category of stipulation is akin to civil law and overlaps with it at points (cf. 21:10–22:4). However, its principal interest was in regulating proper conduct among the vassal-citizens in one-to-one relationships in distinction to that between citizens and foreigners. One could not levy interest charges on a loan to a fellow Israelite, though it was permitted in dealing with a foreigner (23:19-20). Vows made to Yahweh had to be carried out faithfully (vv. 21-23). A neighbor's produce could be plucked by hand without penalty (vv. 24-25). Divorce was also carefully regulated (24:1-4), as was the release from responsibility accorded to the newlywed (24:5).

Other laws dealt with millstones used as pledges (v. 6), kidnapping (v. 7), leprosy (vv. 8-9), pledges for loans made to the poor (vv. 10-13), fair treatment of the helpless (vv. 17-18), gleaning the fields and orchards (vv. 19-22), fair punishment for crime (25:1-3), muzzling the working ox (v. 4), the levirate law (vv. 5-10), unfair physical conflict (vv. 11-12), fair weights and measures (vv. 13-16), and the destruction of Amalek (vv. 17-19). The last proviso appears to be a summation of all the previous legislation concerning hostile elements and a preparation for the next section that pertains to the Conquest and the carrying out of the festivals in the land of promise.[106]

(6) The establishment of the law of covenant celebration and confirmation (26:1-15). The covenant renewal document, synonymous with Deuteronomy itself, was not created for the benefit of the pre-Conquest generation only. It was to be the foundation for covenant thought and life in the land of promise from that day onward, to the end of the Old Testament experience of Israel. Regularly and without fail the covenant community must gather to recite and celebrate the meaning of their task as the special people of Yahweh.

This section contains the occasion for this annual convocation, a theological event closely associated with the festival of the firstfruits (Deut. 26:1-4). A highlight of the gathering was the recitation of the historical covenant relationship

106. Craigie, pp. 317-18.

between Yahweh and Israel, an association traced back to Abraham, through the Egyptian sojourn and the Exodus, up to the present hour (vv. 5-9).[107] The firstfruits of the harvest testified to God's unfailing promises and prompted (or should prompt) His people to renewed commitment (vv. 10-11).

Further evidence of commitment (vv. 10-11) would be seen in the offering of the third-year tithe for the Levites and the disadvantaged of Israel (vv. 12-15). As this was being done, the benefactor would affirm before Yahweh that he had been faithful to the covenant requirements and he would invoke the continued intervention of Yahweh on His land and people.

Exhortation and Narrative Interlude (26:16–27:10). The stipulation sections having been fully unfolded, Moses urged the people to keep them with all their heart and soul. This led to the actual ceremony of covenant acceptance and affirmation, an indispensable part of covenant-making if it were to have any validity (cf. Ex. 24).

Though there must have been such a ceremony even in Moab, there is no record of it. Rather, Moses enjoined the hosts assembled before him to engrave the covenant texts on plastered stones as they entered the land and to take those stones with them to Shechem (Deut. 27:4). There they would build an altar on the exact site of Abraham's ancient shrine, and they would offer the *šᵉlāmîm* (fellowship) offerings, the very ones associated with covenant-making (v. 7; cf. Ex. 24:5).

Then in a remarkable statement Moses and the Levitical priests cried out to the people, "You have become the people of the Lord your God" (Deut. 27:9). By virtue of their having committed themselves to the terms and claims of this covenant (renewal) text they became as much the people of Yahweh as had their fathers at the initial giving of the covenant at Sinai. This, of course, is what covenant renewal was all about.

The Curses and Blessings (27:11–28:68). Continuing to look forward to the ceremony of covenant renewal at Shechem, Moses addressed the next major element of covenant content—curses and blessings. With six tribes on Mount Ebal, six on Mount Gerizim, and the Levites in the valley between them, the curses for covenant violation and the blessings for obedience would be solemnly recited and affirmed by the nation.

First are those curses for disobedience of specific covenant stipulations (Deut. 27:15-26). Presumably the unwritten blessings would complement these and thus be well understood. Then follow the blessings for the obedience of the basic covenant principles (28:1-14). Next are the curses that attend the violation of these so-called general stipulations (vv. 15-68). It is important to note the conditional and motive clauses, especially in verses 15, 20, 45, 47, 58. These suggest that judgment comes because of a disregard for the great fundamental truths on which Yahweh's covenant blessings depend. In fact, there is no blessing list of compara-

---

107. For the connection of the firstfruits with this "Old Credo," see Gerhard von Rad, *Old Testament Theology* (New York: Harper & Row, 1962), 1:297.

ble length here precisely because blessing is implied in the obedience to which
God calls His people.

A Concluding Charge (chaps. 29-30).[108] After a brief narrative statement documenting the existence of the Deuteronomic Covenant as the successor to the
Sinaitic (29:1), Moses once more rehearsed Israel's sacred history (vv. 2-9) and
emphasized the significance of that present moment in which she stood before God
to pledge her fealty to Him (vv. 10-13). The future, he said, would be bright with
opportunity to serve the Lord. If the people failed, however, they could expect
God's chastening, even to the extent of being cast out of the land of promise (vv. 14-
29). But even this could not frustrate the covenant promise and hope, for they could
(and would) repent and be restored to the land and to a position of covenant privilege once more (30:1-10).

Then in a kind of appeal to witnesses (the heavens and the earth—Deut.
30:19) Yahweh called on His people to affirm their commitment and to choose
life and good rather than death and evil (v. 15). To do the former was to receive the
blessing of the Lord, the blessing of "many years in the land He swore to give to your
fathers, Abraham, Isaac, and Jacob" (v. 20).

Covenant Deposition and Continuity (chap. 31). Obviously covenant documents retained no permanent value if they were not preserved for reference regularly or as the need required. So provision was made for their safekeeping in the
palace archives or other depositories of public record.

The Exodus account of the Sinai Covenant makes clear that at least the Ten
Words must be placed in the Ark of the Covenant (Ex. 25:16). The book of
Deuteronomy (and possibly the entire Torah) may have been preserved in some
special place in the later Temple as the story of Josiah's reformation suggests (2
Kings 22:8). Clues as to the disposition of the Deuteronomic Covenant text are
sparse in Deuteronomy itself, though the statement that "Moses wrote down this law
and gave it to the priests, the sons of Levi, who carried the Ark of the Covenant of
the Lord" (Deut. 31:9, 26) may support the notion of text deposit, specifically in the
Temple.

Related to the deposit of the covenant document was the need for continuing
implementation of its stipulations by generations to follow. Thus, it was incumbent
on Moses as covenant mediator that he appoint a successor who would stand
between Yahweh and the people until they were safe in the land of promise and a
new, monarchic order could be established. Joshua filled that role (Deut. 31:1-8),
a ministry so awesome and important that he, like Moses, had to be confronted
with Yahweh in all His glory so that he might understand that it was the Sovereign
of heaven and earth whom he was to serve (31:14-15).

The "Song of Moses" as Witness (chap. 32). The deposit of the text was also
to be accompanied by the oaths of the contracting parties. In the case of Yahweh the

108. Thompson sees this section as "a kind of recapitulation of the total covenant demand" (p.
278).

oath was His own promise of curse and blessing, a promise to be remembered by Israel in connection with the "Song of Moses" (Deut. 32). As they sang it in years to come it would continually testify as a witness for the Lord against them (31:19, 21) just as the heavens and the earth did so in that day of assembly (v. 28).[109]

The "Song of Moses," which celebrates the glory of the Sovereign, was enjoined on the people for it and all the fullness of the covenant message were not idle words but, as Moses stressed, were life itself (32:47). Ironically enough, however, Moses himself would not live. He had broken faith with Yahweh at Meribah and had not upheld the holiness of Yahweh among the Israelites (v. 51). His own experience thus testified to the importance of knowing and doing the will of God as a servant charged with the privilege of representing Him on the earth. The failure of Moses to enter the land spoke most emphatically of the need for Israel as a people to keep covenant faithfully if they hoped to enter into God's fullness of blessing.

The Blessing of Moses (chap. 33). In anticipation of his death Moses pronounced a blessing on the twelve tribes in his role of covenant mediator. The blessing took the form of a prophetic declaration of favor to be expected by the tribes as recipients of Yahweh's grace. Clearly the intent of this address is to assure the chosen nation that it would continue, long after Moses' death, to be the channel of Yahweh's salvific outreach to the nations of the earth.

Narrative Epilogue (chap. 34). Though not technically an element of the covenant text, the narrative of Moses' death is theologically significant: it documents a portent of God's faithfulness to His promise to the fathers (34:1-4); it recounts the death and burial of Moses as the end of the era of initial covenant making (vv. 4-8); and it restates the fact of Joshua's succession to Moses (vv. 9-12). Though Moses was without peer as a prophet whom Yahweh knew "face to face," Joshua, the prophet and covenant spokesman for the next generation, was filled with the same Spirit of God who had empowered Moses to accomplish the ministry of mediation between the great King in heaven and His vassal people on earth.

CONCLUSION

A theology of the Pentateuch founded on and organized around the great kingdom principle of Genesis 1:26-28 is able to integrate the multifaceted materials of universal, patriarchal, and Mosaic revelation in an eminently satisfying manner. The mandate that man should "be fruitful and increase in number; fill the earth and subdue it" (Gen. 1:28), although expressive of the fundamental purposes of the divine creation of man, was frustrated at once by man's obstinate rebellion and fall. A way then needed to be found for that lapse to be redressed and for the pristine conditions and objectives to be undertaken once more and ultimately fulfilled.

That way took the form of a covenant arrangement whereby (1) the seed of the woman would crush the head of the enemy (Gen. 3:15), (2) the postdiluvian race

109. Craigie, p. 372.

headed by Noah would carry out the original mandate in spite of the fallenness of humanity (9:1-7), and (3) Abraham and his descendants would constitute a chosen people who would demonstrate to the world of nations what it means to be the people of the Lord and who would also provide the channel of redemptive grace whereby the world might hear the message of reconciliation and be brought back into covenant fellowship with Yahweh (12:1-3; 15:1-19; 17:1-14; 22:15-18).

In other words, the unilateral promise and covenant commitment made to the patriarchs was that they would sire a nation that would be a servant to the Sovereign God, a servant charged with the privilege and responsibility of bridging the gap between that transcendent Lord of creation and the creatures in His image whom He proposed to restore to the purposes for which He had brought them into existence. That promise at last found expression in Israel with her people, her land, and her ministry.

The elaborate Mosaic Covenant revealed at Sinai is the instrument whereby this servant people became the fulfillment of promise and the vehicle of the redemptive message. Though of a suzerain-vassal type and therefore theoretically conditional, it was inaugurated by the unchanging God, who made it clear that His promises to Israel were eternal and irrefragable no matter what Israel might or might not do in days to come. The election of Israel and her redemption from hostile Egypt were acts of divine grace without precondition and without the possibility of retraction (Ex. 2:24-25; 3:15-17; 4:21-23; 6:2-8). It was only the acceptance of servanthood with all its blessings that was conditional (19:4-6). The creation of Israel as a servant people was a fait accompli, an act of the sovereign God in accord with His own eternal promises. The function of Israel within that framework depended on Israel's obedience to the terms of servanthood spelled out in the Sinai revelation.

Most of Exodus-Deuteronomy is an explication of those terms. The very forms of the great covenant texts—Exodus 20-23 and all of Deuteronomy—are in the mold of the sovereign-vassal treaties so well known in the ancient Near East. By that form alone they reveal their function. They set before Israel the guidelines within which she must conduct herself in order to discharge her God-given responsibilities properly. Obedience to them would result in blessing; disobedience or covenant violation would result in judgment.

Even Israel's failure, however, would not imperil the purposes of God, for, as New Testament revelation makes clear, the Lord Jesus Christ—the suffering Servant of Isaiah—is in Himself a "new Israel," as is His Body the church. Until its era is done, the church has been commissioned to transmit the message of redemption— a task Israel failed to do. But praise be to God, His promise to Israel is not abrogated—not by Israel's Old Testament disobedience or by the subsequent role of the church. For He will regenerate His ancient people and thus qualify them in ages to come to bring to fruition the grand design for which He had called and elected them (Lev. 26:40-45; Deut. 30:1-10; Jer. 31:27-34; 33:19-26; Ezek. 36:22-38; Rom. 11:25-32). This is the theology of the Pentateuch.

2

A THEOLOGY OF
JOSHUA, JUDGES, AND RUTH

THOMAS L. CONSTABLE

INTRODUCTION

How can someone reading the text of Scripture determine which revelations are major and which are minor? Is not everything God has preserved in Scripture important? Should one presume to rank revelation in terms of significance?

The only basis for making this distinction should be the text itself. What did the writers of Scripture, led by the Holy Spirit, emphasize as they wrote? One can answer this question only by discovering the words, phrases, ideas, themes, and structural patterns they used as they wrote. These identify the major motifs in any given piece of literature. By observing the motifs it is possible to discover what was of importance to the writers.

Since the books of Joshua, Judges, and Ruth record a segment of Israel's history it is important to consider the historical context in which that history occurred. How is what the books contain related to what precedes (the Pentateuch) and to what follows (Samuel, Kings, etc.)? The answer to this question constitutes

THOMAS L. CONSTABLE, Th.M., Th.D., is director of D.Min. studies and professor of Bible exposition at Dallas Theological Seminary.

the first part of this chapter. Then the contents of these books will be examined more particularly. It will become apparent that certain major emphases occur in all three books. Then the particular emphases of each of the three books will be pointed out.

JOSHUA, JUDGES, AND RUTH IN THE CONTEXT OF BIBLICAL REVELATION

How the period of Israel's history recorded in these books fits within the larger scope of God's dealings with Israel must be noted to assess accurately what God wanted His people to learn from these writings.

The Israelites regarded God's dealings with them in history just as revelatory as any verbal message delivered by a prophet of God. This is clear from their placement of Joshua and Judges in the Former Prophets section of their Bibles.[1] They regarded these historical records as authoritative revelation of events chosen by God to teach important spiritual lessons. Only certain events were chosen to be included in the historical books of the Old Testament by the divine author—those with permanent spiritual significance (2 Tim. 3:16-17).

THE CULMINATION OF PREVIOUS REVELATION

God created mankind to glorify Himself by giving human beings the opportunity and privilege of enjoying an intimate relationship with Himself. The Creator produced a perfect environment in which man could live (Gen. 1). Then He lovingly and carefully formed man out of humble material and shared His own life with him (Gen. 2).[2] However, man doubted God's goodness, denied His Word, disobeyed His will, and consequently suffered alienation from his Creator (Gen. 3). God proceeded to seek out man in grace and provided for him what he could not produce himself, making renewed fellowship possible (3:21).

As history unfolded, the majority of humanity chose to seize the initiative from God and live independently of Him rather than following Him and experiencing maximum blessing. But God always reached out to the rebels, offering a relationship with Himself and blessing. When man's refusal was complete, God brought cursing and death as punishment.

In the Flood God judged the race of rebels, but in His grace He preserved a remnant of worshipers in Noah and his family. At Babel, God again judged mankind's disobedience (cf. Gen. 1:28) and scattered the population over the earth

---

1. Ruth was also regarded as a book of history and was believed by the Jews to have been written by Samuel, along with the book of Judges and Samuel (*Baba Bathra* 14b). It was placed in the Rolls subsection of the Writings section of the Hebrew Bible rather than in the Prophets only because it was used in the liturgies of Judaism (D. R. G. Beattie, *Jewish Exegesis of the Book of Ruth* [Sheffield: Journal for the Study of the Old Testament. 1977], p. 5, n. 3).

2. God's special interest in mankind is reflected in the Hebrew word *yaṣar,* translated "formed" in Genesis 2:7. The same word describes the careful work of a potter as he shaped the clay on his wheel (Isa. 29:16).

(which was both a curse and a blessing). These early incidents in human history demonstrate God's desire to bless man with a relationship with Himself and mankind's refusal to walk with God and be blessed. Man chose to seek his own way apart from God.

God then offered blessing to mankind through the mediation of one man, Abraham, and his descendants. God purposed to make Abraham the channel of His blessing to the rest of mankind (Gen. 12:1-3). In the process Abraham himself was blessed. The means God covenanted to use for mediating His blessing were Abraham's descendants and a specific geographical land.

In time, as a result of God's grace to Abraham, his family became numerous. It was protected from annihilation and assimilation in Egypt, but later his descendants, the Israelites, were enslaved in that same land where God was protecting them. To judge their oppressors as well as to liberate His chosen people, God brought Israel out of Egypt with a great demonstration of His sovereignty over all the so-called "gods" of Egypt. At Mount Sinai He adopted the fledgling nation as His "firstborn son" (cf. Ex. 19:5-6). The covenant He established with the Israelites there was a provision whereby they could maximize the blessings promised their forefathers by walking in fellowship with God. The Mosaic law was God's revelation of how they were to express their obedience; the Tabernacle and its ritual were His revelation of how they were to express their worship—worship and obedience being the Godward and manward expressions of trust in God.

In Genesis, Moses laid the foundation for Israel's trust in God by demonstrating His infinite power and His complete faithfulness. This book of the Torah was produced under divine inspiration to encourage God's people to exercise faith in Him.[3] Genesis demonstrates that only people who trust and obey God experience His blessings.

The revelation of God in the Mosaic law helped the Israelites realize two things: what it meant for them to be associated with a God who is holy, and how sinful they were. This revelation was designed to bring them into intimate fellowship with God so that they would become His instruments to teach all mankind how glorious it can be to live in fellowship with Him and in submission to His authority.

In the wilderness, Israel learned how stubborn and rebellious she was and also how graciously God deals with sinners. For the older generation the years of wandering were years of judgment for lack of trust and obedience. But for the younger generation they were years of education, a time of preparation for entering the life God had graciously chosen for Israel to enjoy as His mediators of blessing to the world. The Israelites learned that everything depended on their attitude

---

3. Whether Moses wrote Genesis before the Exodus, at Mount Sinai, during the wilderness wanderings, or on the plains of Moab, the choice of material in Genesis clearly seems designed to build Israel's trust in God so that she would obey Him, go forward in His will, and experience the blessing He purposed for her. See Allen P. Ross, *Creation and Blessing* (Grand Rapids: Baker, 1988), pp. 88-91.

toward God. Trust would express itself in worship and obedience and would be crowned with many forms of blessing. But unbelief would lead to divine cursing and death. God's purposes would not be defeated, though His plans would be delayed by the failure of His instruments. In Egypt they had seen that His purposes could not be stopped by His enemies.

In the book of Deuteronomy Moses addressed the new generation of Israelites about to enter the Promised Land. He reviewed God's past faithfulness in spite of Israel's unfaithfulness. He reiterated the basic stipulations of the Mosaic Covenant with emphasis on the principles underlying those commands. And he called on the people to recommit themselves to the Lord and to the Mosaic Covenant, realizing the consequences of obedience and disobedience. Throughout his addresses Moses stressed motivation. God's love for His people had led Him to deal with them as He had, and their love for Him should move them to follow Him faithfully in the future. Only the loving commitment of Yahweh to Israel and of Israel to Yahweh would make possible the fullest blessing of mankind and Israel. Israel would be blessed by possessing the Promised Land and being made fruitful. Their descendants and possessions would multiply.

The Pentateuch reveals all the principles necessary for man to enjoy the intimate relationship with God for which he was created. He must trust and obey God who is strong enough and faithful enough to bring to pass what He has promised. Those who trust and obey God are blessed, and from God's viewpoint they succeed. Those who do not are cursed and fail. Faith in God is manifested in worship and obedience. The motivation of God's universal government is His love for man, and the motivation of man's obedience to God should be his love for God.

In Genesis, God is seen as omnipotent and faithful. In Exodus the emphasis is on His sovereignty, in Leviticus, on His holiness, in Numbers, His grace, and in Deuteronomy, His love.

In Genesis, man is presented as made in the image of God but rebellious, sinful, and unable to come to God on his own. In Exodus, he is seen as enslaved, needing to be redeemed, and the object of God's liberation and adoption. In Leviticus, the sinfulness of man contrasts with the holiness of Yahweh. Here he learns what it means to be a sinner. In Numbers, redeemed man's nature as disobedient, rebellious, and complaining stands out. And in Deuteronomy, man is viewed as the unworthy object of God's loyal love. He is the servant of the King of the Universe but also God's son.

In Joshua, Judges, and Ruth the basic principles of human relationship with God are worked out as the history of Israel began to unfold. In Joshua the account is mainly positive. Victory and success accompany God's people when they follow Him faithfully. The book of Joshua validates Moses' claims in Deuteronomy 28:1-14 that God would bless His people when they remained faithful to the Mosaic Covenant. In Judges the course of events is mainly negative. When God's people do what is right in their own eyes, as opposed to what is right in God's eyes, they experience defeat and failure. Judges proves Moses' warning in Deuteronomy

28:15-68 that God would curse Israel when she defected from the covenant. The book of Ruth demonstrates that, even in the midst of an apostate environment, when individuals choose to trust God and commit themselves to Him He will bless them and mediate blessing through them.

Joshua, Judges and Ruth validate the revelation given in the Pentateuch, so in this sense they are the culmination of what precedes. They also set the stage for later revelation in Samuel, Kings, and other historical books of the Old Testament.

THE PREPARATION FOR SUBSEQUENT REVELATION

God had promised to bring His people into the Promised Land. Canaan would be a base of operations for them to achieve their God-given purpose in history. Joshua records God's fulfilling that promise. Israel entered the land, broke the military might of the native Canaanite tribes, and began to occupy the land. She was effective to the extent that she trusted and obeyed God. But since her trust and obedience were only partial, Israel did not completely drive the Canaanites out or possess the land fully. Pockets of Canaanite resistance remained (in Jerusalem, Shechem, the Jezreel Valley, the coastal plain, and elsewhere). The continuing presence of Israel's enemies in the land proved to be a source of constant frustration throughout the period of the judges and until David finally subdued them (as recorded in 2 Samuel). The promises and incentives God held out to Joshua as he anticipated entering the Promised Land (Josh. 1:2-9) were not fully realized in his lifetime nor in the lives of the leaders who outlived him (24:1-28).

The book of Joshua, therefore, prepared for later revelation by recording Israel's entrance into the land where she was to be a light to the other nations of the world (Isa. 42:6) and a testimony of how glorious it can be to live under Yahweh's governing hand. Her entrance into Canaan was essential to God's further plans and purposes of His kingdom of priests (Ex. 19:6) who were given the privilege of bringing other peoples to the true God. But Israel's failure to drive out the Canaanites completely made her commission more difficult to fulfill.

The land west of the Jordan was divided among the tribes. These territorial divisions became home to most of the various tribal groups within the nation until the captivity of the Northern Kingdom of Israel in 722 B.C. and that of the Southern Kingdom of Judah in 586 B.C.

The book of Joshua records a period of about 40 years of Israel's history.[4] Judges, on the other hand, covers approximately 265 years.[5] Whereas Joshua gives

4. If the Exodus took place in 1446 B.C. (see 1 Kings 6:1), the Israelites entered the land in 1406 B.C. (Num. 14:33-34). The conquest lasted till 1399 (Josh. 14:10; cf. Num. 14:24), and Joshua died about 1366 (Josh. 24:29), assuming Caleb and Joshua were about the same age.
5. The elders who entered the land with Joshua would have been younger than him and Caleb, but probably not more than about ten or fifteen years younger, in view of God's judgment on the older generation at Kadesh-Barnea. Thus, the period of the judges began about 1350 B.C. Samson's death, the last event recorded in Judges, evidently took place around 1084 B.C. (Eugene H. Merrill, *Kingdom of Priests* [Grand Rapids: Baker, 1985], pp. 173-74).

a record of victory and success, Judges documents Israel's spiritual, national, and social defeats and failures. The period of the judges can be visualized as a descending spiral. In the cycles of history recorded in the book, Israel departed further and further from God.

There were six periods of oppression by Israel's foes during the 265 years spanned by the book of Judges. The first of these was an 8-year oppression by the Mesopotamians, which was finally broken by Othniel (Judg. 3:7-11). The second prolonged oppression came from the Moabites and lasted 18 years. Ehud was the judge who ended this domination (3:12-21). This was followed by 20 years of oppression by the Canaanites mainly in northern Israel (chaps. 4-5). Barak and Deborah were God's deliverers in this instance. Then came 7 years of oppression by the Midianites, which Gideon terminated (6:1–10:15). The fifth oppression came from the Ammonites on the east and the Philistines on the west (10:6–12:15).

Israel's most prominent deliverer from the Ammonite foe was Jephthah. After Jephthah's defeat of the Ammonites, the Philistines continued to oppress Israel on the west (the sixth oppression), and Samson began to deliver Israel from this enemy (chaps. 13-16). Conflict with the Philistines continued, however, throughout the ministry of Samuel, on through the reign of Saul who died fighting them, and well into the reign of David who finally subdued them. The record of Israel's oppression by her enemies begins in the book of Judges and continues through 2 Samuel 10.[6] Thus, the book of Judges prepares for future revelations by documenting the downward course of Israel's national affairs, which resulted finally in the people becoming frustrated with rule by judges and demanding a king like the other nations (1 Sam. 8:5).

The reasons for Israel's decline during the judges period are clearly set forth in Judges 2:6–3:6. Beginning from a position of enjoying God's blessing, the Israelites turned from the Lord to the gods and practices of the Canaanites. To bring them back to Himself, God disciplined His people by allowing them to fall under the oppressing domination of their enemies. When they eventually cried out to Him for salvation, He graciously delivered them by raising up a judge. As a result of God's deliverance, the Israelites rededicated themselves to Yahweh. This led to enjoying God's blessing once more. But after a time of blessing the people again apostasized and the cycle began anew. Judges records this cycle of experiences as having taken place six times during the 265 years of history related in the book. Spiritual apostasy led to national disorganization and social chaos, but repentance resulted in deliverance and blessing.

One of the purposes for which Judges was recorded seems to have been to provide apologetic justification for Israel's monarchy.[7] The people did not recognize

---

6. David's defeat of the Philistines, Jebusites, and Ammonites resulted in the consolidation of his kingdom. The last of these battles, the Ammonite wars, ended about 990 B.C. So Israel experienced major threats from neighboring kingdoms for about 360 years (ca. 1350-990 B.C.).

7. Arthur E. Cundall, "Judges—An Apology for the Monarchy," *Expository Times* 81 (October 1969–September 1970): 178-81.

or were not willing to deal with the real causes for decline during the time of the judges, namely, their lack of trust in and obedience to God. Instead, they blamed their form of government and demanded a king and a monarchy. Their desire was not contrary to the will of God. God had long before promised to raise up a king in Israel (Gen. 17:6; 49:10; etc.). And He had made provision in the Mosaic law for a king (Deut. 17). But the peoples' reason for wanting a king was wrong and their timing was wrong. God had purposed to give them a king—namely, David— who would rule as His "son." But the Israelites insisted on a king prematurely and ended up with one who proved to be a great disappointment. Judges sets the scene for the monarchy.

Another purpose for which Judges seems to have been written was to show God's sovereign grace in preserving Israel in spite of herself.[8] Why did Israel continue as a nation in spite of repeated failings and apostasies? Because God had chosen her as His instrument to bring blessing to the rest of mankind (Gen. 12:1-3). Even though Israel failed (cf. Ex. 19:5-6), God remained faithful. The breaking of the reciprocal Mosaic Covenant did not destroy the unilateral Abrahamic Covenant. The book of Judges clarifies God's continued dealings with Israel that are unfolded in the later historical books.

The contribution of Ruth as a foundation for later revelation is also significant. Ruth provides the background of God's anointed king, David. It is a book of roots, whose genealogy at the end ties David with Judah, to whom the promise of God's future ruler was given (Gen. 49:10).

According to the Talmud, Ruth was regarded in Jewish tradition as having been originally part of the book of Judges.[9] Along with the two incidents in the appendix of the book of Judges (chaps. 17-18 and chaps. 19-21), Ruth forms a part of the "Bethlehem trilogy," so called because in each story Bethlehem figures significantly.

In the first story Moses' grandson, Jonathan from Bethlehem, formally established idolatry in Dan.[10] This put Bethlehem in a bad light. In the second story another Levite, on the way home to Ephraim after persuading his concubine to return with him from her family home in Bethlehem, was attacked by residents of Gibeah, Saul's hometown, and they brutalized and murdered the concubine. He then carved her body into twelve pieces and sent them throughout Israel as a summons to the other tribes to bring those responsible for the atrocity to justice. This resulted in civil war and the tribe of Benjamin was almost completely wiped out. Again the connection of Bethlehem with this tragedy put the town in a bad light. The third story, that of Ruth, tells of another man who "left Bethlehem" (Ruth 1:1; cf.

---

8. William J. Dumbrell, "'In those days there was no king in Israel; every man did what was right in his own eyes.' The Purpose of the Book of Judges Reconsidered," *Journal for the Study of the Old Testament* 25 (1983): 30-31; Robert G. Boling, *Judges*, The Anchor Bible (Garden City, N.Y.: Doubleday, 1975), p. 293.

9. "Samuel Wrote . . . the Book [sing.] of Judges and Ruth" (*Baba Bathra* 14b).

10. See G. F. Moore, *A Critical and Exegetical Commentary on Judges* (New York: Charles Scribner's, 1895), pp. 401-2.

Judg. 17:7-8; 19:10), namely, Elimelech. But in contrast to the other two men this one brought honor on Bethlehem. Saul's ancestors had humiliated Bethlehem by their treatment of the concubine from Bethlehem. In view of this apparent weakness, Bethlehem did not have a good reputation. But God raised up from Bethlehem a king who was far superior to Saul. This choice was in harmony with God's typical method of choosing to use and bless the least promising people, viewed naturally, as His instruments.[11]

The book of Ruth, therefore, testifies brilliantly to God's choice of David.[12] Even though David came from Bethlehem, his immediate ancestors were people of sterling character and spiritual commitment, as Ruth reveals. Whereas Judges justifies Israel's monarchy by showing the inadequacy of the tribal confederacy, which degraded into anarchy (Judg. 21:25), Ruth justifies the monarchy by showing how David fit the pattern of God's anointed servants. Saul proved to be cut out of the same cloth as the Gibeonites, who disregarded the will of God to satisfy their own ambitions. David proved to be a true Bethlehemite looked down on by others in Israel because of apparent weakness, but in reality strong in character and spiritual fiber.

Another purpose of the book of Ruth was to connect the Davidic dynasty with the promises of the unconditional Abrahamic Covenant rather than with the conditional Mosaic Covenant.[13] To accomplish this, the writer traced David's genealogy back to Perez, the son of Judah (Ruth 4:18). It was from Judah that a king for Israel would arise (Gen. 49:10). He would be the main channel of God's blessing to Israel—and through Israel to the world. The provision of this king was not conditioned on Israel's obedience to the Mosaic Covenant but was guaranteed on the basis of God's faithfulness to His promise to Judah. When David reigned, he functioned as a priest as well as a king (1 Chron. 15-17). He was able to do so because his right to rule was rooted in the Abrahamic Covenant rather than in the Mosaic Covenant. Had it been rooted in the Mosaic Covenant David could not have served as a priest since he was not a Levite. But because his right to rule went back to the Abrahamic Covenant, obviously antedating the Mosaic Covenant, he could serve as a priest. David functioned according to the order of Melchizedek, not the order of Aaron (cf. Pss. 2, 110). The book of Ruth then links David with the promises of a king that were given to the patriarchs and so prepares for the record of his reign that follows in 1 and 2 Samuel.

THE SHARED EMPHASES IN JOSHUA, JUDGES, AND RUTH

Martin Noth was one of the first Old Testament scholars to point out that the books from Joshua through 2 Kings all view the history of Israel from the per-

---

11. God chose Abraham, though he was from pagan stock and was not the eldest son in his family. He chose Sarah, Rebekah, and Rachel, even though they were barren. He chose Isaac over Ishmael, Jacob over Esau, Joseph over his older brothers, and the Israelites over other nations. Even today He often selects the ignoble rather than the noble (1 Cor. 1:26-29).

12. Oswald Loretz, "The Theme of the Ruth Story," *Catholic Biblical Quarterly* 22 (1960): 391-99.

13. Merrill, *Kingdom of Priests,* pp. 185-87.

spective of the revelation given in Moses' speeches to the Israelites in Deuteronomy.[14] His conclusion that Joshua through 2 Kings was produced in its final form during the Babylonian Exile has been questioned by many conservative scholars. However, few have denied his contention that Israel's history was being evaluated against the standard of the Mosaic law. Deuteronomy in particular is the seed plot from which the major theological ideas in Joshua through 2 Kings arise, wherein Moses expounded the covenant sermonically to the generation of Israelites about to enter the Promised Land. What Moses said was no doubt in the minds of the writers of the books of Joshua through 2 Kings. Several major motifs run through Joshua, Judges, and Ruth.

GOD

When God called Moses and commissioned him at the burning bush, Moses asked God what he should say to the Israelites when they asked him who had sent him to them (Ex. 3:13). God replied that Moses should tell them, "I Am has sent me to you" (v. 14). The ambiguous name "I am that I am" has been clarified as meaning, "I am who I will show Myself to be as history unfolds."[15]

As the history of Israel unfolded from the plagues on Egypt onward, God continued to reveal Himself to His people. By the time the Israelites crossed the Jordan River and entered the Promised Land, they had learned through experience as well as through verbal instruction the kind of God they served.

Joshua 1 is important theologically because God, in appealing to Joshua to enter the land, reminded His general of what he had learned about Him. That memory would give him strength and courage (cf. Deut. 31:23). God reminded Joshua that the land of Canaan was His to give the Israelites because He is the possessor of all things (Josh. 1:2-3). He assured Joshua that He would faithfully fulfill His promise to the patriarchs to give Israel that full territory He had promised, not just the land she would possess initially during the seven-year conquest (v. 4). He promised to be with Joshua as He had been with Moses; God would not just send him out but would *lead* him forth (v. 5; cf. 5:13-15). The basis of Joshua's confidence and strength was God's promised presence and power (1:6). But the key to Israel's success in the Conquest, Joshua's effective leadership, and God's saving presence with His people would be Israel's fidelity to the book of the law (the Mosaic Covenant—Josh. 1:8). The chiastic structure of God's charge to Joshua clarifies the essential importance of obedience to the covenant.

---

14. "Schriften der Konigsberger Gelehrten Gesellschaft," *Geistewissenschaftliche Klass* 18 (1943): 43-266. For an English translation, see *The Deuteronomistic History,* trans. Jane Doull, rev. John Barton, ed. David J. A. Clines (Sheffield: Journal for the Study of the Old Testament, 1981).

15. Sigmund Mowinckel, "The Name of the God of Moses," *Hebrew Union College Annual* 32 (1961): 127; Charles R. Gionotti, "The Meaning of the Divine Name YHWH," *Bibliotheca Sacra* 142 (January–March 1985): 45. See also Umberto Cassuto, *A Commentary on the Book of Exodus* (Jerusalem: Magnes, 1983), pp. 36-37; Brevard S. Childs, *The Book of Exodus* (Philadelphia: Westminster, 1974), p. 75.

A   I will be with you (1:5)
   B   Be strong and courageous (vv. 6-7)
      C.   That you may have success (v. 7)
         D   The Book of the Law (v. 8)
      C′   Then you will have success (v. 8)
   B′   Be strong and courageous (v. 9)
A′   The Lord your God is with you (v. 9)

God's power is emphasized repeatedly in Joshua, Judges, and Ruth. Yahweh gave victory over the Canaanites in the conquest of the land. He also enabled the judges to overthrow Israel's oppressors. He sent famine, but in Ruth's day He removed it. He providentially directed Ruth into Boaz's life; He provided a redeemer for her and eventually a king for Israel.

The faithfulness of God to His promises received regular notice by the writers of these books, just as Moses had stressed it in Deuteronomy. God gave His people the land He had promised their forefathers (Josh. 1:6; 11:23; 21:45; 24:2-13; Judg. 2:1). He did not break His covenant with Abraham (Judg. 2:1; Ruth 4:13-14). He disciplined the people for disobedience but blessed them for obedience (Judg. 2:13-18). He raised up deliverers for them when they cried out for salvation (3:9; 6:6-8; 16:28-30; Ruth 4:13-14). And He went with them into battle (Judg. 6:16).

God continued to reveal Himself as sovereign over all the universe. All the earth belongs to Him (Josh 1:3; 14:1-2; 21:43; 24:4). He is sovereign over His people (Judg. 1:1; 2:3), and He sovereignly rules over their decisions (Ruth 1:6-22; 2:3).

Whereas the holiness of God is not a matter of special instruction in these books, they do reveal God's holiness and show the consequences of God's being holy. The Canaanites were judged in part because their extreme sinfulness could no longer be tolerated by the holy God. God dealt even more severely with sin among His own people than He did with sin among the Canaanitess (e.g., Josh. 7). Because the Israelites compromised with the unholy Canaanites, God disciplined them by subjecting them to enemy oppressors as recorded in Judges. And God blessed Boaz and Ruth for their holy conduct.

God's grace shines forth in these books as in all of Scripture. He graciously did not abandon His people for their sin but disciplined them to bring them back into the place of blessing. He was gracious to the Canaanites by waiting for centuries before judging them (cf. Gen. 15:16). He tolerated six cycles of apostasy in the period of the judges. He brought Rahab the Canaanitess and Ruth the Moabitess not only into the nation of Israel but also into the line of David and the Messiah. The story of practically every major character in Joshua, Judges, and Ruth evidences God's grace in His dealings with these people.

Besides being gracious, God is also loving. Repeated evidence of this characteristic is found in these books. God's loyal love (*ḥesed*) can be seen in His commitment to all the descendants of Abraham. Never did God completely abandon or cast away the people He had chosen to love. And even individuals outside the nation of Israel, such as Ruth, were loved by Him. His love is seen when He reached out to help those who trusted Him. He was committed to the welfare of those on whom He set His love. In Joshua, Judges, and Ruth these aspects of God's character receive major emphasis.

MAN

These books likewise reveal much about the character of man. The rebelliousness of humans toward God stands out in all three books.

According to Joshua, the Canaanites had advanced to such a state of rebellion that they steadfastly opposed God's instrument of discipline, namely, Israel. Even when the Gibeonites submitted to Israel, they did so only to save their own lives.[16] Achan rebelled against God's will concerning "the ban" (*ḥērem*, Josh. 7).

In Judges, the Israelite tribes for the most part rebelled against God by not driving out the Canaanites who remained after Joshua's conquest (Judg. 1-2). Even some of the judges, including Gideon and Samson, were not completely committed to God. In Samson's day no other Israelites are said to have supported him as Israel's judge in his conflicts with the Philistines.

In Ruth, the theme of rebellion is weak. Naomi's attitude seems at first to have been rebellious (Ruth 1:20), but in time she softened (2:20). Orpah also went her own way (1:14). Human rebelliousness against God is another way of viewing man's unfaithfulness to Him.

The limited power of human beings is another motif in these books. Except for divine enablement the Israelite conquest of Canaan would have failed. Whenever the Israelites forgot their natural helplessness and presumed to go against their enemies in their own strength and wisdom, they failed (see Josh. 7:2-5; 9:14). When God withdrew His angel as leader of Israel's forces, the people could no longer drive out their enemies (Judg. 2:1-5). The judges were all weak individuals made powerful only by God's Spirit. Since Gideon recognized his extreme vulnerability, God was able to grant a miraculous deliverance through him and his handful of soldiers. Ruth was blessed not because she was intelligent, aggressive, and strong but because she committed herself to the Lord, who then began to work on her behalf. These books consistently reveal that human power is limited. Only as people submit to God's authority does He work in and through them to demonstrate His supernatural strength.

Man is not only weak; he is enslaved to sin. The evidence of this in these books, as in all of Scriptures, is man's natural inability to overcome evil influences and to break out from the domination of his own sinful nature. The Canaanites and

16. This has been the conclusion of most Jewish and Christian commentators, though some believe the Gibeonites' profession of faith in Yahweh was genuine (e.g., Francis A. Schaeffer, *Joshua and the Flow of Biblical History* [Downers Grove, Ill.: InterVarsity, 1975], pp. 148-51.

the Israelites in the book of Joshua consistently went the way of the flesh except for the grace of God. In later years this tendency is even more clearly revealed in the Israelites and in their judges. And though Ruth the heroine was redeemed by another, Boaz, she could not redeem herself.

Even the redeemed people of God were in need of divine revelation. The book of Joshua shows they needed special revelation from God on how they were to relate to Him, to the Canaanites, and to each other. Redeemed people remain dependent on God. In Judges the Israelites asked God who should go up against which group of their enemies first (Judg. 1:1). As long as the people proceeded on this basis they succeeded, but when they stopped seeking God's direction they failed. The judges who sought and followed God's word flourished (e.g., Gideon), but those who paid little attention to God failed (e.g., Samson). Ruth succeeded because she was open to learning and following God's word made known to her by Naomi and Boaz.

The importance of loving and trusting God is another major theme. Moses had told the Israelites that they should love God because He loved them (Deut. 4:32-40, etc.). As seen in Joshua, when Israel expressed love for God by remaining loyal to His Mosaic Covenant, they prospered, and when they disregarded His will, they floundered. This same pattern is observed in Judges. Ruth's love for Yahweh and Naomi is seen in her commitment to live under their authority. For this she was blessed. Love for God is fueled by remembering (giving heed to) His faithfulness and love in the past. It is based on confidence in Him. Love is more than a *feeling* toward God. Basically it is a *commitment* to honor and glorify Him. As people pursued this commitment loyally, feelings of love for God followed. These books emphasize commitment more than feelings, a commitment rooted in faith (cf. Heb. 11).

COVENANTS

The covenants (formal promises) are another major motif in Joshua, Judges, and Ruth. They are the commitments that bind God and man together in relationship. In the books under consideration, two covenants are constantly in view: the Abrahamic and the Mosaic.

The promises God gave Abraham in Genesis 12:1-3 are the basis for the Abrahamic Covenant. God promised Abraham seed, blessing, and land.[17] These promises were formalized into a covenant in Genesis 15. This chapter makes it clear that what God promised Abraham did not depend on anything Abraham was obligated to do. It was unconditional in this sense. Furthermore, nothing in the

---

17. Walter C. Kaiser has called them heir, heritage, and inheritance (*Toward an Old Testament Theology* [Grand Rapids: Zondervan, 1978], pp. 35, 84-99). David J. A. Clines referred to them as posterity, relationship with God, and land (*The Theme of the Pentateuch* [Sheffield: Journal for the Study of the Old Testament, 1978], pp. 29, 45-60). Compare J. Dwight Pentecost, *Things to Come* (Findlay, Ohio: Dunham, 1958), pp. 65-94.

covenant indicates a time limitation on what was promised. God bound Himself to do these things, but He did not say when complete fulfillment would be realized. The relationship God established with Abraham's descendants in this covenant was that of a Father with His firstborn son.

The other covenant in view in Joshua, Judges, and Ruth is the Mosaic Covenant. This was made with the nation Israel at Mount Sinai following their deliverance from Egyptian bondage (Ex. 2–Num. 10). In the Exodus, He purchased the nation for Himself. At Sinai He revealed how His people could enjoy a close spiritual relationship with Him. The Mosaic covenant clarified how Israel could enjoy to the fullest the blessings promised in the Abrahamic Covenant. They could do so by obeying what God prescribed. The analogy God used to describe His relationship with Israel under the Mosaic Covenant was that of a King (suzerain) over His subjects (vassals).[18]

The relationship of these two covenants to one another is also important to distinguish. Though both covenants were made with the Israelites, they had significant differences. The most obvious of these is the fact that fulfillment of what was promised under the Abrahamic Covenant was not at all conditioned on Israel's actions, whereas fulfillment of the blessings promised in the Mosaic Covenant depended on Israel's obedience. Later Scriptures reveal that the Mosaic Covenant was terminated at the cross of Christ (Rom. 7:6; 10:4; 2 Cor. 3:7-11; Gal. 5:1; Heb. 7:11-12). But no indication is given that the Abrahamic Covenant has ever been terminated. Consequently the Mosaic Covenant does not seem to be a restatement or expansion of the Abrahamic Covenant. The Mosaic arrangement was, so to speak, brought in alongside the Abrahamic Covenant to give Israel guidance so she might enter into what was promised to Abraham as soon and as fully as possible.

The analogies of God's relationship to Israel as a father to a son and as a king to a servant underlie Joshua, Judges, and Ruth as well as the rest of the Old Testament. As mentioned previously, from creation onward God's purpose has been to bless mankind with an intimate relationship with Himself.[19] This is the greatest blessing human beings can experience.

Joshua referred to God's election of Abraham and his descendants for blessing in Joshua 24, where he called on Israel to recommit to the Mosaic Covenant. The relationship analogies are not major motifs in Joshua, Judges, and Ruth in the sense that they are referred to often. But they are foundational to understanding God's relationship with Israel in these books. The themes that do receive emphasis are the great realities promised to Abraham: seed, blessing, and land.

In Joshua, the Israelites are the promised seed (descendants) of Abraham. Their numbers increased, as God had promised Abraham, though not as greatly as they might have, in view of the Kadesh Barnea rebellion. During the Conquest

18. Meredith Kline, *Treaty of the Great King* (Grand Rapids: Eerdmans, 1963).

19. This divine desire will be fully and finally realized in the new heavens and the new earth at the end of history (Rev 21:1–22:5).

Abraham's seed acquired a place in which to settle and multiply in the years to come. The land was divided among the tribes on the basis of the number of Israelites in each tribe in order to accommodate future growth. In Judges, the seed continued to increase. For 265 years Israel grew and became established in her homeland. In Ruth, the seed promise is primary. Here a specific descendant of Abraham, who would come through Judah and rule Israel (Gen. 49:10), is identified. This seed would be God's instrument in solidifying Israel's possession of Canaan and bringing blessings of many kinds to Israel and to the world.

God's promise of blessing to Abraham was twofold. God would bless Israel, and all the nations of the earth would be blessed through Israel (Gen. 12:3). That is, they would be blessed as a result of their contacts with Israel. In Joshua, we have evidence of Israel's being blessed by God. She was given the land and possessions of the Canaanites. She achieved status in the community of nations as she defeated the people of the land and established a homeland and all that goes with national identity.

There is also evidence in Joshua that Israel was a blessing to other nations. All the nations that cooperated with Israel prospered (e.g., the Gibeonite city-state), as did individuals (e.g., Rahab). In Judges, Israel was blessed by God's Spirit to give peace and prosperity to the people. Likewise, Israel became a blessing to others, as can be seen in the desire of many foreigners to intermarry and become part of God's people. Chief among them was Ruth. However, during the period of the judges Israel was not obeying the Mosaic Covenant carefully, so the extent of both her personal blessing and her missionary blessings were limited. In Ruth, too, God blessed Israel with godly ancestors from whom would come His greatest blessing thus far, namely, David.

The greatest evidence of God's blessing in these books, as in all Scripture, is His provision of salvation. In Joshua, God saved His people from their enemies. In Judges, He did the same through several deliverers. In Ruth, He provided salvation for Ruth, He delivered Naomi from heirless barrenness, and He delivered Israel by providing a king.

The land promise receives most attention in Joshua, which contains the record of God's giving the land of Canaan to Israel, His son and servant. Though occupation of the land was not complete, it did begin in Joshua's day. For this reason Joshua could say later in his life that God had fulfilled the land promise to Abraham (Josh. 21:43).[20] In Judges, Israel's enjoyment of the land and her full occupation of it were restricted due to her limited obedience to the Mosaic Covenant. The Abrahamic Covenant promised possession of the land unconditionally, but the Mosaic Covenant warned that occupation of the land would depend on obedience. In Ruth, the land does not figure as strongly as in Joshua and Judges except that it is the place of bless-

20. That it was not completely fulfilled is clear from later statements that there was yet much land to be possessed (Josh. 23:1-13; 24:1-28). See also John Calvin, *Commentaries on the Book of Joshua,* trans. Henry Beveridge (Edinburgh: Calvin Translation Society, 1854), p. xxii; and George Bush, *Notes on Joshua* (reprint, Minneapolis: James & Klock, 1976), p. 189.

ing for Ruth. Her entrance into Israel meant entrance into the Promised Land and its blessings.

One aspect of the land motif deserves special attention: the emphasis on rest reflected by Israel's entrance into the land. Moses had promised rest from the wilderness wanderings in the Promised Land (Deut. 3:20; 12:8-11; 25:19; Josh. 1:13; cf. Ps. 95:11). Possession of the land gave the Israelites rest from their pilgrim wanderings and from the harassment of their enemies (Josh. 1:14-15; 11:23; 18:1; 21:44; 23:1). Compromise with the Canaanites during the period of the judges interrupted the Israelites' rest in the land. They were oppressed and afflicted. But when God's people rededicated themselves to Him, He brought rest to the land for fairly long periods of time (Judg. 3:11, 30; 5:31; 8:28). The land was a place where the Israelites could rest, but their enjoyment of rest depended on their obedience to God. Through Joshua, Canaan was part of the inheritance God passed on to His firstborn son, Israel. Naomi was concerned that Ruth enter into rest as well (Ruth 1:9, 3:1). This she did when she was redeemed by Boaz.

The writer to the Hebrews picked up this rest theme and applied it to the rest Christians are destined to enjoy when they finally cease their pilgrim journey and spiritual battles and enter into that place of security God has promised as an inheritance (Heb. 4).

THE SPECIAL EMPHASES OF JOSHUA, JUDGES, AND RUTH

Having drawn attention to some of the most important themes running through Joshua, Judges, and Ruth, it will be helpful now to turn to emphases that are prominent in each of these books but that do not characterize all three.

JOSHUA

The major theological points stressed in the book of Joshua seem to be two. One of its great revelations is the faithfulness of Yahweh in giving Israel the Promised Land. The other is the revelation of God's hatred of sin.

God's faithfulness in giving Israel the land. The book of Joshua has often been seen as having two major divisions: the *conquest* of the land (chaps. 1-12) and the *division* of the land (chaps. 13-24). Actually the record of the division of the land ends with chapter 21. What follows is instruction for settlement in the land (chaps. 22-24). Clearly the whole book deals with Israel's entrance into the inheritance God promised her in Canaan. The land was promised to the patriarchs, anticipated thereafter, and finally claimed by Joshua. Even though the full extent of the land promised was not occupied in Joshua's day, Israel began to fill it.[21] This record of God's giving the land to Israel is a major revelation of His faithfulness to His

---

21. As many scholars have pointed out, the whole area promised to the patriarchs has never yet been occupied by Israel. For example, see Peter C. Craigie, *The Book of Deuteronomy* (Grand Rapids: Eerdmans, 1976), p. 267; C. F. Keil and Franz Delitzsch, *Joshua, Judges, Ruth, Commentary on the Old Testament* (3 vols.) trans. James Martin (reprint; Grand Rapids: Eerdmans, n. d.), p. 216.

covenant promise. When God speaks, His word can be relied on. When He promises, believers can expect fulfillment no matter how unlikely it may seem. God's people should be encouraged by the book of Joshua to rely on the faithfulness of God.

The book of Joshua also records memorials to God's faithfulness. The Israelites built one memorial in the Jordan River and another memorial beside it after God had enabled them to cross on dry ground (Josh. 4:3-9, 18). The crossing itself would have reminded them of God's deliverance from Egypt through the Red Sea (Ex. 14). The stone monuments would have kept the memory of God's faithfulness to His promise alive in the hearts of succeeding generations of Israelites. The monument built on Mount Ebal would likewise commemorate God's faithfulness in bringing them into the land (Josh. 8:30-35). This altar, located near the geographic center of the Promised Land, was close to the spot where Abraham first received God's promise to give his descendants the land (Gen. 12:6-7) and where Jacob buried his idols after returning to Canaan from Paddan-Aram (33:18-20; 35:1-4). The building of this altar signaled a rededication to the Mosaic Covenant, but the altar itself was also a memorial to God's faithfulness in fulfilling His promise to the patriarchs. The Transjordanian tribes built an altar on the banks of the Jordan River later in an attempt to preserve the unity of the tribe (Josh. 22:24-25). It was a memorial that also looked back and honored God's faithfulness. The stone set up at Shechem by Joshua later in his life (24:26-27) also served as a memorial. The record of the burial of Joseph's bones (24:32) likewise testifies to God's faithfulness in giving His people the land Joseph believed they would fully occupy some day.

Whereas these memorials enabled future generations to look back and remember God's faithfulness, they also constituted statements of commitment to follow God faithfully in the future. This emphasis on the importance of fidelity to the written Mosaic Covenant in order to receive future blessing also receives major emphasis in Joshua. The book opens with a reminder of the importance of observing the law of God faithfully (1:7-8), and it closes with Joshua urging the people to do the same (24:14-27). Other instances in which careful attention to the law was stressed occurred at Shechem (8:30-35) in Joshua's charge to the Transjordanian tribes (22:1-6), and in Joshua's address at the end of his life (chap. 23). Infidelity to the word of God resulted in setbacks in the conquest of the land (chap. 7; 9:3-15). The circumcision of the males and the celebration of the Passover were steps of obedience to the law that enabled Israel to enter into the land (5:2-12).

God had been faithful to bring Israel into the land as He had guaranteed in the Abrahamic Covenant, but occupation of all the promised territory and the accompanying defeat of its native inhabitants depended on Israel's faithfulness to the Mosaic Covenant.

God's hatred of sin. Joshua is perhaps best known as a book of war. Israel was at war with the Canaanites, but behind these human soldiers God was waging war against sin. Earlier in Israel's history God was compared to a warrior (Ex. 14:14;

15:3; Deut. 1:30; 3:22; 20:4). But now Israel experienced His leadership in war as never before. God is constantly at war with sin because it is an affront to His holiness and because it destroys people whom He loves and desires to bless (cf. Rom. 6:23).

In the book of Joshua, God waged war with sin wherever He found it. The Ras Shamra tablets, discovered at the site of ancient Ugarit in northwest Syria, throw light on Canaanite culture and have helped us understand its vile character.[22] When God commanded the Israelites to wipe out the Canaanites, He was using Israel like a broom to sweep a filthy society off the map. The Canaanite spectre had hatched in Noah's tent (Gen. 9:20-27), had evolved for generations, and now in Joshua's day would be tolerated by God no longer. In judging the Canaanites God was performing surgery on the human race to remove a malignancy. After waiting centuries for the Canaanites to repent—which they should have done as a result of godly influences among them, like that of Abraham and Melchizedek—God's severe treatment of these people was entirely justified.[23] But God was not unnecessarily brutal in dealing with His enemies as were the Assyrians, for example.

God also dealt severely with sin in Israel (Josh. 7). Given more spiritual privilege, His people shouldered more spiritual responsibility. God's love for Israel led Him to purge out the sin in the camp so that it would not destroy the whole nation. God evidently dealt with Achan as severely as He did in order to give His people a clear demonstration of His hatred for sin at the beginning of this new era in their national life.[24] God was not slow to judge sin at other times because He felt less hatred for it, but because He chose to be merciful to sinners (cf. 2 Pet. 3:9). God was less merciful in Achan's case because of the significance of his act of rebellion at that particular time in Israel's history.

The book of Joshua also shows *how* God wages war against sin. He Himself takes the initiative. The appearance of the Lord to Joshua before the conquest of Jericho (Josh. 5:13-15; cf. Ex. 3:5) reminded Joshua of his true relationship to God and Israel. Joshua was simply the servant of the captain (prince) of the vast armies of Yahweh (Josh. 5:14). God Himself, though unseen by the people, would lead the Israelites against their foe. Besides being transcendent, He was also immanent.

God led the Israelites by His angel, and He also marshalled the forces of nature to fight for His people. He restrained the waters of a river (Josh. 3:14-17), He shook the walls of a city (6:20), He sent hail from heaven (10:11), He lengthened the hours of a day (10:13-14), all to accomplish His purpose. These instances of

---

22. See Charles F. Pfeiffer, *Ras Shamra and the Bible* (Grand Rapids: Baker, 1962); Peter C. Craigie, "The Tablets from Ugarit and Their Importance for Biblical Studies," *Biblical Archaeology Review* 9 (1983): 62-72; idem, *Ugarit and the Old Testament* (Grand Rapids: Eerdmans, 1983).

23. See Peter C. Craigie, *The Problem of War in the Old Testament* (Grand Rapids: Eerdmans, 1978).

24. Compare God's dealings in a similar fashion with Ananias and Sapphira at the beginning of the church age (Acts 5).

divine intervention are powerful demonstrations of the might of God unleashed against the forces of evil (cf. Rev. 6-19).

The book of Joshua further reveals that God uses people of faith as His partners in combating sin and its malignant influence (cf. Heb. 11:30). To gain what God offered them as an inheritance, the Israelites had responsibilities to carry out. God's methods of providing what He has promised are unpredictable and often seem strange, even foolish, to His servants. But God asked the Israelites simply to trust and obey Him. They needed to refrain from what was forbidden, as well as to do all He directed. The book of Joshua is one of the clearest evidences in Scripture that consistent trust in and obedience to the revealed Word of God results in victorious, powerful, successful living.

Three characteristics marked the people God used to bring victory in Joshua. First, they submitted to His standard of holiness. In undergoing the operation of circumcision, they ritually demonstrated their renunciation of reliance on the flesh and their commitment to God (Josh. 5:2-9). They also separated from the defiling influences of the Canaanites (6:21). Second, they served as God directed. It must have seemed absurd to the Israelites to follow the unusual and strange strategy God ordered for the defeat of Jericho (chap. 6). His plans for the defeat of Ai proved abnormal too (8:1-8). But when the Israelites decided to do as God directed, rather than what seemed most likely to be successful, they won. Third, they succeeded because of God's might. By prescribing unusual strategy and by limiting their own ability (11:6-9) God taught His people that their victories were the work of their God, not of themselves. There should have been no doubt in the minds of the people when the conquest was complete that deliverance had been supernatural, though it took them some time to learn this lesson (cf. 7:3-5). Caleb, an important character in this book, models the person of faith, for he fully followed the Lord (14:8, 9, 14).

With such mighty confrontations as those recorded in Joshua it is not unusual that the book emphasizes both courage and fear. Moses charged Joshua to be courageous (1:6, 7, 9, 18). And Joshua in turn challenged the Israelites to have courage (10:25; 23:6). Rahab told the spies that the Canaanites feared when they heard what mighty things Yahweh had already done for Israel (2:9-11). But she herself manifested great courage in identifying with and remaining loyal to Israel. Both fear and courage were based on the record of what God had done. But those who chose to trust and obey Him became courageous while those who chose to oppose Him became fearful.

A few polemics against the Canaanite gods are recorded in Joshua. When Yahweh sent hail and lengthened the daylight hours to support the Israelite soldiers, He was showing Himself to be the true Lord of the natural elements and the heavenly bodies (Josh. 10:11-14). The Canaanites believed their gods controlled these things.[25] These events demonstrated Yahweh's sovereignty. God's control of the

---

25. See George Saint-Laurent, "Light from Ras Shamra on Elijah's Ordeal upon Mount Carmel," in *Scripture in Context,* ed. Carl D. Evans et al. (Pittsburgh: Pickwick, 1980), pp. 123-39; Leah Bronner, *The Stories of Elijah and Elisha* (Leiden: E. J. Brill, 1968).

Jordan River may have conveyed a similar message to the Canaanites. Every Canaanite defeat in battle would have been perceived as a demonstration of the superiority of Israel's God.

JUDGES

Joshua and Judges resemble two sides of one coin. The former is essentially a positive revelation and the latter a negative one. Joshua demonstrates that victory, success, and progress result when God's people trust and obey Him consistently. Judges, on the other hand, shows that defeat, failure, and retrogression follow when God's people fail to trust and obey Him consistently. Whereas Joshua reveals God's faithfulness in giving Israel the Promised Land, Judges emphasizes Israel's unfaithfulness in subduing the land. Joshua highlights God's hatred of sin, but Judges magnifies God's grace toward sinners.

Israel's unfaithfulness in subduing the land. In the generations following Joshua and the elders who followed him, the Israelites failed to drive the remaining Canaanites out of the land (Judg. 1:8-10). This situation came about because the older generation did not pass the knowledge of Yahweh on to their children (1:10). So the new generation failed to remember what God had done for His people and what He had said to them in the past (3:7; 8:34). Instead of destroying the Canaanites God's people permitted these enemies to live among them (1:27-33; 2:2; 6:10). Ironically instead of destroying the Canaanites the Israelites began to fight among themselves and to destroy each other (5:17-18, 23; 8:5-8; 12:1-6; 18:24-25; 20:8–21:25).

Disobedience to God's command regarding the Canaanites constituted spiritual apostasy. Instead of remaining loyal to Yahweh and worshiping Him exclusively, as He had commanded, the Israelites tolerated, then began to admire, and finally worshiped the gods of the Canaanites (cf. chaps. 17-18). Rather than exterminating the Canaanites, God's people made covenants with them (2:1-2). Rather than destroying their pagan altars, the Israelites worshiped at them (2:11-13, 17, 19). The syncretistic nature of Canaanite religion encouraged Israel's apostasy. The Canaanites did not demand that the Israelites forsake Yahweh worship. They simply encouraged God's people to join with them in worshiping their gods along with Yahweh. But the Lord regarded this as abandonment of Him (3:7).

Spiritual apostasy bore bitter fruit in Israelite culture. Politically Israel began to disintegrate. Instead of continuing to function as a group of twelve tribes united in life and purpose, tribal hostility and self-interest became more and more pronounced (5:17-18, 23; 8:5-8; 12:1-6). National unity deteriorated, and political disorganization increased.

Furthermore, social chaos marked the period of the judges. Disregard for the law grew. People were no longer safe going out in public (Judg. 5:6). They took the law into their own hands (18:24-25). And immorality increased. Practices that characterized Sodom and Gomorrah in Abraham's day now marked Israelite society (chap. 19; cf. Gen. 19). Even one of Israel's judges, Samson, lived an immoral life.[26] The writer of Judges summarized their condition by saying, "Every man did what was right in his own eyes" (Judg. 17:6; 21:25, NASB). Anarchy prevailed.

As a result of these conditions a movement developed in Israel to elect a king who could bring order out of chaos. Some of the people thought Gideon would make a good king (8:22). But Gideon wisely declined their offer and urged the people to commit themselves to following Yahweh as their king in harmony with the Mosaic law (8:23). Gideon's son, not as wise as his father, took advantage of Gideon's popularity to set himself up as king over a segment of the Israelites in the north with headquarters in Shechem (chap. 9). He proved to be a bad ruler and was killed by his own people soon after he began to rule (9:50-57).[27] As conditions worsened in Israel because of the people's continuing apostasy, the movement for a king gained strength. Later the people demanded a king from Samuel (1 Sam. 8:5) and received Saul, who turned out to be another disappointment.

What was the cause of all this trouble during the period of the judges? It was Israel's unfaithfulness to God in refusing to subdue the Canaanites in the land. Israel's unfaithfulness to God is one of the major emphases in the book of Judges.

God's grace toward sinners. Another important revelation, standing in shocking contrast to Israel's unfaithfulness, is God's graciousness as He dealt with His rebellious people. Why did God not allow the Israelites to be absorbed into Canaanite life and lose their national identity? Because of His covenant promise to Abraham to bring blessing to the whole earth through his descendants (Gen. 12:3). God's gracious dealings with His people rested on His faithfulness to his covenant promises to Abraham.

Manifestations of God's grace abound in Judges. God periodically warned His people against continued apostasy (Judg. 2:1-4; 6:7-10; 10:10-14). These warnings were a gracious provision from the Lord.

When the Israelites called out to Yahweh in desperation, He delivered them from their oppressors. The repeated cycle of sin, servitude, supplication, and salvation emphasizes the grace of God lavished on sinful rebels. As in Joshua, God the warrior led His people in battle against their foes. The writer of Judges emphasized that it was He who delivered them (3:9, 15; 7:2, 9; 10:12; cf. 18:10). God did not wait until His people had cleaned up their lives (i.e., repented) before He saved them. He delivered them when they cried to Him for help (3:9, 15; 4:3; 6:6-9; 10:10, 12; 16:28; cf. Rom. 10:13).[28]

26.. For a discussion of why God chose to use spiritually weak and even immoral individuals as His instruments, see Arthur E. Cundall, "Judges," in *Judges and Ruth,* by Arthur E. Cundall and Leon Morris, Tyndale Old Testament Commentaries (Downers Grove, Ill.: InterVarsity, 1968), pp. 42-45.

27. Dumbrell has proposed that "the total effect of Judges 9 is to present kingship to us as a humanistic alternative to the great series of divine initiatives which maintained Israel's position throughout the activity of the successive hero figures" ("'In those days . . .'", p. 28).

28. Frederick E. Greenspahn, "The Theology of the Framework of Judges," *Vetus Testamentum* 36 (1986): 391-95.

The judges God raised up as His instruments of deliverance and leadership were also a provision of His grace (Judg. 2:16).[29] The judges were variously strong or weak spiritually, male or female, and came from various tribes and sections of Israel. In most cases they were leaders who stood alone. In Samson's case the text suggests that he was opposed not only by the Philistines but also by the Israelites (15:11). Yet God used these lone figures to reverse the tide of affairs in Israel on many occasions. God did not need a large Israelite army (cf. 7:1-8). One individual was often adequate in His hand, a testimony to His power and wisdom.

Another manifestation of God's grace that forms a significant motif in Judges is the Spirit of God. God enabled His instruments, the judges, in various ways. He granted them the power of His presence (2:18; 6:16) and the authority of His commission (6:14). But most important His Spirit came on the judges, clothing them with Himself as it were (3:10; 6:34; 11:29; 13:25; 14:6, 19; 15:14, 19). This was a special endowment with supernatural power that was not given to all believers at that time nor was it always given permanently to all who received it (cf. 16:20). Enabled by God's Spirit, the judges overcame opposition and provided deliverance for the Israelites.[30]

The discipline God sent the Israelites for their apostasy was a blessing in disguise. Each foreign oppressor made life difficult for God's people. But by afflicting the Israelites, the foreigners caused Israel to turn back to Yahweh eventually. God's discipline was educative as well as punitive. When God's people departed from Him, He did not abandon them; He afflicted them to bring them back to Himself (cf. Heb. 12:1-13).

RUTH

In Joshua and Judges, the focus of revelation is on the land God promised to the descendants of Abraham. In Ruth, the focus shifts to the seed He promised. In particular, the seed in view is the one who would come from Judah's tribe to rule over God's people (Gen. 49:10).

In general the principal theological motif in Ruth is the outworking of divine purpose through human instrumentality.[31] More specifically God's irresistible sovereignty and His boundless grace receive much attention in Ruth.

God's irresistible sovereignty. God promised Abraham He would make his descendants a great nation (Gen. 12:2). Later He revealed to Judah that through his branch of Abraham's family He would raise up a ruler (Gen. 49:10). In Ruth, the writer related David to the promise of that ruler. He traced David's ancestry to

29. John Bright has given a particularly helpful and concise explanation of what a judge was in *A History of Israel*, 3d ed. (Philadelphia: Westminster, 1981), pp. 167, 178.

30. For further discussion of the work of the Holy Spirit in the Old Testament, see Leon J. Wood, *The Holy Spirit in the Old Testament* (Grand Rapids: Zondervan, 1976), pp. 39-63.

31. Ronald Hals, *The Theology of the Book of Ruth* (Philadelphia: Fortress, 1969); W. S. Prinsloo, "The Theology of the Book of Ruth," *Vetus Testamentum* 30 (1980): 330-41.

Judah and Bethlehem and connected the Abrahamic (not the Mosaic) Covenant with the Davidic dynasty, tying together the partriarchical and monarchical eras.[32]

How God provided David is a major theme in Ruth and a significant demonstration of God's irresistible sovereignty in Scripture. In the period of the judges Naomi's generation encountered many difficulties, some of which were God's discipline of His people for their sins. In Deuteronomy, God promised that if His people turned away from Him He would make their land unproductive (Deut. 28:24, 38-40, 42, 48). As the book of Ruth opens, a famine was in the land (Ruth 1:1). This situation led Naomi's husband, Elimelech, and his family to migrate to Moab. There Elimelech and his two sons died.

When the famine in Canaan lifted, probably due to the Israelites' return to God (Deut. 28), Naomi decided to move back to Israel. She encouraged her daughters-in-law to remain in their homeland because she could not provide them with husbands in keeping with the levirate custom because she was too old to bear any more children (Ruth 1:12; Deut. 25:5-10). She could not expect an heir. The calamity motif is strong in the first part of Ruth. Hongisto has shown that Naomi's statement "I am indeed too old to conceive" (Ruth 1:12, author's translation) is at the center of the chiasm that constitutes Ruth 1.[33] Her inability to bear children presented the major obstacle to God's providing a seed for her (cf. 4:17).

Ruth's determination to trust in and commit herself to Yahweh and to move to Israel with her mother-in-law offered a glimpse of hope, and it is that determination that God blessed. Clearly Ruth was not simply moving physically from Moab to Israel. She was leaving the people and gods of Moab and transferring her allegiance to the people of God and to Yahweh Himself (1:16-18). Ruth, a descendant of Lot (who chose to leave the Promised Land in the hope of greater blessing elsewhere), reversed her ancestor's decision and moved into the Promised land looking for blessing from Yahweh.[34] Because of this decision, God blessed her abundantly.

Having settled in Bethlehem, Ruth and Naomi agreed on a plan whereby they might legitimately experience God's blessing (2:2).[35] Initial blessing did indeed follow. Boaz took notice of Ruth, and she found favor in his sight (2:13, 19). Encouraged by God's loyal love (*hesed*—2:20; cf. 1:8, 3:10), Naomi and Ruth

32. Eugene H. Merrill, "The Book of Ruth: Narration and Shared Themes," *Bibliotheca Sacra* 142 (April–June 1985): 130-41; idem, *Kingdom of Priests*, pp. 182-88.

33. Lief Hongisto, "Literary Structure and Theology in the Book of Ruth," *Andrews University Seminary Studies* 23 (1985): 22.

34. Harold Fisch, "Ruth and the Structure of Covenant History," *Vetus Testamentum* 32 (1982): 425-37.

35. Eugene Merrill has observed that the first use of Bethlehem and Ephratah together in Scripture (which is the case in Ruth) occurred when Rachel struggled to give birth to Benjamin (Gen. 35:16-19). Merrill raised the question whether the writer of Ruth may have intended the reader to make a connection between that old conflict that arose in Jacob's family over Benjamin's birth and the conflict that would arise between Benjamin's descendant Saul and Ruth's descendant David ("The Book of Ruth," p. 133).

embarked on a further plan to obtain rest (3:1; cf. 1:9; 3:18), primarily for Ruth but also for Naomi (3:1-8). The laying of this plan is the pivotal point in the story, the center for the chiastic structure of the book.[36] The plan essentially involved Ruth's redemption by Boaz in which Boaz would provide blessing for Ruth and Naomi by purchasing Elimelech's land and hopefully raising up an heir for him through Ruth (3:13; 4:3-12). This redemption motif is, of course, strong in Ruth.

Ruth and Naomi's plan found fulfillment in Ruth's marriage to Boaz (4:13). Ruth 4:13 seems to be the key verse in the book because it records God's greatest blessing to Ruth, Boaz, Naomi, and all Israel ultimately. God enabled Ruth to conceive and to bear a son. Here the blessing motif reaches its climax. Part of God's blessing involved material property for Ruth, Naomi, and Boaz as God had promised the godly in the Mosaic Covenant (2:1; 3:11; 4:11; cf. Deut. 28). God's blessing also involved rest for Ruth (1:9; 3:1), Boaz (3:18), and Naomi. Other references to God's blessing on Boaz (2:19) and Ruth (3:10) connect it to their experiences. For these blessings Naomi blessed God Himself (2:20; 4:14). Through Boaz and Ruth all Israel was blessed. And God's blessing of the entire world through Israel was made possible by the union of Boaz and Ruth. This was prefigured in the blessing of Ruth, who was originally a stranger to the covenants of Israel.[37]

How God provided an heir for Elimelech who could fulfill in part the promise concerning Judah's ruling descendant constitutes both the fascination of the story of Ruth and the great proof of God's sovereignty. So many seemingly impossible situations had to be overcome that the reader can readily identify with Naomi in her initial despair in chapter 1. But God amazingly brought His will to pass. Certainly the book of Ruth testifies that God's plan cannot be frustrated even by the selfish anarchy of His people that dominated the period of the judges. His sovereignty is irresistible.

God's boundless grace. The book of Ruth reveals much about the plan of God. But it also makes a major contribution to our understanding of how God deals with people.

One of the characteristics of God's dealings with people is His willingness—one might even say His preference—to work with and through individuals other people often regard as unlikely material. The book of Judges shows this too. Several of the judges were individuals one would not expect God to use because of their sex (Deborah), weak faith (Gideon), family background (Jephthah), or moral laxity (Samson). But Ruth was specially unpromising. She was a woman and a foreigner, a member of a nation that was an enemy of the Israelites. Furthermore, she was a poor widow. Why did God not use a rich Israelite woman to bear David's grandfather?

Ruth entered the land because of her faith in Yahweh (1:16). She submitted

36. Hongisto, p. 23.
37. The writer's frequent references to Ruth as "the Moabitess" emphasize her alien status (1:22, 2:2, 6, 21: 4:5, 10).

to the laws of Israel as an expression of her commitment to God (2:3; 3:9). Consequently she was respected by the Israelites and also used by God in His program of bringing blessing to the whole world. The key was her faith in Yahweh. She may have had more faith than many other women in her day. Her confidence in the Lord overcame all other limitations and qualified her for God's use.

The fact that Ruth was incorporated into Israelite life has been a problem for many students of the book of Ruth. God had previously stated in the Mosaic Law that no Moabite was to be admitted into the covenant community (Deut. 23:3).[38] Why then was Ruth admitted into Israel and treated as an equal? One explanation might be that Boaz simply overlooked the Mosaic proscription because he loved Ruth. But this view does not do justice to Boaz, who everywhere else in the book of Ruth is seen as carefully fulfilling the provisions of the Mosaic law. Another possibility is that Deuteronomy 23:3 pertained only to male Moabites, since the male gender of the noun is used in the Hebrew text. But the male gender would have been the normal one to use in describing all Moabites regardless of gender. There are no indications elsewhere that the exclusion applied only to male Moabites. Probably Ruth was admitted because she had placed her faith in Yahweh. This was the essential requirement for entrance into the covenant community as God explained to Abraham when He gave him the rite of circumcision (Gen. 17:9-14, 23). The Mosaic Covenant that was added to Israelite life generations later specified, among other things, the naturalization requirements for people who wanted to immigrate into Israel from other nations. The proscription against Moabites in Deuteronomy seems to have pertained to people who were not believers in Yahweh yet who wanted to become Israelites. There would have been many such cases. According to previously given instructions (Gen. 17), anyone who became a believer in Yahweh could become an Israelite.[39] It was Israel's purpose in the world, after all, to bring the nations into a saving relationship with God (Gen. 12:1-3; Ex. 19:5-6). In harmony with His promise to Abraham God received anyone who became a believer in Him regardless of race, sex, or national origin. This fact shows the boundless grace of God.

Ruth would have been looked on disapprovingly by the other Israelites because she was a Moabitess but also because she was needy and a widow.[40] Boaz

---

38. Deuteronomy 23:3 states that no Ammonite or Moabite could enter the assembly of the Lord to the tenth generation. Entering the assembly of the Lord was a way of saying "becoming a true Israelite and sharing in the worship of Yahweh" (Craigie, *The Book of Deuteronomy,* p. 296). To the tenth generation meant forever (C. F. Keil and Franz Delitzsch, *The Pentateuch, Commentary on the Old Testament* (3 vols.), trans. James Martin (reprint; Grand Rapids: Eerdmans, n.d.), 3:414.

39. In ancient Near Eastern patriarchical societies, of which Israel was one, a female was identified with the father or husband in authority over her. For males circumcision was the sign of identification with the Abrahamic Covenant. Females did not bear the sign of the covenant though they could and did identify their hearts with the covenant. Faith in Yahweh was primary, and circumcision was secondary. Ruth, of course, had neither father nor husband in authority over her since she was a widow.

40. Gleaning the fields was a task reserved for the needy in Israel (Lev. 19:10; 23:22; cf. Deut. 24:21).

saw beneath her needy exterior and lower social status to her sterling character, which was purified, we may assume, by her faith in Yahweh. Like God, Boaz was willing to make Ruth part of his plans because of her faith and what it had accomplished in her life. Thus, Boaz and God overrode not only the Mosaic law but also tradition and social conventions because of Ruth's faith. God's grace superabounded in the case of Ruth.

The last section of the book of Ruth refers to Perez (Ruth 4:18). Perez was the son of Judah, who was born of a Canaanite woman, Tamar, who like Ruth valued the promises of God and became a believer in Yahweh (Gen. 38).[41] The reference to Perez relates David to Judah's branch of Abraham's family. The reference to Perez also magnifies the grace of God further by reminding the reader that God earlier in history was gracious to another outsider and incorporated her into the family of Israel and even into the special line of blessing just as He now did for Ruth.[42]

CONCLUSION

The books of Joshua, Judges, and Ruth are full of rich revelation. During the approximately 300 years in which the events recorded in these books took place, God taught the Israelites much. In His Word, He has preserved major lessons of this period for people of all subsequent ages.

These books show that God does indeed deal with people as He has said He will. He faithfully, inexorably brings to pass what He has unconditionally promised. And He patiently deals with people, providing blessing to any who trust and obey Him and disciplining those who do not.

Whereas certain emphases run through all three of these books, in each of them God makes special points. God's faithfulness, His provision of salvation, and the importance of faith are among the most important common themes. In Joshua, God's faithfulness in giving Israel the Promised Land and His hatred of sin stand out. In Judges, Israel's unfaithfulness in subduing the land and, by contrast, God's grace toward sinners constitute major emphases. In Ruth, the sovereignty of God in working out His plan and His grace in dealing with people dominate the revelation.

These three books also point forward to and prepare for future events and future revelation. They constitute an important segment of God's full self-disclosure.

---

41. Though the text nowhere states that Tamar was a believer in Yahweh, it is likely that she was, on the basis of her unusual zeal to produce an heir for the chosen family.
42. In Matthew's genealogy of Jesus Christ, four (and only four) women are mentioned: Tamar, Rahab, Ruth, and Bathsheba (Matt. 1:3, 5, 6). Each of them was a non-Israelite who came to faith in Yahweh. (Bathsheba was evidently a Hittite like her husband Uriah.) Each one, because of her faith in Yahweh, was made both a member of the chosen nation and an ancestor of Him who completely fulfills the prophecy of Judah's heir in Genesis 49:10, namely, Jesus Christ.

3

A THEOLOGY OF SAMUEL AND KINGS

HOMER HEATER, JR.

HISTORICAL SETTING OF SAMUEL AND KINGS

The beginning date for the events of 1 and 2 Samuel is early in the eleventh century B.C. At that time the Hittite, Mitannian, and Babylonian kingdoms were in decline or complete defeat. The Arameans or Syrians began to move into the northern area in large numbers, but did not consolidate until after David's time. The "sea people" (from the Aegean) had invaded the entire levant in the preceding century. They were defeated by the Egyptians but at great cost to the latter who were weak during the time of the Judges. The sea people became the Philistines.[1] They may have brought with them the secret of iron smelting, which they kept for themselves and by which they dominated the Israelites. The Canaanites were subdued by the Israelites and the Philistines. Pockets of Canaanites were probably under Philistine control as they had previously been under Egyptian control. Some Canaanites moved to Tyre and Sidon and became great maritime people, establishing colonies in northern Africa and southern Spain. There were small king

---

1. There were Philistines in "Palestine" during the time of the Patriarchs. This later wave joined and dominated an older group. See Moses H. Segal, *The Pentateuch* (Jerusalem: Magnes, 1967), p. 34.

HOMER HEATER, JR., M.A., Th.M., Ph.D., is professor of Bible exposition at Dallas Theological Seminary.

doms on the eastern border called Ammon, Moab, and Edom. There were continual clashes between them and Israel.

During the time of the judges, Israel was struggling to consolidate her power, particularly in the central hill country. Her religious state as a whole was abysmal. She had adopted many of the practices of the Canaanites. Constant tension existed between the tribes as they strove for independence on the one hand and unity on the other. However, under David and Solomon Israel moved rapidly to become the most powerful nation in the Middle Eastern arena.[2]

THE THEOLOGICAL PERSPECTIVE OF SAMUEL AND KINGS

The theology of Samuel and Kings must be read on two levels. Both books are compilations of historical material brought together from an editorial point of view. Much as Luke set out to present an account of the ministry and message of Christ and the early church, so an unknown historian or historians have, under divine inspiration, given us these two marvelous compositions showing God's rule among men and, more specifically, the men and women of Israel.

The first level of theology is to be found in the original events and statements themselves. Samuel's godly priestly life and ministry as a judge witness to a faith (somewhat rare—the word of God was scarce in those days) in Yahweh, the covenant-keeping God of Israel. The virile faith of a young David in the face of humanly insuperable odds stands out in contrast to the impotent and uncertain conduct of Saul. In the lives of such men, living, trusting, failing, and sinning, Yahweh is seen powerfully directing the events on the stage of life to effect His eternal purposes as outlined and promised to Abraham, Isaac, Jacob, Joseph, Moses, and Joshua, and as reiterated in the dismal and struggling era of the judges.

The second level of theology is that of the historian who brought together these great strands of divine history, originally composed by such prophets as Samuel, Nathan, and Gad, into a historical-theological treatise on the faithfulness of the Lord in implementing all the facets of His various covenants. In Samuel the reader is left to understand somewhat intuitively God's work by observing the events described in some of the most beautiful and effective literature in the world's history.[3] (What greater piece of literature exists than the story of David's sin with Bathsheba and Nathan's confrontation of David?) On the other hand, 1 and 2 Kings contain long sermons detailing the reasons for the calamities that happened (e.g., 2 Kings 17:7-23). These are the inspired explanations by a sixth-century believer of the events that devastated the people of Israel and Judah through the destruction of their supposed inviolable Temple and city, Jerusalem. For example, the "high places" that had become, through syncretism, so corrupt by the end of the monar-

---

2. See G. Ernest Wright, *Biblical Archaeology* (Philadelphia: Westminster, 1962), pp. 86-96.

3. There are editorial comments throughout 1 and 2 Samuel, but they tend to be terse statements rather than fully developed sermonic material (e.g., 1 Sam. 1:6; 2:12, 17, 25; 3:19-21; 7:13; 10:9; 15:35).

chial era are uniformly criticized by this historian who saw them as destructive to his people, as indeed they came to be. In the earlier period, however, the high places served a legitimate role in the worship of Yahweh and, in the accounts rendered, are accepted as proper by the characters of the story.

First Samuel represents a transition from the era of the judges to the monarchy. This shift is far more dramatic and far-reaching than appears on the surface. There are two forces continually at work in Israel. The centrifugal force was a tendency to fragment into the individual tribal organizations. Some of this is evident in the Exodus and wilderness accounts; in the settlement of Reuben, Gad, and Manasseh; in the Benjamite war; in the Absalom rebellion; and finally in the schism brought about by Jeroboam I. The centripetal force, drawing together people who were disparate culturally and geographically, was the centering of worship on the dwelling place of Yahweh: the Tabernacle and later the Temple. Jeroboam went so far as to establish a rival religious system to offset that force.

The inauguration of the monarchy complicated this tension even further. Saul sought to bring unity to the nation. He achieved this to a certain extent and began the defeat of the Philistines in the process, but he never had the character to solidify his leadership position. That was left to the popular young David, but it took all his personal persuasion and political acumen to unite the tribes and then only after seven years of a rival rule in Mahanaim.

David's firm hand and dynamic leadership kept the cracks plastered over until his son Absalom almost created a permanent rupture. The rest of David's reign was weakened as the internecine strife continued up to and after his death. Solomon's rule caused the cultural and political status of Israel to soar, but the crash came suddenly and permanently after his death.

The theological thread running through Samuel and Kings is God's choice of a leader to represent Him as He implements His covenants with Israel. Israel existed in the land because of the unconditional covenant God made with Abraham. The Abrahamic Covenant was implemented by Yahweh when He redeemed His people from Egypt and made them a nation. The land blessing, however, was conditional: God's blessing was determined by obedience, as clearly stated in Deuteronomy.

The place of David in this thread was already established by the writer of the book of Ruth. Ruth should probably be considered the third "appendix" to the book of Judges, providing light in an otherwise dark corner. However, that its purpose reaches into Samuel and Kings is evident in the genealogy of Ruth 4 that ties Ruth and Boaz into David, the fourth generation from Ruth. The author's hints about David show up in Samuel long before his anointing in chapter 16. In Hannah's magnificat (1 Sam. 2:10), she refers to God's king or anointed one. In the context of her prayer, this was prophetic. The possibility of a king was presented in Deuteronomy 28:36, and her reference is in light of that possibility. To the writer of 1 and 2 Samuel, however, that king could only be David. In this sense, the transition in the book of 1 Samuel is not merely from judges to kings, but from judges to David. Saul figures as a necessary interim king,[4] but the entire movement of the book is toward David.

THE DAVIDIC COVENANT

Given this theology, it is imperative that the place of David in God's program for Israel be seen as set forth in the Davidic Covenant. This covenant underlies all of God's dealings with the monarchy after David as well as with the eschatological "David."[5] Consequently it will be helpful to anticipate the covenant in 2 Samuel and develop it here.

Second Samuel 5-8 summarizes and recapitulates David's achievements. They include his being made king, his capture of the Jebusite fortress, the bringing up of the Ark, the Davidic Covenant, and the defeat of all his enemies. The transfer of the Ark to Jerusalem led David to contemplate the status of Yahweh's dwelling. Since David had a luxurious house, he could not accept the fact that Yahweh was living in a tent (2 Sam. 7:2). He therefore approached Nathan, the court prophet, about the possibility of building a temple. To Nathan, the plan seemed a noble one, and he gave his blessing. However, during the night the Lord informed Nathan that David would not build a house for Him; quite the contrary *He* would build a "house" for David. The contents of the covenant are then given. (Other references to the Davidic Covenant are 1 Chronicles 17 and Psalm 89.)

THE CHOICE OF DAVID (2 SAM. 7:8A)

Yahweh pointed out to David his insignificant beginnings (a similar reference is made to Saul in 1 Sam. 15:17). David was a rustic, a shepherd, a nobody. God emphasized His sovereign choice of David.[6]

THE ELEVATION OF DAVID (2 SAM. 7:8B)

Yahweh placed David in the position of leadership over His covenant people. The clause "you will shepherd My people Israel, and you will become their ruler (*nāgîd*)" was in the mouths of the people when they made David king over all Israel (2 Sam. 5:2). It is also part of the "cumulative exegesis" of Matthew 2:5 in which several Old Testament verses are brought together exegetically to point to the Messiah (Gen. 49:10; 2 Sam. 2:5; Mic. 5:2). Here then is the seedbed of the idea of

---

4. See A. F. Campbell, *Of Prophets and Kings* (Washington, D.C.: Catholic Biblical Association, 1986), pp. 47-62, for a discussion of Saul as prince (*nāgîd*), which Campbell believes has the meaning "king-designate."

5. R. E. Clements rightly says, "Clearly if there is one passage in the Old Testament which can deserve the title of the seed-bed of the messianic hope it is that of 2 Sam. 7:1-17 and especially v. 16 itself" ("The Messianic Hope in the Old Testament," *Journal for the Study of the Old Testament* 43 [1989]: 12).

6. This is indicated by the fact that David was chosen over his apparently more qualified brothers (1 Sam. 16:6-13).

a specially chosen ruler over God's inheritance that reached its culmination in the Lord Jesus Christ.

THE VICTORIES OF DAVID (2 SAM. 7:9-10)

Yahweh promised David that He would be with him. His presence would assure David's victories over his enemies (recounted in 2 Sam. 8). This language is similar to the Lord's words to Joshua (Josh. 1:1-5). Furthermore, He said He would cause David to be well recognized. Yahweh's ruler, therefore, would know the presence of the Lord in his rule, and he would have victory over all his enemies. This should be noted in connection with Isaiah's prophecy of the "Shoot" (Isa. 11:1). This Davidic ideal ruler will know the Spirit of the Lord resting on him. He will rule all people and His place of rest will be glorious.[7] The point in placing the discussion of the Davidic Covenant here rather than in 2 Samuel is to show that 1 Samuel can only be understood in the light of God's covenant with this ideal ruler. The theology of 1 Samuel is built around David, but it goes subtly beyond David to Christ, the greater David.

RESTING PLACE FOR THE PEOPLE OF GOD (2 SAM. 7:10)

That the Davidic "theology" is already in view in 2 Samuel 7 is evidenced by the promised "place" for the people of God. This phrase is echoed in Isaiah 11:10, which describes the "second Exodus." The royal ruler will have a resting place that is glorious. God also promised to "plant" His people, a phrase picked up again in the New Covenant (Jer. 31:27-28). There is a subtle movement in 2 Samuel 7 to the eschatological future. Incipient in these verses is Israel's hope of restoration from troubles and her glorious establishment in the future under Yahweh's hand.

DAVID'S HOUSE (2 SAM. 7:11-16)

This unit contains the core of the Davidic promise: David was not to build a house for God, but God would build one for David. Up to this time, there had been no dynasty in Israel. Saul's son had generously and spiritually submitted himself to David. Now God promised David an eternal seed and an eternal throne. One of David's own sons would succeed him to the throne, and his throne, like David's, would be established forever. Much of the rest of 2 Samuel deals with the identification of that son. Early on it is learned that it would be Solomon (Jedidiah, "whom Yahweh loves/chooses"). Furthermore, this offspring was to build the Temple David wanted to build. This offspring would be treated with filial affection, which includes discipline. Yet, in contrast to Saul, he would never be outside the covenant love of God. God's sovereign choice of David's line will never be abrogated even though discipline must come when disobedience takes place. This theme underlies much of the argument of 1 and 2 Kings. The concluding statement brings

---

7. For this "resting place" see Deuteronomy 12:8-9.

the prophecy to a crescendo: "Your house and your kingdom will endure forever before me; your throne will be established forever" (2 Sam. 7:16).

The Davidic Covenant is the centerpiece of Samuel and Kings. David, as a type of the ideal king (both in position and often in practice), appears "between the lines" in chapters 1-15 and dominates the lines in chapters 16-31. Seeing the centrality of the Davidic Covenant enables the reader to pick up the argument of 1 Samuel and to see how it moves inexorably toward 2 Samuel 7.

THE PRIESTHOOD IN SAMUEL AND KINGS

Three institutions provided leadership for Israel throughout the books of Samuel and Kings: the priesthood, an officially established office from the days of Moses; the prophetic office, an unofficial ministry filled by leaders raised up spontaneously (at least in the earlier era); and the monarchy or kingship.

THE PRIESTHOOD IN 1 AND 2 SAMUEL

There was a certain amount of overlap in the three offices. Samuel himself, as we will develop later, is a case in point. He acted as prophet, judge, and priest. The king, who in many ways supplanted the judge, was given the task of leading his people in battle and adjudicating their causes (2 Samuel 15:1-6).[8] It was ironic that David, the protector of justice, would so pervert justice in the Uriah-Bathsheba incident. King David was also involved in priestly functions when he brought the Ark to Jerusalem (6:14), and some of his sons are even called priests.[9] The king's role was very limited, however, as shown when Uzziah was rebuked by the priests for carrying a censer, and God struck him with leprosy as punishment for intruding into the priest's office (2 Chron. 26:16-21).

THE ROLE OF THE SHILONITE PRIESTHOOD

Eli, as the high priest in Shiloh, was a godly man who sought to please the Lord. As a priest, the morality of the people was his concern. Consequently he rebuked Hannah when he thought she was drunk (1 Sam. 1:12-14). He also rebuked his sons for their immoral conduct at the Tabernacle. Their sin was particularly egregious since they were supposed to be teaching morality and representing the people of God (2:22-25; cf. 2 Chron. 17:7-9).[10]

8. Frank M. Cross distinguishes between the "charismatic" and the "routinized," or dynastic, kingship of David and Solomon (*Canaanite Myth and Hebrew Epic* [Cambridge, Mass.: Harvard University Press, 1973], pp. 219-20).

9. Carl Armerding, "Were David's Sons Really Priests?" in *Current Issues in Biblical and Patristic Interpretation,* ed. G. F. Hawthorne (Grand Rapids: Eerdmans, 1975), pp. 75-86. He argues for a royal priesthood based on a Melchizedekian pattern alongside the Levitical priesthood. Consequently, according to him, David and Solomon both functioned as king-priest.

10. See Walther Eichrodt, *Theology of the Old Testament* (Philadelphia: Westminster, 1961), 2:398-402, for a discussion of functions of the priesthood.

First Samuel gives an early glimpse of the ritual of the sacrifice when Elkanah and his family came to Shiloh to worship Yahweh. The fellowship meal accompanying the sacrifice is the setting for Hannah's sorrowful behavior. By contrast, the corruption of the Shilonite priesthood is seen in the arrogant behavior of Eli's sons toward the humble people who came to offer to the Lord. God blessed Hannah and Elkanah, but He judged Eli's sons for their unethical conduct.

Sometimes priests were advisers in military matters and even accompanied the people into battle (1 Sam. 4:1-11; 2 Kings 3:11-20). The two sons of Eli were killed in the Philistine war when they followed the Ark. Young Abiathar followed David in all his vicissitudes after fleeing from Saul and advised him on courses of action (1 Sam. 23:6-12 and 1 Kings 2:26).

The Shilonite priesthood was judged by God because of the wickedness of Hophni and Phinehas and Eli's failure to discipline them. Eli's family continued to serve through David's time, but when Abiathar was removed, the line of ministry came to an end. "To Abiathar, the priest, the king said, 'Go back to your fields in Anathoth. You deserve to die, but I will not put you to death now, because you carried the ark of the Sovereign Lord before my father David and shared all my father's hardships.' So Solomon removed Abiathar from the priesthood of the Lord, fulfilling the word the Lord had spoken at Shiloh about the house of Eli" (1 Kings 2:20-27). And 1 Kings 2:35 states, "The king put Benaiah son of Jehoiada over the army in Joab's position and replaced Abiathar with Zadok the priest." These verses indicate that the books of Samuel are designed not only to show that David would become God's chosen representative but also that the house of Zadok would succeed the house of Eli in the priesthood. So the first four chapters of 1 Samuel are seen as judgment-writing on the Eli family. The finale to Eli's line is given in chapter 4. The army was defeated twice, Eli's sons were killed, and the Ark was taken. God judges those who refuse to obey Him. The name given to Eli's grandson, Ichabod, is a telling one. The glory of Yahweh had departed from Israel, and for that matter from Eli's house.

THE ROLE OF SAMUEL AS PRIEST IN CONTRAST TO ELI'S HOUSE

Samuel's mantle overshadows all of 1 Samuel from his Nazirite youth to his recall in chapter 28 to give Saul his final rejection. A purpose of 1 Samuel is to show the ideal person God was looking for to lead His people. In the priesthood, He wanted godly people who revered Him and respected His people. In the Eli family neither of these characteristics was present. So God raised up a faithful priest from the godly Levitical family of Elkanah and his especially godly wife.[11] This beautiful story of a faithful mother in Israel whom God honored by giving her a son is the

---

11. The opening verses of 1 Samuel indicate that Elkanah was an Ephraimite. However, 1 Chronicles 6:26-27 indicates that he was a Levite. This should be understood to mean that Elkanah lived as a Levite among the Ephraimites (as the young Levite lived among the Danites in Judg. 18).

crown jewel in the argument of the book. Yahweh looks for faithful, godly men and women whom He can set over His people.[12] Samson the judge was a Nazirite, but his personal life continues to be an enigma. Samuel was also a Nazirite[13] judge, but his life was exemplary in every way as he publicly averred in 1 Samuel 12.

Samuel wore three hats. He was a prophet above all; the man through whom the word of God came. As such he spoke judgment on Eli's house (3:1-18), anointed Saul and David (10:1; 16:13), rebuked Saul for his disobedience (13:13; 15:22-23), and encouraged David (19:18). His prophetic office was exercised even after his death when Saul rendezvoused with him via the witch of Endor (chap. 28). As a prophet he was also involved in writing the history of the Acts of God in Israel (1 Chron. 29:29).

Samuel was also a priest. When he was a boy, he wore a linen ephod, the sign of priesthood.[14] He led in the worship of Yahweh at the high place in one of the Benjamite towns (1 Sam. 9:11-24). Samuel practiced the teaching role of the priest when he addressed the people in 1 Samuel 10:17-27; 12:1-25. The chronicler stated in a short note that Samuel was involved in the original establishment of gatekeepers (1 Chron. 9:22).

Samuel became, strictly speaking, the last of the judges of Israel. Like the judges of old, he led the people in battle against the Philistines. First Samuel 7 draws a contrast between the way the sons of Eli went to battle against the Philistines and the way Samuel led the people. There is no indication in 1 Samuel 4 of a spiritual preparation. They simply went into battle and lost. Then they brought the Ark into the battle as sort of a talisman, and as a result, the battle and the Ark were lost. In 1 Samuel 7, Samuel, God's spokesman, prepared the people to go into battle against the Philistines. He first convinced them to get rid of their idols (vv. 2-4). Then he led them in confession of sin (vv. 5-7). Finally, he offered up sacrifices, and the Lord routed the Philistines. After the victory, Samuel erected a memorial stone reminding the people that Yahweh (when He is properly obeyed) provides help. The "stone of help" (Ebenezer) was erected at the very site the Israelites lost the war with the Philistines under the Elide family (4:1).[15] The text does not state that Samuel was

12. Hannah named her son "Samuel, saying, 'Because I asked the Lord for him.'" The Hebrew word for Samuel may be a reduction of the Hebrew word *šᵉmûʻa ʼēl* ("heard of God"). The name itself bears witness to the godly prayers of Hannah.

13. A Qumran fragment (4QSamᵃ) has a phrase at 1:22 not found in either MT or LXX that says, "And I will dedicate him as a nazirite forever, all the days of his life." McCarter is probably correct in accepting the first part of the reading as genuine (P. Kyle McCarter, Jr., *I Samuel*, The Anchor Bible [Garden City, N.Y.: Doubleday, 1980], p. 56).

14. A contrast between Samuel even as a boy and Eli's house is drawn in the early chapters of 1 Samuel. The boy Samuel was ministering (*mᵉšārat*) before the Lord under Eli the priest (1 Sam. 2:11), but the "boys" of Eli in their priestly office were abusing the people (1 Sam. 2:12-17). Their indictment is given in 1 Samuel 2:17, "This sin of the young men was very great in the Lord's sight, for they were treating the Lord's offering with contempt." In contrast Samuel was ministering (*mᵉšārat*) to the Lord as a little priest (1 Sam. 2:18).

15. Segal observes the links in the Samuel narratives between Samuel and Eli's sons (p. 197, n. 18).

directly involved in the military activities, but he dominated the preparation for battle. While Samuel was offering the burnt offering, God supernaturally routed the Philistines.[16]

THE ROLE OF LATER PRIESTS IN 1 AND 2 SAMUEL

The Shilonite priesthood is represented again when Saul opened his campaign against the Philistines. He inquired of Yahweh through the priest about going to battle, but Yahweh did not answer him.

A dark page in Israel's history is found in 1 Samuel 21 where David received innocent help from Ahimelech, the high priest at Nob. Nob, in the territory of Benjamin, is called a "priestly city" (1 Sam. 22:19). Apparently the Tabernacle was rebuilt there after the destruction of Shiloh, and the Eli family continued in office.[17] In his rage Saul killed eighty-five priests and the residents of the city (vv. 18-19). Abiathar escaped and served David. He was the last of Eli's family to serve as priest.

Zadok served jointly as high priest with Abiathar under David. This arrangement is most unusual, and after David's death, Abiathar, who sided with Adonijah, was dismissed and Zadok served alone.[18] Zadok is the ancestor to whom the priests serving in Ezekiel's eschatological temple trace their lineage.

THE ROLE OF THE PRIESTS IN 1 AND 2 KINGS

The ministry of the priests is mentioned in 1 Kings 8 in conjunction with the dedication of the Temple, but almost in a passing way. The record states that they brought the Ark and other priestly equipment to the new Temple. In 1 Kings, Solomon is center stage. His prayer of dedication is long, and he and all Israel are the ones offering sacrifices (1 Kings 8:62).

When Jeroboam I broke away from Judah and formed an independent kingdom in the north, a primary concern was the attraction of the centralized worship in Jerusalem to the northern Israelites. So he set up a rival religious system utilizing ancient centers with religious significance.

Solomon's son, Rehoboam, was forced to go to Shechem to be questioned about becoming king. Shechem had religious significance, going back to the patriarchs. Jeroboam rebuilt Shechem as a worship center (12:25) as well as Penuel, where Jacob wrestled with the angel. He also adopted the ancient calf cult, setting

16. It was for this priestly preparation that Saul was to wait when he began to attack the Philistines.

17. See McCarter, p. 349.

18. Some critical scholars argue that Zadok was a pagan priest of the Jebusite fortress who went over to David and became his priest and the priest of the sanctuary at Jerusalem (see, e.g., Christian E. Hauer, Jr., "Who was Zadok?" *Journal of Biblical Literature* 101 [1963]: 89-94, for the position and the literature), but Saul Olyan ("Zadok's Origins and the Tribal Politics of David," *Journal of Biblical Literature* 101 [1982]: 177-93) argues cogently that he was an Aaronic priest. For an earlier defense of Aaronic ancestry for Zadok, see Cross, pp. 207-15.

up one calf in Bethel (another ancient religious center) and one in Dan, where the Danites had set up their own religious system in the days of the judges with a descendant of Moses as priest (Judg. 18:30-31).

The priests chosen to function at these centers were not from the tribe of Levi (1 Kings 12:31).[19] The idolatry of Jeroboam led the historian to develop a theme around his sinfulness: "This was the sin of the house of Jeroboam that led to its downfall and to its destruction from the face of the earth" (13:34).

God's attitude toward the priestly religious system of Jeroboam is seen in the prophetic statement by the prophet from Judah who pronounced judgment on the altar and predicted the rise of Josiah who would tear it down (13:1-10; 2 Kings 23:15-16). The priesthood was reconfirmed, as it were, after 722 B.C. when the Assyrians returned a priest to assist the new mixed population in coping with local disasters (17:24-33).

The word "priest" does not occur again until in 2 Kings 10:11, 19 when Jehu killed the priests of Ahab, and 2 Kings 11, when Jehoiada, Joash's mentor, took center stage. The prophets dominate the section from 1 Kings 13 to 2 Kings 10.

Jehoiada carried out a *coup d'état* and unseated the usurper Athaliah (2 Kings 11). His activity was much like that of a prophet. Though there is no mention of anointing, it must have accompanied the placing of the crown on Joash (v. 12). Jehoiada also gave the "testimony" (*'ēdût*) to him. Some take this word to mean "jewels," but others (NIV) translate it "a copy of the covenant," deriving it from the root meaning "witness" or "testimony."[20] Deuteronomy 17:18-20 indicates that the king is to "write for himself on a scroll a copy of this law, taken from that of the priests, who are Levites." Could this be some modified form of that ritual?

Jehoiada became the *de facto* king during the minority of Joash and led him to follow the law of the Lord. He was no doubt influential in the repair and refurbishing of the Temple carried out by the king. This advisory capacity gave Jehoiada considerable influence in national affairs.

The apostate King Ahaz, perhaps as part of his allegiance to Tiglath-pileser, sent the pattern of an altar at Damascus to Jerusalem.[21] At the king's bidding the priest Urijah (Uriah) made an altar like it and set it in the holy place, changing some of the ritual to accommodate it (2 Kings 16:10-16).

Hilkiah the high priest was a significant person in the reform movement of young King Josiah (2 Kings 22-23). There are many parallels between Jehoiada/Joash and Hilkiah/Josiah. Both kings were quite young when they began to reign, both were

---

19. Cross argues that Jeroboam actually installed priests from two ancient priestly groups ("Mushites and Aaronites"), but to do so he must dismiss the biblical statement as a "deuteronomistic polemic" (p. 199).

20. See Mordechai Cogan and Hayim Tadmor, *II Kings,* The Anchor Bible (Garden City, N.Y.: Doubleday, 1988), p. 128.

21. Cogan and Tadmor dispute this and see the practice of Ahaz/Uriah (the latter a friend of Isaiah—8:4) as merely culturization (ibid., pp. 192-93). The text, however, sees the process in a negative light.

involved in the repair of a neglected Temple, both entered into a covenant with the Lord (11:17, 23:2-3); and the covenant in both cases was followed by a purge of pagan priests (11:18; 23:4-5). The historian's purpose in 2 Kings 12 was to highlight the ministry of Jehoiada in the enthronement of Joash, but in 2 Kings 22-23 the central place of the law and Josiah's obedience are featured. So Hilkiah is not emphasized as much as Jehoiada.

Several important distinctions were made in the priesthood at this time. Space does not permit the development of the ideas, but the pagan priests of 23:5 (*kᵉmārîm*) were different from Yahweh priests in 2 Kings 23:8 (*kôhănîm*). The latter were barred from their priestly service because they served at rural shrines, not because they were not legitimate priests.

The last word about priests in 2 Kings refers to the deportation to Babylon of the high priest Seraiah and the second priest Zephaniah (25:18-19).

THE THEOLOGY OF A PLACE OF WORSHIP IN SAMUEL-KINGS

A major facet of Israel's theology revolved around her places of worship. During all of Israel's preexilic history, a Tabernacle or a Temple existed side by side with other places where God's people worshiped. However, with the passing of time, a polemic developed against the high places that culminated in their violent removal by King Josiah.

The tension between a required centralization of worship with the practice of diversity of places of worship forms a cornerstone in the critical approach to the Old Testament. The theory is as follows: Since Deuteronomy (chaps. 12, 14, and 16 in particular) seems to limit all worship to one locale, and since the actual practice of worship from the judges to Josiah was in several places, most of the book of Deuteronomy must have been composed in the time of Josiah to authenticate a new tradition and to authorize the Josianic reform.[22] However, Segal argues that Deuteronomy is not insisting that worship can be conducted in one place only but that the place must be divinely sanctioned as a holy place for the worship of Yahweh.[23]

The Tabernacle stood for some time in Shiloh. After the Philistine war of 1 Samuel 4, the Ark had an independent existence.[24] The Tabernacle was apparently re-erected at Nob, whose priests Saul slaughtered, without the Ark. David erected some kind of a tent (perhaps the full Tabernacle) for the Ark when he brought it to Jerusalem and made that city the central site for the dwelling place of God.

22. See, e.g., Otto Eissfeldt, *The Old Testament: An Introduction,* trans. P. Ackroyd (New York: Harper & Row, 1965), pp. 219-33. See also McCarter, p. 177.
23. Segal, pp. 87-88. Peter Craigie (*Deuteronomy,* NICOT [Grand Rapids: Eerdmans, 1976], p. 217), and Marten Woudstra (*Joshua,* NICOT [Grand Rapids: Eerdmans, 1981], p. 320), concur with Segal's conclusions.
24. Second Chronicles 1:3 speaks of "God's tent . . . which Moses the servant of the Lord had made in the wilderness." This may mean that the Tabernacle survived the Philistine war, or it may mean only that the same *pattern* was followed when the Tabernacle was rebuilt.

THE HIGH PLACES IN SAMUEL

The word "high place" (*bāmāh*) appears in only two places in Samuel, and both are connected with Samuel the prophet and the anointing of Saul.[25] Here the high place was clearly legitimate, for it is sanctioned by no less a person than Samuel. There is not even an editorial comment about the "house not being built for the name of the Lord." These two high places are mentioned without criticism in spite of the previous existence of the Tabernacle at Shiloh and its later existence at Nob.

The worship at the high place in Samuel seems to feature the sacrificial meal as much or more than the sacrifice. We learn that thirty men were gathered for the meal and that Saul was put at the head of the table in the place of honor. A cook prepared the meal and served Saul a special piece of meat. Samuel's presence was required before the meal could proceed.

These passages in 1 Samuel indicate that the writer of Samuel had no problem with high places so long as they were dedicated to Yahweh. McCarter argues in a circle when he says, "The present passage [1 Sam. 9] with its unflinching association of Samuel and a high place is pre-Deuteronomic in origin and has escaped editorial censorship."[26]

In spite of the interest in worship in the remainder of 1 and 2 Samuel, there is no further mention of high places as centers of worship until 1 Kings. In Kings, however, the attitude of the historian is clearly hostile to high places. He concedes the necessity of the people worshiping there (and by inference Solomon also) because of the lack of a temple. However, the historian was writing from a later perspective when religion had become syncretistic, and the high places were a snare to the people.

There were high places dedicated to false gods (1 Kings 11:7) and others that were possibly dedicated to Yahweh but no doubt used for both Yahweh and Baal or some other deity. Jeroboam I's high places were condemned by the historian even though they may have had some connection with Yahweh, and a prophet came from Judah specifically to denounce the altar at Bethel (chaps. 12-13).

A stock phrase occurs in connection with the godly kings Asa (15:14), Jehoshaphat (22:44), Jehoash (2 Kings 12:4), Amaziah (14:4), Azariah (15:4), and Jotham (15:30). Each of these kings is commended, but some form of the phrase "but the high places were not take away" occurs with each one. Only with Hezekiah and Josiah was more drastic and revolutionary action taken to remove the high places (18:4; 23:8).

THE ARK IN SAMUEL

Worship was practiced at the high places under Levitical priests, but the Ark also was special as the symbol of God's presence. When David brought the Ark to

---

25. First Samuel 9:12, 13, 14, 19, 25; 10:5, 13. The plural form is used poetically in 2 Samuel 1 and 22.

26. McCarter, p. 177.

Jerusalem, the centralization of worship began. The high places, legitimate places of worship, continued throughout the history of the monarchy, but Jerusalem, the home of the Ark, increasingly became the center of worship.

The bringing of the Ark to Jerusalem was an event of major theological significance. If Merrill is correct, some twenty-seven years lapsed between the conquering of Jerusalem and the transfer of the Ark to that city.[27] David wanted to make the Jebusite city not only the center of his rule but also the center of the worship of the Lord. Yahweh had met His people at Gilgal, Shiloh, Mizpeh, and Nob. When Solomon began his reign, he went to Gibeon to offer sacrifices (1 Kings 3:4) in spite of the presence of the Ark and at least some form of the Tabernacle at Jerusalem. After Solomon built the Temple, however, Jerusalem became the chief meeting place.

In the theology of 1 and 2 Samuel, the Ark figures largely. It was lost through misuse by the house of Eli; Yahweh's sovereignty was manifested in the impact it had on the Philistine cities; the holiness of Yahweh is indicated by the way the Beth Shemeshites treated it; and it was in the house of Abinadab in Kiriath Jearim for several decades. David wanted to move it to Jerusalem so that his city could become the center of the worship of Yahweh. By bringing the Ark to his new Jebusite capital, David was attempting to bind the tribes and the central government more firmly.[28]

David first tried to move it on a cart as the Philistines had done. The prescribed method was to carry it with staves on the shoulders of the Levites (Num. 4:1-16). God's unhappiness with this breach of Levitical protocol is evidenced in the death of Uzzah (2 Sam. 6:1-8). David's second attempt was successful,[29] and acting in his royal capacity he offered up burnt offerings and fellowship offerings.

The movement of the Ark by David as the symbol of the presence of Yahweh is posed in contrast to its loss by the Eli family. The Ark section (2 Sam. 5-6) also leads up to the Davidic Covenant. In bringing the Ark to Jerusalem, David created the setting for the message from Yahweh about David's eternal house. Solomon completed the Temple, and with a permanent structure, the priesthood at Jerusalem under Zadok took on even greater significance.

THE PLACE OF THE TEMPLE

Since Yahweh is universal and omnipresent, it would be foolish to assume that He could be confined to a local shrine (1 Kings 8:27). At the same time Yahweh had graciously conceded to place His name in the Temple. Since this was true, people should be able to pray toward the Temple and expect a response from the God

27. Eugene H. Merrill, *Kingdom of Priests* (Grand Rapids: Baker, 1987), pp. 244-45.

28. Olyan, pp. 177-93.

29. This is made quite clear in the Chronicles: "Then David said, 'No one but the Levites may carry the ark of God, because the Lord chose them to carry the ark of the Lord and to minister before Him forever'" (1 Chron. 15:2).

who had identified Himself with the Temple. Since Yahweh's true Temple is heaven, it is from there that He will hear the prayers directed toward the Temple on earth (1 Kings 8:30). Unfortunately this concept of a universal God, manifesting Himself in a local shrine, became corrupted. The shrine itself took on larger-than-life proportions; the people were convinced that as long as the shrine stood, God would not judge the city (Jer. 7).

Small wonder that the Temple during the Exile became significant in memory and prospect. Daniel prayed three times a day with his windows opened toward Jerusalem (Dan. 6:10). The city attracted his attention because it was the place where the Temple had been. The decree of Cyrus to the Jews in 538 B.C. concerned the rebuilding of the Temple in Jerusalem (Ezra 1:2-4), and the first official act of the returning exiles in 536 B.C. was to lay the foundation of the Temple (3:9-10).

The Temple was to be a place where justice was carried out. People who had been wronged were to be able to come to this place where Yahweh put His name and cry out for justice and expect vindication (1 Kings 8:21). This statement reflects the strong emphasis placed on justice in the theology of the Old Testament. Since God is just, He expects His representatives to be just also. The Temple was to be a place where this was recognized.

The people of God were to construe defeat by enemies to be a sign of Yahweh's displeasure with them. When this happened, they were to come to the Temple and confess their sins. Solomon prayed that Yahweh would forgive them and "bring them back to the land you gave to their fathers" (8:34).

In the same way they were to interpret a drought as a sign of Yahweh's judgment for sin. Then they were to pray toward the Temple and confess their sin. Solomon urged Yahweh, when He answered their prayer, to teach His people the right way to live (v. 36). The same principle applied to other catastrophes, such as famine, plague, blight, mildew, locusts, or grasshoppers, or even when an enemy besieged them or their cities (vv. 37-40). God's favorable response to these prayers was to cause the people to fear the Lord (v. 40).[30]

The universality of Yahweh is indicated by the reference to the foreigner who came to identify with the people of God (vv. 41-43). People would hear of Yahweh's great name and come from many parts of the earth. Answering the foreigner's prayer would be a vindication of His name among the people of the earth. This is also reflected in the theology of Isaiah 2:2-5, part of which reads, "Many people will come and say, 'Come, let us go up to the mountain of the Lord, to the house of the God of Jacob. He will teach us his ways, so that we may walk in his paths.' The law will go out from Zion, the word of the Lord from Jerusalem."

The issue of the Exile, first systematically promulgated in Deuteronomy, is also anticipated here (1 Kings 8:46-51). Sin will result in captivity. Solomon expected that in the Exile there would be genuine repentance. Then they would pray

---

30. Compare the book of Joel, which speaks of a locust plague being removed by the intercession of the priests and people.

toward the Temple for forgiveness. Solomon prayed that Yahweh would forgive them and cause their conquerors to show them mercy. Daniel surely had this prayer of Solomon in mind when he prayed to Yahweh for the forgiveness of his people (Dan. 9). Furthermore, God did indeed work on the heart of Cyrus, who in turn allowed the Jews to return to Jerusalem to rebuild the Temple.

THE PROPHETIC MOVEMENT IN SAMUEL AND KINGS

The second office God used to mediate His kingdom was that of the prophet. From the time of Samuel on, the prophets dominated the pages of Scripture. The priests no doubt played a larger role than the space attributed to them by the historian would indicate, but the prophets were the ones to bring a new dimension to the relationship between Yahweh and His people.

THE PROPHETIC MOVEMENT IN 1 AND 2 SAMUEL

The first mention of a prophet in these books occurs in 1 Samuel 2:27-36.[31] He is called a "man of God," and his task was to tell Eli, in the name of Yahweh, that the house of Eli was to be replaced by a "faithful priest." As we have seen, a major theme in Samuel and Kings is the removal of the Elide priesthood and its replacement with Zadokites.

The prophet par excellence was, of course, Samuel. From the beginning it was clear that he would be a prophet. When God first spoke to him, the writer noted that "the word of the Lord was rare; there were not many visions" (3:1). According to 1 Samuel 3:19-20, "The Lord was with Samuel as he grew up, and he let none of his words fall to the ground. And all Israel from Dan to Beersheba recognized that Samuel was attested as a prophet of the Lord." Samuel's name is noticeably absent from the account dealing with the first Ebenezer battle, which was a debacle. It was later that he came to the people as priest and prophet and led them to victory.

Samuel also set the precedent of prophets anointing kings. This laid the groundwork for later conflict when some kings refused to submit to the direction of the prophet. But the procedure was divinely directed, since it was Yahweh who told Samuel all about Saul and later directly instructed him to anoint David (1 Sam. 16).

Also in 1 Samuel "bands" (*ḥebel*) of prophets are referred to for the first time. Samuel's relationship to these prophets is not explicit. However, when David fled Saul (chap. 19), Samuel was "standing *and* presiding" over a group of prophets who were prophesying. It seems plausible, therefore, to attribute to Samuel the development of the prophetic movement in a formal sense. Certainly it was always

31. For an excellent discussion of prophets and prophecy, see Edward J. Young, *My Servants the Prophets* (Grand Rapids: Eerdmans, 1952). From a critical perspective, see also Gerhard von Rad, *The Message of the Prophets* (New York: Harper & Row, 1962); K. Koch, *The Prophets: The Assyrian Period* (Philadelphia: Fortress, 1983); and idem, *The Prophets: The Babylonian and Persian Period,* trans. Margaret Kohl, 2 vols. (Philadelphia: Fortress, 1984).

God who raised up the true prophet, but the structure itself had its inception with Samuel and was developed further by Elijah.

Samuel's practice of anointing and advising kings led in some cases to a close relationship between the prophet and the king. These prophets are often referred to as "court prophets." The first of these, Gad, is seen in 1 Samuel 22, advising David about where to flee from Saul. Many years later, he brought God's word to David regarding the plague as punishment for David's census (2 Sam. 24:11). He also told David to erect an altar on the threshing floor of Araunah and so was involved in the selection of the Temple site (24:18). These court prophets did much more than advise kings. They also kept records (1 Chron. 29:29). Samuel, Nathan, and Gad are all mentioned as writers of court records. Thus, when Samuel, Kings, and Chronicles were written, some of the source material came from these prophets.

Nathan was the prophet who first encouraged David to build a temple and later, at the command of Yahweh, rescinded that direction (2 Sam. 7). This indicates that prophets could give advice based on their own common sense as well as give divine direction from God. It was also Nathan who delivered the poignant condemnation of David in the sin against Bathsheba and Uriah (2 Sam. 12). Nathan was further involved in the anti-Adonijah movement to keep Solomon in the line of succession (1 Kings 1:11-14). Nathan knew that Yahweh had chosen Solomon to succeed David (2 Sam. 12) and therefore believed he should move to consolidate Solomon's position since David had reached a point of indifference to the whole situation. Nathan also anointed Solomon to be king. This status of "adviser to the king" continued in Judah with uneven success. Some prophets were beaten, imprisoned, or even killed, but there was always a tacit recognition that the prophet had a right to speak for Yahweh. However, in the north the prophetic office was usually adversarial. This was partly due to the attempt by the prophets of Baal to legitimate their prophecy. The prophets of Yahweh were bound to respond and refute them. The classical example of this is Elijah on Mount Carmel (1 Kings 18).

The word "prophet" translates the Hebrew *nābî'*. The etymology is obscure. Some argue for the meaning "to bubble forth," more a reflection of their idea of a prophet than an etymology. Others argue that it means "to be called."[32] The word most certainly means to be a spokesman for God, but its precise etymology cannot be determined. The classical passage on the Old Testament prophet is Deuteronomy 18, when Moses was preparing the people to enter Canaan, where they would encounter all kinds of occult practices. In contrast to this false activity, Israel was to listen to her prophets. Amos was told by Amaziah to go home and prophesy in Judah rather than in Israel (Amos 7:10-17). Likewise, Ezekiel was told to "prophesy to these bones and say" (Ezek. 37:4). This implies that the idea of prophesying means basically to communicate what God says. This practice can be observed in

32. William F. Albright, *From the Stone Age to Christianity* (Baltimore: Johns Hopkins, 1957), p. 303.

the life of Nathan and Gad. On the other hand, some of the references to prophesying in 1 Samuel (1 Sam. 10:5-7; 19:18-24) indicate that sometimes bizarre behavior accompanied prophesying. Certainly it means that God overpowered the prophet so that he was no longer acting of his own accord.[33] As one of his authenticating signs, Saul prophesied. He was prevented from capturing David when God caused him to lie all night stripped down. God seized on men to carry out His divine purposes as He did the seventy elders working with Moses to help in judging.

The priestly and Levitical movements were instrumental in leading the people in the worship of Yahweh, both in sacrifice and song. The prophetic movement, however, led the way in understanding the mind of God (often given directly through the prophet) and in calling on the people to worship Yahweh in holiness and obedience. The prophetic movement is perhaps the most significant in the history of Israel. Both kings and priests were to submit to the word of the prophet for the simple reason that he was speaking not on his own behalf but for God.

THE PROPHETIC MOVEMENT IN 1 AND 2 KINGS

Several nonwriting prophets are mentioned in 1 and 2 Kings. They will be discussed to determine the theology they present.[34]

Nathan. The old court prophet and friend of David appeared for the last time as Solomon was being made king in the midst of opposition. Nathan received messages from God and even acted as the accuser when David sinned against Bathsheba and Uriah. In 1 Kings, however, he appears as a mere adviser plotting the ascension of Solomon. Certainly, he was following the plan set out by Yahweh when He chose Solomon at his birth, but he does not appear as a man speaking for God so much as one carrying out what he knew to be right.

It is striking that in the entire account of Solomon (drawn from the book of the annals of Solomon), no mention is made of a prophet speaking to Solomon. This is especially so when it is recognized that part of the source for the biblical account came from the "records of Nathan the prophet . . . the prophecy of Ahijah the Shilonite and . . . visions of Iddo the seer concerning Jeroboam son of Nebat" (2 Chron. 9:29). Twice Yahweh appeared directly to Solomon: once at the beginning of his reign (1 Kings 3:5-14), and once after the dedication of the Temple (9:1-9). In addition to these direct appearances, the historian wrote that the word of Yahweh came to Solomon encouraging him to obey Him so that He might fulfill His promise to David (6:12-13). In the chapter in which Yahweh indicted Solomon (chap. 11), the phrase "So the Lord said to Solomon . . ." appears with the promise of removing part of the kingdom from Solomon's son. With this kind of judgment oracle, one might expect to encounter a prophet, but even here no prophet is mentioned. The his-

---

33. For the use of the Hebrew reflexive verb in these cases of ecstatic prophecies, see *Theological Dictionary of the New Testament,* s.v. προφήτης, by Rolf Rendtorff, p. 797.
34. The theology of the writing prophets is discussed later in this volume.

torian presented the idea that Solomon had more direct access to Yahweh than either David his father or any of his successors. The special wisdom God gave him provided greater insight into judicial activities than any other king possessed. While prophets were surely involved in Solomon's rule, the historian emphasized Solomon's direct information. Therefore, the theology found in 1 Kings 3:4-10, which records Yahweh first appearing to Solomon, and 1 Kings 9:3-9, which records the Lord's response to his prayer, would also reflect the theology of the prophets themselves.

Ahijah the Shilonite. The first prophet to appear in Kings (apart from Nathan) is Ahijah. He did not appear before Solomon, though his message certainly concerned Solomon. He appeared before Jeroboam I (1 Kings 11:29-40). The prophetic word, mentioned obliquely in 1 Kings 11:11-13 (and probably delivered by Ahijah), contains the following elements: (1) in fulfillment of the Davidic Covenant, punishment would be brought on the Davidic dynasty by removing the northern part of the kingdom, and (2) again because of the Davidic Covenant (and for the sake of Jerusalem), one tribe would be left to David's family.

Ahijah reiterated the same message to Jeroboam with the added promise that if Jeroboam would walk before the Lord as He had urged David to do, another "Davidic" or "Jeroboamic" covenant would be fulfilled in the north. This raises an interesting question. If Jeroboam had indeed been a righteous man, how would the "sure house" promised him have affected the relations between Israel and Judah in the future? In fact, since he was most unrighteous, the issue is a moot one. The historian says of Rehoboam's obstinacy, "So the king did not listen to the people, for this turn of events was from the Lord, to fulfill the word the Lord had spoken to Jeroboam son of Nebat through Ahijah the Shilonite" (12:15). It was necessary to God's purposes that Rehoboam reject sound counsel and cause the northern tribes to separate. This brought about the prophecy against Solomon.

In the enigmatic story of the prophet who came from Judah to Bethel and spoke against Jeroboam's altar, Yahweh revealed His hostility to pagan altars. The predictive element (essential for authentication) included the young King Josiah, whose reform would extend into this very area some 200 years later (1 Kings 13). Further, the Lord's demands for complete obedience were evidenced when the young prophet was killed (by Yahweh) for failing to carry out His word even though a man professing to speak in the name of Yahweh had deceived him.

Ahijah's message to Jeroboam when the latter's son became sick compared Jeroboam's conduct to David's. This sounds as though Ahijah, in light of his prophecy about a "sure house" for Jeroboam, may have thought that Jeroboam's dynasty would replace David's in some sense.[35] In any event, Jeroboam's failure to walk in the ways of David was the basis of Yahweh's judgment on his house. The

35. The language of 1 Kings 14:7-8 is similar to the language of Yahweh to David in 2 Samuel 7:8-9 and 2 Samuel 12:7-9.

great evil committed by Jeroboam was his idolatry and rejection of Yahweh (14:9-10).

Shemaiah. The chronicler tells us about Shemaiah's confrontation with Rehoboam charging him with spiritual apostasy. Rehoboam humbled himself, and Yahweh gave Judah deliverance but allowed them to be "servants" to the Egyptian king Shishak (2 Chron. 12:1-8). This Shemaiah, along with Iddo the Seer, also wrote an account of the acts of Rehoboam (v. 15).

Azariah and Hanani. Asa's reform (to be discussed later) is passed over rather lightly in Kings whereas Chronicles gives several pages to it and details Azariah's prophecy (2 Chron. 15:1-7). Likewise, the prophecy of Hanani the Seer, who rebuked Asa for seeking an alliance with Syria (vv. 7-9), is passed over in Kings.

Jehu. Yahweh's judgment came on the northern king Baasha through the prophet Jehu the son of Hanani for two reasons: (1) his own personal evil in the sight of Yahweh, and (2) his destruction of the house of Jeroboam (even though this itself was a prophesied judgment) (1 Kings 15:7). Again Baasha was held to the code of righteous conduct expected of Yahweh's kings. Though David is not mentioned in the account, his standard looms in the background.

From here on, the historian of Kings will use this formula of the northern monarchs: "because of his sins he had committed, doing evil in the eyes of the Lord and walking in the ways of Jeroboam and in the sin he had committed and had caused Israel to commit" (16:19).

Elijah and Elisha. The ministry of Elijah and Elisha stands unique in the midst of unique ministries. Their task was formidable for they had to resist a hostile and virulent form of Baalism. Baalism was being promoted strongly by the king and queen of Israel, and the people themselves were caught up in a syncretism of worship of Yahweh and Baal. The fertility cult of Canaan contained cultural ideas, terminology, and practices in common with Yahwism that made cross-over rather easy. The fact alone that Yahweh could be called Baal (lord or master) made separation difficult. The task of Elijah and Elisha was to turn the Northern Kingdom back to a pure, single-minded worship of Yahweh.

Elijah's theology was simple: Yahweh is the God of the universe who can make it rain or withhold rain. The nature religion with which the Israelites were involved was being challenged. Consequently Elijah told Ahab there would be no rain until Yahweh said so (1 Kings 17:2). Yet this God of the universe deigned to meet the simplest needs of His prophet. Elijah was sustained at Cherith and at Zarephath. There, also, Yahweh the God of Israel decreed that the widow's meager food supply would not disappear until He sent rain again on the earth (v. 14). That Yahweh is the God of all life was also proved in the resurrection of the widow's son. This miracle brought the woman to say, "Now I know that you are a man of God and that the word of the Lord from your mouth is truth" (v. 24).

Elijah faced the horde of Baal prophets with equanimity. His trust in Yahweh was so simple and complete he could even mock them in their foolish efforts to win the favor and action of Baal. Then he repaired the ruined altar of Yahweh. He took a stone for each of the 12 tribes of Israel with which to build the altar. Throughout the Elijah account, including his flight to Sinai, the historian emphasized the importance of the pristine revelation of Yahweh in the wilderness. The twelve-tribe organization around the altar of Yahweh with the necessary animal sacrifice was the simple faith of the Israelites in the wilderness to which Elijah was demanding that the people return. When Yahweh responded with the miracle of fire on the altar, the people cried out, "The Lord—he is God! The Lord—he is God!" Baal the storm god should have been able to bring fire, but it was Yahweh, God of all nature, who harnessed the lightning bolts.

Elijah's "pilgrimage" to Sinai was a search for the roots of Yahwism. There Yahweh had appeared to Moses when he was herding sheep, and there He appeared to him when he gave the law. Elijah needed reaffirmation. What he thought he saw happening on Mt. Carmel did not happen, namely, the repentance of Israel. So he went to Mount Sinai (also known as Mount Horeb) to chide Yahweh for forsaking him. Yahweh reassured Elijah of His sovereign control, even as He spoke with a still, small voice. Elijah was recommissioned and returned to the fray (19:15-18).

First Kings 20 does not refer to Elijah, but it is from the same prophetic circle. In this case the wicked King Ahab was permitted to win a battle over the Syrians. A prophet came to Ahab and said that God would give a great victory so that they might know that He is Yahweh (20:13). Later the prophet told Ahab that because the Syrians supposed that the Lord was limited to certain locales, Yahweh would give a great victory, again so that Ahab might know that He is Yahweh (v. 28).

The most heinous act of Ahab came in the matter of Naboth. A king's primary responsibility was to render justice in the land. Ahab egregiously violated this requirement by stealing from a man he had murdered (through Jezebel). God's word of condemnation came through Elijah the Tishbite (21:20-22). The historian added a footnote about the wickedness of Ahab, showing the necessity for his judgment (vv. 25-26).

The last chapter of Ahab's life was, as one might expect, a confrontation with a prophet of Yahweh. Jehoshaphat, an otherwise good king, chose to ally himself with Ahab. He even went so far as to seal his alliance with the marriage of his son to Ahab's daughter. First Kings 22 relates that he had decided to join Ahab in one of his perpetual battles against the Syrians at Ramoth Gilead. Jehoshaphat wanted advice from Yahweh, and Ahab tried to appease him by bringing out the court prophets, lackeys for the king. Jehoshaphat sensed the farce before him and asked for a prophet of Yahweh. Micaiah (whose name means "Who is like Yahweh") ben Imlah was brought out. In this poignant vignette the sovereignty of Yahweh, including His control over the false prophets who were luring Ahab to his death, is clearly set forth. Yahweh's purposes cannot be thwarted. Ahab died and the dogs licked up his blood, as Yahweh had said they would.

Yahweh's control of life is again the question when Ahaziah, Ahab's son, was injured in a fall and sent to Ekron to consult Baal-Zebub the god of Ekron (2 Kings 1). An angel of the Lord told Elijah to challenge Ahaziah and his messengers: "Is it because there is no God in Israel that you are going off to consult Baal-Zebub the god of Ekron?" (v. 3). The punishment for such syncretism was that Ahaziah would not recover from his injury. As happened on other occasions, the king tried to overthrow the word of the prophet by force. He sent messengers to capture Elijah, but they were killed by fire falling from heaven. When Elijah did come to Ahaziah, he simply repeated the dire report he had made before: that Ahaziah would die. Thus, Yahweh was again seen as being in charge of the entire universe.

The miracles by Elisha were often in the sphere of nature: the healing of the water (2 Kings 2:19-22); the miracle in the battle of Moab of the supply of water (3:14-26); the multiplication of oil for the prophet's widow (4:1-7); the restoration of the Shunammite's son (vv. 8-36); the purification of the poisonous stew (vv. 38-41); and the multiplication of the food for 100 people (vv. 42-43). The intense emphasis on the fertility cult in the north required a response on the part of Yahweh that would prove His superiority over the false deities worshiped by the Israelites. There were other effects of the miracles, but the struggle for the minds of the people took place in the arena of nature. Elisha was used to show that the Lord has no peer.

The spectacular healing of the Aramean general, Naaman, showed that Yahweh was capable of restoring life to dead flesh (his "flesh" was "restored," 2 Kings 5:10), that He was gracious to foreigners, and that His prophet was not a mercenary as were most of the prophets of Israel. Nowhere is it better illustrated that the prophet was free from the control of people than in Elisha's refusal to receive remuneration from the wealthy general. His servant was made an example of the foolishness of a mercenary attitude toward the ministry (2 Kings 5).

The universality of Yahweh is demonstrated in Elisha's ability to control the Aramean armies by telling His servant where they were located. This is similar to the situation recorded in 1 Kings 20 when the Arameans thought that Yahweh was limited to certain locales. Elisha's awareness of the Arameans shows that Yahweh knows what is going on in other countries. In the pagan religions the deities were limited to certain spheres (a town, the sea, the hunt, etc.). The reputation of Elisha as Yahweh's prophet was well established in Syria as one who knew the secret things of even the Arameans (2 Kings 6:12).

When the Aramean king came to capture Elisha, the prophet had deep confidence in his Lord. He was aware that "those who are with us are more than those who are with them" (6:16). Furthermore, he prayed to Yahweh to open the eyes of the servant so that he could see the divine army encamped around the mountain.

The story of the Aramean siege of Samaria (2 Kings 6:24-7:20) includes a number of important theological issues. The responsibility for the famine (resulting from the siege) is attributed to Yahweh, and its alleviation must come from the same source. The king (Jehoram?) knew that Yahweh alone could provide for the needs of the people (6:27). He also knew that Yahweh had brought this calamity on the people (v. 33).[36] Also revealed is the rebellion of the Israelite king who refused to submit to Yahweh's authority.[37] The arrogance of the royal house is indicated in the response of the king's adviser, who said, "Look, even if the Lord should open the floodgates of the heavens, could this happen?" (7:2) The lifting of the siege came about through a miracle, and both Yahweh and His prophet were vindicated in the deliverance that came to Israel.

The universality and international nature of God became evident when Elisha went to Damascus, and Ben Hadad inquired of Yahweh through the prophet of God.[38] In the process of the inquiry Elisha revealed to Hazael, the king's messenger, that he would become the next king in Damascus. This was the fullfillment of Elijah's original commission (1 Kings 19:15). Yahweh is certainly the God of the nations.

The syncretism of the north had reached such proportions that a bloody purge was necessary. Yahweh had originally commissioned Elijah to anoint Jehu for this purpose (1 Kings 19:15-17). Ahab and Jezebel had been successful in developing a state cult centered in Baal worship. In spite of the purge carried out by Elijah on Mount Carmel, there had been a great resurgence of Baal worship. Jehu now represented Yahweh in carrying out a new purge. He brought an end to the dynasty of Ahab and to the life of Jezebel, who was brazen and arrogant against Yahweh until the end.

Jehu himself was not an outstanding example of a worshiper of Yahweh. He shared the attitude of his troops toward the prophets. They were "mad men," and Jehu said, "You know the man and the sort of things he says" (2 Kings 9:11). Above all Jehu "did not turn away from the sins of Jeroboam son of Nebat, which he had caused Israel to commit—the worship of the golden calves at Bethel and Dan" (10:29). He was condemned further by the prophet Hosea for unstated reasons beyond the fact that he committed a massacre in Jezreel (Hos. 1:4). In spite of Jehu's personal spiritual failure, Yahweh promised him a four-generation dynasty (2 Kings 10:30) and that promise was fulfilled when Zechariah became king (though he was soon assassinated).

Nothing good is said about Jehoash, grandson of Ahab, but there is an account of a visit he paid to Elisha when the latter was dying. He showed great respect for

---

36. The Hebrew in verse 33 is ambiguous as to the subject of this sentence. Presumably it was the king.

37. He was wearing sackcloth (6:30), but his attitude toward Elisha—he was going to kill him—indicates a rebellious heart against Yahweh.

38. A deliberate contrast is being made here with the actions of Ahaziah, king of Israel, who went to Ekron to inquire of a foreign deity (Baal-Zebub) about whether he would get well. The same phraseology is used here, except that the pagan king knew to inquire of the God of Israel. T. R. Hobbs relates the query of Ahaziah with that of Ben Hadad to Elisha in 2 Kings 8:8 (*II Kings,* The Anchor Bible [Garden City, N.Y.: Doubleday, 1985], p. xix).

Elisha, calling him "my father" and "the chariots of Israel." The latter phrase means that Elisha was more important to Israel than chariots of war. In that instance Elisha, through the symbolism of a bow and arrows, predicted that Jehoash would defeat Syria (13:14-19).

Jonah son of Amittai. Jonah is best known for the prophecy that bears his name and that pertains to his mission to Nineveh. However, a terse statement from the time of Jeroboam II reveals that the prosperous expansion of the Northern Kingdom in the ninth century took place under Jonah's prophetic ministry (13:25).

Isaiah son of Amoz. One of the longer sections in 2 Kings concerns the godly king Hezekiah whose accolade says, "There was no one like him among all the kings of Judah, either before him or after him. He held fast to the Lord and did not cease to follow him; he kept the commands the Lord had given Moses. And the Lord was with him; he was successful in whatever he undertook" (2 King 18:5b-7a). Even the good kings, in the eyes of the exilic historian, were marred by their failure to tear down the high places. Hezkiah did just that and consequently is given extensive space in Chronicles as well as in Kings. Since the Assyrian invasion saw considerable interaction with the prophet Isaiah, this event is discussed here.

The place of the law of Moses ranked high in Hezekiah's life. He was able to separate the tangible witness to Moses (the bronze serpent), which the people superstitiously worshiped, from the intangible reality (18:4). Hezekiah was probably following the advice of Isaiah in throwing off the Assyrian yoke. Isaiah had warned Ahaz, Hezekiah's father, against going to Assyria and had urged him to trust in Yahweh (Isaiah 7-8). But Ahaz refused to listen. Now Hezekiah had chosen to trust in Yahweh and not accept Assyrian overlordship. He must have been bitterly disappointed when Sennacherib, the Assyrian king, came west and devastated the land of Judah and threatened the capital city of Jerusalem.

Sennacherib's officers went to Jerusalem in an effort to intimidate Hezekiah. Their theological insight is revealing. They told Hezekiah that his trust in Yahweh would be to no avail. They then appealed to the common people by saying that Yahweh was offended because Hezekiah had torn down His high places (2 Kings 18:22). Furthermore, the Rab Shakeh said that Yahweh Himself told him to march against Judah and destroy it (v. 25). Assyrian intelligence had well informed them. Hezekiah had told the people to trust in Yahweh. He would deliver the people from the hand of the Assyrian. This was the age-old promise. It was given when the Israelites left Egypt, threatened by the Egyptian army, and was repeated under Joshua and later the judges. Now the Rab Shakeh said in a moment of arrogance that Yahweh would *not* deliver them. Rather, the king of Assyria would deliver them and give them possessions and life. He had attempted to take the place of Yahweh (vv. 31-32). Yahweh, he said, was no different from any other national god. The gods of Hamath, Arphad, and others, were unable to deliver their people, so why should Yahweh do any more for the Judeans? This direct challenge to Yahweh's universality, omnipotence, and covenant-keeping grace to His people had to be answered.

Hezekiah told Isaiah about the reproach and ridicule heaped on God's people. He asked Isaiah to pray for the remnant that survived (19:4). Yahweh promised to send a spirit on the Assyrians so that they would believe a rumor and leave the country. When Sennacherib withdrew, he sent letters to Hezekiah containing more blasphemous language (vv. 9-13). Hezekiah's prayer (vv. 15-19) contains a number of important theological issues.

He began by witnessing to the uniqueness of Yahweh. He alone is God over all the kingdoms of the earth. This argued against the Rab Shakeh's claim that the local gods could not deliver their people, and therefore that Yahweh was incapable of delivering His people. Furthermore Yahweh is the Creator of heaven and earth. He is not some idol to be carried about and dragged into captivity—He is *the* great Creator. The claim of the Assyrians that they had defeated the local gods was a true claim, said Hezekiah, but Yahweh was not a local god. Therefore, a divine deliverance would bear witness to all the kingdoms of the earth that Yahweh was the only true God.

The wonderful theology of Isaiah found in his extensive prophecy is glimpsed in Yahweh's answer to Hezekiah's prayer (19:21-34). Yahweh wanted Sennacherib to know that he operated only by God's divine direction. Actually Yahweh ordained Sennacherib's activity long before. As the great Creator and ordainer, Yahweh knew all about Sennacherib, and his insolence would not go unpunished. The miracle took place that night; 185,000 men died by the hand of the angel of the Lord. Yahweh was vindicated.

Isaiah also predicted the Babylonian Captivity. The placement of this prophecy in the book of Isaiah relates it to the second part of the book about the Babylonian Captivity. Here the historian stated that there were many reasons for the Exile, but the process was begun by Hezekiah's failure to trust in Yahweh by forming an alliance with the newly rising Chaldeans from Babylon (20:12-18).

Huldah. When the law book was found in the Temple, Huldah was consulted about its significance. She declared in words echoed in Jeremiah that the people would be judged. However, Josiah would not personally be involved in the judgment (2 Kings 22:14-20).

Unnamed prophets. Manasseh's long and wicked reign was the basis for much of the judgment of Yahweh on Judah. Here the historian made clear that the disaster of 586 B.C. was brought about because of the wickedness of the people, led and represented by Manasseh, and so he recorded the words of His servants the prophets (2 Kings 21:10-15). Judah is linked with Samaria in judgment (v. 13). As Samaria had already been carried away to Assyrian cities, so Judah would be carried to Babylonian cities. This conquest was the consummation of all the evil of Yahweh's people from the time He brought them up from Egypt.

THE MONARCHY IN SAMUEL AND KINGS

The third office used by God to mediate His kingdom among His people was that of the monarchy, or kingship. The shift in the leadership from judges to kings was dramatic and traumatic. The rule by judges allowed the tribes to maintain a greater independence. The judges arose spontaneously and with a few weak exceptions did not perpetuate their rule through their children. The kings, however, would rule all Israel continuously and would be succeeded by sons whether they were worthy or not. Even so, Yahweh would deal with the king about his worthiness and measure him against the Davidic Covenant and the Davidic ideal. Eventually, the ideal Ruler would become a major theme in the prophets, a Ruler who would judge the people equitably and in justice.[39] In that great eschatological future, this ideal King will even be called David, since He will more than fill out the Davidic ideal (Ezek. 34:23-24).

THE MONARCHY IN 1 AND 2 SAMUEL

The conclusion of the Samuel story comes in 1 Samuel 7:15-17. He obviously figures prominently in the rest of the book, but his own career, in the theology of 1 and 2 Samuel, is completed with the selection of a king. First Samuel 8, therefore, begins a new chapter in that theology: God will select a king, but He is looking for a king meeting the criteria of godly leadership.

Two main questions are raised by 1 Samuel 8-15. Does the discussion in chapter 8 represent an ambivalence toward the monarchy on the part of the writer,[40] and why was Saul chosen at all? If David is the focus of the theology of 1 Samuel, then perhaps it should be noted that the historian was concerned with the *kind* of leader to be appointed. Samuel was the epitome of a godly leader such as Yahweh wanted to rule his people. David would likewise be that kind of leader (a man after God's heart, i.e., a man chosen by God). Saul was brought onto the scene by a sovereign act of God to allow the people to see what a king would be like who does not meet God's standards. The rejection of Samuel was the rejection of godly leadership; the choice of Saul was the choice of ungodly leadership. In many ways Saul was the foil for the godly David, just as the sons of Eli were a foil for Samuel.

Saul had a good beginning. He was humble (although his humility may have been a form of lack of self-confidence). He was from a rustic background, from the reduced Benjamite tribe,[41] and from an insignificant family. These are some of the external aspects of leadership that are presented as ideal. Saul functioned at the first much as a judge. His anointing by Samuel and the signs that followed to confirm the choice were more that of a charismatic judge than a king. His first battle and victory at Jabesh Gilead are described in terms reminiscent of the era of the judges.

In Samuel's farewell address the gauntlet was thrown down: "If you fear the

39. E. g., Isaiah 9:6 (the divine child and son); 11:1-10 (the root from Jesse's stump); Jeremiah 23:5 (the Branch).
40. See Martin A. Cohen, "The Role of the Shilonite Priesthood in the United Monarchy of Ancient Israel," *Hebrew Union College Annual* 36 (1965): 59-98.
41. It may be that in the movement toward a monarchy, it was essential that a nonthreatening tribe be the matrix for the first king. Furthermore, the Benjamite tribe faced the greatest danger from the Philistines.

Lord and serve and obey him and do not rebel against his commands, and if both you and the king who reigns over you follow the Lord your God—good! But if you do not obey the Lord, and if you rebel against his commands, his hand will be against you, as it was against your fathers" (1 Sam. 12:14-15).

The evidence of Saul's lack of the godly criteria for leadership is seen in 1 Samuel 13 when Saul failed to wait for Samuel. The standing order to wait seven days was given in 1 Samuel 10:8. Saul's primary task was to begin to overthrow Philistine domination (9:16). Saul was to wait seven days for Samuel to come and launch the invasion with sacrifice as he had done earlier in 1 Samuel 7. Saul's failure was not that he intruded into the priest's office (he probably offered *through* priests) but that he failed to wait for Samuel and thus on the blessing of God. As God rejected the Elide priesthood, so he rejected Saul: "You have not kept the command the Lord your God gave you; if you had, he would have established your kingdom over Israel for all time. But now your kingdom will not endure; the Lord has sought out a man after his own heart and appointed him leader of his people, because you have not kept the Lord's command" (13:13-14).

Saul's crippled leadership was evidenced in his foolish vow concerning the ensuing Philistine battle. Jonathan, Saul's son, modeled the very qualities looked for in Israel's leadership: he was brave, humble, and trusted in Yahweh. Saul's foolish vow almost cost Jonathan his life. God's failure to answer Saul when he inquired about attacking the Philistines was further evidence of his rejection (14:36-37).

The second evidence of failure was in the Amalekite *ḥērem* war. The key issue in this discussion is the matter of obedience. Saul had a clear mandate from Yahweh, but he failed to carry it out. Thus Samuel's doleful pronouncement: "To obey is better than sacrifice, and to heed is better than the fat of rams. For rebellion is like the sin of divination, and arrogance like the evil of idolatry. Because you have rejected the word of the Lord, he has rejected you as king" (1 Sam. 15:22-23).

And so the era of Saul ended. He remained in the story, but from the theological point of view he was finished when Yahweh "was grieved that he had made Saul king over Israel" (15:34). Henceforth the ideal king—the young, humble, god-fearing rustic—would take center stage. All that Saul was expected to be and even wanted to be, David was. He was young, dynamic, charismatic, beloved by the people. He was humble, courageous, and above all had a simple, durable trust in Yahweh. The rest of 1 Samuel is designed to show the contrast between the failed ruler and the ideal ruler.

THE CHOICE OF A GOOD RULER (1 SAM. 16-31)

The account of David's anointing is classic. The elements people tend to look for in a king were rejected by Yahweh. The boy with the simple confidence in himself and in the Lord was chosen to be the next king. He was the ideal to be emulated by all subsequent Israelite and Judean kings.

The contrast with Saul began immediately. The Spirit of Yahweh came on

David in power from that day on (16:13). The presence of the Spirit was evidence of the blessing and direction of God. Small wonder that David prayed after his sin with Bathsheba that God would not remove His Spirit from him (Ps. 51:11). On the other hand, the Spirit of the Lord had departed from Saul, and an evil spirit had come on him (1 Sam. 16:14). Ironically it was the pious young David who was called in to placate Saul's spirit when he was under attack.

A second contrast is provided in 1 Samuel 17. As the leader of the people, Saul should have been the man to confront Goliath. However, it was the God-fearing youth who vanquished the blasphemous giant. Furthermore, Saul's son Jonathan, who would have succeeded him to the throne, became fast friends with young David. Later, Saul's daughter Michal would defend David to her father. It was obvious to everyone that Yahweh had chosen David, but Saul in the obduracy of his heart continued to resist the inevitable.

A series of vignettes of Saul and David contrast the ideal ruler with the fallen one. Saul's paranoia stands out in contrast to David's trust. Saul's vindictiveness is opposite David's forgiving spirit. David refused to come to the throne by his own devices; he could be brought there only by the Lord.

David's nobility was marred a bit during his sojourn among the enemies of God. His actions in Gath (1 Sam. 27) and lying about his raiding activities do not speak well of him. Yet he was in these straits because of a rebellious Saul, and even in exile God was protecting him. How easily he could have been drawn into the war against Saul and forever vitiated his ability to rule the people of Israel. However, Achish sent him back when the other Philistine rulers refused to allow David to join them.

The last scene in Saul's life is a bitter and sad one. Rejected by Yahweh for failing to be the kind of ruler and man Yahweh demands, he could find no one to answer him in his distress. Faced with a military encounter of gigantic proportions, he needed a word from God but could not get one. He finally went to the witch[42] of Endor, where, probably to the surprise of the witch herself, Samuel returned to speak to the distraught Saul. The answer was the same: "Why do you consult me, now that the Lord has turned away from you and become your enemy? The Lord has done what he predicted through me. The Lord has torn the kingdom out of your hands and given it to one of your neighbors—to David. Because you did not obey the Lord to carry out his fierce wrath against the Amalekites, the Lord has done this to you today. The Lord will hand over both Israel and you to the Philistines, and tomorrow you and your sons will be with me. The Lord will also hand over the army of Israel to the Philistines" (28:16-19). These words are similar to the ones addressed to Eli when his house was rejected. The recurring theme has been restated: Those who disobey Yahweh are not worthy to be His rulers, and they will be replaced by people who will obey Him. And so Saul died, disgraced and deserted by Yahweh, and the kingdom was given to another.

42. The Hebrew word *'ôb* designates a person with an apparent ability to consult the dead.

THE WISE RULER

The ideal king acted wisely all the time Saul was alive. Now that Saul was dead, David continued to act wisely in ascending the throne over all the tribes. This involved biding his time in Hebron for seven years. The wise acts of David were several. First was his treatment of the Amalekite who had either finished off Saul or lied about killing him. David said that Saul was the "Lord's anointed." Just as he had shown restraint in his treatment of Saul, so he expected others to do. Then he lamented the death of Saul and Jonathan. After he had been anointed king over Judah, he sent a word of commendation to the Jabesh Gileadites who had rescued Saul's body from Beth Shan. He acted wisely in responding favorably to Saul's old general Abner, and when Abner was treacherously killed, he publicly mourned his death. Finally, David did not receive kindly the murderers of Ishbosheth. They were sure they would be rewarded for removing this last obstacle in David's path to kingship, but they were wrong. In all these acts David proved himself the wise, godly leader God had chosen as the ideal king.[43]

The core unit of the books of Samuel is 2 Samuel 5-8. The Davidic Covenant has already been discussed. The following discussion shows the theological perspective of these four chapters and their significance to the argument and theology of both books.

Summary of David's rule. Second Samuel 5-8 summarize David's reign. He began in Hebron with Judah (where he spent seven years) and was then made king over all Israel by the elders of Israel. He ruled over the entire nation thirty-three years. A key phrase is found in 2 Samuel 5:2. As the people recognized Yahweh's hand in the selection of David, they said, "And the Lord said to you, 'You will shepherd my people Israel, and you will become their ruler.'" When Herod the Great called the scribes together to ascertain the birthplace of the Messiah, they responded, "In Bethlehem in Judea for this is what the prophet has written: 'But you, Bethlehem, in the land of Judah, are by no means least among the rulers of Judah; for out of you will come a ruler, who will be the shepherd of my people Israel'" (Matt. 2:5-6). The part of the reference that comes from Micah 5:2 speaks of Bethlehem as the birthplace of the Ruler, but the words "who will be a shepherd of my people Israel" are from 2 Samuel 5:2. There is also a possible allusion to Genesis 49:10 as well. This shows that David is the type of the coming ideal ruler, the Messiah.[44] It is not likely that the writer of 2 Samuel was fully aware of the prototypical significance of David, but he began to move in that direction in 2 Samuel 7 and later writers viewed David in this way.[45] David's person became more and more a type of the Messiah,

---

43. These chapters (1 Sam. 31–2 Sam. 4) may even be showing that David followed wisdom practices long before the theology of wisdom was idealized in Solomon.

44. See my comments in "Matthew 2:6 and Its Old Testament Sources," *Journal of the Evangelical Theological Society* 26 (1983): 395-97.

45. The eschatological "David" is referred to in Jeremiah 30:9 and Ezekiel 34:23-24; 37:24-25.

and by New Testament times, he was a major link between the prophecy of Genesis 49:10 and its fulfillment in the Lord Jesus Christ.

The capture of the Jebusite fortress was the next major event in David's life. It also had theological significance. This Canaanite fortress lay on the border between Judah and Benjamin (Josh. 15:8; 18:16). Its unique position and occupation by foreigners made it an ideal city for David's government. Furthermore, the city was quite defensible and had a good water supply. Henceforth this city would be called the City of David and Zion. The spiritual significance of the name Zion is evidenced in the frequency of its use in the Psalms and the Prophets.[46] Zion became the dwelling place of God (Ps. 2:6). Zechariah indicated that "the Lord will again comfort Zion and choose Jerusalem" (Zech. 1:17). At other times Zion designated the people of God (Isa. 52:1) and sometimes Zion was personified as God's people (Jer. 6:23).[47] Hiram, king of Tyre, sent materials for David to build a palace, and David then knew that the Lord had "established him as king over Israel and exalted his kingdom for the sake of his people Israel" (2 Sam. 5:12).

The task of subduing the Philistines, begun by Saul, was finished by David. These Philistine battles are benchmarks in evaluating leadership. First, the house of Eli was judged in the battle in which the Ark was lost; then Samuel won a battle by seeking God's face; finally Saul was judged for not waiting for Samuel the seven days. Jonathan showed his great valor and good character in his encounters. David won over Goliath and in subsequent battles. In two strokes David broke the back of the Philistines (2 Sam. 5).

The next major event of theological significance was the bringing up of the Ark to Jerusalem. This movement of the Ark has already been discussed in the section on the central sanctuary. Suffice it to say here that by establishing a place of worship in his new capital, David made one of his most lasting impressions on the people of God. Even the plague that Yahweh sent to punish him for taking a census had positive results, for the place where he made his propitiatory sacrifice became the site of the Temple (1 Sam. 24:25; 1 Chron. 21:18–22:2).

The Davidic Covenant (2 Sam. 7) was discussed at the beginning of this chapter because it is the fabric out of which the books of Samuel are woven. This important covenant is placed here in the unit on David's achievement to show God's choice of the person through whom He would be working throughout the rest of the Old Testament and into the eschatological future.

The final chapter in this condensation of David's rule is a summary of David's military victories. David defeated the nations on the east (Moab, Edom, Ammon, Amalek), on the west (the dreaded Philistines), and in the north (the newly rising Arameans). This is what 2 Samuel 7:9 means: "I have been with you wherever you have gone, and I have cut off all your enemies from before you. Now I will make

---

46. It is used forty-six times in Isaiah alone. For a discussion from the perspective of the new Jerusalem, see von Rad, pp. 258-63.

47. At Qumran, an entire psalm (11QPs[a], an apostrophe to Zion) is addressed to Zion.

your name great, like the names of the greatest men of the earth."

David's rule was firmly established. Furthermore, he was doing what was "just and right for all his people." This is what a proper king is to do. Christ, the great descendant of David (Isa. 11), will do this to perfection. To show that the kingdom was stable, the writer then listed the members of David's "cabinet." After the upheavals of the revolts of Absalom and Sheba, a similar list was given to show that the king was back in place in Jerusalem (2 Sam. 20:23-25). Just as Samuel's place in the theology terminated with a summary of his ministry in 1 Samuel 7:15 and Saul's in 1 Samuel 15:34-35, so David's summary is given here. All that follows is less concerned with the Davidic ideal than the question of who will succeed David as God's promised seed. The theme of the writer in the rest of 2 Samuel is twofold: (1) the issue of the successor of David who will thus come under the Davidic Covenant promises, and (2) the development of the Temple as the central sanctuary.

The Bathsheba interlude occurs in 2 Samuel 11-12 primarily to indicate the birth and choice of Solomon, but much is learned about God's covenant dealing with His king. David's sin with Bathsheba draws a series of contrasts. David, the man God chose to be the leader of His people, failed to live up to the requirements of his office. Not only did he not judge righteously but his own conduct grossly violated all sense of justice. The foreigner Uriah, who had accepted the faith of David (Uriah's name means "Yahweh is my light"), conducted himself in an exemplary way, in contrast to David. The story is full of irony, culminating in Uriah's carrying his own unopened death warrant to Joab.

The confrontation by Nathan, God's spokesman who had delivered the oracle of David's dynasty, dramatically illustrated the violation of God's covenant. God warned David that while the ultimate fulfillment of the covenant was unconditional, the immediate blessings were conditioned on obedience. David, the first recipient of the covenant, was grossly disobedient in committing the sins of adultery, lying, stealing, and murder. Through Nathan, the Lord said that the covenant stipulations must be enforced, and David must be punished.

David was punished when his first child died, when his son Amnon was murdered, and when his son Absalom was killed in battle. Yahweh's sword had two edges: one to punish David and the other to eliminate Solomon's competitors. The Absalom rebellion was exceptionally traumatic. David had been established as Yahweh's *ḥāsîd* ("chosen one"), but he was almost unseated by Absalom. By 2 Samuel 20:23-25 he had been reestablished. Yahweh's covenant was being worked out.

The selection of Solomon. There had never been a transfer of kingship from father to son in Israel's history. Consequently, the issue of succession is taken up in 2 Samuel 13-20 and 1 Kings 1-2.[48] Clearly Solomon was to be the next king in spite of the seemingly insuperable odds against him.

Second Samuel 10-12 forms a unit designed to show that God had chosen

48. See Moses H. Segal, "The Composition of the Books of Samuel," *Jewish Quarterly Review* 55 (1965): 319.

Solomon to be the successor to David. The Ammonite war brackets the story (10:1–11:1 and 12:26-31). The Ammonites were dealt with in a summary fashion in 2 Samuel 8 along with other surrounding peoples, so they are reintroduced here in detail to provide the setting for the sin of David with Bathsheba and Uriah.

While this unit gives much information about several issues, the author drew attention to the fact that the child born from the union of David and Bathsheba was Solomon. Lest there be any question about the legitimacy of the next king, it was the second son born after Uriah's death who was chosen. Second Samuel 12:24 says of Solomon: "The Lord loved him." This is the Hebrew way of saying the Lord chose him. Furthermore, the Lord sent word through Nathan the prophet stating that the other name of Solomon was to be Jedidiah ("Yahweh loves"). Clearly, then, this unit is designed to show that the next successor to David would be Solomon, and since 2 Samuel 7 indicated that David's son would build the Temple, Solomon became the builder.

The unit composed of 2 Samuel 13-20 (1 Kings 1-2 is included in the whole narrative) shows how God judged David for his sin (the negative part of the Davidic Covenant) but also how he eliminated the contenders for the throne who would threaten Solomon. Amnon, Absalom, and Adonijah were all from David's earlier marriages and therefore in line for the throne by birth. Amnon showed his unworthiness to rule and was killed by his brother. Absalom, because of rebellion against his father, was killed, and finally Adonijah, who decided to "buck the odds," was killed in a foolish bid for the kingship. The way was now clear for Solomon to rule without opposition.

Thus, the purposes of God were being worked out through His *ḥesed* ("covenant love") to David, His anointed. David's seed would be blessed in obedience and disciplined in disobedience. The first "seed" of David would be Solomon, whom God chose over his older brothers, as David was chosen over his older brothers. David chose the city and the site for the Temple, but to Solomon went the task of building it. Henceforth the worship of Yahweh in Jerusalem at the Temple was a main issue to the author of Kings. Further, the successors of David would be judged in light of the Davidic Covenant. The rest of 2 Samuel is devoted to bringing together events in David's life that show God's grace and also to look forward to the work of Solomon in establishing the Temple as the ultimate place of Yahweh's worship in Jerusalem.

David's closing words. Since Yahweh had established David and his dynasty, a psalm was sung in celebration. Second Samuel 22 (parallel to Ps. 18) is appropriately chosen from all the possible psalms of David because it deals with the Lord's deliverance from the hand of all his enemies and from the hand of Saul. It is appropriate because it follows 2 Samuel 21, which refers to the virtual termination of the house of Saul and the defeat of the Philistine giants.

There are nine epithets for God in 2 Samuel 22:2-3: rock (*selaᶜ*), fortress, deliverer, rock (*ṣûr*), shield, horn, stronghold, refuge, and savior. Each of these titles refers to the protective aspect of Yahweh's work on behalf of David. David's refuge was not in his own prowess, nor did he attempt to usurp the throne for him-self (as did his son Absalom). Instead, he chose to trust in Yahweh to work out His divine purposes. This is evident in David's flight from Jerusalem when he responded to the cursing of Shimei. "Leave him alone; let him curse, for the Lord has told him to. It may be that the Lord will see my distress and repay with good for the cursing I am receiving today" (2 Sam. 16:11-12).

The psalm then speaks of Yahweh's deliverance in cosmic terms. This imagery is often referred to as "storm theophany." However one describes this vivid poet-ic language, it is designed to show that Yahweh delivered His servant David from all his enemies. The psalm concludes with a reference to the Davidic Covenant: "He gives his king great victories; He shows unfailing kindness to His anointed, to David and his descendants forever" (2 Sam. 22:51). Yahweh's work on behalf of David was complete. He had defeated all David's enemies, including the house of Saul, and had established His covenant forever. The "last words of David" in 2 Samuel 23 likewise pursue the idea of the establishment of David's kingdom. The righteous rule of Yahweh in the universe is the theme of this unit. When righ-teousness prevails, then all is well (v. 4). In the same vein David's house is a righ-teous dynasty that God established with an everlasting covenant. Yahweh's bless-ing would be evident in David's house and rule. The period of the monarchy following David's reign would be measured in these terms. Kings would be judged by the measure of God's righteous rule in the universe. They would be expected to rule with equity and justice (cf. Ahab and Naboth), and when they failed to do so they would be judged. Furthermore, even though David's dynasty would fail, Yahweh promised a coming King who will rule with equity and justice (Isa. 11; Jer. 23; Ezek. 34).

Interestingly many of the elements in Hannah's psalm (1 Sam. 2:1-10) are found in David's psalm (2 Sam. 22). Yahweh is unique; He is a deliverer; He is a rock (1 Sam. 2:1-2). He controls the destiny of the human race, humbles the proud, strengthens the weak, and takes delight in turning the normal expectations of life on their head (vv. 3-10a). Hannah concluded with the promise that God will give strength to His king and exalt the horn of His anointed. The books of Samuel thus begin with a psalm exalting Yahweh the God of the universe and referring to God's anointed king. They close with a psalm honoring the same God of the universe and referring to Yahweh's covenant with His anointed king.

The broad theology of 1 and 2 Samuel is that God rules justly in the affairs of men. Furthermore, He requires that men live justly under His rule. The leader (whether judge or king) must represent Yahweh's justice in the rule of God's peo-ple. Failure to follow the patterns of righteousness established by God led to chas-tisement of the ruler and the people he ruled. This message was usually presented by a prophet who stood between God and the king as well as the people.

THE MONARCHY IN 1 AND 2 KINGS

To understand the historian's attitude toward the monarchy after David, it is necessary to observe his theological perspective. The books of 1 and 2 Kings were composed from a number of sources. The first two chapters are a completion of the succession narrative, showing that God had chosen Solomon to succeed his father David. The section on Solomon (1 Kings 3-11) is probably derived from the book of the annals of Solomon (11:41). The court records of the northern and southern kingdoms provide much of the data for the books. Some suggest that the statement in the Septuagint in 8:53 (MT, 8:12) was taken from the book of Jashar (the righteous?), which is also mentioned in Joshua and 2 Samuel.[49] The unique sections about Elijah and Elisha probably came from a single source. The *terminus ante quem* for the final composition of 1 and 2 Kings is 560 B.C., the last dated event in the book, which refers to the elevation of Jehoiachin in captivity by Evil Merodach. LaSor and others argue that the composition probably took place just after the fall of Jerusalem in 586 B.C., and that the last event is a later appendage.[50]

Thus, more than 500 years are covered in this historical survey. There were dramatic changes in Israel and in the Middle Eastern world during that half millennium. Yet all this material was brought together and commented on by a writer who spoke from the perspective of the terminus of the monarchy and the destruction of the Temple and citadel of David. One of the purposes of 1 and 2 Kings is to explain the disaster and to provide hope for the future. There is an extensive set of references to the Davidic Covenant or to the Davidic ideal (some sixteen passages). The evaluative comments made throughout the work are from a prophetic point of view.[51] However, Keil is probably right in emphasizing the "prophetico-historical" rather than the "prophetico-didactic" point of view. "The historical development of the monarchy, or, to express it more correctly, of the kingdom of God under the kings, forms the true subject-matter of our books."[52] The theological emphasis of the books is reflected primarily in the comments of the prophetic writer, but it will also be seen in the actions and words of the participants.

THE COMPLETION OF THE SUCCESSION NARRATIVE

The issue of David's immediate successor, begun in 2 Samuel 2, is now brought to a completion. Jedidiah, or Solomon, came to the throne. For the first time in Israel's history, a son succeeded his father to the throne. The accession to the purple was not without its problems, however. The old regime had to go. Adonijah, the last threat to Solomon, was thwarted in his ambitions and ultimate

---

49. Cf. William S. LaSor, *Old Testament Survey* (Grand Rapids: Eerdmans, 1982), p. 253. See also Simon J. DeVries, *1 Kings,* Word Biblical Commentary (Waco, Tex.: Word, 1985), p. 125. DeVries argues for the originality of the Septuagint reading, which reads *'ōdēs,* and presumes a reading of *šîr.* Many assume this to be a corruption of *yāšār.* See H. B. Swete, *an Introduction to the Old Testament in Greek* (Cambridge: University Press, 1900), pp. 247, 514, for an early discussion.

50. LaSor, p. 253.

51. The point of view is often referred to as "deuteronomistic," meaning a movement after the Exile to reconstruct Israel's history from the beginning.

52. C. F. Keil, "The Books of the Kings," in *Biblical Commentary on the Old Testament* (Grand Rapids: Eerdmans, 1950), p. 5.

ly killed. Joab, the fashioner of David's powerful army and in many ways a foil for David, died ignominiously at the altar. The curse on Eli's house was finally enacted in the banishment of Abiathar. God's promise to David was carried out.

THE SOLOMONIC IDEAL

The narration in 1 and 2 Samuel is refreshing in its straightforwardness and simplicity. By contrast, the narrative of Solomon's reign, taken from a source called the book of the annals of Solomon (1 Kings 11:41), is much more stylized and formal. Solomon did not go to the throne as a charismatic judge; he did not even seem to have the personal charisma of his father. What he did have was wisdom (*ḥokmâ*). Though Solomon's greatest contribution was in building the Temple and developing the Temple worship set in place by his father, he is perhaps best known for his wisdom. The author indicated the pleasure of God with Solomon's request for wisdom rather than other obvious things (1 Kings 3:10). Solomon requested a wise heart in order to render justice to the people of God. This is the characteristic of kingship promoted in 1 and 2 Samuel. It reached ideal proportions in Solomon. Further, he developed the concept of wisdom in Israel in a nonjudicial sense: he had encyclopedic knowledge (1 Kings 4:34) and wrote proverbs and songs. Ironically the man who was used by God to develop the idea of court wisdom and royal conduct (reflected in Proverbs) in the end practiced so little of it. Solomon, like David, became a symbol of the ideal king in later Old Testament literature. So the chronicler dealt with him differently than did the writer of Kings.[53]

The construction and dedication of the Temple occupies a large portion of the Solomon memoirs. The two major tangible items in Israel's history, Jerusalem and the Temple, were provided by the first two kings. Jerusalem was Zion, the place where God chose to make His name dwell. The Temple was the edifice in which He dwelt. The destruction of the Temple in 586 B.C. was devastating to Judah's faith. In the theology of 1 and 2 Kings the centrality and uniqueness of the Temple are stressed. The attitude of a king toward the high places, where popular Yahwism was practiced syncretistically, was one basis for the historian's criticism of him.

Much of the theology of 1 and 2 Kings is found in 1 Kings 8 in the prayer of Solomon. Since some of that theology was discussed in the earlier section on the Temple, only three items will be discussed further.

The uniqueness of Yahweh (1 Kings 8:23). Solomon began his prayer by affirming that Yahweh is the God of Israel. There is no God like Him in the entire universe. This does not mean that gods exist who are different from Him; it means no other gods exist. This theme is echoed throughout Kings in the battle between the prophets and the syncretistic people.

The covenant keeping God (1 Kings 8:24-26). In making covenants with His people the Lord shows His grace in reaching down from His holy heights to the

---

53. See Raymond B. Dillard, *2 Chronicles,* Word Biblical Commentary (Waco, Tex.: Word, 1987), pp. 1-7.

inhabitants of the world. Furthermore, unlike the pagan deities He is utterly pre-dictable with regard to His covenants. When He gives His word, He keeps it. Proof of this for Solomon (v. 24) is that he was sitting on David's throne. That was what God promised in the Davidic Covenant, and He had now brought it to pass.

The Davidic Covenant (1 Kings 8:15-21, 24-26). The marvelous, gracious covenant made with David permeates the rest of Old Testament theology. It continues between the Testaments and influences the theology of the Messiah in the New Testament. Furthermore, David himself became a paradigm for all other kings. The kings in the South are compared with the dynastic head and are considered successes or failures based on that comparison. And the eschatological King, who will rule in justice, is even called "David" (Ezek. 34:23-24). Small wonder that Jesus is referred to as the great son of David who will sit on David's throne (Luke 1:31-33).

At the beginning of Solomon's rule he "showed his love for the Lord by walking according to the statutes of his father David" (1 Kings 3:3). The only thing for which Solomon is faulted is his use of high places for sacrifice. Solomon praised God for the great kindness (*ḥesed*, "covenant love") He had shown him, the same kindness and loyalty He showed his father David. God responded to Solomon's request by promising him long life if he would walk in His ways and obey His laws as David had done (v. 14).

David's desire for the Temple is reflected in Solomon's letter to Hiram. Again Solomon referred to the Davidic Covenant and the fact that David's off-spring would build the Temple (5:5). Yahweh appeared to Solomon during the construction of the Temple to reaffirm His promises (6:12). If Solomon would obey God, then the promises made to David about God dwelling among the people (symbolized by the Temple) would come to pass.

When Solomon blessed the people and praised the Lord at the dedication of the Temple (8:15-26), he spoke of the fact that Yahweh had fulfilled His promise made to David (regarding the Temple). No place was ever chosen for a Temple, but David was chosen (v. 16). Furthermore, it was David's desire to build the Temple for God's name, and even though God did not allow him to build it, He did promise that David's offspring would build it. The Ark, in temporary quarters under David's regime, was now housed in a more permanent dwelling. A strong link was thus being made between Solomon's Temple and the Ark that belonged to David's Zion (v. 1).

In his prayer of dedication Solomon urged Yahweh to keep His promises relative to David's descendants: if they were obedient, they would be allowed to sit on the throne (v. 25). In the same vein are the words of Yahweh to Solomon when He appeared to him after the completion of the Temple, and delivered a prophetic statement (9:4-9). Yahweh reiterated the promise of continuity for Solomon and his seed if they obeyed, but He also included promised judgment on Israel for disobe-dience. From the exilic perspective Israel's reproach was shown by the destroyed Temple. The reason for the devastation is given: "because they have forsaken the

Lord their God, who brought their fathers out of Egypt, and have embraced other gods, worshiping and serving them—that is why the Lord brought all this disaster on them" (v. 9). For an exilic or postexilic reader these would have been encouraging words, for they proved that Yahweh did not act capriciously. He was consistent with His promises to David.

Solomon came under the negative aspect of the Davidic Covenant in 1 Kings 11. Contrasting Solomon to David, the historian stated that Solomon failed to meet the standard (v. 4). Because of Solomon's syncretistic activity, Yahweh told Solomon that the kingdom would be torn from him. However, for David's sake, Solomon would not lose the kingdom during his lifetime, and even when it was wrested from David's descendants, one tribe would be left for David's sake (vv. 12-13).

When God addressed Jeroboam I, He reiterated the same promise about leaving one tribe for David's sake. Interestingly Jeroboam, though a Northern king, was compared with David and was promised that he would be judged by that standard. Thus, even though God's covenant with David could not extend to the North, David himself was the standard of excellence by which the Northern kings would be measured. Jeroboam failed to meet the Davidic standard, and so God rejected him and his family (14:8).

Solomon's son Rehoboam is soundly criticized by the historian, who wrote, "His heart was not fully devoted to the Lord his God, as the heart of David his forefather had been" (15:3). Even so, God did not wipe out the dynasty (v. 4). On the contrary, Asa was a godly king. His conduct was compared favorably to that of David (v. 11).

The historian makes no further reference to the covenant with David until 2 Kings 8:19, where he wrote, "Nevertheless, for the sake of his servant David, the Lord was not willing to destroy Judah. He had promised to maintain a lamp for David and his descendants forever." He said this in connection with the rule of Jehoram, Jehoshaphat's son who had married Ahab's daughter. Joash, the Temple repairer, had a son named Amaziah, who did the right thing in the sight of the Lord, but not as his ancestor David had done (14:3). How he failed to measure up to David is not made clear, unless it was with regard to the high places (v. 4). King Ahaz, who ruled during Isaiah's time, is starkly contrasted to David. "Unlike David his father, he did not do what was right in the eyes of the Lord his God" (16:2). Hezekiah, on the other hand, "did what was right in the eyes of the Lord, just as his father David had done" (18:3) This included removing the high places, and, from the historian's point of view in or after the Exile, this may have been the deciding factor in comparing him to David.

The final reference in Kings to the Davidic Covenant is 2 Kings 21:7. There Manasseh who was infamous for his wickedness, went so far as to bring a carved Asherah pole into the Temple. This was the Temple that was part of the Davidic Covenant. Yahweh had decided to cause His name to dwell there forever. Obedience would bring perpetual blessing on His people, but because Manasseh led them astray, Yahweh's judgment had to come on them. The historian then gave a summary of the message of several prophets regarding this severe judgment (2 Kings 10-15).

Thus, a major thrust of the theology of 1 and 2 Kings is that the Exile and the devastation of Jerusalem and the Temple are to be explained in light of the conduct of the kings and people. David was the standard by which the subsequent kings were measured, and David was the reason for God's continued faithfulness to His people in spite of their sin. However, flagrant departure from such a standard could not go forever unpunished, and so Israel went into exile.

THE ISSUE OF THE DIVIDED KINGDOM

The attitude of the chronicler toward the Northern Kingdom is rather clear. All references to the monarchy begun by Jeroboam I were omitted except when necessary to explain something about the Davidic dynasty. The chronicler was focusing on the returning Jews and developing the history that led to the Exile and the return. The future restoration of the Northern tribes, on the other hand, is clearly set out by the exilic prophet Ezekiel. The vision of the two sticks in Ezekiel 37 explicitly affirmed the future of the Northern tribes (called Ephraim and Joseph). Apparently the chronicler was not aware of the future of the Northern Kingdom; that fact simply does not fit into his purposes.

The theology of 1 and 2 Kings about the Northern Kingdom can be seen in the historian's discussion of the relationship of the two kingdoms and in his theological statements about Yahweh's judgment on the nation.

Ahijah the Shilonite, when he conveyed Yahweh's message to Jeroboam I, set out the idea that a rival dynasty to David's was being established (1 Kings 11:29-39). The Davidic Covenant, because of its unconditional aspects, assured the continuity of David's dynasty. However, the conditional aspect was fulfilled in the tearing away of the ten tribes, which were then given to Jeroboam I. Promises made to Jeroboam were similar to those made to David: "If you do whatever I command you and walk in my ways and do what is right in my eyes by keeping my statutes and commands, as David my servant did, I will be with you. I will build you a dynasty as enduring as the one I built for David and will give Israel to you. I will humble David's descendants because of this, but not forever" (vv. 38-39).

What would have happened if Jeroboam had been obedient to Yahweh as David had been? The answer to that question will never be known, because Jeroboam rebelled against Yahweh and even established a rival cult center that was pagan in its structure. Ahijah's second prophecy, given when Jeroboam sent his wife to ask Ahijah about the health of his son, contains the message of destruction to Jeroboam's dynasty and the end to eternal possibilities for his seed (14:10-11). Jeroboam's son Nadab lasted only two years. He was assassinated by Baasha. The language of Ahijah used with Jeroboam is not repeated with any of the other Israelite kings.

Yet, in spite of the sinfulness of the Northern kings,[54] the people of Ephraim were always viewed as Yahweh's people. This is especially evident in such prophets as Amos and Hosea,[55] but it is also prominent throughout the historical account.

When Jehu's son Jehoahaz sought Yahweh because of the terrible oppression of Syria, Yahweh heard him and "provided a deliverer for Israel, and they escaped from the power of Aram" (2 Kings 13:4-6). Likewise, when his son Jehoash sought out Elisha, he was promised victory over the Arameans (vv. 14-19).

One of the most theologically significant statements relative to Yahweh's covenants is made in connection with the rule of Jehoahaz (vv. 22-24). The grace of Yahweh and the compassion of Yahweh in delivering them from the powerful oppressor, Hazael, was based on his covenant with Abraham, Isaac, and Jacob. Obviously the Davidic Covenant cannot come into play here, but the promises made to Abraham (Gen. 12) and confirmed to Isaac and Jacob must be kept. Consequently the historian could say, "To this day he has been unwilling to destroy them or banish them from his presence" (2 Kings 13:23). The historian tells about migrations of people from the north to the south. In a sense, then, all twelve tribes are preserved in Judah, but the historian says more than that. Even though in his time many of the northern people had been deported, he viewed the remaining Jews, even with their intermixture, as the people of the covenant. Yahweh's promises cannot be abrogated.

Jeroboam II was not a godly king, yet Yahweh was gracious to him and, speaking through Jonah the prophet, allowed him to restore the boundaries of Israel. The historian again gave a theological explanation (14:26-27). Yahweh had seen the bitter oppression of His people. "And since the Lord had not said he would blot out the name of Israel from under heaven, he saved them by the hand of Jeroboam son of Jehoash." He brought about deliverance and blessing through Jeroboam II. It was about this time that Hosea was prophesying.

THE REFORM MOVEMENT IN KINGS

The reigns of Asa, Jehoshaphat, Joash, Uzziah, Hezekiah, and Josiah saw significant contributions to the spiritual state of the people of Judah.

Asa was characterized by the Kings historian as a good man. Chronicles devotes to Asa more than thirty verses that are not found in Kings. Asa was extolled for his spirituality and excoriated for trusting in foreign powers rather than in Yahweh. He died in shame. Kings has a brief but positive statement about him: "And Asa did what was right in the eyes of the Lord, as his father David had done" (1 Kings 15:11). He removed the male cult prostitutes (part of the fertility religion of the Canaanites) and the idols his predecessors had made. Chronicles states that he removed the high places from the cities of Judah (2 Chron. 14:3-5). This would

---

54. Only Jehu was zealous for Yahweh, and his evaluation is mixed since he continued the cult center set up by Jeroboam I.

55. Note especially Hosea's "not my people," "my people" prophecy in Hosea 1–2.

be a major undertaking and accounts for the unqualified endorsement of Asa by the historian of Kings, but it seems to contradict 2 Kings 15:14 and 2 Chronicles 14:17. Apparently, Asa attempted to remove the high places, but was only partially successful. Knowing how entrenched the high places were in the religion of the people, it is not surprising that he was not ultimately successful.

Jehoshaphat ruled for twenty-five years and was treated with approval by the historian. Chronicles, again, has a long section on Jehoshaphat regarding his teaching of the law of Yahweh throughout the land as well as many other activities of reform (2 Chron. 19-20). The main theological emphasis in Kings is the fact that he did what was right in the sight of Yahweh (1 Kings 22:42-44). He also removed the cult prostitutes left over from his father Asa's purge.

Joash came to the throne as a child under the tutelage of the priest Jehoiada. The major theme of his reform centers on the Temple (2 Kings 11-12). It was in a sad state of repairs, having been neglected by Athaliah. This indicates the importance placed on the purification of the Temple even though the high places were not removed.

Amaziah, Uzziah, and Jotham continued the reforms of Jehoshaphat and the earlier activity of Joash. Amaziah's adherence to the Mosaic law is indicated by the historian in that Amaziah killed the assassins of his father but did not kill their children (14:6). Uzziah continued the godly emphasis in Judah. Uzziah's intrusion into the priest's role is overlooked in Kings. The historian laconically wrote, "The Lord afflicted the king with leprosy until the day he died, and he lived in a separate house" (15:5).

The most extensive reform was carried out by Hezekiah. Both Kings and Chronicles detail considerable activity on behalf of the true worship of Yahweh. Chronicles, with its emphasis on the Temple and worship, provides three chapters on the liturgical reform in both Judah and Israel. However, even Kings devotes an unusual amount of space to the reform. This time the king was apparently successful in neutralizing the high places. Hezekiah's faith and theology are dealt with elsewhere (pp. 137-38).

Reform must have always been fairly superficial. As is often the case, a religious patina overlay the continuing practice of paganism. Therefore, it was probably rather easy for Manasseh to reverse the spiritual successes of his father. Jerusalem, the city of Yahweh's name, was polluted with idolatry (21:4-5). Even the sacred Temple was defiled. The Assyrian deities (hosts of heavens) were now worshiped at altars in the two courts of the Temple (v. 5).

The final reform movement before the Exile was effected by another boy king, Josiah. Though his work was aborted at his death, his contribution was significant. Like his ancestor Joash, he set about repairing the Temple that had been neglected during the wicked rule of Manasseh and Amon (22:3-7). In the process of the repair, the workmen found a copy of the Torah. When Josiah read it, he was convicted of the fact that failure to obey the law of God was bound to bring reprisals (he was probably referring to the latter chapters of Deuteronomy). Huldah, the prophetess, reassured the anxious young king that though Yahweh would indeed bring judgment on the city, Josiah's pure desires would be honored and he would not see the disaster the city was destined to endure (vv. 15-19). Aware that obedience to the law of Yahweh was essential, he brought the people into a covenant to obey "the Lord and keep his commands, regulations and decrees with all his heart and all his soul, thus confirming the words of the covenant written in this book" (23:3). He was able even to break the guild of the priests in the countryside and to force them to come to Jerusalem (v. 8). The importance of the Torah is seen in Josiah's continued efforts to carry out the instructions regarding purity of worship and the extirpation of the pagan religion, which by this time so totally penetrated the lives of the people of Judah and Israel.[56]

With Josiah's death, the reformation ceased. Swiftly the weeds of paganism grew again. Josiah's sons did not share his interest in spiritual things. The prophet Jeremiah unrelentingly confronted the religious practice of the people who adopted not only the Canaanite fertility religion but also the astral religion of the Assyrians.

THE THEOLOGY OF THE EXILE AS REPRESENTED BY THE HISTORIAN

The great question of the Exile was, How could Yahweh desert His people and allow them to suffer the reproach of domination by a people worshiping pagan gods? Reflection on that question led the believers to recognize the reason for the disaster of 722 and 586 B.C. In 2 Kings 17:7-41 the historian summarized the reasons for the fall of Samaria in 722 B.C.

The first and foremost reason for the fall of Samaria was their sin against Yahweh their God. This is the same God who brought them from Egypt and revealed Himself to Moses and the people. This "rehearsal of the acts of Yahweh" is to call to mind the foolishness of the people in turning their backs on the one who redeemed them (2 Kings 17:1-8). It is striking that the primary sin referred to again and again in this chapter is the sin of idolatry. Idolatry came about because the people had rejected the Torah and the covenant of Yahweh (vv. 14-15). One might expect to see some reference to horizontal sins such as are seen throughout the book of Hosea (abuse of the poor, drunkenness, prostitution, abuse of the Nazirites), but it was enough for the historian to note that the vertical sin of idolatry is the ultimate sin. From it flowed all the abominations and abuses practiced by the Israelites against one another. To reject Yahweh and His covenant was to leave a vacuum in com-

---

56. The emphasis on the law of Moses—and particularly the latter part of the book of Deuteronomy that promises the judgment of captivity and the earlier part insisting on worship at a central sanctuary—leads critics to believe that much of the "deuteronomic" legislation was developed at this point. As already seen, there was a running controversy between the Temple and the high places from the beginning. Under Solomon the high places, once used to worship Yahweh alone, were corrupted into a syncretized religion of Yahweh/Baal or some other deity. This was such a strongly entrenched practice and the priests were so powerful that the attempts of other kings to rid the land of the high places had failed. Josiah was the first to be successful in forcing the rural priests (who were probably involved in popular syncretism) to come to Jerusalem or to leave the priesthood (2 Kings 23:8-9).

munity life that could be filled only by mutual abuse and destructiveness. Thus, the captivity of 722 B.C. was inevitable. In spite of the hopeful view of the Northern Kingdom as part of the people of God, the concluding words of the historian are pessimistic. Even after the deportation and the importation of foreigners, the people of the land persisted in their paganism. It was even exacerbated by the newcomers who brought their own religions with them. He concluded by saying, "They would not listen, however, but persisted in their former practices" (2 Kings 17:40).

Likewise, the historian said, Judah suffered the debacles of 605, 597, and 586 B.C. with the destruction of the Temple being the most ignominious blow of all. In spite of Josiah's efforts to turn Israel back to the law of Moses, "the Lord did not turn away from the heat of his fierce anger, which burned against Judah because of all that Manasseh had done to provoke him to anger. So the Lord said, 'I will remove Judah also from my presence as I removed Israel, and I will reject Jerusalem, the city I chose, and this temple, about which I said, there shall my Name be'" (23:26-27). No long peroration is given after the fall of the city as was the case for Samaria. A perfunctory recitation of the fall and deportation is given, but the final note in the book pertains to the elevation and honor of the last legitimate king of Judah, Jehoiachin, some twenty-five years after the fall. A ray of hope grew into a bright beam with the return of a large group of Jews under Zerubbabel in fulfillment of Yahweh's promises not to forsake His people.

4

A THEOLOGY OF CHRONICLES

Eugene H. Merrill

One of the major areas of discussion in Old Testament scholarship is the "synoptic problem" of 1 and 2 Chronicles vis-à-vis Samuel-Kings.[1] Whereas these great historical works coincide and agree in many respects, their differences are nevertheless profound and must be explained. It is impossible to enter the debate here in any detail, but it should at least be emphasized that the variations existing in the accounts are fundamentally to be attributed to different emphases and purposes. Samuel-Kings, described by some scholars as a part of the "Deuteronomistic history," has as its principal concern the history of the nation from the rise of the first "institutional" prophet, Samuel, to the exile of Judah by the Babylonians. It was a history punctuated by prophetic evaluations and indictments of the monarchy and the political and religious institutions of Israel. Thus the fall of the covenant people is attributed to covenant violation by king, priest, and people. Even David is not excepted, as a major section of 2 Samuel is devoted to an exposé of his personal sins and those of his children.[2]

Chronicles, on the other hand, though not oblivious to the above-mentioned

---

1. W. E. Lemke, "The Synoptic Problem in the Chronicler's History," *Harvard Theological Review* 58 (1965): 349-63; Roddy Braun, *1 Chronicles,* vol. 14 in Word Biblical Commentary (Waco, Tex.: Word), pp. xix-xxi.

2. Martin Noth, *Deuteronomistic History, JSOT* Supplement Series (Sheffield: U. of Sheffield, 1981).

concerns, focuses on the Davidic monarchy as a theocratic expression of God's sovereign elective and redemptive purposes for His people and ultimately for all nations. Having drawn heavily upon Samuel-Kings for historical and even theological documentation, the chronicler nonetheless approached his historiographical task with his own understandings and interpretations and produced a work marked by his own theological stamp. The result is an account parallel and even identical to Samuel-Kings in important respects but sufficiently different to make Chronicles a worthy object of study in and of itself. Nowhere is this more the case than in a theological sense, for basically the uniqueness of Chronicles lies precisely in the uniqueness of its theological message.[3]

Proper biblical theology method demands that any proposed center or structure of theological analysis be derived from the material itself and that it not be imposed on that material. It likewise requires that such an organizing principle be in harmony with theological categories inherent in the totality of biblical revelation, Old Testament and New Testament alike. Careful attention to these guidelines has led to the conclusion that the principle of the kingdom of God as the outworking of His creation purposes best accommodates the multiplicity and variety of biblical revelation and best serves to integrate that revelation around a common theme. With that in mind, it seems that an appropriate statement of the theme and purpose of Chronicles is "the sovereignty of God revealed through the Davidic monarchy in Old Testament times."[4]

This monarchy, as an expression and development of the kingdom of priests of the Mosaic/Sinaitic Covenant, was created to model God's theocratic rule over the earth in history and to anticipate the rule of David's dynastic son, the Anointed One, in the days to come. Thus Chronicles addresses the person and character of God, His theocratic people, the relationship(s) that bound them together, and His present and future work among and on behalf of them.

THE GOD OF THE KINGDOM

In common with the rest of the Old Testament, Chronicles offers no systematic, propositional definition of God and His attributes. Rather, those have to be discovered in the course of narrative and through observations made by persons in those narratives who reflect on these matters. It is clear from such an approach that the traditional rubrics that distinguish God as a person from His activity in history, although not mutually exclusive, are quite satisfactory.

THE PERSON AND ATTRIBUTES OF GOD

The self-disclosure of God in Chronicles is mediated through prophets, priests, kings, and others who reflect on Him and His character as they address the

---

3. For various recent understandings of the purpose of Chronicles, see Brevard S. Childs, *Introduction to the Old Testament as Scripture* (Philadelphia: Fortress, 1979), pp. 643-55.
4. James D. Newsome, Jr., "Toward a New Understanding of the Chronicler and His Purposes," *Journal of Biblical Literature* 94 (1975): 207.

circumstances of their lives and God's appearance to them in those circumstances. It is in His relationships with them, in an understanding of His nature, in His own self-expression, and in His station among them and on their behalf that His spokesmen come to understand who He is and begin to know something of His ineffable attributes.

God in His relationships. By this is meant the possibility of the divine-human encounter. Solomon asked the question, "Will God really dwell on earth with men?" (2 Chron. 6:18), and went on to affirm that even the heavens cannot contain God. Can this God, so transcendent as to stand wholly outside His creation, relate to it in any way? The answer lies in metonymy[5] and theophany. In the same prayer of Solomon, he petitions the Lord that He might, in days of trouble, turn His eyes toward the Temple, the place where He said He would put His name (v. 20). His name is particularly associated with the Ark of the Covenant (1 Chron. 13:6), and as long as it remained in the Temple, Yahweh Himself was there (23:25; 28:2).

Another sign of the immanence of their God was Israel's recognition of His theophanic splendor in the cloud and fire. As the Ark was transported into Solomon's completed Temple, it was filled with the cloud of God's glory, the so-called Shekinah (2 Chron. 5:13-14). Similarly, as soon as Solomon had finished his prayer of Temple dedication, fire descended from heaven and the glory of God filled the Temple once more (7:1-2). So awesome was this tangible manifestation of God's residence among them that the king and people alike prostrated themselves in worship and praise (v. 3).

God in His nature. These matters of divine accessibility and inaccessibility cannot be separated from the nature of God Himself, three aspects of which the chronicler especially singled out. First, He is absolutely holy, a point made not by affirmation but by deduction. This is graphically apparent in the indiscretion of Uzzah who, to steady the holy Ark of God, died for transgressing that holiness (1 Chron. 13:9-10). To violate the sanctity of the Ark, the symbol of God's presence, was to trample on holy ground. In the next place, God is just or righteous, a quality that provides a moral dimension to holiness. To Shemaiah the prophet, who delivered the awful word that Shishak would ravage Judah, Rehoboam and his cohorts cried, "The Lord is just" (2 Chron. 12:6). Their sins had brought divine retribution, a fact commensurate with Yahweh's own integrity. Finally, and in line with His holiness and righteousness, the Lord is omniscient, specifically in regard to the thoughts and motives of human hearts (1 Chron. 28:9). He who is upright demands the interior integrity of His servants.

God in His expression. The holy God, who can and does relate to His creation, does so in ways that are perceptible. For example, David confessed that Yahweh is

---

5. By this is meant the use of some attribute or adjunct of Yahweh, such as His Name, to represent Yahweh Himself. Cf. Gerhard von Rad, *Old Testament Theology,* 2 vols. (New York: Harper & Row, 1962), 1:179-87.

merciful[6] (1 Chron. 21:13), a facet of His character that was demonstrated to the king over and over again. His mercy cannot be separated from His compassion, the quality that makes mercy possible and understandable. Hezekiah understood this, and in a letter to his Israelite brethren of Samaria he offered them hope for reconciliation with their captive countrymen, a hope founded on God's great compassion (2 Chron. 30:9). The second underpinning of the mercy of the Lord is His faithfulness, or *ḥesed*, a self-imposed commitment to His people inherent in His covenant relationship to them. This will be discussed in detail later, but it is interesting to note that Solomon's first appeal to Yahweh in his famous Temple prayer was to His dependability, His faithfulness, a virtue attested to throughout the life of his father David (6:14-15; cf. 21:7).

God in His station. On the borderline between God's person and attributes and God's action in time and space are characteristics that overlap. For example, Chronicles extolls His incomparability, indeed, His exclusivity. In David's prayerful response to Yahweh's covenant promises he exclaims, "There is no one like you, O Lord, and there is no God but you" (1 Chron. 17:20). Solomon too confesses that "our God is greater than all other gods" (2 Chron. 2:5) and that "there is no God like you in heaven or on earth" in keeping covenant with His people (6:14). This incomparability manifests itself in many ways, not least in Yahweh's immeasurable power. David praises Him as the one through whom strength and power come (1 Chron. 29:12). Confronted by Jeroboam I of Israel, Abijah, son of Rehoboam, asserted the derived power of David's dynasty and reminded his foe not to fight "against the Lord, the God of your fathers, for you will not succeed" (2 Chron. 13:8, 12).

The fullest expression of God's power is His sovereignty, an aspect of His person emphasized throughout Chronicles.[7] This note needed to be sounded at that very moment in Israel's history, for the Northern and Southern kingdoms had both been defeated and largely deported, and the prospects for restoration appeared bleak indeed. The paramount question was whether Yahweh, God of Israel, was able to overturn the great empires of the world and pave the way for His people's return to Palestine and restoration to covenant privilege and blessing.

David clearly had no doubt as to the the the sovereignty of Yahweh, as he attests in his prayer on the occasion of the Temple preparation (1 Chron. 29:11-12):

> Yours, O Lord, is the greatness and the power
> and the glory and the majesty and the splendor,
> for everything in heaven and earth is yours.

---

6. The Hebew term used here, *raḥămîm,* is cognate to the noun *reḥem,* "womb," a fact that gives unusual tenderness to Yahweh's character. See R. Laird Harris, Gleason L. Archer, Jr., Bruce K. Waltke, eds., *Theological Wordbook of the Old Testament,* 2 vols. (Chicago: Moody, 1980), s.v. *raḥămîm,* pp. 842-43.

7. So J. Barton Payne, "1, 2 Chronicles," in *The Expositor's Bible Commentary* (Grand Rapids: Zondervan, 1988), 4:316-17.

> Yours, O Lord, is the kingdom;
>   you are exalted as head over all.
> Wealth and honor come from You;
>   you are the ruler of all things.
> In your hands are strength and power
>   to exalt and give strength to all.

Jehoshaphat likewise proclaimed to Yahweh, "You rule over all the kingdoms of the nations. Power and might are in your hand, and no one can withstand you" (2 Chron. 20:6).

The sovereignty of the Lord is implied in many of the narratives as an explanation for otherwise inexplicable turns of events. The chronicler stated that Rehoboam did not listen to the advice of his counselors, for the resulting division of the kingdom was within the purpose of God (2 Chron. 10:15). Shemaiah the prophet followed this up by relaying the message to Rehoboam that the division was indeed by divine sanction (11:4). Nearly a century later Ahaziah, king of Judah, died at the hands of Jehu along with his uncle Joram, king of Israel, a calamity the chronicler specifically attributed to God (22:7). Joash, son of Ahaziah, suffered defeat by a greatly outnumbered Aramean army because the Lord delivered him into Aramean hands (24:24). Uzziah, however, gained victory over the Philistines, Arabs, and Meunites because God was with him (26:7). Conversely, the Lord was against wicked Ahaz and handed him over to the the king of Aram (28:5). In all these episodes it is obvious that all the nations, not just Israel and Judah, moved in response to the sovereign purposes of the Lord.

THE WORKS AND ACTIVITY OF GOD

Central to the position of many contemporary biblical theologians is the notion that Yahweh, if He revealed Himself at all in Old Testament times, did so through history, through His activity among and on behalf of His people.[8] There is truth in this observation, to be sure, but as critics of the "history as revelation" school have pointed out, act or event without confirming and interpretive word is incapable of verification or even meaning. The prophetic explanation must accompany the revelatory act in history.[9]

The biblical historians and prophets did not, however, deny that their God revealed Himself in His works. They saw Him not only as the sovereign initiator of historical processes but as disclosing Himself in them, particularly in acts of election, redemption, and salvation. In the case of Chronicles, these acts are viewed as those on behalf of God's people and those performed with special reference to the nations.

As for Israel, its thinkers understood that she was the peculiar people of

---

8. See, as an example, the essays by Pannenberg, R. Rendtorff, and Wilkens in W. Pannenberg, ed., *Revelation as History* (London: Macmillan, 1968).

9. John Goldingay, *Approaches to Old Testament Interpretation* (Downers Grove, Ill.: InterVarsity, 1981). pp. 74-77.

Yahweh by virtue of a great redemptive act, a magnanimous and magnificent display of His grace. David, in response to the covenant granted him, asked in wonder, "Who is like your people Israel—the one nation on earth whose God went out to redeem a people for himself, and to make a name for yourself, and to perform great and awesome wonders by driving out nations from before your people, whom you redeemed from Egypt?" (1 Chron. 17:21). The historical act and fact of the Exodus thus attested to Yahweh as Redeemer.

The redemption, as the record makes clear, was effected in order to bring Israel out from the chains of Egyptian bondage to the easy yoke of Yahweh's lordship. This transfer of allegiance was made formal at Sinai where Israel accepted the generous terms of the Mosaic Covenant, terms that identified the redeemed people as a kingdom of priests submissive to the Great King of all the earth.

Chronicles does not elaborate on the Sinaitic Covenant but stresses rather the Davidic Covenant, that monarchic expression of the rule of God anticipated by both the Abrahamic and Sinaitic (and Deuteronomic) covenants. This will be elaborated on presently. For now it is important to see how Yahweh disclosed Himself as Lord of the nation, the monarchy, and the cult.

That the kingdom was His to bestow is clear from the fact that Yahweh, having rejected Saul, turned the kingdom over to David (1 Chron. 10:13-14). David understood this transfer and understood further that Judah was the theocratic nation chosen to model and mediate God's saving grace and that he was its elect undershepherd. In a remarkably concise yet comprehensive juxtaposition of these twin ideas of realm and regent, David declared, "The Lord, the God of Israel, chose me from my whole family to be king over Israel forever. He chose Judah as leader, and from the house of Judah He chose my family, and from my father's sons He was pleased to make me king over all Israel" (28:4). These acts of election testify eloquently to Yahweh's sovereign dispositions.

The choice of David simultaneously marked the selection of his dynastic succession. His rule was a prelude to that of his descendants after him, a line that would culminate at last in one whose dominion would never end. As Nathan so eloquently predicted, David would die but his seat would be occupied by a son who would build the house of the Lord (1 Chron. 17:11-12). Beyond him, however, would be One whose throne "will be established forever" (v. 14). The sovereignty of Yahweh will coincide with and be expressed eternally by this scion of David.

The initiation and maintenance of the kingdom was not and will not be without opposition, for anti-theocratic forces have always been at work to frustrate God's saving purposes. The ground of kingship must be gained through war and struggle, and so fearsome are the foes that God Himself must engage in battle as the warrior of this people. Chronicles is not oblivious to this concept of "holy war" or, as most modern scholars prefer, "Yahweh war,"[10] as the following passages indicate.

10. Peter C. Craigie, *The Problem of War in the Old Testament* (Grand Rapids: Eerdmans, 1978), pp. 45-54.

The original conquest of the land of Canaan necessitated divine intervention, a fact repeatedly emphasized in Deuteronomy and Joshua. The chronicler alluded to this in describing the overthrow of the Transjordanian populations as the battle of God (1 Chron. 5:22). This is a theme pervasively found in the military exploits of David and his dynasty. It was the Lord who gave victory over the Philistines (11:14; 14:10, 15, 17) and all other enemies (17:8; 18:6, 13; 22:18).

More or less detailed accounts of Yahweh war appear in the record. In the battle between Jeroboam I of Israel and Abijah of Judah, the Judahites cried out to the Lord, the priests blew the trumpets, the battle cry was sounded, and Yahweh routed Jeroboam and his hosts (2 Chron. 13:14-16).[11] Asa achieved victory over Zerah and his myriads through God's intervention (14:11-13). When Jehoshaphat was about to march against Moab and her allies, the Spirit of God came upon Jahaziel, a Levite, who reminded the king that "the battle is not yours, but God's" (20:15). Then, led by the Levites in song and praise, the forces of Judah advanced to the front lines, where they witnessed the carnage of self-inflicted destruction and death as the Moabites, Ammonites, and Meunites turned on one another (20:20, 22-23). Noteworthy is the reference to the role of the Levites, for this was a clear hallmark of Yahweh war.[12] The result of this campaign puts this interpretation beyond doubt: "The fear of God came upon all the kingdoms of the countries when they heard how the Lord had fought against the enemies of Israel" (20:29).

Hezekiah understood this role of Yahweh in Judah's national affairs. In what perhaps was Judah's greatest crisis, the siege of Jerusalem by the Assyrian Sennacherib, Hezekiah rallied his people with the cry "With him is only the arm of flesh, but with us is the Lord our God to help us and to fight our battles" (2 Chron. 32:8). Then in a mighty vindication of that confidence, Yahweh struck the Assyrian host, annihilating officer and infantryman alike (32:21).

That Yahweh revealed Himself in His deeds on behalf of His own people is crystal clear, but His sovereignty and self-disclosure were not limited to them. The chronicler teaches that He is not only the God of Israel but also the God of the nations. Quoting a psalm of David (Ps. 96:9-10), he wrote,

> Tremble before him, all the earth!
> The world is firmly established; it cannot be moved.
> Let the heavens rejoice, let the earth be glad;
> let them say among the nations, "The Lord reigns."
> (1 Chron. 16:30-31)

As their Sovereign—whether they recognize that fact or not—Yahweh uses the nations to accomplish His purposes, especially with regard to His own covenant

---

11. Dillard points out that "Abijah's speech and the following battle narrative show many of the motifs common in holy war ideology" (Raymond B. Dillard, *2 Chronicles*, vol. 15 in Word Biblical Commentary [Waco, Tex.: Word, 1987], p. 109).

12. Ibid., pp. 157-58.

people. He stirred up the Philistines and Arabs against Jehoram, king of Judah (2 Chron. 21:16), and brought Neco of Egypt against Josiah. The language here is remarkable in that Neco claimed to speak for Israel's God, warning Josiah not to attempt to interdict his march to Carchemish (35:21). That the claim is authentic is seen in the chronicler's complaint that Josiah "would not listen to what Neco had said at God's command" (v. 22). The result, of course, was Josiah's tragic and untimely demise.

The most striking evidence of God's sovereignty over the nations and His use of them to effect His saving objectives is that associated with Cyrus, king of Persia. Writing in the late exilic period, the chronicler offered to the community of exiles the hope that the end was in sight and that the return to the land of promise was about to get underway. The most amazing feature about the restoration was that it would be accomplished under the aegis of a heathen Persian king, the mightiest monarch the world had seen.

And so the historian noted that the Lord, in response to the prophetic word of Jeremiah, "moved the heart of Cyrus king of Persia" to make a proclamation as follows: "The Lord, the God of heaven, has given me all the kingdoms of the earth and he has appointed me to build a temple for him at Jerusalem in Judah. Anyone of his people among you—may the Lord his God be with him, and let him go up" (2 Chron. 36:23). One should not, of course, conclude from this declaration that Cyrus was a convert to Yahwism. But this does not detract from the truth that Cyrus, unwitting or not, was merely an agent of the God of Israel, the sole and incomparable Sovereign of all nations.

THE PEOPLE OF THE KINGDOM

In the theology of Chronicles the people of the kingdom are defined narrowly and precisely—they were the citizens of Israel, the theocratic community. Even more particularly, they were the subjects of the Davidic monarchy, that entity elected and commissioned to model and mediate the sovereignty of God over all creation. As a kingdom of priests called to that task, their very political and cultic structures served both to regulate the fullness of their national life before God, and to articulate how all men, as a result of their witness, should conduct themselves as creatures of God. One cannot therefore understand the theology of Chronicles without understanding the centrality of worship and its formal apparatus to the life of the theocratic people.

On the other hand, Israel did not exist in a vacuum, without roots or reference to universal history. It was therefore the burden of the chronicler to link the elect nation to creation and history in such a way as to show that the Davidic monarchy was far from an ad hoc afterthought in the regnal purposes of God. To the contrary, it was the long-promised expression of God's salvific intentions for a fallen, alienated creation. Man was created to be the image of God and in that capacity to have dominion over all things. The crippling of that mandate because of man's rebellion called for a mighty act of atonement and redemption, one sufficient in its effect to reestablish the pristine purposes of God. Thus was set in motion the history of salvation, a history that in Old Testament times anticipated that act of reconciliation and that in Christ and the gospel saw its accomplishment.

The focal point of salvation and sovereignty in the Old Testament is David and the Davidic dynasty.[13] Abraham, called to be father of a people who would bless the whole earth, understood that he would beget kings, indeed, a nation of kings. These came to be circumscribed in Israel (the chosen nation) and to be epitomized in David (Israel's first legitimate king) and in the line that followed him, culminating in that Son who will reign forever. It is necessary now to see how Chronicles establishes these lines of connection.

THE ORIGIN OF THE NATION

The book of Chronicles begins with a collection of genealogies whose purpose is to provide the very linkages suggested above. The solidarity of the human race and Israel's place within it is evident from the very first list, which traces mankind from Adam to Noah's three sons, Shem, Ham, and Japheth (1 Chron. 1:1-4).[14] Then attention is riveted on the Shemites (i.e., Semites) one of whose members, Eber, gives his name to the offspring of Abraham, namely, the Hebrews. The line of Shem culminates in Abraham (vv. 17-27), in whom originates the seed that will be the channel of universal blessing. It is at this point, then, that a branch of the race becomes chosen to mediate grace to the remainder of the race.

The transmission of the promise of a nation and kingship passes through Isaac on to Jacob (or Israel as the chronicler nearly always describes him). It is then apparent that the chronicler had a special theological concern in his casting of the material for he immediately focused on Judah, the fourth son of Israel (1 Chron. 2:3–4:23), and then on Simeon (4:24-43), a tribe that affiliated with Judah to make up the Davidic kingdom.[15]

THE ORIGIN OF THE MONARCHY

After a most cursory listing of the sons of Israel (1 Chron. 2:1-2), the author addresses Judah and his descendants and in the space of twelve verses arrives at David (vv. 3-15). It is most apparent that he was eager to establish the connection between the chosen tribe (cf. 5:2) and the "man after [God's] own heart" (1 Sam. 13:14). It is not the nation of Israel that is important to him, but her king and her royal descent. Like the genealogy of Ruth 4:18-21, this of 1 Chronicles 2:3-17 bypasses any reference to Moses and the Sinaitic Covenant, which made Israel a national enti-

---

13. For a good discussion of this point see Willem VanGemeren, *The Progress of Redemption* (Grand Rapids: Zondervan, 1988), pp. 230-37.
14. Braun, *1 Chronicles,* pp. 17-18.
15. H. G. M. Williamson, *1 and 2 Chronicles,* The New Century Bible Commentary (Grand Rapids: Eerdmans, 1982). pp. 48-49.

ty.[16] Instead, both lists make the connection between the tribe to whom dying Jacob promised the royal sceptre (Gen. 49:10) and the sovereign who would rule God's people under its sway.

That the linkage is not complete in David alone is clear from the genealogy of 1 Chronicles 3:1-24, which lists all his dynastic successors to the time of the Babylonian exile and beyond. In fact, as the covenant promise to David makes apparent, the throne of his royal descendant will be occupied forever (17:14). The dominion that springs from him is everlasting (2 Chron. 13:5).

Two theological foci that have so far emerged in the analysis of Chronicles are the God of the kingdom and the people of the kingdom. Though intimations of their relationship have suggested themselves even in their separate treatments, it is necessary next to see how and why God, through the chosen community, brought His sovereign purposes to bear on His creation. This gives rise to a consideration of the charter of the kingdom.

THE CHARTER OF THE KINGDOM

In recent decades the idea of covenant has become the subject of much biblical and theological discussion. Some scholars in fact have centered their entire theology on covenant, a center which, though having much in its favor, seems too narrow to serve as the fulcrum upon which all the biblical material can best be integrated and understood. The problem is that covenant itself has been perceived as the *essence* of God's work and witness in the world rather than as the *instrument* by which He has set out to accomplish His creation objectives. That is, it seems best to view covenant in functional and not essential terms.[17]

The thesis has already been advanced that the theological theme or center of Chronicles is the sovereignty of God revealed through the Davidic monarchy in Old Testament times. The centrality of divine sovereignty and its corollary, creation as the arena of dominion, is evident throughout the Bible. It is this bipolarity of King and realm that necessitates consideration of relationship, for the King must have in place an apparatus through which He discloses His intentions, and by means of which they are effected. Covenant is such an apparatus.

The history of covenant originates in creation.[18] God had created all things and then made man to be His image, charging him to "be fruitful and increase in number; fill the earth and subdue it. Rule over the fish of the sea and the birds of the air and over every living creature that moves on the ground" (Gen. 1:28). Sin drastically affected man's ability to fulfill this creation mandate or covenant, but it was not

16. Eugene H. Merrill, "The Book of Ruth: Narration and Shared Themes," *Bibliotheca Sacra* 142 (1985): 135.

17. For an excellent treatment of the role of covenant in Old Testament theology see W. J. Dumbrell, *Covenant and Creation* (Nashville: Thomas Nelson, 1984).

18. Eugene H. Merrill, "Covenant and the Kingdom: Genesis 1-3 as Foundation for Biblical Theology," *Criswell Theological Review* 1 (1987): 295-308.

rescinded, as its repetition to Noah both before (6:18) and after the Flood (9:1-7) attests. The Fall did, however, call for a resolution of the dilemma that resulted. How could a holy God reign over all things, particularly fallen things, through a human vassal who also was fallen? The answer lay in the promise of atonement by One whose perfection could more than compensate for the sins of humankind for all time. Thus the redemptive program was set in place and through a series of covenant arrangements was made efficacious for all who would avail themselves of it.

The reigning and saving purposes of God are inextricable and mutually dependent. God created man to have dominion, but sin rendered that impossible. God therefore initiated a means of salvation whereby man could be restored to his covenant-keeping capacity. Salvation is thus prerequisite to reigning but is not tantamount to it. It is the means of achieving the sovereignty for which man was created at the beginning.

It is crucial that these distinctions and relationships be understood, for otherwise the covenant thread of biblical theology loses its proper significance. It must embrace both aspects—reigning and redemption—if it is to be correctly assessed. This first becomes clear in the call of Abraham to covenant service. The dominion facet is expressed in the promise, "I will make you into a great nation and I will bless you" (Gen. 12:2), and the salvific word in the sequel, "I will bless those who bless you, and whoever curses you I will curse; and all peoples on earth will be blessed through you" (12:3). Abraham would produce a kingdom, a nation that would become the channel of God's saving work in the world.

In increasing detail the Lord continued to reveal these promises of nationhood and saving intercession. The land of the kingdom would be Canaan (Gen. 15:18-21), and the rulers of the kingdom would be kings descended from Abraham (17:5-8), rulers whose reign would know no end. As tokens of His faithfulness, the Lord repeated His covenant pledges to Isaac (26:3-5) and Jacob (28:13-15; 35:11-13; 46:3-4). To the latter, in most explicit terms the promise came that the coming kingdom would find its orientation in his son Judah, for from his tribe the king par excellence would rise:

> The scepter will not depart from Judah,
>   nor the ruler's staff from between his feet,
> until he comes to whom it belongs
>   and the obedience of the nations is his.
>   (Gen. 49:10)

The purpose of the Sinaitic Covenant was to fulfill the promise to the patriarchs concerning a nation and to provide a kingdom over which the Judahite sovereign could reign. It is important to note that the election and redemption of that nation (Israel) was not for the sake of the nation itself but was for the purpose of creating a people who could model among the kingdoms of the earth what it meant to be the dominion of the Lord, and who could serve as a channel by which His salvation could be mediated to them. The role of Israel, then, was twofold, paradigmatic and redemptive. This is why the Mosaic Covenant was a conditional sovereign-vassal type and not like that made with Abraham, namely, an unconditional royal grant. So long as Israel discharged her covenant mandate faithfully, she would continue to exist and be blessed. If and when she failed to do so, however, she could anticipate the termination of her role and its benefits. In any case, the reigning and saving purposes of the Lord would continue unimpaired, for what the nation could not do collectively in history could and would be done by its greatest scion individually and with eternal repercussions. Thus Israel the servant and the Messiah the Servant find perfect harmonization in Isaiah.[19] What the former failed to achieve as the light to the nations the latter accomplished by His vicarious suffering and death.

Though Chronicles has virtually nothing to say about the Mosaic Covenant, it is important to remember that the Davidic monarchy, so central to the theology of Chronicles, cannot be understood apart from the recognition that David and his dynasty did, after all, reign over the nation brought about by means of the Mosaic Covenant. It is therefore necessary to make that connection between the covenants of Sinai and Moab and that which created the Davidic monarchy.

Having remembered His pledge to the patriarchal fathers, Yahweh took note of the sufferings of their offspring in Egypt (Ex. 2:23-25; 3:7-10, 15-17) and promised to bring them out (6:6-8), a promise that resulted in the mighty Exodus deliverance. This deed, which did not make Israel the people of the Lord but only confirmed that status, led to the crucial moment of covenant offer in which Yahweh invited His redeemed people to become the instrument by which He could display His reigning and saving intentions before all the earth:

> You yourself have seen what I did to Egypt, and how I carried you on eagles' wings and brought you to myself. Now if you obey me fully and keep my covenant, then out of all nations you will be my treasured possession. Although the whole earth is mine, you will be for me a kingdom of priests and a holy nation.
>
> (Ex. 19:4-6)

Their acceptance of this offer brought Israel into the twin roles of model and mediator, a role whose practical function was regulated by the covenant instrument with all its principles and stipulations. The Ten Commandments, the Book of the Covenant (Ex. 20:22–23:33), the cultic and ceremonial laws (Exodus 24-40; Leviticus; much of Numbers), and the covenant reaffirmation at the plains of Moab (Deuteronomy)—all constitute the corpus of covenant legislation designed to guide the servant nation in its task of representing its Sovereign and mediating His grace. Not least important among its provisions was that of kingship. In Deuteronomy Moses instructed the nation that when the time would come for a king, "be sure to appoint over you the king the Lord your God chooses. He must be

19. Willis J. Beecher, *The Prophets and the Promise* (Grand Rapids: Baker, 1963), pp. 285-88.

from among your own brothers" (Deut. 17:15). Moreover, he must carefully attend to the terms of the national covenant, for in so doing, "he and his descendants will reign a long time over his kingdom in Israel" (17:19-20).

This King is more specifically identified in the Oracle of Balaam as a star who will come out of Jacob, a scepter out of Israel, One who will lead Israel to great strength at the expense of her enemies (Num. 24:17-19). The juxtaposition of this passage with the blessing of Jacob (Gen. 49:10) makes it certain that the conquering star is to rise out of Judah. From Moses to Samuel, then, the covenant people awaited their king, a human ruler who would hold in his hand the scepter of the King of kings.

With this covenant setting and history in view, it is necessary now to look at the covenant of kingship in Chronicles, a covenant that serves as the charter for the Davidic administration.

THE SOURCE OF THE COVENANT

As stated repeatedly, the chronicler gave little heed to the covenant that brought his nation Israel into existence. His concern was instead with the Davidic monarchy and its historical and theological origins. Because the covenant that established the monarchy finds its roots in the promises to the fathers, Chronicles reaches back to that era to describe its source.

The genealogies of 1 Chronicles 1-9, as noted already, commence with Adam himself, the founder of the human race and the recipient of the original covenant mandate to "have dominion over all things." It is obvious that the chronicler wanted to make the connection between Adam, the first "king," and David, the epitome of earthly, human kingship. David may have been king of Judah, but he was a direct descendant of the primal man and therefore represented a dominion that transcended the narrow perimeters of Judah or any one nation. One might even say that David was king of the whole world inasmuch as he traced his lineage back to the king of the whole world.

The broadening and yet ever narrowing line of descent from Adam leaves no room for doubt that the prism of world history at last focused all its rays on the son of Jesse. Noah, the "second Adam," produced three sons, one of whom, Shem, was set apart from the other two as an example of God's elective strategy. The Semites then must bear the name of Yahweh (Gen. 9:26). The tenth generation of Shem consisted of three sons of Terah—Abram, Nahor, and Haran—of whom again only one, Abram, was chosen. This father of the Hebrews passed the covenant promises on to only one son, Isaac, who handed them on to only one of his, Jacob. At last the national configuration was in place, but it was a nation of twelve tribes, scores of clans, and thousands of families. The narrowing process must go on until one family and one member of that family could be singled out and set aside.

The chronicler wasted no time in arriving at his objective, and by his second chapter he had identified Judah as the tribe in question. Judah, again, had three surviving sons only one of whom (Perez) continued the covenant line. The tenth generation of Perez eventuated in not three but seven sons of the family of Jesse of Bethlehem. The last of these, young David, proved to be the long expected king, though his suitability was not at all apparent. It is only because the Lord looks at the heart (1 Sam. 16:7) that Samuel was finally able to say, "Rise and anoint him; he is the one" (16:12).

David himself was aware that he stood in the covenant tradition. On the occasion of the retrieval of the Ark and its procession into Jerusalem, he recalled the promises to the fathers to give them Canaan (1 Chron. 16:14-18). In the same psalm of thanksgiving he drew attention to the regal sovereignty of Yahweh his God (v. 31), intimating thereby his own role as king. The link between the ancient pledges and the (to him) present kingship is even more forcefully articulated in David's prayer wherein he addressed the Lord as "God of our fathers Abraham, Isaac, and Israel" and invoked Him to give his son Solomon the dedication requisite to successful rule (29:18-19).

David's consciousness of being the object of special and particular elective grace is related in the starkly bold statement to his assembled officials: "The Lord, the God of Israel, chose me from my whole family to be king over Israel forever. He chose Judah as leader, and from the house of Judah he chose my family, and from my father's sons he was pleased to make me king over all Israel" (1 Chron 28:4). This choice, he said later, extended to his son Solomon as well (29:1), a fact that even the heathen queen of Sheba recognized (2 Chron. 9:8). Abijah, son of Rehoboam (and therefore great-grandson of David), stated flatly that Yahweh had given the kingship of Israel to David and his descendants forever (13:5).

That the chronicler himself shared this notion of the election of David and the perpetuity of his dynastic succession is evident from his comment that despite the evil reign of Jehoram of Judah, more than 130 years after David's death, "because of the covenant the Lord had made with him, the Lord was not willing to destroy the house of David. He had promised to maintain a lamp for David and his descendants forever" (21:7). Even when the dynastic thread was at its weakest with the slaughter by Athaliah of all the Judean royal family, the baby Joash was preserved because, as Jehoiada the priest affirmed, "The king's son shall reign, as the Lord promised concerning the descendants of David" (23:3).

THE NATURE OF THE COVENANT

Those scholars who identify the Davidic Covenant form-critically as a royal grant similar to the Abrahamic Covenant appear to be correct.[20] The narrative describing his choice by Yahweh and his anointing by Samuel (1 Sam. 16:1-13) leaves no doubt that David became king by an act of pure grace and with no conditions attached or presupposed. The Lord had rejected Saul and, in Samuel's words, had "sought out a man after his own heart and appointed him leader of his

20. Thomas E. McComiskey, *The Covenants of Promise* (Grand Rapids: Baker, 1985), pp. 62-63.

people" (13:14). That man was one of the sons of Jesse, unnamed at first to Samuel but described to him as one chosen by God (16:1). Nowhere in the narrative or anywhere else in biblical literature is the monarchy of David viewed in any other light than as an unmerited, unconditional gift of God to him and his descendants forever.

The most important information relative to the nature of the covenant in Chronicles is, of course, in the revelation to Nathan in which the Davidic Covenant is spelled out (1 Chron. 17:4-14). The Lord here says that He had taken David "from the pasture and from following the flock, to be ruler over My people Israel" (v. 7). There is no hint of reward or conditionality here. Through the years of David's reign the Lord had affirmed it by giving him victory and success. Then in a glorious climactic pledge the Lord swore to His servant David, "When your days are over and you go to be with your fathers, I will raise up your offspring to succeed you, one of your own sons, and I will establish his kingdom. He is the one who will build a house for me, and I will establish his throne forever. . . . I will set him over my house and my kingdom forever; his throne will be established forever" (vv. 11-14). Again, one looks in vain for anything but an unvarnished declaration of grace, a boon granted by divine initiative alone.

Though there can be little argument that the covenant with David was unconditional both in its granting and in its perpetuity, the benefits of that covenant to David and to the nation depended on their obedience to the terms of the Mosaic Covenant within which the monarchy functioned.[21] In this respect and only in this respect was the Davidic Covenant conditional.

David himself made this clear to Solomon when he promised him that "you will have success if you are careful to observe the decrees and laws that the Lord gave Moses for Israel" (1 Chron. 22:13). He shortly thereafter addressed the officials of the nation and told them that the kingdom of Solomon would last forever provided "he is unswerving in carrying out [God's] commands and laws" (28:7). One might suggest that only the continuance of the nation, and not the monarchy, is at stake here. But David, addressing Solomon, went on to say, "If you forsake [the Lord], he will reject you forever" (v. 9).

That the endurance of the nation as a model and mediator is conditioned on obedience is obvious from the fact that the covenant made with Israel at Sinai was of the sovereign-vassal type and therefore inherently conditional. What is to be said, however, of the possibility of the cessation of the Davidic monarchy in light of the previously advanced arguments that it is unilateral and unconditional? The answer no doubt lies in the singular pronoun. The warning is not to the dynasty as a whole, but to Solomon alone. His obedience to the Lord will bring success, but his disobedience will result in personal rejection and in judgment upon his kingdom (cf. 2 Chron. 7:19-20). The kingship will nonetheless survive and go on forever.[22]

21. Dumbrell, *Covenant and Creation,* pp. 150-51.
22. Braun, *1 Chronicles,* p. 271.

Further evidence of the contingency of blessing on obedience may be seen in the historical narratives of Chronicles where the author constantly made that point. Azariah the prophet came to Asa, for example, and reminded him that if he forsook the Lord the Lord would forsake him (2 Chron. 15:2). The Lord was with Jehoshaphat, the chronicler wrote, because he "sought the God of his father and followed his commands" (17:4). Zechariah the priest warned the people of his day that the Lord had forsaken them because they had forsaken Him (24:20). As long as Uzziah sought the Lord, so wrote the historian, "God gave him success" (26:5). The same kinds of commendations and rebukes pepper the pages of the inspired record (cf. 2 Chron. 27:6; 28:6, 9; 29:6-9; 33:8; 34:24-27).

THE FUNCTION OF THE COVENANT

As a "kingdom of priests and a holy nation" (Ex. 19:6), Israel was called into covenant to undertake the ministry of a priest, namely, to represent the nations of the earth before the Lord God and to model before them the submissive dominion to which all men had been called by virtue of creation.[23] Or to put it another way, Israel must exhibit in her social, political, and religious life what it means to be a redeemed people so that she might attract all other peoples to the sovereign God who created them and who desired to restore them to covenant-keeping capacity.

This concept is most clear in Chronicles as an ideal and as a matter of practical outworking in both the political and cultic forms of Israel's life. The principle of Israel's covenant role as a kingdom of priests and a holy nation should be addressed first.

The kingdom as a mediator/model. It is only with Solomon's accession and the building of the Temple that this idea first finds expression in Chronicles, for Yahweh had at last come to dwell on the earth in a more visible, lasting way and in a political and religious framework that allowed the nation to express fully its covenant witness. Solomon, in fact, viewed the Temple as a focal point of that witness when he prayed, on the occasion of its dedication, that the foreigner, attracted to it by "your great name and your mighty hand and your outstretched arm," will come and pray toward the Temple and in so doing "may know your name and fear you, as do your own people Israel" (2 Chron. 6:32-33). Israel, and the Temple specifically, is designed to be a magnet drawing the nations to a knowledge of the Lord.[24]

The classic example of this actually taking place is the visit of the queen of Sheba to Solomon at Jerusalem (2 Chron. 9:1-8). Having heard of Solomon's famous wisdom, she came to test him. Instead, she was overwhelmed by what she saw and could only exclaim, "Praise be to the Lord your God, who has delighted in you and placed you on his throne as king to rule for the Lord your God" (v.8). And

23. VanGemeren, *The Progress of Redemption,* pp. 146-48.
24. Williamson, *1 and 2 Chronicles,* p. 219.

she was only typical, for the chronicler related that "all the kings of the earth sought audience with Solomon to hear the wisdom God had put in his heart" (v. 23).

Clearly, then, Israel and her God became attractive to the curious peoples near and far who were forced to confess that Yahweh was indeed among His people and was the secret of their blessing and prosperity. But those who would not submit to the God of Israel out of religious conviction often submitted through political or military coercion as a testimony to His sovereignty through His people. Solomon, for example "ruled over all the kings" from the Euphrates to the border of Egypt (2 Chron. 9:26). This rule epitomized and anticipated the dominion by the Lord over the whole creation in line with His creation purposes.

In Jehoshaphat's time all the nations surrounding Judah likewise submitted to him because the fear of the Lord fell on them (2 Chron. 17:10-11). As a result, they brought the king tribute, a sign of their submission to him as the representative of Yahweh. This fear arose particularly when the nations saw that Judah's successes were not to be attributed to human skill and courage, but that success came because Yahweh fought for Judah and gave her victory (20:29).

The kingdom in its political and historical form. The ideal of the theocratic rule had to be translated into and expressed by actual political institutions, most notably the monarchy and specifically that of David and his dynasty. The function of the covenant was to call David to the headship of the priestly kingdom that in turn, as is now clear, was to serve as mediator/model among the nations. Though David was no doubt aware of his special role from the time of his anointing by Samuel (1 Sam. 16:13), any lingering doubts were removed by the time he had succeeded Saul and had begun to rule from Jerusalem. Flushed by success of every kind, "David knew that the Lord had established him as king over Israel" (1 Chron. 14:2). More important, he knew that his personal exaltation was for the sake of the covenant nation Israel.

Nowhere is the role of the king more clearly elaborated than in the so-called Davidic Covenant passage (1 Chronicles 17:7-14). Here Yahweh reminded David that he had been taken from the position of one who followed a flock of sheep to that of leader of a people. He had prevailed over his enemies and would become famous the world over. More important, even after he died he would continue on in a dynastic succession that would last forever. Thus the monarchy was more than a single man—it was an institution that would never end, the result of an unconditional covenant arrangement designed to implement divine rule through a human instrument.

David (1 Chron. 28:4), Solomon (2 Chron. 6:6), Abijah (2 Chron. 13:8), and the whole line of Davidic kings were aware of Yahweh's elective grace in having chosen the founder of their line, and they likewise understood that it would continue forever through them. David relayed this promise to Solomon (1 Chron. 22:10) and confirmed it before the leaders of the nation in a most remarkable statement: "Of all my sons—and the Lord has given me many—he has chosen my son Solomon to sit on the throne of the kingdom of the Lord over Israel" (28:5). This statement affirms the principle of election that is at the very heart of covenant relationship, and it conjoins the kingdom of the Lord and the kingdom of Israel. In fact, Solomon sat over Israel on the very throne of Yahweh Himself. This important theological idea will be developed later.

The kingdom in its cultic form. The function of the Mosaic and Davidic Covenants is expressed by the chronicler more, by far, in terms of their cultic shape and significance than in any other way. Again, this is quite in keeping with the dual capacity of Israel and her monarchy as mediator/model. As a kingdom of priests, it is fitting that her role in that capacity be described in categories appropriate to the cultus. Furthermore, Israel's covenant status as vassal to the Great King required that the relationship effected by covenant be maintained and articulated by the stipulations characteristic of such arrangements, stipulations that in the case of divine-human relationships must of necessity be expressed in religious forms.

The first of these forms has to do with holy places and holy objects. A God who is transcendently holy and apart cannot be approached without mediation. One aspect of that mediation is the selection and sanctification of locales that exclusively provide access to the presence of the Holy One. In pre-Solomonic times these shrines were altars, high places, the Tabernacle, and the Ark. Then, as part of the promise to David, Yahweh deigned to come among His people and dwell on the earth in the Temple entrusted to Solomon. The theology of Chronicles gives considerable attention to this development.

The first step in effecting the localization of Yahweh among His people following their unification under David was the retrieval of the sacred Ark from Kiriath Jearim, where it had rested since its return from Philistia a century earlier. The Mosaic Tabernacle, having moved about from Shiloh to Nob to Gibeon, could not, for various reasons, be brought by David into Jerusalem, so he prepared on Mount Zion his own temporary facility to house the Ark (1 Chron. 15:1). This tent would eventually be replaced by the great Temple of Solomon.

The significance of the Ark as a holy object is clear in the account of its procession into Jerusalem. David first of all desired to bring the Ark into the city because it had been neglected through all the long years of Saul's reign (1 Chron. 13:3). There is little wonder that the nation had fallen to such spiritual depths under those conditions. Moreover, the Ark was the tangible evidence that Yahweh ruled among and over His people, and it even bore His Name (v. 6). In a real sense Yahweh was wherever His Ark was. It crystallized His immanence, bearing witness to both His nearness and His sovereignty.

From the time of the covenantal convocation at Sinai, Yahweh's Ark and hence He Himself had dwelt among His people in a tabernacle, a portable and temporary tent-shrine suitable to a nomadic style of life. Even after the conquest of Canaan the instability of Israel's life in the land precluded the possibility of a permanent structure. As long as the occupation of assigned territory was incomplete and the nation was subject to internal and external disorders, the Tabernacle was subject to frequent and unexpected dislocation. This condition existed throughout the days of Joshua and the judges and even into the reign of David, in all a period of more than four centuries.

Located first at Gilgal (John. 4:19; cf. 10:15, 43), the Tabernacle appeared next at Shiloh (Josh. 18:1; cf. Judg. 21:19; 1 Sam. 1:3), then Nob (1 Sam. 21:1; cf. 22:19), and finally Gibeon (2 Chron. 1:3). Once David had secured Jerusalem as the political capital of united Israel he wanted to make it the religious center as well, a plan that apparently was considered radically novel by the leadership of the nation since hitherto the political and religious foci of the nation had been scrupulously separated. In fact, even after David established the seat of government at Jerusalem, he left the old Mosaic Tabernacle at Gibeon, choosing to erect a new shrine on Mount Zion in which to house the Ark. How and why he eventually concluded that it was appropriate to shift the cultic center of the nation from Gibeon to Jerusalem is not clear, but that it was acceptable to Yahweh is obvious from the lack of any prophetic rebuke.

What was precluded, however, was the logical next step, namely, to construct a permanent house for Yahweh on a magnificent and glorious scale. Struck by the disparity between the opulence of his own royal palace and the comparative meagerness of the Zion Tabernacle, David shared with his prophetic confidante Nathan his desire to build a temple commensurate with the majesty and glory of his God (2 Sam. 7:1-2). But precisely because full stability had not yet been achieved and David was a man of war ("You are not to build a house for my Name because you have shed much blood on the earth in my sight," 1 Chron. 22:8), the privilege of temple building was reserved for his son Solomon, whose very name means "peace" (v. 9).[25]

But David was not excluded completely from the transition from Tabernacle to Temple for he purchased the site on which the Temple would be built (1 Chron. 21:18-27), going so far as to name the place "the house of the Lord God" (22:1) as a synecdoche for the reality that he anticipated. In fact, David built an altar there on which he offered burnt offerings and fellowship offerings to atone for his sin of pridefully numbering his military hosts. God responded to this act of worship by answering David with "fire from heaven" (21:26), a sign that not only the sacrifices but also their venue were sanctioned by Him. Clearly the threshing floor of Araunah on Mount Moriah was the site on which God's permanent earthly residence would take form.

David also took the initiative to prepare labor and materials for the construction (1 Chron. 22:5). Peace was imminent and Yahweh could now take up His eternal dwelling place (23:25). Short of actually doing the work of fabrica-

---

25. The context seems to favor this interpretation over against those who view the shedding of blood as a ritual violation of some kind. See C. F. Keil, *The Book of the Chronicles* (reprint, Grand Rapids: Eerdmans, n.d.), p. 245.

tion, David was involved in the conception and execution of the project in its every stage. What must be observed and emphasized is that no detail of the project arose from the originality or creativity of David or Solomon or any other human designer. The chronicler was insistent in pointing out that David gave to Solomon "the plans of all that the Spirit had put in his mind" (28:12). David himself related to his son, "All this [preparation for building the Temple] is in writing because the hand of the Lord was upon me, and he gave me understanding in all the details of the plan" (1 Chron. 28:19).

Before the theological concept of the Temple as a holy place receives further elaboration, it is necessary to deal briefly with the significance of temples in the ancient Near East as a background to their role in the Old Testament.[26] The intra-Semitic word for temple finds its etymology in the Sumerian vocable E.GAL, an ideogram meaning "great house." A temple then was nothing more or less than the house of the god who was associated with it. Even the Sumerians, however, recognized the symbolic character of their temples, for their epic and mythic literature makes most clear that their native deities were cosmic and not earth-bound. Nevertheless the temple did serve as a focus in which was concentrated the spatial, immanent aspect of the divine-human relationship.

The Akkadian term for temple, *ekallu,* is obviously borrowed from Sumerian and bears the same meaning. The same is true for Ugaritic (*hkl*), Aramaic (*hêkal*), Syriac (*hayk^{e}lā'*), Arabic (*haikal*) and, of course, Hebrew (*hêkāl*). In all these languages the word in question is used to describe either the palace of a king or the temple of a god. The difference between a palace and temple, then, is only in the latter's having become "sanctified" or "cultified" by virtue of its association with deity.

Unfortunately for biblical theology this distinction has caused most students to lose sight of the fact that the Temple of Old Testament Israel was not essentially a "religious" center where religious activities such as sacrifice and worship were carried out; it was the house of Yahweh, the palace of the Great King who could and must be visited there by His devoted subjects.[27] Losing sight of this downplays the centrality of covenant as a fundamental theological principle. When one understands that Yahweh had redeemed and made covenant with His elect people Israel as a great king makes covenant with a vassal, the role of the Temple as the focal point of Israel's faith becomes immediately apparent. It is the palace of the Sovereign, the place to which they make periodic pilgrimage to proffer their allegiance and to offer up their gifts of homage. Seen as such, the care with which even its most minute details are revealed and executed is most intelligible, for as the visible expression of the invisible God, the Temple with all its forms and functions becomes a sublime revelatory vehicle of the character and purposes of the Almighty.

---

26. See G. J. Botterweck and H. Ringgren, eds., *Theological Dictionary of the Old Testament* (Grand Rapids: Eerdmans, 1978), s.v. *hêkhāl,* 3:382-88.

27. This understanding of temple-building to provide a seat of kingship is well stated by Meredith G. Kline, *The Structure of Biblical Authority* (Grand Rapids: Eerdmans, 1972), pp. 79 84.

Thus such matters as the courts, the treasuries, the divisions of priests and Levites, the gold and silver articles of Temple service, the lamps and furniture, and even the "chariot" or cherubim of gold are not meaningless trivia but are objects and places invested with profound theological truth, whether or not that truth can always be divined by modern man.

Solomon, fully aware of the hermeneutical significance of the Temple, was also aware of his inability to achieve its construction without outside help. He therefore engaged the services of the Phoenicians, celebrated worldwide for their architectural and building skills (2 Chron. 2:6-7), always careful to ensure that the heavenly blueprints and specifications were implemented to the letter (v. 14). That this was done is evident from Yahweh's reaction to the completed project—"the temple of the Lord was filled with a cloud, . . . for the glory of the Lord filled the temple of God" (5:13-14). He was pleased with the obedience of the king and people and showed His pleasure by choosing it as a place of sacrifice (7:12), a place where His Name would abide forever (v. 16).

Finally, one cannot overlook Jerusalem itself as a holy place, for just as the Temple housed the Ark, so Jerusalem was the home of the Temple and for that reason was forever after designated "the Holy City." Though the city had from antiquity remained a Canaanite or Jebusite enclave, it finally fell to David's attack. He wanted to take advantage of its neutrality between Israel and Judah by making it the seat of government. His rationale may appear (and might have been) political and self-serving, but the choice was not without divine sanction and even divine anticipation. A thousand years before David, Abraham had encountered Melchizedek, king of Salem (Jerusalem) and priest of El Elyon (Gen. 14:18), and had offered him tribute. David saw himself as successor to Melchizedek at Jerusalem, both as king (Ps. 110:1-2) and as priest of the same non-Aaronic order (v. 4).

In light of this preparation of Jerusalem as a holy place, it is not surprising that Solomon is able to repeat the words of Yahweh: "I have chosen Jerusalem for my Name to be there, and I have chosen David to rule my people Israel" (2 Chron. 6:6). The chronicler affirmed this selection of Jerusalem as the city of the Lord when he referred to it as "the city the Lord had chosen out of all the tribes of Israel in which to put his Name" (12:13). From holy Ark to holy city Yahweh concentrated His presence among His people in circumscribed places, places made holy because He had set Himself apart there and nowhere else.

The kingdom in its cultic form finds expression also in holy times, stated occasions when God's people met Him in celebration and worship. This suggests that He is not only the Lord of space (hence holy places) but also the Lord of time. In broadest terms the God of Israel was sovereign of universal history, not only that of His own elect nation but of all nations. More narrowly, He was inextricably associated with the years, the months, the weeks, and the days. The seasonal cycles, the phases of the moon, and the rising and setting of the sun were tokens of His unflagging interest in creation and bespoke His dominion over nature and all its processes.

Chronicles presupposes this aspect of the cult, an aspect spelled out fully in the Torah (Ex. 23:14-17; 34:18-24; Lev. 23:1-44; Num. 28:1–29:40; Deut. 16:1-17). In only one passage, 1 Chronicles 23:30-31, is the sacred calendar addressed. There David instructed the Levites to observe the daily services of thanksgiving and praise as well as the sabbaths, new moon festivals, and appointed feasts. That this was not done faithfully in the ensuing years is clear from the accounts of reformation in which the people were called back again and again to the observance of holy times. Particularly noteworthy were the efforts of Hezekiah and Josiah, both of whom centered their religious revivals on the Passover, that festival that first marked Israel as the elect recipient of Yahweh's covenant favor. Following Hezekiah's Passover, he reaffirmed the ministry of the Levites, including their participation in the regular festivals (2 Chron. 31:2-3). It was neglect of these, in fact, that the chronicler, citing Jeremiah, addressed as the reason for the seventy-year captivity of Judah. Because the land had not enjoyed its sabbaths as covenant law prescribed, it would do so after the covenant people were uprooted from it and sent into a distant land (36:21).

The final aspect of the cultic form of the kingdom has to do with holy persons, those individuals set apart to administer the religious affairs of the covenant community. These consisted of the priests and Levites and, in a way emphasized especially in Chronicles, the Davidic kingship.

Just as holy places mediated between heaven and earth, so holy persons must mediate between a sinless God and a sinful, fallen humanity. This is evident from the initial descriptions of the inauguration and function of Israel's priesthood. Once the covenant had been effected at Sinai and its stipulations clearly delineated, Moses received instruction about the Tabernacle and its furnishings (Ex. 25:1–27:21). Immediately thereafter Aaron and his four sons were selected, clothed in the garments indicative of their priestly vocation, and consecrated to that holy office (28:1–29:46). The Lord informed Moses that they were "to serve Me as priests" (28:1, 4), a service that was to include bearing the names of Israel's tribes on their shoulders (v. 12) and over their hearts (v. 29) so that they could, at least as high priest, determine the will of God for His people.

The priests also interceded in the presentation of the offerings of the people to the Lord. Whether these gifts be animals or produce, the priest accepted them on behalf of Yahweh and disposed of them on the altar, or otherwise as the occasion dictated (cf. Lev. 1:1–7:37).

The third fundamental ministry of the priesthood consisted of the teaching of Torah to the community. This is spelled out clearly in Deuteronomy where Moses commanded the priests to "read this law" so that the people "can listen and learn to fear the Lord your God and follow carefully all the words of this law" (Deut. 31:11-12). He underscored this injunction in His blessing to the tribe of Levi where He said of the priest, "He teaches your precepts to Jacob and your law to Israel. He offers incense before you and whole burnt offerings on your altar" (Deut. 33:10).

As suggested already, Chronicles is very much concerned with Israel's reli gion and religious institutions as vehicles by which her mediatorial role among the nations can be articulated. The critical ministry of the priests and Levites as part of the cultic apparatus is evident from the beginning of the chronicler's work where he devoted a long chapter (1 Chron. 6) to this matter.

To establish first the legitimacy of the Zadokite priesthood of his own con- temporaries, the chronicler traced its genealogy back through Zadok, Eleazar, and Aaron to Levi himself (1 Chron 6:1-15).[28] He ended the list with Jehozadak, the priest who accompanied the exiles into Babylon and who was also the direct ancestor of Joshua, the high priest of postexilic times (Zech. 6:11). The Exile, then, as traumatic as it was, did not bring the ancient Aaronic priesthood to an end.

The next section of the genealogy (1 Chron. 6:16-30) commences again with Levi but it traces the nonpriestly descendants, that is, the Levites. Their tasks were multifaceted but primarily consisted of assisting the priests in their mediatorial work. Specifically they were in charge of music in the Tabernacle and Temple (vv. 31-48) and, except for actually making offerings on the altars (vv. 48-53), occupied themselves with worship at the house of the Lord. To make themselves accessible to the whole population of Israel, the Levites settled in towns and villages strate- gically located throughout the land (vv. 54-81). Holy place and holy person are thus juxtaposed once more.

When David became king and made preparation for the centralization of worship at Jerusalem, he ordered the priests and Levites to consecrate themselves to the assignment of moving the Ark into Jerusalem, a task that must explicitly follow Mosaic regulation (1 Chron. 15:11-15; cf. Ex. 25:14). He then appointed the Levitical singers according to their orders (1 Chron. 15:16-24), defining their min- istry as one of making petition, giving thanks, and praising the Lord (16:4-6). On the eve of temple building, David again organized the Levites to oversee the work of the Temple (23:4), to serve as officials and judges (v. 4), to be gatekeepers (v. 5), and to praise the Lord in music (v. 5). In sum, "the duty of the Levites was to help Aaron's descendants in the service of the temple of the Lord" (23:28).

The priests and Levites obviously played an important part in the cultic life of Israel, serving as they did, within the context of the Sinaitic Covenant, as mediators between the vassal nation and its Great King. What must be remem- bered, however, is that this ministry was restricted to that covenant and to that nation, though lessons in holiness and intercession of eternal application may be seen in it.

This is not the case with the second kind of holy person, the king, as he is revealed in Chronicles in his twin roles as priest and son of God. In fact, Chronicles makes an unusual contribution to biblical theology in precisely these concepts. As this study has repeatedly argued, biblical theology most clearly and consistently finds integration around the theme of sovereignty, that of Yahweh over all His creation and that of man, His vice-regent, over all things delegated to him. That derived

28. Braun, *1 Chronicles,* p. 83.

dominion, though impaired by the Fall, is still in force and will find unimpeded perfection in the ages to come.

In the meantime, in human history Yahweh elected a nation, Israel, to mediate His saving purposes to the world and also to provide a model of sovereignty on the earth. Thus Abraham was called and received a promise that through his descent all the earth would be blessed. A corollary promise was that he would sire kings, a promise narrowed in the blessing of Jacob to a ruler who would come from the tribe of Judah. Picking up on this line of expectation, the chronicler made the direct connection between Adam and Abraham and then between Abraham and David, his purpose being to show that David and his royal house were the physical and historical expression of the dominion mandate given to Adam and channeled through Abraham and his seed. The king of Israel was therefore more than a mere political figure; he was the messianic ruler who stood as second Adam in dominion over all things but who, because he was human, stood also as a type of anticipation of the sinless One who would climax and complete the line of David.[29]

As such a king, then, David was an intercessor, a priest, but one not limited to Israel and the Aaronic line. He was, in fact, of the line of Melchizedek, priest of El Elyon, who, the author of Hebrews emphasizes, was "without father or mother, without genealogy, without beginning of days or end of life," one who "like the Son of God . . . remains a priest forever" (Heb. 7:3).[30] This was the understanding of David himself for, referring to himself, he wrote, "The Lord has sworn and will not change His mind: 'You are a priest forever, in the order of Melchizedek'" (Ps. 110:4).

This extravagant claim finds abundant confirmation and illustration in the accounts of David's reign, particularly in Chronicles. The first attestation appears in connection with the transfer of the Ark into Jerusalem from Kiriath-jearim. Leading the procession is David himself, "clothed in a robe of fine linen, as were all the Levites who were carrying the ark" (1 Chron. 15:27). In fact, above that he wore the linen ephod, a garment reserved to the Aaronic high priest alone (v. 27). Since he was not of Levi but Judah, David could not have worn the habiliments of the Levitical priesthood. Thus his was a priesthood of a different kind (cf. Heb. 7:11-17).[31]

Once David had placed the Ark in the Zion Tabernacle, he sacrificed burnt offerings and peace offerings, rites reserved to the priesthood, and he bestowed on the people a priestly blessing (1 Chron. 16:1-2). Again, only as a priest could even the king qualify to discharge these functions.

That this office of royal priest was transmissible by David is evident in the intercessory ministry of Solomon, his son. After he completed the Temple and it was invested with the glorious presence of the Lord, Solomon offered burnt offerings and

29. Walter C. Kaiser, Jr., *Toward an Old Testament Theology* (Grand Rapids: Zondervan, 1978), pp. 143-64.
30. Dumbrell, *Covenant and Creation*, p. 152.
31. Roland de Vaux, *Social Institutions*, vol. 1 of *Ancient Israel* (New York: McGraw-Hill, 1965), pp. 113-14.

fellowship offerings (2 Chron. 7:7). These were not just offerings sanctioned by him or offered on his behalf, but as his leadership of the religious convocation shows (5:2–7:10) Solomon was himself participating and was doing so in a priestly capacity.

Negative support for the royal priesthood concept appears in the story of Uzziah (2 Chron 26:16-20). Having become powerful, he arrogated to himself priestly prerogatives that lay exclusively in the domain of the Aaronic priests and entered the Temple to burn incense. While in the act he was confronted by the high priest Azariah who chided him for usurping ministry reserved for the Levitical priesthood.[32] "It is not right for you, Uzziah, to burn incense to the Lord," Azariah warned. "That is for the priests, the descendants of Aaron, who have been consecrated to burn incense." The identification of the priests as the descendants of Aaron presupposes another order of priests, that to which Uzziah himself belonged. His sin was not in functioning as a priest but rather in intruding into the domain of the priests of Israel.

Even more remarkable is the chronicler's description of David and his dynasty as sons of God. This bold metaphor is in keeping with the connection between David and Melchizedek as established in Psalm 110, and in fact that psalm of David states explicitly, "The Lord says to my Lord [i.e., David]: 'Sit at my right hand until I make your enemies a footstool for your feet'" (Ps. 110:1).

When this elevated language is viewed in light of another psalm of David (Psalm 2) it is most evident that the priestly king is none other than the Son of God.[33] The relevant lines read, "He said to me, 'You are my son, Today I have become your father. Ask of me, and I will make the nations your inheritance, the ends of the earth your possession'" (Ps. 2:7b-8).

This obviously refers to adoptive sonship, as most scholars agree, but it suits most admirably the One who someday would be the Son of God in human flesh, David's greatest scion. David himself is never described as the son of God in the Old Testament narrative texts, but Solomon is in Chronicles. In discussing with his son the plans for the Temple, David said to Solomon, speaking for the Lord, "He [Solomon] will be my son, and I will be his father" (1 Chron. 22:10). The same statement appears in 1 Chronicles 28:6.

Finally, there may be a hint of divine sonship in the reaction of the people of Israel to David on the occasion of his presentation to them of Solomon to be his successor. The record states that they praised the Lord God of their fathers and then "bowed low and fell prostrate before the Lord and the king" (1 Chron 29:20). This unusual linking of the Lord and the king as subjects of homage suggests more than ordinary kinship between them.[34]

32. Keil, *The Books of the Chronicles*, p. 429.
33. Kaiser, *Toward an Old Testament Theology*, pp. 158-62.
34. Braun points out that the "note of a common obeisance . . . to Yahweh and Solomon is surely striking" (*1 Chronicles*, p. 290), but he fails to follow up on this observation. Obviously it is because the king is seen by the people as Yahweh's representative.

It has already been proposed that the theology of Chronicles focuses on the Davidic monarchy as a theocratic expression of God's sovereign elective and redemptive purposes for His people and ultimately for all nations. This initial programmatic thesis finds abundant confirmation in the role of David and the Davidic dynasty as both priest and son of God. It is certainly of interest that Jesus Christ, offspring and heir of David, is revealed also as royal priest and Son of God (Heb. 5:1-10).

THE COURSE OF THE KINGDOM

Chronicles, like all the books of the Bible, is a theological treatise, but it is one whose form and content is historiographical. It reveals the Person and works of God and the nature of His relationship with His people in narrative terms, in the context of the events of history. This does not diminish its theological value in any sense whatsoever for it is precisely in His involvement with nations and individuals that His elective and redemptive purposes are best demonstrated and understood. The discussion must now be directed therefore to the chronicler's presentation and assessment of sacred history in both its completed and anticipated aspects, that is, to the course of the kingdom in retrospect and in eschatological hope.

THE COURSE OF THE KINGDOM IN HISTORY

Chronicles commences its account of the history of the kingdom at the very beginning with Adam, because its interest is universal and its intention is to demonstrate that the theocratic people Israel are a part of and find their source in the common history of all mankind. This is a theological prerequisite to Israel's ability to perform her dual ministry of mediator and model of God's salvific grace to the world. The theocratic kingdom cannot therefore be divorced from the course of universal human events.

At the same time Israel, the Old Testament expression of the kingdom, is not synonymous with the nations but separate and distinct from them. This is what is meant by her designation "a kingdom of priests and a holy nation." In fact, Israel's history (and that of God's theocratic program even before) is one of constant struggle to survive as the "light of the nations" in a world hostile to it and to its message. The chronicler therefore arranged his material relative to this aspect of this theology in terms of opposition to the kingdom, affirmation of the kingdom, and judgment on the kingdom.

Opposition to the kingdom. From the very beginning of God's program of redemption sinful man has either ignored it or attempted to frustrate it. Chronicles draws attention to this in both overt and subtle ways. Thus, in the pre-Davidic era, in the genealogies themselves, there are reminders that the course of covenant transmission was not a smooth one.

The first example is that of Nimrod, "a mighty warrior on earth" (1 Chron. 1:10). The mere reference to his name evokes the antitheocratic spirit of Babel, for it was Nimrod, according to Genesis 10:8-10, who founded that infamous symbol of covenant resistance. This same rebellion is no doubt hinted at in the reference to Peleg, descendant of Shem, in whose time "the earth was divided" (1 Chron. 1:19; cf. Gen. 10:25). Most scholars associate this division of the earth with the scattering of the nations that followed Yahweh's judgment of the Tower of Babel.[35] The mandate to "be fruitful and increase in number; fill the earth and subdue it" (Gen. 1:28), the prerequisite to man's dominion over all things under God, was in danger of subversion at Babel, but this hostile opposition was overcome.

Further antitheocratic tendencies emerge in the genealogies with the mere listing of Ishmael (1 Chron. 1:28) and Esau (v. 34), for these names speak of the near-disruption of the Abrahamic promises by the impatience of Abraham and Isaac respectively to wait for the Lord to bring His own purposes to pass. These references too presuppose familiarity with the Genesis narratives that provide the background (Gen. 16:1-6; 25:19-26). Most significant is the preoccupation with the Ishmaelite and Esauite (i.e., Edomite) genealogies, for subsequent Old Testament history attests to the bitter opposition to Israel that arose from their descendants, especially Edom.

As for the Davidic monarchy itself, it was threatened by none other than Judah, its tribal source, when he violated his daughter in-law Tamar (Gen. 38:13-30). Nevertheless despite that illicit union, God passed on the theocratic hope through their child Perez, ancestor of David (1 Chron. 2:4-15). That this was not an unencumbered process the chronicler made clear by his brief reference to Achan (2:7), the Judahite who nearly aborted the conquest of Canaan by his greedy appropriation of the spoils of Jericho (cf. Josh. 7:1). Opposition to Yahweh's saving work did not always come from without, then. In fact, as the record shows, it more often came from within the covenant people.

The final illustration of kingdom opposition appears in the account of the very first ruler of Israel, Saul. The story of Samuel's resistance to the choice of Saul is well known (1 Sam. 8:4-22) and should be sufficient to show that his monarchy was in fact a premature, nonsanctioned expression of antitheocratic sentiment. Everywhere it is clear that David was the man after God's own heart (1 Sam. 13:14), and the selection of any other constituted covenant infidelity. The words of divine indictment that summarize the chronicler's version of Saul's reign speak for themselves: "Saul died because he was unfaithful to the Lord; he did not keep the word of the Lord and even consulted a medium for guidance, and did not inquire of the Lord. So the Lord put him to death and turned the kingdom over to David son of Jesse" (1 Chron. 10-:13-14).

The establishment of the true monarchy under David did not bring an end to kingdom opposition. It was, in fact, intensified in many respects both at the hands of external enemies and from within, the very division of the kingdom into two

---

35. Thus with some hesitation Allen P. Ross, *Creation and Blessing* (Grand Rapids: Baker, 1988), p. 243.

parts being the most grievous example. It is impossible (and unnecessary) here to recount the episodes of David's warfare against aggressors, such as the Philistines (1 Chron. 14:13-17; 18:1), Moabites (18:2), Arameans (18:3-11), and Edomites (18:12-13) except to note that "the Lord made all the nations fear him" (14:17). Because the kingdom of David was in fact the kingdom of God, He "gave David victory everywhere he went" (18:6). These successes were tokens of God's favor and signs of His ultimate dominion over the nations.

Even more serious assaults against the theocratic community occurred in the days of the divided monarchy. First was the campaign of Shishak of Egypt, primarily against Judah (2 Chron. 12:2-4). This came as a judgment from Yahweh because of Rehoboam's covenant disobedience. When Judah and the king repented, Yahweh delivered them but allowed them to remain under Shishak's hegemony for a time so that "they may learn the difference between serving me and serving the kings of other lands" (v. 8). This succinctly expresses the essence of what it meant for Israel to be the special people of Yahweh—a people devoted exclusively to Him in servanthood.

•The responsibility this entailed for Israel must be constantly balanced by the overriding conviction that the kingdom is really that of Yahweh, that He created it, rules over it, and comes to its side in times of opposition. King Asa of Judah understood this and when overrun by Zerah, ruler of Cush, he entreated Yahweh to deliver him so that mere man might not prevail over the Lord (2 Chron. 14:9-11). In even more striking language Jehoshaphat, under attack by Moab and Ammon, appealed to Yahweh as the one who rules "over all the kingdoms of the nations" (20:6). His plea found response in the word of the prophet Jahaziel who reminded him that "the battle is not yours, but God's" (v. 15) and that "the Lord will be with you" (v. 17). Opposition to the kingdom was in fact opposition to Yahweh and therefore could have no permanent effect.

As noted above, the most grievous attack on the kingdom purpose of the Lord was not from the wicked nations but from within the body of the chosen people. Thanks largely to the intemperate fiscal policies of Solomon the northern tribes revolted under Jeroboam and against Rehoboam and formed the separate Northern Kingdom of Israel (2 Chron. 10:16-19). This obviously handicapped the mission of the twelve-tribe nation of Israel to be the mediator and model of divine sovereignty, but it left the Davidic Covenant promise in full effect because that promise was centered in Judah and David alone. Thus the chronicler was able to assert that the division of the kingdom was not an unforeseen and irreparable blow to Yahweh's redemptive design, for "this turn of events was [in fact] from God" (v. 15). The distinction between Israel as a whole as the vassal people of Yahweh and the Davidic kingdom as a part of and yet transcending that role was clear even to the rebel Northern tribes, as is evident from their famous "declaration of independence": "What share do we have in David, what part in Jesse's son? To your tents, O Israel! Look after your own house, O David!" (10:16). The Davidic monarchy as the vehicle of Yahweh's saving and sovereign rule on earth did not depend, then, on its connection with all Israel. Most instructive in this regard is Abijah's address to his northern foes: he reminded them that the Lord gave the kingship to David and his descendants forever, and he scolded them because they planned "to resist the kingdom of the Lord, which is in the hands of David's descendants" (2 Chron. 13:4-8).

Affirmations of the kingdom. Opposition to the kingdom cause was matched by Yahweh's consistent expressions of favor. It was His kingdom, after all, and therefore its eventual success was a foregone conclusion.

In a charming little vignette, whose inclusion in the inspired text can hardly be explained otherwise, the chronicler tells of Jabez, a Judahite, who petitioned God to enlarge his territory, a petition that was granted (1 Chron. 4:9-10). As a Judahite and ancestor of David, it seems quite likely that Jabez was a type of David and that his fervent appeal was made in anticipation of God's selection and blessing of the yet unborn house of David.

The description of David's reign is replete with evidence of God's affirmation. Even more so is this the case with Solomon, who was the recipient not only of wisdom and knowledge but of unsurpassed wealth, riches, and honor "such as no king who was before you ever had and none after you will have" (2 Chron. 1:11-12). The fulfillment is attested to in the enormous amount of riches described as a summary to his reign (9:13-21) and especially in the acknowledgement that "King Solomon was greater in riches and wisdom than all the other kings of the earth" (v. 22). Similar sentiments describes the reign of good King Hezekiah (32:27-29).

New Testament theology sees no necessary correlation between physical, material prosperity and godly obedience, and rightly so. Yet the Old Testament makes clear that the covenant uprightness of nation was well as individual will inevitably result in blessing and abundance, whereas the converse is equally true— absence of success is indicative of spiritual and moral failure. Hence Yahweh's affirmations of the kingdom took the form of tangible compensation.

Judgment on the kingdom. The book of Chronicles was written in the postexilic period to explain why the Exile had come to be in the first place and to provide hope that the restored community would be the beginning of a new theocratic kingdom, one able to complete the mission that the preexilic nation had failed to accomplish.[36] It is from that historical perspective, then, that the chronicler deals with the judgment of Yahweh on the two kingdoms and the root causes for their failure.

Once again embedded in a genealogy is a brief narrative that draws attention to itself precisely because of its interruptive character. This concerns the destiny of the Transjordanian tribes of Reuben, Gad, and Manasseh, who "were unfaithful to the God of their fathers and prostituted themselves to the gods of the peoples of the land" (1 Chron. 5:25). This egregious act of covenant violation resulted in the

36. William J. Dumbrell, "The Purpose of the Books on Chronicles," *Journal of the Evangelical Theological Society* 27 (1984): 226.

deportation of the people by the Assyrians, a captivity from the land that continued to the day of the chronicler himself (v. 26).

In an even more startling juxtaposition, the historian noted, following his extensive genealogical lists (1 Chron. 1:1–9:1*a*), that "the people of Judah were taken captive to Babylon because of their unfaithfulness" (9:1*b*). This statement, so out of place at first blush, is followed by a list of the returnees to Jerusalem (9:2-34) and then the genealogy of Saul (vv. 35-44). As Braun notes, however, the message is one of continuity.[37] All Israel came crashing to the ground in the Exile, a disaster attributed directly to covenant failure, but Yahweh, true to His everlasting promises, brought His people back and gave them a new beginning.

Finally, at the very end of his account, the sacred writer summarizes the whole history of his people as one that inexorably led to judgment (2 Chron. 36:15-19). Again and again Yahweh had sent His prophets with words of warning, words that were received with mocking and ridicule. At last the judgment of Babylonian destruction and deportation fell, for "all the leaders of the priests and the people became more and more unfaithful, following all the detestable practices of the nations and defiling the temple of the Lord" (36:14). The word rendered "unfaithful" (*mā'al*) occurs also in 1 Chronicles 5:25 and 9:1 and speaks of an act of treachery, of covenant disloyalty. Chronicles therefore ends on a rather bleak note.

THE COURSE OF THE KINGDOM IN ESCHATOLOGY

Forgiveness and restoration. Despite the note of pessimism sounded by the Exile, there are throughout Chronicles rays of hope, for the God of covenant is reliable—He cannot deny Himself. In his famous prayer of Temple dedication Solomon entreated the Lord that, on the occasion of His people's sin and exile, He might "hear from heaven and forgive the sin of Your people Israel and bring them back to the land You gave to them and their fathers" (2 Chron. 6:24-25). This of course would require repentance, a change of heart, for which the king fervently prayed (6:37-39).

Eternal establishment. The conditions of restoration stated clearly in Solomon's prayer are perhaps implied in Nathan's word from God to David on the occasion of the revelation of the Davidic Covenant, but the emphasis there is on the gracious initiative of the Lord Himself to be faithful to His own covenant word. Thus God said, "I will provide a place for my people Israel and will plant them so that they can have a home of their own and no longer be disturbed" (1 Chron. 17:9). His kingdom, embodied in His people Israel and particularly in the house of David, will be established forever (v. 14). Even after the kingdom was divided it was clearly understood that the sovereignty of Yahweh through His servant David would endure forever (2 Chron. 13:5).

37. Braun, *1 Chronicles,* p. 143.

CONCLUSION

The great theological burden of Chronicles is the assertion that Yahweh, through covenant establishment with the Davidic dynasty, has offered to all peoples a model of His dominion and a means of their participation in it. David, the royal priest and son of God, was chosen both to reign over Israel, "a kingdom of priests and a holy nation," and to typify that messianic sovereign of his descent whose dominion would be forever. Every effort is bent, therefore, to the task of centralizing this integrating theme. The genealogies provide for David by linking him to creation and the patriarchal promises; the campaigns and conquest of the king validate his election to his redemptive role; the establishment of an elaborate cultus witnesses to the priestly nature of that calling; and the promises of historical and eschatological restoration of the nation and its Davidic kingship attest to the permanency of God's saving purposes. The people of the covenant might (and did) fail in Old Testament times, but Yahweh has reserved a day when, as He said, "I will restore David's fallen tent. I will repair its broken places, restore its ruins, and build it as it used to be" (Amos 9:11). This is the message of Chronicles.

5

A THEOLOGY OF EZRA-NEHEMIAH
AND ESTHER

EUGENE H. MERRILL

A THEOLOGY OF EZRA-NEHEMIAH

In its original composition Ezra-Nehemiah was one book, so it is appropriate that a theological analysis deal with it as such.[1] Moreover, as one reads both parts at one sitting he comes to appreciate their common historical and religious setting, their concern with the same issues, and their reflection of identical points of view. These factors are so strong that one is almost compelled to admit not only unity of composition but single authorship or redaction.

Before this can be addressed further, it is important to note that Ezra 1:1-3*a* is an exact repetition of 2 Chronicles 36:22-23, the conclusion of the chronicler's history. Thus a deliberate bridge connects these two books, a link that suggests either that the chronicler was author of both Chronicles and Ezra-Nehemiah or that he added the latter to his own work. It is impossible here to enter the debate concerning sources and the process of composition, but it seems most likely that both Ezra and Nehemiah kept careful records and memoirs and that these were taken *en bloc* or adapted to the books of Chronicles by the anonymous historian conven-

---

1. For an excellent discussion of introductory matters such as unity, authorship, and composition of Ezra-Nehemiah, see Edwin M. Yamauchi, "Ezra-Nehemiah," in *The Expositor's Bible Commentary* (Grand Rapids: Zondervan, 1988), 4:573-79.

tionally designated "the chronicler." Thus Ezra-Nehemiah is a sequel to Chronicles, a narrative picking up where Chronicles left off, thereby carrying the history of the theocracy down to the end of Nehemiah's governship.

This last remark presupposes the chronological priority of Ezra to Nehemiah, a priority that is implied in the canonical structure as it now stands but one that has been criticized by many modern scholars. This debate also is beyond the confines of this study,[2] but the theology of the books is little affected in any event by the chronological sequence. Taking the record at face value (which is the way the tradition intends to be taken), one can assign a date of 458 B.C. for Ezra's arrival in Jerusalem (Ezra 7:1). His appearance in the narrative as late as the time of the arrival of Nehemiah (Neh. 8:1) extends his ministry to at least 444 B.C. As for Nehemiah, his final fixed date is 432 B.C. (Neh. 13:6), so his memoirs must have been completed shortly thereafter. The chronicler's work came to an end by the beginning of the fourth century (i.e., about 400 B.C.), so by then Ezra-Nehemiah had become part of the longer historiographical work.

Regardless of one's view of the authorship of Ezra-Nehemiah and its relationship to Chronicles, the theological viewpoint of the whole collection is essentially the same. The message is addressed to the postexilic community of Jews who wonder if there is any hope of political and religious restoration. Its central thrust is that there indeed is hope but that hope must be incarnated in the rebuilding of the Temple, the cultus, and the priesthood. Only as the remnant people became the theocratic nation, founded on and faithful to the covenant Yahweh made with their fathers, could they revive the Davidic house and anticipate the resumption of their mediatorial role among the nations of the earth.[3] Ezra and Nehemiah are therefore burdened to clarify (1) the Person and works of God, (2) Israel's own identity and function as a covenant people, and (3) the nature of that covenant in postexilic times.

THE PERSON AND ACTIONS OF GOD

God's Person and attributes. Fundamental to Israel's faith is the confession that Yahweh, her God, is one and that He and He alone exists and is to be worshiped (Deut. 6:4-5). Even the Babylonian Exile, which exposed that captive people to the impressive polytheism of Mesopotamia, could not alter the fact that there is only one God. In fact, Cyrus, king of Persia, acknowledged at least the superiority if not exclusivity of Israel's God and in His name allowed the Jews to return to their homeland (Ezra 1:1-4).[4] This uniqueness of Yahweh provided the basis for

2. For the traditional view and responses to the contrary position, see Eugene H. Merrill, *Kingdom of Priests: A History of Old Testament Israel* (Grand Rapids: Baker, 1987), pp. 502-6.

3. William J. Dumbrell, "The Theological Intention of Ezra-Nehemiah," *The Reformed Theological Review* 45 (1986): 65.

4. This obviously does not suggest that Cyrus was a convert to Yahwism; rather, he was manifesting a syncretistic spirit known to be characteristic of Persian religion of the time. See T. Cuyler Young, Jr., *The Cambridge Ancient History*, 2d ed., ed. John Boardman et al. (Cambridge: Cambridge U., 1988), 4:102.

covenant renewal later on when the Levites led the assembly to exclaim, "You alone are the Lord" (Neh. 9:6).

Even more pronounced is the emphasis in Ezra-Nehemiah on the sovereignty of God, a regency inherent in His sole legitimate claim to deity. Again, against the background of rampant polytheism or even the dualism of newly emerging Zoroastrianism it was important to affirm that Yahweh is Lord of all in heaven and on earth. To their enemies the Jews affirmed this when they announced that they were building the second Temple as the "servants of the God of heaven and earth" (Ezra 5:11).

The phrase "God of heaven " is typical of postexilic language. It occurs with reference to Yahweh in the decree of Darius I (Ezra 6:9-10), as well as in that of Artaxerxes I (7:12, 21, 23). Nehemiah, in his famous prayer in the presence of this same Artaxerxes, addressed Yahweh in the same terms. The reason is obvious, for the setting of the accounts is no longer the narrow confines of Palestine and the chosen people but it is international. The miraculous return and restoration of the pitiful exile community against overwhelming odds certified that Israel's God is no parochial deity; rather, He is God of heaven itself.[5]

In more practical and political terms it was evident that Yahweh was sovereign over the political structures of the time. Cyrus acknowledged that his power was derivative for it was Israel's God, he said, who "has given me all the kingdoms of the earth" (Ezra 1:2). Ezra himself realized that Artaxerxes had allowed his return from Babylon and had authorized the refurnishing of the Temple because God had put it in the king's heart to do so (7:27). A similar sentiment was expressed by the joyful congregation who celebrated the great Passover following the completion of the second Temple. The Lord had "changed the attitude of the king" (6:22), thus allowing the project to be brought to finality.

The sovereignty of the Lord also is manifest in the leading of His people in various ways. The return under Cyrus was prompted by the moving of their spirit to do so (Ezra 1:5). Ezra and Nehemiah both refer to the lordship of Yahweh over them by the interesting expression "the hand of the Lord his God was upon him/me" (7:6, 9; 8:18, 22, 31; Neh. 2:8). The hand of God, as is particularly clear in Ezekiel,[6] is a metonymy for His power. Translated into ultimate terms it is a way of referring to divine sovereignty, the control by Yahweh over all facets of life.

True dominion demands that one's foes also comply with its dictates. When Tattenai, governor of Trans-Euphrates, tried to interdict the building of the Temple he failed because "the eye of their God was watching over the elders of the Jews" (Ezra 5:5). More directly, Ezra asserted that he hesitated to seek protection from King

---

5. This seems preferable to the opinion that the epithet, typical of Persian religion, was employed by Ezra-Nehemiah to show openness to other religious views. It seems, to the contrary, to be polemical against those views. For the standard position that this is a statement of accommodation, see F. C. Holmgren, *Ezra & Nehemiah*, International Theological Commentary (Grand Rapids: Eerdmans, 1987), pp. 8-10.

6. Ezekiel 1:3; 3:14, 22; 8:1; etc.

Artaxerxes in his journey to Jerusalem because he had already testified to the king that his God was well able to deal with his foes (8:22). When under great pressure from Sanballat and his co-conspirators, Nehemiah urged his people to keep building the wall for Yahweh their God would deliver them (Neh. 4:14).

In addition to His exclusivity and sovereignty, other attributes of Yahweh receive attention in Ezra-Nehemiah. Nehemiah, in the passage just cited (4:14), described Yahweh as One who is "great and awesome." Pagan Artaxerxes extolled His wisdom as the source of Ezra's ability to make sound decisions (Ezra 7:25). Yahweh was also the righteous One before whom the nation stood impure and condemned (9:15; Neh. 9:33). The chasm occasioned by that righteousness in contrast to the wickedness of rebellious mankind can be redressed, however, by another aspect of the character of God, His grace and mercy. Ezra, in his great priestly intercessory prayer, spoke of the grace of God in preserving a remnant of His people, a remnant that also found favor in the eyes of the king of Persia (Ezra 9:8-9). The words the narrator used here are *hēn* and *hesed* respectively, terms suggestive not just of kindly disposition but also of covenant fidelity.[7] Nehemiah described the mercy of the Lord by the term *raḥămîm* (Neh. 9:27-28, 31), a more anthropopathic way of communicating the emotional side of Yahweh's nature. Yet, since this passage is in the context of a covenant statement, one must be sensitive to the term as a technical one relating, once more, to Yahweh's covenant commitment. In fact, Nehemiah praised God (v. 32) as the one who "keeps his covenant of love" (*habbᵉrîth wᵉhesed*), perhaps better rendered, "keeps His covenant faithfully."[8]

God's works and actions. The Old Testament consistently affirms that God is known not only by (or perhaps not chiefly by) His stated attributes but by His involvement in the affairs of His people. By His work in history He declares who He is. Obviously the act alone cannot communicate unambiguously, so the interpretive word, the proposition, is also mandatory. Therefore Ezra and Nehemiah, like the rest of the canonical witness, speak of God's actions but also give them meaning in the spoken and written word.

From a logical and theological standpoint the first revelatory act of God was creation, an event that receives but scant attention in Ezra-Nehemiah because the focus of the material is on the restoration of the theocratic community, a restoration necessarily predicated on creation but not directly linked to it in postexilic thought. It is precisely when the linkage is needed, namely, in rehearsing covenant history, that Nehemiah grounded God's covenant power and faithfulness in His initial work of creation (Neh. 9:6).[9] This will receive more adequate treatment below.

---

7. F. Charles Fensham, *The Books of Ezra and Nehemiah,* The New International Commentary on the Old Testament (Grand Rapids: Eerdmans, 1982), p. 130.

8. This is close to the rendering of the new Jewish Publication Society translation. See *The Writings: A New Translation of the Holy Scriptures* (Philadelphia: Jewish Publication Society of America, 1982).

9. Joseph Blenkinsopp, *Ezra-Nehemiah: A Commentary* (Philadelphia: Westminster, 1988), p. 303.

Yahweh is also the revealer of His purposes (Ezra 5:1-2), especially through His prophets—purposes that focus particularly on His role as Covenant-maker and Covenant-keeper (Neh. 1:5). Historically this has come to pass as He fought for His people in holy war (4:20; 9:24) and worked on their behalf in achieving His objectives for them (6:16). Occasionally, however, He acted as judge, for as His people transgressed His holy covenant He brought on them its awful sanctions, especially and climactically in the form of deportation and exile (Ezra 5:12; 9:7, 13; Neh. 9:27).

THE PEOPLE OF GOD

The division of Israel into the Northern and Southern kingdoms followed by the permanent exile of the former under the Assyrians left Judah alone as the covenant people of Old Testament times. This was not as devastating to covenant promise and hope as might appear because the Davidic monarchy originated in Judah and continued to exercise rulership there, at least until the fall of Jerusalem to the Babylonians in 586 B.C. This constituted a lethal blow against the viability of the covenant for despite prophetic voices that offered words of comfort and promises of restoration, the fact remained that Jerusalem was conquered, the Temple razed, and the people with their Davidic monarch had been taken captive to far-off Babylon.

A ray of optimism continued to shine forth, however, in the person of Jehoiachin, the last surviving descendant of David to sit as king. Exiled in 598 B.C. as a boy of 18, Jehoiachin continued to live in Babylon until at least 562 B.C. There he was well treated and remained, as long as he lived, a link between the Davidic lineage of the past and the promised resumption of that line in ages to come. The book of 2 Kings closes with reference to Jehoiachin as though to say that the terrible judgment of God on His people did not nullify His commitment to restore the house of David to the royal throne (2 Kings 25:27-30; cf. Jer. 52:31-34).

How long Jehoiachin survived cannot be known, but the decree of Cyrus followed the last reference to him by only a little more than twenty years. The genealogies indicate that Jehoiachin was followed by Shealtiel and he by his nephew Zerubbabel,[10] the principal leader of the first return from Babylon (1 Chron. 3:17-19; cf. Ezra 3:2). Zerubbabel thus furnished tangible, physical evidence that the pledge to restore the Davidic dynasty had found fulfillment though Zerubbabel never actually functioned as king in the Persian province of Judea.

The restoration of the community. What was the theological significance of the restoration as set forth in Ezra-Nehemiah? This first takes the form of extensive genealogical lists (Ezra 2:1-70; 8:1-14; Neh. 7:5-65) whose purpose was at least twofold: (1) to legitimize the returnees by identifying them with their tribal ances-

---

10. For the conflicting data that Zerubbabel was a son of Padaiah (1 Chron. 3:19) and of Shealtiel and a reasonable reconciliation, see D. J. Clines, *Ezra, Nehemiah, Esther*, New Century Bible Commentary (Grand Rapids: Eerdmans, 1984), p. 64.

try, and (2) to demonstrate by that linkage that the Exile, though it had been traumatic and terribly disruptive, had not severed the line of promise that originated in
Abraham and would continue forever. Included in these lists were the lineages of
the priests, Levites, and other religious functionaries (Ezra 2:36-54; 8:1-14; Neh.
7:39-56), for the theocratic kingdom, as a kingdom of priests, was a worshiping people who expressed their vassalage in cultic form.

The genealogies suggested, then, that the very nation that had been so violently
uprooted from the land of promise had returned again. And yet it was not the identical people but their offspring, chastened and greatly reduced in number. Nehemiah
knew well the pledge of the Lord to Moses (Deut. 30:2-4) that even if His disobedient people were exiled to the ends of the earth He would gather them from thence
and bring them to the place inhabited by His Name (Neh. 1:8-10). Nehemiah also
knew, however, that it would be almost like beginning again, for the restored people would be only a remnant (*niš'ārîm*) (v. 3). It is from such humble beginnings that
Ezra too knew the restored community must spring up again (Ezra 9:15).

The doctrine of the remnant is pervasive in the Old Testament.[11] It was a fact
that the people of the Lord would always tend to fall away from Him except for a
small minority, the remnant, who would remain faithful to their covenant responsibilities. In other words there was always an Israel within Israel, the true kernel surrounded by the husk of an external national entity. The saving purposes and promises of Yahweh could not, therefore, find fulfillment in the nation as such but only in
that godly core that He preserved through the ages.

What marked the remnant off from the people at large was its determination
to be a separated people, one whose allegiance was exclusively to the Lord. Against
the backdrop of the Exile, a judgment that had taken place precisely because the
covenant nation had abandoned this principle of exclusivity, it is most evident why
Ezra-Nehemiah gives evidence of such interest in the purity of the postexile remnant. They must come out from among the unbelievers of their age and exhibit in
their own godliness what it means to be a holy nation and a kingdom of priests.

Zerubbabel faced this issue early on when the work of the temple building got
underway. The Samaritans and other adversaries of the returnees tried to join them
in temple construction but the Jewish leaders saw at once that the syncretism
implied in this cooperative effort was blatantly contrary to the covenant spirit.
Thus Zerubbabel replied, "You have no part with us in building a temple to our God"
(Ezra 4:3).

The exclusivity implied in this response is echoed repeatedly in the warnings
of Ezra and Nehemiah to the remnant people to separate themselves from the surrounding populations, especially in the practice of marriage. Ezra heard the complaint that people, priests, and Levites alike had begun to intermarry with their
ungodly neighbors, an abomination that resulted in the mingling of the holy race with

---

11. Gerhard Hasel, *The Remnant: The History and Theology of the Remnant Idea from Genesis to
Isaiah,* Andrews University Monographs, 5 (Berrien Springs, Mich.: Andrews U., 1975).

those around them (Ezra 9:2). Like their ancestors centuries before them, they entered the land of promise only to take up the evil practices of its Canaanite inhabitants (vv. 11-12).

Ezra was so incensed by this breakdown of the lines of demarcation that he commanded wholesale divorce where mixed marriages were concerned (Ezra 10). Some years later Nehemiah took up the cause. He enjoined those who had separated themselves from their pagan neighbors to renew their covenant vows to Yahweh (Neh. 9:2) and to refrain from such intermarriage thenceforth (10:28).

Of special concern to Nehemiah was the problem of Jewish marriages to the women of Ashdod, Ammon, and Moab. He compared those alliances to the ones of Solomon that had eventually spelled the demise of the united monarchy (13:23-27). This was particularly offensive to him because the Mosaic law specifically forbade Ammonites or Moabites from entering the assembly of Israel (Deut. 23:3-5),[12] a prohibition that clearly was undermined by mixed marriages. When this was understood by the Jews involved, they quickly removed the mixed multitude from their midst though Nehemiah apparently did not go so far as Ezra in demanding a termination of the already established marriages (Neh. 13:1-3).

The final expression of community restoration was the rebuilding of the physical structures of the city and nation. This was necessary not only for practical reasons of housing and community resources but also as a symbol of continuity with the past and confidence in the future. Immediately on their return, then, the people under Zerubbabel and Joshua commenced their building projects, in particular the Temple of the Lord (Ezra 3:8-13). Slowly the work progressed under these leaders and others, including Ezra and Nehemiah, until it was finished and stood as a monument to the faithfulness of Yahweh to His people.

The restoration of worship. The remnant people were more than just an ethnic or national entity—they were the vassal people of Yahweh elected and redeemed by Him to serve Him as a light to the nations. As such, they must both model His sovereign and saving purposes and mediate them to the world. This is in line with the central thrust of the Mosaic Covenant that Israel must take up the challenge to be a kingdom of priests and a holy nation (Ex. 19:4-6).

The clearest demonstration of the theocratic character of the community was its faithful commitment and to and practice of the terms of the covenant, a practice inextricably connected to the national worship system with its holy places, holy persons, holy actions, and holy times.[13] It was Israel in worship that best modeled the dominion of Yahweh over all aspects of human life. Just as the destruction of the Temple and its ministries signaled the true beginning of the Exile, so its rebuilding and the renewal of its ministries would make the reestablishment of God's

---

12. For the rationale, see Peter C. Craigie, *The Book of Deuteronomy,* The New International Commentary on the Old Testament (Grand Rapids: Eerdmans, 1976), pp. 297-98.

13. F. C. Fensham, "Some Theological and Religious Aspects in Ezra and Nehemiah," *Journal of Northwest Semitic Languages* 11 (1983) : 64-66.

people to their redemptive role. The community without worship could serve no effective function.

Not surprisingly then the first event of Judah's postexilic life was the celebration of the Feast of Tabernacles, a celebration that obviously preceded the rebuilding of the Temple itself (Ezra 3:1-7). How fitting that the Feast of Tabernacles, which commemorated God's provision for His people in the Sinai wilderness, should now be the occasion of rejoicing in His care during the seventy years of their Babylonian exilic wilderness. Sixteen years later, the Temple having been completed, the people again celebrated Yahweh's gracious provision in a massive service of dedication followed at the turn of the year by the great Passover observance (6:16-22).

It was the Temple, however, that provided the central focus of the community's life and witness. Early in the second year of the return Zerubbabel, eager to restore God's house to that crucial role, guided the people to the laying of its foundations (Ezra 3:8-13). As meager as it appeared to be in the eyes of those who had seen the magnificence of the Temple of Solomon, it nevertheless sufficed to show that Yahweh once more was pleased to live among His people. After sixteen years of interruption, the work proceeded again, thanks to the prophetic inspiration and encouragement of Haggai and Zechariah (5:1-2). The Persian kings also lent their support (6:12, 14-15) until at last the Temple was finished in 515 B.C.

Though the Temple was the very dwelling place of God, Jerusalem, its site, was the city of God. Its reconstruction was also necessary in order for the full expression of Yahweh's regnal purposes on the earth to be realized. Thus Temple and city were joined (Ezra 4:24), so much so that it was possible to speak of them interchangeably (7:15-17, 19). Nehemiah sensed the need not only to rebuild the city but to be sure it was adequately repopulated. Describing it as "the holy city," he sought volunteers to move into it so that it might have the size and splendor requisite to the capital of the theocratic kingdom (Neh. 11:1-2).

Worship required holy times, sacred seasons, along with temples and services. Though Ezra-Nehemiah is sparing in its description of these as well as other details of actual cultic performance, there are references to the Feast of Tabernacles and the Passover as has been noted (Ezra 3:4; cf. Neh. 8:13-18; Ezra 6:19). Nehemiah also makes reference to Rosh ha-Shanah, or New Year's Day (Neh. 8:2), though its significance as such was not emphasized until postbiblical times.

Ezra-Nehemiah certainly does not go into detail concerning public worship that was so important to the chronicler, though one should not therefore conclude that the cult was not important to the postexilic community. What is more likely is that such details need not be repeated in a work that the chronicler might have had a hand in shaping. There is, however, the lingering impression gained from both Ezra-Nehemiah and the postexilic prophets that the restored Temple and its worship was but a dim shadow of what it had been in Israel's glorious past. Moreover, their message seems to be that the postexilic stage of Israel's life was only an anticipation of something much more wonderful to come. As Haggai put it, clearly looking to the distant (to him) future, "I will fill this house with glory" (Hag. 2:7).[14]

Opposition to the kingdom. The history of God's kingdom on the earth, no matter at what time and in what form, is a history of struggle and conflict because its establishment is at the cost of subduing the hostile elements arrayed against it. The Exile itself, though a judgment of the Lord, was at the hands of wicked Babylon, a perennial foe of the theocratic program. But the end of the Exile did not usher in the end of kingdom conflict, for the postexilic community, in its efforts at restoration, continued to face obdurate, unrelenting counteraction.

As soon as the exiles returned home and commenced the Temple construction their enemies sought to frustrate their work, first by illicit collaboration (Ezra 4:1-2) and then by overt resistance (vv. 4-6). When Nehemiah came on the scene ninety years later to rebuild the walls of Jerusalem, the antagonism was still there. Accusing the Jews of treason against the Persian king, Sanballat and his colleagues first ridiculed the efforts of God's people (Neh. 2:19). Then they became angry when they saw the work was still going on (4:1-3), and they decided the only recourse was military intervention, a strategy that was overcome by the prayers and watchfulness of Nehemiah and his associates (vv. 8-9). Thus the work was completed and Yahweh triumphed through His obedient servants. The theological message is most apparent. Jerusalem, the focal point of God's habitation and saving work on the earth, is a symbol or perhaps even a microcosm of His kingdom. As such, it is the home of God's people but also the object of the attack of antitheocratic forces that try to obliterate it from the earth. But Jerusalem, like the eternal kingdom of God itself, cannot fall forever. From the ashes of human history it will arise like a phoenix, restored to pristine purity as the eternal dwelling place of the Lord and all His royal subjects.

History of the covenant. Without any doubt the most theologically traumatic event of the history of the theocratic people was the destruction of Jerusalem and the Temple and the deportation of the covenant people to far-off Babylon. It was not the physical displacement that was so tragic, however, but the apparent disruption of the covenant that had bound God and His people together for nearly a millennium. What would happen now? Was the Lord through with Israel? Was there any prospect that the ancient promises could be renewed and the exiled nation restored?

Many of the preexilic prophets had anticipated this calamity and had already gone on record as extending hope to those who, in bondage, would seek the Lord's forgiveness and thus be reinstated as the servant nation. Now that the return from captivity had taken place the postexilic prophets added their words of confirmation and, indeed, looked to even more glorious days ahead. God's people had egre-

---

14. Ralph L. Smith, *Micah–Malachi,* vol. 32 in Word Biblical Commentary (Waco, Tex.: Word, 1984), pp. 157-58.

giously broken their covenant vows, to be sure, but the commitment to the fathers had been unequivocally eternal. There would never lack a royal nation or a Davidic ruler to provide it leadership. Israel would fail again and again but the Lord would have the last word. His covenant obligations to His people were as certain as His very Name and reputation.

With this in mind, Nehemiah led his people in one of the most well-documented and significant ceremonies of covenant renewal in all the Old Testament (Neh. 8-10).[15] Its centrality in his book shows beyond question that the covenant relationship was very much intact. All that was needed was for the people to repent and to reaffirm their allegiance to the covenant's provisions and demands. Then and only then could they pick up the mantle of theocratic privilege that had marked them from Sinai onward as God's special priestly nation.

The renewal account begins with a history of the covenant relationship from the beginning (Neh. 9:5-35). In standard treaty form the Initiator of the covenant, Yahweh, God of Israel, is introduced as the only God, the Creator and Preserver of heaven and earth (vv. 5-6). Next follows the historical prologue, a lengthy recitation of God's dealings with His people from the time of Abraham to the present hour (vv. 7-35). The father of the nation had been elected and then, having been found faithful, became the recipient of covenant promises concerning land and seed (vv. 7-8). Then ensued the sojourn in Egypt and the miraculous deliverance of Israel through the Red Sea, an act of redemption that resulted in the gracious covenant provisions at Sinai (vv. 9-15).

Since that time, however, no matter the goodness of the Lord, Israel had sinned. This was true in the wilderness (Neh. 9:16-21), the Transjordan (v. 22), and in Canaan itself (vv. 23-25). They rejected the admonitions of the judges (vv. 26-29) and gave no heed to the prophets (vv. 30-35). The Lord therefore had brought judgment over and over again but did not totally destroy His people because He was "gracious and merciful," that is, true to His unconditional, eternal promise (vv. 31-32).

Judah as a servant people. Now that the Exile was over and the community restored, the covenant remnant once more had come to place itself before the Great King as a servant people (Neh. 9:36). This was the essence of what it meant to be in covenant with Yahweh. In fact, the sovereign-vassal character of the Mosaic Covenant led to the inescapable conclusion that Israel's exclusive role was that of servant.

The returnees long before Nehemiah understood this clearly, for when they were interrogated by the Trans-Euphratean governor Tattenai as to their motives in building the second Temple they had justified it by declaring, "We are the servants of the God of heaven and earth" (Ezra 5:11). Nehemiah identified himself as the servant of Yahweh but also described his people Israel in those terms (Neh.

15. Dennis J. McCarthy, "Covenant and Law in Chronicles-Nehemiah," *Catholic Biblical Quarterly* 44 (1982) : 34.

1:6). In language reminiscent of the Exodus and the Sinaitic Covenant, he went on to speak of the remnant nation as "your servants and your people, whom you redeemed by your great strength and your mighty hand" (1:10). The continuing force of the covenant relationship is crystal clear from these statements.

Covenant violation. As already noted, the history of God's covenant dealing with His people was punctuated by their constant disobedience to its requirements. Unfortunately even the destruction of Jerusalem and deportation to Babylon had not cured this addictive propensity, for Ezra and Nehemiah both had to deal with covenant violation in their respective postexilic situations. When informed about the Jews' intermarriage with the neighboring peoples, Ezra saw this as just one more example of Israel's infidelity. With bitter lament he remembered the history of his people's unfaithfulness (Ezra 9:6-7) and then confessed to the Lord, "We have disregarded the commands you gave through your servants the prophets" (v. 10), just as their fathers had done. Though He had graciously left a remnant before, the Lord might not do so again, Ezra concluded (v. 14).

The response was as he had hoped, for Shecaniah spoke on behalf of the people and said, "We have been unfaithful to our God by marrying foreign women from the peoples around us" (Ezra 10:2). That this is perceived as the epitome of covenant violation is apparent from Shecaniah's appeal to the people that they make a covenant with Yahweh to dissolve the illegitimate marriages and restore the purity of the community (v. 3).

Even more specifically covenantal in its tone is Nehemiah's language in his first prayer. Addressing Yahweh as "the great and awesome God, who keeps His covenant of love with those who love Him and obey His commands" (Neh. 1:5), Nehemiah confessed for his people that they had not obeyed the "commands, decrees and laws" He had given Moses (v. 7). The technical terms employed here speak clearly of covenant violation in a formal sense.[16]

On his return to Jerusalem after a twelve-year absence, Nehemiah was confronted with at least two glaring examples of covenant disobedience by the people—Sabbath-breaking and intermarriage. The first of these he identified as one of the principal causes of the destruction of Jerusalem itself, for the Sabbath was the very sign of the Sinaitic Covenant (Neh. 13:15-18; cf. Ex. 31:12-17). Intermarriage with pagans testified to complete breakdown of the separation demanded of the covenant people, so it too was especially odious to the Lord. When Nehemiah returned to Jerusalem, he found that not only had the general population married among the neighboring peoples (Neh. 13:23-27) but even the son of the high priest himself had done so. This act of special sacrilege Nehemiah described as a defiling of the priestly office and of "the covenant of the priesthood and of the Levites" (v. 29).

Covenant violation, then, was not something limited to Israel's distant past. It continued on into exilic and postexilic times and had to be addressed over and over by the prophets and other theocratic spokesmen such as Ezra and Nehemiah. The only

16. Fensham, *The Books of Ezra and Nehemiah,* p. 155.

remedy was renewal, both personal and corporate. Until the covenant foundations were rediscovered and their principles reappropriated, Israel's role as kingdom model and mediator remained constantly in jeopardy.

Covenant renewal. Though no ceremony of covenant renewal as such occurs in Ezra, renewal is suggested in Ezra's condemnation of mixed marriages and the steps that needed to be taken to make things right again (Ezra 10:11-17).[17] He first insisted on confession and then urged the guilty to do God's will (v. 11). Specifically this called them to separate themselves from the peoples around them and from their foreign wives. This reached the heart of the covenant relationship, the notion that Israel was a holy people elected and commissioned to be God's own possession. As such she must be pure from all entangling alliances, serving only Yahweh and representing His dominion on the earth.

Covenant renewal under Nehemiah has already received some attention. Now it is important to look at some if its technical aspects. It is introduced by the reading of Torah by Ezra at the beginning of the great autumn festivals (Neh. 8:2). Then Nehemiah and Ezra proclaimed that the occasion was a holy one, one in which the people were to celebrate the Feast of Tabernacles in commemoration of Yahweh's provision for their ancestors in the wilderness (vv. 13-18). Finally, on the twenty-fourth day of the seventh month, two days after the Tabernacles festival,[18] the assembly, separated "from all foreigners" (9:2), stood and confessed their sins before the Lord. At this point the Levites officiated in the ceremony of covenant renewal.

The various elements just observed—Torah, Tabernacles, and confession— clearly set the stage for what followed. The sovereignty and exclusivity of Yahweh were affirmed (Neh. 9:6), the history of His covenant relationship with Israel was recited (vv. 7-35), and the confession that the present assembled community is the servant of Yahweh was gladly confessed (vv. 36-37). The whole occasion ended with a covenant commitment in these remarkable words of the assembly: "In view of all this, we are making a binding agreement, putting it in writing, and our leaders, our Levites and our priests are affixing their seals to it" (v. 38). In the great tradition of reformation and revival in the past, Israel's postexilic community thus bound itself once more to the pledge to be the covenant people of Yahweh.

CONCLUSION ON EZRA-NEHEMIAH

The books of Ezra and Nehemiah reflect some of the bleakest and most difficult days of Israel's long Old Testament history. Though the Exile was over and a remnant people was in process of rebuilding the superstructures of national life, the prospects for success paled in comparison to the halcyon days of the past when

---

17. McCarthy, "Covenant and Law," pp. 32-33.

18. For a helpful discussion of the problems of a joyous festival being followed by this (otherwise unattested) day of penitence, see Clines, *Ezra, Nehemiah, Esther*, p. 189.

the Davidic kingdom dominated the entire eastern Mediterranean world. What was needed was a word of encouragement, a message of hope in the God who had once blessed His people above all nations of the earth and who had promised to do so again.

But this word of hope was conditioned on the willingness of the community to reestablish the covenant foundations on which they had been built and to take seriously the mandate to be a kingdom of priests and a holy nation. The great theological theme of the books lies, then, precisely in this nexus between the ancient promises of Yahweh and the present and future expectations of His chosen people. The postexilic community was small but its God is great. Reliance on such a God will assure a future more glorious than anything in the days gone by.

A THEOLOGY OF ESTHER

On the basis of Hebrew style, Persian vocabulary, and an apparently firsthand acquaintance with the life and times of mid-fifth-century Persia, it seems quite clear that the book of Esther, in its Masoretic version at least, is to be dated no later than the end of the fifth century B.C.[19] Its authorship is unknown, but whoever wrote or compiled it possessed information quite in keeping with whatever historical records exist from Persian and classical sources. There is no reason, then, to view Esther as fiction, a historical romance, or something other than an account of actual events.[20]

Such matters in any case have little to do with the central theological message of the book, for Esther, like all other historical texts of the Bible, exists in order to reveal something about God, His people, and His purposes for them and the world. That the writing reflects a genuine involvement of God in documentable events of human history simply enhances the theological significance. Were Esther shown to be only an apocryphal creation (which is emphatically not the case), its revelatory value would not in any sense be diminished.

THE PERSON AND ACTIONS OF GOD

The book of Esther shares with the Song of Solomon the distinction of being the only Old Testament book that fails to mention God by name. This omission, in fact, was the occasion for much discussion as to Esther's canonicity. Such an arbitrary criterion, however, betrays enormous insensitivity to the presence of God in the book, a presence without which the book cannot be explained. In short, absence of the divine name only serves to emphasize the transcendent quality of God's self-revelation. That things happen as they do testifies to His sovereign control over all matters of life and death. The eye of faith can see providence at work even

19. E. J. Young, *An Introduction to the Old Testament* (Grand Rapids: Eerdmans, 1958), p. 375.
20. J. Stafford Wright, "The Historicity of the Book of Esther," in *New Perspectives on the Old Testament,* ed. J. Barton Payne (Waco, Tex.: Word, 1970), pp. 37-47; and William H. Shea, "Esther and History," *Concordia Journal* 13 (1987) : 234-48.

(or especially) when normal channels of divine self-disclosure are absent. In Esther the Lord is manifested especially in His sovereignty, His demand for exclusive allegiance and homage, and His deliverance of His chosen people.

Esther herself, in almost fatalistic terms, informed Mordecai that she was about to appear before King Xerxes on behalf of her people. Not knowing the outcome, she committed herself to the Lord with the words "if I perish, I perish" (Esther 4:16). Her life, she clearly understood, was in God's hands and things would turn out according to His purposes for her and her people.

The sovereignty of God naturally entails His incomparability and His insistence that He be given exclusive recognition as Lord. Again the reference is veiled, but when Mordecai stubbornly refused to prostrate himself before Haman, the highest of the royal officials, one may conclude that it was not out of sheer recalcitrance but because of his monotheistic faith that Mordecai stood his ground (Esther 3:2). He would not kneel down and honor (the Hebrew word suggests an act of worship) a mere man, nor would he tremble in fear before him (3:5), because to do so would render homage to a godless system, one antithetical to the dominion of his God.[21]

It is commonly recognized that a major motif of Esther is that of reversal.[22] The social and political structures of this world, epitomized in this case of Persia, seek to destroy God's people, but these efforts are overcome as He intervenes and reverses the course of events. Deliverance thus becomes the hallmark of God's presence in history, an attestation to His sovereignty and power.

When Mordecai appealed to Esther to use her good offices as queen to save her people, he knew full well that she might refuse. But this turn of events could not frustrate or preclude the survival of the Jews for, as Mordecai so confidently expressed it, "If you remain silent at this time, relief and deliverance for the Jews will arise from another place" (Esther 4:14). That place, of course, was God Himself.

Even Zeresh, wife of Haman, knew this, for she counseled her husband that resistance to Mordecai was futile since, as a Jew, he could not be withstood (Esther 6:13). This fear of the Jews (cf. 8:17; 9:2) can be explained only by the fact that their enemies acknowledged that there was a supernatural hedge about them, a God who intervened on their behalf and who could enable them to prevail no matter the odds against them.

THE KINGDOM OF GOD

The theology of the Old Testament finds focus in great measure in the nation Israel, the covenant people of Yahweh, whom He elected, redeemed, and commissioned to serve Him among the nations of the earth. As a kingdom of priests and

---

21. Carey A. Moore, *Esther,* The Anchor Bible, vol. 7B (Garden City, N.Y.: Doubleday, 1971), pp. 36-37. Moore suggests that Mordecai refused to bow to Haman because of Haman's Amalekite ancestry.

22. So Clines, *Ezra, Nehemiah, Esther,* p. 269.

a holy nation (Ex. 19:46), it was Israel's task to model the dominion of God over His creation and to mediate His saving grace to fallen and alienated humanity (Gen. 1:26-28; 12:1-3). This role found historical expression most forcefully in the glorious Davidic monarchy with its eternal covenant provisions (1 Chron. 17:1-15). The Exile, however, had effectively brought that monarchy to an end, especially for the exiles like Mordecai and his cousin Esther, who remained in the Diaspora. Even the Jews who returned to Jerusalem under Sheshbazzar, Zerubbabel, Ezra, and Nehemiah found only a truncated version of the earlier kingdom glory. The issue of Israel as the servant people was as much concern to them as to the Jewish community scattered across the Persian Empire.

The feeling of despair regarding the covenant hope was only exacerbated by the sense of awe the Jewish exiles felt as they witnessed the magnificence of human achievement all around them. The book of Esther unabashedly marvels at the glory of Persia and her remarkable king Xerxes (Esther 1:4-6). He demonstrated the kind of sovereignty that characterized the reigns of David and Solomon in the distant past and that should be reserved for the dominion of the Lord alone. Thus Xerxes issued commands and decrees that kept the fate of friend and foe alike in the grasp of his hand (1:8, 19; 3:9, 12; 4:11; 9:14; 10:1-2).

Such sheer power had the capacity for either enormous good or incalculable evil. As an extension of fallen humanity it was inherently antitheocratic and therefore naturally in opposition to the Jewish community over which it held sway. Mordecai certainly was aware of this animus and for this reason he disguised his own identity as a Jew and counseled Esther to do so as well (Esther 3:4; cf. 2:10, 20). Ironically, however, it was the disclosure of Mordecai's ethnic affiliation that precipitated an overt and concerted effort to destroy the Jews (Esther 3:6). Having persuaded Xerxes that the peculiar, "stand-offish" ways of the Jews constituted a threat to the unity of his realm, Haman advised him to undertake a thorough pogrom against them (3:9-11).

Nowhere is the hand of God more apparent in the story than in the reversal of this whole chain of events, for the very king who set it in motion inexplicably (from the human vantage point) counteracted it. The way it came about is a marvelous example of human cooperation with divine initiative, for it was through an ordinary man and his cousin that the saving power of God on behalf of a whole nation found expression.

Even before Xerxes took Esther as his wife he was advised to replace Vashti, his queen at the time, with "someone else who is better than she" (Esther 1:19). In this way Xerxes' attitude toward his future consort, and thus the Jewish people, is favorably inclined. When at last Esther appeared before the king, she "pleased him and won his favor" (2:9, 17), a reaction shared by the entire royal court (v. 15).

Mordecai too rose quickly in the ranks and in the esteem of the king. Having uncovered a plot against the king, Mordecai disclosed it and as a result received honor and reward, ironically enough from the hand of his arch-enemy Haman (Esther 6:10-11). To add insult to injury, Mordecai then took over the office (8:1-2) and estate of Haman (v. 7) after that villain's execution. This was only the beginning of his rise to power, because before long Mordecai's reputation spread throughout the extent of the empire (9:3-4). The book of Esther ends with the epitaph that "Mordecai the Jew was second in rank to King Xerxes, preeminent among the Jews, because he worked for the good of his people and spoke up for the welfare of all the Jews" (10:3).

One might cynically conclude that it was sheer human genius, or even duplicity, that brought Mordecai to such a glorious position, but the theology of the book of Esther will not allow that interpretation. It was God and God alone who worked, secretly to be sure, through human agency on behalf of His kingdom program. This explains the ability of the Jews to protect themselves (Esther 8:11) even to the extent of turning the tables (9:1) and doing as they pleased to those who hated them (v. 5).

THE COVENANT OF GOD

Israel's identity and role in Old Testament times is tied into her covenant relationship with Yahweh and in fact is totally incomprehensible apart from that relationship. This is so evident throughout the Old Testament as a whole that many scholars view covenant as the single most important strand of Old Testament theology.[23] While this undoubtedly is an overstatement, it is nevertheless true that most of the books of the Old Testament emphasize covenant to some degree so that when a composition such as the book of Esther ignores covenant and the complex of technical terms that accompany it one finds himself seeking explanation.

What must be kept in mind is that Esther concerns the Jewish community of the Diaspora and not the restored nation of Judea. This distinction is important because the covenant was made not with a heterogeneous and scattered people but with the nation gathered and worshiping as a corporate entity. The Temple and Jerusalem were still at the center of the theocratic program, and it was there and there only that Yahweh promised to meet with His covenant people as a collective expression of His kingdom on earth. Covenant, therefore, was crucially important in the theology of Ezra-Nehemiah but of only marginal interest in Esther.

This should not suggest, however, that there are no overtones of covenant in Esther for, as has been suggested, Israel in whatever form—gathered or scattered—understands itself and indeed exists only in reference to covenant. Fundamental to her character as a covenant people was Israel's separation from all other peoples, her distinctiveness as God's special servant among the nations. Haman recognized this aspect of Israel's life when he referred to the Jews as "a certain people dispersed and scattered among the peoples . . . who keep themselves separate" (Esther 3:8).

The reason for the separation, of course, was that Israel might exhibit a puri-

---

23. For several examples see Gerhard F. Hasel, *Old Testament Theology: Basic Issues in the Current Debate* (Grand Rapids: Eerdmans, 1982), p. 138, n. 107.

ty of life that modeled the kingdom of God on earth and that would attract the nations to the redemptive grace of God who desires all men to be reconciled to Him. A remarkable statement attesting to the success of that mission by scattered Israel appears in Esther 8:17 where the narrator relates that following the reversal of the fortunes of the Jews "many people of other nationalities became Jews because fear of the Jews had seized them" (cf. 9:27). Although one should not overpress the matter, it is a fact that fear is sometimes an epithet for Yahweh so that Yahweh used his people here as a means of bringing other people to Himself.[24]

On a more individual level, Mordecai served a mediatorial role when he disclosed an assassination plot against King Xerxes (Esther 2:21-23; 6:2-3), a role that ingratiated him with the king and led to the blessing of his people. Esther even more epitomized the intercession God expected His servant nation to undertake. When Mordecai first learned of the edict of annihilation that doomed the Jewish community, he implored his cousin Esther to go before the king and to plead with him for her people (4:8). It may be, he said, "that you have come to royal position for such a time as this" (v. 14). Subsequent events reveal just how successful she was as she stood between her people and those forces that threatened to eradicate them. Mordecai and Esther thus demonstrated in their own faithfulness as mediators something of the task assigned to their nation as intercessor between a holy and just God and all the peoples of the earth.

CONCLUSION ON ESTHER

Though nameless and working behind the scenes, Yahweh is very much the central character of the book of Esther, for only the presence and power of deity can account for the radical reversal of circumstances that form the central plot of the book. The Jewish people, scattered in exile, remained His servant nation, called and commissioned to serve Him in the work of universal redemption. Because of their disobedience and the unrelenting hostility of the world against them their very existence was placed in jeopardy over and over again. The lovely story of Esther provides the great theological truth that the purposes of God cannot be stymied because He is forever loyal to His covenant with His eternally elected nation.

---

24. See Isaiah 8:12-13 and Psalm 76:11 (Heb. v. 1). Thus H. Ringgren, as cited by Moore, *Esther*, p. 82.

6

A THEOLOGY OF THE WISDOM BOOKS AND THE SONG OF SONGS

ROY B. ZUCK

INTRODUCTION

Job, Proverbs, and Ecclesiastes are commonly referred to as the wisdom books of the Bible. This is because of the frequent occurrence of the words "wisdom" (*ḥokmāh*) and "wise" (*ḥākām*) in these books, and because of their topics related to the subject of wisdom or wise living. The Song of Songs,[1] not always considered part of the Bible's wisdom literature, may be included in the wisdom corpus because its authorship, like that of Ecclesiastes and much of Proverbs (see Prov. 1:1; 10:1; cf. 25:1),[2] is ascribed to Solomon, because Solomon is mentioned

---

1. "Song of Songs," the title in the *New International Version,* follows the Hebrew *šîr haššîrîm* in verse 1. Other versions, such as the King James Bible and the *New American Standard Version,* have "Song of Solomon," based on the last two of the four Hebrew words in verse one, *'ăšer lišlōmōh* ("which is Solomon's").
2. Of course some portions of Proverbs were composed by Agur (chap. 30), Lemuel (31:1-9), and anonymous "wise men" (22:17–24:34; see 22:17 and 24:23).

ROY B. ZUCK, Th.M., Th.D., is vice-president for academic affairs, academic dean, and professor of Bible exposition at Dallas Theological Seminary.

six times in the book (Song of Songs 1:5; 3:7, 9, 11; 8:11-12),[3] and because it addresses how to live wisely in one's courtship and marriage.

The order of the books in many Hebrew Bibles is Job, Proverbs, Ruth, Song of Songs, Ecclesiastes. The order in the Vulgate is Job, Psalms, Proverbs, Ecclesiastes, and Song of Songs. Perhaps the Vulgate considered these three books a Solomonic collection, following a loose chronological order—Job (in patriarchal times), Psalms (mostly written by David), and Proverbs, Ecclesiastes, and Song of Songs (composed largely by David's son Solomon).

Some scholars also attribute the authorship of the book of Job to Solomon,[4] arguing that this justifies its inclusion in the wisdom corpus. However, the authorship of Job is much debated. Several factors suggest that the book may have been written centuries earlier.[5] Its inclusion in the Bible's wisdom literature is to be based not on its supposed Solomonic authorship, but on its wrestling with the perplexities of life—a factor that also explains why Ecclesiastes is called a wisdom book, even though it repeatedly challenges the value of wisdom (Eccles. 2:13-16; 7:11-12, 19; 9:1-2, 11-12, 16; 10:1).

Some psalms include wisdom themes and are called "wisdom psalms." These include at least Psalms 1, 19, 32, 34, 37, 49, 73, 78, 112, 119, 127, 128, and 133.[6] Bullock suggests that certain themes in these psalms show why the psalms are considered wisdom psalms. These themes include retributive justice (Pss. 37, 49, 73), the rewarding of righteousness (Pss. 1, 112, 127, 128, 133, 144:12-15), and the emphasis on the law of the Lord as the basis for instruction for life (Pss. 1, 19, 119).[7] Also Psalm 49 has a number of parallels to statements in Ecclesiastes.

The Bible's wisdom books are to be distinguished from the poetic books. The latter are more inclusive, embracing the book of Psalms, which is entirely poetry, but which, as already stated, only occasionally deals with wisdom themes. Large portions of the prophetic books are written in poetic style, as the format of the *New International Version* makes clear. As Hubbard suggests, wisdom literature was "a literary genre common in the ancient Near East in which instructions for successful living are given or the perplexities of human existence are contemplated."[8] The

3. Audet suggested that the book was included with the wisdom books because it was "adopted" by the "wise men" who appreciated its teaching on marital fidelity (J.-P. Audet, "Le sens du Cantique des Cantiques," *Revue Biblique* 62 [1955]: 197-221, esp. 202-3).

4. For example Gregory of Nazianzus; Martin Luther; Hugo Grotius (1583-1645); and F. Delitzsch, *Biblical Commentary on the Book of Job* (Grand Rapids: Eerdmans, 1949), p 20-26. Andersen suggests that it was written in the time of Solomon, (Francis I. Andersen, *Job: An Introduction and Commentary* [Downers Grove, Ill.: InterVarsity, 1976], p. 63).

5. See Albert Barnes, *The Book of Job* (Glasgow: Blackie & Son, 1847), pp. xxv-xxvi; and Roy B. Zuck, *Job* (Chicago: Moody, 1978), pp. 8-11.

6. Scholars differ on the number of wisdom psalms. Others include Psalms 25, 31, 39, 40, 50, 62, 78, 90, 91, 92, 104, 105, 106, and 111 because all or parts of these psalms seem to reflect at least some wisdom influence.

7. C. Hassell Bullock, *An Introduction to the Old Testament Poetic Books* (Chicago: Moody, 1979), p. 26.

8. *The New Bible Dictionary*, s.v. "Wisdom Literature," by David A. Hubbard, p. 1334.

instructions are given in pithy sayings, as in Proverbs, and in speculative wisdom books (Job and Ecclesiastes). According to Crenshaw, wisdom literature consists of a marriage of a certain form ("proverbial sentence or instruction, debate, intellectual reflection") and content ("instructions about mastering life," "gropings after life's secrets with regard to innocent suffering, grappling with finitude, and quest for truth concealed in the created order").[9]

The wisdom books have universal appeal, dealing as they do with topics of concern and relevance to people everywhere and in all eras of history. Proverbs deals with issues of daily life, including relationships and standards of proper conduct. The Song of Songs addresses one of these areas, namely, marital love and fidelity. Job and Ecclesiastes speak more to the ultimate meaning of human experience.

Job faces the problem of the existence of evil and suffering; Proverbs discusses how to have a successful existence; and Ecclesiastes probes the problem of a meaningful existence. The questions these books probe are these: How is man to satisfy his conscience and his thirst for God? (Job). How is a man to make a success of life? (Proverbs). How can he make his existence bearable? (Ecclesiastes).[10] "Proverbs seems to say, 'Here are the rules for life; try them and see they will work.' Job and Ecclesiastes say, 'We did, and they don't.'"[11]

The subjects dealt with in these books are amazingly broad in scope, intriguingly profound in depth, and unusually practical in nature.

THE MEANING OF WISDOM

Ḥokmāh. In the Old Testament the noun *ḥokmāh* ("wisdom") and its related forms (the adjective *ḥākām,* "wise"; the verb *ḥākam,* "to be wise"; and the abstract plural noun *ḥokmôt,* "wisdom") are used frequently in the Old Testament, and are especially prominent in Job, Proverbs, and Ecclesiastes. According to Whybray, the root *ḥkm* is found in these three wisdom books 189 times out of the 346 occurrences in the Old Testament (including the 22 Aramaic occurrences of *ḥokmᵉtā'* and *ḥakkîm*).[12] This frequency—more than half (54.6 percent)—explains why these books are designated "wisdom literature."

In books other than the wisdom books, "wisdom" refers to skills in relation to the working of crafts, the giving of advice or shrewd counsel, the managing of people or tasks, or intellectual acumen. Tailors who made garments for Aaron (Ex. 28:3), and Tabernacle workers—including metalworkers, stonecutters, wood-

9. James L. Crenshaw, *Old Testament Wisdom: An Introduction* (Atlanta: John Knox, 1981), p. 19.

10. R. B. Y. Scott, "The Study of the Wisdom Literature," *Interpretation* 24 (1970): 20.

11. David A Hubbard, "The Wisdom Movement and Israel's Covenant Faith," *Tyndale Bulletin* (1966): 66.

12. R. N. Whybray, *The Intellectual Tradition in the Old Testament* (New York: Walter de Gruyter, 1974), p. 75, n. 20. Louis Goldberg, however, states that the verb *ḥākam* and its derivatives occur 312 times, excluding the Aramaic forms (*Theological Wordbook of the Old Testament,* ed. R. Laird Harris, Gleason L. Archer, Jr., and Bruce K. Waltke, 2 vols. [Chicago: Moody, 1980], 1:284).

carvers, embroiderers, weavers, and designers (35:30–36:2), and women who spun yarn and linen (35:25-26)—all had wisdom for their tasks. "Skilled" in Exodus 28:3 and "skill" in 35:35 translate the Hebrew *hokmat-lēb*, "wise of heart or skillful of heart." "Skilled" in 36:1-2 renders the similar *hăkam-lēb*.

Huram of Tyre, hired by Solomon to work on the Temple, was a skilled craftsman (possessing *hokmāh*) in bronze (1 Kings 7:13-14). The various artisans and craftsmen for the Temple were likewise skilled (1 Chron. 22:15; 2 Chron. 2:7, 13-14).

Workmen who made idols (Isa. 40:20; Jer. 10:9) were also said to be wise because of their skilled craftsmanship. Sailors of Phoenicia were "skilled men" (Ezek. 27:8). Seamen in a storm at sea "were at their wits' end" (Ps. 107:27, literally, "all their wisdom [*hokmāh*] was swallowed up"). Their usual skill in piloting ships was useless in the distress of the disastrous storm. Women skillful (*hăkāmôt*) in mourning were hired to wail in times of desolation (Jer. 9:17).

Hokmāh referred not only to ability or skill in craftsmanship but also to skill in advising and/or administering. Elders of the tribes (Deut. 1:13, 15), Joseph and Daniel in their high administrative posts (Gen. 41:33-39; Dan. 5:11, 29), Joshua (Deut. 34:9), and King Solomon (1 Kings 3:12, 28; 5:7, 12; 10:23-24) were all men of wisdom, with the responsibility to exercise justice, make correct decisions, and provide leadership. Also the king of Tyre possessed wisdom (Ezek. 28:4-5, 17; the NIV translates *hokmôt* "wisdom" in v. 4 and "skill" in v. 5).

Hokmāh sometimes suggested shrewdness or craftiness, as in the counsel given by Jonadab (2 Sam. 13:3), a woman of Tekoa (14:2), and a woman of Abel Beth Maacah (20:14-16).

Egypt had her wise men in Joseph's day (Gen. 41:8) and in Moses' time (Ex. 7:11), and Babylon had wise men in Daniel's day (Dan. 2:12-14, 18, 24, 48; 4:6, 18; 5:7-8, 15). These men in the king's court were associated with sorcerers and diviners, men who had learned the skills of interpreting dreams and using occultic powers. Pharaoh also had his wise counselors in later times (Isa 19:11). *Hokmâ* is also used of intellectual acumen as in Solomon's composing of proverbs and songs, and teaching of botanical and zoological subjects (1 Kings 4:29-34). Intelligence in Joseph was recognized by Pharaoh (Gen. 41:33, 39).

These occurrences of *hokmāh* outside the wisdom books speak of the "practical art of being skillful and successful in life,"[13] of "superior intelligence which knows how to achieve success."[14] As will be discussed later in this chapter, this expertise in practical concerns of life constitutes an essential element in wisdom in Job, Proverbs, and Ecclesiastes.

Synonyms of hokmāh. Additional indications of the meaning of wisdom can be seen by examining the synonyms of *hokmāh*, words that point to shades

---

13. William Dyrness, *Themes in Old Testament Theology* (Downers Grove, Ill.: InterVarsity, 1979), p. 189.

14. Whybray, *The Intellectual Tradition in the Old Testament,* p. 10.

of thought close in meaning to that of *ḥokmāh*.

Bînāh, "understanding," occurs twenty-two times in the wisdom books (eight in Job and fourteen in Proverbs) and fifteen times elsewhere. The adjective *nābôn*, "intelligent or discerning," occurs nine times in Proverbs, once in Ecclesiastes, and eleven times in other books. In most of its occurrences (eighteen of twenty-one) *nābôn* is used parallel to or in close association with *ḥokmāh*[15] For example, Joseph was a "discerning" (*nābôn*) and "wise" (*ḥākām*) man (Gen. 41:33, 39). The idea of intelligence is clearly seen in David, who was literally "intelligent [*nābôn*] of speech" (1 Sam. 16:18).

Of its forty-two occurrences, *tebûnāh*, "understanding or insight," is used twenty-three times in the wisdom books, four in Job, and nineteen in Proverbs). Like *ḥokmāh*, *tebûnāh* is sometimes used of manual skills; they occur together in Exodus 31:3; 35:31; 36:1; and 1 Kings 7:14. In the three Exodus references the NIV renders *tebûnāh* "ability," a close parallel to *ḥokmāh*, "skill." In seventeen of its forty-two occurrences *tebûnāh* is used in parallel to or in close association with *ḥokmāh*.

Of the ninety occurrences of *da'at*, the common word for "knowledge" (from *yāda'* "to know"), fifty-nine are in the wisdom literature: eleven in Job, forty in Proverbs, and eight in Ecclesiastes.

Proverbs 1:2-7 uses several of these words (*ḥokmāh* in vv. 2, 7; *bînâh* in v. 2; *da'at* in vv. 4, 7; and *ḥākām* and *nābôn* in v. 5). Other synonyms in the passage are *musār*, "discipline" (vv. 2-3, 7); *'sākēl*, "prudence" (v. 3); *'ormāh*, "shrewdness" (v. 4); *mᵉzimmāh*, "discretion or wise planning" (v. 4); and *taḥbūlôṯ*, "guidance" (lit. "steerings," like the tackle for directing a ship, (v. 5). This rich vocabulary for wisdom—skill, understanding, discernment, insight, knowledge, discipline, prudence, shrewdness, planning, guidance—points to the practical nature of Old Testament wisdom. It is utilitarian, not theoretical. It promotes guidance through the labyrinth of life's experiences.

Definition of wisdom. Scholars have long struggled with how to define wisdom in view of its variegated uses. Von Rad's classical definition is that wisdom is "the essence of what man needs for a proper life" and the "practical knowledge of the laws of life and of the world, based on experience."[16] As early as 1933 Fichtner spoke of wisdom as man's search for a mastery of life, a search that was then handed down orally and in writing in the form of admonitions.[17] Schmid related this concept of mastery to the Egyptian idea of *ma'at*, "justice," "truth," "order." As man lives in harmony with *ma'at*, he helps maintain this divine order in the world, and

---

15. Ibid., p. 138.

16. Gerhard von Rad, *Old Testament Theology*, 2 vols. (New York: Harper & Row, 1967), 1:418.

17. J. Fichtner, *Die alt orientalische Weisheit in ihrer israelitisch-jüdischen Ausprägung*, BZAW 62 (Giessen: Alfred Töpelmann, 1933), pp. 12-13.

18. Hans H. Schmid, *Wesen und Geschichte der Weisheit*, BZAW 101 (Berlin: Alfred Töpelmann, 1966), p. 156.

he finds order in his own life.[18] Von Rad acknowledged the existence of order in the universe, but did not base it on the Egyptian concept of *ma'at*. He wrote, "Wisdom thus consisted in knowing that at the bottom of things an order is at work, silently and often in a scarcely noticeable way, making for a balance of events. One has, however, to be able to wait for it, and also be capable of seeing it."[19] Von Rad also wrote that the goal of pursuing wisdom is to "wrest from the chaos of events some semblance of order in which man is not continually at the mercy of the incalculable."[20]

Crenshaw states that by discovering this order hidden in the universe, the wise can "secure their existence by acting in harmony with the universal order that sustained the universe."[21] Proper conduct strengthens the order, whereas improper conduct threatens it. Wisdom then is "man's search for specific ways to assume well-being . . . in daily existence."[22] In wisdom, man maintains a "proper attitude toward reality, a world view."[23] Crenshaw also suggests that wisdom is "the quest for self-understanding in terms of relationships with things, people, and the Creator."[24]

Whybray rejects the notion that wisdom is a search after order for the purpose of mastering life. Wisdom, he says, is "a set of ideas, or an attitude to life."[25] It is intelligence, enabling individuals to cope with life. Murphy also disagrees that biblical wisdom is the search for order in human life.[26] He suggests that it would be "better to speak of man's imposing an order (however provisory) upon the chaotic experience of life," for wisdom's sayings convey "a respect for the complexity of what is, rather than a search for a (hidden) order."[27] In other words, as Bergant states it, Murphy's point is that in biblical wisdom man does not search *for* order in human life; he seeks to *put* order in human life.[28] However, can man place order in his life without first searching for and observing what contributes to order?

The idea that wisdom is a search for creation's order so as to master life is summarized by Kenworthy as "the ability to cope."[29] Others go beyond the sense of

19. Von Rad, *Old Testament Theology,* 1:428.
20. Gerhard von Rad, *Wisdom in Israel* (Nashville: Abingdon, 1972), p. 308.
21. Crenshaw, *Old Testament Wisdom: An Introduction,* p. 66.
22. Ibid., p. 24.
23. Ibid., p. 17.
24. James L. Crenshaw, *Studies in Ancient Israelite Wisdom* (New York: KTAV, 1976), p. 484.
25. Whybray, *The Intellectual Tradition in the Old Testament,* pp. 72-73.
26. Roland E. Murphy, "Wisdom Theses," in *The Papin Festschrift: Wisdom and Knowledge* ed. Joseph Armenti (Philadelphia: Villanova U., 1976), 2:197. Cf. Roland E. Murphy, "Wisdom— Theses and Hypotheses," in *Israelite Wisdom: Theological and Literary Essays in Honor of Samuel T. Terrien,* ed. John G. Gammie et al. (New York: Union Theological Seminary, 1978), pp. 35-36.
27. Murphy, "Wisdom Theses," pp. 197-98.
28. Diane Bergant, *What Are They Saying about Wisdom Literature?* (New York: Paulist, 1984), p. 15.
29. Alexander W. Kenworthy, "The Nature and Authority of Old Testament Wisdom Family Ethics: With Special Reference to Proverbs and Sirach" (Ph.D. diss., University of Melbourne, 1974).

merely coping, to the more positive idea of succeeding. To Hubbard, wisdom is "the art of being successful,"[30] and Cazelles writes that it is "the art of succeeding in human life."[31]

Certainly the uses of *ḥokmāh* in relation to skills would suggest that biblical wisdom includes the art of being skillful and successful in one's relationships and responsibilities in life.[32] Wisdom, according to Paterson, is "capacity; to be wise is to possess the requisite capacity for a particular task.[33] Skill or proficiency leads to success, success in the sense of accomplishment or ease of operation or conduct.

An individual is "successful" as he directs his life in accord with God's divine design, His plans for the world. Seeing God's moral order, sensing from divine revelation what God desires and has planned for mankind, one is then challenged by the wisdom literature to conduct his life in line with those principles established by the Creator. To the extent an individual follows these principles or rules of God's order or pattern for life, to that extent he is able to cope with realities, and to enjoy inner order and harmony. Neglecting God's order leads to disorder and chaos; heeding God's design results in satisfaction and peace.

Source of wisdom. Proverbs encourages man to pursue wisdom. He is to listen for it (Prov. 1:33; 2:2), acquire it (4:6-7), love it (4:6; 8:17), esteem or value it (4:8), and seek it (8:17).

Where is this wisdom to be found? Asking this question twice (Job 28:12, 20), Job answered that God alone knows (v. 23). Wisdom belongs to God, Job had said earlier (12:13). His wisdom is profound (9:4). He possessed wisdom in the beginning (Prov. 8:22), He created the earth in wisdom (3:19), and He counts the clouds in His wisdom (Job 38:37). Therefore wisdom is more than a humanly contrived trait. It is a divine enabling, an ability to cope and succeed, based on God's provisions. Only He has "endowed the heart with wisdom" (v. 36).

This divine source of wisdom means that life is not to be dichotomized into the intellectual and the practical, the religious and the secular. "The whole of life was thus connoted in terms of religious experience, and wisdom was held to be relevant at all points of existence."[34] Wisdom literature deals with ethical conduct, conduct seen in light of man's relationship to God. Life takes on a spiritual dimension, for godliness is the key to practical living. A person's relationship to others—his family, neighbors, employees, strangers—is affected by his relationship to His Creator and Lord. The person with biblical wisdom has more than secular, intellectual

30. *The New Bible Dictionary,* s.v. "Wisdom," by David A. Hubbard, p. 1333.
31. Henri Cazelles, "Bible, sagesse, science," *Religious Studies Review* 48 (1960): 42.
32. Although "skill" includes superior intellectual ability (Whybray, *The Intellectual Tradition in the Old Testament,* p. 11), it seems to go beyond it in meaning to embrace the idea of proficiency in various functions in life.
33. John Paterson, *The Book That Is Alive* (New York: Scribner's, 1954), pp. 50-51.
34. R. K. Harrison, *Introduction to the Old Testament* (Grand Rapids: Eerdmans, 1969), p. 1008.

insight; he has a spiritual perspective that pervades all his life. The truly wise person is the godly person.

THE PLACE OF WISDOM

How do the wisdom books relate to the rest of the Old Testament? They seemingly differ so significantly in content and style from the Law and the Prophets that many Bible students have pondered what place wisdom literature has in the Hebrew canon. Since the wisdom books focus more on universal and individualistic than national (Israelite) concerns and are more reflective than prophetic, they seem at first glance to be out of place. Themes such as God's covenant relationship to Israel, the Exodus, and the prophets' messages to Israel and surrounding nations regarding judgment and repentance are missing from the wisdom books. In view of this observation Zimmerli wrote that "wisdom has no relation to the history between God and Israel."[35]

Therefore Wright wrote in 1952 that "the proper place to treat the Wisdom literature is something of a problem,"[36] for there seems to be no room in the general stream of Old Testament theology for a wisdom emphasis.[37] Gese[38] in 1958 and later Preuss[39] in 1970 both felt wisdom literature was foreign to Old Testament thought.

Can that view be substantiated? Is there no way to view the wisdom books as an integral part of the Old Testament? Is there some focus or "center" in Old Testament theology that can embrace the wisdom literature? Can the wisdom books be viewed as essential to the Old Testament revelation rather than optional or contradictory? Is there nothing that ties Job, Proverbs, and Ecclesiastes with the Law and the Prophets?

Wisdom and the fear of the Lord. The fear of the Lord is hereby suggested as a unifying principle in Old Testament theology, "as one of the formal connectors between the wisdom writers and the theology of the *tora* and prophets."[40] "The fear of the Lord" is central to the wisdom literature, occurring as it does fourteen times in Proverbs, and also occurring several times in Job. This "fear" (*yir'at*) of

---

35. Walther Zimmerli, "The Place and Limit of Wisdom in the Framework of Old Testament Theology," *Scottish Journal of Theology* 17 (1964): 147.

36. G. Ernest Wright, *God Who Acts* (London: SCM, 1952), p. 115.

37. Ibid., pp. 103-4.

38. Hartmut Gese, *Lehre und Wirklichkeit in der alten Weisheit* (Tübingen: J. C. B. Mohr, 1958), p. 2.

39. H. D. Preuss, "Erwägungen zum thelogischer Ort altestamentlicher Weisheitsliteratur," *Evangelische Theologie* 30 (1970): 412-17.

40. Walter C. Kaiser, Jr., "Integrating Wisdom Theology into Old Testament Theology: Ecclesiastes 3:10-15," in *A Tribute to Gleason Archer,* ed. Walter C. Kaiser, Jr., and Ronald F. Youngblood (Chicago: Moody, 1986), p. 199. Also see Henri Blocher, "The Fear of the Lord as the 'Principle' of Wisdom," *Tyndale Bulletin* 28 (1977): 3-28.

Yahweh is the "beginning" (*rē' šît*) of knowledge (Prov. 1:7), and the "beginning" (*tᵉhillat*) of wisdom (9:10; Pss. 111:10). Besides being the starting point or inception of wisdom,[41] the fear of the Lord is also "the first and controlling principle."[42] or "essence and heart"[43] of wisdom.

Proverbs also refers to "the fear of the Lord" in 1:29; 2:5; 8:13; 9:10; 10:27; 14:27; 15:16, 33; 16:6; 19:23; 22:4; and 23:17. The command to fear the Lord occurs in 3:7 and 24:21, and four times the verbal form "fears the Lord" occurs (14:2, 16, 26; 31:30). Job 28:28 equates the fear of the Lord with wisdom, and several times the verbal form is used ("feared God," 1:1; "fears God," v. 8; 2:3, "fear God," 1:9; "fear him," 23:15; "revere him," 37:24) and related nominal phrases ("the fear of the Almighty," 6:14; "fear of his splendor," 31:23).

Ecclesiastes uses the noun *yir'āh* and the verb *yārē'* six times ("revere him" 3:14; "stand in awe of God," 5:7 [Heb., 5:6]; "fears God," 7:18; "are reverent before God," 8:12; "fear God," 8:13; and "fear God," 12:13). The conclusion or summation (*sôp̱*) of the discussions in Ecclesiastes is that man should fear God. Fearing the Lord is thus seen to be prominent in the wisdom literature,[44] and several times fearing the Lord is associated with wisdom (Job 28:20; Prov. 1:7, 29; 2:5; 8:13; 15:33).

To fear God means to acknowledge His superiority over man, to recognize His deity and thus respond in awe, humility, worship, love, trust, and obedience.[45] The fear of God, "properly understood, was no mere 'attitude,' [it] involved the full range of humanity's response to the deity."[46] Such response to God results in wisdom, in wise, skillful living.

Is the theme of the fear of the Lord limited to wisdom literature? Indeed not! The subject of fearing God reverberates throughout the Old Testament, starting with the patriarch Abraham. Having obeyed God's directive to sacrifice his son

41. Walter C. Kaiser, Jr., "Wisdom Theology and the Centre of Old Testament Theology," *Evangelical Quarterly* 50 (1978): 138.

42. Derek Kidner, *The Proverbs: An Introduction and Commentary*, Tyndale Old Testament Commentaries (Downers Grove, Ill.: InterVarsity, 1964), p. 59. Interestingly Proverbs 4:7 also uses *rē' šît* in reference to wisdom. The NIV renders the words *rē' šît ḥokmāh*, "Wisdom is supreme," and the NKJV has, "Wisdom is the principal thing."

43. Kaiser, "Wisdom Theology and the Centre of Old Testament Theology," p. 138.

44. The book of Psalms also refers frequently to fearing the Lord (Pss. 15:4; 22:23, 25; 25:12, 14; 31:19; 33:8, 18; 34:7, 9, 11; 36:1; 55:19; 61:5; 66:16; 67:7; 76:7, 11-12; 89:7; 90:11; 96:4; 102:15; 103:11, 13, 17; 111:5; 112:1; 115:11, 13; 118:4; 119:38, 74, 79, 120; 128:1, 4; 130:4; 135:20; 145:19; 147:11), and four times the phrase "the fear of the Lord" occurs in the Psalms (19:9; 34:11; 36:1; 111:10).

45. R. N. Whybray, *Wisdom in Proverbs* (London: SCM, 1965), p. 96. Dubarle points out that humility is a basic component in the fear of the Lord, an awareness of the sense of distance between the Creator and the creature, of God's transcendence and man's finitude (A. M. Dubarle, *Les Sages d'Israel* [Paris: Cerf, 1946], p. 45). This is seen in Job 28:28; 37:24; Proverbs 15:33; 22:4; Ecclesiastes 3:14; and 12:13.

46. Michael L. Barré, "'Fear of God' and the World View of Wisdom," *Biblical Theology Bulletin* 11 (1981): 43.

Isaac, Abraham heard God's words of approval, "Now I know that you fear God" (Gen. 22:12). Job, who may have lived in the time of the patriarchs, feared God (Job 1:1, 8-9; 2:3).

Joseph told his brothers, "I fear God" (Gen. 42:18). The Hebrew midwives feared God (Ex. 1:17, 21) more than they feared Pharaoh. The Israelites, seeing God's great power in delivering them across the Red Sea on dry ground and in destroying the Egyptian soldiers, "feared the Lord and put their trust in him" (14:31). One of the qualifications of leaders to whom Moses delegated responsibility for handling disputes was that they be "men who fear God" (18:21). After God gave Moses the Ten Commandments, He said that fearing Him would keep His followers from sinning (20:20). Five instructions in Leviticus against taking advantage of others are coupled with the command to "fear your God" (Lev. 19:14, 32; 25:17, 36, 43).

In Deuteronomy the Lord through Moses repeatedly challenged the people to fear Him (4:10; 5:29; 6:2, 13, 24; 8:6; 10:12, 20; 13:4; 14:23; 17:19; 28:58; 31:12-13). The Israelites were also responsible for communicating to their children this response to the Lord (4:10; 5:29; 6:2; 31:12-13). Fearing God was frequently associated with obeying the commands of the law (5:29; 6:2, 24; 8:6; 13:4; 17:19; 28:58; 31:12-13) or with serving Him (6:13; 10:12, 20) or loving Him (10:12).

References to fearing the Lord appear in connection with major events in Israel's history: soon after the crossing of the Jordan River and entering the Promised Land (Josh. 2:24), in Joshua's farewell address in the renewal of the covenant at Shechem (24:14), in Samuel's farewell speech to the nation (1 Sam. 12:14, 24), in Solomon's prayer of dedication for the Temple (1 Kings 8:40, 43; 2 Chron. 6:31, 33), in the reigns of several kings (Jehoshaphat, 2 Chron. 17:10; 20:29; Uzziah, 2 Chron. 26:1-5; Hezekiah, Jer. 26:19), and in the postexilic community (Neh. 1:11; 5:9).

Several prophets spoke of fearing the Lord (Isa. 50:10; Jer. 5:22, 24; 10:7; Hag. 1:12; Mal. 3:16). Isaiah said the Messiah delights in the fear of the Lord (Isa. 11:2). Four prophets spoke of people from various nations fearing the Lord in the Millennium (Isa. 25:3; 33:6; 59:19; Jer. 32:39-40; Mic. 7:17; Mal. 4:2). Interestingly, Micah associated fearing God with wisdom: "To fear your name is wisdom" (Mic. 6:9).

The fear of the Lord, then, is a dominant concept not only in wisdom literature but also throughout the Old Testament. It served to link these segments of the Old Testament that otherwise may seem disparate.

Wisdom and the law. Rather than seeing wisdom as distant from the Torah, we should view it as closely aligned with it. Obeying the law is an evidence of wisdom. "The statutes of the Lord are trustworthy, making wise the simple" (Ps. 19:7). "Whoever is wise, let him heed these things" (107:43). Moses told the people, "Observe them [God's decrees and laws] carefully, for this will show your wisdom and understanding" (Deut. 4:6).

At least five of the Ten Commandments are addressed in the wisdom literature. For example, the truth of the fifth commandment, "Honor your father and your mother" (Ex. 20:12), is addressed in negative and positive ways in verses such as Proverbs 15:20; 19:26; 20:20; 23:22; 28:24; 30:11, 17. The act of murder (the sixth commandment, Ex. 20:13) is mentioned in Job 24:14 and Proverbs 28:17. The consequences of adultery, which is forbidden by the seventh commandment (Ex. 20:14), are frequently mentioned (Job 24:15; 31:1, 1; Prov. 2:16-19; 5:3-6, 20:23; 6:23-29, 32-35; 7:1-27; 22:14; 23:27; 30:20). Theft (the eighth commandment, Ex. 20:15) is mentioned in Job 24:14 and 16 as a sinful act. Giving false testimony against a neighbor (ninth commandment, Ex. 20:16) is denounced in Proverbs (6:19; 12:17; 14:5, 25; 19:5, 9, 28; 21:28; 25:18).

Accepting bribes is prohibited in the law (Ex. 23:8; Deut. 16:19; 27:25) and is also viewed as sin in the wisdom books (Job 15:34; 36:18; Prov. 15:27; 17:8, 23; 29:4). Exercising justice, a standard in the Torah (Ex. 23:2, 6; Lev. 19:15; Deut. 16:19-20; 24:17; 27:19), is a subject mentioned frequently in the wisdom literature (Job 29:14; 31:13; Prov. 8:20; 17:23; 18:5; 19:28; 21:15; 24:23-25; 28:5; 29:4, 7, 26; Eccles. 3:16; 4:1; 5:8; 8:9). Kindness to the poor, admonished in Deuteronomy 15:11; 24:14, is addressed in Job 24:4, 14; 29:16; 31:19; Proverbs 14:21, 31; 19:17; and 31:9, 20.

Ecclesiastes 12:13 clearly related the principle of wisdom—fearing the Lord—to the law: "Fear God and keep His commandments." Thus there can be no question that many themes in the Torah find further elaboration in the wisdom books, thus demonstrating that the latter hold an essential and unified place in the Old Testament canon.

Wisdom and creation theology. Wisdom literature is also linked to the rest of the Old Testament canon by its emphasis on creation. As Zimmerli suggested in his classical, often-quoted sentence, "Wisdom thinks resolutely within the framework of a theology of creation."[47] This relationship is seen in a number of ways. First, wisdom, as discussed earlier, is involved in man's search for order (or regularity and purpose[48]) in the natural realm and in human experience. Successfully coping with reality (i.e., being wise) involves (1) seeing the design God has put into the created realm and (2) living in accord with that design. Many proverbs, for example, are based on observations of the multiple phenomena in nature and the complexities of human experience. Those proverbs thus enunciate general truths based on those observations. Noting the patterns in God's creation made the formulation of proverbs possible.[49]

Second, the world was brought into existence by God's wisdom. "By wisdom

47. Zimmerli, "The Place and Limit of Wisdom in the Framework of Old Testament Theology," p. 148. This article originally appeared as "Ort und Grenze der Weisheit im Rahmen der alttestamentichen Theologie," *Gottes Offenbarung* (Munich: Kaiser, 1963):302.

48. Hans-Jürgen Hermisson, "Observations on the Creation Theology in Wisdom," in *Israelite Wisdom*, p. 44.

49. Leslie J. Hoppe, "Biblical Wisdom: A Theology of Creation," *Listening* 14 (1979): 20.

the Lord laid the earth's foundation, by understanding he set the heavens in place; by his knowledge the deeps were divided, and the clouds let drop the dew" (Prov. 3:19-20). (Compare Ps. 104:24, "How many are your works, O Lord! In wisdom you made them all; the earth is full of your creatures.") In Proverbs 8 wisdom is personified as being with God at the time of creation. "I [wisdom] was there when he set the heavens in place" (Prov. 8:27). Verses 27-29 refer to five aspects of God's created work that were accompanied by the presence of wisdom. Wisdom is then pictured as cavorting with God, "rejoicing always in his presence, rejoicing in his whole world" (vv. 30-31).

When God established the wind, the waters, the rain, and thunderstorms (Job 28:25-26), He "looked at wisdom and appraised it; he confirmed it and tested it" (v. 27). When Job spoke of God's wonders in the created universe (9:5-10), he introduced the subject by affirming, "His wisdom is profound" (v. 4). God told Job that He, not man, by His wisdom counts the clouds (38:37), and gives hawks instinct to fly southward (39:26).

Third, in wisdom literature man expresses appreciation for the beauty of and variation in the created world. Lessons from animate and inanimate nature abound in the wisdom books. As Solomon wrote, God "has made everything beautiful in its time" (Eccles. 3:11). Praise for God's creative work stems from an awareness of nature all around man.

Fourth, order in creation buttresses belief in divine justice.[50] As Creator, God sees all He made and all man does and has "created the universe in such a way that sin is punished [and] virtue rewarded,"[51] even though this exercise of justice may be delayed or seemingly perverted. Job struggled with God's seeming injustice toward him, and Solomon in Ecclesiastes was disturbed by the many injustices he observed in life. And yet neither Job nor Solomon cursed God or abandoned Him.

Fifth, creation's order prompts man to recognize his inadequacies and limitations. He, along with nature, is created. Therefore he is incapable of grasping all God has done and planned, and he cannot fully understand the ways of the infinite Creator. In spite of observed harmony in the universe, much remains unpredictable and incomprehensible. Job said to God, "He performs wonders that cannot be fathomed" (Job 9:10). Zophar asked, "Can you fathom the mysteries of God?" (11:7). After hearing God's speeches, in which He spoke extensively about nature, Job responded, "I spoke of things I did not understand, things too wonderful for me to know" (42:3). Solomon wrote that man "cannot fathom what God has done from beginning to end" (Eccles. 3:11).

This fact of man's limitations does not contradict the concept of order, for as Bergant explains, "wisdom does not enable one to transcend the ambiguous, but to deal with it appropriately. Neither contingency nor ambiguity need undermine a ver-

---

50. *The Interpreter's Dictionary of the Bible,* s.v. "Wisdom in the OT," by James L. Crenshaw, 4:956.

51. Ibid.

satile theory of order. . . . There is indeed a cosmic order but the human mind cannot grasp all of its ramifications."[52]

Sixth, though man is seen in creation theology as a created being—one who can observe order, can question and wrestle with apparent contradictions in that order, and must admit to his finiteness and limitations—he is also seen as one who is challenged to revere, love, obey, and trust the Lord, who in His sovereignty works all things according to His purposes (Job 42:2; Prov. 16:4; Eccles. 3:14-15).

Seventh, wisdom literature views God's creative work as providing for man's enjoyment. Work, pleasure, relaxation, and joy are part of God's design for man.[53] The righteous, though part of the finite, creaturely world, can experience joy as part of God's design in creation (Job 33:26, 28; Prov. 5:18; 10:1, 28; 11:10; 12:20; 13:2; 15:20, 23, 30; 21:15; 23:16, 24-25; 27:9; 27:11; 29:2-3; Eccles. 3:22; 5:19; 8:15; 9:9; 11:8-9; Song of Sol. 1:4; 3:11). As Hoppe observes, "Even Qoheleth's skepticism does not end in bitterness or resignation. He calls upon his readers to act in spite of life's uncertainties (Qo 11:1-6)."[54]

Wisdom literature, then, relates inexorably to the doctrine of creation. And in this linkage, wisdom literature stands as an integral part of Old Testament theology. Without the wisdom books, the biblical canon would be woefully impoverished.

A THEOLOGY OF JOB

GOD

The book of Job deals essentially with man's relationship with God, centering on two questions. The first question is, Why does man worship God? Satan suggested the motive behind Job's worship was self-focused aggrandizement (Job 1:9-11). This issue strikes at the very heart of the man-to-God relationship. Satan's point was that God has no way of inducing man to worship Him except to bribe him, to pay him in return for his devotion. If that were true, then worship is adulterated; it is no longer man's willful adoration of God. Self-serving worship is no worship at all.

The second question is, How will man react to God when God seems unconcerned about his problems? Job, the exemplar of underserved suffering, demonstrates both right and wrong responses to God in times of adversity. Job questioned God, longing for an explanation of his painful experience. And yet he did not curse God as Satan had twice predicted (1:11; 3:4). Job's attitude was at first commendable. "May the name of the Lord be praised" (1:21), and, "Shall we accept good from God, and not accept trouble?" (2:10). Immediately after both attacks by Satan, Job "did

---

52. Bergant, *What Are They Saying about Wisdom Literature?* p. 17.
53. Kaiser, "Integrating Wisdom Theology into Old Testament Theology: Ecclesiastes 3:10-15," in *A Tribute to Gleason Archer,* pp. 202-3.
54. Hoppe, "Biblical Wisdom: A Theology of Creation."

not sin" (1:22; 2;10). Later, however, his attitude toward God became abrasive and sinful. He accused God of constantly gawking at him (7:17, 19; 13:27), oppressing and terrorizing him (9:33; 10:3; 13:21, 25; 16:7-14; 19:8-11; 23:14-16; 30:18-19, 21-22), considering Job His enemy (13:24; 19:11-12), hiding from him (13:24), being unjust (19:6-7; 27:2), and ignoring him (30:20). Because Job developed a bitter attitude toward God, He confronted him with his inadequacies and ignorance in light of God's sovereign power and wisdom. Job then acknowledged that his sin had led him to an attitude of pride, and he repented of his ways (42:1-6). Unmerited pain, while not understood, can be accepted as from God's hand, the book of Job indicates. Job's experience demonstrates that when a believer faces the mystery of unexplained and undeserved misery, he ought not shake his fist in God's face, for God may have other purposes in the suffering that are not immediately apparent.

Job's three friends, however, asserted repeatedly that his suffering could be explained in only one way—as punishment for wrongdoing. By adhering so firmly to this concept, they unknowingly were limiting God's ways. They were truncating His sovereignty, suggesting that He could use suffering for only one purpose, namely, discipline for sin. For this reason they each suggested that Job repent (5:8; 8:5; 11:13-14; 22:21-24). Job insisted, however, that he was innocent of any known sin (6:24; 9:21; 10:7; 13:18-19; 16:17; 23:11-12). The subject of man's relationship to God—in worship, submission, and repentance—is paramount in the book of Job. Therefore it is fitting that each protagonist's view toward God be examined.

Eliphaz's views of God. Eliphaz viewed God as existing in the heavens (22:12), being righteous and pure (4:17), being aware of sin on the part of angels (4:18-19; 15:15), creating man as his Maker (4:17), being superior to man (4:17), and independent of and uninfluenced by man (22:2-3), judging the wicked and causing them to perish (4:9, 18-21; 15:30), judging fools (15:2-7), having miracle-working power (5:9), bringing about justice by reversing the fortunes of the innocent and the wicked (5:11-16), bringing blessing to man (vv. 18-26; 22:18-21), answering prayer (5:8; 22:27), disciplining man (5:17), and benefiting the earth with rain (v. 10).

Bildad's views of God. Job's second antagonist emphasized the justice of God (8:3), particularly in punishing sin (v. 4). In addressing the fate of the wicked, Bildad in his second speech spoke of the calamities and losses the wicked experience (18:5-21). He did not say in that speech that God metes that judgment but it is implied (e.g., "The lamp of the wicked is snuffed out," 18:5; he "is banished from the world," v. 18). God is mentioned only once in chapter 18.

God is fair, Bildad maintained, because He does not reject people who are blameless and does not bless sinners (8:20), and because He extends mercy to the repentant (vv. 5-7). God is also sovereign in ruling over the universe (25:2) and angels (v. 3), and He is omnipresent (v. 3). God is righteous and pure (v. 4), far excelling His creation in the sky (moon and stars, v. 5), and His creation of man (v. 6). Bildad's words in 25:4 about man's being less righteous than God and not being pure echo Eliphaz's words in 4:7.

Zophar's views of God. To Zophar, God is lenient (11:6), forgetting some of Job's sin. God is mysterious beyond man's comprehension (vv. 7-8), He is unapproachable (v. 10), and He notices man's sins (v. 11). He responds to man's devotion to God and his forsaking of sin (vv. 13-14) by blessing him (vv. 15-20). According to Job's third so-called friend, God causes a rich, wicked person to relinquish his riches (20:14-15; cf. vv. 20-22), just when he is enjoying them (vv. 13-14). In His anger at the wicked (vv. 23, 28) God punishes their sin severely (vv. 23-28) for their judgment is determined (v. 29).

Elihu's views of God. Elihu, younger than the three and angry with both the three and Job (32:2-3, 5), had much to say about God. Job had questioned God's silence, but Elihu defended God's right to speak to man (33:13-16) as well as His right to be silent (34:29). Also since Job had questioned God's justice, Elihu defended His justice (chap. 34; 36:3; 37:23). And since the three had said God's only purpose in suffering is retribution for sin (e.g., 4:8-9; 8:4), Elihu pointed up another purpose in suffering, namely, to help prevent man from sinning and destroying himself (36:16-18, 29-30).

Elihu spoke of several attributes of God. One attribute is His sovereignty. He is greater than man (33.12), sovereign over individuals and nations (34:29; 36:22), and is great (v. 26) and majestic (37:22). His sovereignty is also seen in His work in nature, including evaporation (36:27), rain (v. 28; 37:6), clouds and thunder (36:29-33; 37:2, 4-5, 15-16), lightning (36:30, 32; 37:3, 11-12), snow (v. 6), ice (v. 10), and summer skies (vv. 17-18, 21).

A second attribute mentioned by Elihu is God's infinity, for He cannot be understood (36:26; 37:5, 15-16) or seen by man (34:29). A third attribute is His eternality (36:26, 29). A fourth is God's justice (34:12, 17; 36:3, 23; 37:23). He judges sin (34:11), punishing sinners (v. 26), shattering the mighty (v. 24), bringing sinners to death (v. 20; 36:6), correcting kings who oppress the righteous (v. 7), judging godless rulers (34:30), and punishing flattery (32:22). A fifth attribute is His holiness, for He does no evil (34:10).

God is impartial (34:19), and does not reward on man's terms (v. 33). Sixth, God is omniscient, for He sees man's every step (v. 21) and never needs to examine their hearts (v. 23). Sinners can never hide from God (v. 22), for He sees their deeds (v. 25; 35:15). Also He sees the righteous at all times (36:7). No wonder Elihu twice referred to Him as "perfect in knowledge" (v. 4; 37:16).

Omnipotence is a seventh divine attribute Elihu mentioned. God is man's Creator, for man is "the work of his hands" (34:19), and He is the "Maker" (35:10; 36:3), who has made all men "out of clay" (33:6). Six times Elihu called God "the Almighty" (32:8; 33:4; 34:10, 12; 35:13; 37:23), and three times he said God is "mighty" (34:17; 36:5, twice). Twice he said God is "exalted in power" (36:22; 37:23). In referring six times to God as "the Almighty," the young protagonist used the word *šadday*. Interestingly *šadday* is used in Job thirty-one times and only seventeen times elsewhere in the Old Testament. Job used the word fourteen times; Eliphaz, seven (in all three speeches); Bildad, twice (8:3, 5); Zophar, once

(11:7); Elihu, six; Job, fourteen (in five speeches); and God, once (40:2). *Šadday* may be related to the Akkadian word *šadû* that means mountain or breast or both. As a title of God, it refers either to His strength (like the stability of a mountain) or His providential care (like that of a mother for her infant).

Elihu stated a number of facts about God's relations with man. He gives man life (33:4) and keeps him alive (34:14-15). He provides food (36:31) and gives man insight (32:8-9). He sets up rulers (34:24), and despises the proud (37:24). His love for people, as well as His punishment for sin, are seen in nature (v. 13). He hears the cries of the needy (34:28), but refuses to respond to prayers of arrogant sinners (35:12-13). He communicates with man sometimes through dreams (33:14-15), giving man warnings to keep him from sin (vv. 16-17) and death (vv. 18, 22, 30).[55] But He can also be silent if He so chooses (34:29). God uses trouble to woo man from distress (36:16), He blesses the needy (v. 6) and those who obey Him (v. 11), He gives songs in the night (35:10), teaches man (v. 11; 36:22), and He restores those who repent (33:26), delivering them from death (v. 28). It is obvious that Elihu had a deep understanding of God's character and actions. His statements about God far exceeded those of the three friends.

Job's Views of God. Job said more about God than any of his counselors. In his speeches he often turned from responding to the three advisers and spoke directly to the Lord. In addressing God, he commented on His attributes and actions, particularly in relation to Job himself. The following attributes were referred to by the sufferer from Uz.

Sovereignty. No one can stop God or challenge what He is doing (9:12) or thwart His plans (40:2), Job recognized. No one can oppose Him for He does what He pleases (23:13). He is above man so that Job sensed he could not dispute with Him, though he desired to do so (9:14-16, 32, 35).

Omniscience. Job sensed that God was watching him constantly, dogging his steps to accuse him (7:19-20; 10:14; 30:20). And yet Job found consolation in God's knowledge, for he sensed God knew of his innocence (23:10; 31:4, 6). God sees man's "ways" (24:23) and in fact "sees everything under the heavens" (28:24).

Omnipotence. God's power was frequently mentioned by Job. He spoke of God's power as "vast" (9:4), "awesome" (10:16), and "great" (30:18). His power is seen in His giving or holding back rain (12:15; 26:8), shaking mountains (9:5-6), covering the sun, stars, and moon with clouds (9:7; 26:9) and then clearing the sky (v. 13), stripping leaders of their power and wisdom (12:16-21, 24-25; 24:22), building up and destroying nations (12:23), performing miracles (9:10), causing earthquakes (26:11), and churning the sea (v. 12). Because God is mighty, Job said He could teach his three opponents about God's power (27:11).

55. In the Old Testament the pit is often used as a synonym of death or the grave, the place of the dead. The parallel lines in Job 33:22 makes this clear: "His soul draws near to the pit and his life to the messenger of death." Also see Job 33:24, 28, 30; Psalms 55:23; 88:3-4; Isaiah 38:18; Ezekiel 31:14, 16; 32:18, 24, 29-30.

God's power is also seen in His work of creation, according to Job. He made the stars (9:9) and wind, water, rain, and thunderstorms (28:25-26). Three times Job attested to God's having formed him in his mother's womb (10:8-12; 14-15; 31:15). God sustains life for all creatures by giving them breath (12:10; 27:3), and He takes away life (v. 8). After God's two speeches to Job, the man from Uz responded by acknowledging the Lord's power: "I know that you can do all things" (42:2).

God's strength is also indicated by Job's frequent use of the title "the Almighty" (6:4; 21:20; 27:2, 10-11, 13; 29:5; 31:2, 35). Job also frequently spoke of God as *'Ělôah,* apparently an older form of *'Ělōhîm* ("God"). Job used that word for God twenty-three times, whereas others in the book used it far less frequently (Eliphaz, six times; Bildad, not at all; Zophar, three times; Elihu, six times; and God Himself, twice). Interestingly, these usages account for forty of the fifty-five occurrences of *'Ělôah* in the Old Testament.

Wrath. God's anger and wrath are against the wicked (21:17, 20) and against Job (10:17; 14:13; 16:9; 19:11). In God's anger He overturns mountains (9:5) and opposes "cohorts of Rahab" (9:13).

Justice. Three times Job refers to God as Judge (9:15; 21:22; 23:7). But Job vacillated in his sense of God's justice. At times he felt God was acting in justice by punishing sin and sinners (9:4; 10:14; 13:16; 27:13-23; 31:2-3). Other times Job felt God was not exercising justice (10:3; 12:6; 21:7-15, 17-28; 24:12), neither in the lives of others (21:7-15, 17-18; 24:12) or in his own experience. He cried, "God has wronged me" (19:6), "There is no justice" (v. 7), and, "As surely as God lives, [He] has denied me justice" (27:2). God ignored Job's plans for justice: "I get no response" (19:7), and, "I cry out to you, O God, but you do not answer" (30:20).

Wisdom. Though God was seemingly unfair to Job, the sufferer recognized God's wisdom ("His wisdom is profound," 9:4). Man cannot find wisdom by his machinations (28:12-13) nor purchase it with precious jewels (vv. 15-19) because it is hidden (v. 21). Only God knows where it is to be found (v. 23).

Others. A few other attributes Job mentioned are the Lord's righteousness (9:2), holiness (as suggested by the title "Holy One," 6:10), eternality (10:5), kindness (v. 12), distance (23:3, 8-9), and life (19:25).

Actions. God is viewed by Job as giving and taking away blessings (1:21) and giving trouble as well as good (2:10). He had blessed Job in his pre-calamity days, when God watched over him (29:2), blessed him (God's "lamp shone upon my head," 29:3), and He had close fellowship with Job (vv. 4-5). God forgives and pardons (7:21; 14:16-17). On the negative side, Job said God strips rulers of their power and wisdom (12:14-21, 24-25), puts up nations and destroys them (vv. 23), rebukes partiality (13:10), overpowers man (14:20), and brings him to death (vv. 21-22).

Most of Job's comments about God's actions pertain to the Lord's oppression against him. Job frequently lamented that his sad condition resulted from the Lord's opposition to him. God was against him! This is expressed in numerous ways: hedging him in (3:23), shooting poisoned arrows at him (6:4; cf. "target" in 7:20; 16:12-13), frightening him (7:14; 9:34; 11:19; 13:21; 23:16), keeping His hand of oppression on him (6:9; 12:9; 13:21; 19:21; 23:2; 30:21), crushing him (9:17-18; 16:12), gawking at him (7:18-20; 10:14; 13:27; 31:4), wearing him out (16:7), devastating his family (16:7), tearing at him like an animal (16:9), attacking Job like a warrior (16:14; 19:12), blocking his way (19:8), stripping him of his armor (v. 9), making him a byword (17:6), unstringing his bow (i.e., making him defenseless, 30:11), reducing him to dust and ashes (v. 19), turning against him (v. 21), tossing him about (like a leaf) in a storm (v. 22), and considering Job His enemy (13:24; 19:11; cf. 33:10). In addition God kept watching over Job (7:19-20; 10:14; 30:20), searching into his sins (13:26), and was angry with him (14:13; 16:9; 19:11). Clearly Job felt intensely the antagonism of God against him. This action on the part of God continued to confuse and frustrate Job in his agony. This relentless problem is seen in that he spoke of God's animosity in almost every one of his speeches.

God's view of Himself. When God addressed Job (chaps. 38-41), He revealed a number of truths about Himself. He spoke of His power in creation, including making the earth (38:4-7), separating the land from the sea (vv. 8-11), and establishing day and night (vv. 12-15, 19-21). He made the oceans (v. 16), and various atmospheric elements including snow, hail, lightning, wind, rain, thunder, dew, and ice (vv. 22-30, 34-35, 37-38). He is also the Creator of the stars (vv. 31-33), of man, giving him wisdom (v. 36), and of animals including beasts and birds (38:39–39:30; 40:15–41:34). He gives strength to the wild ox (39:9-12), unusual speed to the seemingly stupid ostrich (vv. 13-18), strength and animation to the horse (vv. 19-25), instinct to the hawk and the eagle (vv. 26-30), unusual physical strength to the behemoth (40:15-19), and fierceness and strength to the leviathan (41:1, 9, 12, 22, 25).

God's dozens of questions to Job were designed to point up Job's ignorance in contrast to God's knowledge.

God's providential care of the animal world is clearly stated. He feeds lions and ravens (38:39-41), cares for young goats and deer (39:1-4), gives desertland and hills for wild donkeys to roam (vv. 5-8), and provides food for the behemoth (40:20). His providence is also seen in His regulating the rising of the sun (38:12-19), and the movements of the heavenly bodies by "the laws of the heavens" (v. 33).

God's questioning of Job also reveals the Lord's sovereignty. God is sovereign over the world because He created it and cares for it. Job acknowledged that sovereignty by admitting his own unworthiness (40:3-5) and ignorance ("I spoke of things I did not understand," 42:3) and by repenting (v. 6). By questioning God's way, Job had put himself up as a rival to God. But through God's repeated questioning of Job, the plaintiff came to recognize that challenging God and defending his own innocence were inappropriate and useless. Job had charged God with "wrongful deprivation," with unlawfully taking away his wealth, family, and health. Job had accused God of having committed an offense (*ḥāmās*, 19:7, an act of unlawful conduct).[56]

---

56. Sylvia Huberman Scholnick, "Poetry in the Courtroom: Job 38-41," in *Directions in Biblical Hebrew Poetry,* ed. Elaine Follis (Sheffield: JSOT Press, 1987), p. 187.

God responded to this charge by affirming that He had the right of ownership because of His creative work. "Everything under heaven belongs to Me" (41:11). God's many references to creation are highly appropriate because by them He was addressing His ownership of the universe while at the same time refuting Job's accusation of deprivation.[57] God did not actually deprive Job of anything, because He, as Creator, owns all that is in the universe. The Founder is the Owner; the Creator is the Ruler.

God also revealed His justice: "Would you discredit my justice [*mišpāṭ*]? Would you condemn me to justify yourself?" (40:8). *Mišpāṭ* here may suggest sovereignty or rulership as well as judgeship. Divine justice, in other words, is to be viewed not as a human judicial system, but as a system of divine kingship.[58] "What Job learns is that the divinely ordained justice in the world is God's governance."[59] Accusing God of injustice was presumptuous because God as Ruler has a system of justice that exceeds what Job sensed in the human legal forum.

Why did God speak of the behemoth (40:15-24) and the leviathan (chap. 41), usually considered the hippopotamus and the crocodile?[60] In the ancient Near East those animals were symbols of cosmic power and chaos.[61] By numerous rhetorical questions and statements of irony, God demonstrated to Job that he could not possibly subdue these ominous and fierce creatures. Therefore he had no right to challenge God. Since he thought God was allowing chaos in his life and since he questioned what God was doing, Job was challenged to defeat the symbols of chaos. Only then could he have the right to discredit God and to replace the moral chaos in his life with order and justice.

Since Job could not conquer the symbols of chaos, mere animals, he could not possibly assume God's role and bring order into the moral realm. "If Job cannot subdue them, he is in no position to discredit God, his Creator and Maker, for treating him unjustly."[62]

Job learned that pride has no place before God. Even a crocodile looks down on the haughty (41:34), bringing fear to man's heart (vv. 9, 25). How then could Job

57. Ibid., p. 191.
58. Ibid., pp. 194-96.
59. Sylvia Huberman Scholnick, "The Meaning of *Mišpāṭ* in the Book of Job," *Journal of Biblical Literature* 101 (1982): 529.
60. For a defense that the behemoth and the leviathan are real creatures and not mythological, and that they are the hippopotamus and the crocodile, see Roy B. Zuck, "Job," in *The Bible Knowledge Commentary, Old Testament* (Wheaton, Ill.: Victor, 1985), p. 771; and Zuck, *Job*, pp. 70-80.
61. Othmar Keel, *Jahnes Entgegnung an Ijob: Eine Deutung von Ijob 38-41 vor dem Hintergrund der zeit-genössischen Bildkunst* (Göttingen: Vanderhoeck und Ruprecht, 1978); Torgny Säve-Soderbergh, *On Egyptian Representations of Hippopotamus Hunting as a Religious Motive* (Uppsala: C. W. K. Gleerup, 1953); and Gregory W. Parsons, "A Biblical Theology of Job 38:1-42:6" (Th.D. diss., Dallas Theological Seminary, 1980), pp. 31, 33, 199-201, 336-48.
62. John E. Hartley, *The Book of Job*, New International Commentary on the Old Testament (Grand Rapids: Eerdmans, 1988), p. 534.

hope to stand in defiance against God, the Maker of the crocodile? As God asked, "Who then is able to stand against me?" (v. 10).

MAN

The book of Job raises numerous questions about the nature and destiny of man. Since man is a mere mortal, how can he have a relationship with God? What effect does sin have on a person's lot in life and his relationship with God? What relationship exists between sin and suffering? Is it possible to worship and serve God unselfishly? How can man reconcile his suffering with God's love and care? Is there hope beyond the grave?

Job's view of man. Job's suffering led him to reflect intensively and agonizingly on man's nature, destiny, and relationship to God.

Man's Origin. Job acknowledged that at birth he was "naked" (1:21), that is, he possessed no earthly goods. Moaning in physical and emotional agony, he wished he had never been born (3:3-10), or had died a stillbirth (vv. 11-19) so that he would have avoided the troubles of his life on earth and be at peace in the grave. Since neither of those occurred, he longed to die then (vv. 20-26). Death would end his misery and bitterness (v. 20), and he would be glad (v. 22). Otherwise he would continue to be without peace, quietness, and rest (v. 26).

Thinking of God's careful forming of Job in his mother's womb, Job asked God how He could now destroy him (10:8). Since God, like a potter, had molded Job in the womb (v. 9) and since that intricate embryonic development was like the curdling of milk into cheese and like a weaver knitting him with skin, flesh, bones, and sinews, how, Job asked, could God turn against him now (vv. 10-11)? This was inconsistent, it seemed to Job. Once again he lamented ever have been born (v. 18). Being a stillbirth ("carried straight from the womb to the grave," v. 19) would have been preferable to his present misery.

Man's Nature. Being "born of a woman" (14:1) speaks of man's frailty (cf. 15:14; 25:4). Yet he is God's "creature" (14:15), having been made by His hands (v. 15; cf. "hands" in 10:3, 8) in the womb (31:15), and having breath from God (27:3). In man's mortality he cannot discover wisdom apart from fearing God (28:12-13, 21, 28). When Job spoke of man's being "a mortal," he used *'ĕnôš,* a word used thirty times in the book of Job and which means man in his weakness, finitude, or frailty. Job recognized that before God's holiness, man is impure (14:4). And man is wicked (3:17; 9:22, 24; 10:3; 16:11; 21:7, 16, 28; 24:6, 27:7, 13; 29:17; 31:3), godless (13:16; 27:8), and without hope (6:11; 7:6; 14:19; 17:15; 27:8). Job recognized that sin can occur in one's heart (1:5; 31:7, 9), or thoughts (v. 1). Sin can take the form of deceit (27:4; 31:5), injustice (vv. 13, 16, 21), lack of compassion (v. 17), or gloating (v. 29).

Life's Brevity. Job repeatedly and in a variety of ways spoke of the brevity of man's life. He compared the shortness of his own life to the quick movements of the weaver's shuttle (7:6), a breath (v. 7), a cloud (v. 9), a swift runner (9:25), boats of papyrus (v. 26), eagles swooping down on their prey (v. 26),[63] and a flower and a shadow (14:2). His life, he said, seemed like a few days (10:20), a few months (21:21), and a few years (16:22). Since his life was cut short (17:1), with the number of his days already determined (14:5), he felt his life was ebbing away (30:16).

Man's Suffering. Job's suffering was multifaceted. It was physical, social, emotional, and spiritual. He was in pain and torment (13:25; 16:6; 30:17) and had great trouble (*'āmāl*, "sorrow, misery," 3:10; also used in 4:8; 5:6-7; 11-16; 15:35). In the physical realm he suffered insomnia (7:4), he had lost weight (16:8), his eyes were red and deep shadows were around his eyes (v. 16), he was emaciated (17:7; 19:20), trembling (21:6), with pain in his bones (30:17); he had blackened, peeling skin (vv. 28, 30), fever (v. 30), and itching boils (2:7). Socially, people rejected him. They jeered and mocked (12:4; 16:10; 17:2, 6), and even children mocked him (30:1, 9-11). So he had no joy (9:25; 30:31). In his anguish and bitterness (7:11; 10:1) he sensed he was in darkness (19:8; 30:26) and despair (6:14, 20). All his friends and relatives had forsaken him (19:17-29).

Before God, he was spiritually without hope (14:13; 19:10). God was silent and seemingly unconcerned about Job (19:7; 30:20), even though the sufferer cried for help (vv. 24, 28).

In spite of all his suffering, Job insisted he was undeserving of his calamities, that his suffering far exceeded any known sin deserving of such calamities (6:10, 29-30; 13:19; 16:17; 23:7, 11-12; 27:4-6; 31:6).

Man's Relationship to God. The focus of the book of Job is man's relationship to God, and especially, as stated earlier, the question of how man should relate to God when injustice, in the form of undeserved suffering, prevails. Man is capable of worshiping God (1:20), based on fear of Him (1:1, 8; 2:3; i.e., recognizing all His splendor and responding accordingly), which is the essence of wisdom (28:28). God accepts man's sacrifices on behalf of others (1:5; 42:8). Though man is capable of cursing God (1:5, 11; 2:5, 9). Job never did. He challenged God, decrying his seeming injustice, but he never renounced God or cursed Him as Satan had predicted.

Does God punish man for his sin? Job's three self-appointed counselors affirmed repeatedly that God always punishes sin—quickly and in this life. Job challenged that view, stating that the wicked often continue to live prosperously with apparently no experience of judgment (21:7-15, 17-18) and continue to sin in various ways without being punished (24:1-17). Job, however, did affirm that *eventually* the wicked do get what they deserve (vv. 18-24; 27:13-23; 31:2-3). Many scholars prefer to see 24:18-24 and 27:13-23 as words spoken by Bildad or Zophar, because, it is argued, those verses seem to contradict Job's statements about God's indifference toward sinners. However Job's point is that although the wicked live on (21:7, in opposition to Zophar's words in 26:5 that the wicked die young), sinners will ultimately be punished. "Job's position was that *both* the righteous and the wicked

63. The Hebrew *nešer* may refer to falcons and vultures as well as eagles. The peregrine falcon can swoop on its prey at an an unbelievable speed of 120 miles per hour.

228   Biblical Theology of the Old Testament

suffer and *both* prosper. This differs drastically from the insistence of the three disputers that only the wicked suffer and only the righteous prosper."[64]

Death. Since Job's suffering, as already stated, resulted in such physical dissipation, he sensed that he would soon die. In fact he even preferred death to the intense suffering he was undergoing (6:8-9; 7:15). Death is final, Job stated, for there is no return from it (7:9; 10:21; 16:22), and at death man is "no more" (7:21; 14:10), "he is gone" (v. 20), and he has no hope (vv. 10-12; 17:15-16) of returning to his former life. The days of "all the living" (30:23) "come to an end" (7:6) and the living are not remembered (24:20). Both the prosperous and the poor die (21:23-26). Lying dead in the dust (7:21; 17:16; 21:26), man is in darkness (10:21-22; 17:13) and his body is subject to decay by worms (17:14; 21:26; 24:20).

"The dead," who "are in deep anguish" (26:5), are literally the repā'îm. The NASB renders this word "departed spirits," and the NIV translates the word as "spirits of the departed" in Isaiah 14:9. The Rephaites, descendants of Rapha, were an ethnic group (Gen. 14:5; 15:20; Deut. 2:11; 3:13; Josh. 17:15) who were tall in stature (Deut. 3:11; 2 Sam. 21:16, 18-20). In Ugaritic, the Raphaites were the chief gods or noble warriors. When used in Ugaritic of the dead, the word referred to the elite among the dead.[65] Job's point was that even the elite dead "are in deep anguish" because God is over them. This hints at conscious torment in death. Verses that speak of the dead being in darkness point to the physical aspect of death. In Job 26:6 Job stated that "death is naked before God," that is, He sees all that goes on in Sheol, the place of the dead.

Another reference to death from Job's lips is recorded in Job 19:26. The word *death* is not used, but he did say, "After my skin has been destroyed, yet in my flesh I shall see God." "Destroyed" means "flayed or stripped off." That is, he would die from the constant peeling away of his skin (2:7; 30:30).[66] Some, however, suggest this means that after his skin had become shriveled up or marred beyond recognition,[67] while he was still alive, he would see God vindicate his cause. Others say Job meant he would see God in a resurrected body. Whether this is the meaning hinges on the Hebrew word *min* ("in," NIV, "without," NASB). If it is translated "in," then the idea is "from the vantage point of," and the verse means in his resurrected body *or* in his flesh while still living. If it is translated "from," then the verse means "apart from" his flesh (i.e., after death). Favoring the second view is that *min* normally means "without" (cf. 11:15), and that because 19:26a speaks of death, one would normally expect to find verse 26b in Hebrew parallelism to refer to death also. Job then was not saying he would see God *in* his flesh, but without or apart from his flesh. He would see God in his state of death. This points not to bodily resurrection

64. Zuck, "Job," p. 747.
65. Conrad L'Heureux, "The Ugaritic and Biblical Rephaim," *Harvard Theological Review* 67 (1974): 265-74.
66. Marvin H. Pope, *Job,* The Anchor Bible (Garden City, N.Y.: Doubleday, 1973), p. 147.
67. Hartley, *The Book of Job,* p. 297.

after death but to conscious awareness after death. He himself would see God (v. 27) face to face, and God would then stand as his vindicator. Such an anticipated fact was a grand climax of faith in the midst of Job's agony of physical and emotional pain and social ostracism.

The counselors' view of man. Whereas Job's view of man focused on the brevity and misery of life, his unfriendly trio each concentrated on man's sin and its consequences (though they too mentioned the brevity of life). This is understandable because the three were committed to explaining Job's circumstances as the result of his evil conduct.

Eliphaz. Eliphaz said man plows evil (4:8), is unrighteous and impure (v. 17; 15:14), is guilty of resentment and envy (5:2), is crafty and wily (vv. 12-13), vile and corrupt (15:16), evil (vv. 16, 35; 22:15), wicked (15:20), defiant against God (vv. 25-26; 22:17), godless (15:34), and deceitful even from birth (v. 35). Eliphaz accused Job of sinning with his words (vv. 5-6, 13), of being ignorant of God (vv. 7-9), of raging against God (v. 13), of being of no benefit to God (22:2-3), and of being guilty of great wickedness (v. 5). He accused Job of demanding security from others for no reason (v. 6), and of ignoring the needs of the tired, hungry, widowed, and orphaned (vv. 7, 9). In the Mosaic law, demanding security pertained to the practice of a creditor accepting a borrower's cloak as a pledge of payment if the latter was unable to pay his debt. The clothing, however, had to be returned before sundown (Ex. 22:26-27). So to accuse Job of requiring such pledges and not returning them in the evening suggested that he was heartless, greedy, and a thief. Interestingly Eliphaz had no basis for making those allegations in 22:6-9; in fact Job later denied those very accusations (31:16-22, 32).

Trouble, the consequence of sin, is brought by man himself, not by external conditions (5:6), and is as inevitable as sparks flying upward from an open fire (v. 7).[68] In fact man conceives trouble (15:35, *'āmāl*, the same word used in 3:10; 4:8; 5:6-7). Eliphaz, like Job, also spoke of the frailty of man, suggested by the fact that he was "born of woman" (15:14).

Numerous claims and statements were made by the eldest of Job's verbal enemies to describe the consequences of sin. He spoke of sinners perishing and being destroyed (4:7, 9; 22:20), being crushed as easily as a moth is crushed (4:19), being "broken to pieces" and unnoticed (v. 20), and suffering torment (15:20). The Hebrew for "suffers torment" can be rendered "writhes in pain," referring to a woman's labor pains. In addition, the children of the wicked person are defenseless (5:4), and the craftiness of the wicked is thwarted (vv. 12-14). The godless will be attacked (15:22), hungry (v. 23), terrified (v. 24; 22:10), homeless (15:28), unsettled and insecure (v. 30; 22:16), and ruined and mocked (v. 19). Their wealth and possessions will vanish (5:5; 15:29-34; 22:20). Eliphaz likened the confusing state

---

68. The word "sparks" is literally "sons of Resheph," perhaps a poetic allusion to the Ugaritic god of lightning, pestilence, and flames.

of the wicked to darkness (5:14; 15:22-23, 30; 22:11), and stated that fire and floodwaters would destroy their possessions (15:34; 22:11, 16, 20).

Bildad. Bildad, like his elder counselor Eliphaz, stressed that calamities are the consequences of man's sin. Man is frail ("born of a woman," 25:4; cf. 15:24), weak (*'ĕnôš*, 25:4, 6, and "a son of man," v. 6), impure and unrighteous (vv. 4-5; cf. 8:6), and as useless and disgusting as a maggot or worm (25:6). His life is brief, moving quickly from birth to death like a shadow (8:9) and as if he were born yesterday. The godless are destroyed, withering like papyrus without water or dying like a well-rooted plant pulled up by the roots (vv. 11-19; 18:16). Their tents are burned (v. 15) and gone (8:22), and they die (spoken of as being in darkness, 18:5-6, 18). They are trapped in all kinds of difficulties (vv. 8-10), facing terror, disaster, insecurity, and disease (vv. 11-14). No one remembers them (v. 17), and they have no survivors (v. 19).

Zophar. Eliphaz spoke of the distance of the wicked, Bildad said the wicked are trapped, but Zophar stressed that wicked men lose their wealth. Zophar accused Job of two sins: wrongfully claiming to be innocent (11:4) and depriving the poor (20:19). This third disputant, more vitriolic than his two companions, called man deceitful (11:11), evil (vv. 11, 14), stupid (v. 12), godless (20:5), and proud (v. 6). Therefore sinners experience trouble (11:16; 20:22), and terror (v. 25), their joy is short-lived (v. 5), and life is passing and ephemeral like a dream (v. 8). Job was ignorant of God (11:7-8), and wicked men die without hope (v. 20) and perish like their own dung (20:7). Under God's anger and wrath (vv. 23, 28), the wicked experience darkness, fire, and flood (20:26, 28), the same three calamities Eliphaz had mentioned (5:14; 15:34; 22:11). The wealth of the godless, acquired wrongfully, will be lost suddenly (20:10, 15-18) and completely (v. 21) before he can enjoy it (v. 18).

Elihu. With Job's critics stalemated, Elihu, an onlooker, spoke up. Young and angered by the impasse of the debates, Elihu was amazed that they, men older than he, were not wise (32:6-7). He too spoke of man's sinful nature, though he stressed man's inability to know and influence God. Speaking less of the results of sin than did the other three, he saw a different purpose in suffering, namely, to prevent man from destroying himself (33:17-28, 30; 36:16). Suffering can help keep man from sin rather than being a club to punish him for his sin. To Elihu, Job's suffering led to an attitude of pride before God. Job's complaining to God (33:13; 34:17) meant that he needed to humble himself before God (33:27; 36:23; 37:24).

Created by God (33:6; 34:19; 35:10; 36:3; 37:7),[69] man is dependent on God for his very breath (33:4; 34:14-15), and obviously is inferior to God ("God is greater than man," 33:12-13). Man is answerable to God, not vice versa (v. 13). Man

---

69. In the clause "I too have been taken from clay" (Job 33:6) the word "taken" (*gāraṣ*) means "to be pinched or nipped." This figuratively pictures the fact that all men are made from a lump of clay, suggesting the commonality and lowliness of man. The cognate Akkadian word is used in the same way to mean "pinched" or "nipped."

cannot condemn God (34:17, 29), see God (v. 29; 35:14), challenge God (36:23), reach God (37:23), or understand God (36:26) and His ways in nature (v. 29; 37:15-16). The youthful theologue-counselor said that Job perceived God's communications with him, though He spoke in dreams (33:15-18) and pain (vv. 18-22; 36:15). And yet God sees man (34:21-22; 36:7).

Besides being unable to understand God, Job was also presented by Elihu as a sinner. He was guilty of pride (33:17; 35:12; 36:9; 37:24), wickedness (34:36-37), rebellion (v. 37), and speaking against God (v. 37). And yet man's sin does not affect God adversely nor does man's righteousness accrue to God's benefit (35:6-8). Like the trio of protagonists, Elihu associated punishment with wrongdoing, though he was not as specific or harsh as they were in their pronouncements (34:11, 26; 36:6).

Elihu spoke of death, as did the other four ashheap debaters. Each day man's soul draws nearer to the pit (33:22), a reference to death, as discussed earlier, and a man dies suddenly (34:20-25) with his body returning to the dust (v. 15).

God's view of man. In His first speech to Job, God's numerous rhetorical questions were designed to point up Job's inadequacies and weaknesses in view of God's sovereignty and strength, and Job's ignorance in light of God's omnipotence. The Lord's questions varied: "Where were you . . .?" "Who . . .?" "Have you . . .?" "What is . . .?" "Can you . . .?" "Does . . .?" "Do you know . . .?" "Will you . . .?" Since man was created on the last day of creation, Job obviously had no role in and knew nothing about God's creative work on the preceding days. The earth and the sea, the clouds and the dawn, the darkness and the light, snow and hail, lightning and wind, rain and dew, ice and frost, stars and planets (38:4-38)—all aspects of inanimate nature—were made by God without Job's help or knowledge. Unquestionably that truth underscores the finite nature of man. Lions and ravens, mountain goats and deer, wild donkeys and oxen, ostriches and horses, hawks and eagles (38:39–39:30) are all made and cared for by God's hand of creative power and loving providence. Here too man is incompetent and ignorant. No wonder Job responded to this first speech by acknowledging his unworthiness and inability to respond (40:4-5).

God's second speech, in which He described the anatomy and ways of the behemoth (40:15-24) and the leviathan (chap. 41), also pointed out Job's inabilities and suggested his need to repent of pride. Significantly Job, having been "reduced to dust and ashes" (30:19), to a position of lowly disgrace, now repented "in dust and ashes" (42:6), acknowledging that he was as worthless as the dust and ashes in which he had been sitting. Job, having complained that God had molded him out of clay only to turn him to dust again (10:9), now accepted his lowly position at the ash pile as symbolism of his own worthlessness. Therefore he resolved to change his attitude of defiance toward God and in humility to withdraw his allegations against God's supposed injustice. God's colloquies clearly point out that man is finite (40:9; 41:10-11), that pride has no place before God, that God deals with sin, and that accusing God of injustice is absurd (40:8).

ANGELS

The angels mentioned in Job 1:6 and 2:1 are literally "the sons of God." They are His sons in the sense that they were created by Him and are His servants. Though Eliphaz considered the angels to be God's servants (4:18) and His "holy ones" (5:1), He did not view them as without error (4:18; cf. 15:15). They have access to God's presence, to account for their work as His courtiers (1:6; 2:1). Existing before the earth's creation, they rejoiced at God's creative work (38:7). The morning stars, mentioned in poetic parallelism in this same verse, may also refer to angels,[70] or they may be planets like Venus and Mercury spoken of figuratively as if they sang.

Eliphaz had said that no angel could respond to Job's need (5:1), but Elihu disagreed (33:23-24). He said in sickness God may send an angel as a mediator to remind him of what is right (i.e., the right path to lead him back to God) and to intercede with God to keep him from the pit (death). As "one out of a thousand" this is a special angel sent to help restore the one who has strayed, and by paying a ransom (some unspecified compensation to satisfy God's justice) to direct the angels of death (called "messengers of death" in 33:22) from taking his life.

Satan too has access to God's presence (1:6; 2:1) along with the angels. He roams throughout the earth, apparently looking for those whom he may accuse before God. Satan, unable to question God's assessment of Job as a blameless and upright man who feared God and shunned evil, challenged Job's *reason* for being righteous. Instead of impugning Job's character, Satan attacked Job's motives, suggesting that he was serving God selfishly for monetary gain.

The book of Job makes an outstanding contribution to the theology of God and man. God is seen as sovereign, omniscient, omnipotent, and caring. By contrast, man is seen as finite, ignorant, and sinful. And yet, even in the face of suffering, man can worship God, confident that His ways are perfect and that pride has no place before Him.

A THEOLOGY OF PROVERBS

THE DOCTRINE OF WISDOM

Wisdom and creation order. As stated earlier, wisdom means being skillful and successful in one's relationships and responsibilities. It involves observing and following the Creator's principles of order in the moral universe. This order manifests God's wisdom, which is available to man. So to the extent man follows this order, he is wise. Heeding the wisdom of the book of Proverbs, then, brings harmony to one's life. By contrast, failure to heed God's divine design results in disorder. Lack

70. On the ancient Near Eastern veneration of morning stars as gods see Hartley, *The Book of Job*, p. 495, n. 21.

of compliance with God's wise ways brings unpleasant and disastrous consequences on oneself and others.

In identifying the wise with the righteous, and the unwise with the foolish, the book of Proverbs demonstrates that wisdom is more than intellectual. It encompasses the moral and the religious. Two paths are set before the reader: the path (or conduct and character) of the righteous/wise, and the path (or conduct and character) of the wicked/foolish. Each path bears certain consequences. The path of wisdom leads to life, and the path of folly leads to death.

The value of wisdom. Because of its value to the character of the wise person, wisdom is likened to silver and hidden treasure (2:4). In fact its value exceeds that of gold, silver, or rubies (3:14-15; 8:10-11, 19; 16:16). The wise person understands what is right, just, and fair (2:9; 8:15-16), is protected from harm (2:8, 11-12, 16; 4:6; 6:24; 7:5; 14:3), and has prosperity and wealth (3:2, 16; 8:18, 21; 9:12; 14:24; 16:20; 21:20-21; 22:4), health and nourishment (3:8; 4:22), favor and a good reputation (3:4; 8:34-35; 13:15), honor (3:16, 35; 4:8-9; 8:18; 21:21), security and safety (1:33; 3:22-23; 4:12; 12:21; 22:3; 28:26), peace (1:33; 3:17-24), confidence (3:25-26), guidance (6:22), life (3:2, 16, 18, 22; 4:10, 22; 6:23; 8:35; 9:11; 10:16-17, 27; 11:19; 16:22; 19:23; 22:4),[71] health (4:22), and hope (23:18; 24:14).[72]

Others also benefit from an individual's wisdom. For example the wise person brings joy to his parents (10:1; 15:20; 23:15-16, 24-25; 27:11; 29:3). Righteous/wise living results in a tree of life (11:30; 13:12; 15:4; cf. 3:18), that is, like a tree it is a source of benefit to others. And wisdom is also a fountain of life (10:11; 13:14; 15:27; 16:22) bringing rejuvenation to others.

No wonder wisdom is to be sought after (2:3-4), attained (4:5, 7), loved (v. 6), chosen (v. 8), grasped and guarded (v. 13), heard (vv. 32-34), and found (v. 35). Wisdom is to be valued like a necklace (1:9; 3:3, 22; cf. 6:21) and a garland or crown on one's head (1:9; 4:9).

Similarly *ma'at*, the Egyptian goddess of justice, order, and truth, is pre-

---

71. "Life" may refer to length of years, the continuation of life, as in 3:2, 16; 9:11; 10:27, or to quality of life, as in 11:19; 19:23; 21:21. Walter Brueggemann refers to life in Proverbs as "all the assets—emotional, physical, psychological, social, spiritual—which permit joy and security and wholeness" (*In Man We Trust* [Richmond, Va.: John Knox, 1972], p. 15). Death, by contrast, may refer to physical loss of life (10:27), or figuratively to the loss of blessing in life.

72. These benefits of wisdom do not suggest so-called prosperity theology, which teaches the way to become wealthy and healthy is to serve God. The book of Proverbs points up, instead, the normal though not guaranteed consequences of wisdom. Exceptions may occur, but these are not stated. Furthermore, wisdom was to be pursued for its own sake, not for the sake of its benefits. The benefits were bestowed as a by-product of acquiring wisdom. In addition, as Scott points out, other motivations for conduct, besides material rewards and punishments, are mentioned in Proverbs. These include the pleasure or displeasure of the Lord (12:22), honor or shame brought to one's parents (10:1), effect on others (10:12, 21; 11:10), and the desire for wisdom (12:1; 13:14) (R. B. Y. Scott, *Proverbs, Ecclesiastes,* The Anchor Bible [Garden City, N.Y.: Doubleday, 1965], p. 25).

sented in ancient Egyptian literature as providing protection,[73] giving a garland or wreath of victory to the gods,[74] and is pictured as a chain around the neck of judges and the vizier.[75] In addition *ma'at* carries an *ankh,* as the sign of life, in one hand and a scepter, as a symbol of riches and honor, in the other hand (cf. 3:16).[76]

Does wisdom always result in these and other blessings? The experience of many people seems to present a challenge to these assurances of long life, well-being, and prosperity. Three answers to this problem may be suggested. First, these statements present what is usually and normally true. Though not everyone who is "upright" (2:7) is protected from harm (vv. 7-8, 11), physical protection *is* often experienced more by the wise, godly person than the foolish, wicked person. Living wickedly leads to risk-taking, which often results in harm, a sense of insecurity, restlessness, and/or lack of honor. Even casual observations of wicked people confirm this fact. True, some exceptions may be noted, but the proverbs are pointing to what is normal and usual, what is recurring enough to be considered normative.

Second, many proverbs are intentionally written in contrastive modes to underscore the vast differences of conduct and consequences. This teaching device is designed to motivate toward proper action and away from improper action.

Third, circumstances may introduce exceptions to the statements otherwise seen as absolutes. Or one's own conduct may alter the outcome. The self-will or disobedience of a child may alter what would otherwise appear to be the statement of guarantee in Proverbs 22:6, "Train a child in the way he should go, and when he is old he will not turn from it." While this verse is *generally* true, folly, which "is bound up in the heart of the child" (v. 15), may introduce a situation which is an exception to the norm.

The personification of wisdom. Ascribing personal traits to inanimate objects or to abstract ideas is common in the Old Testament. Mountains singing and trees clapping their hands (Isa. 55:12), truth stumbling (59:14), and the tongue hating (Prov. 26:28) are examples of personification. It is not surprising to see wisdom personified in Proverbs. The fact that wisdom is personified as a woman is partly explained by the fact that the noun *ḥokmāh* is feminine. Another reason is that wisdom, like a woman, is said to be attractive. Just as a man may be attracted to and desire a woman's beauty, so he should respond to and desire wisdom. The personified figure of wisdom also heightens the contrast between wisdom and folly. Folly, also personified as a woman (9:13-18), seeks to attract male followers. Just as immoral women can lead men into illicit conduct and dire consequences ("death"), so folly can lead people to pursue improper conduct that results in defeat and death.

Wisdom is presented as a prophetess (1:20-23; 8:1-21), a sister (7:4), a child

73. Christa Kayatz, *Studien zu Proverbien 1-9* (Neukirchen-Vluyn: Neukirchener Verlag, 1966), p. 103.

74. Ibid., p. 112, n. 1.

75. Ibid., p. 108.

76. Ibid., p. 104.

(8:22-31), and a hostess (9:1-6). As a prophetess, she cries out in the streets, where people are traveling, public squares where people are buying and selling, and gateways, where business is transacted (1:20-21). She admonishes "simple ones" and "mockers" because of their love for naive ways and mockery of others, and "fools" because of their hatred of knowledge (v. 22). Because they fail to heed her rebuke and to learn from her (vv. 23-25), she will ignore their cries for help when they are overtaken by calamity and distress (vv. 26-27). Their ignoring her cry will result in her ignoring their cry. Refusing to fear the Lord and spurning wisdom's advice (vv. 28-30), they will suffer the consequences of their actions ("the fruit of their ways," v. 31), including death (v. 32).

An intimate relationship with wisdom is suggested by wisdom's being personified as a sister (7:4). Being closely related to wisdom is a means of protection from the adulteress (v. 5). As one enjoys wisdom like a sister, he is deterred from the allurement of adultery. Wisdom, accompanied by godliness, is contrasted to adultery, the height of folly and wickedness.

Proverbs 8 is the classic chapter on personification of wisdom. Again wisdom, like a prophetess, calls out to the "simple" and the "'foolish" (8:5), urging them to heed her words, which are true, just, and right (vv. 7-9) and priceless in value (vv. 10-11). She gives discretion (vv. 12-14), hated of evil (v. 13), justice for rulers (vv. 15-16), and wealth, honor, and righteousness (vv. 17-21). Wisdom is to be loved (vv. 17-21), again suggesting the appropriateness of personifying wisdom as a woman.

Wisdom had a special role in God's creative work (8:22-31). She existed before the creation of the world (vv. 22-26), and she rejoiced as she by His side beheld Him create the world (vv. 27-31). The fact that wisdom preceded the creation of the universe is shown by a plethora of phrases: "At the beginning of his work" and "before his deeds of old" in verse 22, and "from eternity," "from the beginning," and "before the world began" in verse 23. Wisdom existed when there were no oceans or springs, mountains or hills, or earth with its fields and dust (vv. 24-26). She was acquired (or created, v. 22), appointed (v. 23), and given birth (vv. 24-25).

Does the verb *qānāh* mean "to acquire" or "to create, to give birth to"? Elsewhere in Proverbs the verse means to acquire or possess ("get," 1:5; 4:7; 16:16; 23:23; "gains," 15:32; "get," 19:8). On the other hand the verb in Genesis 4:1 and Psalm 139:13 does seem to mean "to create." These two passages use this verb in a context of birth, which aligns with the references to wisdom being given birth in Proverbs 8:24-25. Therefore it may be preferable to render the verb *qānāh* by the word "create." Metaphorically, then, God "created" wisdom. It did not exist apart from Him.

Continuing to speak in the first person, wisdom stated that, having existed *before* creation (8:24-26), she was present *at* creation (vv. 27-31). Wisdom witnessed the Lord's making the heavens (v. 27; Gen. 1:1-5) and also the separating of waters on the second day of creation (Prov. 8:27b-28; cf. Gen. 1:6-8) and the forming of the land and sea on the third day of creation (Prov. 8:29; Gen. 1:9-10).

Being "at His side" (Prov. 8:30), wisdom was intimately associated with the

Lord as an *'āmôn*. This word is rendered "craftsman" (or "master craftsman" or "workman") by some interpreters[77] and "nursing child" by others.[78] Several factors indicate a preference for the latter translation. (1) Verses 30-31 refer to wisdom rejoicing, not working. God did the creative work. (2) The context of childbirth (vv. 22-25) suggests the translation "nursing child." (3) A verbal form of this word is used in Lamentations 4:5 to refer to those "brought up" or nursed as children. (4) *Ma'at*, the Egyptian goddess, is likened to a child playing before *Re-Atum*.[79] In chiasm, wisdom is said to be (a) "filled with delight," (b) rejoicing in God's presence, (c) rejoicing in God's world, and (d) delighting in mankind, the apex of His creative genius. Cavorting as a child, wisdom is pictured as being overjoyed with all God made.

Because of wisdom's ancestry, existing before creation, and because she witnessed the creation of the world (cf. Eliphaz's taunt against Job in Job 15:7-8), wisdom has unequaled authority in appealing to men to follow her. Those who listen to her and heed her ways are blessed and become wise. In Proverbs 8:32-34 the words "listen" and "blessed" are used alternately ("listen," v. 32; "blessed," v. 32; "listen," v. 33; "blessed," v. 34; "listens," v. 34). Finding wisdom brings life (v. 35) and rejecting wisdom brings harm and ultimately death (v. 36).

When God created the world, wisdom was at His side, that is, His creative work was a wise work. There was nothing foolish about what he did. He made it all "in wisdom." This truth is also stated in 3:19-20. This again points to the fact, as stated earlier, that wisdom theology is creation theology. The created world was brought into existence by the *wise* God.

Not a separate, independent, entity (hypostasis),[80] nor a mythical goddess,[81] nor an adumbration of Christ, wisdom in Proverbs 8 is best seen as a poetic personification of God's attribute of wisdom.[82]

In Proverbs 9:1-6 wisdom is personified as a virtuous hostess. Having built a house of seven pillars (v. 1), that is, a large, spacious house suggestive of prosperity, and having prepared a banquet (v. 2), she instructed her maids to call out (cf. 1:21; 8:1-3) to the naive to share her banquet (9:4-5). By doing so, they would live (enjoy

---

77. For example, Mitchell Dahood, "Proverbs 8:22-31: Translation and Commentary," *Catholic Biblical Quarterly* 30 (1968): 518-19. *'Āmôn* is thought to be from an Akkadian loanword *ummānu*.

78. For example, Crawford H. Toy, *A Critical and Exegetical Commentary on the Book of Proverbs,* The International Critical Commentary (Edinburgh: T. & T. Clark, 1899), pp. 177-79.

79. Kayatz, *Studien zu Proverbien 1-9*, pp. 93-98.

80. This view is proposed by Helmer Ringgren, *Word and Wisdom: Studies in the Hypostatization of Divine Qualities and Functions in the Ancient Near East* (Lund: Hakan Ohlssons Boktryekei, 1947).

81. This view is suggested by William F. Albright, "Some Canaanite-Phoenician Sources of Hebrew Wisdom," *Vetus Testamentum Supplement* 3 (1960):8.

82. Von Rad, *Wisdom in Israel,* pp. 144-70.

life to the fullest) and have understanding (v. 6). Three lines (vv. 7-8*a*) point up the dangers of rebuking sinners, whereas three lines (vv. 8*b*-9) point up, by contrast, the response of a wise person to rebuke and instruction. Wisdom's final words in 9:10-12 summarized several truths in chapters 1-9. (1) The essence of being wise is fearing the Lord. (2) Being wise results in blessings, including long life. (3) The opposite of being wise—actively rejecting wisdom as a mocker—brings suffering. Lady Wisdom is then contrasted with Lady Folly, who also invites men to her house but who is boisterous, deceptive, and disastrous (9:13-18). Again death results from folly (v. 18), whereas life comes from wisdom (v. 6).

Some Bible students also see wisdom personified by the "wife of noble character" in Proverbs 31:10-31. This is based on statements made about this wife that are familiar to statements made earlier about wisdom.[83] The wife "is more precious than rubies" (31:10) as is wisdom (3:15; 8:11; cf. 8:10, 19; 16:16). The noble wife laughs (in confidence and security) at any future threat (31:25), and wisdom too laughs at disaster (1:26). Her lamp (*nēr*) does not go out at night (31:18), and the light (*nēr*) of the righteous continues to shine (13:9). In 31:10-31 she is a wife of virtue and industry, and in 9:1-6 wisdom is pictured as a young, virtuous woman preparing a banquet for young men. In 31:26 the noble wife gives instruction, and numerous passages in Proverbs 1-9 refer to wisdom giving instruction.

It is also argued that the position of the passage, at the end of the book of Proverbs, suggests that the noble wife represents wisdom, the topic of the book. Because wisdom was personified in several other passages in Proverbs, it is argued that the woman here is also a personification of wisdom. And the position of the passage makes a fitting inclusion, it is suggested, with chapters 1-9, in which wisdom is personified as a woman. This view, however, has several problems. (1) The activities of the wife suggest more than wisdom. When wisdom is personified in chapters 1-9, she is not pictured as having a husband (31:11), or as one who sews (vv. 13, 19, 22), cooks (v. 15), purchases food and real estate (vv. 14-16), plants (v. 17), trades (v. 18), sells (v. 24), provides for the various needs of her husband, children, and servants (vv. 15, 21, 27), and helps the needy (v. 20). She is energetic, hard-working, well-to-do, compassionate, strong, confident, and spiritual. (2) Wisdom in chapters 1-9 is not pictured as a mother, as is the woman in 31:15, 28. (3) The noble woman speaks with wisdom (v. 26). If this woman is wisdom, then the verse would be stating that "wisdom speaks with wisdom." This seems to make no sense.

Therefore it seems preferable to see the woman in 31:10-31 as a wife and mother. She is a *wise* woman, not wisdom personified. This finds support in verse 30, "a woman who fears the Lord is to be praised." Since fearing the Lord is the essence of wisdom, the ideal woman, the one who fears God, is indeed wise. She is a model or example of a wise woman. In contrast to a foolish, adulterous woman

---

83. Thomas P. McCreesh, "Wisdom as Wife: Proverbs 31:10-31," *Revue Biblique* (1985): 41-43.

(2:16-19; 5:20; 6:23-34; 7:4-27) this woman is faithful to her family and is therefore praised (31:30-31) by her children and her husband (v. 28) and the public (v.
31). As a wise woman, she is in contrast to "woman Folly" (9:13-18). Rather than
a personification of wisdom, the woman in 31:10-31 is an embodiment or model of
wisdom, a woman who is wise because she is living skillfully.

THE DOCTRINE OF GOD

His names. The name *Yahweh* is used of God in Proverbs eighty-seven times,
'Ĕlōhîm occurs only seven times (2:5, 17; 3:4; 14:31; 25:2; 30:5, 9) and *'Ĕlōah*
occurs once (30:5). God is also called the Holy One (9:10; 30:3), the Righteous
One (21:12), the Defender (23:11), and the Maker (14:31; 17:5; 22:2).

His attributes. The attributes of God presented in the book of Proverbs include
his *holiness* ("the Holy One," 9:10; 30:3), *omnipresence* (5:21; 15:3), *omnipotence*
(as the Creator of the universe [3:19-20; 8:22-31; 30:4] and of man's ears and eyes
[20:12; 29:13], and the Maker of the poor [14:31; 17:5; 22:2] and the rich [22:2]),
and *omniscience* (in examining and knowing death [15:11], man's conduct [5:21;
21:2], man's motives [16:2], and heart [17:3; 20:27; 24:12] and in seeing good
and evil [15:3], and those who gloat over others' misfortunes [4:16-17]).
God also possesses *sovereignty,* working everything for His purposes (16:4;
19:21), even determining man's decisions (16:33) and course of action (v. 9),
directing the hearts (or interests and decisions) of kings (21:1), and superseding
every plan of mankind (19:21; 21:30). God has *wisdom* (3:19-20) and *justice.* In His
justice (29:26) He is the Righteous One (21:12) who thwarts and punishes the
wicked (3:33; 10:3; 11:8; 21:12; 22:12), the crafty (12:2), and the proud (15:25), and
He upholds the poor and afflicted (22:22-23; 23:10-11). His justice is equitable
for He repays man in accord with his conduct (20:22; 24:12), and rewards the righteous (19:17; 25:22).
In His justice God hates perversity (3:32; 11:20), pride (6:17; 16:5), lying
(6:17-19; 12:22), violence ("hands that shed innocent blood," 6:17), wicked schem-
ing and actions (v. 18), dissension (v. 19), dishonesty (11:1; 20:10, 23), hypocrisy
("the sacrifice of the wicked," 15:8; 21:27; the prayers of the lawless, 28:9), and injustice (17:15).
God's *personality* is evident in that He loves and disciplines (3:12), hates
(6:16-19), delights (in honest business dealings, 11:1; in the conduct of the blameless, v. 20 [cf. 16:7a]; in people who are truthful, 12:22; and in the prayers and
righteous conduct of the godly, 15:8-9).

His actions. The preceding paragraphs show that God's attributes reveal a
number of His actions. These include creating, seeing, examining, purposing, influ-
encing, directing, punishing, defending, rewarding, hating, loving, and delighting.
Other actions include giving wisdom (1:7; 2:6), giving grace to the humble (3:34),
protecting the righteous (2:7-8; 3:26; 10:29; 14:26; 15:25; 18:10; 19:23; 29:25;

30:5), providing for the righteous (10:3), delivering the righteous (20:22), blessing the righteous (3:33; 10:22; 12:2), giving life (10:27), giving men prudent wives (18:22; 19:14), directing those who trust Him (3:5-6), giving people words to say (16:1), guiding man's ways ("steps," v. 9; 20:24) and decisions (16:33), and hearing the prayers of the righteous (15:29).

THE DOCTRINE OF MAN

Proverbs frequently uses the metaphor of the way or the path, as already stated. By metonymy a way or path came to represent the conduct of the person walking in that direction or along that path.[84] This figure of speech suggests a choice, a decision as to which one of two kinds of life a person will lead. The two contrasting invitations—to follow wise conduct or to follow foolish conduct (8:1; 9:1-6, 13-18)—call for a choice. This figure also calls attention to the contrasting terminations of the paths, the resulting consequences of the two kinds of conduct.

The two paths are those of righteous living and wicked living, which are also identified as wise conduct and foolish conduct. All people are either righteous/wise or wicked/foolish. The path of righteousness or wisdom is the path of virtue, whereas the path of wickedness or folly is the path of vice. The lifestyle of the former leads to blessing, and the lifestyle of the latter leads to bane. Since wise living means following the principles or rules of God's order or pattern for life, harmony or blessing comes to the extent a person heeds the admonitions and observations in Proverbs pertaining to the path of wisdom. Conversely, as a person neglects or disdains wise living, pursuing the foolish path, he experiences disorder and chaos.

Wickedness takes a person on a path of darkness and crookedness (2:13-15; 4:19). It is a deviant path, leading to loss of blessing, including death (2:18; 8:36; 11:19; 14:12).[85] Righteousness, however, takes a person along a path that is straight (2:13; 4:26) and bright (v. 18). It leads to fullness of life (2:20-21; 8:35).

Proverbs points out the many different circumstances and relationships of the righteous/wise course of action, and many different contrasting circumstances and relationships of the wicked/foolish course of action. The righteous/wise path begins with a right relationship and response to God. As discussed earlier, fearing the Lord is the starting point of wisdom and also the controlling principle or essence and heart of wisdom.[86] The righteous/wise way of life begins by fearing God, that is, recognizing His superiority, and responding in awe, humility, worship, love, trust, and obedience to God.[87] Fearing God results in life (10:27; 14:27; 19:23; 22:4). Trusting God, part of the response in fearing Him, is enjoined several times

84. "Way" and "ways" occur sixty times; "path" and "paths" twenty-nine times; and "walk," "walks," and "walking," seventeen times.
85. See note 70.
86. See notes 40-42.
87. See note 44.

in Proverbs. It results in guidance (3:5), prosperity (28:25), and safety (29:25). Fearing God also involves committing one's conduct to the Lord (16:3), and in hating and spurning evil (3:7; 8:13; 16:6; cf. v. 17).

Several terms are used in Proverbs to describe the foolish person. *Petî,* used fourteen times in Proverbs,[88] means one who is naive, gullible, open to influence, easily persuaded. *Kᵉsîl,* used forty-nine times in Proverbs and twenty-one times elsewhere, means to be stupid or thickheaded. The word *'ewîl,* found nineteen times in Proverbs[89] and several times elsewhere, speaks of a fool who is coarse, hardened, or obstinate in his ways. *Nābāl,* used only three times in Proverbs (17:7, 21; 30:22) and nine times elsewhere, describes a person lacking ethical or spiritual perception, one who is morally insensitive. *Ḥăsar lēb,* "lacking in heart," means to be without any sense. It occurs only ten times, all of them in Proverbs,[90] where the NIV renders it "lacks judgment" or "lacking in judgment."

Moral uprightness, extolled in numerous ways in Proverbs, stems from being rightly related to God (by fearing, trusting, and obeying Him) and being wise. Apart from a right relationship to God, moral excellence is not possible. One of the virtues commended in Proverbs is *diligence* (10:4-5; 12:24, 27; 14:23; 24:27), with its benefits of profit (10:4; 14:23), food (12:11; 20:13; 27:18; 28:19), responsibility (12:24), self-satisfaction (13:4), ease (15:19), and honor (22:29). Another quality commended in Proverbs is *humility,* which increases one's wisdom (11:2) and brings honor (15:33; 29:23), wealth and life (22:4), and grace (3:34). Being "lowly in spirit" is to be preferred to having wealth with proud people (16:19).

Patience and *self-control* are desirable virtues for they are associated with wisdom and understanding (14:29; 17:27; 19:11; 29:11), and they help calm quarrels (15:18). *Courage* (28:1); *love* (10:12; 16:6; 20:28); *reliability* (11:13; 25:13); *truthfulness* (12:17, 19, 22; 14:5, 25; 16:13); *kindness* (11:17) to animals (12:10) and to the poor and needy (14:21, 31; 19:17; 31:9, 20); *generosity* (11:25; 22:9); *honesty* in giving witness in court (12:17), in answering questions (24:26), and in business transactions (11:1; 16:11; 20:10, 23); *teachableness* (10:8, 17; 12:1; 13:1, 13, 18; 15:5, 31-32; 19:20); *moderation* in eating (23:1-3; 24:13; 25:16, 27), and *sobriety* (20:1; 23:20-21; 31:4)—all these are characteristics of the wise and godly person.

In addition, Proverbs says much about the proper use of one's *words.* Right words can encourage and uplift (10:11, 21; 12:18, 25; 18:21), impart wisdom (10:13; 15:7; 16:21, 23; 20:15), and protect (21:23). Words should be spoken with restraint (10:19; 11:12; 13:3; 15:28; 16:23; 17:27; 21:23; 29:20), and should be fitting or appropriate to the occasion (10:32; 15:1, 23; 16:24; 25:11, 15).

Many vices or undesirable qualities discussed in Proverbs present exact opposites of the foregoing virtues. For example, opposite to diligence stands *laziness,*

---

88. 1:4, 22, 32; 7:7; 8:5; 9:4, 6, 16; 14:15, 18; 19:25; 21:11; 22:3; 27:12.
89. 1:7; 7:22; 10:8, 10, 14, 21; 11:29; 12:15-16; 14:3, 9; 15:5; 16:22; 17:28; 20:3; 24:7; 27:3, 22; 29:9.
90. 6:32; 7:7; 9:4, 16; 10:13; 11:12; 12:11; 15:21; 17:18; 24:30.

which is strongly chided (22:13; 26:13-15) because it results in poverty (6:10-11; 10:4; 13:4; 20:13), disgrace to one's parents (10:5), frustration (v. 26), hunger (12:27; 19:15, 24; 20:4; 21:25-26; 26:15), problems (15:19; 24:33-34), and even death (21:25). *Pride* is condemned repeatedly as a sin (21:4). God hates pride (6:16-17; 16:5). It leads to disgrace (11:2), loss of one's possessions (15:25), one's downfall (16:18; 18:12; 29:23), quarrels and strife (13:10; 28:25), and punishment (16:5). Pride is foolish (14:16; 26:12; 30:32). Seeking one's honor or boasting of one's accomplishments is detestable (25:27; 27:2).

Anger and loss of temper are repeatedly denounced as foolish (14:16-17, 29; 15:18; 19:19; 22:24-25; 29:11, 22), for a person without self-control is vulnerable to many kinds of problems, much as a city without walls in Bible times was insecure and subject to enemy attacks (25:28).

The wrong uses of one's *words* include lying (26:28), which God hates (6:16-17; 12:22); slander (10:18; 30:10); gossip, which betrays confidences (11:13; 20:19), separates friends (16:28; 17:9), and is not easily forgotten ("they go down to a man's inmost parts," 18:8; 26:22); chattering (10:19; 19:7; 20:19); false witnessing (12:17; 14:5, 25; 19:5, 28; 21:8; 25:18); mocking (13:1; 15:12; 22:10; 24:9; 30:17); perverse or harsh talk (10:13, 31-32; 12:18; 13:3; 15:1, 28; 19:1, 28); boasting (17:7; 25:14; 27:2); quarreling (17:14, 19; 20:3); flattery (26:28; 28:23; 29:5); and foolish talk (14:7; 15:2, 14; 18:6-7).

Greed (15:27; 28:25; 29:4), *envy* and *jealousy* (3:31; 6:34; 14:30; 23:17; 24:1, 19; 27:4), *drunkenness* (20:1; 21:17; 23:20-21, 29-35; 31:4-7), *hypocrisy* (10:18; 12:20; 13:7; 21:27; 23:6-7; 26:18-19, 24-26; 27:6), *oppression* of the poor (3:27-28; 13:23; 14:31; 22:22-23; 28:3, 8; 29:7; 31:4-5, 9), *injustice* (10:2; 16:8; 17:15, 26; 18:5), *bribery* (6:35; 15:27; 17:8, 23; 21:14; 29:4), and acquiring money by *dishonesty* (10:2; 13:11; 28:20, 22) are all condemned.

The godly, wise person also honors God in societal relationships, including the family. Husbands and wives are to be faithful to each other (5:15-19; 31:10-11), assiduously avoiding sexual misconduct or immorality (2:16-19; 5:20; 6:23-29, 32-35; 7:4-27; 22:14; 23:27-28; 30:20). Wives are not to be contentious or quarreling (19:13; 21:9, 19; 25:24; 27:15-16). A disgraceful wife is a problem (12:4), but a prudent, noble wife is a blessing from God (12:4; 18:22; 19:14; 31:10). For a woman, being wise and fearing God is far more virtuous than possessing physical beauty (11:22; 31:30).

Sons are challenged to heed parental teaching (1:8-9; 4:1-9, 20; 5:11-12; 6:20-22; 13:1; 15:5, 32; 19:27; 23:22), including the instruction given by their mothers (1:8; 6:20; 31:1). Child discipline, while painful for parents to apply, benefits the child (3:12; 13:24; 19:18; 22:6, 15; 23:13-14; 29:15, 17). Wise, obedient sons bring joy to their parents (10:1; 15:20; 23:15; 24; 27:11; 29:3), whereas unwise, unruly children cause parental grief (17:21, 25; 19:13; 28:7; 29:15). Children who disregard or dishonor their parents will suffer serious consequences (11:29; 15:20; 19:26; 20:20; 28:24; 30:11, 17). Parents who live righteously give their children a sense of personal security (14:26; 20:7).

Grandparents who lead upright lives can be glad for long life and grandchildren (13:22; 16:31; 17:6; 20:29). Even servants in the home can benefit from being wise (14:35; 17:2) and diligent (27:18). Outside the family, one must choose his friends carefully (12:26; 22:24). True friends are faithful (17:17; 18:24; 27:10), can give wise counsel (27:9), and even, when needed, reproof (27:6). Gossip, on the other hand, can spoil friendships (16:28; 17:9). Neighbors, too, should be treated properly, avoiding betrayal (25:8-10), false testimony (24:28; 25:18), deception (26:18-19), thoughtlessness (27:14), and flattery (29:5). Getting advice from others marks a person as wise (12:15; 13:10; 19:20) for it can lead to success in one's endeavors (11:14; 15:22; 20:18; 24:6).

Friends and associates must be chosen carefully. The wise avoid being around fools (13:20; 14:7; 17:12; 23:9), the proud (16:19), talkers (20:19), the wicked (1:10-19; 22:5; 24:1-2), the rebellious (24:21) and violent (3:31; 16:29), drunkards (23:20), gluttons (28:7), thieves (29:24), and immoral women (2:16-19; 5:8; 6:24-26; 29:3).

Proverbs also includes standards for kings and rulers. Their qualifications include honesty (16:13), humility (25:6), justice (16:10, 12; 25:5; 29:4; 31:8-9). reliability (20:28), sobriety (31:4-5), and self-control (16:14; 19:12; 20:2; 28:15).

Any society must transact business using money as a means of exchange. Therefore it is not surprising that Proverbs, with its emphasis on interpersonal and societal relationships, says much about business and finances. Hunger (16:26) and profit (14:23) motivate people to work. Money provides a degree of protection (like a "fortified city," 10:15; 18:11), keeps one alive (10:16), attracts friends (14:20; 19:4), and grants a degree of influence (22:7). However, the power of money is limited, for it cannot divert God's wrath (11:4), and it is temporary (23:4-5), especially if it is gained dishonestly (10:2; 13:11; 20:17; 21:6) or foolishly (17:16). Money acquired by wicked means brings trouble (1:13-14, 18-19; 15:6), whereas money properly acquired brings long life.

Wealth is no substitute for integrity (10:9; 16:8, 19; 19:1, 22; 22:1; 28:6), fear of the Lord (15:16), or wisdom (16:16). True, using money to bribe others may be influential (17:8; 21:14), but bribery is wrong (15:27; 17:23; 29:14). Money should be shared with the poor and needy (11:24-25; 14:31; 19:17; 21:13; 22:9, 22; 28:27), for the one who does so honors God and in turn will be blessed. Get-rich-quick approaches are condemned (20:21; 28:20, 22), as is partiality (18:5; 24:23; 28:21), unfair pricing of products (11:1; 16:11; 20:10, 23), and providing guarantees for loans that have exorbitant interest rates (6:1-5; 11:15; 17:18; 20:16; 22:26-27).[91]

Emotions addressed in Proverbs include anxiety (12:25), disappointment

---

91. These verses against putting up "security" for someone else's loan do not say borrowing or lending is wrong. Instead they speak against being held accountable for others' loans with high interest rates. In Israel lending was a means of helping a fellow Israelite, but interest was not to be charged (Ex.22:25; Lev. 25:35-37). Loans to non-Israelites could include interest (Deut. 23:19-20), but not with excessively high rates (Prov. 28:8; cf. Ezek. 22:12).

(13:12), satisfaction from hopes fulfilled (13:12, 19), and joy and heartache (14:10, 13, 30; 17:22; 18:14; 25:20; 27:6). Man's heart (his inner being) is referred to seventy times in Proverbs. "Soul" is mentioned fourteen times; "spirit," ten times; and "body," four times.

In its theology, the book of Proverbs, amazingly broad and inclusive in its topics, clearly delineates the two paths (kinds of conduct) of wisdom/righteousness and folly/wickedness.[92] And it does so with startling variety, intricately spelling out the characteristics and consequences of the two paths. No one can be truly wise (skillful in living) without fearing the Lord and heeding the direct commands, stern admonitions, keen observations, and probing maxims presented in the book of Proverbs.

A THEOLOGY OF ECCLESIASTES

Through the centuries many people have questioned whether the book of Ecclesiastes belongs in the biblical canon, and especially in the wisdom corpus. Since it seems to underscore the futility and uselessness of work, the triumph of evil, the limitations of wisdom, and the impermanence of life, Ecclesiastes appears to be a misfit.

Because it apparently contradicts other portions of Scripture and presents a pessimistic outlook on life, in a mood of existential despair, many have viewed Ecclesiastes as running counter to the rest of Scripture or have concluded that is presents only man's reasoning apart from divine revelation. Smith wrote, "There is no spiritual uplift embodied within these pages. . . . Ecclesiastes . . . accomplishes only one thing, confusion. Reason is elevated throughout the whole work as the tool with which man may seek and find truth."[93] Scott affirms that the author of Ecclesiastes "is a rationalist, a skeptic, a pessimist, and a fatalist. . . . In most respects his view runs counter to his religious fellow Jews."[94] Crenshaw speaks of the "oppressiveness" of Ecclesiastes, which conveys the view "that life is profitless; totally absurd."[95] Since "virtue does not bring reward" and since God "stands distant, abandoning humanity to chance and death," this book, Crenshaw asserts, contrasts "radically" with earlier teachings expressed in the book of Proverbs."[96] "Qoheleth discerns no moral order at all,"[97] for "life amounts to nothing."[98]

---

92. Other topics not mentioned in this chapter but discussed in Proverbs include, but are not limited to, death, encouragement, enemies, failure, prayer, purity, reputation, sacrifices, success, and worry.

93. L. Lowell Smith, "A Critical Evaluation of the Book of Ecclesiastes," *Journal of Bible and Religion* 21 (April 1953): 105.

94. Scott, *Proverbs, Ecclesiastes*, p. 192.

95. James L. Crenshaw, *Ecclesiastes: A Commentary* (Philadelphia: Westminster, 1987), p. 23.

96. Ibid.

97. Ibid.

98. Ibid., p. 34.

Elements in the book that supposedly suggest this outlook of secularist despair include (1) the repeated refrains, "everything is meaningless"[99] (1:2; 2:11, 17; 3:19; 12:8); "this too is meaningless" (2:15, 19, 21, 23, 26; 4:4, 8, 16; 5:10; 6:9; 7:6; 8:10);[100] "chasing after wind" (1:14, 17; 2:11, 17, 26; 4:4, 6, 16; 6:9); and "under the sun," which occurs twenty-nine times; (2) death's finality, which removes any advantage or gain man may have acquired in life (2:14, 16, 18; 3:2, 19-20; 4:2; 5:15; 6:6, 12; 7:1; 8:8; 9:2-5, 10; 11:7-8; 12:7); (3) the fleeting, transitory nature of life (6:12; 7:15; 9:9; 11:10); (4) life's inequities, including the frustrating nature of work (2:11, 18, 20, 22-23; 4:4), the uselessness of pleasure (1:17; 2:1-2, 8; 10-11), the inadequacies of wisdom (1:17-18; 2:14-17; 8:16-17; 9:13-16), and uncorrected injustice (4:1, 6, 8, 15-16; 6:2; 7:15; 8:9-10; 9:2, 11; 10:6-9); and (5) the puzzle of life with its many enigmas of unknowable elements (3:11, 22; 6:12; 7:14-24; 8:7, 17; 9:1, 12; 10:14; 11:2, 5-6).

Is this the total picture of the message of Ecclesiastes? Is it true that the book presents "no discernible principle of order"[101] in life? How does this skeptical approach square with statements (1) that life is a gift from God (2:24; 3:13; 5:19; 8:15; 9:7, 9); (2) that life is to be enjoyed (2:24-25; 3:12-13, 22; 5:18-20; 8:15; 9:7-9; 11:8-9); (3) that injustices *will* be corrected (3:17; 8:12-13; 11:9; 12:14); (4) that God is in control (3:14; 5:2; 7:14; 9:1); and (5) that man is challenged to please God (2:26), remember Him (12:1, 6-7), and fear Him (3:14; 5:7; 7:18; 8:12-13; 12:13)? Can one ignore these counterbalancing ideas? When Qoheleth[102] *five times* enjoined his readers to fear God, are we doing justice to the book's message to say that only man's reasoning is presented, that the book provides no answer to life's anomalies and enigmas? Is it adequate simply to view Ecclesiastes as presenting

99. "Meaningless" is the NIV's translation of *hebel*, literally "a vapor or breath." This suggests brevity or transience and emptiness of content. See *Theological Dictionary of the Old Testament,* ed. G. Johannes Botterweck and Helmer Ringgren [Grand Rapids: Eerdmans, 1978], s. v. "[*hebhel*]," by K. Seybold, 3:313-20. Other Bible versions translate the word "vanity" or "futility." Ogden suggests that *hebel* can best be translated "enigma" or "mystery" (Graham S. Ogden, "'Vanity' It Certainly Is Not," *The Bible Translator* 38 (July 1987): 301-7.

100. "Meaningless" is also used in 2:1; 4:7; 5:7; 6:2, 4, 11-12; 7:15; 8:14; 9:9; 11:8, 10. More than half the Old Testament usages of this word *hebel* are in Ecclesiastes—thirty-eight of its seventy-three occurrences!

101. Crenshaw, *Ecclesiastes: A Commentary,* p. 28.

102. "Qoheleth" transliterates the Hebrew word rendered "teacher" or "preacher" in 1:1-2, 12. Stemming from the verb *qāhal,* "to call an assembly," the noun *qōheleth,* suggests one who calls an assembly to address them. Some scholars argue that the anonymous author called himself "son of David, king in Jerusalem" (1:1; cf. vv. 12, 16; 2:9) to give his book a ring of authority as having been written in the tradition of Solomonic wisdom. Others (including me), however, argue that the author is indeed Solomon. For a discussion of the arguments on each side of this issue see Donald R. Glenn, "Ecclesiastes," in *The Bible Knowledge Commentary, Old Testament,* pp. 975-76; Louis Goldberg, *Ecclesiastes,* Bible Study Commentary (Grand Rapids: Zondervan, 1983), pp. 19-20; and Gleason L. Archer, "The Linguistic Evidence for the Date of 'Ecclesiastes,'" *Journal of the Evangelical Theological Society* 12 (1969): 167-81.

thoughts and counterthoughts that stand in unresolved tension,[103] or as stating contradictions without solving them so that life is viewed as absurd and irrational?[104] To conclude that Qoheleth recommended enjoyment of life only to make existence endurable on one's "journey into nothingness"[105] fails to account for the positive side of the book.

Why then does Ecclesiastes paint a dark picture of life? Why does the writer present the gloom and doom of life? How can the seeming contradictory elements in the book be reconciled? Four answers may be given to these questions.

First, Qoheleth was demonstrating that life without God has no meaning. He was demolishing confidence in man-based achievements and wisdom to show that earthly goals "as ends in themselves lead to dissatisfaction and emptiness."[106] Solomon recorded the futility and emptiness of his own experiences to make his readers desperate for God, to show that their quest for happiness cannot be fulfilled by man himself. Qoheleth "shocks us into seeing life and death strictly from ground level, and into reaching the only conclusions from that standpoint that honesty will allow."[107]

Second, Solomon was affirming that since much in life cannot be fully understood, we must live by faith, not by sight. Unexplained enigmas, unresolved anomalies, uncorrected injustices—life is full of much that man cannot comprehend or control. Like the book of Job, Ecclesiastes affirms both the finiteness of man and the fact that man must live with mystery. Life "under the sun," that is, down here on earth, "does not provide the key to life itself" for the world in itself "is bankrupt."[108] Man therefore must have more than a horizontal outlook; he must look upward to God, fearing and trusting Him. What are to us enigmas and injustices must be left in His hands to resolve and to correct.

Third, Ecclesiastes and its realistic view of life counterbalances the unqualified optimism of traditional wisdom. According to Proverbs 13:4, "the desires of the diligent are fully satisfied," but Ecclesiastes 2:22-23 challenges whether this is always true. Proverbs 8:11 extols wisdom, whereas Ecclesiastes 2:15 questions its value. Proverbs 10:6 affirms that justice is meted to the righteous and the wicked, but Ecclesiastes 8:14 observes that this is not always the case.

Are these contradictions? No. As stated in the section on Proverbs, that book

103. J. A. Loader, *Polar Structures in the Book of Qohelet* (Berlin: Walter de Gruyther, 1979; and Loader, *Ecclesiastes: A Practical Commentary* (Grand Rapids: Eerdmans, 1986).
104. Michael V. Fox, *Qohelet and His Contradictions* (Sheffield: Almond Press, 1989).
105. Crenshaw, *Old Testament Wisdom: An Introduction,* p. 144.
106. Roy B. Laurin, "Ecclesiastes," in *The Wycliffe Bible Commentary,* ed. Charles F. Pfeiffer and Everett F. Harrison (Chicago: Moody, 1962), p. 585.
107. Derek Kidner, *The Wisdom of Proverbs, Job, and Ecclesiastes* (Downers Grove, Ill.: InterVarsity, 1985), p. 94.
108. J. Stafford Wright, "The Interpretation of Ecclesiastes" in *Classical Evangelical Essays in Old Testament Interpretation,* ed. Walter C. Kaiser, Jr. (Grand Rapids: Baker, 1972), p. 142.

usually looks at the opposites in life without noting exceptions. Ecclesiastes, however, points out that while a righteous order does exist, as affirmed in Proverbs, it is not always evident to man as he views life "under the sun" from his finite perspective. "God is in heaven and you are on earth" (Eccles. 5:2). Job and Ecclesiastes, both wisdom books, demonstrate exceptions to what Proverbs often states in black-and-white fashion. The books then are complementary, not contradictory. Even though the affirmations in Proverbs are normally true, exceptions, as observed in Job and Ecclesiastes, do exist. As Williams has well observed,

> Proverbs affirms by *faith* (not by sight as is commonly assumed) that a righteous order exists in the world, but Qohelet contends that righteous order cannot be discerned by *sight*. This latter premise, that even the wise cannot explain the apparent lack of order in the world, is simply Qohelet's way of expounding on the limitations of wisdom. But these limitations were even admitted by the sages: "Do you see a man wise in his own eyes? There is more hope for a fool than for him" (Prov. 26:12). . . . Ecclesiastes was intended to balance the optimism of faith with the realism of observation.[109]

Job and Ecclesiastes both present the frustrations and futilities of wise, wealthy men. Both books demonstrate that wealth does not provide lasting satisfaction, that many people experience injustice, that death is inevitable, that man must live with the mystery of suffering.

Fourth, Ecclesiastes affirms that the only answer to the meaning of life is to fear God and enjoy one's lot in life. Qoheleth shows that man, left to his own machinations, finds life empty, frustrating, and mysterious. The book, however, does not mean that life has no answer, that life is totally useless or without meaning. That meaning is found, he explained, in fearing God—a point that clearly justifies a place for Ecclesiastes in the Bible's wisdom literature—and in enjoying life. Accepting what God has given and rejoicing in those gifts brings substance to a life that otherwise would be viewed as one of hopelessness and despair. Frustrations can thus be replaced with contentment. While recognizing the vanity of empty human pursuits, Solomon went beyond them and affirmed that "there is a bigger truth to live by," that we should "set our hearts not on earthly vanities themselves but on our Creator."[110] True, life has its puzzles, but with God life *is* worth living. Life is fleeting and death is coming, but with God life can be accepted and enjoyed.

GOD

Forty times Ecclesiastes uses the word *'Ĕlōhîm*, and no other name, in speaking of God. As the transcendent God ("God is in heaven," 5:2), He is the Creator (12:1), "the Maker of all things" (11:5). His created works include man, giving

---

109. Neal D. Williams, "A Biblical Theology of Ecclesiastes" (Th.D. Diss., Dallas Theological Seminary, 1984), pp. 85-86 (italics the author's).

110. Kidner, *The Wisdom of Proverbs, Job, and Ecclesiastes*, p. 94.

him life (8:15; 9:9) and a spirit (3:21; 12:7), making him upright (7:29), and setting eternity in his heart (3:11).[111] In His sovereignty God has planned the timing of all things (3:1-8), which timing is beautiful (v. 11), though incomprehensible (v. 11; 8:17; 11:5) and unalterable by man (3:14; 7:13). The events and activities God has under His control include positive elements of life such as birth, planting, healing, upbuilding, joy, searching, keeping, mending, speaking, loving, and enjoying peace—and all their negative opposites (3:1-8). All of life is under divine appointment and timing. Qoheleth was not approving man's killing, tearing, hating, or engaging in war; he was simply affirming that these things occur in human experience (because of man's sin, 7:29) and that man cannot alter what God has planned.

God in his sovereignty and providence controls the rising and setting of the sun, the cyclic movements of the wind, the flowing of rivers, and the evaporation of water (1:5-7). He is called the Shepherd, a term used only a few times of God in the Old Testament (Gen. 48:15; 49:24; Pss. 23:1; 28:9; 80:1; Eccles. 12:11).

Ten times God is said to give and ten times to do. Man's burden, because of his finite wisdom, is given by God (1:13; 3:10). God gives man opportunity to enjoy food and work (2:24; 3:13; 5:19-20; 9:7). He gives man wisdom, knowledge, and happiness (2:26), and wealth, possessions, and honor (5:19; 6:2). God's work, which man cannot fully understand (11:6), includes both good and bad times (7:14). What He does has endurance (3:14) and cannot be altered (7:13).

Other divine attributes evident in Ecclesiastes include God's personality (He hears, 5:2; He despises, 5:2; He can be pleased, 2:26; 7:26; or angered, 5:6), goodness (2:24-26; 3:13; 5:18-19; 6:2), holiness (5:1-2), and inscrutability (3:11, 8:17; 9:1; 11:5). In addition, His justice will be exercised against wickedness. Even His judging the righteous and the wicked is included in God's control of the timing of events (3:17). Though the punishment of the wicked may seem delayed, it will occur (8:13). Young people, challenged to enjoy the energy of their youthful days, should also be sobered by the fact that they are accountable for their actions under the scrutiny of God's judgment (11:9). In fact, every act, whether overt or hidden, good or evil, will be judged by God (12:14) and either rewarded or punished.

Though God cannot be fully understood, some of the motives for His actions are mentioned. These motives include seeking to get people to fear Him (3:14) and testing man to show him his finiteness (v. 18).

All these truths about God are consistent with the rest of Scripture, thus affirming the validity of the place of Ecclesiastes in the Bible.

---

111. That is, God has given man an awareness that he is an eternal creature. He has a God-given "longing to know the eternity of things . . . but, try as we will, we cannot see it. . . . That eternal WHY hangs over our lives" (Wright, "The Interpretation of Ecclesiastes," p. 141). This is "a deep-seated, compulsive desire to know the character, composition, beauty, meaning, purpose, and destiny of all created things" (Kaiser, "Integrating Wisdom Theology into Old Testament Theology: Ecclesiastes 3:10-15," p. 205). Others say the word '*ôlām* rendered "eternity" means (1) the world, or (2) ignorance (revocalizing the word to be read '*elem*), or (3) darkness (from a related Ugaritic root). "Eternity," however, is preferable, in light of the reference to forever ('*ôlām*) in 3:14 and its contrast to time (3:1-17).

MAN

Man's nature. Man's finiteness is seen in the fact that he is created (11:5; 12:1), earth-bound (5:2), and subject to death (3:19-20; 6:6; 7:2; 9:5). He is a rational creature, for he can be guided by his mind (2:3), he can evaluate (v. 11), understand (1:17), investigate (v. 13), observe (v. 14; 2:12, 24; 3:10; 5:13; 6:1; 7:15; 8:9-10; 9:11, 13; 10:5, 7), reflect (1:16; 2:1, 12, 15; 8:9; 12:9), and draw conclusions (2:14, 15; 5:18).

Human emotions, according to Ecclesiastes, include joy (2:10; 9:7, 9; 11:9), love (9:1, 6, 9), hatred (2:17-18; 9:1, 6), contentment (4:8), despair (2:20), grief (v. 23), envy (4:4), anger (7:9), and sadness (v. 4).

Qoheleth referred to the material part of man by by word *bāśār,* normally translated "flesh" or "body." The body can experience "troubles" (11:10) and weariness (12:12). It can also be cheered, figuratively speaking (2:3), or ruined (4:5), that is, dissipated. The NIV translators thought of *bāśār* in 2:3 and 4:5 as a metonymy (a part for the whole) because they translated it "myself" and "himself" in these verses respectively.

The immaterial part of man includes his soul (*nepeš*), spirit (*rûaḥ*), and heart (*lēb*). The soul is the center of desires for fulfillment (6:2-3, 7, 9; see NASB), the seat of inner satisfaction (NIV's "find satisfaction in his work" in 2:24 is literally "causes his soul to see good in his labor") or joy ("depriving myself of enjoyment" in 4:8 is literally "depriving my soul of enjoyment"), or the seat of inner contemplation ("while I [lit. 'my soul'] was still searching," 7:28).

The spirit is used of mood or temperament ("patience" in 7:8 is literally "length of spirit," and "provoked in your spirit," 7:9, speaks of anger). "Spirit" also speaks of man's animating principle of life, which returns to God at death (3:19, 21; 12:7).[112]

Man's "heart" is referred to in Ecclesiastes more often than his soul or spirit. Consistent with its usage elsewhere in the Old Testament, "heart" represents the inner part of man, either his intellect, his emotions, or his will. The intellect is

---

112. Ecclesiastes 3:19-20 affirms that all animate creation, including men and animals, face death. The bodies of each expire and disintegrate into the earth. The spirit (*rûaḥ*) is the life principle in both men and animals (Gen. 7:22). However, Ecclesiastes 3:21 indicates, by means of a question, that no one can observe what happens to the spirit of man, "which ascends upward" (NASB) and the spirit of animals "which descends downward" (NASB). The NIV rendering "who knows *if* the spirit of man" casts doubt on whether man's spirit goes upward. It seems preferable to render the verse, "Who knows *that* the spirit of man goes upward," as suggested by Goldberg (*Ecclesiastes,* p. 69; cf. Michael A. Easton, *Ecclesiastes: An Introduction and Commentary* [Downers Grove, Ill.: InterVarsity, 1983], p. 87). Understood in this way, the verse is pointing up the difference in the destiny of men and beasts. Because they are different, man's spirit goes upward to God and the animal's spirit does not. Only in man's nostrils did God directly breathe the breath of life (Gen. 2:7) and only man was made in God's image (1:26-27). Therefore the breath or animating principle of men and animals has different destinies, but, as Ecclesiastes 3:21 indicates, no one can *see* or observe where their spirits go.

suggested in 1:13, 16-17, in which the NIV translates the Hebrew "I said in my heart" by the words "I applied myself" or "I devoted myself." The idea in these verses is inner determination to complete an intellectual pursuit. The NIV renders "heart" by "mind" in 7:25; 8:9, 16—verses that clearly suggest an intellectual exercise. "Take this to heart" (7:2), "you know in your heart" (v. 22), and "the wise heart will know" (8:5) all suggest the intellect. "I reflected on all this" (9:1), another instance of the exercise of the mind, is literally "I have taken all this to heart."

"Heart" also speaks of the emotional side of the immaterial part of man, as seen in 5:2 ("do not be hasty in your heart"), 7:3 ("a sad face is good for the heart"), 7:4 ("The heart of the wise is in the house of mourning, but the heart of fools is in the house of pleasure"), 9:7 ("a cheerful heart," NASB), 11:9 ("follow the ways of your heart"), and 11:10 ("banish anxiety from your heart").

The willful aspect of the heart is seen in these verses: 7:7 ("a bribe corrupts the heart"), 7:26 ("the woman . . . whose heart is a trap"), 8:11 ("[their] hearts . . . are filled with schemes to do wrong"), 9:3 ("the hearts of men . . . are full of evil"), and 10:2 ("the hearts of the wise inclines to the right, but the heart of the fool inclines to the left").

Man's sin. Sin is universal (7:20) and inward (9:3, "full of evil"). Man's inner pull toward sin accelerates if he feels he, like others, can get away with sin without immediate punishment (8:11). The sinful nature shows itself in specific acts of sin. In Ecclesiastes these acts include oppression of the poor (4:1, 3; 5:8), envy (4:4), greed (v. 8; 5:10), insensitivity in worship (vv. 1-2), unfulfilled vows (vv. 4-5), uncontrolled talk (v. 6), pride (7:8), anger (v. 9; 10:4), discontentment (7:10), sexual seduction and adultery (v. 26), and foolish talk (10:13). Man's injustice to others is described several times (3:16; 4:1; 5:8; 7:7; 8:9, 14).

This wisdom literature repeatedly underscores human finiteness by pointing to man's ignorance. He does not know God's ways (3:11; 8:17; 11:15) nor does he know the future (6:12; 7:14; 8:7; 9:1, 12; 10:14; 11:2, 6).

Sin has its consequences. It holds sinners in its grasp (8:8), it brings them trouble (v. 13), it can undo much good (2:26; 9:18; 10:1), and it can even lead to an untimely death (7:17; 8:13). After man dies, God will punish his sin (3:17; 11:9; 12:14).

Man's work. The word *'āmāl* ("labor, trouble, turmoil, work") occurs frequently in Ecclesiastes.[113] No lasting profit (*yiṭrôn*, "gain" or "advantage" 1:3; 3:9; 5:8-19, 15; 7:12; 10:10-11) comes from one's labor or toil (1:3; 3:9). The fact that work brings pain (2:17, 23) is said to be *hebel*, that is, meaningless or enigmatic,[114] as is the fact that the results of one's labors must be left to someone else (2:19, 21, 26; 4:7-8). Many people find no end to the toils of life (2:22-23; 4:8; 8:16), sometimes because they are driven by envy of what others have (4:4). Though

---

113. The noun occurs 21 times, the verbal form 8 times, and the adjective 5 times.
114. See notes 99 and 100.

work may bring despair (2:20), it can be enjoyed (vv. 10, 24; 3:22; 5:18-19; 8:15; 9:9) when seen as a gift from God.

Man's death. Life is fleeting ("few days," 2:2; 6:12), and death is certain. All will die (2:14-16; 3:18-20; 6:6) including sinners (8:10, 12-13; 9:2-3). Since God has appointed the time of each person's death (3:2), man cannot influence when it will occur (8:8) or even know when it will occur (9:12). Nothing can be taken from this life when a person dies; his exit is like his entrance (5:15-16). The dead go to Sheol (9:10), that is, the grave,[115] where they have no more opportunity to participate in this life's activities (9:5-6). Death is final. To be dead is said to be preferable to a life of oppression (4:1-2) or to nonenjoyment of one's prosperity (6:3-5), and yet the living do have an advantage over the dead (9:4). The dead will eventually be forgotten (1:11; 2:16; 9:5). Old age brings physical problems (12:1-5)[116] and eventuates in death (vv. 6-7), in which a person's spirit goes to God (3:21; 12:7) and he enters eternal consciousness ("his eternal home," v. 5).

A number of truths about man in Ecclesiastes are consistent with truths elsewhere in Scripture, particularly the early chapters of Genesis. Man was originally created good (Gen. 1:31; Eccles. 7:29), but fell into sin (Gen. 3:1-19; Eccles. 3:16; 4:1; 7:29), with the consequence of toil (Gen. 3:14-19; Eccles. 1:3, 8; 2:11, 17, 22) and death (Gen. 3:19, 24; 4:5, 8; Eccles. 2:14-16; 3:20; 4:2; 9:5; 12:6-7). Made from dust and breath (Gen. 2:7; 3:19; Eccles. 3:20; 12:7), man has limited knowledge (Gen. 2:17; Eccles. 8:7; 10:14; 11:5). He was created to live in companionship with others (Gen. 1:27; 2:21-25; Eccles. 4:9-12; 9:9).[117]

Man's responsibilities. What responsibilities does man have in light of the futilities and mysteries of life? What actions did Qoheleth say will aid man in his pursuit of life? At least six suggestions are given in the book.

Be Wise. Although wisdom has its drawbacks (1:18), can be nullified by a little folly (10:1), is transitory (4:13-16; 9:13-16), and does not prevent death (2:14), it does have advantages. It is better to be wise than foolish (v. 13) or famous (4:13-16), for it can help preserve life (7:11-12), gives strength (v. 19), causes one to reflect on the seriousness of life and death (v. 5), and can brighten a person's countenance (8:1). Mere human wisdom, wisdom acquired by intellectual pursuits, is inadequate, but divine wisdom enables man to rest in the sovereign ways of God and in His providential timing (8:5).

---

115. See R. Laird Harris, "The Meaning of the Word Sheol as Shown by Parallels in Poetic Texts," *Bulletin of the Evangelical Theological Society* 4 (December 1961): 129-34.

116. Views on this passage include these four: (a) the decreasing health of organs of the body, (b) old age depicted by a Palestinian winter or approaching storm (Franz Delitzsch, *Commentary on the Song of Songs and Ecclesiastes* [reprint, Grand Rapids: Eerdmans, 1979], pp. 403-5, and Christian D. Ginsburg, *The Song of Songs and Coheleth* [1857; reprint, New York: KTAV, 1970], p. 458); (c) old age depicted as the ruin of an estate (Robert Gordis, *Qoheleth— The Man and His World* [New York: Shocken, 1968], p. 329), or (d) a combination of these views.

117. C. C. Forman, "Koheleth's Use of Genesis," *Journal of Semitic Studies* 5 (1960): 256-63.

Worship and Please God. Proper worship entails a sense of caution and apprehension in God's presence (5:1-2). Making a commitment to the Lord should be done thoughtfully and without haste, but once having made it the worshiper should follow through on his promise (vv. 4-6). Pleasing God should be man's deepest desire (2:26; 7:26).

Remember God. More than a mental exercise, this means to acknowledge His authority and respond with loyalty (12:1, 6) and obedience (v. 13, "keep his commandments").

Fear God. As already discussed, fearing God stands at the heart of wisdom literature. Hence it is no surprise that in Ecclesiastes man is commanded five times to fear God (3:14; 5:7; 7:18; 8:12-13; 12:13), to recognize who He is, and to respond accordingly in worship, awe, love, trust, and obedience.

Be Diligent. Life with its many uncertainties (9:11-12) means man knows comparatively little. "You do not know" is stated three times (11:2, 5-6) to point up man's ignorance of which disasters may come and when, where the wind will blow, how the human embryo develops in the womb, or which enterprise or investment will be successful. This ignorance need not paralyze us or stifle us into laziness. Instead we should forget trying to change things that cannot be changed (v. 3) or trying to predict what cannot be known (vv. 4, 6), and should be hard at work all day (v. 6), working wholeheartedly (9:10) and leaving the results to the Lord. Laziness results in increased problems (e.g., sagging rafters and leaking roofs, 10:18).

Enjoy Life. The fact that Solomon admonished his readers not to look for the answer to life in the pleasures of life itself did not rule out his encouraging them to accept their lot (*heleq*) in life and to be glad for the simple pleasures of life including food, warmth, marriage, and doing good. This theme occurs seven times in the book: 2:24-26; 3:12-13, 22; 5:18-20; 8:15; 9:7-9; 11:8-9. "These modest pleasures are not goals to live for, but bonuses or consolations to be gratefully accepted."[118] The fact that these pleasures are for man's joy and contentment rules out asceticism, and the fact that they are given by God rules out sinful hedonism.

Castellino well summarizes the message of Ecclesiastes: "Therefore: (a) set aside all anxious striving and labor (*'āmāl*); (b) avoid all speculations on God's ruling of the world; and (c) be thankful to God for whatever satisfaction he gives you, valuing and measuring everything as a gift from him and enjoying it, never forgetting that you shall have to render strict account to God Himself."[119]

A THEOLOGY OF THE SONG OF SONGS

THE PLACE OF THE SONG OF SONGS IN WISDOM LITERATURE

Though the canonicity of the Song of Songs has been challenged from time to time,[120] generally Jewish and Christian writers have regarded it as canonical.

---

118. Kidner, *The Wisdom of Proverbs, Job, and Ecclesiastes,* p. 100.
119. George A. Castellino, "Qohelet and His Wisdom," *Catholic Biblical Quarterly,* 30 (1968): 28.
120. Two who argued against its inclusion were Rabbi Hillel and Theodore of Mopsuestia.

The Talmud (*Baba Bathra* 14) included it in the sacred books, as did Melito, Bishop of Sardis, in the latter part of the second century. The canonicity of the book was reaffirmed at the Council of Jamnia in A.D. 90. Defending its place in the Scriptures, Rabbi Akiba (A.D. 50?-132) exclaimed, "The whole world is not as worthy as the day on which the Song of Songs was given to Israel, for all the Writings are holy, but the Song of Songs is the Holiest."[121]

A related concern is why the Song of Songs should be included with the wisdom literature. As suggested earlier, one reason is the fivefold mention of Solomon in the book (1:5; 3:9, 11; 8:11-12). Gordis argues that the Song of Songs belongs in the body of wisdom literature also because it was written as a song.[122] Since Solomon, the wisest of his day (2 Chron. 9:22), was noted for having spoken 3,000 proverbs and 1,005 songs (1 Kings 4:31) and since Ethan and Heman, wise men (1 Kings 4:30-31), were associated with the Temple music (1 Chron. 15:19), it is not surprising that one of Solomon's songs should be associated with wisdom.

The extensive usage of symbolism places the Song of Songs squarely within the poetry of the Bible. "It is the essence of poetry that it employs *symbolism* to express nuances beyond the power of exact definition. This is particularly true of love poetry."[123] Drawing his imagery from nature, Solomon compared the Shulamite to a lily (Song 2:2), and she spoke of him as an apple tree (v. 3). Their love-making was like the enjoyment of fruit (vv. 3-4), wine (1:2; 5:1), honey and milk (5:1), and the delights of a garden (4:12, 16; 5:1; 6:2) and a vineyard (8:12). She spoke of him as a gazelle (2:9, 17; 8:14), quick, agile, handsome in appearance, and strong. He was as attractive and desirable as hennah blossoms (1:14). He called her a dove (2:14; 5:2) and likened her eyes to doves (1:15; 4:1), her hair to a flock of goats (4:1; 6:5, black and flowing), her teeth to sheep (4:2; 6:6, white), her temples to pomegranates (4:3; 6:7, red), her breasts to fawns (4:5, attractive in form and delightful to touch; cf. Prov. 5:19), and her lips to honey (Song 4:11). Using symbolism of him, the Shulamite compared his hair to a raven (5:11), his eyes to doves (v. 12), his lips to lilies (v. 13), his arms, torso, and legs to precious metals (vv. 14-15). In turn, he said her legs were like jewels (7:1), her navel like a goblet (v. 2), her waist like wheat with lilies (v. 2), her breasts like fawns and clusters of fruit (vv. 3-7), her eyes like pools (v. 4), and her head like Mount Carmel (v. 5).

The world *ḥokmāh* does not appear in the Song of Songs, nor does the phrase "the fear of the Lord." In fact neither the word "God" (*'Ĕlōhîm*) nor "Yahweh" appears in the book.[124] Yet the subject of the book legitimizes its place in the wisdom corpus of the biblical canon. The wise person is successful or skillful in his rela-

---

121. Mishnah, Tractate *Yadaim*, 3, 5.
122. Robert Gordis, *The Song of Songs and Lamentations* (New York; KTAV, 1974), pp. 13-16.
123. Ibid., p. 37 (italics his).
124. Some suggest, however, that the suffix *yah* on the word "mighty" in the phrase "like a mighty flame" refers to Yahweh so that the phrase should be rendered "like the flame of the Lord."

tionships, including the relationship of marriage. Directing one's life in accord with God's divine design, the wise person is committed to a life of virtue and marital faithfulness.

The book of Proverbs frequently admonishes its readers to maintain the highest standards of ethical conduct in relation to the opposite sex. Negatively this includes avoiding the adulterous, prostitute, and wayward wife (Prov. 2:16-19; 5:3-14, 20; 6:24, 29, 32-35; 7:4-27; 22:14; 23:27-28; 30:20), with her dangerous sexual entanglements. Positively this involves enjoying and being faithful to one's wife, which is likened to drinking water from one's own cistern, well, or fountain (5:15-19). With more than mere coincidence Solomon spoke to his bride on their wedding night as a fountain and a well of flowing water (Song 4:12, 15).

"The way of a man with a maiden" (Prov. 30:19), that is, his affectionate courting of the woman he loves, is mysterious and involves an element of mystery over what is seemingly difficult, as is the case with the other "ways" in that same verse: the way of an eagle in the sky, the snake on a rock, and a ship on the high seas. Does not the Song of Songs illustrate the way of a man (Solomon) with his maiden (the Shulamite)? The confidence in and admiration of the husband for his "wife of noble character" (Prov. 31:10-12, 20-30) are redolent of the mutual love of Solomon and his bride.

The frequent emphasis in Ecclesiastes on the enjoyment of life also helps prepare the biblical reader for the picture of the delights of marital love in the Song of Songs. Ecclesiastes 9:9 encourages the physical enjoyment of marriage ("Enjoy life with your wife, whom you love"), which is then presented in detail in the Song of Songs. Proverbs 5:18 is similar: "May you rejoice in the wife of your youth."

Still another point of association between the Song of Songs and wisdom literature is creation theology. God created man and woman to enjoy each other in nuptial love (Gen. 2:24). A male-female union in marriage is part of God's design for the world. Should it then be of any surprise that He would include a book in the Scriptures that demonstrates the purity and wholesomeness of the deepest and most intimate of all human relationships? Companionship instead of loneliness (Gen. 2:20), union instead of isolation (vv. 21-23), dependence instead of self-reliance (v. 23), spiritual and physical identity ("one flesh," v. 24) instead of separation, enjoyment of each other's physical charms without shame (v. 25)—these aspects of love within the marriage bond, sketched in Genesis, are depicted and developed in the Song of Songs. Appropriately then, we may think of the Song of Songs as "a commentary on Genesis 2:24 ['they will become one flesh'] and a manual on the blessing and reward of intimate married love."[125]

The Song of Songs has been subjected to numerous and varied interpretations, including (1) an allegory—God's love for Israel (taught by the Jewish medieval rabbis Rashi and Ibn Ezra), of Jesus' love for the church (first suggested by Hippolytus

125. Walter C. Kaiser, Jr., *Toward an Old Testament Theology* (Grand Rapids: Zondervan, 1978), p. 180.

of Rome), of God's love for the virgin Mary (the view of Ambrose), of the mystical union of the soul with God (the view of Origen and Gregory of Nyssa); (2) a collection of poems sung at peasant weddings (first suggested by Bossuet in 1693 and later propounded by Renan, Wetzstein, and Budde); (3) a liturgy for celebrating the cultic wedding of the goddess Ishtar and the god Tammuz (suggested by Meek, Margolis, Snaith, and others); (4) an anthology of disconnected love songs (the view of Gordis, Rowley, Eissfeldt, and many others); (5) a funeral love feast (held by Pope), and (6) a drama (held by Jacobi and others).[126] Rejecting these views, I believe the book is to be considered an expression of normal married love between Solomon and the Shulamite, a peasant girl who became his wife. Many evangelical scholars hold this view. Young wrote that "the Song does celebrate the dignity and the purity of human love."[127] Ginsburg, a Jewish scholar, traced this view in modern times back to Moses Mendelssohn (1729-1786) and held this view himself.[128]

A THEOLOGY OF MAN IN THE SONG OF SONGS

Viewing the Song of Songs as presenting the courtship, wedding, and marriage of Solomon and the Shulamite, we can see a number of aspects of the theology of man. As already stated, God's creation of man and woman included their sexuality, in which husband and wife are seen as enjoying each other in the wholesomeness of sex. As in Genesis, sex in marriage in the Song of Songs is pure and delightful. Husband and wife, physically attracted to each other, are partners who find fulfillment in giving themselves to each other. In admiring each other, the Shulamite and Solomon gave descriptions before the wedding that are general (4:1-15) and after the wedding the descriptions were more explicit and intimate (5:10-16; 6:4-7; 7:1-9).

This appreciation for and delight in each other physically is genuine love, not lust. Their nakedness on their wedding night was not the nakedness of shame, as in Genesis 3:7, but the intimacy of union, as in Genesis 2:25. Though without inhibitions, they were also delicate and without offense in their descriptions of each other. "Here we have none of the crassly physical references to be found in the Akkadian love-charms, in Sumerian love-poems, or in contemporary Arabic love-songs."[129]

Solomon and the Shulamite portray a number of other aspects of the marital relationships besides the purity of their mutual physical attraction. Obviously marriage is viewed as monogamous. In referring to her as "my perfect one" and his

126. For an explanation of these and other views see Gordis, *The Song of Songs and Lamentations*, pp. 2-13; Marvin H. Pope, *Song of Songs,* The Anchor Bible (Garden City, N.Y.: Doubleday, 1977), pp. 89-229; H. H. Rowley, *The Servant of the Lord and Other Essays on the Old Testament* (London: Lutterworth, 1952), pp. 189-234; and C. Hassell Bullock, *An Introduction to the Poetic Books of the Old Testament* (Chicago: Moody, 1979), pp. 224-32. The purpose of this chapter excludes a discussion of these views.
127. Edward J. Young, *An Introduction to the Old Testament* (Grand Rapids: Eerdmans, 1949), p. 327.
128. Ginsburg, *The Song of Songs and Coheleth,* pp. 58-59.
129. Gordis, *The Song of Songs and Lamentations,* p. 40.

"unique" wife (Song 6:9), he was pointing up his sole affection for only her. She reserved her fruit exclusively for him (7:13). In fact she had kept herself a virgin, inaccessible to others, suggested by her description of herself as a private garden and a sealed-up fountain (4:12) and a wall (8:10).

Also their attraction was more than physical; they delighted in the beauty of each other's personality. In humility she spoke of herself as "a rose of sharon," probably a crocus, a mere flower of the meadow (2:1). He responded to this expression of humility by extolling her as "a lily among thorns" (v. 2). He turned her words into a compliment—compared with other women, she was indeed beautiful and they were brambles. Her entire personality was attractive like a lily.[130]

The Song of Songs also depicts the steadfastness that is to be present in marital love. "Love is as strong as death. . . . Many waters cannot quench love; rivers cannot wash it away. If one were to give all the wealth of his house for love, it would be utterly scorned" (8:6-7). True love is "invincible, steadfast, victorious."[131] It endures and it is priceless. The Song of Songs also points up the importance of (1) maintaining premarital chastity (2:1-7; 3:5; 8:4), (2) the bride leaving her family to cleave to her husband (3:6-11; cf. Gen. 2:24), (3) the husband and wife giving each other verbal compliments and visual stimulation, (4) the use of perfumes to enhance the desire for love (4:10-11), (5) the husband's patience in waiting for his wife's sexual excitement to grow (4:12-16), (6) selflessly continuing to love one's spouse (6:4-10; 7:1-9) when conflict arises in marriage (5:7-8),[132] and (7) lifelong commitment to each other ("my lover is mine and I am his," 2:16; "I am my lover's and my lover is mine," 6:3; and, "I belong to my lover, and his desire is for me," 7:10).

The exultation of marital love in the Song of Songs communicates a much-needed emphasis in modern-day societies that promote premarital and extramarital sex, that substitute lust for love, and that denigrate the beauty of sex in permanent, monogamous marital relations. Certainly the engaged or married person who would be wise will follow the principles set forth in the Song of Songs. Being wise or successful in one's marriage calls for a recognition of the sexual morality between husband and wife, presented in Genesis 2 and spelled out in Solomon's courtship, wedding, and marriage in the Song of Songs.

As purity, fidelity, privacy, intimacy, ecstasy, and permanency are present in a marriage, a husband and wife can then enjoy God's approval, as He says to them, "Drink your fill, O lovers" (5:1). Only that kind of marital relationship can be truly wise or successful in the biblical sense.

130. Robert B. Laurin, "The Song of Songs and Its Modern Message," *Christianity Today,* August 3, 1962, p. 11.

131. Ibid.

132. Apparently Song of Songs 5:2-7 records a dream in which the bride fears her husband had left her and then was indifferent about letting him in when he returned. Many evangelical commentators suggest that 1:2–3:5 presents the courtship: 3:6–5:1, the wedding (with 3:6-11 describing the wedding procession, and 4:1–5:1 presenting the wedding night); 5:2–8:4, the maturing of the marriage; 8:5-7, the power of love; and 8:8-14, how love began. (See, e.g., Jack S. Deere, "Song of Songs," in *The Bible Knowledge Commentary, Old Testament,* pp. 1010-11).

7

A THEOLOGY OF THE PSALMS

ROBERT B. CHISHOLM, JR.

The book of Psalms testifies to the vibrant relationship that existed between the God of Israel and His ancient covenant people. Though the Old Testament often portrays the people of Israel in a negative light, the Psalms demonstrate that there were many in the covenant community who trusted in the Lord and obediently served Him. The Psalter contains the prayers and hymns of such people who looked to God as a refuge in the midst of turmoil and experienced His personal intervention in their lives time and time again.

The Psalms differ from the rest of the Old Testament. There one finds God's law proclaimed by Moses, inspired accounts of God's historical dealings with His people, divine advice on practical living revealed through wise men, and messages of judgment and salvation delivered by divinely commissioned prophets. Rather than being God's direct word to His people, the Psalms contain their expressions of faith in God and their responses to God's self-revelation in word and deed.[1] At the

---

1. Psalm 19 speaks of the basic twofold nature of God's revelation to ancient Israel. The first six verses relate how God's creative work "silently" declares His glory. Verses 7-11, which at first glance might seem unrelated to the preceding context, expound on the Lord's revelation through His written Word, the Mosaic law. Psalms 97:6 and 98:2 attest to the revelatory character of God's creative and salvific deeds, respectively. The former states: "The heavens proclaim his righteousness, and all the peoples see his glory." The latter declares: "The Lord has made his salvation known and revealed his righteousness to the nations."

ROBERT B. CHISHOLM, JR., M.Div., Th.M., Th.D., is associate professor of Old Testament studies at Dallas Theological Seminary.

same time, these prayers and hymns *offered to God* must also be understood as *God's word to men and women,* albeit in an indirect sense. God Himself moved the psalmists to pray and sing as they did. Through their words one can learn much about His character and how He relates to His world and His people. Like the other portions of Scripture mentioned above, the book of Psalms is fully inspired (or "God-breathed") and thereby "useful for teaching, rebuking, correcting, and training in righteousness" (2 Tim. 3:16).

Several types of psalms appear in the Psalter. The most common are the laments, or psalms of petition, and the songs of praise. The latter include thanksgiving songs, offered in response to a specific and usually recent act of divine intervention, and hymns, which praise God in more general terms for His goodness throughout history. Many psalms deal with particular themes, such as the royal psalms (which focus on the king and his relationship to God), the so-called enthronement psalms (which depict the Lord ruling over His world), the songs of Zion (which celebrate the greatness of Jerusalem, the city chosen by God as His earthly dwelling place), and the wisdom psalms (which, like Proverbs, contrast the lifestyles and destinies of the righteous and the wicked). As one might expect, this great formal and thematic variety makes the Psalter a rich source for biblical theology.

Like many other portions of the Old Testament, the Psalms are written in poetic form. They are characterized by a correspondence in thought between lines (known as parallelism) and an abundance of literary figures. The use of poetic imagery gives the Psalms a concreteness and vividness which engages the imagination, moves the emotions, and allows the reader to sympathize more easily and even empathize with the psalmists. Because of the emotional and personal qualities of these ancient prayers and hymns, one can readily apply them to his own experiences and appreciate more personally and fully the relevance of the theological truths they affirm.

From her own experience with monarchy and her contacts with foreign nations, ancient Israel was well aware of kingship and its accompanying concepts (cf. 1 Sam. 8). The central theme of the book of Psalms, which its prayers assume and its songs of praise affirm, is God's kingship. For example, Psalm 103:19 declares; "The Lord has established his throne in heaven, and his kingdom rules over all." Several psalms refer specifically to the Lord as king (Pss. 5:2; 10:16; 24:7-10; 29:10; 44:4; 47:2; 48:2; 68:24; 74:12; 84:3; 95:3; 98:6; 145:1; 149:2) or speak of His dominion (22:28; 59:13; 66:7; 89:9; 93:1; 96:10; 97:1; 99:1; 103:22; 114:2; 145:11-13; 146:10). Many psalms depict God as a just judge, a caring shepherd, a mighty warrior, and a covenant overlord, all of which were royal functions or roles in the ancient Near Eastern world.

The book's theological message may be summarized as follows: As the Creator of all things, God exercises sovereign authority over the natural order, the nations, and Israel, His unique people. In His role as universal King God assures order and justice in the world and among His people, often by exhibiting His power as an invincible warrior. The proper response to this sovereign King is trust and praise.

GOD THE CREATOR: THE BASIS FOR HIS KINGSHIP

THE CREATOR OF THE NATURAL ORDER

In agreement with the very first verse of the Bible, the Psalms affirm that God made the heavens and the earth (121:2; 124:8; 134:3; 146:6). His verbal command brought them into existence (33:6, 9; 148:3-5) and they are regarded as the work of His hands (8:3; 19:1; 95:5), formed with infinite understanding and skill (136:5). The Lord separated the sea from the dry land (95:5) and established the earth on its foundations (104:5). He made all living creatures (104:24-26) and placed man and woman, the pinnacle of His creative work, as rulers over the earth (8:6-8). Though humankind may seem to be a small and insignificant part of God's vast universe (8:4), their position is actually a highly exalted one, being just below God Himself (8:5).[2]

Even the surging sea, a symbol of chaos and disorder in ancient pagan thought, is the product of God's creative work. In Ugaritic mythology the storm god Baal, in his quest for kingship, is forced to fight Yam, the god of the sea. After a vicious struggle Baal emerges victorious. The battle is described as follows: "And the club danced from the hand of Baal, (like) an eagle from his fingers. It struck the crown of prince (Yam), between the eyes of judge Nahar. Yam collapsed (and) fell to the earth; his joints quivered and his form crumpled. Baal dragged out Yam and laid him down, he made an end of judge Nahar."[3] In other texts a creature named Leviathan, apparently one of Yam's attendants, opposes Baal's rule (another possibility is that Leviathan is an alternate name for Yam). By way of contrast, some psalms simply affirm that God made the sea (*yām*, 95:5; 146:6). Rather than being viewed as forces that oppose God, the sea and its creatures, including Leviathan, are presented as prime examples of God's creative skill (104:24-26).

However, the motif of the battle with the sea does appear in conjunction with God's creative work in Psalm 89:9-12, perhaps to buttress the psalm's assertion of the Lord's incomparability (cf. vv. 5-7).[4] Contrary to the claims of the pagan nations, the Lord, not Baal or some other god, subdued the forces of chaos (symbolized by the surging sea in v. 9 and the sea monster Rahab in v. 10[5]) when He ordered the uni-

2. Psalm 8:5a is best translated, "You made him a little lower than *God*" (NIV margin). The translation "heavenly beings" (NIV text), though finding support in the form of the passage quoted in Hebrews 2:6-8, is highly unlikely in the literary context of the psalm. The word in question (*'ĕlōhîm*) is a common title of God in the Old Testament, but rarely, if ever, refers to angelic or heavenly beings. Reading "God" in verse 5 is also consistent with Genesis 1:26-28, where God formed humankind in His own image and designated them as His vice-regents over the newly created world.

3. See John C. L. Gibson, *Canaanite Myths and Legends*, 2d ed. (Edinburgh: T. & T. Clark, 1978), p. 44.

4. The motif of the battle with the sea also appears in Psalms in conjunction with God's creation of Israel and His subjugation of historical enemies that threaten His people and seek to disrupt the order He has established. See discussion below.

5. References to Rahab also appear in Job 9:13 and 26:12. In the former "the cohorts of Rahab" are described as cowering before the Lord, who is depicted as the creator and sovereign king

verse.[6] The Lord alone is the sovereign Ruler over the world by reason of His mighty creative act and He alone deserves the acclaim of humankind (cf. vv. 14-15). Having established the earth and subdued the chaotic seas, He rules over His world from His eternal throne (93:1-5).

THE CREATOR OF ISRAEL, HIS COVENANT PEOPLE

The Lord created the nation Israel to be His special covenant people (95:6; 100:3; 149:2). As He promised Abraham and the patriarchs, He miraculously delivered their descendants from bondage in Egypt, formed them into a nation, and led them into the Promised Land (cf. 105:6-11, 42-45). Several psalms rehearse the basic historical events leading to the creation of Israel, highlighting the judgments on Egypt (78:12, 43-51; 105:27-36; 135:8-9; 136:10) and the supernatural deliverance at the Red Sea (77:14-20; 78:13; 81:10; 136:11-15). As Israel's Creator, God was entitled to rule over the nation (114:1-2 declares that Israel became God's "dominion" when He delivered them from Egypt, and in 149:2 "their Maker" stands in poetic parallelism with "their King").

In Israel's case God's creative work was also an act of redemption. The two themes are closely related in Psalm 74:12-17, where the psalmist praised God as the eternal King who brings salvation on the earth (v. 12), recalls God's victory over the sea creature Leviathan (vv. 13-14), and describes some of His creative acts (vv. 15-17). The reference to "salvation" in verse 12 and the description of Leviathan being given "as food to the creatures of the desert" (v. 14; cf. Ex. 14:30) suggest the author is alluding to the crossing of the Red Sea and the destruction of Pharaoh's armies in its waters. At the same time, the association of God's victory with His act of creation (Ps. 74: 15-17) would seem to indicate that the subduing of the primeval sea is in view (cf. 89:9-12). Perhaps it is unnecessary to choose between creation and exodus here, as if they were distinct concepts. The redemptive event at the Red Sea was also an act of creation whereby God brought order (a nation) out of disorder (slavery in Egypt) by subduing the forces of chaos (the Egyptian armies), just as He had done when He subdued the primeval sea and brought the ordered universe into existence. Consequently the language of Psalm 74:12-14, while tailored to reflect the redemptive character of the Exodus event, also alludes to God's victory over chaos at creation.[7]

---

of the universe (cf. Job 9:1-12). These cohorts of Rahab remind one of the allies of Tiamat, whom the creator god Marduk subdued, according to the Babylonian creation account. Job 26:12, like Psalm 89:9-10, refers to God's victory over Rahab in conjunction with His creative work. Other references in Job to a sea creature which promotes disorder appear in 3:8 (Leviathan) and 7:12.

6. The reality behind the imagery would seem to be the "deep" of Genesis 1:2, which, in combination with the primeval darkness, characterized the "formless and empty" condition of the world before God's creative activity, whereby He brought into existence an ordered universe (i.e., "heavens and earth").

7. Isaiah 51:9-16 also closely associates creation and redemption. Verses 9-11 recall the Exodus from Egypt, when God destroyed the monster Rahab (symbolic of the Egyptian armies) so that His redeemed people might cross the sea in safety. In verses 12-16 the Lord speaks as the creator of both the universe and His covenant people (see. vv. 13, 16). As in Psalm 74, Israel's

THE SPHERES OF GOD'S DOMINION

THE NATURAL ORDER

As the sovereign creator and ruler of the universe, the Lord sustains and controls the natural order. By His decree the heavenly bodies carry out their designated functions (19:4-6; 104:19-23; 148:3-6), the earth's foundations remain immovable (93:1; 96:10; 104:5), and the sea stays within its assigned boundaries (93:3-4; 104:6-9). The natural elements, including the thunder, lightning, hail, snow, clouds, and winds do His bidding (29:3-9; 104:3-4; 135:7; 147:15-18; 148:8). As the one who controls the rain, the Lord is the source of life for all creatures (65:9-13; 104:10-15). Life and death are in His hands (104:27-30) and even the underworld, the dwelling place of the dead, is within His jurisdiction (33:19; 95:4; 103:4).[8]

God's sovereignty over His created natural order demonstrates His infinite superiority to the idol gods of the nations (96:5; 97:9; 135:5-7). The Lord's work in creation is evidence of His glory (8:1; 19:1; 96:5-6; 104:1), power (65:6), wisdom (104:24; 136:5), concern for order and justice (96:10; 97:6), reliability (119:89-91), and goodness (104:28; 145:9). All of creation is called on to praise Him (148:1-13). In contrast to the mighty Creator, the pagan idol gods are nothing but the products of human craftsmen (135:15). Though the images have mouths, eyes, and ears, they are incapable of speaking, seeing, hearing, or breathing. They bring only shame to their worshipers (97:7; 135:16-18).

God's control of the natural order is especially significant against the background of ancient Canaanite beliefs. In Ugaritic mythology Baal was the god of the storm who rides the clouds and uses the elements of the storm to bring fertility to the land.[9] He boasts, "I alone am he that is king over the gods, (that) indeed fattens gods and men, that satisfies the multitudes of the earth."[10] Baal was supposedly the source of life's staples, bread (Ugar. *lḥm*), wine (*yn*), and oil (*šmn*).[11] In direct contradiction to this, the psalmists asserted that the Lord softens the earth with showers (65:10) and brings forth "food [Heb. *leḥem*] from the earth; wine [*yayin*] that gladdens the heart of man, oil [*šemen*] to make his face shine, and bread [*leḥem*] that sustains his heart" (104:14-15).

The myths also depict the elements of the storm, especially the thunder and lightning, as Baal's weapons. One text speaks of Baal's arsenal as including his "seven lightnings" and "eight storehouses of thunder."[12] Another describes Baal's

---

redemption from Egypt is viewed as a creative act, and poetic imagery and symbolism associated with the creation of the universe are applied to the Exodus.

8. In 95:4 the parallelism with "mountain peaks" suggests that the "depths of the earth" refer here to the subterranean regions, where the dwelling place of the dead was localized in ancient thought.

9. Gibson, *Canaanite Myths and Legends*, pp. 77-78, 98.

10. Ibid., p. 66.

11. Ibid., p. 98. See text, 16 iii 14-16.

12. On this text see John Day, *God's Conflict with the Dragon and the Sea* (Cambridge: Cambridge U., 1985), p. 59.

mighty storm theophany as follows: "Then Baal opened a slit in the clouds, Baal sounded his holy voice, Baal thundered from his lips . . . the earth's high places shook. Baal's enemies fled to the woods, Hadad's [an alternate name for Baal] haters took to the mountains. And Baal the Conqueror said: 'Hadad's enemies, why are you quaking, assailers of the Valiant One?' Baal's eye guided his hand, as he swung a cedar [i.e., a lightning bolt] in his right hand. So Baal was enthroned in his house."[13] In direct opposition to this mythological portrayal of Baal, Psalm 29 presents the God of Israel as the lord of the storm who sits enthroned over the chaos waters. The psalmist focuses on the destructive power of God's thunderous voice, which shatters even the tallest trees and causes the earth to shake violently (vv. 3-9). Seven times "the voice of the Lord" is specifically mentioned, emphasizing the fullness and magnitude of its awesome power.

In Ugaritic mythology Baal's two major enemies are Yam, the god of the sea (see discussion above), and Mot, the god of death and the underworld. As the god of life and fertility, Baal engages in an ongoing struggle with Mot, which reflects either the seasonal cycle or the threat of prolonged drought to seasonal regularity. Baal initially submits to Mot's authority and is forced to enter the realm of death. Sometime later, Baal returns and finally subdues Mot after a fierce struggle. By way of contrast, the Psalms never depict the Lord as subservient to death, nor do they view death as presenting any real danger to His dominion. Though death is sometimes portrayed as a hostile force which threatens God's people (18:4-5; 116:3) and as a place where one is separated from the worshiping covenant community and no longer experiences the mighty acts of God (6:5; 30:9; 88:10-12; 115:17), even this dark realm is ultimately under the sovereign control of God, who holds the "depths of the earth" in His hand (95:4). He possesses the power to deliver His people from death's grip (16:10; 18:15-19; 33:18-19; 103:4) and He alone determines the life span of His creatures (90:3-12; 104:27-30).

THE NATIONS

As the creator of humankind, the Lord also rules over the world of nations (22:28; 47:8-9; 66:7; 113:4). He does "whatever pleases Him" on earth (135:6; cf. also 115:3), thwarting the plans of the nations (33:10). Throughout Israel's history He demonstrated His sovereignty over the nations. In delivering His people from Egypt and giving them the Promised Land, He defeated powerful kings, including Pharaoh, Sihon of the Amorites, Og of Bashan, and all the kings of Canaan (135:9-11; 136:17-20). Later He enabled David to conquer the surrounding nations and make them vassal states of Israel (18:43-45). In a salvation oracle directed to David, the Lord declared; "Moab is my washbasin, upon Edom I toss my sandal; over Philistia I shout in triumph" (60:8; 108:9). However, when His people rebelled against Him, He raised up nations as instruments of punishment (66:12;

13. The translation is that of Michael D. Coogan, *Stories from Ancient Canaan* (Philadelphia: Westminster, 1978), p. 105.

106:40-43). Though the nations are hostile to the Lord and worship false gods (74:10, 18, 22; 135:15), His desire is that they cease their rebellious ways, recognize His sovereignty, and offer Him genuine worship (2:10-12; 47:1; 96:7).

ISRAEL

Israel's position and obligations as the Lord's vassal kingdom. Though He is king over the natural order and the world of nations, God chose one nation, Israel, to be His unique covenant people. Israel became God's "inheritance" (*naḥălāh*; cf. 33:12; 78:62, 71; 94:5, 14; 106:5, 40) and His "treasured possession" (*sᵉgullāh*; cf. 135:4). Both of these words are used in Deuteronomy as technical terms indicating Israel's special status as God's vassal kingdom (Deut. 4:20; 7:6; 9:26, 29; 14:2; 26:18).[14] In an unique sense then, the Lord is the "God of Jacob" (Ps. 46:7-11).

As the Lord's vassal nation, Israel was entrusted with His law (147:19), which they were to love and obey (103:18; 105:45; 111:10). The most basic demand of the law was absolute allegiance to the Lord. God's people were to place their faith in Him alone (37:3, 5; 44:4-8; 62:8; 115:9-11) and reject the gods of the nations (40:4; 81:9). Neither were they to trust in their own strength or in foreign alliances (20:7; 33:16-17; 118:8-9; 146:3).

The author of Psalm 119 exemplifies an attitude toward the Mosaic law which was the ideal for all Israel (cf. also 19:7-11). In this lengthy prayer the psalmist employed a variety of expressions and metaphors to describe his devotion to God's commandments. Over and over again he affirmed his great love for the law (vv. 47-48, 97, 113, 119, 127, 140, 163, 167) and declared his faithful obedience to it (vv. 17, 44, 55-57, 60, 67, 69, 88, 100-101, 106, 112, 115, 129, 134, 145-46, 166-68). He chose (v. 173), remembered (v. 52), longed for (vv. 20, 40, 174), sought after (vv. 45, 94), held fast to (v. 31), meditated on (vv. 11, 15, 23, 27, 48, 78, 95, 97, 99, 148), delighted and rejoiced in (vv. 14, 16, 24, 47, 70, 77, 92, 111, 143, 174), ran in (v. 32), spoke of (v. 46), found comfort in (v. 52), hoped in (vv. 74, 81, 147), and stood in awe of (v. 120) God's law. On the negative side he did not forget (vv. 61, 93, 109, 141, 153, 176), forsake (v. 87), or depart from (vv. 102, 110, 157) it. As an act of praise he lifted his hands up and thanked God seven times a day for the law (vv. 48, 164), which was a light to guide him through the sometimes

14. Semitic cognates of the relatively rare word *sᵉgullāh* are also used in treaty or covenant contexts to refer to a vassal or servant. Akkadian *sikiltum* apparently signifies a vassal/servant in a seal impression from Alalakh where Abba-El is called the *sikiltum* of a goddess. See Moshe Weinfeld, "The Covenant of Grant in the Old Testament and in the Ancient Near East," *Journal of the American Oriental Society* 90 (1970):195, n. 103. In a text from Ugarit the Ugaaritic cognate *sglt* means "vassal" or "property." H. Huffmon and S. Parker translate the text (UT 2060:11-12) as follows: "Now you belong to the Sun your lord; you are his servant, his property (*sglt*)." See Herbert B. Huffmon and Simon B. Parker, "A Further Note on the Treaty Background of Hebrew *Yāda'*," *Bulletin of the American Schools for Oriental Research* 184 (1966):37.

treacherous path of life (v. 105). For the psalmist God's law was more valuable than material wealth (vv. 72,127) and more satisfying than honey (v. 103).

God's presence with His covenant people. As Israel's covenant Lord, God lived among His people. In Moses' day He guided and protected them with a cloud and a pillar of fire (78:14; 105:39). He later dwelt in the Tabernacle at Shiloh (78:60) and eventually chose the Temple in Jerusalem as His permanent sanctuary (78:68-69; 87:1-2; 132:13-14).

Several psalms, especially the songs of Zion (Pss. 46, 48, 76, 84, 87, 122), exalt Jerusalem as the Lord's dwelling place. Zaphon, located north of Israel, was the sacred mountain of the Canaanites from which their high god El supposedly ruled. However, Zion was the real "Zaphon," for it was here that the Lord God of Israel, the "Great King" of the universe, lived and ruled (48:2). As the capital of God's universal kingdom, Zion enjoyed His protection and blessing. God's presence within the city made it immune from the raging nations outside its walls (46:1-11). When they advanced against the city, they were swiftly destroyed by His devastating power (48:3-8; 76:3-6). Mount Zion would endure forever, unshaken by its foes (125:1). God provided the city's residents with the necessities of life, causing them to sing with joy (132:15-16). His abundant blessings were like life-giving streams flowing through the city (46:5; cf. 36:8). Eventually even the pagan nations would be forced to recognize Zion's greatness and the privileged position of its residents (87:3-7).

Zion was the focal point of ancient Israelite religion and faith, both before and after the Exile. God's people, especially religious pilgrims approaching the city (84:5-7), found comfort and delight in its very physical structures (48:12-13; 84:1; 122:3) for they were tangible reminders of God's protective presence. Psalm 84 extols the Temple in particularly glowing terms, even romanticizing it as a place of safety for a mother bird and her little ones (v. 3). In his exhilaration the author cried out, "Better is one day in your courts than a thousand elsewhere; I would rather be a doorkeeper in the house of my God than dwell in the tents of the wicked" (v. 10). All those who loved Jerusalem were to pray for its continuing welfare and prosperity (122:6-9). Even when they were taken captive to Babylon and mockingly asked to sing one of the songs of Zion for their captors, fear-stricken exiles continued to vow their loyalty to the city (137:1-6). Writing after the fall of Jerusalem, the author of Psalm 102 prayed for the restoration of Zion and anticipated a day when the Zion ideal would be fulfilled (vv. 13-22). In that day the nations and their rulers would fear the Lord (v. 15) and assemble in Jerusalem to worship His name (vv. 21-22).

Of course, mention of the Exile and the fall of Jerusalem reminds one that the hymnic ideal of Zion as the city of God stands in stark contrast to the historical reality of the city's violent overthrow and total ruin. According to the psalms surveyed above, Zion, as God's permanent (cf. 132:14) residence, was immune from the attacks of the nations. However, other psalms describe in vivid detail its destruction at the hands of pagan armies. The author of Psalm 74 lamented that Babylonian soldiers entered the Temple and hacked it to bits with their axes before burning it to the ground (vv. 1-11, esp. vv. 4-8). Were those who celebrated God's protective presence in Zion mere wishful thinkers carried away to ridiculous extremes by their unrealistic expectations? Did not Jeremiah denounce the citizens of Jerusalem for placing false hope in the city's defenses and the Temple's courts (Jer. 7:4; 8:19; 21:13)?

To resolve this tension one must recognize that the songs of Zion, with their at times extravagant language and optimistic viewpoint, are not unconditional prophetic guarantees or promises, but rather expressions of an ideal which was only partially realized in the preexilic period. The Zion portrayed in the songs is what Jerusalem should and could have been had its leaders and citizens remained loyal to the God who dwelt in their midst. Jerusalem's miraculous deliverance from the Assyrians in 701 B.C. even provided a glimpse, however brief, of what God was able and willing to do for the city in response to genuine repentance and faith on the part of His people (Isa. 36–37). However, Hezekiah's trust in the Lord at that time was a rare exception in Israel's history. The utter lack of faith displayed on an earlier occasion by his father Ahaz (Isa.7) was the norm among God's people. Eventually the people's obstinate disobedience forced the Lord to remove His protective presence from the sinful city, leaving it open to enemy invaders and destruction (cf. Ezek. 10-11). On that day the Zion ideal suffered a serious setback.

However, the authors of the songs of Zion should not be ridiculed as dreamers or be associated with the idolatrous, unjust rebels who transformed the Zion ideal into a false guarantee of divine protection and brought the prophets' criticism down on them. Rather they should be admired as loyal followers of the Lord who delighted in the reality of His presence in preexilic Jerusalem and who in faith anticipated the realization of the full potential it afforded. Though they chose to focus on the ideal, rather than the moral-ethical prerequisites for its realization, they certainly did not overlook or repudiate the latter (cf. Ps. 84:11*b*-12). Someday the ideal which they longed for and even to a small degree had experienced will materialize. The same prophets who announced the downfall of ancient Jerusalem also looked forward to a day when God would purify and restore Zion and again make it His dwelling place. At that time the city and its inhabitants will receive universal recognition as the "city of God" (cf. 87:3-7). For this reason the Zion ideal continued to inspire Israelites, even when they were confronted by the realities of God's judgment (cf. 102:13-22).[15]

15. The ideal of God dwelling among His people, which ancient Israel experienced in part and future Israel will realize in full, stirred the imagination of the early church. In the New Testament the motif of an ideal Zion, which included the assurance of God's protective presence and ongoing blessing, is expanded to include realities beyond the literal restoration of Zion. The author of Hebrews used Zion in a figurative sense in reference to the heavenly city populated by God, His angelic hosts, and the "church of the firstborn" (Heb. 12:23; cf. also 16; 13:14, and Gal. 4:26). The apostle John envisioned a new Jerusalem descending from heaven following the final judgment (Rev. 21:1–22:6). This city, called "the bride, the wife of the Lamb,"

God's gift of a mediator to His covenant people. In addition to giving His covenant people His protective presence, God gave them the Davidic king to serve as a mediator between Himself and the nation. He took David from tending sheep and made him "the shepherd of his people Jacob" (78:70-72; cf. 89:20), responsible for guiding them in righteousness and assuring peace and justice in the land.

God established a covenant with His anointed ruler, which elevated David and his descendants to a special position before Him (2 Sam. 7). The Davidic king enjoyed the status of God's "son" (Ps. 2:7) and "firstborn" (89:26-27).[16] As the Lord's vice-regent over Israel, he sat, as it were, at God's right hand (110:1, though see discussion of this psalm below) and was even addressed as "God" (45:6).[17]

is inhabited by the people of God from all ages (cf. Rev. 21:12-14, the symbolism of which alludes to both the tribes of Israel and the church). This extension of the Zion ideal beyond its Old Testament limits illustrates how the full potential of biblical motifs is sometimes realized in the progress of revelation as the motifs are utilized as figures and symbols. There is a sense in which the Zion ideal is already being fulfilled through the church. However, when the nation Israel is restored (cf. Rom. 11:25-32) the ideal will be more fully (and literally!) realized as God establishes His earthly rule from Jerusalem. Nevertheless, John's use of the motif in Revelation shows that even this literal millennial fulfillment of the Zion ideal does not exhaust its potential. A day will come when all of God's people from all ages will together enjoy His protective presence as He rules over His new creation from the new Jerusalem.

16. Another reference to the Davidic king as God's "son" may appear in Psalm 2:12*a*, though several problems arise here. The Masoretic text has been traditionally interpreted to read "Kiss the son," but the word for "son" is not the normal Hebrew term *bēn* (as in v. 7), but *bar*, the Aramaic form of the word. Some defend the reading by pointing out that the exhortation is addressed to the kings of the surrounding nations, which would have included Aramean rulers. However, others prefer to read, "Kiss (i.e., do homage) with sincerity," understanding the form in question as a noun or adjective related to the verb *bārar*, "purify." This reading fits well with the parallelism of the preceding verse (cf. "Serve . . . with fear" and "rejoice with trembling"). Another possibility is that the text of verses 11*b*-12*a* is corrupt and should be reconstructed, one suggested reading being "with trembling kiss his feet."

17. Though it is possible to argue that Psalm 82:6 is addressed to God, not the king, this is improbable in this psalm, which seems to be addressed to the king from the outset (cf. v. 2). To propose a shift in addressee from the king to God somewhere between verses 2-6 (and then back again between vv. 6-7) has no justification in the text and harms the literary integrity of the opening verses. The "scepter of justice" mentioned in verse 6 is most naturally the king's, whose love for righteousness is applauded in verse 7, where he is clearly addressed. Referring to or addressing the king as "God," while rare, should be taken neither as blasphemy, on the one hand, nor as proof of the king's deity, on the other. As God's chosen vice-regent, the king represented God on the battlefield (cf. vv. 3-5) and on the throne of the nation. When God energized him for war or accomplished just deeds through him, it was as if God Himself were fighting on the battlefield or making pronouncements from the throne.

Various parallels to the phenomenon in Psalm 45:6 (a king or official being addressed or referred to as "God") have been proposed. In Exodus 4:16 and 7:1 Moses, as a divine representative to Aaron and Pharaoh, is referred to as "God," but the figurative use of the title is clearly delineated in the context (hence NIV's *"like* God"). Some understand human judges to be the referent of *'ĕlōhîm* in Exodus 21:6; 22:8-9, 28, and 1 Samuel 2:25, but there is no reason why God should not be understood as the direct referent in these texts. In Psalm 82:1, 6 the "gods" addressed are probably human rulers who entertain delusions of deity for themselves and are thus appropriately (and sarcastically!) referred to as divine beings (see discussion below). Perhaps the closest parallel to Psalm 45:6 is Isaiah 9:6, where one of the coming warrior king's titles is "Mighty God" (*'ēl gibbôr*). See p. 312 for a discussion of Isaiah 9:6.

The background for the Davidic Covenant and the sonship imagery associated with it is the ancient Near Eastern covenant of grant, whereby a king would reward a faithful servant by elevating him to the position of "sonship" and granting him special gifts, usually related to land and dynasty. Unlike the conditional suzerain-vassal treaty, after which the Mosaic Covenant was patterned, the covenant of grant was an unconditional, promissory grant which could not be taken away from the recipient.[18] Consequently God's covenantal promises to David were guaranteed by an irrevocable divine oath (89:3, 28-37; 132:11). Obligations were attached, of course, to the covenant. Each king was responsible to obey God's law (132:12). If he failed in this regard, he would be severely disciplined and forfeit full participation in the benefits of God's promise (89:30-32). However, even under these circumstances, God would not revoke His promise to the house of David (89:33-34). The Davidic line would continue and the benefits attached to the covenant would remain available to those who faithfully adhered to God's demands. God's solemn oath to David was as certain as the continuing existence of the sun and moon, which never fail to make their regular appearances in the sky (89:35-37).

God promised His chosen king a continuing dynasty, victory over his enemies, and universal dominion. The central promise of the covenant was that of an everlasting dynasty. The Lord declared to David, "I will establish your line forever and make your throne firm through all generations" (89:4). However, the Davidic kings lived in a hostile world where internal foes would seek to usurp their position and foreign kings would threaten their kingdom. Therefore the Lord promised to strengthen the king with His very own arm, enabling him to defeat would-be oppressors and enemies (20:6; 21:8-12; 63:9-11; 89:21-23; 132:18). In Psalm 18 David described in detail how God supernaturally energized him for battle (vv. 29, 32-35; cf. 144:1) and enabled him to subdue his enemies (18:36-42). As his protector the Lord was like a rocky cliff, a fortress, a shield, and the horn of a wild ox. (vv. 2, 30-31; cf. 144:2). Overwhelmed by the greatness of David and his God, nations willingly submitted to his authority (18: 43-45), in accord with God's covenantal promise to give His anointed ruler dominion over the whole earth (2:8; 72:8-11; 89:25).

The king's success in battle was essential to the entire nation's well-being. This

18. See Weinfeld, "The Covenant of Grant in the Old Testament and in the Ancient Near East," pp. 184-203, for a thorough study of this type of covenant and its biblical parallels, including the Davidic Covenant. A particularly informative illustration of the favored servant being elevated to "sonship" is found in a second millennium treaty between the Hittite king Šuppiluliuma and his subject Mattiwaza. The latter recalls the words of his lord and benefactor, "(The great king) grasped me with his hand . . . and said: 'When I shall conquer the land of Mitanni I shall not reject you, I shall make you my son, I will stand by (to help in war) and will make you sit on the throne of your father'" (Weinfeld, p. 191). The following excerpt from a treaty between the Hittite ruler Hattušiliš III and his subject Ulmi-Tešup of Dattaša illustrates the unconditional nature of a royal grant: "After you, your son and grandson will possess it [the land and dynasty granted by the lord], nobody will take it from them. If one of your descendants sins the king will prosecute him at his court. Then when he is found guilty . . . if he deserves death he will die. But nobody will take away from the descendant of Ulmi-Tešup *either his house or his land* in order to give it to a descendant of somebody else" (cf. Weinfeld, p. 189, italics his).

is perhaps most clearly seen in Psalm 144, which records the king's prayer for God's intervention on his behalf (vv. 1-11, esp. vv. 5-8) and describes the national consequences of a positive response (vv. 12-15). The king asked God to come down from heaven in all His splendor and deliver him from the enemy armies which surged against him like "many waters." When the nation's security was assured through victory, signs of prosperity and fertility would be everywhere, including strong young men, beautiful young women, barns filled with food, and fields teeming with flocks and herds.

The royal psalms clearly outline the essential obligations and responsibilities of the Davidic king. As noted above, his most basic responsibility was to obey the law of God (89:30-31; 132:12). More specifically the king was to promote righteousness and justice in the land (72:1) by personal example and deed. This is perhaps most clearly seen in Psalm 101, which is a royal confession of loyalty to God (cf. also 18:20-24). The king declared, "I will be careful to lead a blameless life. . . . I will walk in my house with blameless heart. I will set before my eyes no vile thing" (101:2-3*a*). He also vowed to choose faithful, godly men, rather than deceitful slanderers, for his royal court (101:3*b*-7), and to make every effort to eliminate evil men from the land (101:8). Psalm 72 describes the ideal king as one who actively promotes justice in the land by defending the cause of the afflicted, weak, and needy, and by crushing those who oppress them (vv. 2, 4, 12-14). It was through this kind of ruler that the nation would experience peace, prosperity, and international prestige (cf. vv. 3, 5-11, 15-17).

The messianic fulfillment of the Davidic ideal. As with the Zion ideal discussed above, the ideal of a godly, just Davidic king portrayed in the royal psalms was never fully realized in ancient Israel. Solomon ruled over a vast kingdom, but his introduction of foreign religious practices ultimately led to its downfall. When his foolish son Rehoboam sought to intensify his father's oppressive treatment of the Northern labor force, the kingdom was permanently divided, with the Davidic king exercising authority over only a southern remnant of the nation. Although a few kings exhibited godly traits, the ideal of a just king who would bring the nation lasting peace and prosperity remained just that, an unfulfilled ideal.

When God judged the nation for its rebellious deeds, the Davidic kings even experienced humiliation. The author of Psalm 89, after reminding God of His ancient promises to the house of David (cf. vv. 1-37), lamented the catastrophe which had fallen on the dynasty in his day (vv. 38-51). He observed that God in His anger had "rejected" and "spurned" His anointed king and "renounced" the covenant. The king's crown lay in the dust, his palace was in ruins, and the king himself was an object of scorn. The Lord had removed His support from the king and allowed his enemies to defeat and mock him. In agony the psalmist asked, "How long, O Lord? Will you hide yourself forever? How long will your wrath burn like fire? . . . O Lord, where is Your former great love, which in Your faithfulness you swore to David?" (vv. 46, 49). This picture of shame and ruin stands in stark contrast to the beautiful royal portrait painted in Psalm 72.

Though the Exile seemed to deliver the death blow to the Davidic ideal, the words of the prophets continued to echo through Jerusalem's ruins. Before the Exile, Isaiah, Micah, Jeremiah, and others had announced the downfall of the Davidic throne. However, they had also looked forward to a day beyond judgment when God would raise up an ideal ruler and fulfill His promises to David of eternal, universal dominion. In the postexilic period Haggai and Zechariah revived this hope by attaching the Davidic promises to the person of Zerubbabel, the governor of Judah under the Persians and a descendant of David. Eventually God raised up the "Anointed One," or Messiah. Jesus Christ, son of David par excellence, came as Israel's Messiah, but was rejected and crucified. However, He will someday return to earth and establish the kingdom foreseen by the prophets. In that day the Davidic ideal of the royal psalms will become reality as Jesus rules "from sea to sea" and brings blessing to all nations (Ps. 72:8. 17).

Because the Davidic ideal portrayed in the royal psalms is fully and finally realized through Jesus, these psalms are often classified as messianic psalms. The label is appropriate but in need of qualification. The royal psalms, by their literary nature, are not inherently prophetic and should not be understood as *direct* predictions of Jesus' messianic reign. As already noted, they express an ideal which, though probably attached with renewed hope to many historical Davidic kings on the occasion of their accession to the throne, is ultimately and fully realized in and through Jesus. As such, these psalms are to be understood as messianic in an indirect sense, in contrast to the messianic predictions of prophetic literature, which, though also rooted in the Davidic covenantal ideal, may be classified as directly messianic on the basis of the literary genre in which they appear.

A closer look at several of the royal psalms supports this conclusion in that various details of the psalms more naturally reflect the historical background of ancient Israel, not the future reign of Christ. At the same time, the ideal expressed in the psalm as a whole finds its realization in Jesus, not in a mere human ruler.

For example, Psalm 2 reflects the period of the Davidic-Solomonic empire when many of the surrounding vassal nations must have sought to free themselves from Israelite rule. The psalm begins with a description of the nations' desire to rebel against the Lord and His anointed ruler (vv. 1-3). Verses 4-6 then give the Lord's response. He laughs in mockery and reminds the kings that He has installed His ruler on Zion. The king speaks in verses 7-9, recalling the Lord's decree whereby he was elevated to the position of sonship and granted universal dominion. Finally the kings are warned to exercise wisdom by submitting to the Lord and His king before they are swept away by divine judgment (vv. 10-12). Perhaps the psalm was used when representatives of subject nations were brought to Jerusalem to vow their loyalty and pay their tribute. Its rehearsal of God's decree would have made it suitable for coronation ceremonies as well.

As time passed and the glory of the Davidic empire began to fade, there was little if any correspondence between the psalm's ideal of universal dominion and the political realities of Israel's world. Israel was left to look for a future king through whom the ideal might be realized. In the progress of history and revelation Jesus emerged as that king (Rev. 9:15 quotes Ps. 2:9 in describing Jesus' descent from heaven to destroy His enemies). Recognizing Jesus as the Messiah, the apostle Peter saw His rejection by the rulers of the day as a manifestation of the rebelliousness described in Psalm 2 (cf. Acts 4:25-28, which quotes Ps. 2:1-2). Others saw the words of verse 7 as being especially applicable to the resurrected and ascended Christ who sits at the right hand of the Father (Acts 13:33; Heb. 1:5; 5:5).

Psalm 45 is another example of a royal psalm which reflects the historical situation of ancient Israel, but which ultimately applies to Christ in that He is the one through whom the primary aspects of its idealistic portrayal of the Davidic ruler are fully realized. This psalm was written for the king (cf. v. 1) on the occasion of a royal wedding. Verses 2-7 praise the king as "the most excellent of men" who subdues enemy armies by his military might and establishes justice in the land. Verses 8-15 focus on the king and his bride, while the conclusion (vv. 16-17) promises the king a lasting dynasty and continuing fame. In this psalm one sees the Davidic king at his finest—a handsome, robust warrior concerned with justice and assured of a continuing dynasty on the occasion of his marriage to a beautiful princess. The eventual demise of the Davidic dynasty threatened to reduce the psalm to the status of an irrelevant, albeit romantic, relic of the distant past, but through Christ its portrayal of the ideal king will be realized. The author of Hebrews thus applied the words of verses 6-7 to Jesus (Heb. 1:8-9).[19] In so doing he utilized the passage that most readily pertains to Christ, namely, the portion of the psalm dealing with the king's special status and just character. At the same time, the New Testament avoids drawing any allegorical connection between the ancient royal wedding and Christ's relationship with His church.

Psalm 72 is another indirectly messianic royal psalm. The psalm begins and ends with prayers (vv. 1, 15-17) offered on behalf of the king (perhaps Solomon or his son, cf. the heading).[20] The intervening verses describe the conditions that will prevail in the kingdom if the Lord responds positively to these petitions for blessing.[21] The idealistic portrayal of the king as one who establishes justice, peace, and prosperity in his realm and achieves lasting fame has striking parallels in western

19. In its original setting the title "God" was applied to the king as God's vice-regent and earthly representative (see. n. 17), but in Hebrews 1:8-9, where it is addressed to Jesus as God incarnate, it takes on a heightened, or literal, sense.

20. The petitionary framework is clearly established by the imperative form in verse 1 (*tēn*, "Endow") and the jussive forms in vv. 15-17 (*wîhî*, "may he live," and *yᵉhî*, "Let abound," and "May . . . endure"). Verses 18-20 conclude Book II of the Psalter (Pss. 42-72), not Psalm 72 per se.

21. It is not certain whether the verbal forms in verses 2-14 should be translated with the future tense (NIV text) or as jussives (NIV marginal note with v. 2). Even if one uses the future tense, the realization of the situation described is conditional on a positive response to the introductory prayer and concluding blessing. The verses should not be taken as an unconditional prophecy of a future age.

Semitic royal inscriptions from the early first millennium B.C.[22] Certain features of the description, such as the geographical extent of the kingdom (v. 8) and the references to visitors and tribute arriving from distant lands, including Sheba (vv. 10-11, 15), seem to reflect the Solomonic era (cf. 1 Kings 4:21; 10:1-15, 23-25). Nevertheless the ideal expressed in the psalm was never fully realized in Israel's history, not even during the reign of Solomon. The psalm may be labeled messianic because only during the millennial reign of Christ will Israel and the nations enjoy the peace and prosperity for which its author longed.

Some label Psalm 110 as an indirectly messianic royal psalm, but in this case the classification is more uncertain because of the way the psalm is utilized in the New Testament. To appreciate the complexity of the problem a survey of both the psalm's contents and its use in the New Testament is necessary.

Psalm 110 begins with a formal decree, spoken by the LORD God (NIV "the LORD," which translates *yhwh*, "Yahweh") to the psalmist's "Lord" (*'ādōn*), who is clearly a royal figure (cf. v. 2, "your mighty scepter from Zion" and "you will rule"). Neither the author nor his "Lord" are precisely identified. If one understands the phrase *l^edāwîd* in the heading as indicating authorship (NIV "of David"), then David's "Lord" would be some other royal figure to whom even he is subordinate. If one takes the heading in the sense of "for " or "pertaining to David," then David himself would be the "Lord" referred to and the psalmist would be one of David's subjects, perhaps a member of his royal court. At any rate, the psalmist observed that Yahweh had granted his "Lord," the king, a privileged position at the divine right hand and has promised to subdue the king's enemies (v. 1). In verses 2-3 the psalmist speaks to his "Lord." He reiterated the content of the preceding oracle and anticipated the king's being supported by his subjects or troops (the precise meaning of v. 3 is not clear). Verse 4 reports another divine decree (cf. v. 1) whereby Yahweh elevates the psalmist's "Lord" to the status of a king-priest patterned after Melchizedek. Verse 5*a* may be addressed to God (cf. "at your right hand" with "Sit at my right hand" in v. 1), in which case verses 5*b*-7 describe the king's victories over his enemies and sustenance in battle. Another possibility is that the king is addressed in verse 5*a* and that "the Lord" (*'ǎdōnāy*) is Yahweh. In this case verses 5*b*-6 probably describe God's, not the king's, actions. Unless verse 7 is anthropomorphic, it probably depicts the reviving effects which God's intervention produces for the king.

Psalm 110 was utilized by Jesus, Peter, and the author of Hebrews. In a debate with the Pharisees, Jesus, assuming that David spoke the words of verse 1 about his Lord, the Messiah, asked His opponents how the Messiah could be both David's son and Lord (Matt. 22:41-45; Mark 12:35-38; Luke 20:41-44). Understanding the language of verse 1 in a literal sense, Peter concluded that David could not be the one addressed since he did not ascend into heaven and sit at God's

---

22. See especially the Azitawadda inscription, a translation of which appears in James B. Pritchard, ed., *The Ancient Near East*, 2 vols. (Princeton: Princeton U. Press, 1958-75), 1:215-17.

right hand. Peter assumed, like Jesus, that David spoke these words about the Messiah and concluded that Jesus is "both Lord and Christ" (Acts 2:34-36). The author of Hebrews understood Jesus as the recipient of both of the decrees recorded in Psalm 110 (Heb. 1:13; 5:6-10; 6:20; 7:11-22) and even developed an elaborate theology of Christ's priesthood based on the second oracle. In short, the New Testament assumes that Jesus the Messiah is at least the ultimate referent of "my Lord" in Psalm 110:1 and the recipient of the oracles recorded in Psalm 110:1, 4. Furthermore, Jesus and Peter understood David as at least the speaker of the words of Psalm 110:1, if not their original author.

In light of the New Testament evidence, one could easily and perhaps rightly conclude that Psalm 110 is a uniquely prophetic royal psalm which contains a direct prediction of the Messiah's reign and ministry uttered by David himself. However, in fairness one must acknowledge that this is not the only explanation that satisfies the biblical data. Another possibility is that the psalm is indirectly messianic like the others surveyed above. David may have written the psalm for Solomon's coronation (or applied to Solomon a psalm originally written for him[23]) in order to authorize the succession (what better way to do this than actually call the chosen heir one's "Lord"?) and attach the covenantal promises to his son's person (cf. 1 Chron. 28-29 for an historical account of Solomon's succession). Of course, despite Solomon's greatness, the ideal portrayed in the psalm did not materialize fully or permanently in Israel's history. Because Jesus is the one in whom it is realized (and the one whom the idealized historical king foreshadowed), he could declare that David spoke of him, and Peter and the author of Hebrews could understand the oracles of Psalm 110 as addressed to Jesus.

If one interprets Psalm 110 as indirectly messianic, then it is apparent that both Peter and the author of Hebrews, in applying the psalm's two oracles to Jesus, gave the language a heightened, or literal, sense (the author of Hebrews does the same with Ps. 45:6; see note 19). Viewed against the background of the Davidic promises and ideal, the command in the first oracle ("Sit at My right hand," Ps. 110:1) is a figurative expression emphasizing the king's election and special position in relation to God. However, both Peter and the author of Hebrews understood a more literal fulfillment in the case of Jesus, who ascended into heaven and took up His place at the right hand of the Father (Acts 2:34-35; Heb. 1:3; 8:1; 10:12-13; 12:2). In the context of ancient Davidic kingship, the second oracle (Ps. 110:4) refers to the Davidic ruler's dual status of civil and religious leader, likening it to that of Melchizedek, the ancient king-priest of Salem (Gen. 14:18). Although certain priestly duties were strictly limited to the Levites (2 Chron. 26:16-18), the Davidic ruler did oversee many aspects of Israel's religious institutions and worship system and, as a

---

23. The New Testament stops short of attributing authorship of the psalm to David. It states only that David *spoke* the words of Psalm 110:1, not that he was their original author (Matt. 22:43, 45; Mark 12:36-37; Luke 20:42, 44; Acts 2:34).

mediator between God and the people, could be called a "priest."[24] In their ancient Israelite context the words "You are a priest *forever* " were likely understood as hyperbole or as a promise of enduring priestly status for the king's dynasty, not as a promise of literal eternal life for the king as an individual.[25] However, the author of Hebrews elevated the language to a new level. As the final and ideal royal (or "Melchizedekian") priest, Jesus does not simply exercise authority over the Levites, but rather, supersedes them and makes the old order obsolete (Heb. 7-10). In establishing his case, the author of Hebrews emphasized that Jesus is literally an eternal priest (7:3, 16-17, 24-25), in contrast to the Levites, who attained office through ancestral succession (7:16, 23).

GOD'S ROYAL FUNCTIONS

JUDGE

Ancient Near Eastern background. Preserving order and justice was a chief responsibility of kings in the ancient Near Eastern world. Egyptian royal names from the twelfth dynasty frequently contain the elements *ma'at*, "justice," or *ma'a*, "just."[26] Mesopotamian rulers referred to justice in their royal year formulas. For example, Hammurabi's second year was known as "the year in which he set forth justice in the land."[27] In the interest of justice a release of debts was sometimes proclaimed.[28] Kings were also responsible for helping the weak and destitute elements of society, which included widows, orphans, and the poor. Richard Patterson writes, "Throughout the Babylonian legal stipulations and wisdom literature the care of the widow, the orphan, and the poor is enjoined, since the ideal king, as the living representative of the god of justice, the sun god Šamaš, is expected to care for the

---

24. For a convenient summary and helpful discussion, see the remarks of John H. Stek in *The NIV Study Bible* (Grand Rapids: Zondervan, 1985), p. 907 (note on Ps. 110:4). A survey of the pertinent texts shows that the Davidic king superintended the worship system of Judah, exercised authority over the Levites, and at times performed worship functions. David instructed the Levites to bring the Ark to Jerusalem (1 Chron. 15:11-15), participated in the procession, offered sacrifices, danced before the Lord in a linen ephod, and pronounced blessings on the people (2 Sam. 6:12-19). At the dedication of the Temple Solomon led the ceremony by offering sacrifices, pronouncing blessings on the people, and praying to the Lord on behalf of the nation (1 Kings 8). Several kings, including Asa, Joash, Hezekiah, and Josiah, commissioned the priests to repair and/or rededicate the Temple (2 Kings 12:4-16; 22:3-7; 23:4; 2 Chron. 15:8; 24:4-14; 29:3-36; 35:15-19). David and Hezekiah appointed musicians to lead in worship (1 Chron. 6:31-32; 25:1; 2 Chron. 29:25, 30) and assigned the Levites their various duties (1 Chron. 23:2-32; 31:2). Jehoshaphat appointed priests to teach the people (2 Chron. 17:7-9) and settle disputes (2 Chron. 19:8-11).
25. Eternal life is hyperbolically ascribed to human kings in Psalm 21:4-6; 61:6-7; 72:5 (LXX).
26. John A. Wilson, *The Culture of Ancient Egypt* (Chicago: U. of Chicago, 1956), p. 133.
27. H. W. F. Saggs, *The Greatness That Was Babylon* (New York: New American Library, 1962), p. 198.
28. For example, see the edict of Ammiṣaduqa in Pritchard, *The Ancient Near East*, 2:36-41.

oppressed and needy elements of society."[29] In a text from Ugarit, Yaṣṣib denounced King Keret as follows: "You do not judge the cause of the widow, you do not try the case of the importunate. You do not banish the extortioners of the poor, you do not feed the orphan before your face (nor) the widow behind your back."[30] In his role as guardian of justice, the king was regarded as the shepherd of his people.[31] For example, the Assyrian Tukulti-ninurta I stated, "When Ashur, my lord, faithfully chose me for his worshiper, gave me the scepter for my office of shepherd, (presented) me in addition the staff for my office of herdsman . . . (at that time) I set my foot upon the neck of the lands (and) shepherded the extensive black-headed people like animals. He (Ashur) taught me just decisions."[32]

God as universal judge. In typical ancient Near Eastern fashion several hymns in the Psalter depict the Lord as a royal judge who preserves order and executes justice throughout His universal kingdom. He loves righteousness and justice (33:5; 99:4), which form "the foundation of his throne" (97:2). The Lord executes justice on behalf of the needy and/or oppressed, including the poor (113:7), the barren woman (113:9), hungry captives imprisoned in dark dungeons (146:7-8), those living as aliens in foreign lands, orphans, and widows (146:9).

Unfortunately reality conflicts with these hymnic affirmations of God's justice. While one can certainly find evidence of God's concern for the needy throughout human history, examples of gross injustice and cruel oppression are far more plentiful. How is one to harmonize reality with the psalmists' assertions? Were the ancient hymn writers guilty of overgeneralizing about God, while closing their eyes and ears to the misery in the world around them?

Though no easy or completely satisfying solution is available for this problem, at least three factors must be considered in discussing it. First, despite the universal flavor of the hymns (cf. 113:4-5; 146:6), they derive from an Israelite context where God's involvement in the life of His covenant people was uniquely personal and revelatory, setting this community apart from the world at large. In this respect it is significant to note that two of the hymns are addressed to "the servants of the Lord" (113:1) and to Zion (146:10), who had repeatedly experienced His help (146:5).

The barren woman motif provides a good illustration of how Israel's experience, and therefore perspective, were capable of differing from those of humankind at large. Generally speaking, many barren women have never experienced the joy of childbirth, but in the history of God's covenant people barren women were often

---

29. Richard D. Patterson, "The Widow, the Orphan, and the Poor in the Old Testament and the Extra-Biblical Literature," *Bibliotheca Sacra* 130 (1973):226.
30. Gibson, *Canaanite Myths and Legends*, p. 102 (see text, 16 vi 45-50).
31. See Wilson, *The Culture of Ancient Egypt*, pp. 132-33, and Saggs, *The Greatness That Was Babylon*, p. 353.
32. A. K. Grayson, *Assyrian Royal Inscriptions*, 2 vols. (Wiesbaden: Otto Harrassowitz, 1972-76), 1:102.

the Lord's instruments in fulfilling His promises and delivering His people. God miraculously allowed barren Sarah (Gen. 11:30) to have a son, even though by her own admission she was "worn out" (18:12). Other barren women who gave birth to important figures in Israel's history were Rebekah (25:21), Rachel (29:31), Samson's mother (Judg. 13:2-3), and Hannah (1 Sam. 1-2). With this tradition in view, it is little wonder that the author of Psalm 113 reminded the Lord's servants that their God "settles the barren woman in her home as a happy mother of children" (v. 9).

Several other hymnic elements also reflect Israel's experience. God released them from prison in Egypt (cf. 146:7-8) and gave them food in the wilderness (146:7). Through the Mosaic law He expressed His concern for the poor, the alien, the widow, and the orphan (113:7; 146:9; cf. Ex. 22:21-23; 23:6, 11; Lev. 19:33-34; Deut. 15:7-11; 24:14).

Second, one must recognize the literary character of these hymns. They are not historical narratives, but songs designed to celebrate God's kingship in largely typical ancient Near Eastern terms. In this genre, characterized as it is by stereotypical language and hyperbole, one cannot expect an exact correspondence to reality in all details. The psalmists were convinced that their God is the just ruler of the world because He had given them adequate experiential and historical evidence of that fact. Their assertions need not imply that they believed justice was in fact realized in every instance on a worldwide scale.

Third, the Psalms, like the Bible as a whole, indicate that God has delegated the task of maintaining justice to human rulers, who, for the most part, have failed to implement His wishes and consequently are destined for judgment. Psalm 82 deals directly with this theme. This psalm denounces a group of unjust rulers for showing favoritism to the wicked (v. 2) and neglecting the rights of the poor and destitute (vv. 3-4). Because of their failure to promote justice, "all the foundations of the earth are shaken" (v. 5) and these rulers, despite their elevated position, will die (vv. 6-7). The psalm concludes with a prayer asking God personally to ensure justice in His worldwide kingdom (v. 8).

The precise identity of the rulers addressed in Psalm 82 is debated. Certain features of the psalm suggest they are pagan gods. They are specifically called *'ĕlōhîm*, "gods," and the phrase "great assembly" (v. 1, *'ădat 'ēl*, lit. "assembly of God/El") reminds one of the divine assembly of Canaanite myth headed up by the high god El. Verse 7 might also support this interpretation, since it calls the rulers "gods," but then states that they will die *like* men (NIV's "like *mere* men" and "like every *other* ruler" are interpretive), perhaps implying that they are not actually human. If one follows this approach, then the psalm would be a bold polemic against Canaanite religion, depicting God as marching into the assembly and denouncing the gods as unfit rulers. Perhaps it even includes the confession of a former worshiper of the Canaanite gods who has come to realize their impotence vis-à-vis the God of Israel (cf. vv. 6-7).

A more traditional interpretation understands the rulers as human kings. Verses 2-4 support this view in that the responsibility of maintaining justice is associated more naturally with human kings than pagan deities in the context of the Old Testament. Also the Hebrew comparative preposition k^e- does not always indicate a true comparison of unlike objects, but sometimes has the force of "in every respect like."[33] Consequently the NIV translation of verse 7, though interpretive, is certainly grammatically possible, in which case the rulers may be understood as human. Finally, proponents of this view attempt to show that human judges appear as the referent of '*ĕlōhîm* in several other passages (cf. note 17).

The most likely solution to the problem combines the strengths of these two views. The rulers are actual human kings (cf. vv. 2-4) who, for rhetorical effect and in accord with their arrogant self-perception, are addressed as if they were members of the divine assembly known from Canaanite myth (vv. 1, 6-7). Parallels to this phenomenon occur in Isaiah 14, where the king of Babylon is likened to a petty god who tried to ascend El's mountain and usurp His authority, and in Ezekiel 28, where the proud king of Tyre is described in terms of a cherub who has access to God's holy mountain but is cast down because of his hubris. Thus Psalm 82 attests to the general failure of human rulers to fulfill adequately God's desire for justice. The psalmist longs for the day when God will take matters into His own hands (see also Ps. 58).

Indeed the so-called enthronement psalms anticipate, almost in prophetic fashion, a time when God will come and establish justice on the earth. Psalm 96:13 declares, "He comes to judge the earth. He will judge the world in righteousness and the peoples in his truth" (cf. 96:10; 98:9). His advent is greeted by an explosion of song and praise in the natural order (96:11-13; 98:7-8) and by worldwide recognition of His sovereignty (96:1-8; 98:4-6).

To summarize this section, the Psalms, in accord with the typical ancient Near Eastern ideal of the just ruler, portray God as One who preserves order and justice in the world and defends the cause of the needy and oppressed. Though this portrait conflicts with the hard realities of a world populated by evil men and plagued with unjust rulers, it is consistent with God's concern for justice and reflects His just decrees and deeds, especially as revealed to and experienced by His covenant people. A day is coming when God will personally establish justice on earth and the generalized, somewhat hyperbolic, hymnic descriptions of His just rule will be fully realized on a universal scale.

---

33. For discussion of this grammatical point see E. Kautzsch, ed., *Gesenius' Hebrew Grammar*, trans. A. E. Cowley, 2d Eng. ed. (Oxford: Clarendon, 1910), p. 376, sect. 118x; and Ronald J. Williams, *Hebrew Syntax: An Outline*, 2d ed. (Toronto: U. of Toronto, 1976), p. 47, sect. 261. For examples of this use of a simile, see E. W. Bullinger, *Figures of Speech Used in the Bible* (1898; reprint, Grand Rapids: Baker, 1968), pp. 728-29. Job 31:33*a* reads, "If I have concealed my sins like men." The phrase "like men," which is the same construction used in Psalm 82:7*a* (k^e'*ādām*), is not truly comparative here, but rather has the force of "in every respect like men" or "like other men do" (NIV, "as men do"). If one understands Psalm 82:7 in the same way, then the text would not be comparing the rulers to men, but warning that the rulers would die just as all other men do.

God as Israel's judge. Having God as their just king was a two-edged sword for Israel. God executed justice for His covenant people by protecting them from hostile would-be oppressors. However, when Israel rebelled against God's authority, He was forced to bring disciplinary judgment on His own people. Nevertheless even when God's people experienced the just consequences of their rebellion, they continued to look to Him as their vindicator before the scoffing nations.

Throughout Israel's history God protected His people from hostile nations. The author of Psalm 95 exhorted his listeners: "Come, let us bow down in worship, let us kneel before the Lord our Maker; for he is our God and we are the people of his pasture, the flock under his care" (vv. 6-7; cf. 100:3). As the "Shepherd of Jacob" (80:1), the Lord led His people out of bondage in Egypt, guided them safely through the wilderness, and settled them in the Promised Land (136:10-22). He planted them like a vine in the land and enabled them to spread out, like the branches of a vine, and fill the entire land (80:8-11). Like any good farmer, He erected a protective wall around His "vine" so that its produce might be safe from passersby and wild beasts (cf. 80:12). The Lord watched over Israel unceasingly (121:4) and destroyed hostile nations by their very own schemes (9:5-6, 15). Having observed God's just punishment of such nations, the author of Psalm 9 concluded, "The Lord is known by his justice; the wicked are ensnared by the work of their hands" (v. 16). Various nations sought to oppress and humiliate God's people, but in retrospect Israel was able to declare, "the Lord is righteous; he has cut me free from the cords of the wicked" (129:4).

The Psalms contain several national prayers for God's protection in the face of unjust attacks by enemy nations. For example, Psalm 59:5-8 describes the hostile nations as vicious wild dogs who seek Israel's destruction. However, the psalmist appealed to God as a just king and urged Him to punish the oppressive nations.[34] The author of Psalm 83, after describing the plots of the surrounding nations (ten of which are specifically named) to destroy God's people (vv. 1-8), asked the Lord to intervene once more for Israel in a mighty way, just as He had done in the days of Gideon and Deborah (vv. 9-18).

While many psalms praise or look to God as Israel's just king and protector, others indicate that this divine protection was sometimes withheld because of the people's rebellious deeds. When Israel was guilty of wrongdoing, the Lord, as their just ruler, was forced to repay them for their evil. Psalm 78 recites God's mighty acts on behalf of Israel, but also laments that the nation had been "stubborn and rebellious" (v. 8). Though the people had experienced a mighty deliverance at the Red Sea, they complained in the wilderness, bringing God's wrath

34. The heading of Psalm 59 attributes it to David on the occasion of one of Saul's many attempts to take his life. Although much of the psalm suggests the circumstances alluded to in the heading, verses 5-8 appear to reflect a different background, namely, a threat directed by foreign nations against Israel. Perhaps the Holy Spirit led a later writer to reapply a Davidic prayer to the nation's experience by adding verses 5-8 (or perhaps just verses 5 and 8) to the psalm. See Stek's comments in *The NIV Study Bible*, p. 845.

down on them (vv. 9-31). Subsequent generations followed in the sinful footsteps of their fathers, rousing God's anger and causing Him to allow surrounding nations to conquer His people (cf. esp. vv. 56-67). Psalm 106 likewise describes how Israel rebelled in both the wilderness and the Promised Land (vv. 13-39), forcing God to punish them severely and eventually hand them over to oppressive foreign rulers (vv. 41-42). In Psalm 81 the Lord Himself laments that Israel had forfeited His protection by disobeying His will: "But my people would not listen to me; Israel would not submit to me. So I gave them over to their stubborn hearts to follow their own devices. If my people would but listen to me, if Israel would follow my ways, how quickly would I subdue their enemies and turn My hand against their foes!" (vv. 11-14).

Many psalmists, having witnessed the effects of God's disciplinary judgment on Israel, continued to look to Him to vindicate and restore the nation. While acknowledging that God had been angry with His covenant people, they pleaded for a cessation of wrath (74:1; 79:5; 80:4; 85:5) and waited expectantly for His merciful forgiveness (79:8; 85:2-7; 130:1-8). They reminded God of His ancient covenantal commitment to Israel (74:2, 12, 19-20) and emphasized the atrocities carried out by the nations (74:21; 79:2-3, 7, 10; 137:7-9). The enemy desecrated the Temple (74:3-9; 79:1), scoffed at His people (79:4; 80:6), and even mocked God Himself (74:10, 18, 22-23; 79:6, 10). Such actions demanded a response from the just ruler of the universe. The author of Psalm 79 appealed for divine justice in no uncertain terms: "Why should the nations say, 'Where is their God?' Before our eyes, make known among the nations that you avenge the outpoured blood of your servants. May the groans of the prisoners come before you; by the strength of your arm preserve those condemned to die. Pay back into the laps of our neighbors seven times the reproach they have hurled at you, O Lord" (vv. 10-12). The author of Psalm 137 went so far as to pronounce a blessing on the Lord's instrument of vengeance against the cruel Babylonians (vv. 8-9).

God as the vindicator of His righteous servants. In His role as judge, God also protected righteous individuals within the covenant community from wicked men who opposed Him and sought to destroy His servants. This conflict between good and evil is played out dramatically on the pages of the Psalter. Many psalms (known as laments) contain the prayers of the righteous in which they describe the threats of the wicked, protest their innocence, and appeal to God for justice. Thanksgiving songs recall God's intervention in such a crisis and praise Him for His deliverance. Wisdom psalms contrast the lifestyles and destinies of the righteous and wicked.

In the world view of the psalmists, there were but two categories of men—the righteous and the wicked. The righteous exhibit genuine fear of the Lord by obeying His commandments (112:1; 128:1; cf. 1:2; 18:20-24; 37:31). Their words and actions are characterized by justice and integrity (15:2-5; 24:4; 34:12-14; 37:30; 112:5) and they give generously to those in need (37:21, 26; 112:5, 9). They shun the company and practices of evil, godless men (1:1-2; 17:3-5; 26:4-5; 31:6; 139:19-22). By way of contrast, the wicked are arrogant and live as if God and His law were nonexistent (10:2-11, 13; 12:3-4; 14:1; 31:18; 36:1-2; 73:6, 9, 11; 75:4-5; 94:4, 7; 119:155). Several psalms contain quotations from the wicked which illustrate their practical atheism. The wicked man thinks to himself, "God has forgotten; he covers His face and never sees. . . . He won't call me to account" (10:11, 13). He asks, "How can God know? Does the Most High have knowledge?" (73:11) and assuredly states, "The Lord does not see; the God of Jacob pays no heed" (94:7). Confident that God is not actively involved in the world and that they will not be held accountable for their actions, the wicked set out to promote their own interests with no regard for the well-being of others. They fail to repay debts (37:21) and accumulate wealth at the expense of others (52:6). They use slander and deceit to destroy and exploit others (5:6, 9; 10:2; 12:2; 28:3; 31:18; 36:3-4; 37:7, 12; 52:2-4; 73:7; 109:2) and think nothing of resorting to violence and bloodshed (5:6; 10:8-10; 73:6; 94:5-6; 140:4).

In the psalmists' world the righteous and the wicked do not peacefully coexist in the name of pluralism. Rather the wicked marshal all their cunning and power in an effort to annihilate the righteous (31:13; 56:5-6; 71:10; 143:3). Vivid imagery is employed to describe their attacks. The wicked are pictured as archers waiting to ambush their unsuspecting victims (11:2; 64:3-4) and as hunters who lay traps and snares for their prey (35:7; 38:12; 57:6; 64:5; 140:4-5; 141:9; 142:3). They are likened to dangerous bulls (22:12), wild dogs (22:16, 20), and ferocious lions (10:9; 17:12; 22:13, 16 [cf. MT], 21; 57:4). Their deceitful words are as deadly as a poisonous snake's venom (58:3-4; 140:3).

Because they pose a deadly threat to the righteous, the attacks of the wicked are sometimes viewed as an assault by death itself. In Psalm 18 David compares the attacks of his enemies (vv. 3, 17-18) to the cords and snares of death (vv. 4-5; cf. 116:3). To rescue him the Lord had to blast open the underworld with a powerful shout and pull him from its raging, chaotic waters (18:15-16). The author of Psalm 69 (David according to Acts 1:16, 20 and Rom. 11:9) likened his enemies (cf. Ps. 69:4) to surging waters that had reached his neck and threatened to drown him (vv. 1-2). In desperation he cried out to God, "Rescue me from the mire, do not let me sink; deliver me from those who hate me, from the deep waters. Do not let the floodwaters engulf me or the depths swallow me up or the pit [a name for death and the underworld in the Psalms; cf. 30:3; 88:3-4] close its mouth over me" (vv. 14-15).

Confronted by such hostile and seemingly invincible enemies, the righteous presented their just cause to God. To emphasize the seriousness of their situation and the urgency of their request they described the physical and emotional effects of the enemy's attack in graphic and at times exaggerated fashion (6:2-3, 6-7; 22:14-15; 31:9-13; 42:10; 55:4-5; 109:24; 143:4). To make it clear that they were worthy recipients of God's justice, they referred to themselves as weak, helpless, and oppressed (10:2, 9, 17; 12:6; 25:16; 69:33), and compared themselves to destitute socio-economic elements, such as orphans (10:14, 18) and the poor (35:10; 37:14; 40:17; 86:1; 109:16, 22; 140:12). Despite being falsely accused by their enemies

(27:12; 35:11, 20) and even rejected by friends (31:11-12), the righteous protested their innocence and appealed to God for vindication. For example, the author of Psalm 17, when surrounded by his proud and vicious enemies (vv. 10-12), prayed; "May my vindication come from you; may your eyes see what is right. Though you probe my heart and examine me at night, though you test me, you will find nothing; I have resolved that my mouth will not sin. . . . I have kept myself from the ways of the violent. My steps have held to your paths; my feet have not slipped" (vv. 2-5). In a similar manner the author of Psalm 26 asked: "Vindicate me, O Lord, for I have led a blameless life; I have trusted in the Lord without wavering" (v. 1). As proof of his assertion he pointed out that he had rejected evil companions and had offered the Lord genuine worship (vv. 4-7).

Because vindication and deliverance necessitated the destruction of the enemy, the righteous frequently called down God's vengeance on their tormentors. The author of Psalm 5 requested: "Declare them guilty, O God! Let their intrigues be their downfall. Banish them for their many sins, for they have rebelled against you" (v. 10; cf. 3:7; 7:6-9; 28:4; 31:17-18; 35:26; 54:5; 58:6-8; 140:7-11). Psalm 109 contains a lengthy imprecation (or curse) in which the author (David according to Acts 1:16) called God's judgment down on his wicked enemies (vv. 6-10). In rather typical Semitic fashion he prayed that his enemies be cut off in the prime of life and that their families be reduced to poverty and suffer eventual extinction.[35]

The psalmists could place their destiny in God's hands because they were convinced that He was "not a God who takes pleasure in evil" (5:4), but rather "a righteous judge" who "searches minds and hearts" (7:9, 11) and defends "the fatherless and the oppressed, in order that man, who is of the earth, may terrify no more" (10:18; cf. 140:12). The author of Psalm 11 pictured God as the sovereign ruler, enthroned in heaven, who carefully "observes the sons of men" and repays the wicked for their violent deeds (vv. 4-6; cf. 28:5; 94:23). In Psalm 18 David declared

---

35. One might think the punishment should be confined to the individual and that his family should not have to suffer for his crimes. However, in ancient Semitic thought a man and his offspring were inseparably bound together so that the actions of the former could influence the destiny of the latter. Of course, one sees this principle at work in the world every day and, not surprisingly, it permeates the Bible as well. A few examples will suffice. The sin of the first man adversely affected the entire human race (Rom. 5:12, 18-19). In the Ten Commandments God warned that He would punish "the children for the sins of the fathers to the third and fourth generation of those who hate" Him (Ex. 20:5). In the wilderness the earth swallowed up the families of Korah, Dathan, and Abiram, including even the "children and little ones" (Num. 16:27). When Achan sinned against the Lord, the entire nation suffered and he and his children were stoned to death (7:15, 24), even though the text gives no indication that his sons and daughters were aware of his act (the text, in fact, suggests just the opposite, v. 21). In the days of David God brought a famine on Israel which was not lifted until seven of Saul's sons were handed over to the Gibeonites for execution as retribution for their father's atrocities against that city (2 Sam. 21:1-9). Ezekiel 20:14-20 balances out this picture to some degree. Here the Lord declares that an individual who rejects the evil ways of his father will be spared and his own righteousness credited to him.

that the Lord treats both the righteous and the wicked in an appropriate manner (vv. 25-26; cf. 62:12). Those who are faithful find the Lord to be faithful, but those who are deceitful find Him to be more than their match.[36]

> *Excursus on the psalmists' protestations of innocence and prayers of imprecation.* Certain elements of these prayers appear to be at odds with other portions of Scripture. The psalmists' protestations of innocence (see, e.g., 17:3; 18:20-24; 26:1) sound like self-righteous affirmations of sinless perfection and seem to conflict with the biblical doctrine that all men are sinful and stand guilty before God [cf. Rom. 3:23]. The imprecations contain several troublesome statements [see, e.g., 109:9-12], especially when set alongside the biblical injunctions to bless one's enemies (cf. Matt. 5:44; Luke 6:28; Rom. 12:14; 1 Cor. 4:12). Can these aspects of the psalmists' prayers be harmonized with other biblical teachings, or should they be dismissed as excesses characteristic of desperate men living in a less enlightened era?
>
> In protesting their innocence the psalmists were not issuing universal theological propositions (such as those laid down by the apostle Paul in his letter to the Romans), but rather were claiming to possess a practical and relative degree of righteousness, especially vis-à-vis their wicked oppressors. According to Psalm 15, righteousness, as viewed by the writers of the psalms, entailed speaking honestly, not slanderously, treating fellow human beings fairly, despising the godless, but giving the godly their proper respect, keeping one's word, and rejecting all forms of dishonest gain (vv. 2-5). For the author of Psalm 17 righteousness meant having pure motives, guarding one's tongue, and shunning the practices of the wicked (vv. 3-5). According to Psalm 26, leading a "blameless life" meant avoiding evil companions, offering the Lord the praise due Him, and longing to be in the presence of the Lord (vv. 4-8). These psalms make it clear that those who protested their innocence were

36. NIV's translation "shrewd" (v. 26) may be a bit weak in this context. (The Hebrew verb *pātal* carries the literal idea of "twist" or "wrestle" in Genesis 30:8, where Rachel used the word to describe her "struggle" with her sister Leah for Jacob's affections. [As a play on the word, she even named her concubine's son "Naphtali."] In Job 5:13 the word refers to the schemes of the "wily" which are thwarted by God. In Proverbs 8:8 wisdom declares her advice to be sound and right, not crooked or "perverse.") Through word repetition Psalm 18: 25-26a emphasizes that God responds to the faithful, blameless, and pure in accord with their character. His actions toward them are the mirror reflection of their own deeds. Even though the literary form varies in verse 26b (the Hebrew words translated "crooked" [*'iqqēš*] and "shrewd" are from different roots, which nevertheless are closely associated elsewhere; cf. Deut. 32:5; Prov. 8:8), the point seems to be the same. Like the righteous, those whose actions are "crooked" (i.e., deceitful; cf. the use of the root *'qš* in Ps. 101:4; Prov. 2:15; 10:9; 11:20; 17:20; 19:1; 28:6; Isa. 59:8) finds God's treatment of them to be the mirror image of their own deeds. In their case He appropriately used deception to bring about their downfall. An illustration of this principle occurs in 1 Kings 22:19-22, where the prophet Micaiah describes a heavenly scene in which God authorized a lying spirit to "entice" (or "deceive") evil, deceitful Ahab and lead him to his demise.

not addressing the Pauline theme of humankind's spiritual standing before God. Rather they were affirming that their lifestyle and values were evidence of their essential devotion to God and His standards. As such they were innocent of their enemies' slanderous accusations and were worthy recipients of God's protection.

For further proof that the psalmists were not claiming to be sinless in an absolute sense, one need only consider several psalms where the righteous acknowledged that they had been tainted by sin, which in some cases had even occasioned the crisis they faced. For example, the author of Psalm 25, when confronted by his fierce enemies (v. 19), declared his trust in God (vv. 1, 21), asked the Lord not to hold his youthful sins against him (v. 7), and begged for forgiveness (vv. 11, 18). The author of Psalm 38, though claiming to have pursued what is good (v. 20), confessed his sin (vv. 3, 18) in conjunction with his request for deliverance from his foes (vv. 16, 19-22). Likewise the author of Psalm 40, while asserting his unwavering devotion to the Lord in no uncertain terms (vv. 6-10) and asking for deliverance from his oppressors (vv. 15-17), admitted that his sins had "overtaken" him (v. 12). The author of Psalm 41 referred to both his sin (v. 4) and his integrity (v. 12).

The psalmists' imprecations against their enemies pose a greater challenge for the biblical theologian. Jesus commanded His followers to bless and pray for those who cursed them. On the surface at least, such a response seems to be exactly the opposite of what one encounters in the Psalter, where prayer after prayer asks God to bring about the enemies' demise. Perhaps Jesus was calling for a new way of responding to mistreatment, but before one is too quick to dismiss or condemn the psalmists' imprecatory prayers, several observations are in order.

First, the psalmists should not be understood as expressions of personal vindictiveness. Rather they attest to the psalmists' confidence in and concern for God's just character. The psalmists, when encountering enemies who threatened their reputations and lives, refused to take matters into their own hands, but instead turned in faith to God as their righteous judge and vindicator. In so doing, their response was in accord with the teaching of Moses and the Proverbs (cf. Lev. 19:18; Prov. 20:22; 24:29), which in turn influenced Paul's instruction on the subject (cf. Rom. 12:17, 19). The psalmists were as concerned for the reputation of God as they were for their own well-being. If God was indeed the just ruler of the universe, then He must intercede for the innocent and oppressed. If He failed in this regard, there would be reason to question His sovereignty and the wicked would grow even more complacent and arrogant (140:8). This explains why the author of Psalm 58, after asking God to break the teeth of the wicked (v. 6), declared: "The righteous will be glad when they are avenged, when they bathe their feet in the blood of the wicked. Then men will say, 'Surely the righteous still are rewarded; surely there is a God who judges the earth'" (vv. 10-11). In a similar way the author of Psalm 35 anticipated that his deliverance and the destruction of his enemies would lead observers to declare: "The Lord be exalted, who delights in the well-being of his servant" (vv. 26-27).

Second, the specific judgments called down on the wicked, while at times sounding unduly harsh and suggesting a vindictive spirit, attest instead to the psalmists' strong sense of justice and their concern for God's character. The demise of the wicked had to be decisive and appropriate, so that observers would be impressed with the certainty and exactitude of divine justice. This is why the author of Psalm 109 could call a curse down on his enemies and ask that their children be reduced to poverty (vv. 9-12). The form of the prayer and desired punishment are appropriate, for the wicked "loved to pronounce a curse" on others and "hounded to death the poor and the needy and the brokenhearted" (vv. 16-17).

Third, such appeals to divine justice are not limited to the Psalter or even the Old Testament. In Revelation 6:10 the souls of the martyrs are described as crying out to God to avenge their shed blood. Later in this same book God is praised for avenging the wrongs committed against His saints (Rev. 16:5-6; 19:2) and His people are urged to rejoice over the fact (18:20). In his second letter to the Thessalonians, Paul encouraged persecuted believers by reminding them that God is just and would "pay back trouble" to their enemies in the day of judgment (2 Thess. 1:6-9). In his second letter to Timothy he declared that the Lord would repay Alexander the metalworker for the harm he had done (2 Tim. 4:14).

The Psalter supplies ample evidence that the psalmists' confidence in God's justice was not misplaced or unrewarded. The psalmists testified that God heard their prayers and delivered them from their enemies (22:24; 34:4-7, 17-20; 92:10-11; 116:1-6), often in dramatic fashion (18:3-19; 30:1-3; 40:1-2). They proclaimed Him to be their savior and protector (18:1-2; 25:5; 27:9; 31:4; 38:22; 40:17; 54:4 59:16; 62:6; 91:9), comparing Him to a mother bird sheltering her young beneath her wings (17:8; 36:7; 57:1; 91:4), a shield (5:12; 7:10; 18:2; 28:7), and a rocky cliff or fortress (18:2; 27:1; 28:1; 31:2-3; 59:16-17; 61:3; 62:7; 71:3). Secure from the threats of their enemies, the righteous have access to God's presence (11:7; 15:1, 5; 16:11; 23:6; 26:12; 27:6; 73:23-26; 140:13) and enjoy His blessings of peace, prosperity, and long life (1:3; 37:11, 18-19, 29; 52:8; 112:2-3).

In contrast to the righteous, the wicked are swept away by God's judgment like chaff before a strong wind (1:4; 35:5). Though the wicked might prosper for a time (10:5-6; 52:7; 73:3-5), God sends sudden destruction on them (64:7; 73:18-20) like fire from heaven (11:6; 140:10) and they shrivel up like withered grass (37:1-2, 20). In the prime of life they disappear into the underworld (31:17; 37:10, 35-36; 52:5; 55:15, 23: 141:7) and their offspring are cut off from the earth (34:16; 37:28, 38; 69:25; 109:13).

Several psalms emphasize the appropriate nature of the evildoers' demise. In many cases they are portrayed as being destroyed by their own schemes and instruments. For example, the author of Psalm 7 (David according to the heading) observed, "He who digs a hole and scoops it out falls into the pit he has made. The trouble he causes recoils on himself; his violence comes down on his own head" (vv. 15-16; cf. 35:7-8; 57:6; 141:9-10). According to Psalm 37:15, "their swords will pierce their own hearts, and their bows will be broken." Psalm 64 combines irony and wordplay to emphasize the fitting nature of God's punishment of the wicked. The wicked fearlessly prepare to ambush the innocent psalmist suddenly with their arrows (vv. 3-4). They are confident that no one will detect them (vv. 5-6). Little do they realize that the divine archer will destroy them suddenly with His arrows (v. 7). Ironically those who boast that no one sees them will experience public humiliation as passersby shake their heads in scorn (v. 8). Though the wicked fear no retribution, those who witness their demise will be struck with fear as they consider the Lord's righteous deeds (v. 9).

Some of the statements describing the vindication of the righteous have been taken as proof that the psalmists anticipated an enjoyable afterlife in the Lord's presence and eventual physical resurrection. For example, the author of Psalm 49, after contemplating the destiny of the proud (vv. 13-14), affirmed; "But God will redeem my life from the grave; he will surely take me to himself" (v. 15). Similarly the author of Psalm 73, after describing the demise of the wicked (vv. 18-20), boldly asserted; "Yet I am always with you; you hold me by my right hand. You guide me with your counsel, and afterward you will take me into glory" (vv. 23-24). It is tempting and natural for those living after the resurrection of Christ to interpret these passages in accord with the great affirmations of the New Testament concerning the afterlife and resurrection.

However, others have challenged such an interpretation of these and other passages, arguing that the psalmists' understanding of realities beyond death was limited and that statements of confidence like those mentioned above reflect their hope for vindication in this life. They contend that only late in the progress of revelation were God's people given a more detailed and positive picture of what to expect after death.

Before looking at the key psalms more closely, it is necessary to observe the psalmists' general attitude toward death. In so doing it quickly becomes apparent that they did not look at death with the same anticipation and confidence as did the apostle Paul (cf. Phil. 1:21-23). On the contrary, in many of the laments the psalmists begged the Lord to deliver them from physical death at the hands of their enemies. In presenting his case before God, the author of Psalm 6 even declared: "No one remembers you when he is dead. Who praises you from the grave?" (v. 5). Likewise the author of Psalm 30, through the literary device of the rhetorical question, suggested that the dead are cut off from the worshiping community: "What gain is there in my destruction, in my going down into the pit? Will the dust praise you? Will it proclaim your faithfulness?" (v. 9; cf. 115:17). With another series of rhetorical questions the author of Psalm 88 indicated that the dead no longer witness or praise God's mighty deeds: "Do you show your wonders to the dead? Do those who are dead rise up and praise you? Is your love declared in the grave, your faithfulness in Destruction? Are your wonders known in the place of darkness, or your righteous deeds in the land of oblivion?" (vv. 10-12).[37] Does this generally negative attitude toward death represent a less enlightened view of the afterlife which conflicts with the statements of confidence cited above? Or does it instead provide an interpretive clue for understanding the expressions of confidence as pertaining to this life? To answer these questions we must look at the key psalms in more detail.

As indicated above, the affirmation of confidence in Psalm 49:15 is often used as proof that at least some psalmists anticipated resurrection.[38] In this wisdom psalm (cf. vv. 1-4) the author observed that all men, even the rich and the wise, die like animals (vv. 7-13). Consequently the rich are not to be feared or envied (vv. 5-6, 16-20). Furthermore a time will come when "the upright will rule over them" (v. 14). In light of these facts the psalmist expressed his assurance that God would redeem him from the grave (v. 15).[39]

What is one to make of the affirmations of confidence in verses 14-15? It is possible that the psalmist is looking at ultimate eschatological realities, anticipating his own resurrection and a time when the righteous, not the rich, will rule on earth. However, it is more likely that the ascendancy of the righteous refers to their vindication in this life, a well-attested theme in the Psalter, especially in the wisdom psalms (see, e.g., Pss. 1, 34, 37, and 112, as well as the discussion above). In this case verse 15 refers to God's preserving the psalmist through "evil days" (cf. v. 5) by keeping him from premature, violent death at the hands of the oppressive rich and from the calamity that overtakes them.[40] "Morning" (v. 14), which brings to mind the dawning of a new day after a night of darkness, aptly symbolizes the cessation of these "evil days."

Psalm 73:24 has been understood as alluding to an afterlife in God's presence.

---

37. A similar attitude toward death is found outside the Psalms (cf. Eccles. 9:4-6, 10; Isa. 38:10-11, 18).

38. An alternative view is that the psalmist expected to escape death by being suddenly carried away to heaven, like Enoch and Elijah. Proponents of this view point out that the Hebrew verb translated "take" in 49:15 (*lāqaḥ*) is used to describe the translation of both Enoch and Elijah (Gen. 5:24; 2 Kings 2:10).

39. To provide better balance in the Hebrew poetic structure, verse 15 should be translated, "But God will redeem my life; from the grave he will indeed take me." This eliminates the need for NIV's questionable interpretive addition "to himself."

40. The verbs used in verse 15 (*pādāh*, "redeem" and *lāqaḥ*, "take") speak generally of deliverance and are not technical terms for resurrection. *pādāh* carries the idea of "ransom, redeem, buy back," and by extension "rescue, deliver." In 1 Samuel 14:45 it is used of Jonathan's being rescued from physical death. Job used the word in pointing out to his friends that he had never asked them to ransom him "from the clutches of the ruthless" (Job 6:22-23). *Lāqaḥ*, while used twice for the translation of individuals (Enoch and Elijah), is hardly a technical term for that idea, as a survey of its broad range of usage makes clear. In Psalm 18:16 it describes the Lord's deliverance of David from his enemies (symbolized by the raging waters of death).

The author of this psalm recalled how he envied the wicked because of their prosperity (vv. 2-12). He questioned whether it really paid to follow the paths of righteousness until he entered the sanctuary of the Lord (vv. 13-17). Whether through a divine oracle or reflection on the truths uttered by the worshipers there, the psalmist realized that the prosperity of the wicked was shortlived, for God's judgment would sweep them away suddenly (vv. 18-20). The psalmist committed himself anew to God and declared his confidence in God's protective hand (vv. 23-28).

Two interpretive options exist for the psalmist's statement of confidence in Psalm 73:24b. It is possible to understand the statement as a reference to the psalmist's being ushered into God's presence in heaven following his life on earth.[41] However, in the context of the Psalms it is more likely that he is referring to God's ability to preserve him through the time of calamity that would destroy the wicked. Though "glory" sometimes refers figuratively to heaven or the afterlife in Christian hymnic and poetic idiom, the Hebrew word so translated in verse 24 (*kābôd*) is not used in this way. In the context of Psalm 73:24 the word probably carries its commonly attested meaning of "honor." In contrast to the proud, who are swept away in judgment, the psalmist was confident that God's protective hand would guide him to a place of honor.[42] Verses 25-28 conform nicely to this interpretation. In verse 25 the psalmist affirmed that nothing else in the universe (note the merism "heaven" and "earth") could replace God as the object of his desire.[43] Even if his body grew weak and he was on the verge of death,[44] God would sustain and protect him (vv. 26, 28), while the wicked would perish (v. 27).

Other alleged references to a belief in an afterlife in God's presence are also better interpreted along the lines suggested above for Psalms 49:15 and 73:24. For example, the author of Psalm 17 concluded his prayer by confidently affirming; "And I—in righteousness I will see your face; when I awake, I will be satisfied with seeing your likeness" (v. 15). It is improbable that the idiomatic language refers to awaking from the sleep of death to behold the Lord's face. The psalmist challenged the Lord to examine his motives during the dark hours of the night (v. 3), pleaded his innocence, and asked for divine retribution against his enemies. Assured that God's examination of his heart would reveal only righteousness, he was confident

41. Because of the use of *lāqaḥ*, "take," in verse 24, some also see this passage as referring to translation. See note 38 above.
42. In this interpretation *lāqaḥ* is understood in the sense of "lead, conduct, guide," in accord with the synonymously parallel line. The verb also has this nuance in Numbers 23:14, 27-28; Joshua 24:3; and Proverbs 24:11.
43. Because of the proximity of the question in verse 25a to the declaration of verse 24b, one might think that "glory" is a metonymic reference to heaven. However, verse 25b indicates that this is not the case. "Heaven" does not explicate "glory," but rather combines with "earth" to refer idiomatically to the entire universe.
44. The opening statement of verse 26 ("My flesh and my heart may fail") does not refer to physical death, but to physical weakness characteristic of those approaching death (cf. Job 33:21; Pss. 71:9; 143:7; Prov. 5:11).

that the dawning of a new day would bring a fresh experience of God's presence and blessing (cf. v. 14).[45]

It is also unlikely that Psalm 23 refers to an afterlife in God's presence, though verses 4 and 6 in particular have sometimes been so understood. Verse 4 refers to the divine shepherd guiding his lamb (the psalmist) through a dangerous dark valley (a symbol for the danger posed by his enemies, cf. v. 5).[46] In verse 6 the psalmist expressed his confidence that he would have access to God's presence (the "house of the Lord" refers to the earthly Tabernacle or Temple; cf. Judg. 19:18; 1 Sam. 1:7, 24; 2 Sam. 12:20; 1 Kings 7:12, 40, 45, 51) throughout his lifetime. NIV's "forever" translates a Hebrew phrase (*'ōrek yāmîm*, lit. "length of days"), which, when used elsewhere of men, usually refers to a lengthy period of time (such as one's lifetime), not eternity (cf. Deut. 30:20; Job 12:12; Ps. 91:16; Prov. 3:2, 16; Lam. 5:20).[47]

Because of its use in the New Testament, Psalm 16:10 is often understood as referring to resurrection. However, the New Testament attributes the words to Christ, not the psalmist (David according to the Old Testament). If the psalm is taken as exclusively messianic, then it only attests to the psalmist's confidence in the Messiah's resurrection, not a general Old Testament expectation of resurrection (in this regard note that Peter and Paul contrasted the experiences of David and Jesus; Acts 2:29-31; 13:35-37). If the psalm is taken as indirectly messianic (i.e., as being applicable in a lesser sense to the psalmist and in a heightened sense to the Messiah), then David, like so many other psalmists, was probably expressing his confidence that God would keep him from a violent, premature death and give him continual access to His presence (cf. v. 11).[48]

In conclusion, the psalmists had a limited and somewhat negative view of the

---

45. In this context the idiom "to see [*ḥāzāh*] the face" refers to receiving God's favor. The expression also occurs in Psalm 11:7 ("upright men will see his face"), where the vindication of the righteous following God's judgment on their wicked oppressors is in view. A related expression (using Heb. *rā'āh*, rather than *ḥāzāh*) appears in Job 33:26, where seeing God's face is closely associated with the renewing of divine favor.

46. The phrase "valley of the shadow of death" may be better translated "the darkest valley" (cf. NIV margin). The traditional reading understands *ṣalmāwet* as a rare compound word. Etymology and usage suggest the word is more likely an abstract noun meaning "deep darkness." Note its frequent association with darkness/night and (by contrast) light/morning in poetic texts (Job. 3:5; 10:21-22; 12:22; 24:17; 28:3; 34:22; Ps. 107:10, 14; Isa. 9:1; Jer. 13:16; Amos 5:8). In some cases the darkness described is associated with the realm of death (Job 10:21-22; 38:17), but this nuance is derived contextually and is not inherent in the meaning of the word itself.

47. Psalm 21:4, where the phrase is followed by "for ever and ever," may be an exception, though the juxtaposition of the phrases may be an example of intensification (where the second phrase goes beyond the limits of the first), rather than synonymity. Even if one takes both expressions as referring to eternal life, the language is part of the king's hyperbolic description of the Lord's blessings and should not be taken literally.

48. Psalm 16 is discussed in more detail below, in the section entitled "The Messianic Fulfillment of the Righteous Sufferer Motif."

afterlife. For them death was an unwelcome intruder because it separated one from God's revelatory deeds and from the worshiping community. Rather than being exceptions to this concept of death which display a more positive view of the after-life, the statements of confidence examined above more likely pertain to the vin-dication of the righteous in this life, a theme widely attested in the Psalter and wisdom literature in general.

This theme, like others we have examined in this survey of the theology of the Psalms, conflicts with reality in many respects. Despite the affirmations of the psalmists, the wicked usually prevail over the righteous in this sinful world where survival of the fittest, not the most godly, seems to be the operating principle. The experience of many is just the opposite of that of the seemingly naive author of Psalm 37, who declared: "I was young and now am I old, yet I have not seen the righteous forsaken or their children begging bread" (v. 25).

In the progress of revelation the tension between reality and the ideal expressed in the Psalms is eased. Further revelation, especially passages dealing with escha-tological events, makes clear that the faith of the psalmists was not misplaced. One learns of a final judgment whereby God will examine and repay the deeds of the wicked. The wicked will indeed be swept away by God's wrath and the righteous vindicated. The righteous need not fear death, for it cannot separate one from God and even its hold on one's physical body is temporary. In short, the psalmists' statements of confidence are important building blocks in the gradual unfolding of the biblical principle that the righteous will be vindicated by the just ruler of the universe.

It is natural for a Christian to see more in the Psalter's statements of confidence than the psalmists intended. Although the author of Psalm 23 may have been con-fessing his trust in God's ability to protect him from the enemies he encountered in this life, the Christian, who understands that God's protection extends beyond this life, finds its words comforting and relevant in all circumstances, especially when the inevitable reality of physical death has invaded one's family or is about to be per-sonally experienced. While the psalmist may not have been speaking specifically of an afterlife in God's presence, in the progress of revelation his words come to express such a hope for God's people, who now understand the full ramifications of the psalm's affirmation that God protects His own. In the same way the statements in Psalms 17:15; 49:15; and 73:24 become, on the lips of a Christian, a testimony of faith in God's final vindication of the righteous, even beyond the grave.[49]

49. The preceding discussion illustrates how the tasks of the exegete, biblical theologian, and preacher are distinct yet interrelated. For example, in dealing with Psalm 23 the exegete, who is concerned with the meaning of the psalm in its literary and cultural context, understands the psalmists' words as referring to God's protection in this life. The biblical theologian, who is concerned more with the psalm's major principle (God protects His own) and its development in Scripture, discovers that later revelation broadens the scope of the principle. The preacher, while not neglecting the intent of the author or blurring the distinctions between exegesis and theology by failing to account for the progressive nature of God's revelation, focuses on the psalm's contribution to the totality of biblical revelation and shows how its unique artic-

The messianic fulfillment of the righteous sufferer motif. In its portrait of Jesus as God's suffering Servant, the New Testament utilizes many statements from the Psalms depicting the agony, loyalty, and vindication of God's righteous followers. The psalms used in this way are appropriately labeled messianic, but, as with the royal psalms discussed above, this classification needs to be qualified and explained. By their very nature as laments and songs of praise, these psalms should not be understood as direct predictions of Jesus' ministry. In fact a close examination of their contents shows that they refer directly to the experiences of their ancient authors, not those of Jesus. Nevertheless these psalms present an ideal of the innocent sufferer who is persecuted for the sake of righteousness and is ultimately vindicated by God, an ideal attached to an eschatological figure by the prophet Isaiah and realized in Christ. As the New Testament writers reflected on Jesus' teaching and experience, they correctly identified Him as Isaiah's suffering Servant and realized that He brought to culmination the long line of righteous sufferers, so many of whom speak on the pages of the Psalter. In applying statements from the Psalms to Jesus, they followed the lead of the Lord Himself and employed a recognized hermeneutical principle of their day, which involved reasoning from the lesser to the greater. Certain descriptions of the psalmists' suffering, hope, and vindication were even more applicable to Jesus, God's suffering Servant par excellence. When applied to Jesus such statements sometimes even take on a more literal or heightened sense, as if to erase any doubts that He is the One toward whom they ultimately point. In light of the foregoing discussion, psalms utilized by the New Testament in this way should be labeled indirectly messianic. A survey of such psalms follows.

Psalm 22 begins with a lengthy lament in which the author bemoaned the fact that God had seemingly abandoned him (vv. 1-10). Though the psalmist, like previous generations of faithful Israelites, had once experienced God's favor, he now felt abandoned as his tormentors mocked his faith in God. After a brief cry for help (v. 11), he described his desperate situation in vivid detail (vv. 12-18). His enemies surrounded him like powerful bulls, roaring lions, and ferocious wild dogs. His physical strength was gone and onlookers were so certain of his impending death that they were eager to divide up his possessions among them. Finally, in response to his plea (vv. 19-21*a*) God delivered him from his enemies (v. 21*b*; cf. NIV margin). In gratitude for God's mighty act of salvation, the psalmist vowed to praise the Lord in the assembly of Israel (vv. 22-26). In his exhilaration he even anticipated a time when all nations would recognize the greatness of God (vv. 27-31).

As Jesus hung on the cross He used the words of Psalm 22:1 to express the agony and abandonment He felt (Matt. 27:46; Mark 15:34). Because Jesus Himself associated His experience with that of the ancient psalmist, it comes as no surprise

ulation of the larger principle relates to the audience's situation. In the case of Psalm 23, the preacher will emphasize the theological principle of God's protection and point out that the words of the psalm, when read by Christians, provide comfort in all situations, including those not directly in view by the author.

that the gospel writers saw certain aspects of Jesus' crucifixion as fulfilling the language and imagery of Psalm 22. Onlookers hurled insults at Jesus, shook their heads, and mocked His faith in God the Father (Matt. 27:39, 43; Mark 15:29; cf. Ps. 22:7-8), while soldiers divided up His clothing and cast lots for His seamless undergarment (Matt. 27:35; Mark 15:24; Luke 23:34; John 19:23-24; cf. Ps. 22:18).[50]

Psalm 69 is another indirectly messianic psalm that is widely used in the New Testament. In this psalm the author asked the Lord to deliver him from his enemies, who threatened to overwhelm him like raging waters (vv. 1-4, 13-18). Acknowledging his folly and guilt (v. 5), he also affirmed his zeal for God and His Temple (v. 9). He lamented his rejection by his relatives (v. 8) and the humiliation heaped on him by those who witnessed his plight (vv. 10-12). When he looked for relief, he received only scorn, like a starving, thirsty man who is given gall and vinegar (vv.19-21). He called down God's wrath on his enemies, asking that their tents be deserted (vv. 22-28, esp. v. 25). He concluded with another petition for help and a vow to praise God when deliverance finally arrived (vv. 29-33).

The New Testament draws several parallels between the experiences of the psalmist and Jesus. When Jesus drove the moneychangers from the Temple, His disciples recalled the words of Psalm 69:9 (John 2:17). The night before His crucifixion the Lord Himself explained to His disciples that the world's unjustified hatred of Him fulfilled the words of Psalm 69:4 (John 15:25). While on the cross, Jesus was offered gall and vinegar in accord with the words of Psalm 69:21 (Matt. 27:34, 48; Mark 15:23, 36; Luke 23:36; John 19:28-30). Paul viewed Jesus' self-sacrificial devotion to God as an illustration of the words of Psalm 69:9*b*. (Peter's application of v. 25 to Judas [Acts 1:16, 20] is discussed below.)

Two observations are in order. First, certain statements in Psalm 69 (cf. the admission of imperfection in v. 5 and the formal curse in vv. 22-28) make clear that the ancient psalmist (David; cf. Acts 1:16, 20; Rom. 11:9) was describing his own plight, not that of Jesus. Nevertheless since Jesus is the perfect example and fulfillment of the typical sufferer portrayed in the psalm, some of the psalmist's statements can be applied to His experience. Second, the application of verse 21 to Jesus' experience on the cross illustrates how poetic imagery can materialize when the Old Testament ideal is realized in Jesus. The psalmist was comparing the scorn

---

50. The New Testament does not cite Psalm 22:16 in describing Jesus' crucifixion. The traditional translation of the final line (NIV, "they have *pierced* my hands and my feet") is misleading. The Masoretic text reads literally, "Like a lion, my hands and my feet." Though this reading is usually rejected as meaningless, the psalmist's words may refer to a lion's pinning its human victim's hands and feet to the ground with its paws, a scene depicted in ancient Near Eastern art. In this case the elliptical statement might be paraphrased: "Like a lion they have pinned my hands and my feet to the ground." Following several ancient versions, others prefer to emend "like a lion" to a verb, such as "to bind" or "to dig." The latter would be more descriptive of a dog's gnawing and tearing at one's hands and feet (cf. v. 16*a*) than the piercing or boring associated with crucifixion. Because of the New Testament's silence and the textual problems surrounding the passage, it is best not to associate verse 16*b* with Jesus' crucifixion in any specific or direct way.

of his enemies to bitter food and drink (cf. vv. 19-20); Jesus was literally offered these items, as if to demonstrate that the psalmist's rejection foreshadowed His own.

While Psalms 22 and 69 are the most extensively used psalms in the New Testament description of Christ's suffering, statements from other psalms are utilized as well. The apostle John applied Psalm 34:20 to Jesus' crucifixion. After describing how Jesus' legs, unlike those of the criminals crucified with Him, remained unbroken, John declared: "These things happened so that the scripture would be fulfilled: 'Not one of his bones will be broken'" (John 19:31-37, esp. v. 36).

Psalm 34, attributed to David (cf. the heading), is a song of thanksgiving for God's deliverance. The psalmist recalled his time of need and praised the Lord for saving him (vv. 4, 6). He exhorted his audience to trust in the Lord, promising them that their faith would not be misplaced (vv. 8-10). He warned them to shun evil (vv. 12-13) for evildoers are cut off from the earth (vv. 16, 21). By way of contrast the righteous experience God's protection (vv. 15, 17-20, 22). Verse 20 describes in figurative terms how the Lord protects the righteous from troubles that descend on them.

On the surface John's application of verse 20 to Jesus' experience on the cross seems strange. John gave the passage a literal sense that is foreign to its literary context by applying its promise of divine protection to a man who had just been brutally and unjustly crucified by His enemies. In light of Jesus' terrible plight, the observation that His legs were unbroken seems irrelevant.

However, further reflection shows that John's observation is quite pertinent. The literal understanding of the psalm's figurative language, as we have seen in other cases, has the effect of drawing attention to Jesus as one in whom an ideal presented in the psalm is realized. In this case, John viewed Jesus as the righteous man par excellence. When given their proper symbolic value Jesus' unbroken bones testified to this fact and become a guarantee of His ultimate vindication, an event which John went on to describe in the context which immediately follows.

The author of Hebrews used Psalm 40:6-8 in his description of Christ's priestly work (Heb. 10:5-7). Though readily acknowledging his sin (Ps. 40:12), the author of this psalm also affirmed his wholehearted devotion to God (vv. 6-10). He praised God for His past saving acts (vv. 1-3) and asked for deliverance from those who sought his life (vv. 11-17). In verses 6-8, which are part of his confession of loyalty, he emphasized that God desires genuine devotion, not empty ritual (cf. 51:15-17).

In the New Testament application of these words to Jesus, one sees the same principles noted above with regard to Psalm 69. First, certain statements in the psalm make clear that the speaker is the ancient psalmist, not Jesus (cf. v. 12). Nevertheless, because Jesus fulfills the ideal of the righteous sufferer portrayed in the psalm, the psalmist's words were also Jesus' words, as seen in Hebrews 10:5-7. Second, when spoken by Jesus the words of verses 6-8 take on a heightened sense. In their Old Testament context the psalmist's statement does not imply a rejection of the sacrificial system, but rather attests to the priority of genuine loyalty. On the lips of Jesus, however, the words take on a new significance and indicate that Jesus' totally sufficient sacrifice for sins has made the Old Testament sacrificial system obsolete (cf. Heb. 10:8-14).

Since Jesus is the fulfillment of the righteous sufferer ideal, then Jesus' enemies brought to culmination the long line of evildoers who opposed God's faithful servants. Since Judas possessed so many of the characteristics of these wicked men (especially greed, deceit, and disloyalty), he could stand as their representative. As such, certain of the psalmists' descriptions of their enemies could be readily applied to him.

The night before His crucifixion Jesus did this very thing. He hinted that one of the twelve would betray Him (John 13:10-11, 18a) and then quoted the words of Psalm 41:9: "He who shares my bread has lifted up his heel against me" (John 13:18b). In their original context, these words do not refer to Jesus and Judas. Rather the psalmist spoke as one plagued by a serious physical illness (Ps. 41:3, 8), which apparently had been brought about by his own sin (v. 4). He lamented the fact that his enemies, including one who had once been his close friend, slandered him and eagerly awaited his death (vv. 5-9). He begged for deliverance and affirmed his essential integrity and loyalty to God (vv. 1a, 10-12). As God's persecuted servant par excellence (unlike the psalmist, Jesus was sinless) who was also betrayed by a friend, Jesus could appropriate the words of verse 9 to Himself. By doing so just before a meal in which He actually shared bread with Judas (cf. John 13:26-27), Jesus made clear that the language of the psalm referred ultimately to His betrayal by Judas.

Peter also applied language from the Psalms to Judas. He observed that the Scripture had spoken of Judas's downfall long beforehand. For support he quoted Psalms 69:25 and 109:8 (cf. Acts 1:15-20). In their literary contexts both statements are formal curses pronounced by David against his enemies. Reasoning from the lesser to the greater, Peter applied the curses to Judas, the enemy par excellence who epitomized the horde of evildoers who had opposed the righteous throughout history. To facilitate his application of Psalm 69:25 to Judas, Peter even altered the grammatical form of the text, changing the plural forms of the passage to the singular. While some might accuse Peter of playing fast and loose with the text, his treatment of the passage is in perfect harmony with the hermeneutical principle that Jesus' death at the hands of His enemies was the culmination of the struggle between the righteous and wicked played out on the pages of the Psalter. As such one may apply (and even adapt) language depicting earlier stages in that struggle to its final episode.

The New Testament also utilizes language from the Psalter in its proclamation that God has vindicated Jesus through the resurrection. In addressing his fellow Israelites on the day of Pentecost, Peter announced that Jesus had risen from the dead in accord with the words of David as recorded in Psalm 16:8-11. Assuming that the psalmists' words refer to resurrection, he explained that they could not apply to David's experience, for he had long since died and his tomb was known to all. Rather David, being a prophet, had spoken of Christ's resurrection (cf. Acts 2:22-

31). In similar fashion the apostle Paul proclaimed that Jesus' resurrection fulfilled the words of Psalm 16:10. As if to demonstrate that the words of the psalm, understood in this sense, did not refer to David, he also contrasted David, whose body had undergone decay, with Christ, who had escaped death through His resurrection (Acts 13:35-37).

In light of Peter's and Paul's statements, it is tempting and perhaps correct to understand Psalm 16 as a directly prophetic psalm in which David, speaking on behalf of his Descendant, anticipated the Messiah's resurrection. After all, Peter specifically called David a "prophet" and stated that David *"seeing what was ahead, . . .* spoke of the resurrection of the Christ" (Acts 2:30-31).

However, some prefer to understand Psalm 16, like so many other psalms used by the New Testament, as indirectly messianic. In light of Peter's seemingly clear statements, is such an interpretation feasible? To answer this question we must look more carefully at the psalm itself and the pertinent New Testament passages, keeping in mind principles observed in our analysis of the indirectly messianic psalms discussed above.

Psalm 16 may be classified as a song of confidence. In the first section of the psalm, the speaker asks for divine protection (v. 1), affirms his loyalty to God in contrast to others who have departed from Him (vv. 2-4), speaks in figurative terms of God's rich blessings (vv. 5-6), and vows to praise the Lord (v. 7). In verses 8-11 (the portion quoted by Peter) he states his confidence in God's protective presence. He will not be shaken because the Lord is at his right hand, allowing him to experience joy and security (vv. 8-9). God will not "abandon" him "to the grave" or let him "see decay" (v. 10). Rather he will enjoy life in God's presence (v. 11).

Because verse 10 is the key verse, it requires special attention. Several observations are pertinent to its interpretation. First, the poetic parallelism of the verse is synonymous, with each of the elements in the first line corresponding to an element in the second. The affirmation "you will not abandon" corresponds to "nor will you let . . . see," while "me" (literally "my life") and "your Holy One," are parallel, as are "the grave" and "decay." Because of the parallel structure of the verse, it is virtually certain that "your Holy One" is the speaker himself, not a distinct individual.

Second, the Hebrew term rendered "Holy One" is not a technical term for the king, but is frequently used in the psalms of God's faithful servants in general.[51] Thus it cannot be understood as inherently messianic.

Third, the translation of Hebrew *šāḥat* as "decay" (cf. NIV) is problematic. This rendering assumes the existence of a noun *šāḥat* "corruption" (derived from the verb *šāḥat*, "to be corrupted, destroyed"), which is understood as a homonym of the well-attested *šāḥat*, "pit."[52] Since *šāḥat*, "pit," frequently refers figurative-

51. Compare the use of the word (*ḥāsîd*) in Psalms 4:3; 12:1; 32:6; 86:2 (singular) and in 30:4; 31:23; 37:28; 52:9; 79:2; 85:8; 89:19; 97:10; 116:15; 132:9; 145:10; 148:14; and 149:9 (plural).
52. The lexical meaning of *šaḥat*, "pit," (which is derived from *šûaḥ*, "to sink down") is well supported (cf. the verbs of making, digging, ascending, and descending associated with it).

ly to death or the grave, it would make excellent sense in Psalm 16:10 parallel to "grave."[53] If one reads "pit" instead of "decay," it becomes more difficult to see a reference to literal death and burial in the text.

Fourth, the verbs used ("abandon" and "let see") could refer theoretically to either deliverance from physical death (especially if one reads "pit" instead of "decay") or to deliverance from the grave after one has experienced physical death. In the context of the Psalter, the former appears to be more likely (see the above discussion of the psalmists' view of the afterlife). In short, an examination of Psalm 16:10 in its literary context does not demand that it be understood as referring to resurrection. Apart from the New Testament use of the passage, verse 10 is more easily understood (in the context of the Psalter as a whole) as the psalmist's confident statement that he would be protected from a premature, violent, unjust death at the hands of those hostile to God and His servants.

Of course, possessing a completed canon of Scripture, we cannot divorce the psalm from its New Testament usage. However, in considering the New Testament one must also be careful not to make quick assumptions as to the nature of the psalm's use and thereby unfairly neglect other interpretive options. Exactly what does the New Testament assume about the nature of Psalm 16? How far can one legitimately press its statements? Does its treatment of the psalm demand that the latter be understood as exclusively and directly messianic?

As already noted, the New Testament assumes that resurrection is in view in Psalm 16:10 and therefore that Jesus Christ is the speaker, as well as the referent of "Holy One." However, in and of itself this does not necessarily mean that the psalm is *exclusively* messianic or directly prophetic. The New Testament's Christological application of the psalm could be accounted for by the hermeneutical principles noted earlier in relation to indirectly messianic psalms. Since the righteous sufferers of the Psalter were vindicated by being delivered from death at the hands of their enemies, one expects Jesus, the righteous sufferer par excellence, to be vindicated as well. When threatened by their enemies, the psalmists did not experience physical death, though they did come face-to-face with its horrors before being rescued from its clutches. As the epitome of the ideal sufferer, Jesus went one step further by actually descending into the grave itself and then rising from it. When given the heightened sense attached to it by the New Testament, Psalm 16:10 describes Jesus' experience. In its heightened sense the language applies exclusively to Him, but this need not mean that the psalm, understood in a less, more typically Old

---

53. *Šaḥat* clearly means "pit" in Job 33:18, 22, 24, 28, 30 (cf. "going down" in vv. 24 and 28); Pss. 30:9 (cf. "going down"); 103:4; Isa. 38:17; Ezek. 28:8 (cf. "bring you down"); Jonah 2:6 (cf. "brought . . . up"). (Note that NIV translates "pit" in each case.) In other texts where *šaḥat* is associated with the realm of death (Job 17:14; Pss. 49:9; 55:23), NIV understands the proposed homonym (it translates *šaḥat* with "corruption" or "decay" in these texts), though "pit" would make just as good sense in each case. In Job 17:14 "pit" is definitely preferable in light of the book's use of the word elsewhere (cf. 9:31 and the verses in chap. 33 cited above). In Psalm 55:23 (*lib'êr šaḥat*, NIV "pit of corruption") one might expect an attributive genitive after "pit," but in this case *šaḥat* may be an explanatory gloss or an emphatic appositional genitive (cf. *ni šmat rûaḥ*, lit. "breath of breath" [NIV "blast of breath"] in Ps. 18:15).

Testament sense, could not refer to David or be applicable to his audience as well. Because the apostles were concerned only with the Christological significance of the psalm, one would not expect them to mention a more immediate (and relatively mundane!) sense which the psalmist's words might have possessed. Their failure to do so does not mean that such a sense did not exist.

In spite of what has just been said, one must acknowledge that certain elements in Peter's statement set it apart from other New Testament contexts which utilize psalms in an indirectly messianic sense. In other cases we are not given such clear and explicit statements that the psalmist himself understood his words as possessing a heightened, prophetic sense. However, according to Peter, David was aware that the words of verses 8-11 were applicable (whether exclusively or ultimately) to one of his descendants. David understood the ramifications of God's promise that one of his descendants would fulfill the messianic ideal and occupy his throne (Acts 2:30). As a prophet (Acts 2:30) David apparently saw that this would entail a divine victory over the power of the grave, which transcended mere deliverance from a premature, unjust death at the hands of one's enemies (the sense of the words if applicable to David himself). Though we are not told exactly how clearly he saw these future developments, one thing is certain in retrospect—in speaking of this future ideal descendant's triumph over death, David spoke of the Messiah's resurrection (Acts 2:31).

To summarize, in light of Peter's statements, it is possible to view Psalm 16 as exclusively and directly messianic. However, nothing in the psalm itself or in the New Testament demands this interpretation. It is possible that Psalm 16:10 was David's own statement of confidence that God would deliver him from a violent death at the hands of his enemies and at the same time a prophetic confession that the Messiah would escape death in an even more dramatic way. If so, Psalm 16 may be labeled indirectly messianic, though Peter's statements about David's awareness of its heightened sense set it apart from others so categorized above. In this case the significance of the psalmist's experience as foreshadowing that of the Messiah did not await unveiling in the progress of revelation, but was understood by the author himself.

WARRIOR

One of the primary roles of ancient Near Eastern kings was that of a warrior. Kings frequently boasted of their military prowess. For example, the Assyrian ruler Ashur-nasir-pal II described himself as the "great king . . . subduer of all princes, fearless in battle, ferocious dragon, the one who breaks up the forces of the rebellious . . . who treads upon the necks of the princes insubmissive to him, mighty flood tide whose conflict cannot be rivaled . . . he who (stirs up) battle (and) conflict, who forces to bow down princes insubmissive to him, who rules all peoples, strong king, who destroys the fortifications of his enemies, who smashes the weapons of princes."[54]

54. Grayson, *Assyrian Royal Inscriptions*, 2:158-59.

The Psalms depict God as a mighty warrior-king who protects His people and, in His capacity of judge, executes justice on their behalf. When threatened by their enemies, individuals appealed to God as a warrior. For example, the author of Psalm 35 prayed, "Take up shield and buckler: arise and come to my aid. Brandish spear and javelin against those who pursue me" (vv. 2-3*a*). Davidic kings testified that God had trained them in the art of warfare and specially equipped them for battle (18:34-35; 144:1). The songs of Zion portray God as an awe-inspiring warrior who devastates hostile forces (cf. 47:2; 76:7, 12). The Lord brings "desolations . . . on the earth," "breaks the bow and shatters the spear," and "burns the shields with fire" (46:8-9; cf. 75:3). When enemy armies march against His chosen city God strikes terror into their hearts with His powerful battle cry (76:5-6; cf. 48:4-6).[55] Just as a mighty wind breaks up sailing vessels, so He shatters His foes outside the walls of Zion (48:7). Psalm 24:7-10 pictures God as "the King of Glory" returning to His city following a mighty victory. He is called "the Lord Almighty" (or "Lord of Armies") who is "mighty in battle." In this militaristic context God's "glory" is the physical radiance which He displays in battle (cf. Pss. 29:3; 97:6). In similar fashion Psalm 68 describes the Lord, accompanied by thousands of chariots, ascending into His sanctuary with captives and tribute (vv. 17-18, 24-31) following His victory over kings and armies (vv. 12, 14).

The most vivid descriptions of God as warrior occur in so-called theophanic passages, which depict the Lord coming in splendor and power to fight for His people. The somewhat stereotypical imagery used in these theophanic descriptions was heavily influenced by the Lord's historical theophanies (see, e.g., Ex. 19; Josh. 10;1 Sam 7; 2 Sam. 5), early poetic accounts of God's mighty deeds (cf. Ex. 15; Deut. 33; Judg. 5), and ancient Near Eastern depictions of warrior-kings and gods, especially the storm god Baal. Though these poetic texts do not describe literal appearances of God, they do reflect the psalmists' awareness of God's very real intervention in history and testify to their faith in His ongoing personal involvement in the life of the nation.

Psalm 18:7-16 is the most detailed of these theophanic texts. David pictured the Lord as breaking through the sky and speeding to his defense on the wings of the wind, personified here as a cherub (vv. 9-10). Breathing out smoke and fire (v. 8), He thunders from heaven and scatters His enemies with lightning bolts (vv. 13-14).[56] The entire cosmos quivers before Him (v. 7) and even the underworld is

---

55. In Psalm 76:6 NIV's "rebuke" is probably too weak a translation for Hebrew *g^e'ārāh*. Usage in other militaristic/theophanic contexts suggests that the word refers to a loud, resounding shout or battle cry (note the corresponding parallel expressions in Pss. 18:15*b* and 104:7) which has devastating physical effects on everyone or everything that hears it (cf. Job 26:11; Pss. 18:15; 104:7; Isa. 50:2). Note also the use of the related verb *gā'ar* in Psalm 106:9; Isaiah 17:13; and Nahum 1:4.

56. The verb translated "routed" in v. 14 (*hāmam*) appears at least five times in early historical accounts of the Lord's victories over Israel's enemies (cf. Ex. 14:24; 23:27; Josh. 10:10; Judg. 4:15; 1 Sam. 7:10). Perhaps David, in using this word, affirmed his confidence that the living God (cf. Ps. 18:46) was still miraculously intervening for His people, just as He had done for earlier generations of Israelites.

blasted open by His battle cry (v. 15). This display of power is all on behalf of His chosen servant, whom He pulls to safety from the raging chaos waters (v. 16).

These same elements appear in other theophanic descriptions. In vivid and frightening fashion Psalm 29 pictures God using the elements of the thunderstorm as He does battle for His people (cf. v. 11). As in Psalm 18, the entire cosmos shakes before Him. Psalm 68 depicts God as the One who "rides the clouds/ancient skies" (cf. 104:3) and "thunders with a mighty voice" (vv. 4, 33). Verses 7-8 of this psalm use theophanic imagery (drawn from Judg. 5:4-5) in conjunction with the conquest of Canaan (cf. vv. 9-10). The same God who shook Mount Sinai marched ahead of His people as He led them into the Promised Land. Psalm 77:16-19 uses theophanic imagery in recalling the crossing of the Red Sea. God's appearance in the storm shakes the earth and incapacitates the sea so that He is able to lead His people safely through its raging waters (cf. also 114:3-7). In Psalm 97:3-5 God's arrival in defense of His people (cf. v. 10) is accompanied by destructive fire (cf. 104:4) and lightning bolts and causes widespread cosmic disruption. Using language and imagery reminiscent of Psalm 18, the royal author of Psalm 144 asked the Lord to descend from the sky, shoot His lightning bolts like arrows, and deliver him from the enemy, which threatened him like raging waters (vv. 5-7).

THE DIVINE KING'S CHARACTERISTICS AND ATTRIBUTES

The preceding discussion of God's royal position and functions has highlighted His sovereignty, incomparability, justice, and power. However, the Psalms also emphasize several of His other characteristics or attributes that require closer examination.

HATRED AND WRATH

According to the Psalms, God hates "all who do wrong" and "those who love violence" (5:5; 11:5) in the sense that He rejects and destroys them (cf. 5:4-6; 11:6). He directs His anger toward those who rebel against His sovereign authority (2:5) and seek to destroy His people (18:7; 69:24; 76:7). God's compassion and love cause Him to be "slow to anger" (86:15; 103:8) and to refrain from sending the full power of His wrath against His people (78:38; 103:9). Though their sin does at times stir up His anger (78:49-50; 95:10; 106:40), God responds favorably to their cries for mercy (cf. 86:3-6; 90:13-17 [cf. v. 7]). Those who experience His restoration can affirm that "His anger lasts only a moment, but his favor lasts a lifetime" (30:5).

GOODNESS

The Psalms frequently affirm that God is "good" (*ṭôb*). While this term seems to be rather vague and general on the surface, the specific contexts in which it appears usually give it sharper focus. For example, God's goodness is often associated with His enduring faithfulness and love (100:5; 106:1; 107:1; 136:1) as exhibited in His protection of and provision for His people (34:8; 54:6; 69:16;

109:21; 118:1, 29; 135:3). God's goodness also encompasses His compassion for
all whom He has created (145:9) and His merciful forgiveness of sin (25:7; 86:5).
For the psalmist, then, God's goodness is like a fountain out of which other more
specific characteristics spring forth.

FAITHFULNESS AND LOYAL LOVE

According to the psalmists, one of God's most fundamental and important
attributes is His faithfulness (cf. the virtually synonymous Hebrew terms *'ĕmûnâ*
and *'ĕmet*), which is established in heaven and surrounds Him as He rules from
His heavenly throne (89:1-2, 5, 8, 14). It knows no limitations geographically
(36:5; 57:10; 108:4; though cf. 88:11) or temporally (100:5; 119:90; 146:6). God's
faithfulness characterizes both His words and deeds (33:4; 111:7-8). His law is
trustworthy (119:86, 138) and His promises to David reliable (89:25, 33, 49).
Perhaps His reliability is most clearly seen in His protection and deliverance of
those who appeal to Him in times of need (31:5; 40:10; 57:3; 61:7; 69:13; 71:22;
91:4; 98:3; 138:2; 143:1).

Closely related to God's faithfulness is His loyal love or devotion (*ḥesed*),
which He extends to His covenant people both corporately and individually.[57] Like
His faithfulness, God's loyal love knows no geographical or temporal limits (57:10;
100:5; 103:7; 138:8). This love played such an important role in Israel's history that
the declaration "His love endures forever" appears as a refrain in all twenty-six
verses of Psalm 136, a hymnic recital of God's mighty deeds on the nation's behalf.
God primarily exhibits His loyal love by delivering (6:4; 21:7; 31:16, 21; 32:10;
44:26; 48:9; 66:20; 85:7; 86:13; 94:18; 98:3; 107:8, 15, 21, 31) and forgiving (25:7;
51:1; 103:8-11) those who acknowledge (36:11), trust (147:11), and fear (103:11,
13, 17) Him.

MERCY AND COMPASSION

The psalms also declare that the Lord is "gracious (or merciful) and compassionate" (*ḥannûm wᵉ raḥûm*, 111:4; 145:8; cf. 86:15; 103:8; 116:5). This word
pair refers to God's favorable disposition toward those whose needs move Him
emotionally. The psalmists frequently appealed to God's mercy and/or compassion when they were overwhelmed by powerful enemies or by their own sinfulness
(4:1; 6:2; 9:13; 25:6, 16; 26:11; 27:7; 30:10; 31:9; 40:11; 41:4, 10; 51:1; 56:1;
57:1; 79:8; 86:3, 16; 119:58, 77, 132, 156; 123:3).

THE PROPER RESPONSE TO GOD'S KINGSHIP: PETITION AND PRAISE

The book of Psalms is the only divinely inspired collection of prayers and
hymns which God's people possess. As such it provides a pattern for His people to

57. Note the close association of *ḥesed* and *'ĕmûnāh* / *'ĕmet* in Psalms 25:10; 26:3; 40:10-11;
57:3; 61:7; 85:10; 86:15; 88:11; 89:2, 14, 24; 92:2; 98:3; 115:1; 117:2; and 138:2.

follow during times of crisis and triumph. Recognizing the Lord's sovereignty, the psalmists looked to Him in faith during their hour of need and found confidence in His revealed character and word. When deliverance arrived, they gratefully praised their divine king for His intervention and exhorted others to learn from their experience and join them in extolling God's virtues. God's ongoing dependability in such times of distress led His people to write hymns of praise which proclaimed His goodness and greatness in general terms.

PETITION: FAITH IN THE KING IN TIMES OF CRISIS

The Psalter is filled with psalms of petition (often called lament psalms) in which God's people cry out to Him for help in the midst of distress. These psalms display certain standard formal features, including an opening cry for help, a lament (or description of one's plight), a petition (or request for help), a statement of confidence in God's willingness and/or ability to deliver, and a vow of praise, in which the psalmist promises to tell others of God's goodness and greatness following his deliverance. Three general characteristics of these psalms are particularly noteworthy in that they provide a model of how God's people should approach their sovereign Lord in times of need. The authors of the laments looked to God alone as their deliverer, they approached Him in a personal way, reasoning with Him and appealing to His emotions, and they placed their confidence in His revealed character and word.

Dependence on God. The very form of these psalms illustrates their authors' dependence on God. The psalms of petition invariably begin with, or contain in their opening statement, an address to God (3:1; 4:1; 5:1; 6:1; 7:1; 10:1; 12:1; 13:1; 17:1; 22:1; 25:1; 26:1; 28:1; 31:1; etc.). Rather than being indirect or investigating other potential sources of deliverance, the psalmists came directly to Him when overwhelmed by trouble.

Approaching God as a Person. The psalmists assumed that God is personal (possessing rational, emotional, and volitional faculties) and consequently capable of being persuaded to act on their behalf. More specifically, in seeking a favorable response the psalmists appealed to God's reputation, His desire for praise, and His personal attributes of justice, faithfulness, love, and compassion.

In lamenting the fall of Jerusalem the author of Psalm 74 argued that the enemy's mistreatment of the nation was actually a challenge to God's reputation. He pointed out that the Babylonians had burned *God's* sanctuary to the ground and defiled *His* dwelling place (v. 7). He asked, "How long will the enemy mock you, O God? Will the foe revile your name forever?" (v. 10: cf. v. 18), and concluded with this prayer: "Rise up, O God, and defend your cause; remember how fools mock you all day long. Do not ignore the clamor of your adversaries, the uproar of your enemies, which rises continually" (vv. 22-23). For further discussion and examples of the psalmists' concern for God's reputation, see pp. 281-83 (excursus).

The psalmists recognized that God was desirous of the praise due Him (cf. Isa. 42:8). Consequently they vowed that, if delivered, they would tell everyone within hearing of God's goodness and greatness (for examples of such vows of praise, see 9:14; 22:22-31; 35:18; 43:4; 51:14-15; 54:6; 56:12; 57:9; 59:16-17; 61:8; 69:30-33; 71:22-24; 79:13). Some even boldly argued that God's failure to deliver them would mean that He would not receive praise, for those who descend into the world of the dead have nothing to rejoice about and are cut off from the worshiping community (cf. 6:5; 30:9; 88:10-12).

The psalmists also appealed to God's just character. As already seen (pp. 279-80) they declared their innocence, sought vindication from their just king, and asked for divine retribution against their enemies.

The psalmists' appeals to God's faithfulness and love (cf. 6:4; 31:16; 44:26; 61:7; 69:13; 85:7; 143:1) presuppose the existence of a binding relationship between themselves and God wherein divine protection is promised to those who remain loyal to the Lord. The psalmists went to great pains to emphasize their devotion. They referred to themselves as God's servants (e. g., 27:9; 86:2, 4, 16: 116:16; 123:2; 143:2, 12), addressed Him as their God, king, and savior (5:2; 25:5; 27:9; 44:4; 74:12; 84:3), and formally proclaimed their trust in Him (e. g., 7:1; 9:10; 25:2, 20; 26:1; 28:7; 31:1, 14; 55:23; 56:4, 11; 57:2; 71:1; 141:8; 143:8). The psalmists' declaration that they have "taken refuge" (*ḥāsāh*) in the Lord is tantamount to a confession of loyalty and, as such, can be offered as a fundamental reason why divine protection should be extended (16:1; 57:1; 71:1; 141:8). Those taking refuge in the Lord are identified as His righteous servants who love and fear Him (5:11; 31:19; 34:22; 37:39-40; 64:10). They stand in contrast to rebels (2:12), idolaters (16:1-4), and those who trust in mere men (118:8-9). Those who exhibit such devotion to God can expect to experience His faithfulness and loyal love in the form of deliverance and protection.

Excursus on Psalm 44. Perhaps the Psalter's boldest appeal to God's faithfulness is found in Psalm 44, a communal lament psalm offered to God during an unidentified national catastrophe. The nation testified to God's mighty historical deeds and confessed its faith in His sovereign protection (vv. 1-8). However, the mood of the psalm then changes abruptly, as the nation lamented that God had handed them over to their enemies and subjected them to humiliation (vv. 9-16). At this point, knowing Israel's propensity for rebellion as outlined on the pages of the Old Testament, one expects a confession of sin, but instead finds a protestation of innocence. The nation claims that it has been faithful to the covenant and loyal to the Lord (vv. 17-22). The psalm then concludes with one of the most shocking requests found in the Psalter: "Awake, O Lord! Why do you sleep? Rouse yourself! Do not reject us forever. Why do You hide Your face and forget our misery and oppression? We are brought down to the dust; our bodies cling to the ground. Rise up and help us; redeem us because of your unfailing love" (vv. 23-26).

The inclusion of this lament among the inspired prayers of the Psalter indicates that it should not be dismissed as an irreverent expression of the nation's self-righteousness and lack of faith. Rather, it is the heartfelt, brutally honest cry of a confused, suffering nation, faced with the fact that one of their primary theological affirmations (God is faithful to His covenantal promise to protect those loyal to Him; cf. Ex. 23:22) has been called into serious question by the reality of national catastrophe. Of course this psalm, like the book of Job, reminds us that the sovereign God cannot be placed in a box. There are times when His larger purposes dictate that even the righteous and innocent must temporarily suffer. Nevertheless the authors of Psalm 44 should not be condemned as theologically shortsighted or as unwilling to submit to God's sovereign purposes. On the contrary, they should be commended for their stubborn faith in God's faithfulness. In the midst of extreme distress they clung to their theological creed (cf. vv. 4-8) and prayed, in accord with that creed, for a fresh display of God's loyal love. One might even view their request as an illustration of the boldness and persistence commended by Jesus (Luke 11:5-13; 18:1-8).

The psalmists also appealed to God's compassion (Pss. 4.1; 6:2; 9:13; 26:11; 31:9; 56:1; 57:1; 79:8; 86:3, 16; 123:3), often buttressing their requests with laments expressing their deep inner emotions and describing their pitiable condition in horrifying detail. In attempting to move God to action some psalmists unreservedly depicted their situation as one of utter disgrace and intense suffering. For example, the author of Psalm 6 declared, "I am worn out from groaning; all night long I flood my bed with weeping and drench my couch with tears. My eyes grow weak with sorrow; they fail because of all my foes" (vv. 6-7). Similarly the author of Psalm 109 lamented, "I am poor and needy, and my heart is wounded within me. I fade away like an evening shadow; I am shaken off like a locust. My knees give away from fasting; my body is thin and gaunt. I am an object of scorn to my accusers; when they see me, they shake their heads" (vv. 22-25). Other vivid descriptions of suffering include 22:12-18; 31:9-13; 35:11-16; 69:1-4; and 102:3-11.

Excursus on the penitential psalms. Though many psalmists offered their innocence, loyalty, and persecuted state as reasons why God should deliver them from their enemies, others appealed to His faithfulness, love, and compassion in the midst of personal spiritual failure. Their prayers for forgiveness and restoration appear in the so-called penitential psalms. Several features of these psalms are noteworthy and instructive for God's penitent people of all ages. The psalmists honestly confessed their sinful condition and deeds, making no attempt to justify themselves or pass blame (25:7, 10-11, 18; 32:5; 38:18; 41:4; 51:3-5). They displayed an attitude of genuine repentance, repudiating empty ritual (51:16-17) and asking instead for a transformation of their character and actions (25:4-5; 51:10, 12-13). As grounds for their request they appealed to God's personal attributes (25:6-7; 51:1) as well as to the debilitating physical and emotional effects of their sin and guilt (32:3-4; 38:2-14; 51:8*b*).

Confidence in God's revealed character and Word. In addition to appealing to God as their sole defender and approaching Him in a personal way, the psalmists placed their confidence in His revealed character and Word. With rare exception (Ps. 88) the mood of the psalms of petition moves from lament to confidence (see, e. g., 6:1-7 [petition and lament]/8-10 [confidence]; 7:1-9/10-17; 10:1-13/14-18; 13:1-4/5-6; 28:1-5/6-9).

In some cases this shift in perspective appears to be due to reflection on God's character as revealed in His past deeds. For example, the author of Psalm 77, after lamenting his distress and expressing his feeling of abandonment by God (vv. 1-9), stated, "Then I thought, 'To this I will appeal: the years of the right hand of the Most High.' I will remember the deeds of the LORD; yes, I will remember your miracles of long ago. I will meditate on all your works and consider all your mighty deeds" (vv. 10-12).

In other cases the shift to confidence is the result of a divine oracle of salvation delivered (probably by an authorized intermediary, such as a prophet or priest) in response to the petitioner's request. Such an oracle appears in Psalm 12:5, where the Lord, in response to the psalmist's lament and petition (vv. 1-4), declared, "Because of the oppression of the weak and the groaning of the needy, I will now arise. . . . I will protect them from those who malign them." Psalm 60:6-8 records an oracle delivered to the nation following a military setback (cf. vv. 1-3). In this case the Lord spoke "from his sanctuary" and promised victory over the surrounding nations. Several other psalms refer indirectly to salvation oracles (6:9; 18:30; 28:6; 56:3-4, 10-11; 130:5).

Whether due to reflection on the historical record of God's mighty deeds or in response to His verbal assurance of deliverance, the psalmists placed their confidence in God (see, e. g., 12:6-8; 60:9-12; 77:13-20). In the same way, God's troubled people in all ages can place their confidence in His revealed character and Word.[58]

PRAISE: DECLARING THE KING'S GOODNESS AND GREATNESS

Thanksgiving songs. Following their deliverance the psalmists composed thanksgiving songs to God in fulfillment of vows made in the midst of their crisis. Though these psalms exhibit much formal variation, they all include a narrative section in which the author recalls his time of need and describes the Lord's saving intervention. The narrative sections, which are usually brief and to the point (Ps. 18

---

58. With the passing of the apostolic age, New Testament Christians do not receive special revelation from the Lord as many of the psalmists did. Nevertheless they can place their confidence in the promises and principles of Scripture, God's written revelation.

being an exception), emphasize the utter helplessness of the psalmists and the invincible power of God. In most cases the psalmists' strength was gone and they faced the prospect of certain death (18:4-5, 15-16; 30:3, 9; 32:4-6; 40:2; 116:3). Miraculously God pulled them from death's raging waters (18:16) and miry pit (30:1, 3; 40:2*a*) and placed them on firm ground (40:2*b*).

On the basis of their experience the psalmists extolled the character of God in general terms and exhorted their audience to learn practical lessons about how men should live before Him. God's mighty deeds on their behalf demonstrate that He is just (18:25-26; 116:5), reliable (18:30; 32:10), capable of protecting His own (18:30; 34:7; 116:6; 118:6-9), incomparable (18:31), forgiving (32:1-2), and compassionate (116:5). Their vindication before their enemies proves that He saves the humble and righteous, but opposes the proud and wicked (18:27; 34:15-22; 138:6). When forced to discipline His people, God's punishment is shortlived and leads to eventual restoration (30:5). Rather than being stubborn (32:9), men should trust and obey God, for those who fear Him receive His blessings (32:1-2, 10; 34:5, 8-14; 40:4; 118:8-9).

As divinely inspired models of how God's people are to respond to His intervention in their lives, the thanksgiving songs provide insight into the nature of genuine praise. The exuberance of the opening proclamations (30:1; 34:1 2; 116:1-2), calls to praise (30:4; 32:11; 34:3; 116:19), and declarations about God's attributes show that public praise is the logical and natural expression of gratitude for God's deliverance. Praise also involves moving beyond the details of a specific experience and discovering in it implications about God's character and how men should live before Him. Praise glorifies God, the sovereign king, and thereby compels others to trust Him more fully (cf. 40:3).

Hymns. The hymnic genre logically grows out of the generalized statements of the thanksgiving songs. The hymns typically contain a call to and basis for praise, with the latter being in the form of general declarations about God's goodness and greatness as exhibited in the world at large and in the history of His covenant people. Perhaps more succinctly than any other portion of Scripture, the hymns declare who God is and what He has accomplished in the world, facts which God's people do well to bring to mind continually.

In many respects, the content of the hymns has been the subject of this essay on the theology of the Psalms, for the hymns, more than any other genre in the Psalter, encapsulate that theology. A summary of hymnic themes is at the same time a convenient conclusion to this study. The authors of the hymns praise God as the sovereign, incomparable king over His creation (29:1-2; 103:19; 145:11-13), including the natural world (8:3; 19:1-6; 33:6-9; 104:1-30; 135:6-7; 136:5-9; 146:6; 147:4, 8-9, 15-18; 148:1-10), humankind (8:4-7; 33:10-11, 13-15; 113:4-6; 148:11-12), and His covenant people Israel (33:12; 100:3; 103:7; 114:1-2). As universal king, God preserves order and executes justice (33:5; 103:6; 113:7-9; 135:14; 145:20; 146:7-9; 147:6), often revealing His power as an invincible warrior (29:3-9; 136:10-

22). Through His mighty deeds God demonstrates that He is holy (He angrily rejects and opposes evildoers), good, faithful, loving, merciful, and compassionate (33:4-5, 18; 100:5; 103:1-5, 8-17; 111:1-9; 113:7-9; 117:2; 135:14; 136:1-22; 145:8-9, 13-19; 147:11-14; 149:4). The king's subjects should trust in Him (33:20-21) and praise Him for His goodness and greatness.

> Clap your hands, all you nations;
> shout to God with cries of joy.
> How awesome is the Lord Most High,
> the great King over all the earth! (Ps. 47:1-2)

8

A THEOLOGY OF ISAIAH

ROBERT B. CHISHOLM, JR.

Isaiah is perhaps best known for his unsurpassed view of our sovereign, almighty God. The prophet's presentation of God is not the abstract description of the philosopher-theologian, but rather a highly personal portrait influenced by his face-to-face encounter with God at the beginning of his ministry. For Isaiah, God is first and foremost "the Holy One of Israel" who possesses absolute sovereign authority over His covenant people and the nations of the earth, but who at the same time personally intervenes in history to accomplish His purposes.

The book's panoramic view of Israel's history also makes it a rich theological source. Isaiah outlined Israel's history from the eighth century B.C., when the prophet lived, to the eschatological age. Israel's future included judgment and exile but also final restoration. According to Isaiah, several key figures would emerge in the outworking of God's plan for His people, the most important being the ideal Davidic ruler (or Messiah) of the eschaton and the Suffering Servant of the Lord. Though their roles overlap to some degree, Isaiah stopped short of directly equating the two, leaving that task to subsequent biblical revelation.

The theological message of the book may be summarized as follows: The Lord will fulfill His ideal for Israel by purifying His people through judgment and then restoring them to a renewed covenantal relationship. He will establish Jerusalem (Zion) as the center of His worldwide kingdom and reconcile once hostile nations to Himself.

The book of Isaiah has been the focal point of intense higher critical debate.

The virtual consensus of modern critical scholarship is that a large portion of the book postdates the eighth-century prophet Isaiah, whose work was revised and supplemented by several later anonymous editors. Chapters 40-66 are regarded as products of the exilic-postexilic periods, with some dividing the section between the so-called Deutero-Isaiah (chaps. 40-55) and Trito-Isaiah (chaps. 56-66). The consistent perspective of these later chapters is indeed exilic-postexilic, as the numerous references to the ruined condition of Jerusalem and Judah and the exilic situation of God's people indicate. For this reason, many scholars argue that chapters 40-66 originated in this later time period.

In response to this position, conservatives have appealed to the authority of the New Testament, which attributes both sections of the book to the eighth-century prophet (cf. esp. John 12:38-41; Rom. 9:27-33; 10:16-21). Admittedly Isaiah's sustained projection of himself into the future, even to the point where he reasons with the exiles as if literally present with them, is unique. However, this section of the prophecy affirms that the Lord's ability to prophesy events long before they occur is proof of His superiority to the pagan gods of Babylon. In this regard a highly rhetorical message directed to the exiles by a long dead prophet of the Lord would be especially effective and provide convincing support for the Lord's argument.[1]

In the following treatment of Isaiah's theology I assume Isaianic authorship of the entire book. At the same time I recognize that the differing perspectives of the book's two major sections (chap. 1-39 and chaps. 40-66) result in distinct thematic emphases, despite the large amount of thematic interplay between them. For this reason my discussion is divided into two parts, in accordance with the book's basic literary structure. The discussion within each section is then arranged under the major headings, "God and His People" and "God and the Nations," reflecting the relational framework and emphases of Isaianic and prophetic theology in general (see my introduction to the later chapter "A Theology of the Minor Prophets.")

THEOLOGY OF ISAIAH 1-39

GOD AND HIS PEOPLE

Breach of covenant. Isaiah's vision of God's holiness, encompassing both His royal transcendence over the world and His absolute authority in the moral-ethical

---

1. One key passage in the debate is Isaiah 48:6-7. Some contend that this passage conclusively proves that chapters 40-55 date to the sixth, rather than the eighth, century. For example, Christopher R. North states with regard to this passage, "If, as those who defend the Isaianic authorship agree, the 'new things' were not to happen for two centuries, it could not be said in the eighth century that 'they are created now.' Nor could sixth-century readers be told that they had never heard of them. They might fairly retort that they had, unless it be that xl-lv was hidden for two centuries, and the defenders of Isaianic authorship do not allege that it was" (*The Second Isaiah* [Oxford: Clarendon, 1964], p. 3). Perhaps here the key is recognizing that the prophet's *rhetorical posture* is the sixth century. He speaks to the exilic audience as if present and does not assume that they have had access to his message for 150 years. This approach is part of the rhetorical genius of the section and makes the message, once it is understood as coming from an eighth-century prophet, all the more powerful.

realm, was foundational to the prophet's ministry and message (cf. 6:1-13). When Isaiah saw this holy God seated on His throne, he became aware as never before of his own, and his people's, sinfulness. When the seraph symbolically cleansed him, he was compelled to volunteer as God's messenger to his sinful countrymen. As he departed from the divine assembly, he went with the full authority of the sovereign king of the universe.

Isaiah's accusations and warnings of judgment must be placed against the background of the Mosaic Covenant established at Mount Sinai and renewed on later occasions (cf. Ex. 24:1-8; 34:10-28; Deut. 29:1–32:47; Josh. 24:1-27). Through this covenant Israel agreed to be the Lord's people and obey His commandments. The Lord promised to reward obedience with agricultural prosperity and national security, but He also threatened to punish disobedience with famine, pestilence, military defeat, and exile (note the lists of "blessings" and "curses" in Lev. 26 and Deut. 28). Like many of the other preexilic prophets, Isaiah came as a specially commissioned messenger of Israel's covenant Lord to accuse the people of rebellion, call them to repentance, and warn them of impending judgment.

The covenantal nature of Isaiah's message is apparent from the outset. The book's first literary unit (1:2-20) takes the form of a covenant lawsuit, in which the Lord accuses His people of rebellion and issues an ultimatum. The Lord is called "the Holy One of Israel" (v. 4), a title that refers to His sovereign authority over Israel and serves as a reminder of His moral-ethical demands. He pictures Himself as a father who has patiently reared his children, only to see them rebel against his authority and repay his devotion with ingratitude (vv. 2-4). Comparing His sinful people to the residents of ancient Sodom and Gomorrah (v. 10), the Lord denounces their empty rituals and warns that only true repentance, in the form of social and economic justice, can save them from total ruin (vv. 10-20). Persistence in sin will bring death by the sword; repentance will bring renewed prosperity (v. 19-20). Word play is used to highlight the alternatives the Lord has placed before His people: they can either "eat [*'ākal*] the best of the land" or "be devoured [*'ākal* again] by the sword." The covenantal violations of God's people fell into several categories, including social injustice, idolatry, foreign alliances, reliance on manmade armaments and fortifications, and rejection of the Lord's messenger and word.

Like his fellow eighth-century prophets Amos and Micah, Isaiah had much to say about socioeconomic injustice. Several passages refer to the widespread exploitation of the poor. In defiance of the covenantal principle that the land belonged to the Lord (Lev. 25:23), the rich accumulated houses and fields (5:8) by instituting oppressive laws (10:1-2) and controlling the judicial processes (1:23; 5:23; 29:21). Enriched by the land and property taken from the poor (3:15-16), the wealthy caroused from morning until evening (5:11-12, 22), while their wives strutted about proudly displaying their luxurious clothes and expensive jewelry (3:16-23). The Lord likens this oppression of the poor to violent acts of murder and bloodshed (1:15, 21; 4:4). When He looked at the richly adorned women, He saw only "filth" (4:4; elsewhere this word refers to vomit [28:8] and excrement [36:12]).

This socioeconomic corruption of the covenant community was particularly upsetting to the Lord. Like a farmer who plants a vineyard, He had gone to great pains to establish His people in their land. He expected them to produce the good fruit of justice (*mišpāṭ*) and righteousness (*ṣᵉdāqāh*), but ironically they yielded only the wild grapes of bloodshed (*mišpāḥ*) and cries of distress (*ṣᵉ'āqāh*; 5:1-7). The literary transformation of this song of the vineyard from a love song (cf. v. 1) to a harsh judgment speech (see esp. vv. 5-7) draws attention to the Lord's sense of loss and disappointment.

Despite their mistreatment of their fellow Israelites, these oppressors of the poor had the audacity to come before the Lord with offerings on various holy days (1:11-15). The Lord rejected their religious rituals, pointing out that when they raised their bloodstained hands in prayer their hypocrisy was obvious. The Lord exhorted them to change their ways by promoting justice and defending the cause of the widow and orphan (vv. 16-17). Seen here is a principle that permeates the Bible: Sacrifice, prayer, and other religious exercises and rituals are meaningless apart from obedience to God's commandments regulating man's relationships with others (cf. 1 Sam. 15:22; Hos. 6:6; Amos 5:21-24; Mic. 6:6-8; Matt. 5:23-24; James 1:27; 1 Pet. 3:7).

Isaiah also denounces idolatry and other pagan religious influences. He alludes to certain pagan worship sites (1:29) and practices, including divination (2:6) and spiritism (8:19). Rather than seeking guidance from their God, the people attempted to contact the spirits of the dead. Such confused thinking would bring only the darkness of judgment on the land (vv. 20-22). In the coming Day of the Lord idolaters would realize the futility of worshiping man-made images (2:8, 18-20; 17:8; 27:9; 31:7) and discard them like a menstruous rag (30:22).

Because of the Assyrian threat looming on the horizon, the leaders of Judah were prone to look to other nations, especially the Egyptians, for assistance. Isaiah warned against this practice and urged his contemporaries to trust in the Lord for help. The leaders of Judah went to great pains to ally with Egypt, thinking that Pharaoh and his chariots could protect them from Assyria (30:1-7; 31:1). However, Egypt was nothing but a blowhard (30:7), doomed to destruction (31:3). Isaiah reminds his listeners of a principle that appears throughout the Old Testament: Victory does not come through soldiers and horses, but through the power of God (31:3; cf. Ex. 15:1; Josh. 11:4-9; 2 Kings 6:14-17; Pss. 20:7; 33:16-19; Prov. 21:31). For an inspiring extrabiblical illustration of the principle, see 1 Maccabees 3:13-26.

In addition to trusting in foreign alliances, God's people also placed their faith in their own armaments (Isa. 2:7; 22:8) and man-made fortifications. The Northern Kingdom was proud of its capital city, Samaria, located on a hill overlooking a valley (28:1). The people of Jerusalem attempted to hold back the Assyrians by refortifying their city (28:8-11). However, their fortifications provided no protection against the Lord's "day of battering down walls" (22:5). The Assyrians captured Samaria in 722 B.C. (2 Kings 17:6) and were on the verge of conquering Jerusalem in 701 when the Lord miraculously delivered the city (2 Kings 18-19).

While trusting in other nations and in their own strength, God's people rejected His prophet and His word of promise. At the beginning of Isaiah's ministry the Lord told him that his exhortations and warnings would fall on deaf ears and would actually have the reverse effect of making the people more and more ingrained in their rebellion (Isa. 6:9-10). The people mocked Isaiah (28:9-10) and demanded that God's prophets bring them messages of salvation, rather than exhortations to holy living (30:10-11). King Ahaz, when challenged by Isaiah to place his trust in God's ancient promise to the house of David, rejected God's offer of a confirming sign (7:1-12). (Fortunately for Judah, Ahaz's son, Hezekiah, proved to be an exception to this general trend of unbelief; cf. chaps. 36-37.)

Because of their foreign alliances and fortifications, the people actually thought they could escape death. Chapter 28 sarcastically depicts the leaders of Jerusalem boasting that they had made a covenant with death and consequently were safe from the "overwhelming scourge" (vv. 14-15). Of course, such presumption was nothing but self-delusion and sheer lunacy. The nation's supposed covenant with death was as meaningless as Neville Chamberlain's 1938 Munich agreement, which the wishful-thinking British prime minister mistakenly thought would prevent war with Hitler's Germany. When the "overwhelming scourge" swept through the land like a destructive flood, it would become apparent to all that true protection comes only through trust in the Lord's faithfulness to His promises and adherence to His just and righteous standards (vv. 16-19).

Judgment. Because of the people's covenantal violations, the Lord warned that judgment would come on them. The Lord Himself would actively oppose them and their allies (5:25; 9:19; 29:2-3; 31:3). He would regard His people as an enemy and take vengeance on them (1:24). They would become the objects of His warfare, just as Israel's enemies had been in earlier days (28:21). At Mount Perazim the Lord miraculously enabled David's armies to defeat the Philistines (2 Sam. 5:20), while at Gibeon He supernaturally intervened so that Joshua's army might destroy the Amorites (Josh. 10:10-13). Now the Lord's ancient "holy wars" would be repeated, but ironically Israel would be placed in the role of her traditional enemies. God's people would experience "the day of the Lord," a day of "tumult, trampling and terror . . . of battering down walls and of crying out to the mountains" (22:5, NIV). In that day once-proud men would run for their lives, in their panic tossing their useless man-made idols aside (2:10-21).

This portrayal of the Lord's day contains several parallels with ancient Near Eastern accounts of the exploits of mighty warrior kings and deities. First, the very concept of the Lord's "day" derives ultimately from the ancient Near East, where conquering kings would sometimes boast that they were able to consummate a campaign in a single day.² Ancient Near Eastern texts also sometimes associate cosmic disturbances and widespread panic with the king's/god's approach (cf. 2:10, 19-21). For example, an Egyptian royal inscription claims that the enemies of Pharaoh Thutmose III "hid in holes" when they heard his battle cry.³ According to a Ugaritic mythological text, the warrior god Baal's voice convulsed the earth and shook the mountains, causing his enemies to flee to the woods.⁴ An Assyrian royal inscription reports that the enemies of Tiglath-pileser I "dreaded" his "fierce battle" and "took to hiding places like bats and scurried off to inaccessible regions."⁵

The Lord's primary instrument of judgment would be the mighty Assyrian army. The Assyrians would come like a hail and wind storm against Samaria and trample her underfoot (28:2-3). They would then sweep into Judah like a flood (7:17; 8:6-8), marching forward speedily and relentlessly, roaring like a mighty lion, and causing a dark cloud of gloom and terror to descend on the land (5:26-30). The Assyrians would besiege and terrorize Jerusalem (29:1-4). Though the Lord would miraculously deliver the city from Assyrian hands, He would eventually raise up another Mesopotamian power, the Babylonians, to punish the royal house of Jerusalem (39:6-7).

Through those enemy armies the Lord would make the judgments threatened in the covenantal curse lists (cf. Lev. 26 and Deut. 28) a reality. The produce of the land would be destroyed (Isa. 1:7; 5:5-6, 9-10; 6:11; 8:21) and its people killed or exiled (3:25; 5:13-14, 24-25; 6:12; 10:4; 39:7).

The Lord would reduce His people to a mere remnant, a motif that has a negative significance in several passages.⁶ Besieged Jerusalem, likened to an isolated hut in the middle of a field (1:8), constitutes the remnant and, as such, is all that stands between survival and total annihilation similar to that of Sodom and Gomorrah. Destruction would be so thorough it would reduce the remnant surviving the first wave of judgment to an infinitesmal number (6:13). This remnant, likened to a lonely flagpole erected on a mountain (30:17), stands in stark contrast to the innumerable host promised in the Abrahamic Covenant (10:22).

God's judgment would be appropriate and just, something Isaiah highlighted through the literary device of irony. Because the people worshiped pagan gods under "sacred oaks" and in gardens, they would become like an oak or garden that is deprived of water (1:29-30). Jerusalem's haughty women would be humiliated,

2. See Douglas Stuart, "The Sovereign's Day of Conquest," *Bulletin of the American Schools of Oriental Research* 221 (1976): 159-64.

3. Miriam Lichtheim, *Ancient Egyptian Literature,* 3 vols (Berkeley, Calif.: U. of California, 1975-80, 2:36.

4. James B. Pritchard, ed., *The Ancient Near East,* 2 vols. (Princeton, N.J.: Princeton U. 1958-75), 1:106.

5. A. K. Grayson, *Assyrian Royal Inscriptions,* 2 vols. (Wiesbaden: Otto Harrassowitz, 1972-76), 2:26.

6. For a thorough discussion of the remnant theme in Isaiah, see Gerhard F. Hasel, *The Remnant.* 3d ed. (Berrien Springs, Mich.: Andrews U., 1980), pp. 216-372.

their luxurious clothing and jewelry replaced by captives' ropes and mourners' sackcloth (3:16–4:1). Those who dishonestly accumulated houses and lands would be deprived of their ill-gotten gains (5:8-10). Their carousing would come to an end as they died of hunger and thirst in exile (vv. 11-13). In that day they would become the main course at Death's feast, while sheep would graze on the ruins of their banqueting halls (vv. 14, 17). The darkness of judgment would descend on those who replaced light with darkness in the moral and ethical realm (vv. 20, 30). Those who derisively mimicked the prophet's words and complained that his message was too childlike would come face to face with foreign invaders, whose words would be unintelligible to them (28:9-13).

Despite its severity, the ultimate purpose of God's judgment was to purify His people. Sin-filled Jerusalem was like good wine diluted by water, or silver mixed with dross (1:22). The Lord's fiery judgment would burn away the dross and reestablish the city as a center of justice (vv. 25-27). By purging out the city's evildoers, the Lord would, as it were, wash away its bloodstains (4:4). These references to the purifying character of God's judgment are a guarantee of God's commitment to His covenant people and lay the foundation for the shift from judgment to salvation in Isaiah's theology.

Deliverance and restoration. Divine judgment would not bring Israel's history to a screeching, permanent halt. As noted, judgment was merely a necessary step toward the realization of God's ideal for the nation. Even through the smoke of judgment, one could discern a ray of hope.

The miraculous deliverance of Jerusalem in 701 B.C., which brought the Assyrians' devastating invasion of the land to an end, became a reminder of the Lord's sovereignty and a guarantee of the city's ultimate exaltation. Though the countryside lay in ruins as a sign of divine displeasure and warning of the consequences of sin (1:7-9), Jerusalem remained intact, the sole survivor among the cities of Judah. As the remnant of Judah (1:9; 37:31-32) the city's very existence was a source of encouragement. After all, the Lord had come short of vaporizing His people—it was not like Sodom and Gomorrah (1:9). Though they were like a mere stump left after a tree has been chopped down, that stump offered hope for the future (6:13; cf. Job 14:7-9). This historical remnant foreshadowed a future remnant that would return to the land from exile (Isa. 10:21; 11:11, 16), populate a purified Jerusalem (4:3-6), experience the Lord's agricultural blessings (4:2), and boast in His strength (28:5).

The Lord's slaughter of the Assyrians outside Jerusalem's walls foreshadowed that future day when He will once and for all deliver the city from hostile Gentile armies (17:12-14; 29:5-8; 30:27-33; 31:4-9). The language of these texts, while clearly reflecting the Assyrian crisis, also transcends that event, as its cosmic tone makes clear. (Note especially the references to "many nations" and "peoples" in 17:12-13 and to "many enemies," "ruthless hordes," "hordes of all the nations," "nations," and "peoples" in 29:5-8 and 30:28.) The association of the Assyrians' defeat with the messianic age (cf. 10:5–11:16 and 31:4–32:2) also indicates the typological nature of the former.

A day of glory and exaltation will eventually come for Jerusalem, fulfilling the ideal expressed in the hymns of Zion found in the book of Psalms (cf. Pss. 46, 48, 76, 84). Purified of evildoers (Isa. 1:21-28), she will become a center of justice (33:5) and enjoy the Lord's constant protection (4:5-6; 14:32; 25:1-5; 27:2-6; 33:17-24). As in the days of Moses, when a cloud and pillar of fire accompanied the people on their journey, there will be tangible signs of God's protective presence (4:5). He will guard the city from enemies, just as a shelter shields one from scorching heat and driving rainstorms (4:6; 25:4-5). In a reversal of the fruitful vineyard imagery of 5:1-7, the Lord likens Jerusalem of the future to a fruitful vineyard that will enjoy His protection and flourish under His care (27:2-6).

In that day the entire covenant community will be transformed. God's people will abandon idols and follow the Lord alone (17:7-8; 29:24; 30:22; 31:7). Wisdom (29:24; 32:5-8; 33:6), spiritual enlightenment (29:18; 30:20-21; 32:3-4; 35:8), justice (29:19-21; 32:1-2, 17-18; 33:5), and gratitude (25:9; 26:1-6) will characterize God's people. In turn they will experience His rich covenantal blessings (4:2; 29:17, 23; 30:23-25; 32:20; 35:1-2, 5-7).

Central to Isaiah's vision of the future covenant community is the Messiah, the ideal king who fulfills God's ancient promises to David. First and foremost, Isaiah depicts this coming king as a mighty warrior who defeats Israel's enemies and inaugurates an exciting new phase of salvation history, which is patterned after early Israel's experience of deliverance and military victory. Out of the darkness and gloom of defeat, this Deliverer emerges like a bright light (8:22–9:2). As in "the day of Midian," when the Lord gave Gideon a decisive victory over Israel's oppressors (cf. Judg. 6-7), this king will violently subdue Israel's enemies (Isa. 9:4-5; cf. 10:26). As in the days of David, the united tribes of Israel will conquer the surrounding nations (11:13-14).

In conjunction with the Messiah's rise to power, the exiles, including those of the Northern Kingdom, will experience a grand new exodus and return to the Promised Land (10:26; 11:11-12, 15-16; 14:1-3; 27:12-13). In response to this awesome display of God's power, this redeemed community will praise God for His salvation, just as Moses did following the miracle at the Red Sea (cf. 12:1-2 with Ex. 15:2). Unlike the days of Moses, when the wilderness symbolized rebellion and postponed blessing, the wilderness will blossom before the returning exiles (Isa. 35:1-10).

The Messiah's royal titles emphasize His military prowess and ability to bring Israel peace (9:6). Four titles are given, each of which contains two elements. The first, "Wonderful Counselor," in this context probably pictures the king as an extraordinary military strategist. Verses 3-4 depict the effects of his warfare and the following title, "Mighty God," points to His role as a warrior. In 36:5 *'ēṣāh*, "counsel" (which is related to the term here translated "Counselor") refers to military strategy (cf. NIV "strategy"). "Wonderful," a term normally used for God and His deeds, indicates the superhuman nature of His strategies.

The second title, "Mighty God" (cf. 10:21) depicts the king as God's representative in battle, whom He empowers in a supernatural way. The divine enablement of warrior-kings has parallels in the ancient Near East. For example, an Egyptian text says of the warrior Ramses II: "No man is he who is among us, It is Seth great-of-strength, Baal in person; Not deeds of man are these his doings, They are of one who is unique."[7] Some understand this title as proof of Messiah's deity. Subsequent biblical revelation, of course, clearly teaches the deity of the Messiah, but whether Isaiah or ancient Israel would have understood this passage in such a way is not certain.

The king's third title, "Everlasting Father," points to His role as protector of His people. The title "Father" should not be understood in Trinitarian terms here. It carries the idiomatic sense of "protector, provider, benefactor," as in Isaiah 22:21 and Job 29:16. Ancient Near Eastern kings often used such language of themselves. For example, Azitawadda of Adana (c. 800 B.C.) declared that Baal had made him "a father and a mother" to his people.[8] Kilamuwa of Samal (c. 850-800 B.C.) boasted, "I, however, to some I was a father. To some I was a mother."[9] In the original context of the prophecy the language may have been understood as idealized royal hyperbole (note especially "everlasting"; cf Pss. 21:4-6; 61:7-8; 72:5 [LXX], which attribute eternal life to earthly rulers). However, in the progress of revelation one discovers that Christ's eternal reign will literally fulfill the ideal expressed in the prophecy.

The Messiah's final title, "Prince of Peace," indicates that the primary benefit of His military successes and benevolent rule will be peace and prosperity for His people. This close association between the king's military might and the prosperity of His people is seen in several royal psalms (see esp. Pss. 72 and 144) and in ancient Near Eastern texts.[10]

To summarize, the messianic ruler's titles depict Him as an extraordinary

---

7. Lichtheim, *Ancient Egyptian Literature*, 2:67. Along these same lines ancient Near Eastern sculpture and literature depict gods training the king for battle (see, e.g., Othmar Keel, *The Symbolism of the Biblical World: Ancient Near Eastern Iconography and the Book of Psalms*, trans. T. J. Hallett [New York: Seabury, 1978], p. 265, and Daniel D. Luckenbill, *Ancient Records of Assyria and Babylonia*, 2 vols. [Chicago: U. of Chicago, 1926-27], 2:362), giving the king special weapons (see, e.g., W. F. Edgerton and J. A. Wilson, *Historical Records of Ramses III: The Texts in Medinet Habu. Volumes I and II* [Chicago: U. of Chicago, 1936], p. 4; Grayson, *Assyrian Royal Inscriptions*, 2:16; and Luckenbill, *Ancient Records of Assyria and Babylonia*, 2:126), and supernaturally intervening on the king's behalf during the battle (see, e.g., James Pritchard, ed., *The Ancient Near East in Pictures*, 2d ed. [Princeton, N.J.: Princeton U. 1969], no. 536 and p. 314; Peter B. Machinst, "The Epic of Tukulti-ninurta I: A Study in Middle Assyrian Literature," Ph.D. diss., Yale University, 1978, pp. 118-20; Lichtheim, *Ancient Egyptian Literature*, 2:70; and Luckenbill, *Ancient Records of Assyria and Babylonia*, 2:83.

8. Pritchard, *The Ancient New East*, 1:215.

9. Ibid., 1:218.

10. See the Azitawadda inscription, ibid., 1:215-17.

military strategist who will be able to execute His plans because of His supernatural abilities as a warrior. His military prowess will ensure His beneficent rule over His people, who will enjoy peace and prosperity because of His ability to subdue all His enemies.

The Lord will specially endow this king with His Spirit, enabling Him to rule wisely and effectively (11:2). Because of the divine Spirit resting on Him, the king will possess extraordinary discernment (cf. the emphatic synonymous word pair "wisdom" and "understanding"), the ability to execute His decisions (cf. "counsel" and "power"), and, most importantly, an unwavering devotion to the Lord (cf. "knowledge" and "fear of the Lord"). The qualities listed in verse 2 are not to be understood as six distinct characteristics. Rather, they are arranged in three pairs. This observation is especially important in understanding the nuance of the word "knowledge." The word does not refer here to knowledge in general, but rather to "knowledge" that results in submission to the Lord, as its parallel expression, "the fear of the Lord," makes clear. The "knowledge" in view is a recognition of the Lord's authority accompanied by a willingness to obey His will. A helpful illustration of this meaning of the word can be found in Jeremiah 22:15-16, where King Josiah's concern for justice is offered as proof that he "knows" the Lord. By defending the poor and needy, Josiah demonstrated that he recognized the authority of God, who commanded His covenant people and their leaders to promote socioeconomic justice in the community.

Because of His wisdom, ability, and allegiance to God's standards, the Messiah's reign will be characterized by absolute justice. His judgments will be based on truth, not superficial appearances or impressions (11:3). He will intervene on behalf of the weak and eliminate their evil oppressors from His realm (v. 4). This cessation of injustice and oppression in human society will be symbolized by a fundamental change in the animal kingdom and in the relationship of mankind with once hostile animals. Predators will lie down in peace with the animals they once attacked and devoured, while children will play with creatures that once endangered their lives (vv. 6-8). Justice and harmony will replace oppression and hostility throughout the Messiah's worldwide kingdom (v. 9).

To appreciate fully the messianic portrait of Isaiah 1-39, it must be viewed against the backdrop of the generally negative presentation of Judahite kingship in these same chapters. Apart from the book's heading, the first reference to a specific king appears in 6:1, where it is noted that Isaiah received his vision of God's glory in the year of King Uzziah's death (740 B.C.). Isaiah saw the true King of the universe (cf. 6:5), whose awesome glory and perfect holiness contrasted starkly with the mortality of the king of Judah.

This negative view of the kings of Judah is developed more fully in chapter 7, where King Ahaz takes center stage. During the Syro-Ephraimitic war (c. 735-734 B.C.), the armies of Aram and the Northern Kingdom invaded Judah, besieged Jerusalem, and threatened to replace Ahaz with the ruler of a local kingdom. Isaiah encouraged the terrified Ahaz to trust in the Lord's covenantal promises to the house of David. The kings of Aram and the Northern Kingdom were virtual nobodies; Ahaz was the descendant of God's chosen ruler. However, when the prophet challenged Ahaz to seek a sign from the Lord, the king refused. Isaiah then delivered the sign of Immanuel. A child would soon be born and named "Immanuel" (meaning "God is with us") because he would serve as living proof of God's ability to deliver Judah from her enemies. Before the child reached the age when he could discern good from evil, the Lord would eliminate the Aramean-Israelite threat. At that time people would be able to point to the child Immanuel as a reminder that the Lord was sovereign over the nation's destiny and had announced in advance the demise of the enemy. However, because of Ahaz's unbelief, this apparent prophecy of salvation was turned into a warning of punishment. The Lord would turn the Assyrians, His instrument of judgment on Aram and the Northern Kingdom, against Judah. Ironically the curds and honey eaten by Immanuel, which initially seemed to symbolize deliverance and prosperity, would actually testify to the desolate condition of the land brought about by the Assyrian invasion. Ahaz's lack of faith would cause Judah to forfeit the blessing that could have been hers.

The immediate fulfillment of the Immanuel prophecy is recorded in chapter 8. Isaiah made careful preparations for the birth of a sign-child, and "the prophetess" gave birth to a child named Maher-Shalal-Hash-Baz (meaning "quick to the plunder, swift to the spoil"). Like Immanuel, this child's growth pattern, when viewed in conjunction with developments on the international scene, would be a reminder of God's providential control over His people's destiny. Before the child could address his parents, the Assyrians would defeat Aram and the Northern Kingdom. However, they would then turn against Judah as well. Certain features of the text suggest that Immanuel and Maher-Shalal-Hash-Baz, despite the difference in names, are one and the same. The juxtaposition of the birth report narrative (8:1-8) with the birth announcement narrative (7:14-25) suggests a close relationship between the prophecy and the birth. The pattern of events (initial deliverance followed by punitive judgment) associated with the growth pattern of the child is the same in both chapters. Also, Immanuel is addressed in the conclusion of the prophecy in chapter 8 (cf. 8:8) as if He were already present on the scene. This address makes excellent sense if one understands the introduction of the same message (8:1-3) as describing his birth.

The differing names present a problem (which, by the way, one also faces in Matthew's application of the Immanuel prophecy to the birth of Jesus). Perhaps Immanuel, understood as a symbolic name, focuses on God's involvement in Judah's history, whereas Maher-Shalal-Hash-Baz, the child's actual name, alludes to the specific purpose or effect of His involvement. (In the same way, when applied to Jesus, "Immanuel" attests to God's personal intervention in history through the Incarnation, whereas the Lord's actual name, Jesus, indicates the specific purpose or effect of that intervention.)

In addition to serving as proof of God's sovereignty and presence, the sign-child Immanuel also pointed ahead to ultimate deliverance for the kingdom of

Judah (cf. 8:9-10). He foreshadowed another child who would someday restore
the glory and honor of the Davidic throne that had disappeared while it was occupied by ineffective rulers like Ahaz. Through the birth formula of 9:6, Isaiah links
the birth of Messiah with that of Immanuel. Immanuel was a sign of God's providential presence with His people and a reminder of His ability to deliver them from
the worst of crises. The Messiah would manifest God's presence in an even more
tangible and impressive way, as His titles indicate (cf. esp. "Wonderful," "God," and
"Everlasting").

To summarize, "Immanuel" was a child born in Isaiah's day (very likely the
prophet's own son Maher-Shalal-Hash-Baz). This child, as a sign of God's presence,
foreshadowed or typified the future Messiah, who, as subsequent revelation makes
clear, would be "God with us" in the fullest possible sense. The announcement of
Immanuel's birth, then, is not a direct or exclusively messianic prediction but,
rather, has typological significance as a divinely intended foreshadowing of the
Incarnation.

> *Excursus on Matthew's use of the Immanuel prophecy.* When Matthew
> applied Isaiah 7:14 to the birth of the God-man Jesus, he was following the lead
> of Isaiah himself, who, as noted above, suggested a typological connection
> between the child Immanuel and the coming ideal Davidic ruler. Matthew's use
> of Isaiah 7:14 is consistent with his use of other Old Testament passages in the
> early chapters of his gospel. In 2:14-15 Matthew draws a connection between
> Hosea 11:1, which refers to the historical Exodus of the nation Israel in the days
> of Moses, and the infant Jesus' exile in Egypt. The Hosea passage can in no way
> be interpreted in its context as prophetic or messianic, but it can legitimately
> provide a pattern for subsequent salvation history. Jesus came as a new or
> ideal Israel (see the discussion of the servant songs later in this chapter) whose
> experience of exile and return followed the pattern of the ancient nation's
> early history. In 2:17-18 Matthew sees Herod's slaughter of the children of
> Bethlehem as a fulfillment of Jeremiah 31:15, which describes the mothers of
> Ramah (not Bethlehem) weeping as their children are carried away into exile.
> Herod's deed "fulfilled" Jeremiah's words in that it corresponded in its basic
> character to the event portrayed by the prophet. Once again, Matthew's use of
> the Old Testament is based on the observation of a pattern or analogy between
> distinct historical events or persons.

With King Hezekiah the Davidic throne experienced a revival of sorts. In
fact, it is possible that Isaiah's generation looked for the prophet's messianic ideal
to be realized in and through him. In contrast to Ahaz, Hezekiah displayed several commendable qualities, most notably trust in God in the midst of crisis. When the
Assyrians threatened Jerusalem, Hezekiah poured his heart out before God and
acknowledged that only the Lord could provide deliverance (chap. 36-37).

However, like Uzziah and Ahaz before him, Hezekiah also proved to be mortal and imperfect. Chapter 38 records how the king became terminally ill. When

notified by Isaiah that he would die, Hezekiah pleaded for his life. The Lord agreed to extend his life an additional fifteen years and even gave him a miraculous sign of confirmation, which ironically took place on the "stairway of Ahaz," named for the one who years before had refused to ask the Lord for a sign. Hezekiah here represents his nation Judah, which, like her king, had been given a new lease on life. However, the days of both Hezekiah and Judah were numbered. Chapter 39 prophesies Judah's eventual demise. Following Hezekiah's recovery, a contingent of Babylonians visited him. Hezekiah unwisely showed his treasures to the emissaries, displaying the same kind of pride that led to the downfall of so many kings before and after him. The Lord used this occasion to announce that the Babylonians would someday loot the palace and even carry some of Hezekiah's descendants into exile. With this account the first major section of the book comes to an end. It is apparent at this point that to varying degrees the contemporary rulers of Judah fell short of the prophet's messianic ideal. One is left longing and looking for someone else. The way is thus paved for the emergence of the Lord's servant in the chapters to follow.

Excursus on Isaiah 4:2. One familiar with discussions of Isaiah's messianic portrayal will notice that 4:2 has been omitted in this treatment of the theme. Many regard the "Branch of the Lord" mentioned here as a messianic title and understand the verse as describing Messiah's eschatological rule over Israel. The word translated "Branch" is used as a royal or messianic title by later prophets (Jer. 23:5; 33:15; Zech. 3:8; 6:12), but in each case the context clearly associates the title with an individual. (Jeremiah even draws the specific connection with David.) Such is not the case in Isaiah 4:2. Here the parallelism of the verse (note the corresponding phase "fruit of the land") suggests that the future agricultural abundance of the land is in view. The word translated "Branch" most often refers elsewhere to literal vegetation or agricultural growth (e.g., Gen. 19:25; Ps. 65:10; Ezek. 16:7), and the picture of restored agricultural prosperity in the eschaton is a common one in the prophets (cf. Isa. 30:23-24; 32:20; Jer. 31:12; Ezek. 34:26-29; Amos 9:13-14).

GOD AND THE NATIONS

Judgment. Much of the book's first major section is devoted to the theme of universal judgment. God would judge the various nations of ancient Israel's world, including the mighty kingdoms of Egypt, Assyria, and Babylonia, as well as the smaller neighboring kingdoms of Philistia, Moab, Aram, Edom, Arabia, and Tyre.[11]

11. The judgment oracles of chapters 13-23 are arranged in two corresponding panels:
   a. Judgment on Babylon and Assyria (13:1–14:27); Judgment on Babylon (21:1-10).
   b. Judgment on smaller neighboring states (14:28–16:5; 21:11-17)
   c. Judgment on Aram and Israel (chap. 17); Judgment on Judah (chap. 22)
   d. Judgment on Ethiopia and Egypt (chaps. 18-20); Judgment on Tyre (chap. 23). Egypt and Tyre were trading partners, which the Tyre oracle mentions (cf. 23:3, 5).

This judgment would culminate with the final defeat of the hostile nations and the establishment of God's earthly rule from Mount Zion. The purpose of these oracles was to demonstrate to God's people that the Lord is sovereign over international affairs and that, despite opposition, His purposes for Israel and the world would ultimately be realized. Consequently God's people should neither fear nor place their trust in the surrounding nations.

Egypt receives special attention in Isaiah's prophecies against the nations (cf. 19:1–20:6; 31:1-7; 31:1-3) because Judah was tempted to form alliances with this southern power in an effort to hold back the Assyrians. This policy was unwise for the Lord would cause the Egyptians to wilt before the Assyrians (19:1, 4, 16). Egypt's gods, wise men, civil leaders, and army would be helpless before the Lord's onslaught (19:1, 3, 11-15; 31:1-3).

Though the Lord would use Assyria as His instrument of judgment against His people and several of the surrounding nations, He would eventually punish this proud empire (10:5-34; 14:24-25; 30:27-33; 31:4-9). The Assyrian king was nothing but a club in the hand of the Lord, but he arrogantly taunted Jerusalem, suggesting the the Lord was unable to deliver His people from the powerful Assyrian army (10:5-14, 32; 36:4-20; 37:9-13, 24-25). Sennacherib's speeches indicate his belief that he was the sovereign ruler of the world before whom none of the gods of the petty western states could stand (cf. 36:18-20; 37:11-13). The Lord compared this proud king to a tool or weapon trying to brandish its user. Once the Lord had used the Assyrians to complete "his work against Mount Zion" (10:12; cf. 28:21), He would direct His judgment against them.

Various metaphors are used to describe this judgment, including disease (10:16), fire (10:17; 30:27, 30, 33; 31:9), the felling of trees (10:19, 33-34), a flood (30:28), a rainstorm (30:30), and an attack by a raging lion (31:4). The appearance of such imagery in conjunction with the Lord's defeat of Assyria is ironic in that the Assyrian kings liked to use many of these same metaphors in describing their conquest and exploits. Assyrian rulers boasted of chopping down the cedars of Lebanon (37:24), but in the day of the Lord's judgment the Assyrians, likened to the tall trees of Lebanon (10:34), would fall by the divine axe. Assyrian kings often portrayed themselves as raging lions, rushing floodwaters, and destructive fires, before which their enemies could not stand. However, in the day of judgment they would be the objects of such an attack as the Lord unleashed His anger and power against them. Just as the Assyrians put hooks into the noses of the unfortunate captives, so the Lord would do to them (37:29). Thus the Lord would demonstrate His sovereignty over Assyria and prove that He, not the king of Assyria, was the most powerful warrior-king in the world.

Isaiah 37:36-38 records the fulfillment of this prophecy of judgment. As the Assyrian army besieged Jerusalem, the angel of the Lord went out and destroyed the army in one night. Sennacherib was forced to return home, where approximately twenty years later he was assassinated by his own sons as he worshiped in the temple of one of his gods.

Babylon, Assyria's successor as the Near East's most powerful empire, would also experience God's judgment (13:1–14:23; 21:1-10). Some understand the Babylonian oracles against the background of the Assyrian period (eighth-seventh centuries B.C.) because the Assyrians controlled Babylon for a good part of Isaiah's career and severely destroyed the city in 689 B.C. (an event referred to in 23:13). However, it is more likely that the downfall of the Chaldean Empire (an empire that reached its peak in the sixth century) provides the historical backdrop. In 13:19 Babylon is specifically called the "glory of the Babylonians" (i.e., Chaldeans), and the "king of Babylon" referred to in 14:4 is to be viewed as a Chaldean in light of 39:1 (where the Chaldean ruler Merodach-Baladan is specifically called "king of Babylon"). Also, 13:17 mentions the Medes as the conquerors of Babylon (cf. Jer. 51:11, 28; Dan. 5:28).

Though some question the authenticity of these judgment oracles and attribute them to a later exilic editor, their eighth-century origin can be adequately defended. Since Isaiah foresaw the Babylonian exile (39:6-7), it is quite natural that he would include Babylon within the scope of God's coming judgment on the enemies of His people. Furthermore, Babylon, because of its symbolic value as a city opposed to God (cf. Gen. 11:1-9), serves as an apt representative of the hostile nations. This representative and symbolic function of Babylon explains why the description of Babylon's fall in Isaiah 13:17-22 (see also 14:23) does not correspond to the historical circumstances surrounding Cyrus's relatively peaceful takeover of the city in 539 B.C. The stylized and hyperbolic description of its judgment transcends the historical fall of the city to the Medes and Persians and foreshadows the final judgment of the nations before the establishment of God's earthly kingdom.[12] In this respect it is instructive to note the cosmic tone of the language that introduces chapter 13 (cf. vv. 1-13; see also 14:26-27). As one might expect, subsequent revelation picks up the Babylon symbol in describing God's final victory over His endtime foes (cf. Rev. 17-18).

The vivid prophecy of Babylon's final demise culminates in Isaiah 14 with a taunt song addressed by the restored exiles to the once-proud king of Babylon. They describe his descent into Sheol, where other deceased pagan kings rise to meet him. These rulers, utilizing imagery from their own mythological traditions, compare the king to the petty deity "Morning Star, Son of the Dawn," who actually tried to ascend the mountain of the gods and rule with El, the high god of the Canaanite pantheon. However, despite his delusions of grandeur, the king of Babylon proved to be just as mortal as all the human kings who walked the earth before him.

A popular interpretive tradition has seen in the language of 14:12-15 an allu-

---

12. The motif of complete, permanent devastation appears elsewhere in the Old Testament (cf. Isa. 34:11-15; Jer. 50:39-40; 51:36-37; Zeph. 2:13-15) and in ancient Near Eastern literature. Examples of the latter include a curse in the Sefire treaty (see Pritchard, *The Ancient Near East*, 2:222) and Ashurbanipal's description of the destruction of Elam (see Luckenbill, *Ancient Records of Assyria and Babylonia*, 2:310-11).

sion to the fall of Satan.[13] However, this subject "seems a bit forced in this chapter."[14] Instead the language and imagery seem to have their roots in Canaanite mythology, which should not be surprising in a quotation ostensibly addressed by ancient pagan kings to another pagan king (the quotation of the kings' words is most naturally extended through v. 15).[15] The most striking mythological parallels include (1) the name of the principal deity, "Morning Star, Son of the Dawn," (2) "stars of God" (*'ēl*, the name of the Canaanite high god who presided over the assembly of the gods), and (3) "the mount of assembly," specifically located on the "sacred mountain" (*ṣāpôn*, the name of the Canaanite Olympus where the gods assembled). A specific mythological parallel to Morning Star's rebellion is not yet known, but similar episodes in Canaanite and Greek myth have been noted.[16]

Like Babylon, Edom also serves a representative and symbolic function in Isaiah's oracles against the nations. Chapter 34 begins with a description of God's universal judgment, the magnitude of which is so great that even the heavenly bodies, perhaps symbolic of spiritual opposition (cf. 24:21), are adversely affected (vv. 1-4). The message then focuses on Edom, a nation that had a long history of hostility toward Israel, despite the close blood ties between the two. When Jerusalem fell to the Babylonians, the Edomites gloated over her defeat, participated in the ransacking of the city, and sold some of her refugees as slaves (cf. Ps. 137:7; Lam. 4:21; Joel 3:19; Obad. 10-14). Consequently the Lord's judgment on Edom is called His "day of vengeance" and "a year of retribution, to uphold Zion's cause" (Isa 34:8). The Lord would carve the Edomites up with His sword as if they were sacrificial animals (vv. 5-7) and turn their land into an eternal heap of ruins inhabited only by desert creatures (vv. 9-17). Once again the dramatic, hyperbolic imagery transcends the historical fall of the Edomites and anticipates the final demise of all the hostile nations that Edom so well epitomized.

Isaiah's oracles against the nations culminate in a description of worldwide judgment that ushers in God's kingdom on earth. Although several passages allude to and foreshadow the Lord's final victory over the hostile nations (8:9-10; 13:1–14:27; 17:12-14; 29:5-8; 30:27-33; 31:4-9; 33:1-4; 34:1-17), chapters 24-27, the so-called Little Apocalypse of Isaiah, give the most thorough and sustained treatment of this event.

---

13. For a history of interpretation of these verses, see Gerald Keown, "A History of the Interpretation of Isaiah 14:12-15," Ph.D. diss., Southern Baptist Theological Seminary, 1979.

14. John A. Martin, "Isaiah," in the *The Bible Knowledge Commentary, Old Testament*, eds. John F. Walvoord and Roy B. Zuck (Wheaton, Ill.: Victor, 1985), p. 1061.

15. Isaiah's use of mythological imagery is not limited to these verses. Several passages in the so-called Little Apocalypse (chaps. 24-27) reflect his awareness of ancient mythological motifs and imagery (cf. 24:21-22; 25:8; 27:1).

16. For further study, see P. C. Craigie, "Helel, Athtar, and Phaethon (Isa. 14:12-15)," *Zeitschrift für die Alttestamenliche Wissenschaft* 85 (1973): 223-25; J. W. McKay, "Helel and the Dawn-Goddess: A Re-examination of the Myth in Isaiah XIV 12-15," *Vetus Testamentum* 20 (1970): 451-64; and W. S. Prinsloo, "Isaiah 14:12-15. Humiliation, Hubris, Humiliation," *Zeitschrift für die Alttestamentliche Wissenschaft* 93 (1981): 432-38.

Picking up on the cosmic tone and imagery of 13:1-13, chapter 24 pictures the whole earth being devastated by a curse (vv. 1-13). According to verse 5 this curse comes on the world because "the earth is defiled by its people; they have disobeyed the laws, violated the statutes and broken the everlasting covenant" (NIV). At first glance the reference to "laws" and "statutes" suggests the Mosaic Covenant, but the universal tone of the context precludes this. The language is best interpreted against the background of God's mandate to Noah (and through him to human society in general), which is viewed here in covenantal terms (Gen. 9:16 uses the phrase "everlasting covenant" in conjunction with God's promise to Noah.) The people of the earth have rebelled (cf. Isa. 24:16, 20) against the mandate to multiply and to respect God's image in mankind (Gen. 9:1-7) by indiscriminately shedding blood (cf. Isa. 26:21) and thereby polluting the land (24:5; cf. Num. 35:33, which refers to a land being "polluted" by bloodshed—the word rendered "pollute" there is translated "defiled" in Isa. 24:5). Further support for this interpretation comes from Isaiah 24:18, where God's judgment is portrayed as a reenactment of the Noahic flood (cf. Gen. 7:11).

The focal point of God's judgment is an unnamed city characterized by strength and pride (24:10-12; 25:2; 26:5-6). Because the fall of this city occurs in the context of worldwide disaster, some conclude that it is typical or representative of the earth's strong cities.[17] In 25:12 Moab (cf. v. 10) is described as having "high, fortified walls," much like the unnamed city (cf. v. 2; 26:5). This suggests that Moab be identified with the city in question, but, even so, Moab in this context represents all hostile Gentile powers. In this respect one should note that 26:1-6, which celebrates the fall of the city and contrasts it with Zion, is a praise response to the fall of Moab described in 25:10-12.

In 24:24 (NIV) God's enemies are specifically identified as "the powers in the heavens above and the kings on the earth below," suggesting some kind of endtime coalition between the spiritual and the human. In 27:1 Isaiah depicts this group of rebels as a great sea creature. Both of these passages utilize mythological motifs and imagery. According to 24:22, the heavenly-earthly coalition will be herded into a prison and eventually punished. This sounds much like the Babylonian creation account in which the god Marduk defeats Tiamat and then imprisons her allies, the forces of chaos.[18] The symbol of Leviathan is drawn directly from Canaanite myth, where this same creature opposes the storm god Baal and his female ally Anat. Isaiah's description of the beast as a "gliding" and "coiling serpent" is virtually identical to its description in myth.[19] In myth Leviathan represents the sea and those forces of chaos that oppose Baal's royal authority. In the Old Testament this sea/sea

17. See, for example, Ronald E. Clements, *Isaiah 1-39,* The New Century Bible Commentary (Grand Rapids: Eerdmans, 1980), p. 202. Clements understands the city "as a pictorial description of the body of organized human society, a kind of 'Vanity Fair.'"

18. See Pritchard, *The Ancient Near East,* 1:34.

19. See John C. L. Gibson, *Canaanite Myths and Legends,* 2d ed. (Edinburgh: T. & T. Clark, 1978), pp. 50, 68. See specifically texts 3. iii. 38-39 and 5. i. 1-3.

monster symbolism is applied to those forces, both cosmic and historical, that oppose the Lord's kingship and seek to destroy the order He establishes. The battle with the sea/sea monster motif is associated with the Lord's victories over chaos at creation and in history (cf. Pss. 74:13-14; 77:16-20; 89:9-10; Isa. 51:9-10). His subjugation of these forces demonstrates His kingship and sovereignty (Pss. 29:3, 10; 93:3-4). Isaiah 27:1 applies the motif to the Lord's final victory over such forces in the endtime (also 17:12-13 depicts the nations as raging, surging waters). In that day all those who oppose the Lord's program and authority will be subdued once and for all.

The Lord will even destroy the ultimate enemy, death itself (25:7-8). Once again mythological antecedents are evident. In Canaanite myth, Baal, in his effort to attain kingship, defeats the sea/sea monster (symbolic of chaos), celebrates his victory with a banquet, but then experiences temporary defeat at the hands of death. In the same way the Lord is depicted as defeating chaos (24:21-22; 27:1) and then celebrating His success with a rich banquet on His royal mountain Zion (24:23; 25:6). However, in contrast to Baal, the Lord subdues death. The statement "he will swallow up death forever" (25:8) is exceedingly ironic in that death is portrayed in both the Old Testament (Prov. 1:12; Isa. 5:14; Hab. 2:5) and Canaanite myth as voraciously swallowing up its prey and enemies. In the myths death has "a lip to the earth, a lip to the heavens . . . and a tongue to the stars."[20] Death describes his own appetite as follows: "But my appetite is the appetite of lions in the waste. . . . If it is in very truth my desire to consume 'clay' [a reference to his human victims], then in truth by the handfuls I must eat it, whether my seven portions [indicating fullness and completeness] are already in the bowl or whether Nahar [the god of the river responsible for ferrying victims from the land of the living to the land of the dead] has to mix the cup."[21]

Restoration. Israel's return from exile will be a vivid demonstration of the Lord's authority over the realm of death. Separated from the Promised Land, the exiles were like lifeless corpses lying in the dust. However, the Lord will miraculously resurrect the nation and bring His people back to their land (Isa. 26:19; 27:12-13; cf. Ezek. 37:1-14, which also employs resurrection imagery for the nation's restoration from exile). In contrast to their oppressors, who will be dead and gone forever (Isa. 26:14), the Lord's revived people will enjoy a new age of glory (v. 15). (Some understand v. 19 as referring to a literal eschatological resurrection of Israelites. The Lord's victory over death mentioned in 25:7-8 would certainly allow for this interpretation, as would Dan. 12:2.)

When the Lord established His universal rule from Mount Zion (Isa. 24:21; 25:6-8; 27:13), He will usher in an age of worldwide peace (cf. 11:10) and pure worship. Distant nations, as well as those who once labored only for self-aggrandizement, will pay tribute to Him in recognition of His sovereignty (18:7; 19:21; 23:18).

20. Ibid., p. 69. See 5. ii. 2-3.
21. Ibid., pp. 68-69. See 5. i.14-22.

Once hostile nations will come to Jerusalem to receive instruction from the Lord and to submit their disputes to His mediation. With the all-wise, all-powerful God justly settling their disagreements, the once warring nations will forget about military preparations and devote their energies to more constructive pursuits (2:2-4). Even nations that were once arch-enemies will join together in worshiping the Lord (19:23-25).

THEOLOGY OF ISAIAH 40-66

GOD AND HIS PEOPLE

God's response to the exiles' condition. As noted earlier, chapters 40-66 presuppose the exile of God's people. Jerusalem and the promised land lay in ruins (40:1-2; 44:26, 28; 45:13; 49:19; 51:3; 52:2; 58:12; 60:10; 61:4; 62:4; 63:18; 64:10-11), and at least some of the people were imprisoned in Babylon and other distant lands, awaiting future deliverance (42:7, 22; 43:5-6, 14; 45:13; 47:6; 48:20; 49:9-12, 22; 51:11, 14; 52:11-12; 56:8; 57:14; 61:1). Understandably the exiles were discouraged by their situation and skeptical about their future prospects (40:27; 41:17; 49:14). Some apparently thought the Lord was no longer interested in their plight, while others even suggested that He had treated them unfairly. Being under the control of the mighty Babylonian Empire, some were tempted to acknowledge the superiority of the Babylonians' gods and to worship their images. Perhaps the God of Israel was only a local deity who, because of geographical limitations, was unable to deliver them from Babylon. In response to such attitudes, the Lord makes certain facts crystal clear.

First, Israel was in exile because of her own sins, not because of some unjust decision or action on His part (50:1). Israel had angered the Lord by breaking His law (42:24; 43:24; 48:18-19; 64:5) and was suffering the just consequences for her unfaithfulness.

Second, the Lord had not abandoned His people. Several passages, especially in the early chapters of the section, reveal that the covenantal relationship and promises of God were still intact. The Lord addresses Israel as His servant (41:8-9; 42:19; 43:10; 44:1-2, 21; 45:4; 48:20), His chosen one (41:8-9; 43:20; 44:1-2; 45:4), and the seed of Abraham, His covenantal partner (41:8). In 44:2 He calls the nation "Jeshurun" (meaning "upright one"), a rare name that appears elsewhere only in Deuteronomy 32:15 and 33:5, 26. In Deuteronomy it is used of Israel as the object of God's rich blessings and protection who, despite His favor, rebelled against His authority. By addressing the exilic generation by this ancient name, the Lord reminds His people of His ideal for them (righteousness) and holds out the possibility of renewed blessing (cf. Isa. 44:3-4). In addition to addressing Israel with names that indicate her covenantal status, the Lord presents Himself as Israel's God (41:13, 17; 43:3; 45:15; 48:1-2), Creator (43:1, 7, 15, 20; 44:2, 24; 46:3), king (41:21; 43:15; 44:6), Holy One (41:14, 16, 20; 43:3, 14-15; 45:11; 47:4; 48:17), and redeemer (41:14; 43:14; 44:6, 24; 47:4; 48:17). He comforts personified Jerusalem, which epitomized the downtrodden condition of the nation, and promises that restoration and covenant renewal were in His future plans for His people.

Third, the Lord affirms His deep concern and love for His people (43:4). To emphasize this fact, several vivid metaphors are used. In 40:11 the Lord is pictured as a shepherd who holds His lambs (His exiled people) closely to His chest with His powerful arm as He leads them back to the Promised Land in triumph (cf. v. 10). The reference to the Lord's arm is an especially important part of the word picture, for elsewhere in Isaiah the Lord's arm usually symbolizes His mighty power that He unleashes against His enemies (30:30; 40:10; 51:9; 52:10; 59:16; 63:5, 12). Here that same strong arm protects His people.

In chapter 49 the Lord employs the figure of a mother to emphasize His devotion to Zion. In response to Zion's charge that the Lord had forgotten her (v. 14), He asks, "Can a mother forget the baby at her breast and have no compassion on the child she has borne?" (v. 15). Under normal conditions, of course not. However, to drive the point home even more forcefully, the Lord adds that even if mothers were to abandon their children, He could never forsake His people.

The Lord also compares Himself to a husband who had for a brief moment angrily divorced the wife of His youth. However, He would restore the marriage, showing His wife "deep compassion" and "everlasting kindness" (54:5-8). Zion had once been called "Deserted" and "Desolate," but someday her name would be changed to Hephzibah (meaning "My delight is in her") and Beulah (meaning "married"), for the Lord would rejoice over her like a bridegroom over his bride (62:4-5).

Finally, the Lord demonstrates His absolute sovereignty over the Babylonians and His infinite superiority to their idol-gods. The Lord created and controls the entire universe without having to consult any advisers (40:12-14; 42:5; 44:24).[22] He determines the destiny of nations and their rulers (40:17, 22-24). The heavenly bodies, associated with various deities in pagan thought, are His servants (40:26). The Lord frustrates the wisdom of pagan diviners and prophets (44:25) but brings His own decrees to pass (44:26). He announces the latter long in advance as a demonstration of His sovereign control of history (41:4, 21-29; 42:9; 45:21; 48:3-7). The man-made pagan idol-gods are incapable of such deeds and so would be unable to prevent God's redemption of His people.

Several contrasts with the pagan idol-gods emphasize God's incomparability. Many keys words found in the idol polemics (40:18-20; 41:5-7, 21-29; 42:17; 44:9-20; 45:16, 20; 46:1-2, 6-7; 48:5, 14) also appear in descriptions of the Lord's activities in such a way as to demonstrate His uniqueness. For example, according

---

22. Isaiah 40:13-14 may contain a polemic against Marduk, the chief god of the Babylonian pantheon, who consulted Ea, the god of wisdom, when creating the world. Cf. Roger N. Whybray, *Isaiah, 40-66*, The New Century Bible Commentary (Grand Rapids: Eerdmans, 1975), pp. 53-54. Also see Whybray's more thorough study, *The Heavenly Counsellor in Isaiah xl 13-14: A Study of the Sources of the Theology of Deutero-Isaiah*, Society for Old Testament Study, Monograph Series, 1 (Cambridge: Cambridge U., 1971).

to 40:19-20 and 41:7, the idol is a product of a human craftsman. By way of contrast, the Lord asserts that He is the creator of the craftsman (54:16). The craftsmen expend their energy and strength in forming their idols (44:12), but the Lord is capable of empowering His weary people with supernatural energy and strength which supersedes that of even the strongest young men (40:29-31). To make an idol, a craftsman chooses wood from a tree (v. 20). However, the Lord is the creator of the trees (41:19) and is portrayed poetically as the object of their worship (44:23).

Rather than being the product of a human decision, the Lord chooses men as instruments to perform His sovereign will (43:10; 44:1-2; 48:10; 49:7). All the trees of Lebanon could not fuel an adequate sacrificial fire for the Lord (40:16), but an idol is made from part of the wood used by a man to cook his food and warm his hands (44:15). Idol worshipers use the refining process (40:19; 41:7; 46:6) to form their gods (44:9-10), but the Lord refines (48:10) and forms (44:2) His people. In making an idol, the worker overlays (*rāqaʻ*) it with metal (40:19) and stretches a measuring line out over his work (44:13); the Lord "spreads out" (*rāqaʻ*) the earth (42:5; 44:24) and stretches out the heavens (40:22). Men set up (*kûn*) idols (40:20) in little shrines (44:13); the Lord establishes (*kûn*) the earth (45:18) and sits on its horizon as He raises up and brings down kingdoms (40:22). An idol is the product of human wisdom or skill (40:20), which the Lord frustrates (44:25). The worshipers of idols should live in fear because their trust in the products of their own hands proves misdirected and unfounded (44:11). However, Israel need not fear, for her God is the true God (44:8). Pagan idols can be carried off into exile by beasts of burden (46:1-2), but the Lord has carried His people throughout history (46:3-4). In these passages the Lord emerges as an active God, with man being the object of His creative deeds. By contrast, the pagan idol-gods are inactive and portrayed as the product of frail man's efforts.

Israel's future restoration. Because God was concerned about His people and powerful enough to deliver them, His promise of restoration can be trusted. Unlike weak man and his unreliable promises, which are here today and gone tomorrow, the Lord's word of promise is dependable (40:6-8).[23] His promises of salvation are accomplished, just as the rain and snow that drop down from the sky and water the earth fulfill the purpose for which they are designed (55:10-11).

As further proof of the reliability of His word, the Lord appeals to the "former things," namely, past events that He predicted and then brought to pass (cf. 41:22; 42:9; 43:9; 44:7; 46:9; 48:3). More specifically, the former things include the Exodus in the day of Moses (43:18). The fulfillment of the former things becomes the guarantee that the coming/new things, the Lord's deliverance of His people from exile and their reinstatement in the land, will also take place (42:9; 43:19; 48:6).

---

23. Isaiah 40:6b should be translated, "All men are like grass, and their *devotion/reliability* [*ḥesed*] is like the flowers of the field."

As in the first half of the book (10:26; 11:11-16), Israel's future deliverance and restoration to the land is portrayed as a second Exodus (43:16-21; 44:26-27; 48:20-21; 49:9-12; 51:9-11; 52:10-12). The God who promises this deliverance is the same One who once made a way through the sea and then destroyed the chariots of Egypt (43:16-17). In 51:9 Egypt is called Rahab (cf. also 30:7 and Ps. 87:4), one of the names given by the Old Testament to the sea monster of ancient myth (cf. Job 9:13; 26:12; Ps. 89:10). The Bible poetically associates God's victory over this monster (also called Leviathan) with His creative work in which He brought order out of disorder and darkness (cf. Job 26:7-14; Pss. 74:12-17; 89:9-12). The Exodus from Egypt was also a creative event whereby God formed a new nation out of the chaos of bondage and oppression (Isa. 43:15). Hence the application of the name Rahab to Egypt in Isaiah 51:9 is quite appropriate.

The second Exodus will surpass the first in several respects, so much so that the Lord can exhort His people, albeit hyperbolically, to forget the former event (43:18; but cf. 46:9). The people left Egypt in haste (Ex. 12:11; Deut. 16:3), but they would leave Babylon at a leisurely pace, being fully assured of God's mighty protective presence (Isa. 52:12). Though God provided for the physical needs of Moses' generation during their wilderness wanderings, that period was essentially one of postponed blessing. However, in the second Exodus signs of God's abundant blessing would accompany the returning exiles all along the way home. He will turn the mountains into a roadway (49:11) and the desert into a lush garden land filled with streams (43:19-20; 48:21; 49:9-10).

All roads out of exile will lead to Jerusalem (49:14-23; 52:11). The suffering city, poetically compared to a wife deserted by her husband (54:6), a widow (54:4), a barren woman (49:21; 54:1), and a mother bereaved of her children (49:21), will witness the miraculous return of her exiled people (49:19-21; 54:2-3). The wealth of nations will flow into rebuilt and beautified Zion, and she will never again be defiled by an enemy army (54:11-17; 60:4-22; 61:4-6; 62:1-2). No longer will the light of the sun and moon be needed, for the bright light of the Lord's glory will emanate from the city (60:19-20).

The early chapters of Genesis provide various illustrations of Zion's future transformation. Renewed Zion will be the focal point of God's new creation (65:17-18). The Lord will turn Zion's suffering into joy, just as He made a mighty nation out of aged Abraham and his barren wife Sarah (51:2). His blessing will replace His curse and Zion's ruins will be changed into a garden land rivaling Eden (51:3). Zion will never again experience God's angry judgment, for the Lord will make an everlasting "covenant of peace" with the city, patterned after His promise to Noah (54:9-10).

Just as God established His rule over Israel through the first Exodus and the conquest of the land (cf. Ex. 15:18; Pss. 47:3-5; 114:1-2), so His return to Zion will cause all to recognize His right to rule (Isa. 52:7). On the basis of analogy with shouts of acclamation associated with human rulers, the statement "Your God reigns!" in 52:7 might be better translated, "Your God has become king!" (cf. 2 Sam. 15:10; 2 Kings 9:13).

God's instruments of salvation. The Lord would use two primary instruments in bringing about the deliverance of His people: the Persian ruler Cyrus, and an unidentified servant depicted as an ideal Israel and a new Moses.

The Lord would raise up Cyrus as a mighty conqueror of nations and one whose military power would be irresistible (41:2-3; 25; 45:1-2). God's ultimate purpose in raising up Cyrus was the release of His people from their Babylonian exile and the rebuilding of Jerusalem (44:28; 45:13; 46:9). In exchange for the release of His exiled people, God would, as it were, give the Persians other nations in return (43:3-4). (Though some object that the specific naming of Cyrus [44:28; 45:1] points to a sixth-century B.C. date for chapters 40-55, such a precise prediction is not without precedent [1 Kings 13:2] and is consistent with one of the major themes of the surrounding context—God's ability to predict events long before they happen.)

These predictions were fulfilled in the sixth century B.C. when Cyrus burst on the scene and extended the Medo-Persian Empire into the west. He conquered Babylon in 539 and decreed that the exiled Jews could return to their land and rebuild the Temple (2 Chron. 36:22-23; Ezra 1:1-4). He also recognized the Lord's contribution to his success (Ezra 1:2; cf. Isa. 45:3), though this should not be interpreted as an affirmation of monotheism. The Cyrus Cylinder suggests that Cyrus attributed his success to various deities, including Marduk of Babylon.[24] In fulfillment of 43:3-4, Cyrus's successors even conquered Egypt.

Cyrus's release of the exiles foreshadowed a more significant act of salvation, which the Lord would bring about through His special servant. The so-called servant songs outline this servant's ministry (42:1-9; 49:1-13; 50:4-11; 52:13–53:12) as one of suffering and ultimate vindication.

The identity of the servant referred to in these songs is probably the most hotly debated issue in Isaianic studies. Some conclude that the servant is the nation Israel, which suffers on behalf of the Gentile nations. Throughout this section of the book Israel is addressed and described as the Lord's servant (cf. 41:8-9; 42:19; 43:10; 44:1-2, 21; 45:4; 48:20). As such the nation is to testify to the Gentiles of God's greatness (43:10; 48:20). The second servant song even calls the servant "Israel" (49:3).

However, the problem cannot be solved this easily. Since one of the tasks of this servant "Israel" is to restore the nation Israel to God (49:5-6), some kind of distinction between the servant and the nation seems necessary. This same distinction between the servant and the nation is evident in 49:8 (see also 42:6), where the servant mediates a covenant for God's people, and in 53:8, where he suffers on behalf of his people.[25] Also, as Harry Orlinsky observes, "it is unheard of in the Bible that Israel . . . should suffer innocently for the sins and in behalf of any non-

24. See Pritchard, *The Ancient Near East,* 1:206-8. In this text Cyrus states that Marduk chose him and commissioned him to march against Babylon. He claims that Marduk "was well pleased with" his "deeds and sent friendly blessings to" him.
25. "His people" (the reading of the Isaª scroll from Qumran) is preferable to "my people" in Isaiah 53:8. The speaker in the song consistently uses the first plural form, whereas God's speech is limited to the introduction (52:13-15) and conclusion (53:11-12) to the song.

Israelite people."²⁶ This section of the book makes clear that Israel was not innocent and consequently was in no position to suffer for others. Furthermore several passages indicate that Israel's suffering was due to her own sins.²⁷ For these reasons many prefer to identify the servant as an individual or as a personified ideal/righteous Israel/remnant within the nation.

Before attempting a more precise identification of the servant, it is necessary to examine the songs in more detail. As already noted, the servant must in some sense be "Israel" while remaining distinct from the nation as a whole. A closer analysis of the songs reveals how this can be so. The servant is a covenant mediator on behalf of the nation Israel (42:6; 49:8). In 42:6 the context suggests that the referent of "people" is all men. The term stands parallel to "Gentiles" (cf. v. 6*b*), and in verse 5 "people" refers to the inhabitants of the earth in general. However, the parallel passage in 49:8 indicates that the people with whom the covenant is made are Israelites, since verses 8*b*-12 associate this covenant with the second Exodus and the repossession of the land. Furthermore in chapters 40-66 God's future covenant is with Israel, not the Gentiles (54:10; 55:3; 59:21; 61:8). As covenant mediator for the nation, the servant also leads a second Exodus out of exile and back to the Promised Land (49:5-12). He "opens eyes that are blind" by releasing captives from their dark prison (42:7). The servant's commission is not limited to Israel. He is also a "light to the Gentiles" (42:6; 49:6) in that he brings deliverance to all of the earth's oppressed (49:6) and establishes justice throughout the world (42:1-4). This aspect of his commission, when examined against its biblical and ancient Near Eastern background, is decidedly royal in nature. In the ancient world, kings were responsible above all others, for promoting and maintaining justice.²⁸

At this point one can make several observations about the servant's role and identity as perceived by Isaiah. The title "Israel" is appropriate because, as a representative group or individual within the nation, the servant embodies God's ideal for His people. In his capacity as covenant mediator and deliverer from bondage, the servant's role is like that of Moses, who led Israel out of Egypt and mediated the covenant at Sinai (cf. esp. Ex. 34:27). Indeed, the book's second Exodus motif would be incomplete without the presence of a second Moses. Through the servant, God's original ideal for Israel with respect to the nations is also fulfilled. By living according to God's law, Israel was to serve as a model of God's standards of justice to the surrounding nations (cf. Deut. 4:6-8). The nation failed, but the servant will succeed by establishing justice throughout the earth. In this respect his function parallels that of the messianic ruler described in Isaiah 11:1-10. To summarize, Isaiah portrays the servant as an ideal Israel who is both a new Moses and, like

26. Harry M. Orlinsky, *The So-Called 'Suffering Servant' in Isaiah 53* (Cincinnati: Hebrew Union College, 1964), p. 10.

27. Ibid., pp. 9-10.

28. See Keith W. Whitelam, *The Just King: Monarchical Judicial Authority in Ancient Israel,* Journal for the Study of the Old Testament, Supplement Series, 12 (Sheffield: JSOT Press, 1979).

the ideal royal figure of chapter 11, the Lord's instrument in bringing justice to the earth. The parallels to Moses and the Messiah suggest that the servant is an individual, not a group.

The songs describe the servant's career in some detail. The first song (42:1-9) emphasizes his special divine commission to establish justice (vv. 1-4) and deliver those who are imprisoned (vv. 6-7). It portrays the servant as one who does not draw attention to himself (v. 2) and who refrains from oppressing those who are already downtrodden (v. 3*a*).

The second song (49:1-13) develops these themes, describing in more detail the servant's special status (vv. 1-3) and his commission to deliver the exiles from bondage (vv. 5-12). This song also indicates that the servant would experience some discouragement and rejection in carrying out his task (vv. 4, 7), thus paving the way for the main theme of the third and fourth songs, the servant's rejection and suffering.

The third song (50:4-11) contains the servant's testimony of faith and endurance in the face of opposition. The servant testifies that God has made him His special spokesman, a responsibility he readily assumed (vv. 4-5). Even when he was mistreated and humiliated, he continued to trust in the Lord, knowing his vindication would come (vv. 6-9).

The fourth song gives a more detailed account of the servant's rejection and suffering (52:13–53:12). The song is filled with irony. Israel admits that she misinterpreted the reason for the servant's suffering. She assumed that his suffering was due to his own sin (53:1-3, 4*b*), but in reality he was suffering on the people's behalf (53:4*a*, 5-6, 11-12). Because he willingly submitted to such unjust treatment (53:7-9), the Lord vindicates him (53:10-12). Even mighty kings, who had considered him a nobody, are forced to acknowledge his greatness (52:13-15). Perhaps the most striking example of irony in the song is that the sinful nation is declared innocent (cf. v. 11*b*, "he will justify many") because of the servant's suffering on their behalf.[29] Such an exoneration of the guilty is forbidden and condemned elsewhere in the Old Testament (cf. Ex. 23:7; Prov. 17:15; Isa. 5:23, all of which use the verb translated "justify" in Isa. 53:11), yet the servant's suffering is of such a unique character that the normal demands of justice are set aside in this instance. This statement implies that the guilty somehow escape punishment because of the servant's identification with them and his suffering on their behalf.

The fourth song raises several exegetical and theological questions. Two of the most problematic and significant are these: (1) Did the prophet indicate that the servant's suffering is substitutionary or merely shared? In other words, Does he suffer in place of, or along with, the nation? (2) Does the song actually intend to pic-

29. The verb translated "justify" probably has the force here of "declare innocent, acquit" (cf. its use in Ex. 23:7; Deut. 25:1; 1 Kings 8:32; Prov. 17:15; Isa. 5:23). Other attested nuances include "administer justice, vindicate" (2 Sam. 15:4; Ps. 82:3; Isa. 50:8), "recognize as in the right" (Job 27:5), and "lead toward righteousness" (Dan. 12:3).

ture the literal death and resurrection of the servant?

Some have questioned the traditional interpretation of the song, arguing instead that the servant's suffering, although shared, undeserved, and redemptive, is not vicarious in the sense that it prevents others from undergoing the punishment for their sins.[30] Both Orlinsky and Whybray identify the servant with the so-called Deutero-Isaiah who supposedly submitted to unjust treatment, rejection, and even imprisonment in order to bring a message of hope to the exiles. Whybray offers a painstaking exegetical analysis of the fourth song in which he attempts to show that none of the language traditionally understood as teaching the servant's vicarious suffering actually does so. The evidence he cites, which is too complex and lengthy to even survey here, would seem to indicate that the language of the text does not *demand* vicarious atonement. However, by insisting that the language precludes such an interpretation, Whybray has overstated his case. Much of the language, although perhaps ambiguous in its original setting, *allows* for the concept of vicarious suffering and paves the way for subsequent biblical revelation's full development of the doctrine of substitutionary atonement in conjunction with the servant's mediation of a new covenant.

If one follows the NIV, several statements and details of the text seem to indicate the substitutionary nature of the servant's suffering: (1) 52:15a, which indicates that "he will sprinkle many nations"; (2) references to the servant bearing the people's sins and their consequences (53:4a, 6b, 11b, 12b); (3) verse 5, which states that his suffering was "for our transgressions/iniquities" and resulted in peace and healing; (4) verse 7, which compares the servant to a lamb led to the slaughter and is sometimes interpreted against the background of the sacrificial system; (5) verse 10, which refers to the Lord making "his life a guilt offering"; and (6) verse 11, which states that the servant "will justify many" by bearing their sins.

However, one must be careful not to draw conclusions from questionable translations or press the language of the text beyond its reasonable contextual limits. Several of these statements are not as clear or determinative as they may seem to be on the surface. The translation "sprinkle" in 52:15 is probably mistaken. In other uses of this verb the object sprinkled is introduced by a preposition, but no preposition appears before "many nations." It is more likely that this is a homonym meaning "spring" or "leap" and that the line should be rendered, "so will he startle (i.e., cause to spring up or leap with surprise) many nations" (the LXX translates the verb as "marvel"). This fits much better with the parallel line, which emphasizes the astonishment that the kings will experience when they witness the servant's exaltation.

The metaphorical references to the servant's bearing/carrying sins are capa-

---

30. See Orlinksy's monograph cited in note 26 and Roger N. Whybray, *Thanksgiving for a Liberated Prophet,* Journal of the Study of Old Testament, Supplement Series, 4 (Sheffield: U. of Sheffield, 1978).

ble of picturing shared or vicarious suffering.[31] The translation *"for* our transgressions/iniquities" in verse 5 is perhaps too interpretive.The Hebrew preposition used here is better rendered "because of." This certainly allows for vicarious atonement, but does not demand it. The lamb simile in verse 7 does not have the sacrificial system as its background. Neither the word translated "slaughter" nor its related verb are technical terms for the sacrificial system. When used in relation to animals, both refer to slaughtering or butchering of animals for food (Gen. 43:16; Ex. 22:1; Deut. 28:31; 1 Sam. 25:11; Prov. 7:22; 9:2; Jer. 11:19; 50:27; 51:40). The NIV translation of Isaiah 53:10 is also problematic. The line literally reads, "Though you make his life a guilt offering" or "though he offers a guilt offering" (the verb *tāsîm* being either second masculine singular or third feminine singular). To understand the verb as being addressed to God (second person) is problematic because verse 10 refers to God twice in the third person and the song nowhere else addresses Him. The verb is better understood as third person with Hebrew *napšô* (from *nepeš*, which is grammatically feminine), with "he" (lit. "his life") as the subject. The resulting statement, while still being capable of an interpretation along traditional lines, does not readily lend itself to such a viewpoint and is in fact quite cryptic and unclear. Exegetical and theological caution dictate that it not be used as a basis for any dogmatic conclusions about the nature of the servant's suffering.

To summarize, the language of the fourth song certainly allows for the servant's suffering to be vicarious (note esp. "he will justify many"), but it does not demand such an interpretation in and of itself. The full import of the language awaits clarification by subsequent revelation (concerning which, see below).

Another interpretive issue concerns the language of 53:8-12. Do these verses portray the death and resurrection of the servant, or do they picture him being delivered at the last moment from an unjust execution?[32] The language of the text seems clearly to refer to his death (cf. esp. "cut off from the land of the living," v. 8; [33] "in his death," v. 9; and "poured out his life unto death," v. 12). However, the

31. In Isa. 53:6 the statement translated by NIV "the Lord has laid on him the iniquity of us all" would be better rendered, "the Lord has caused the iniquity of us all to encounter/attack him." Elsewhere the verb in question (hiphil of *pāga'*) means "make entreaty," a sense that does not apply here. The meaning of the verb in 53:6 should probably be understood in relation to the qal usage of the verb in the sense of "encounter with hostility, fall upon." The precise construction used in 53:11 (*sābal 'āwōn*) occurs elsewhere only in Lamentations 5:7, where it refers to the children suffering the consequences of their fathers' sins. The construction used in Isaiah 53:12 (*nāśā'hēt'*) is used in other passages with the idea of sharing in or bearing the guilt or consequences of sin (Lev. 19:17; 20:20; 22:9; 24:15; Num. 9:13; 18:22, 32; Ezek. 23:49).
32. Whybray has argued at length for the latter interpretation (see note 30).
33. Several passages show that the "land of the living" is the polar opposite of Sheol, the place of the dead (Ps. 52:5; Isa. 38:11; Ezek. 26:20; 32:23-32). Consequently the phrase "cut off from the land of the living" is, technically speaking, a figurative description of physical death, not imprisonment or some other life-threatening crisis. However, as noted in the text, the language and idioms of physical death do frequently refer *poetically* to life-threatening situations that have brought one to the brink of literal death.

matter cannot be solved this easily. Several Old Testament passages hyperbolically use the language of physical death to describe a life-threatening crisis. For example, the author of Psalm 88 laments, "I am counted among those who go down to the pit; I am like a man without strength. I am set apart with the dead, like the slain who lie in the grave. . . . You have put me in the lowest pit, in the darkest depths" (vv. 4-6).[34] Other poets describe themselves as being entangled in death's restricting ropes (Ps. 18:4-6), engulfed in its surging waters (Ps. 18:4, 16), trapped in its deep pits (Ps. 30:3), and surrounded by its bars (Jonah 2:6). Several psalmists asked or gave thanks for divine deliverance from the gates or depths of death (Pss. 9:13; 56:13; 71:20; 86:13). Admittedly the language of the fourth song might be interpreted along these lines, in which case it would indicate that the servant, although coming face to face with death, was delivered at the last moment and vindicated by God. However, at the same time the language allows for literal death and resurrection. Once again, subsequent revelation becomes vital to understanding the full import of the prophet's language (see below).

In the process of time Jesus Christ emerged as the servant of the Lord anticipated by Isaiah's servant songs. This is perhaps most clearly seen in the gospel of Matthew. From the outset Matthew presents Jesus as the ideal Israel (cf. Isa. 49:3) who succeeds where the nation failed (cf. 1:13-15). According to Matthew, Jesus' miracles of physical healing were object lessons that identified Him as the Isaianic servant (Matt. 8:16-17). Matthew 12:15-28 is particularly instructive in this regard. Matthew sees Jesus' warning against publicizing His ministry as a fulfillment of Isaiah 42:1-4 (Matt. 12:15-21). He then notes that Jesus gave sight to the blind, an act that recalls the prophecy of Isaiah 42:7 (Matt. 12:22-23). Jesus' act of healing literal blindness implied that He also had the power to heal the figurative blindness (bondage resulting from breach of covenant) referred to in Isaiah. When the Pharisees attributed His abilities to demons, Jesus convincingly argued that His power came from the Spirit of God (vv. 24-28; cf. Isa. 42:1). Matthew's description of Jesus' death also draws on the Isaianic portrait of the suffering servant (cf. Matt 26:63; 27:12, 14 with Isa. 53:7; 26:67; Matt. 27:30 with Isa. 50:6; and Matt 27:38 with Isa. 53:9, 12). Other New Testament passages also identify Jesus as the Isaianic servant, including Acts 8:32-33; 26:23 (cf. Isa. 53:7; 49:6),[35] and 1 Pet. 2:21-25 (cf. Isa. 53).

Jesus' experience clarifies the somewhat ambiguous language of the fourth servant song. Jesus identified with and shared in the suffering of God's people (cf. Matt. 3:14-15; 8:16-17). But more than that His suffering was vicarious in the sense that it released God's people from the guilt and full consequences of their sins and laid the foundation for the reconciliation that comes through the New Covenant

---

34. For a similar description in a Mesopotamian text, see tablet II of "Ludlul Bel Nemeqi" in Pritchard, *The Ancient Near East*, 2:151-54.

35. In Acts 13:47 Paul and Barnabas, as Jesus' ambassadors, apply the servant's commission as "light to the Gentiles" to themselves.

(Matt. 26:28). In Jesus' death and resurrection, the language of Isaiah 53:7-12, which in its ancient context could be understood merely as stereotypical and hyperbolic, also realizes its full potential.

> *Excursus on Isaiah 61:1-4.* It is possible that Isaiah 61:1-4 should be included among the servant songs. The speaker in these verses is most naturally understood as the prophet, but several details suggest that the servant is in view, especially his possession of the Lord's Spirit (v. 1; cf. 42:1), his role as God's spokesman (vv. 1-2; cf. 49:2; 50:4), his commission to proclaim deliverance and the Lord's favor to the prisoners (vv. 1-2; cf. 42:7; 49:8-9), and his association with the restoration of the land (vv. 3-4; cf. 49:6-12) and the establishment of a new covenant (cf. 61:8 with 49:8). It might seem abrupt for the servant to speak here, but the second and third servant songs begin abruptly with the servant speaking as well (49:1; 50:4). If this passage is a speech by the servant, then it rounds out the sequence of the songs nicely—its closest parallels are with the first and second songs—and also provides further evidence for the royal character of the servant. The proclamation of freedom to the captives is reminiscent of ancient Near Eastern royal edicts and decrees whereby debtors and slaves are released from their obligations and prisoners are allowed to go free.[36] Understanding this passage as a servant song is also consistent with Jesus' statement that His ministry brought its fulfillment (Luke 4:16-21).

Covenant renewal. God announced the future salvation of His exiled people and exhorted them to trust in His promise of deliverance. However, the final restoration promised by Isaiah would not be automatic. The prerequisite to the fulfillment of Isaiah's vision was covenant renewal. Chapter 55 contains an urgent call to God's people to renew their covenant relationship with the Lord. The chapter is arranged in two panels (vv. 1-5 and vv. 6-13), each of which includes exhortations (vv. 1-3, 6-7) supported by motivating promises (vv. 3-5, 7-13).

In the first panel God invites His people to eat and drink the commodities He freely offers (i.e., His covenantal blessings). He promises life and a new, everlasting covenantal relationship that will bring the nation international prominence. The life in view here is not simply physical or spiritual life but, rather, the prosperity and well-being resulting from a proper covenantal relationship to God (cf. Deut. 30:15-21). The everlasting covenant is compared to God's unconditional promise to David. Just as David ruled over nations, so God's people would exercise authority over distant nations.

The precise relationship of the Davidic covenantal promises and the ever-

---

36. Cf. Pritchard, *The Ancient Near East,* 2:36-41, 187-88. Biblical parallels include the Year of Jubilee legislation (cf. Lev. 25:10) and hymnic descriptions of the Lord as a just king who releases prisoners (Pss. 68:6; 146:7-8). (The imagery of release from prison is applied to God's deliverance of oppressed Israel in Pss. 79:11 and 102:20).

lasting covenant is uncertain. Some have argued that the Davidic Covenant is here democratized and viewed as being fulfilled through the nation. However, since Isaiah elsewhere clearly includes an individual Davidic ruler in his eschatological vision, it is more likely that the relationship is simply one of analogy or that Israel's New Covenant and ascendancy over the Gentiles are viewed as the national benefits of the fulfillment of God's promises to David. One must not overemphasize the distinction between the Davidic king and the nation, as many Old Testament passages make clear (e.g., 1 Kings 6:12-13; 9:4-9 and Pss. 72 and 144).

In the second panel the divine appeal takes on greater moral substance as the initial exhortations to "seek" or "call on" the Lord are followed by a demand for repentance. The Lord promises mercy and forgiveness to the repentant, as well as renewed blessing. Many of the key terms used in Isaiah 55:6-7 are found in other passages that speak of an eschatological renewal of covenant with the exiles, including "seek" (Deut. 4:29), "turn" (Deut. 4:30; 30:2-3, 10; 1 Kings 8:47-48), "have mercy" (Deut. 4:31; 30:3; 1 Kings 8:50), and "pardon" (1 Kings 8:50). Israel had experienced the exile foreseen by Moses and Solomon; now the Lord was making available to her the reconciliation anticipated by these two ancient leaders of the nation.

This appeal for covenantal renewal, with its promise of forgiveness, must be harmonized with the earlier declarations that the sins of Jerusalem (the city represents the exiled nation) have been paid for through the Exile (Isa. 40:2) and that God has "swept away" the offenses of His people (44:22). The Exile was the necessary punishment for the nation's rebellion. Once the prescribed period had come to an end, the initial barrier to reconciliation was eliminated. The removal of this initial barrier is in view in 40:2 and probably also in 44:22. However, another barrier to restoration remained: Israel's propensity to rebel, which had brought about the Exile in the first place. Until Israel truly repented and experienced an inner renewal, no true and lasting restoration would occur. Chapter 55 is an appeal for such a change.

Recognizing the relationship between the declaration in 40:2 and the appeal in chapter 55 provides answers for two perplexing questions that arise in the interpretation of Isaiah 40-55: (1) If Israel has already suffered for her own sins in exile, how can the servant's suffering be vicarious? (2) Why did the actual return of the exiles in the sixth–fifth centuries B.C. fall so far short of Isaiah's glorious vision?

As for the first question, it is true that Israel necessarily suffered for her own sins to a degree and that this suffering opened the way for her restoration. However, as noted, something beyond this, namely, covenant renewal, was essential to the completion of the nation's reconciliation. The servant, as the nation's covenant mediator (49:8), plays an important role in the establishment of this New Covenant. More specifically, as subsequent revelation reveals, his suffering provides the sacrificial foundation for the implementation of the covenant (cf. Matt. 26:28; Mark 14:24; Luke 22:20; 1 Cor. 11:25; Heb. 9:15; 12:24). In short, Israel's suffering in exile was not sufficient in and of itself to bring about her complete restoration.

A fundamental change in the nation's moral character was also necessary, a change that comes about through the New Covenant, mediated by the suffering servant.

As for the second question, it is true that the historical return from Babylon failed to live up to Isaiah's magnificent vision. This was partly because the response of the exiles to the Lord's appeal for covenant renewal was less than overwhelming. Indeed, wholesale national repentance and renewal could not occur until the servant actually came and laid the foundation for the New Covenant.[37] Subsequent revelation indicates that, in God's hidden plan for the world, Israel's covenant renewal as a national entity would be postponed so that Gentiles might also be incorporated into His program of salvation and become recipients of the New Covenant (cf. Rom. 11:25-27). The historical return from Babylon, accomplished through the instrumentality of Cyrus, merely foreshadowed the final restoration of Israel effected by the servant. Since Cyrus's release of the exiles set in motion God's program of deliverance, it is closely associated with the full eschatological realization of Israel's salvation. In Isaiah, type and antitype are often blended in this way.

Future purification of God's people. Isaiah himself suggested that the nation's propensity to rebel would delay the complete fulfillment of his eschatological vision. Even in chapters 40-48, the tone of which is overwhelmingly positive and encouraging, there is a recognition that all was not well among the exiles. As the section progresses, the prophet's tone becomes increasingly hortatory and even accusatory. Among the exiles there was a quarrelsome spirit that questioned the wisdom of God (45:9-10). God addresses some, at least, as "rebels" (46:8; 48:8), "treacherous" (48:8), and "stubborn-hearted" (46:12). The exiles' avowed loyalty to the Lord was not wholehearted (48:1-2) and they were prone to attribute the work of God to pagan idols (48:5).

This negative portrayal of the exiles is fully developed in chapters 56-66, where Isaiah anticipates that the community, like its preexilic predecessors, would be corrupted, forcing God once again to purify the nation through judgment.[38] In these chapters the Lord approaches the people as His covenant community and makes clear that they must uphold the righteous standards of His covenant. In 56:1-2 the Lord exhorts the people to promote justice and then pronounces a blessing on the one "who keeps the Sabbath without desecrating it and keeps his hand from doing any evil." To emphasize that He desired genuine loyalty, not mere outward conformity, the Lord even promises that those excluded from His Temple under the old order, such

---

37. In the sermon recorded in Acts 3:12-26, Peter's argument is developed along these lines (cf. esp. vv. 17-20).

38. As noted earlier, Isaiah 56-66 presupposes the circumstances of the Exile. Jerusalem and the land in general are in ruins and a return of the exiles is anticipated. At the same time, certain features of these chapters anticipate that the community would be restored to the land. Note the calls to justice, denunciations of Canaanite religious practices, and predictions of another phase of purifying judgment on the nation. Whereas chapters 40-55 consistently reflect an exilic perspective, chapters 56-66 appear to blend exilic and postexilic perspectives.

as eunuchs and foreigners, would now be allowed access if they displayed devotion to the covenant (56:3-8).

The concern for the Sabbath (cf. also 58:13) should not be understood as a strictly late phenomenon. While later prophets did emphasize Sabbath-breaking in their accusations (Jer. 17:21-27; Ezek. 20:12-13, 20-21; 22:8, 26), the Sabbath was singled out as a special sign of the covenant (Ex. 31:12-17) from the very beginning of Israel's history. An appeal to the Sabbath law is especially appropriate in conjunction with exhortations for social justice because Sabbath observance was to be a reminder of Israel's freedom from bondage and of her responsibility to treat her own servants in a humane fashion (cf. Deut. 5:12-15).

In Isaiah 56-66 the Lord condemns the community for various sins, many of which had been committed by their forefathers and had led to the nation's exile. He specifically denounces idolatry (57:3-13; 65:3-7, 11), injustice and violence (57:1-2; 59:3-8), and religious hypocrisy (58:1-7).

In chapter 57 the denunciation of idolatry is particular vivid.[39] The Lord addresses the idolaters as "adulterers and prostitutes" who lustfully worship their pagan gods "under every spreading tree," a practice with a long history among God's people (cf. 1 Kings 14:23; 2 Kings 16:4; 17:10; Jer. 2:20; 3:6; 17:2; Ezek. 6:13; 20:28; Hos. 4:13-14). The Lord compares their passion for idolatry, which included child sacrifice, to an adulteress who climbs into bed with her lovers and shamelessly looks on their nakedness.

The reference to fasting (Isa. 58:1-7), though not necessarily reflecting an exilic/postexilic background (cf. Judg. 20:26; 1 Sam. 7:6), is consistent with the emphasis on this practice that developed in later times (cf. Zech. 7:1-5; 8:19). As in Zechariah, the Lord makes clear that fasting is meaningless apart from social justice. In and of itself, fasting cannot bring God's favor. The Lord places a higher priority on fairness to one's workers and concern for the poor and homeless. Only when justice replaced oppression would the people and the land experience divine blessing and renewal (cf. Isa. 58:8-12). In that day the people would "ride" in triumph "on the heights of the land," as they did in earlier times (cf. 58:14 with Deut. 32:13).

Isaiah 56-66 sharply distinguishes the wicked and the righteous in their char-

---

39. Several features of the denunciation in 57:3-13 resemble preexilic descriptions of idolatry. So some have understood this appeal as directed to Isaiah's eighth-century audience. Even some who attribute these chapters to a "Third Isaiah" label this particular section preexilic. See, for example, Claus Westermann, *Isaiah 40-66*, Old Testament Library, trans. D. M. G. Stalker (Philadelphia: Westminster, 1969). pp. 301-2. In the larger context of these chapters, the passage is best understood as addressed to the exilic/postexilic community. Perhaps those who remained in the land during the Exile continued the practices of their forefathers and returning exiles may have resumed them as well. (In this regard note Jer. 44:15-19, which shows that the exiles in Egypt remained attached to the pagan gods they had previously worshiped in Palestine.) Then again Isaiah may be simply addressing a future generation in preexilic terms. Unfortunately not enough information is available on the popular religious practices of the early postexilic period to be certain about the precise background in view in the passage.

acter and their respective destinies. The wicked, who practiced the idolatrous and unjust deeds outlined above, would be purged out of the community by the Lord's judgment, symbolized by sword and fire (65:12; 66:15-16). Their smoldering corpses would lie exposed in the sight of all men as a perpetual reminder of the consequences of rebellion against the Lord (66:24).[40]

In contrast to the wicked, the righteous are characterized, first and foremost, by humility and a repentant spirit (57:15; 66:2). The prayers of repentance offered by the righteous are included in these chapters, probably as a model of how the exiles should approach their God. Overwhelmed by the iniquity all around them (cf. 59:1-8), the repentant acknowledge their offenses (59:12-13) and lament the consequences of the nation's rebellion (59:9-11, 14-15). They confess that the nation responded to the Lord's mighty acts with ingratitude (63:7-10) and admit that their sins have brought seemingly total corruption and irreversible destruction (64:5-7). Yet they cry out to the Lord, reminding Him of His special relationship to the nation as its Father/Creator (63:16; 64:8) and redeemer (63:16). They beg that He might relent from His anger (64:9) and no longer give them over to their hardheartedness (63:17). They ask that He might take pity on the desolate land and its destroyed Temple (63:18; 64:10-12) and renew His mighty deeds of old. They long to see a new display of His awesome power against His enemies (64:1-4). The references to His coming down and to the mountains trembling draw on poetic theophanic tradition (cf. Judg. 5:5; Pss. 18:9; 144:5), while "awesome things" recall the divine miracles in conjunction with the Exodus from Egypt (cf. Ps. 106:22).

The righteous will experience God's protection and restorative work (57:19-21; 59:20) and enjoy a special place as His servants (65:13-16). As God's "holy people" (Isa. 62:12; cf. Deut. 7:6; 14:2, 21) they will populate His new creation, the focal point of which is restored Zion (Isa. 65:17-19; cf. also chaps. 60-62). Tangible and vivid signs of God's blessing will highlight this new era as the covenant curses of death and exile are removed (65:20-25). Life expectancy will increase radically and God's people will enjoy the fruits of their labors, free from the threat of invasion. The powerful will no longer prey on the weak (cf. 11:6-9, which employs similar imagery to describe the advent of peace in the coming age) and the New Covenant anticipated and offered in chapters 40-55 will become a reality (59:21; 61:8).

Excursus on Isaiah 65:25. The statement "but dust shall be the serpent's food" has been understood by some as an allusion to Genesis 3:14, where the serpent is punished for its crime by being forced to crawl on its belly and thus "eat dust." In this case, the point might be that in the eschaton, when signs of God's restored blessing are all about, the crawling serpent will remain as a reminder of the consequences of disobedience and of God's suppression of rebellious forces. However, the context suggests a different inter-

---

40. The imagery has left its mark on later extrabiblical and biblical texts (see Judith 16:17; Ec'us 7:17; Mark 9:48).

pretation. The parallel statements in the verse indicate that once dangerous predators will no longer attack their victims. The serpent, like the lion and wolf, will no longer pose a mortal danger to those who once feared it. The parallel passage in 11:8 has this same emphasis. An allusion to Genesis 3:14 is unlikely, despite superficial verbal similarities.

GOD AND THE NATIONS

As the sovereign Creator of the world, God controls the destiny of the nations. As in chapters 1-39, the nations appear as instruments of divine judgment (cf. the references to Cyrus the Persian, discussed earlier), objects of God's anger, and ultimately as His obedient subjects.

Judgment. Through Cyrus, God would bring judgment on many of the nations of the ancient Near Eastern world. In announcing His decree to raise up Cyrus, He challenged the nations and their gods to contest His sovereignty (41:1-7, 21-29; 43:8-13; 45:20-21). None of the gods of the nations were able to decree events and then bring them to pass, and none would be able to resist the fulfillment of God's purposes through the Persian ruler.

Babylon, introduced earlier as an enemy of God's people and as a symbol of those nations hostile to God (cf. chap. 13-14, 39), has a prominent place in chapters 40-55. Like Egypt of old, Babylon was a place of bondage for Israel. However, God announces His absolute sovereignty over this great city and empire. Babylon's man-made idol-gods could not begin to compare to the Lord, the Creator and Ruler of the universe, and would be unable to prevent His redemption of Israel. Because the gods of Babylon had no power, those who sought revelations from them and relied on their protection would be disappointed.

In chapter 47 Babylon is depicted as a once proud and glorious queen who has suffered the humiliation of defeat. She is deposed and forced to perform the harsh labor of a commoner or servant (vv. 1-3). God takes vengeance on her (v. 3) because she overstepped her bounds as His instrument of punishment and showed no mercy to His people (v. 6). She boasted that her reign would never end, claiming she would never experience widowhood or the loss of her children (v. 8). However, the Lord brings both upon her in a single day (v. 9). Her gods fail her in that day and none of her diviners and astrologers are able to resist the destructive power of God (vv. 9-15).

Edom also appears in a representative role as the object of God's angry judgment (63:1-6; cf. chap. 34).[41] Chapter 63 presents one of the most vivid pictures of

---

41. In the symmetrical structure of Isaiah 59:9–64:12, the portrayal of the Lord as warrior in 63:1-6 corresponds to 59:15*b*-21, which describes the Lord going out as a warrior against the nations. The structure of the section is as follows.

   a. Prayer/Lament (59:9-15*a*)
      b. Intervention by the Divine Warrior (59:15*b*-21)
         c. Zion's Future Glory (chaps. 60-62)
      b.' Intervention by the Divine Warrior (63:1-6)
   a. Prayer/Lament (63:7–64:12)

God as warrior in the entire Old Testament. It portrays the Lord as returning from Edom wearing garments so stained with blood that He looks like one who has been trampling grapes in a winepress. His judgment on the nations (cf. v. 6, which uses more universal language) is called His "day of vengeance" and is characterized by "wrath." At the same time, it is a time of redemption (cf. 62:12 with 63:4) and salvation for Israel.[42]

Salvation. As in chapters 1-39, the judgment of the nations leads to their eventual reconciliation to God. Chapter 40-55 refer to this in several places. One of the Lord's servant's major tasks is to bring justice to the nations (42:1-4; 49:6; note that the second servant song is addressed to the distant nations). The nations should respond to this good news with joy and praise (42:10-12). Isaiah's trial speeches against the nations culminate with an appeal for repentance (45:22-25). Having overwhelmed the nations with evidence of His incomparability and sovereignty, the Lord offers them reconciliation. "Turn to me and be saved, all you ends of the earth; for I am God, and there is no other" (v. 22). To motivate a positive response, the Lord informs them that a day is coming when all will acknowledge His sovereignty. Wisdom dictates that one voluntarily make this confession now, rather than be forced in shame to make it later.

Chapters 56-66 also foresee the incorporation of the nations into God's kingdom. They will conduct Israel's exiles back to Palestine, assist in the rebuilding of Jerusalem, and bring their tribute to the Lord (60:3-16; 61:6; 62:2; 66:12, 18-20). God will send ambassadors to the distant nations to proclaim His greatness and glory (66:19). All the nations will worship the Lord on designated holy days (66:23).

CONCLUSION

Genesis 1-11 describes how mankind's rebellion disrupted the created order, bringing curse, death, and societal discord in its wake. God chose Abraham and promised to restore universal blessing through his offspring (Gen. 12). Through Israel's Exodus from Egypt and the giving of the covenant at Sinai, the Lord created a nation from Abraham's offspring. However, as Isaiah and others so clearly pointed out, Israel broke this covenant and failed to be the example of obedience and justice God intended. Consequently the nation also failed to be a channel of God's universal blessing. Despite this history of universal and national rebellion and failure, God's ideal for His covenant people and for the nations will ultimately be realized. According to Isaiah, ideal Israel, God's obedient servant, will lead national Israel, God's blind servant, out of bondage once more and will mediate a New Covenant on her behalf. He will also be instrumental in bringing the nations to a place of submission and blessing. As such He is not only central to the message of Isaiah but also to biblical history and eschatology in general.

42. The warrior motifs of the solitary charge (cf. 63:5) and extensive blood-letting also appear in ancient Near Eastern accounts of warrior kings. On the former, see Ramses II's Kadesh battle inscription, where the king claims to have single handedly defeated thousands of Hittite chariots (Lichtheim, *Ancient Egyptian Literature,* 2:57-72). References to shedding blood in bat-

tle are abundant. A rather vivid example comes from the Assyrian annals of Tiglath-pileser I, who boasted, "I spread out the corpses of their warriors on mountain ledges like (slaughtered) sheep (and) made their blood flow into the hollows and plains of the mountain" (Grayson, *Assyrian Royal Inscriptions,* 2:14-15).

9

A THEOLOGY OF JEREMIAH AND LAMENTATIONS

ROBERT B. CHISHOLM, JR.

A THEOLOGY OF JEREMIAH

Jeremiah lived and prophesied during Judah's final days. Called to be a prophet while still a young man, he denounced the sins of the people and warned that judgment would soon overtake the land. Intense hostility and opposition from kings, priests, and prophets caused him to cry out to the Lord in despair and at times bitterness. Nevertheless, he remained faithful to his prophetic commission and continued to exhort God's people even after the fall of Jerusalem. He was taken to Egypt against his will by a group of Judahite refugees. Jeremiah warned the exiles living there against placing their trust in Egypt.

Like so many of the other preexilic writing prophets, Jeremiah's message focuses on God's relationship to His covenant people, while at the same time including several judgment oracles against the surrounding nations. Jeremiah accused Judah of breaking the Mosaic Covenant and announced that the covenant curses would fall on the nation. In particular, he drew attention to the people's idolatry, which he, like Hosea before him, likened to adultery. However, he also foresaw a day when God would bring down the powerful and hostile surrounding nations, restore His people to the land, and establish a new covenant with them.

One of the unique features of the book of Jeremiah is the large amount of biographical material it contains. The book includes many of Jeremiah's laments, accounts of symbolic actions he performed, and narratives of his encounters with unjust kings, corrupt priests, and lying prophets. This material contributes to the theology of the book by providing insight into the true prophet's relationship to God, concrete illustrations of the prophet's messages, and tangible proof of the degree of the nation's corruption before her fall.

The theology of the book of Jeremiah may be summarized as follows: God's judgment would fall on Judah because she had broken His covenant. The people worshiped other gods, and the religious and civil leaders were hopelessly corrupt. Sword, plague, and famine would devastate the land and many would be carried into exile. However, God would also judge the arrogant nations and eventually restore His people to their land. He would establish a new covenant with the reunited Northern and Southern kingdoms and replace the ineffective kings and priests of Jeremiah's day with an ideal Davidic ruler (Messiah) and a purified priesthood.[1]

GOD AND HIS PEOPLE

Judah rejects her God

The Broken Covenant. Jeremiah reminded the people of their covenant obligations and accused them of breaking their agreement with the Lord. Centuries earlier, in the days of Moses, God had established His covenant with the nation. The Lord warned that the covenant curses would fall on violators, but He promised that obedience would result in His presence and blessing (11:2-5). Throughout Israel's history the people broke the terms of the covenant and experienced God's discipline (vv. 7-8). The people of Jeremiah's generation followed in the footsteps of their rebellious forefathers (vv. 9-10). They rejected God's law (9:13) and blatantly disobeyed its most basic standards by mistreating one another and worshiping other gods (cf. 7:9, which specifically mentions violation of five of the Ten Commandments). Because of their persistent disobedience a severe and inescapable judgment was about to come on them (11:11-17).

To highlight the people's unfaithfulness to God's covenant demands, Jeremiah gave them an object lesson involving the Recabite family (35:1-19). The Recabites were the descendants of Jonadab son of Recab, mentioned in 2 Kings 10:15-23 as a zealous follower of the Lord and opponent of Baal worship. Jonadab commanded his descendants to follow a nomadic and rigidly ascetic lifestyle, which includ-

1. It is beyond the scope of this study to discuss the serious textual difficulties presented by the book of Jeremiah. When the Hebrew text underlying the Greek (Septuagint) version of Jeremiah is reconstructed, it is approximately one-eighth shorter than the traditional Hebrew (Masoretic) form of the book. The placement and order of the oracles against the nations (chaps. 46-51 in the Masoretic text) also differ. The oracles appear after 25:13 in the Septuagint. Evidence from Qumran suggests that two recensions of the book circulated during the intertestamental period. Thus the problem is broader than the scope of textual criticism (traditionally understood) and raises the question of the accepted canonical form of the book. Because the subject is still being debated in scholarly circles, it is best to base this study on the traditional Hebrew form of the book, though making allowances where needed for superior readings in alternate textual traditons.

ed abstinence from wine. More than 200 years later his descendants were still obeying the regulations established by their ancestor. At the Lord's command Jeremiah invited the Recabites to the Temple and offered them wine. They, of course, refused to drink it, pointing out that they must remain faithful to their ancient standard of abstinence. The Lord then instructed Jeremiah to inform the people that the Recabites were an object lesson for them. The Recabites' unwavering devotion to their ancestral commands stood in stark contrast to the people's persistent rejection of God's law and His calls to repentance through the prophets.

Judah's rebellion had made the nation useless to the Lord, a fact that He illustrated through an object lesson (13:1-11). At the Lord's command Jeremiah purchased a linen belt, wore it on his waist, and then buried it in some rocks near a stream. When the prophet later dug the belt up, it was, of course, ruined and useless. Just as a man hopes that a fine belt will bring him attention and compliments, so the Lord intended that His people might bring Him fame and praise by obeying His law and serving as a model of righteousness to the nations (cf. Deut. 4:5-8). However, just as the natural elements ruined Jeremiah's fine belt, so Judah's sins had made her useless as the Lord's servant.

Spiritual Adultery. Judah's breach of covenant took many forms, but the nation's most heinous crime was her rejection of the Lord in favor of other gods. The Lord is the true and living God, the sovereign Creator of the universe (10:10, 12) who sets boundaries for the raging sea (5:22), controls the elements of nature (10:13), and rules over the nations (10:7, 10). He created Israel (10:16), delivered her from bondage in Egypt, and brought her safely into the fertile Promised Land (2:6-7). Despite His goodness to Israel, the people turned to worthless, lifeless, man-made idols formed from wood and metal (1:16; 2:5, 8-12; 10:3-5, 8-9, 14-15; 16:18-20). In rejecting the Lord, who was like a "spring of living water" capable of providing them with continual sustenance, they had, as it were, "dug their own cisterns" (2:13). The idol-gods were like "broken cisterns that cannot hold water," for they were totally incapable of supplying the needs of God's people.

Jeremiah specified certain pagan deities and practices as being especially attractive to the people. They worshiped the Canaanite storm and fertility god Baal (2:8, 23; 7:9; 9:14; 11:13, 17; 12:16; 19:5; 23:13, 27; 32:29, 35) and even burned their children in the fire as whole offerings to this god (19:5) and to Molech (32:35; cf. Lev. 18:21; 20:2-5; 2 Kings 23:10). They also expressed their devotion to the Mesopotamian goddess Ishtar, called in Jeremiah "the Queen of Heaven" (7:18; 44:17-19, 25). The worship of this goddess involved the ritual of baking cakes in her image, burning incense, and pouring out drink offerings. Following the destruction of Jerusalem, the exiles in Egypt even resumed this practice, claiming that the city's downfall was the result of abandoning the ritual (44:15-19).

To emphasize how repulsive the people's idolatrous behavior was in the sight of God, Jeremiah compared it to marital infidelity. Their worship of Baal under the sacred trees of the high places was comparable to an adulteress surrendering herself to her lovers (2:19). Following in the footsteps of her sister, the Northern

Kingdom (3:6-20), idolatrous Judah was like an unfaithful wife who forgets her symbols of marriage (2:32) and shamelessly engages in numerous illicit relationships (3:1-3). In her unbridled lust for pagan gods she was like a she-camel running frantically about, or a wild donkey in heat craving a mate (2:23-24).

Social Injustice. Jeremiah also denounced the injustice that characterized Judahite society. The rich violently oppressed the poor and failed to defend the cause of widows and orphans (2:34; 5:26-28; 7:5-6). The kings of Judah, who were to promote and maintain justice in the land (21:11; 22:2-4), were the worst offenders. Jehoiakim forced his countrymen to build him a fine royal palace and failed to pay them for their labor (22:13-14). Jeremiah contrasted this oppressive act with the just deeds of Jehoiakim's father, Josiah, who had defended the rights of the poor and needy (22:15-17). By obeying God's commandments pertaining to social and economic justice, Josiah had demonstrated that he truly recognized the Lord's authority,[2] but Jehoiakim was interested only in "dishonest gain." Zedekiah, the last king of Judah, also failed to promote justice. During the Babylonian siege of Jerusalem, he and the residents of the city made a solemn covenant before the Lord to release their Hebrew slaves, in accord with the law of Moses. However, when the siege was temporarily lifted, they went back on their agreement (34:8-20).

Hypocrisy and False Hope. Despite these obvious violations of the covenant, the people still offered sacrifices to the Lord and believed the false prophets' promises of salvation. These prophets assured the people that calamity would not overtake them and that the future would be filled with peace and prosperity (5:12; 8:11; 14:13, 15; 27:9; 28:2-4). Apparently this false message of hope was based on the nation's possession of the Mosaic law (8:8) and the presence of the Lord's Temple in its midst (7:4).

In response the Lord emphasized that He did not find their sacrifices acceptable (6:20). From the days of Moses He had always regarded sincere obedience to be more fundamental than sacrificial ritual (7:21-12).[3] The possession of the law was meaningless so long as the priests mishandled it and the people disobeyed

---

2. After pointing out Josiah's concern for justice, the Lord asked, "Is that not what it means to know me?" (22:16). "Know" is here used in its idiomatic and covenantal sense of "recognize one's authority." It is typical of the Old Testament to equate knowledge of God with practical obedience to His will, rather than mere abstract, philosophical understanding of facts about His person or character.

3. The historical observation in 7:22 has been misunderstood by some as an outright rejection of the sacrificial system. The text literally reads, "I did not give them commands about burnt offerings and sacrifices" (NIV's "just" being interpretive). This appears to imply, in contrast to the Pentateuchal narratives, that God gave the Israelites no regulations for worship at the time of the Exodus. Because this was not the case, verse 22 must be understood as an overstatement designed to emphasize the priority of obedience from God's standpoint. One should also note that in the Exodus account of the making of the covenant at Sinai the first regulations given by the Lord deal with the basic covenantal demands of loyalty to God and love for one's neighbor. Only later did the Lord give regulations for the Levitical worship system. (For further discussion, see J. A. Thompson, *The Book of Jeremiah* [Grand Rapids: Eerdmans, 1980], pp. 287-88.)

it (8:8-9). God also made it clear that the presence of the Temple was no guarantee of safety. To support His argument, He pointed to Shiloh, which had once been the site of the Tabernacle, but was later abandoned by God. If the people failed to repent, the Temple mount would be destroyed as Shiloh had been (7:12-14; 26:6, 9).[4]

The false prophets would be a special object of divine wrath. Their primary motive in pronouncing oracles of salvation was greed, for they were apparently richly rewarded when they spoke reassuring words to the people (6:13; 8:10). However, these prophets had not stood in the divine assembly (23:18) or been commissioned by God (14:14; 23:21; 29:9, 31), for if they had, they would have denounced the people's wicked deeds (23:22). Instead they assured the evildoers that no harm would overtake them (23:10-17). Their preoccupation with prophecies of peace marked them as suspect, for the Lord's true prophets from earliest times had been primarily messengers of impending doom (28:8-9).[5] The false prophets' messages were a delusion, derived from their own divination methods and visions (14:14; 23:16, 26-38; 29:8). In contrast to these false prophets, Jeremiah had been chosen by God even before birth and had received a special commission to proclaim God's word of judgment (1:4-19). Unlike the false prophets, who had no genuine divine revelation, Jeremiah devoured, as it were, the word of God (15:16) and was filled with a compulsion to preach it (20:9). He was one of God's "watchmen" (6:17), sent to warn God's covenant people to turn from their evil ways (7:25; 25:4).

Rejection of the Lord's Word. Perhaps the most tangible evidence of the people's rejection of God's authority was their harsh treatment of the prophetic messengers who faithfully proclaimed His word. Jehoiakim actually executed one of Jeremiah's prophetic colleagues, Uriah son of Shemaiah (26:20-23), and Jeremiah's life was also threatened on several occasions.

The book records in detail the persecution Jeremiah faced from his countrymen, including the religious leaders and the civil authorities. Certain men of Anathoth, Jeremiah's hometown (1:1), told Jeremiah not to prophesy in the Lord's name and plotted his death (11:18-21). A priest named Pashhur son of Immer had him beaten and placed in stocks at one of the Temple gates (20:1-2). On another occasion several priests and prophets were ready to execute Jeremiah (26:8-9) before certain officials and elders of the land intervened on his behalf (vv. 10-19, 24).[6] When

---

4. The Old Testament does not specifically refer to the destruction of Shiloh, although 1 Samuel 4-6 records how the Israelites took the Ark from the Tabernacle there and carried it into battle against the Philistines. When the Philistines sent the Ark back, it was not returned to Shiloh.

5. The observation in Jeremiah 28:8-9 does not imply that the Lord was unduly negative in approaching His people. It does accurately reflect the reality of sin among Israel and the nations and the fact that the holy God of the universe must constantly confront and judge sinful and rebellious humankind.

6. This passage is especially interesting because of its reference to the prophecy of Micah (cf. Jer. 26:18 with Mic. 3:12) and the insight it provides into the nature of prophetic judgment speeches. The judgment speech in Micah 3:12 sounds like a straighforward, unconditional announcement of Jerusalem's destruction. However, as seen in Jeremiah 26 this prophecy, despite its

Jeremiah placed a yoke on his neck to illustrate the approaching conquest of the western states by Babylon, the false prophet Hananiah removed it from his neck and broke it before all the people (28:10). Another of the false prophets, Shemaiah the Nehelamite, wrote a letter to the priests accusing Jeremiah of treason and of being a false prophet and strongly advised that they place him under arrest (29:24-28).

Kings also reacted violently to God's word through Jeremiah and failed to show him the respect his position deserved. When Baruch recorded one of Jeremiah's messages and then read it in the Temple, Jehoiakim's officials confiscated the prophetic scroll and took it to the king, who proceeded to cut it up column by column and throw it into the fire (36:1-26). During the reign of Zedekiah, royal officials arrested Jeremiah on charges of treason, beat him, and then threw him into prison for many days (37:13-16). Zedekiah ordered the prophet to be transferred to more comfortable quarters (v. 21), but he eventually succumbed to pressure from Jeremiah's opponents and allowed them to lower him into a cistern filled with mud (38:1-6). Only the intervention of a certain Cushite, Ebed-Melech, saved Jeremiah's life (vv. 7-13). Though the king secretly conversed with Jeremiah in hopes of receiving a word from the Lord, he refused to acknowledge or defend Jeremiah publicly (vv. 14-27). The prophet remained imprisoned until the day the Babylonians conquered the city (v. 28). Even after the downfall of the city, some of the leaders of the refugees accused Jeremiah of treason and rejected his words (43:1-4). They forced Jeremiah to go with them to Egypt (v. 6), where the prophet continued to speak out against the sins of the people (43:8-44:30).

> *Excursus on Jeremiah's laments.* In the face of persecution Jeremiah prayed to the Lord on numerous occasions. He serves as a godly example and source of encouragement for all who suffer oppression at the hands of evil men. Jeremiah affirmed his innocence (11:19; 15:10, 17) and loyalty (15:15-16; 17:16; 18:20), appealed to God as his righteous judge (11:20; 12:1; 20:12) and protector (17:17; 20:11), and asked God to take vengeance on his enemies (11:20; 12:3-4; 15:15; 17:18; 18:21-23; 20:12). Under the pressure of intense opposition and hostility, Jeremiah did vacillate emotionally at times. He questioned why the wicked prospered (12:1-2), cursed the day of his own birth (immediately after praising the Lord as his deliverer; 20:13-18), accused God of being unreliable (15:18) and deceptive (20:7), and complained that his faithfulness to God's work had brought him nothing but trouble (20:8). Though the Lord did rebuke His prophet (15:19), He also encouraged him to remain faithful to his commission, promised him protection, and assured him that his enemies would be punished (11:21-23; 15:11, 20-21).

outward appearance, was conditional. According to the elders of Jeremiah's day, the judgment threatened by Micah had been averted by the repentance of Hezekiah (Jer. 26:19). Of course one should note that when the condition of repentance was not met in Jeremiah's day, Micah's prophecy was fulfilled. In 586 B.C. the Babylonians reduced Jerusalem and the Temple to rubble, just as Micah had warned.

The Possibility of Repentance Fades Away. Through an object lesson the Lord made clear that His relationship to the nations is not fixed and immovable (18:1-11). At the Lord's command Jeremiah went to the potter's house. As the potter was shaping a particular kind of pot, the clay was marred. He then formed it into a different kind of pot. The potter's decision to alter his design illustrated the Lord's relationship to nations. Even if the Lord decrees judgment for an evil nation, that decision can be altered if the nation repents. At the same time, the Lord's decision to bless a nation can also be changed, if that nation rejects the Lord and does evil. This lesson was particularly relevant for Judah. God's ideal for His people had been marred by their sinful behavior. He desired to bless them, but their sin had forced Him to decree judgment. To avert disaster the people must now repent.

The Lord urged His wayward people to abandon their wicked ways and "return" to Him (3:12, 14, 22; 4:1; 18:11; 25:5; 35:15; cf. also 26:3 and 36:3, 7). He demanded that they acknowledge their unfaithfulness, put away their idols, and circumcise their "hearts" (3:9–4:4).[7] Physical circumcision marked an Israelite as a member of the covenant community. The Lord desired something more profound than an external sign of one's attachment to the covenant. He demanded a sign of one's true allegiance to the Lord of the covenant and commitment to the principles He had just laid down. One must demonstrate this wholehearted devotion to the Lord of the covenant by obeying the demands of the covenant, the most basic principle of which was to worship the Lord alone. If the people sincerely returned to the Lord, He would show them mercy (3:12), heal their backsliding (3:22), and refrain from sending disaster on them (26:3). As a tangible test of their sincerity, the Lord commanded them to observe the Sabbath regulations of the Mosaic law (17:19-27).

This call for a change in the heart of the people went unheeded. Repentance, along with the promise of forgiveness and blessing attached to it, proved to be an unrealized ideal. As in the past (3:7, 10), God's people refused to turn to Him (5:3; 8:5-6; 15:7; 18:12; 23:14; 25:7; 35:15; 44:5)[8] and instead returned to the evil ways of their fathers (11:10).[9] Consequently God gave them over to destruction and

---

7. "Heart" in this context refers to one's entire being, including the intellect, emotions, and will. The metaphor of circumcising the heart did not originate with Jeremiah. Moses urged Israel to do the same (Deut. 10:16) and looked forward to the day when the Lord Himself would transform the nation's character in this way (Deut. 30:6; cf. Lev. 26:41).

8. According to Jeremiah 34:15, God considered the release of the Hebrew slaves during Zedekiah's reign as a step in the right direction, but unfortunately this repentant attitude was short-lived (34:16).

9. In 11:10 the verb šûb, "return," is used in an ironic sense to illustrate that the people's actual response was diametrically opposed to the Lord's intent. In several passages the verb is translated "return," "repent," or "turn," referring to a turning back to God (repentance). However, in 11:10 this same verb (cf. NIV "returned") refers to the people's rejection of God and their insistence on following in the evil footsteps of earlier generations. This ironic use of šûb also appears in 34:15-16, where the verb is used of both the people's short-lived repentance (cf. NIV "repented," v. 15) and their turning back to their former unjust practice (cf. NIV "turned around" in 34:16).

announced, ironically, that He would not turn back from judging them (4:28).[10] With a touch of hyperbole, He declared that He would spare Jerusalem if even one honest and faithful individual could be found in the city (5:1). Jerusalem was even more corrupt than Sodom and Gomorrah (23:14), which the Lord had agreed to spare if ten righteous individuals could be found in those cities (cf. Gen. 18:32). He told Jeremiah not to intercede on the nation's behalf (Jer. 14:11) and stated that He would not be moved by religious rites, such as fasting and sacrifice (14:12). When Jeremiah attempted to intercede (14:19-22), the Lord responded: "Even if Moses and Samuel [whose prayers had spared the nation on several occasions; Ex. 32:9-14; Num. 14:11-23; 1 Sam. 7:2-13; 12:19] were to stand before me, my heart would not go out to this people. Send them away from my presence! Let them go!" (Jer. 15:1).

In contrast to the days of Hezekiah, there would be no miraculous divine deliverance. When Zedekiah asked Jeremiah if the Lord might miraculously intervene for His people, as He had done so many times in their history, the prophet announced that the Babylonians would conquer Jerusalem and slaughter its inhabitants (21:1-10).[11] He advised Zedekiah to submit to Babylonian rule, warning that resistance would only bring unnecessary and total destruction on Jerusalem (27:1-22). Resigning himself to the inevitability of judgment, the prophet looked to the exiles as the future hope of the nation (24:1-10) and encouraged them to settle down in Babylon, contribute to the prosperity of their new land, and await their ultimate release (29:1-14).

Judgment comes from the north

God's Instrument of Judgment. From the outset of his prophetic ministry, Jeremiah warned that judgment would sweep down from the north on the unrepentant nation. When God commissioned Jeremiah, He showed him a vision of a boiling pot tilting from the north. He explained that the pot represented the armies of northern kingdoms that would pour into the land as instruments of God's judgment on His sinful people (1:13-15). The ground would shake before these invading hordes (10:22)[12] and the people would melt in fear as they saw the well-equipped masses of the cruel enemy marching swiftly and relentlessly toward Jerusalem (4:13; 6:1-2, 22-26). Like a powerful lion this northern foe would ravage the Lord's flock, lay waste the land, and plunder its treasures (4:5-9; 5:15-17; 13:20; 15:12-13). Various passages, as well as historical developments, identify this northern invader with Nebuchadnezzar's Babylonian armies and their northern allies (note espe-

10. Ironically He would not "turn back" (*šûb*, 4:28) from carrying out judgment against those who had rejected His call to "return" (*šûb*, 3:10, 12, 14, 22, 4:1) to Him.

11. The word translated "wonders" (*niplā'ôt*) in 21:2 is used elsewhere of God's judgments on Egypt (Ex. 3:20; Judg. 6:13; Ps. 78:11; Mic. 7:15), the crossing of the Jordan River (Josh. 3:5), the conquest of the land (Ex. 34:10), and His mighty deeds in general (1 Chron. 16:9, 24).

12. The word *ra'aš*, translated "commotion" in NIV, refers to a shaking or quaking of the ground, caused in this case by the chariots of the invaders (cf. 47:3, where "noise" translates the same word).

cially 25:9, 26), who destroyed Jerusalem and the Temple in 586 B.C.

Covenant Curses Realized. Through this invader, whom God even referred to as His "servant" (25:9), the ancient covenant curses (Lev. 26; Deut. 28) would be realized. As Moses had long ago warned (Deut. 28:49), a distant nation, whose language the people did not understand, would conquer His people (Jer. 5:15). Sword, famine, and plague (14:12, 15) would sweep over the land, destroying its agricultural produce (5:17; 8:13; 14:2-6) and decimating its population (5:17; 9:22; 14:16, 18; 15:2-3, 9). The women of the land would lament that death had crept in through the windows of their homes and robbed them of their children and young men (9:21). God's judgment would culminate in the exile of the survivors (13:19; 15:2), who would be scattered among the nations (9:16; cf. Deut. 28:64). Exile to a foreign land and subservience to foreign kings would be an appropriate punishment for those who had worshiped foreign gods (Jer. 5:19; 16:10-13). Judah's period of servitude to Babylon would last for seventy years (25:11-12; 29:10). While this number may be understood literally (albeit approximate), it may also indicate a typical life span (Ps. 90:10) or be symbolic of an appropriate or complete period of punishment.[13] In any case it would suggest that few of those who witnessed the destruction of the land would live to see its restoration.

Excursus on Jeremiah's prophecy of seventy years. The events that Jeremiah identified as terminating the seventy-year period, namely, the fall of Babylon (25:11-12) and the initial return of Judahite exiles from Babylon (29:10), occurred in 539-538 B.C., approximately fifty years after the fall of Jerusalem in 586. Consequently, those who understand Jeremiah's prophecy as referring to a literal period of seventy years must identify the beginning point of the period with the Babylonian invasion of 605, which involved the exile of some Judahites (Dan. 1:1-7). This harmonizes well with the context of the prophecy in Jeremiah 25:11-12, which was delivered in that very year (25:1). Jeremiah's other reference to the seventy-year period (29:10) occurred in a letter written by the prophet to the exiles sometime after Jehoiachin's exile in 597 (29:2).

Two later passages, Daniel 9:2 and 2 Chronicles 36:21-22, refer specifically to Jeremiah's prophecy of a seventy-year period of exile. In 539-538 B.C. Daniel, living in Babylon, read the prophecy and was moved to pray for the restoration of the exiles. If the period in view began in 605 B.C., when the Babylonians carried away the first group of exiles (including Daniel; Dan. 1:1-7), then this seventy-year period would have been near completion in 539-538, thus prompting Daniel's emotional response. This interpretation, which assumes a literal understanding of the seventy years on Daniel's part, makes

13. Seven is frequently used in the Bible and ancient Near Eastern literature as a symbolic or ideal number, indicating completeness. Multiples of seven are sometimes employed as an emphatic way of expressing this idea (e.g., Gen. 4:24; Matt 18:22). The number seventy may be used in this hyperbolic manner in Judges 1:7 and Isaiah 23:15.

good sense in the context of the book and Daniel's experience. At the same time, there is nothing in the introduction or prayer of Daniel 9 that *demands* this interpretation. Daniel's response is just as easily explained by the other interpretations of the number seventy. It had been almost an entire lifetime since his exile from Judah and he regarded the Lord's judgment to have been thorough and complete (Dan. 9:11-13).

According to 2 Chronicles 36:21-23 "the land enjoyed its sabbath rests" (cf. Lev. 25:1; 26:34-35, 43) during the seventy-year period of judgment prophesied by Jeremiah. The passage in 2 Chronicles then records the edict of Cyrus, who allowed the exiles to return to Judah. Interpreting the seventy years as literal is more problematic in this context. Second Chronicles 36 seems to proceed in chronological sequence, covering in succession the reigns of Jehoahaz (609 B.C., vv. 1-4), Jehoiakim (609-598, vv. 5-8), Jehoiachin (598-597, vv. 9-10), and Zedekiah (597-586, vv. 11-16), the fall of Jerusalem (586, vv. 17-19), the exile of its people(vv. 20-21), and Cyrus's edict (vv. 22-23). The beginning of the "time of its (the land's) desolation" (v. 21) is most naturally associated with the destruction and exile of 586 described immediately before (vv. 19-20). This time of desolation is seemingly equated with the seventy years mentioned immediately after.[14] If so, this suggests that Jeremiah's seventy years were being understood in a figurative sense, since Cyrus's edict and the initial return of the exiles occurred approximately fifty years after the fall of the city.

The seventy-year period referred to in Zechariah 1:12 (cf. also 7:5) should not be associated with Jeremiah's prophecy. The vision recorded in Zechariah 1:7-17 occurred in 519 B.C. (cf. v. 7). The seventy years refer to the approximate length of the period between 586, when Jerusalem fell, and the time of the vision.

Creation Reversed. Jeremiah portrayed the coming judgment as a reversal of creation. He describes the effects of judgment as follows: "I looked at the earth, and it was formless and empty; and at the heavens, and their light was gone. I looked at the mountains, and they were quaking; all the hills were swaying. I looked, and there were no people; every bird in the sky had flown away" (Jer. 4:23-25). The land would become like the world before the time when God brought the light into existence and filled the earth with people and the sky with birds. It would revert to a "formless and empty" condition, as the world had been before creation (cf. Gen. 1:2, where the same Hebrew expression is used). Ironically the

---

14. Proponents of a literal seventy-year period must distinguish between "the time of its desolation" (which began in 586) and the period of seventy years, both here and in Jeremiah 25:11. The latter states that Judah and her neighbors would serve the king of Babylon for seventy years. This period of servitude could be understood as starting in 605, when Nebuchadnezzar marched westward after his victory over the Egyptians at Carchemish. It would then predate the desolation of the land itself by about twenty years.

Creator of the universe (Jer. 10:10, 12), who suppresses the chaotic forces that threaten to destroy the order He has established (5:22), would undo His creative work on behalf of His covenant people (cf. 10:16), causing them to experience the disorder and darkness of judgment.

Object Lessons of Judgment. To illustrate the coming judgment, the Lord gave the people vivid object lessons. He instructed Jeremiah to refrain from taking a wife, mourning over the dead, or participating in feasts (16:1-9). Jeremiah's celibate lifestyle foreshadowed the decimation of the nation's families. The sword and famine would rob families of husbands/fathers, wives/mothers, and children. The prophet's refusal to participate in funerals anticipated the day when people would not have time or opportunity to bury their dead, let alone formally lament over them. Feasting was inappropriate, for God's judgment would soon bring an end to all the land's joyous celebrations.

On another occasion Jeremiah took a clay jar to the Potsherd Gate near the Valley of Hinnom (also called Topheth), which served as a dump for broken pottery, and smashed it before several onlookers (19:1-15). Just as the prophet had broken the clay jar, so the Lord would "ruin the plans of Judah and Jerusalem" and smash them to bits.[15] The Valley of Hinnom was a site for pagan worship, where the people sacrificed to their foreign gods and even offered up their own children as burnt offerings (cf. also 7:31). In the future the corpses of the people would fill this valley and Jerusalem would become, like Topheth, a defiled place.

Prophecy Fulfilled. The book's final chapter (52), which functions as an appendix and is almost identical to 2 Kings 24:18–25:30, describes how Jeremiah's prophecies of judgment were fulfilled. Nebuchadnezzar besieged Jerusalem from January 588 B.C. until July 586. At the end of this period famine had overtaken the city. King Zedekiah and others attempted to sneak out of the city, but they were captured by the Babylonians. Nebuchadnezzar slaughtered Zedekiah's sons before the king's eyes, then blinded him and carried him away to Babylon where he remained for the rest of his life. In August 586 the Babylonians invaded the city, looted and destroyed the Temple, and carried thousands into captivity.

Future restoration. Jeremiah's vision of Judah's future was not entirely dark and gloomy. He foresaw a time when the people would return from exile and rebuild Jerusalem.[16] The Northern and Southern kingdoms would be reunited under the leadership of an ideal Davidic king and a purified priesthood. The Lord would establish a new covenant with His people, enabling them to remain loyal to Him.

Return from Exile. The Lord would reverse the most devastating effect of

---

15. The very designation "clay jar" (*baqbuq*, vv. 1, 10) contributes to the lesson, for it sounds like the word translated "ruin" (*bāqaq*, v. 7) and thereby hints at what the Lord would do to the nation. The "plans" (*'ēṣāh*) referred to in verse 7 may include the people's plot against Jeremiah (cf. 18:23, where "plots" translates the same Hebrew word).

16. Though brief references to the nation's future restoration occasionally qualify oracles of judgment (cf. 3:14-18; 12:15; 16:14-15; 23:3-8; 29:10-14), Jeremiah's messages of future hope appear primarily in chapters 30-33.

judgment by resettling His exiled people in their land. Once the seventy years had passed, the Lord would show compassion on the remnant of His people and, like a watchful shepherd, lead them out of the land of exile back to Palestine, the land He promised to their fathers (12:15; 16:15; 23:3; 29:10). From all directions would come a great throng, including even those normally considered unable or unfit to travel (31:7-8).[17] This mighty act of deliverance would make the nation forget about the ancient Exodus under Moses. No longer would they swear, "As surely as the Lord lives, who brought the Israelites up out of Egypt." Rather they would declare, "As surely as the Lord lives, who brought the Israelites up out of the land of the north and out of all the countries where he had banished them" (16:14-15; cf. 23:7-8).

Perhaps the most moving scene in Jeremiah's portrayal of the return from exile appears in 31:15-22. Looking back to the days when His people were carried off into exile, the Lord describes Ramah (mentioned here as a representative Benjamite town)[18] and Rachel (here a personification of her sons, the tribes of Benjamin [cf. Ramah] and Joseph [cf. the references to Ephraim, one of Joseph's sons, in vv. 18 and 20], which in turn represent the entire Northern Kingdom [cf. vv. 1, 4-7, 9-11, 18, 20-21]) weeping over the loss of their exiled children. The picture reflects the historical reality of helpless Israelite (and later Judahite) mothers crying inconsolably as their little ones were taken from them by foreigners, presumably never to be seen or heard from again. However, the Lord boldly commands Rachel to cease her lamentation and promises that a day would come when the exiled children would return to their land.[19] Ephraim (here representing the Northern Kingdom) was His dear firstborn son, the object of His delight for whom His heart yearned (v. 20; cf. v. 9). Though the Lord must discipline His child, He would hear Ephraim's cries of repentance and shower him with compassion (vv. 18-20).[20]

With a burst of emotion and a change in metaphors (from son Ephraim to wife Israel) the Lord exhorts wayward, exiled Israel to abandon her sinful lifestyle and follow the signs leading home (vv. 20-22a). He promises that something new would

---

17. Jeremiah's description of the return from exile transcends the historical return of the sixth-fifth centuries B.C. and includes the future restoration of the nation. It is typical of prophetic eschatology to blend chronologically distant events into one picture.

18. Ramah was located in Benjaminite territory, about five miles north of Jerusalem.

19. Jeremiah 31:15 is quoted in Matthew 2:18 in conjunction with Herod's slaughter of the innocent children of Bethlehem shortly after the birth of Christ. According to Matthew, Herod's act "fulfilled" Jeremiah's words. This does not mean that Matthew understood Jeremiah 31:15 to be a direct prediction of Herod's deed. Such an interpretation is especially problematic, for Jeremiah 31:15 refers to Ramah (not Bethlehem) and is not predictive (the passage primarily refers to the exile of the Northern Kingdom by the Assyrians in 722 B.C.). Matthew is here making a typological or analogical application of Jeremiah 31:15 to events surrounding the birth of Christ. Herod's act "fulfilled" the words of Jeremiah in that it shared the same basic character as the event portrayed in 31:15. In Herod's day, as in the days of Israel's exile, God's people suffered under the cruel hand of an oppressive ruler. (On Matthew's use of the Old Testament in the early chapters of his gospel, see the discussion of Isaiah 7:14.)

20. The clause translated "I have great compassion" in Jeremiah 31:20 is emphatic in the Hebrew text, drawing attention to the degree of the Lord's love for His son.

come into being: a woman would surround a man (v. 22). Though the statement in verse 22*b* is cryptic and precludes interpretive dogmatism, the context suggests that the "woman" is the virgin Israel (cf. vv. 4, 21). If so, the "man" is probably her husband, the Lord (cf. v. 3). In the day of restoration God's adulterous wife would embrace her husband with vigor (the sense of "surround" in this interpretation).[21]

As proof that the land would again be inhabited, the Lord provided an object lesson through His prophet (32:1-44). While the Babylonian army besieged Jerusalem, the Lord commanded Jeremiah to purchase a field from his cousin Hanamel. Jeremiah then placed the deed of purchase in a clay jar, where it would be preserved, and he announced, "This is what the Lord Almighty, the God of Israel, says: 'Houses, fields, and vineyards will again be bought in this land' "(v. 15). Though he carried out the Lord's instructions, Jeremiah was still somewhat puzzled. He praised the Lord as the sovereign ruler of the universe who had accomplished mighty deeds on Israel's behalf, but he also expressed his confusion over the significance of this latest symbolic act that he had been asked to perform. With the Babylonians waiting outside the city walls as God's instrument of judgment on His sinful people, it made little sense for Jeremiah to be buying land as if life were going to continue in normal fashion in Judah (vv. 24-25). Reminding Jeremiah of his earlier affirmation of faith, the Lord stated, "I am the Lord, the God of all mankind. Is anything too hard for me?" (v. 27; cf. v. 17). The Lord then explained that following the time of judgment He would gather His people, give them the capacity to obey His commands loyally, and make a new, eternal covenant with them (vv. 37-41). God's people would again occupy their land and buy and sell property (vv. 42-44). Jeremiah's symbolic purchase anticipated this day of restoration beyond judgment.

Restored Blessings. God's people would experience spiritual healing and enjoy the divine blessings of peace and prosperity. Both Israelite and Judahite exiles would return to the land (30:10; 31:27; 33:7) and rejoice over their fruitful harvests and abundant flocks and herds (31:4-5, 24; 33:10-13). Northerners would willingly go to Jerusalem (31:6) and celebrate the Lord's blessings (31:12-14). Having received forgiveness (33:6, 8), the returning exiles would no longer lament that they were being forced to suffer for their fathers' sins, but would recognize that God deals fairly with men on an individual basis (31:29-30; cf. Ezek. 18:1-32).

Zion Repopulated. Jerusalem would be the focal point of the restored nation. The city would be rebuilt in its entirety (Jer. 30:17; 31:38-40) and purified in the sight

---

21. Another possibility is that the statement is proverbial or idiomatic, giving an illustration of how new or unusual the future restoration would be. Robert Davidson, in discussing this option, refers to the *Good News Bible*, which paraphrases here, "I have created something new and different, as different as a woman protecting a man." In this case "surrounds" (*sābab*) is taken in the sense of providing protection (cf. Deut. 32:10, where NIV translates the word "shielded"). If one follows this line of interpretation, the unusual development to which the statement refers is probably the renewed devotion of once faithful Israel. (For further discussion, see Robert Davidson, *Jeremiah and Lamentations*, The Daily Study Bible Series, 2 vols. [Philadelphia: Westminster, 1983-85], 2:84.)

of God (31:40). Its once desolate streets would be filled with people (30:17, 19-20). Northerners would make pilgrimages to it (31:6, 12-14) and the people of Judah would pronounce blessings on it (31:23). As the object of God's abundant blessing, the city's fame would spread and bring God glory among the nations (33:9).

New Leadership. With the exception of Josiah, the Davidic kings of Jeremiah's day were displeasing to the Lord (2 Kings 23:32, 37; 24:9, 19). In apparent contradiction of the Davidic promise, God even announced to King Jehoiachin that none of his offspring would occupy the Davidic throne (Jer. 22:28-30). The Davidic dynasty experienced humiliation as three of the last four kings of Judah were carried into exile (2 Kings 23:33-34; 24:15; 25:6-7). Like 1 and 2 Kings, the book of Jeremiah ends with the pathetic picture of Jehoiachin imprisoned in the palace of the Babylonian king (Jer. 52:31-34).

The shame of the Davidic throne would not last forever. The Lord would raise up a new Davidic king, the Messiah, to rule over His people. Though this ruler is specifically called "David" in 30:9, other texts make clear that he is a descendant of David (23:5; 33:15). He is called David because he would rule in the spirit of his illustrious ancestor and be the Lord's instrument in bringing peace to His people.[22] In contrast to the unjust rulers of Jeremiah's day, this king would promote justice in the land (23:5; 33:15). As the protector of God's people, he would be called "The Lord our Righteousness" (or better, "Deliverance" or "Vindication," 23:6).[23] Through this ruler God's eternal, unbreakable oath to David would be realized (33:17, 20-21, 26; cf. 2 Sam 7:16; Ps. 89:36). Its fulfillment was as certain as the cycle of day and night established by God at creation. Using a motif from the Abrahamic Covenant tradition, the Lord even promised to make David's descendants as numerous as the stars of the heavens and the sand of the seashore (Jer. 33:22; cf. Gen. 22:17). In fact, through this Davidic ruler God's promises to Abraham's descendants would also be fulfilled (cf. Jer. 33:26).

In contrast to the corrupt priests of Jeremiah's time (6:13; 20:1-6; 26:11), a purified Levitical priesthood would serve the Lord in the future day of restoration (33:18, 21-22). In fulfillment of His promise to the Levites, they would never "fail to have a man stand before" the Lord "continually to offer burnt offerings, to burn grain offerings and to present sacrifices" (33:18).[24] As in the case of David's descen-

22. Ezekiel and Hosea also referred to the Messiah as "David" (Ezek. 34:23-24; 37:24; Hos. 3:5) and Micah portrayed Him as the second coming of David (Mic. 5:2).
23. The Hebrew text of Jeremiah 33:16 applies this same title to restored Jerusalem of the eschaton.
24. The identity and origin of the covenant referred to in 33:21 are unclear. The "covenant of salt" made with the Levites in Aaron's day (Num. 18:19) seems more limited in scope than the covenant referred to by Jeremiah. Nehemiah 13:29 and Malachi 2:4-5 refer to a covenant between God and the Levites that made provision for God's blessing in exchange for obedient service. Whether this is the covenant mentioned by Jeremiah is uncertain, since the latter focuses on God's promises and does not refer to priestly obligations as a basis for divine blessing. Another possible referent is the Lord's unconditional promise to Phinehas of an everlasting priesthood, given as a reward for the priest's devotion to God during Israel's moral lapse at Shittim (Num. 25:1-13). However, this promise was made only with Phinehas, not the entire Levitical family.

dants, the Lord also applied the Abrahamic covenantal motif of numerous off-spring to the Levitical priesthood of the eschaton (33:22).

New Covenant. The promise of a new covenant is the highlight of Jeremiah's portrayal of the nation's future restoration (31:31-37; cf. also 32:40; 50:5). This covenant would be new in the sense that it would differ from and supersede the ancient covenant established in the days of Moses. The difference would not lie in the basic demand of the covenant itself but in the people's capacity to obey it. Under the Old Covenant, God as Israel's "husband" demanded His people's loyalty, but they rebelled against His authority and disobeyed His commands. In establishing the New Covenant relationship with the reunited northern and southern tribes, the Lord would forgive their former sins. He would again demand their devotion, but this time He would place within them the desire and ability to remain loyal to Him. Under the Old Covenant the people needed to exhort their fellow Israelites to obey the Lord, for the nation's tendency was to drift away from God. However, in the coming era such exhortation would be unnecessary, for all Israelites would possess an innate fear of the Lord (32:40) and the capacity to follow Him.[25] As Moses anticipated long before (Deut. 30:6), the people's hearts would be transformed. The Lord's demands would be, as it were, written "on their hearts," rather than on stone tablets (Deut. 6.6). This loyal future generation would stand in stark contrast to Jeremiah's evil contemporaries, whose hearts were engraved with sin (Jer. 17:1) and whose capacity for evil was hopelessly ingrained (cf. 13:23).

The New Covenant would also contain the promise that God would never again reject His people and cause them to cease as a nation. This promise would be just as reliable as the unchanging divinely decreed laws of nature and the fact that the infinitely vast universe cannot be completely measured or searched out by finite man (31:35-37).

GOD AND THE NATIONS

The Lord is the sovereign King over the nations and their man-made gods (19:6-16). It is understandable, then, that His prophet Jeremiah's commission was more far-reaching than the borders of Judah. When the Lord called Jeremiah, He told him, "See, today I appoint you over *nations* and *kingdoms* to uproot and tear down, to destroy and overthrow, to build and to plant" (1:10, italics added). Jeremiah's oracles against the nations were primarily messages of judgment, designed to remind God's people of His absolute universal sovereignty, warn them of trusting in foreign alliances, and to assure them of eventual vindication before their enemies.

Universal judgment. Though God's judgment would initially fall on Judah, eventually all the surrounding nations would experience its full force, including the mighty kingdoms of Egypt and Babylon (25:15-38). The nations were like a group of men seated around a barroom table. Each in turn would drink from the cup

---

25. As in 22:16, the verb "know" is used in 31:34 in its idiomatic and covenantal sense of "recognize one's authority." (See note 2 above.)

of God's wrath until all were overcome by its intoxicating contents and stumbled in their own vomit. Like a raging lion the Lord would attack the nations, whose "shepherds" (probably a reference to their leaders) would be helpless before His anger and power.

Like Judah, some of the nations practiced the custom of circumcision. Because of its significance as the sign of the Abrahamic Covenant, some might have thought that circumcision gave men, including even foreigners, special status in God's sight and immunity from His wrath. The Lord made it clear that this was not so, for those who practiced physical circumcision, including His own covenant people, were really uncircumcised in His sight (9:25-26). The Lord would punish them, for their rebellious attitudes and actions demonstrated that they were "circumcised only in the flesh" and not "in heart."

Judgment on Egypt. The Lord's judgment would fall on Egypt, a nation in which the people of Judah were tempted to place their own confidence, both before (2:18, 36) and after the fall of Jerusalem (42:14). Using Nebuchadnezzar and the Babylonian armies as His instrument of judgment (43:10; 44:30; 46:13, 26), the Lord would destroy the power and glory of Egypt. Though Egypt possessed a degree of military strength and entertained delusions of world conquest (46:8), she would be unable to withstand the Lord's "day of vengeance," in which He would drench His sword with the blood of His foes (46:10). Pharaoh and his chief god, Amon, would be helpless before Him (46:25). In light of her approaching fate, it was absurd for God's people to place their trust in Egypt. The Lord would eventually deliver and restore His people without the assistance of the Egyptians (cf. 46:27-28).

Judgment on neighboring kingdoms. God would also severely judge the neighboring kingdoms of Philistia (47:1-7), Moab (48:1-47), Ammon (49:1-6), and Edom (49:7-22). These nations were proud and complacent (48:7, 29; 49:4, 16), and they ridiculed and exploited Judah during her time of divine punishment (48:26-27, 42; 49:2).[26] Foreign armies would overrun these kingdoms, leaving bloodshed and destruction in their path.[27] The numerous geographical references in the oracles, especially in the lengthy message to Moab, emphasize the thorough nature of their defeat.

Although many allusions to the invading armies appear, the oracles stress God's direct involvement in the judgment of these nations. The Lord commanded the invasion of Philistia (47:7) and would destroy it with His own sword (47:4, 6).

26. Though the oracles against Philistia and Edom do not specifically refer to those nations' hostility toward God's people, other prophets speak of their exploitation of the people of Judah at the time of Jerusalem's fall (cf. Joel 3:4-6; Obad. 10-14).

27. With the exception of the Philistine oracle, there is no specific reference to the Lord's instrument(s) of judgment. The heading to the message against Philistia mentions an attack of Gaza by Pharaoh, suggesting that the oracle may have been fulfilled, at least in part, by this Egyptian invasion. However, the reference to waters "rising in the north" (47:2) suggests that the Babylonians were also used by the Lord in bringing the decreed judgment to pass.

The Lord decrees the fall of Moab (48:8) and would send enemy soldiers against it (48:12). He would bring an end to Moab's formal worship of its god Chemosh (48:35), causing the people to be ashamed of their exiled deity (48:7, 13). The Lord would shatter Moab, making it like a useless jar (48:38). He would sound the battle cry against the Ammonites (49:2) and cause terror to surround them (49:5). He would bring disaster against Edom (49:8), uncover its hiding places (49:10), decree the fall of one of its major cities (49:13), bring it down from its lofty nest (49:15-16), and attack it like a lion in accord with His plan (49:19-20).

Judgment on distant kingdoms. God would also attack the Aramean states of Damascus, Hamath, and Arpad; the Arab tribes of Kedar and Hazor; and the distant land of Elam.[28] While no specific accusations are made against these kingdoms, one must assume that the Lord's general charge against the nations (mentioned in 25:31) applies in each case. Once more emphasis is placed on God's involvement in the downfall of these kingdoms, especially in the oracle against Elam. The Lord would set fire to the walls of Damascus (49:27; cf. Amos 1:4) and scatter the Arabs to the four winds (Jer. 49:32). In the Elam oracle seven successive poetic units begin with first-person assertions by the Lord (49:35-38, "I will break the bow. . . . I will bring. . . . I will scatter. . . . I will shatter. . . . I will bring. . . . I will pursue. . . . I will set"). The last two units contain first-person verbal forms in both lines (49:37*b*, "I will pursue . . . until I have made," and 49:38, "I will set . . . and destroy").

Judgment on Babylon. The Lord's judgment of the nations would culminate with the overthrow of the mighty Babylonian Empire. Babylon was "a gold cup in the Lord's hand," by which He made Judah and the other nations of the Near East drunk with His wrath (51:7). However, the Lord had also appointed a day in which Babylon would drink the cup of His judgment (51:39).

Babylon's hordes invaded Judah from the north and spread terror and destruction throughout the land of Palestine. Now appropriately the Babylonians would experience defeat at the hands of an invincible northern invader (50:3, 9, 41; 51:48). The Medes, along with their allies from the northern regions of Ararat, Minni, and Ashkenaz, would sweep over the land of Babylon like locusts and strike terror into the hearts of Babylon's once powerful warriors (51:11, 27-32). Babylon would be reduced to an uninhabited heap of ruins (50:3, 12-13, 39; 51:26, 37, 43) like Sodom and Gomorrah (50:40). In that day her idol gods, including her most prominent deity Bel/Marduk, would be put to shame before the angry judgment of the sovereign Creator of the universe (50:2, 38; 51:15-19, 44, 47, 52).

Excursus on the destruction of Babylon. Though the Persians are not specifically mentioned in Jeremiah 50-51, the references to the Medes indi-

---

28. Only the oracle against the Arab tribes identifies the Lord's instrument of judgment as Nebuchadnezzar (49:28, 30).

cate that these chapters look forward to the conquest of Babylon by the Medo-Persian Empire in 539 B.C. However, the portrayal of the Babylonian downfall and utter desolation is difficult to reconcile with the facts of history. Cyrus's takeover of the city was relatively peaceful and even welcomed by some Babylonians. The city was not destroyed in the manner depicted by Jeremiah. How is one to explain this apparent failure of prophecy? It is possible that the description of Babylon's fall is stereotypical and exaggerated, in which case the termination of the Chaldean Empire in 539 might satisfy its poetic and hyperbolic imagery. However, it is more likely that the portrayal of Babylon's fall transcends this historical event and anticipates the final destruction of those nations that oppose God. In this case the historical city of Babylon takes on symbolic value and represents all hostile nations, including those of the endtimes. For further discussion, see remarks on Isaiah 13-14.

As in earlier oracles, emphasis is placed on the Lord's direct involvement in Babylon's fall. Because of His desire for vengeance (50:15, 28; 51:6, 11, 36) He planned and solemnly decreed Babylon's fall (50:45; 51:12, 14, 29). He would stir up and formally commission the northern armies as His instrument of judgment (50:9; 51:1-2, 11, 20-23, 53). Even though this army is described in detail (50:41-42), the Lord is the energizing force behind it and would attack Babylon like a raging lion and bring about her destruction (50:25, 44; 51:24-25, 39-40, 47, 52, 55-57).

The primary reason for Babylon's doom was her arrogant opposition to God (50:11, 14, 24, 29-32). This hostility took tangible expression in the Babylonian's mistreatment of God's people (50:11, 17-18, 33; 51:24, 34-35, 49) and their lack of respect for His Temple (51:11). Like the cruel Assyrians before them, the Babylonians had come like a mighty lion and crushed the bones of God's people (50:17). Nebuchadnezzar devoured Judah like a serpent swallows its prey (51:35). As they gloated over God's defeated people and plundered their wealth, the Babylonians resembled a frisky heifer and a neighing stallion (50:11). They must be repaid for their cruel and excessive treatment of God's people (51:24, 49).

Babylon's fall would bring relief to God's exiled people. The Lord would release them from their captors (50:33-34), demonstrating that He had not forsaken them (51:5) and that He was concerned that they be vindicated (51:10-11). Released from their prison in exile, they would return to Jerusalem (51:50) and experience the Lord's renewed favor (50:4-5, 20).

To emphasize the certainty of Babylon's doom, Jeremiah provided the exiles there with an object lesson of the city's judgment (51:59-64). He sent a scroll to Babylon, on which was written God's decree of judgment against the city. He instructed Seraiah son of Neriah, the one who took the scroll to Babylon, to read it before the exiles, give a short prayer, tie a stone to the scroll, and throw it into the Euphrates River. Seraiah was then to declare, "So will Babylon sink to rise no more because of the disaster I will bring upon her. And her people will fall."

Future hope for the nations. The book of Jeremiah makes very few positive statements about the future of the nations. The Lord spoke of a day when the nations would give God praise and honor because of His great deeds on Jerusalem's behalf (33:9). Four of Jeremiah's oracles against the nations include brief statements about the future restoration of the particular nation under discussion. Despite the disaster that was about to fall on Egypt, God announced that it would someday be "inhabited as in times past" (46:26). He also promised that He would personally "restore the fortunes of" the Moabites (48:47), Edomites (49:7), and Elamites (49:39). The other oracles contain no such positive statements. There is no apparent reason that Philistia, the Aramean states, and the Arab tribes are given no encouraging word. However, the omission of any future hope is understandable in the case of Edom and Babylon, for the crimes of these nations were regarded as excessive, so much so that both are viewed elsewhere as representative of all those hostile nations that oppose God and His people.

A THEOLOGY OF LAMENTATIONS

The book of Lamentations was written in the aftermath of Jerusalem's destruction by the Babylonians in 586 B.C. Many of the people of Judah had either been slaughtered or carried away into exile. Out of the smoke of judgment the author, traditionally identified as Jeremiah, lamented the nation's downfall, acknowledged her sins as the reason for the tragedy, and cried out to God for mercy and restoration. His prayers provide the faithful of all ages with a model of how God's people should approach the Lord after they have experienced His discipline. Although not a theological treatise, this book contains several profound theological insights, illustrating again that it is often in the midst of a crisis that one seriously reflects on and learns the most about God's character and His relationship to His people. The theological message of Lamentations may be summarized as follows: God's angry disciplinary judgment of His people, while severe and deserved, was not final. Even in the aftermath of judgment, Judah's loving, compassionate, and faithful God remained the source of the nation's future hope for restoration.

GOD'S ANGRY JUDGMENT

God as judge. Though the Babylonian hordes had invaded the land and destroyed Jerusalem, the author of Lamentations recognized that they were mere instruments of God's wrath (1:14-15). Over and over again he affirmed that the Lord Himself had decreed (1:17; 2:17; 3:37-38) and sent the calamity (1:5, 12-15; 2:1-8; 3:1, 43-45; 4:11). The Lord had become the enemy of the nation (2:4-5) and had brought "the day of his fierce anger" down on it (1:12).

According to 2:17, this outpouring of divine judgment should not have been a surprise to God's people, for He had decreed it long before. Reference is made here to the warnings that the Lord delivered by His prophets throughout Israel's history, beginning with Moses (Lev. 26; Deut. 28) and culminating with Jeremiah and other late preexilic prophets. The basic message of the prophets had remained the same from the time of Moses: Obedience would result in God's blessings of security and prosperity; disobedience would bring the divine curses of drought, invasion, defeat, and exile. Because of its sin, Judah had experienced the covenant curses in full force.

In his portrayal of God as judge, the author emphasized the Lord's anger (1:12; 2:6) and its destructive consequences. Using a variety of metaphors, he likened the Lord's judgment to being engulfed by fire (1:13; 2:3), entrapped in a hunter's net (1:13), trampled like grapes in a winepress (1:15), shot by an arrow (2:4; 3:12-13), afflicted by an illness (3:4), imprisoned in a dark dungeon (3:2, 6-8), attacked by fierce predators (3:10-11), and ground into the dust (3:16).

The effects of judgment. Perhaps in an effort to motivate a positive divine response to his petitions for mercy, the author described Jerusalem's and the nation's plight with great vividness and detail. Though Jerusalem had once enjoyed prestige, she now suffered the humiliation of defeat. The hymns of Zion described the city as the "perfection of beauty" and the "joy of the whole earth" (2:15; cf. Ps. 50:2 and 48:2, respectively), but her enemies now heaped insults on her and gloated over her defeat (Lam. 1:7; 2:15-16). She who had once been like a queen was reduced to a slave (1:1). She was like a widow (1:1) with no one to comfort her (1:16-17, 21). Her children, once considered as precious as gold, were now treated like common household vessels (4:1-2). Throughout the city and the land atrocities abounded. Many had perished by the sword (2:21; 4:9) or been carried into exile (1:3, 5, 18). Women had been raped (5:11),[29] prominent leaders publicly humiliated (5:12), and young men forced to perform harsh labor (5:13). Many of the unfortunate survivors, including infants, were slowly dying from starvation (1:11, 19; 2:11-12, 19; 4:9; 5:9), while some even ate their own children in desperation (2:20; 4:10; cf. Deut. 28:53-57). The people were like orphans and widows, two of the most economically destitute groups in ancient society (Lam. 5:3). God was no longer listening to their prayers (3:44) and they were regarded as "scum and refuse" in the sight of other nations (3:45). In some ways their punishment was worse than Sodom's, for that ancient evil city had at least been reduced to ashes suddenly and had not been forced to die a slow, agonizing death (4:6).

The religious and civil institutions that had given the nation stability were in shambles. Judah's religious feasts had ceased (1:4; 2:6) and pagan soldiers had even polluted the Temple (1;10; 2:7) and slaughtered priests and prophets (2:20). Divine revelation through the prophets had come to an end (2:9),[30] a fitting pun-

---

29. The parallelism of 5:11 is a prime example of intensification, a fairly common Hebrew poetic technique. The first line describes a horrible stituation—women had been ravished in the very capital of the land. However, the second line intensifies the first by describing something worse—even *virgins* had been raped, not just in Jerusalem, but *throughout the land.*

30. Though Jeremiah constituted an exception to this, one should recall that his prophetic ministry in Jerusalem took place primarily before the downfall of the city and that he was forced to accompany a group of Judahite refugees to Egypt shortly after the city fell (see Jer. 39-44).

ishment for a society whose people had placed their trust in the messages of false prophets (2:14). The civil leaders were humiliated (4:7-8; 5:12) and taken into exile (2:9). Even the Davidic king, to whom the people had looked for protection, had been captured (4:20).[31]

The reason for judgment. The author made no attempt to justify the nation, nor did he accuse God of unfair treatment. He acknowledged that the nation's punishment was deserved due to its sin and rebellion. Jerusalem's "many sins" (1:5, 22) had made her unclean (1:8-9), like a woman ceremonially defiled during menstruation (cf. Lev. 15:19-20, 24-26; 18:19; Ezek. 22:10, where the same word translated "unclean" in Lam. 1:8 also appears). Three times the nation's sins are referred to as rebellion against the Lord (1:18, 20; 3:42). To complain about God's punishment would be inappropriate (3:39), for He is righteous (1:18) and just (3:34-36).[32]

The author specified very few sins. He alluded to the injustice that had permeated Judahite society (3:34-36), as well as to the nation's trust in foreign alliances (4:17). He referred directly to the violent deeds of certain prophets and priests (4:13) and mentioned the misleading promises of the false prophets, which the people found so attractive (2:14).

The basis for the false prophets' messages of hope was the doctrine of Zion's inviolability, the belief that Jerusalem could not be destroyed because it was the dwelling place of God Himself (cf. 4:12, which appears to allude to this doctrine). While the inviolability of the city was a theological ideal expressed in the Zion hymns (cf. Pss. 46, 48, 76), it was perverted by the false prophets. They transformed the ideal into an unconditional promise and ignored the moral-ethical prerequisites for the realization of the ideal. Jerusalem's fall in 586 B.C. exposed their false assurance and illustrates a theological truth of Scripture: Sinful and rebellious people, even if outwardly associated with the covenant community and the promises of God, should not presume on His protection.

THE HOPE OF RESTORATION

Despite the horrors of God's judgment and the pathetic condition of Jerusalem and the people, hope for the future was not abandoned (3:21). Judah's God was the eternal king (5:19), the "Most High" God (3:35, 38) who resides in heaven (3:41, 50, 66) and exercises sovereign control over the affairs of men. Judah's destiny lay in His hands. If He so willed, the nation could again experience His bless-

---

31. Reference is made here to Zedekiah, who was captured while fleeing from Jerusalem, forced to watch the execution of his sons, blinded, taken to Babylon, and imprisoned (2 Kings 25:4-7; Jer. 52:7-11).

32. The word translated "complain" (*'ānan*) in 3:39 does not refer to lamentation such as the author expresses in this book. The verb is used in only one other passage, Numbers 11:1, where it describes the Israelites' complaints against God in the wilderness. It aroused His anger and brought severe punishment on the people. In the context of Lamentations 3:39, the verb probably refers to accusations of unjust treatment against God.

ing. The proper response to God's judgment was genuine repentance and sincere prayer for the restoration of His favor (3:40-42; 5:21).

The people's very existence was a positive sign. The Lord could have totally destroyed the nation, but instead He preserved some through the day of judgment. The author interpreted this as an expression of God's love, compassion, and faithfulness (3:22-23). The word translated "compassions" draws attention to God's emotional response to the needs of His people.[33] The terms rendered "love" and "faithfulness" are closely related in meaning.[34] They refer to God's devotion to His covenant people and to the promises He made to them. Through His covenants with Abraham and David the Lord had committed Himself to the nation and not even the rebellious spirit of the people could break that bond. Though the Lord must discipline sinners and purge out evildoers from the covenant community, His ideal for the nation would be ultimately realized.

Assured that the well of God's devotion and compassion had not run dry, but was still supplying the daily needs of His people, the author expressed his trust in God. He affirmed that the Lord was his "portion" and declared that he would "wait" in faith for the Lord's salvation, strengthened by the knowledge that the "Lord is good to those whose hope is in him" (3:24-26). With the metaphor "portion" the author compared the Lord to an allotment of landed property, which provides the necessities of life (cf. Pss. 16:5-6; 73:26; 119:57; 142:5).

The author's great faith gave him a proper perspective on suffering and discipline. He was able to declare, "It is good for a man to bear the yoke while he is young. Let him sit alone in silence, for the Lord has laid it on him" (3:27-28). He could say this because he realized that the Lord's discipline is neither arbitrary nor permanent (3:31-39). Though the Lord does not delight in sending affliction, His justice demands that sin be punished. When such discipline comes, one must accept it without complaint (3:28-30, 39) and turn to the Lord in repentance (3:40-42).

VENGEANCE ON ENEMIES

His belief in God's just character provided the basis for the author's prayers for divine vengeance against the nation's enemies. Though Judah's demise was brought about by God, the surrounding peoples responded improperly by arrogantly gloating over the nation's tragic downfall (1:21; 3:63) and taking advantage of its vulnerable position (3:52-54). Edom in particular had rejoiced over Judah's defeat (4:21) and exploited her weakness (cf. Ps. 137:7; Obad. 10-14). The author asked the Lord to repay Judah's enemies for their misdeeds (1:21-22; 3:64) by bringing a destructive curse (or formal decree of judgment) down on them

33. In the human sphere the word *rahămîm* describes the emotional attachment of Joseph to his brother Benjamin (cf. Gen. 43:30, where NIV's "deeply moved" literally reads, "his compassion was stirred") and of a mother for her baby (1 Kings 3:26).
34. The terms *hesed* and *'ĕmûnâ* also appear together in Pss. 89:24; 92:2; 98:3; and Hos. 2:19-20.

(3:65-66).[35] Though Edom had rejoiced over Judah's fall, someday the tables would be turned (4:21-22). Judah's period of affliction and exile would come to an end, but Edom would be punished for her sins. Edom would be forced to drink from the cup of divine judgment and her subsequent humiliation would be that of a drunkard who shamefully exposes himself.[36]

35. The proper translation and interpretation of Lamentations 3:65a is unclear. The word translated "veil" by NIV (*meginnāh*) occurs only here. Some understand it to mean "covering" or "veil" and then interpret this as a reference to divine hardening, which precedes and leads to judgment. See, for example, R.K. Harrison, *Jeremiah and Lamentations* (Leicester: InterVarsity, 1973), p. 232. Others prefer "anguish" or "confusion" (cf. Delbert R. Hillers, *Lamentations*, Anchor Bible [Garden City, N.Y.: Doubleday, 1972], pp. 53, 60).

36. The comparison of judgment to drinking an intoxicating beverage is a common one in prophetic speech (see Hillers, *Lamentations*, p. 93, for a list of pertinent texts), probably because one of the effects of judgment (confusion) would resemble the stumbling of a drunkard. The motif of indecent exposure is combined with that of drunkenness in Habakkuk 2:15-16 as well as here.

10

A THEOLOGY OF EZEKIEL AND DANIEL

EUGENE H. MERRILL

A THEOLOGY OF EZEKIEL

Ezekiel, the great prophet of the Exile, delivered his messages of calamity and comfort between 592 B.C. and 570 B.C. according to his own chronological information.[1] He had gone into Babylonian captivity in the second wave of deportation in 598 and evidently spent the remainder of his life among the exiles in Mesopotamia in the vicinity of the Chebar River.[2] Only in vision did he return occasionally to his homeland to witness the tragic defection of his people from their covenant responsibilities, a defection that resulted in the destruction of Jerusalem in 586 and the third and climactic phase of deportation of the Jewish population.

As a priest as well as a prophet, Ezekiel was particularly concerned with matters of Temple and cultus as expressions of Israel's special relationship with Yahweh. Thus he encountered Yahweh in epiphany and theophany, he excoriated the religious leadership of Jerusalem for its abuse of the fabric and forms of worship, he lamented the idolatry that was carried out even in the sacred Temple, and

---

1. See Ezekiel 1:1-2 and 29:17 respectively. For defense of these dates, see Anthony D. York, "Ezekiel I: Inaugural and Restoration Visions?" *Vetus Testamentum* 27 (1977): 82, 92-93. York, however, prefers 567 B.C. as the actual (if unstated) terminus ad quem.
2. The Hebrew n^{e}har k^{e}bār ("river of Chebar") reflects the Babylonian nār kabari and modern šaṭṭ en-nîl, a canal that flows from the Euphrates near Babylon east to Nippur and then back to the Euphrates. See Walther Zimmerli, *A Commentary on the Book of the Prophet Ezekiel, Chapters 11-24* (Philadelphia: Fortress, 1979), p. 112.

he viewed the departure of the glory of Yahweh from the Temple as tantamount to His departure from the land and the rupture of the covenant between Him and His people. On the other hand, the prophet described the entire eschatological restoration of Israel in terms of the rebuilding of the Temple, a theme obviously close to the heart of a priest.

The dashing of the hopes of a continuing Davidic dynasty caused by the collapse of the kingdom of Judah gave rise to the understanding that the unconditional promises of Yahweh to Abraham and David must find their fulfillment at a later, postexilic time. However, the simultaneous rise of great imperialistic powers like Babylonia and Persia offered little encouragement that Judah could ever regain the glory of the days of David and Solomon through ordinary means or in the flow of the currents of ordinary history. What was needed was a radical overthrow of the existing structures of human government in favor of the universal kingdom of God over which the scion of David would reign. This must be accomplished by Yahweh Himself and only at the end of time, in the "day of Yahweh" when all human institutions would fall under divine dominion.

This cataclysmic way of perceiving the eventual sovereignty of Yahweh and the elevation of his people Israel as the head of all the nations is best described as apocalyptic.[3] The term may be used with reference both to the means by which God's purposes are achieved and to the type of literature describing them. Since apocalyptic, among other things, gives universal scope to the activity of God in history (activity necessitated in the face of human incapacity and despair), it is understandable that apocalyptic intensified precisely in the context of the Exile. At no earlier time, including the fall of Samaria in 722 B.C., had the covenant promises been in such jeopardy, for until 586 there remained at least the Temple and the Davidic kingship. But the Babylonian onslaughts hammered away at these promises until it was clear that the only hope of the fulfillment lay in the eschatological day of Yahweh's ultimate triumph.

The message of Ezekiel is therefore couched largely in apocalyptic form and imagery. There had been precursors of this as early as the prophecies of Joel[4] and Isaiah,[5] to be sure, but not until Ezekiel was the essential message one of apocalyptic

3. For Ezekiel as apocalyptic and the characteristics of apocalyptic thought and literature in general, see D. S. Russell, *The Method and Message of Jewish Apocalyptic* (Philadelphia: Westminster, 1964), pp. 89-90, 104-39.

4. H.W. Wolff asserts that "Joel stands at the threshold between prophetic and apocalyptic eschatology," but he dates Joel "in the century between 445 and 343" (*A Commentary on the Books of the Prophets Joel and Amos* [Philadelphia: Fortress, 1977], pp. 12 and 5, respectively). Douglas Stuart, however, describes Joel as "an apocalypticist" but allows apocalyptic (and Joel) to be as early as the beginning of the seventh century (*Hosea-Jonah*, Word Biblical Commentary, vol. 31 [Waco, Tex.: Word, 1987], pp. 225-27). For an even earlier date, see A. F. Kirkpatrick, *The Doctrine of the Prophets* (London: Macmillan, 1892), pp. 57-72.

5. Isaiah 24-27 is universally regarded as apocalyptic, so much so that it has to be denied to Isaiah by scholars who advocate exilic or postexilic origins of apocalyptic. (See Russell, *The Method and the Message of Jewish Apocalyptic,* p. 91.) For a defense of the Isaianic authorship of these chapters and hence pre-Ezekielian apocalyptic, see Edward J. Young, *The Book of Isaiah,* 2 vols. (Grand Rapids: Eerdmans, 1969), 2:146-47.

concern. Daniel, Ezekiel's younger contemporary and fellow exile, also expressed Israel's hope in these categories as did the illustrious postexilic prophet Zechariah. The New Testament message of apocalyptic consummation fell from the lips of Jesus Himself and found climactic triumphalism in the Patmos vision of the apostle John, the book of the Revelation.

Because Israel's hope lay only in Yahweh and not in human power, Ezekiel focused on Yahweh's Person and reputation in a way unparalleled in the Old Testament. In fact, the phrase "you will know that I am the Lord" or "they will know that I am the Lord" or the like may well be the central theological theme of the book.[6] Above all, Ezekiel was concerned to demonstrate that Yahweh is not only the God of Israel (or Judah) but also of all the earth and that His faithfulness to His covenant pledges to His own people will attest to His sovereignty over all creation in the day when He vindicates them. Everything He has done in history, all His powerful acts in the present, and the magnificent displays of His glory to come attest to who He is and what He has done so that all men everywhere will confess His incomparability and uniqueness.

GOD: HIS SELF-DISCLOSURE

This central focus of the prophet emerges at the very beginning of his treatise, in Ezekiel 1-3. In one of the most awesome disclosures of the divine glory in all of Scripture, Yahweh, in intensely apocalyptic imagery, manifests Himself to the prophet in the prophet's thirtieth year, the fifth year of Jehoiachin's captivity (i.e., 592 B.C.). Ezekiel asserted that he "saw visions of God" (1:1), visions accompanied by the interpretive word (v. 3) and by the energizing power of the Lord (v. 3).

These three elements—vision, word, and power (or hand)—appear pervasively in Ezekiel's descriptions of his call and of Yahweh's self-revelation.[7] The vision is the abstract message itself, the word is its interpretation, and the power is the means by which the message is effectually communicated. For the hand of the Lord to come on the prophet is to assure him of the Lord's affirmation and enablement.

The epiphany of Yahweh—His coming in transcendent glory—was in the form of a fiery cloud, a form characteristic of such manifestations elsewhere in the Bible. The apocalyptic elements of the epiphany, however, first appear in Ezekiel. They consist of anthropoid living beings that have four wings and four faces— those of a man, a lion, an ox, and an eagle (1:4-11). Otherwise described as cherubim (Ezek. 10:1-14, 20), it is clear that these creatures represent the invisible God.[8] It was they who overshadowed the Ark of the Covenant in the Tabernacle (Ex. 25:16-22) and who indeed may have been the throne and char-

6. Thus Walther Zimmerli, "Knowledge of God according to the Book of Ezekiel," in *I Am Yahweh,* ed. Walter Brueggemann (Atlanta: John Knox, 1982), p. 88.

7. H. Van Dyke Parunak, "The Literary Architecture of Ezekiel's *Mar' ôt 'Ĕlōhîm,*" *Journal of Biblical Literature* 99 (1980): 62-66.

8. Ralph H. Alexander, "Ezekiel," in *The Expositor's Bible Commentary,* ed. Frank E. Gaebelein (Grand Rapids: Zondervan, 1986), 6:757.

iot on which the Lord figuratively rested (Ps. 80:1; 99:1).

The idea of the cherubim as a royal chariot is suggested by their rapid movement (Ezek. 1:12-14) and their association with omnidirectional wheels (1:15-21).[9] In fact, the life spirit of the creatures was in the wheels themselves, thus identifying them as one and the same (v. 20). Moreover, when Ezekiel later saw the glory of God in a vision, he saw that glory above the cherubim, riding as it were in the chariot they constituted (10:18-19; cf. 2 Kings 2:11-12; 6:17).

The thronelike nature of the cherubim is seen in the prophet's description of the appearance of "a man" (Ezek. 1:26) who sat on a throne above their heads (cf. Rev. 1:13). Such a being of indescribable brightness was identified as "the likeness of the glory of the Lord" (Ezek. 1:28). That is, it is the Lord who is thus enthroned above the cherubim, which are both His chariot and His throne. In the vision of Ezekiel 10 the prophet observes that "the glory of the Lord rose from above the cherubim and moved to the threshold of the temple" (v. 4). The cherubim as a throne is clearly important to their identification.

The complexity of this vision with all its symbolism notwithstanding, the purpose of the epiphany is clear: it is to introduce the living God of Israel and to magnify His terrifying glory. The people had sinned grievously against Him and even now languished in exile because of it. Now they must encounter this One whose trust they have violated and learn from Him what remedial steps to restoration must be taken.

Vision therefore leads to word, for bare epiphany, though it might inspire awe, offers no message of redemption or even of judgment.[10] With this in mind, the Lord revealed Himself in language (Ezek. 2:1–3:11). This is "the word that came" (1:3; 6:1; 7:1; 12:1; etc.). The message is that both houses of Israel had rebelled and must be confronted with their apostasy. The Lord would fill the prophet with His message (2:8–3:3; cf. Rev. 10:8-11), with words of "lament and mourning and woe" (Ezek. 2:10).

The intended initial audience was not the remnant of Judah left behind in Jerusalem but the captives among whom the prophet was numbered (3:4-6; cf. v. 11). They would not receive his message, the Lord said (3:7-9), but he as God's spokesman must speak (2:8) and must bear its tidings faithfully despite all obstacles.

Ezekiel's ability to do this was far exceeded by the intransigence and hostility of his hearers, so the Lord brought to pass the third element of the call and commission—He placed His hand on him (3:14; cf. 1:3; 8:1; 33:22; 37:1). The "hand of the Lord" is always a metaphor for His power.[11] In this case the hand lifted the prophet up (3:12; cf. 8:3; 11:24; 40:1; 43:5) to transport him to the place where

---

9. Moshe Greenberg, *Ezekiel 1-20,* The Anchor Bible (Garden City, N.Y.: Doubleday, 1983), pp. 56-58.

10. For the connection between word and deed as revelation, see Dale Patrick, *The Rendering of God in the Old Testament* (Philadelphia: Fortress, 1981), pp. 90-91.

11. *Theological Dictionary of the Old Testament,* s.v. by *yād,* P. R. Ackroyd, 5:418-23.

the captives lived (3:15) and to provide him encouragement despite the bitterness of his assignment (v. 14). When he was overcome by the anticipation of the task and the burden of being the watchman of the Lord (vv. 15-21), Ezekiel again was revived by the hand of God who raised him up (v. 22), revealed to him his glory (v. 23), and promised to fill his mouth with words when the time of proclamation came (v. 27).

ISRAEL: COVENANT VIOLATION

Though the technical language of covenant is sparse in Ezekiel, the notion of covenant is everywhere presupposed. The glorious epiphanic displays of Yahweh serve the purpose of introducing the covenant God, the sovereign to whom Israel and all the nations of the earth are accountable. The heinousness of Israel's sinful defection becomes all the more apparent in the light of Yahweh's glory and majesty (cf. Isa. 6:1-5). Indeed the very meaning of Yahweh's rebuke of Israel lies in the clear assertion that Israel has rebelled, a term that is central to covenant thought (cf. Ezek. 2:3-5; 3:5-9, 26-27).

Ezekiel described Israel's covenant disobedience under three rubrics: violation as harlotry, violation as idolatry or apostasy, and violation as the breaking of law or stipulation. He reminded his people that from the beginning their history had been one of unfaithfulness to their God. What they had done in recent times was little different from what their ancestors had done in the wilderness, in the days of Moses (20:1-32). In language filled with covenant overtones, the prophet rehearsed that dismal account.

From the day Yahweh had chosen them (20:5) and affirmed that He was their God, they had rebelled by rejecting the first two commandments of the covenant code (vv. 7-8; cf. Ex. 20:2-6). He had then threatened to disinherit them but for his own reputation's sake had forgiven them (Ezek. 20:9). They went on, however, to break the decrees and laws, particularly the sabbaths, so that the adult generation died in the wilderness. Even the younger ones rebelled later on with the result that the Lord promised ultimate exile of His people and the turning of the blessings of the covenant into meaningless ritual (vv. 23-25). Thus, from Moses until the day of the ruin of Jerusalem, the covenant people had refused to submit to their Lord. But just as Zedekiah had broken his covenant with Nebuchadnezzar and was punished for it (17:11-15) so Israel, having proved unfaithful to Yahweh, would suffer the consequences (vv. 16-19).

As already noted, one of the metaphors for covenant violation was harlotry,[12] a figure developed at great length in Ezekiel 16:1-59 and 23:1-49. In the former passage Israel is referred to as a native of Canaan, a descendant of Amorites and Hittites (16:3). She had lain exposed at birth until Yahweh took pity on her, took her to Himself, and made her His wife (i.e., made a covenant with her, v. 8). He then decked her out in sumptuous finery until she became celebrated far and wide for her

---

12. Walther Eichrodt, *Ezekiel: A Commentary* (Philadelphia: Westminster, 1970), pp. 210-12.

beauty (v. 14). It was then that she took up a life of whoredom and in violation of her covenant vows went after strange lovers including the Egyptians, Assyrians, and Babylonians (vv. 26-29).

Though Judah might claim that this indictment was directed only at Israel, Ezekiel is quick to point out that she was as guilty as her older sister, who had already gone into captivity. In fact, Judah was worse than her northern neighbor and even Sodom to the south (v. 46). The marital infidelity that had brought Israel such judgment would produce even more severe repercussions for Judah.

In far more graphic terms Ezekiel describes the two kingdoms as sisters from Egypt who from the beginning were harlotrous (23:1-3). The one sister (Samaria) was named Oholah ("her tent") while the other (Jerusalem) was Oholibah ("my tent is in her"). Both names suggest the covenant relationship of Yahweh to Israel, especially to the Southern Kingdom.

Oholah, because of her dalliance with the Assyrians, had already gone into exile (v. 9). Learning little or nothing from this, Oholibah also took up with not only the Assyrians but with the Babylonians as well, violating the covenant with Yahweh to form alliances with these pagan peoples. Again the result would be catastrophic. Judah would be shamefully exposed to the whole world (v. 29) and she would drink of the cup of her sister's deportation (v. 32). This was because of her harlotry, a figure interpreted by the prophet as desecration of the Temple and violation of the Sabbath, that is, repudiation of the covenant as a whole.

Covenant rupture occurred, in the second place, as a result of idolatry and apostasy. These two ideas cannot be dissociated because apostasy fundamentally is defection from truth. In the case of Old Testament Israel it was a falling away from the true and living God to worship (or as a result of worshiping) false gods, usually represented iconically.

In his first oracle concerning idolatry, Ezekiel addresses the mountains, hills, ravines, and valleys—all places where illicit worship was carried out—and predicts the overthrow of their religious paraphernalia (6:1-7). Their abominable practices would be decimated and the participants themselves slain among their very idols who, obviously, were incapable of protecting them (vv. 11-14).

That Israel's idol-worship was not just a form is clear from Ezekiel 14:3, where the prophet wrote that "these men have set up idols in their hearts." Their apostasy is therefore complete.[13] There is hope, however, for the individual who would separate himself from his idolatry and turn wholeheartedly to the Lord (v. 6). But if he persisted in his rebellion and went so far as to seek endorsement for his apostasy from a prophet, the Lord would destroy both the idolater and the prophet who encouraged him in his unbelief (vv. 7-11). Every member of the covenant community, epitomized by Jerusalem, would fall under the fearsome judgment of God

---

13. As C. F. Keil puts it, "God does not suffer those whose heart is attached to idols to seek and find Him" (*Biblical Commentary on the Prophecies of Ezekiel,* 2 vols. [Grand Rapids: Eerdmans, n. d.], p. 178).

because of the infamy of their abominations (22:1-5).

The most graphic illustration of these detestable practices is that of Ezekiel 8:1-18, where the prophet describes the desecration of the Temple of Yahweh. He had been transported in vision to Jerusalem (vv. 1-3) where he saw, in the Temple court, the "idol [that] provokes to jealousy" (v. 3). The precise identity of this deity is unknown, though it may have been the goddess Asherah.[14] The fact that it provoked the Lord to jealousy attests to what an affront it was to Him who described Himself as a "jealous God" (cf. Ex. 20:3), a God who tolerates no rival. Again covenant violation is, first and foremost, disloyalty to the sovereign God who alone has legitimate claim to worship.

Within the Temple itself Ezekiel saw a multitude of images depicting every form of creature (Ezek. 8:7-13). Their presence was in direct violation of the commandment that forbade the representation of any creature whatsoever in tangible form (Ex. 20:4-6). Ezekiel also saw, on the north side of the Temple, women weeping for Tammuz (Ezek. 8:14-15), the Sumero-Babylonian god of fertility.[15] That this was done at the gate of the house of the Lord suggests not only open and blatant idolatry but also the attribution to Tammuz of the blessings of fertility that only Yahweh could provide. In that sense it was a violation of the commandment prohibiting the use of the Lord's name in an empty manner, for what should have been ascribed to Him was ascribed instead to Tammuz.[16]

The worship of the sun by the religious leaders of Judah who turned their backs on the Temple (8:16) was the final exhibition of Temple desecration observed by Ezekiel. By paying homage to the sun, only part of the material creation of God, these apostates were perhaps guilty of breaking the fourth commandment, which demanded that the Sabbath be observed as a reminder that God had created all things (Ex. 20:8-11).

In total disregard of the great covenant principles they had sworn to uphold, God's people had taken to themselves other gods and other alliances. No wonder the Lord raised up Ezekiel and the other prophets to confront them with their apostasy. To make matters worse, however, many of the prophets themselves led the way into spiritual declension. It is true that in most cases they were self-appointed spokesmen with no message from Yahweh (Ezek. 13:1-7). They had covered over the fissures of Israel's crumbling walls of covenant security (v. 10), preaching peace where there was no peace (v. 16). At last these charlatans, with all the appa-

---

14. As Greenberg points out, the Hebrew word *semel* used here appears as *pesel* in 2 Kings 21:7, where the deity in view is Asherah (*Ezekiel 1-20,* p. 168). Second Chronicles 33:7, 15 combines the two—*pesel hassemel*—in referring to the same goddess. This is the idol set up in the Temple by Manasseh.

15. See especially Thorkild Jacobsen, *The Treasures of Darkness* (New Haven, Conn.: Yale U., 1976), pp. 47-63.

16. This interpretation finds support in Brownlee's suggestion that the article on Tammuz (i.e., "The Tammuz") indicates that it may be a title and therefore is referring to Yahweh by that epithet. In this sense the name of the Lord would indeed be taken in vain (William H. Brownlee, *Ezekiel 1-19,* Word Biblical Commentary, vol. 28 [Waco, Tex.: Word, 1986], p. 136).

ratus of their divination, would be exposed for what they were—the blind leading the blind—and would come to ruin (vv. 8-9, 17-21).

Finally, covenant violation manifested itself in simple disobedience of covenant stipulation. The Lord chided His people with the indictment "You have not followed my decrees or kept my laws but have conformed to the standards of the nations around you" (11:12). Reference to "decrees" and "laws" brings to mind the manifold stipulations of the Mosaic Covenant texts to which Israel had sworn obedience (Ex. 19:8).

Specific examples of these statutes appear in Ezekiel 22:6-12. Here the prophet charged the people with disregard of the laws concerning killing, respect for parents, care for the vulnerable and neglected, profanation of the Sabbath, and fornication and adultery, among other things. All this, he said, suggested that Israel had forgotten God (22:12). Can a people who do these things expect the blessing of the Lord? Can they continue to hope for inheritance of the land (33:23-26)?

GOD: HIS PROCLAMATION

Proclamation concerning Israel. God, revealed in theophany and epiphany as the glorious sovereign of Israel, had prompted His servant Ezekiel to draw attention to the covenant relationship that bound Yahweh to His people and to their egregious violations of its demands. Now it is important to look in detail at God's response to that covenant infidelity. This takes the form of four major themes: judgment, the remnant, restoration, and messianic kingship. Each of these is first of all viewed with reference to Israel alone. There will follow then a brief survey of God's messages to the nations of the earth, for they too are accountable to Him.

The Message of Judgment. Judgment is a pervasive theme of all the prophets of Israel, but none exceeds Ezekiel in the abundance and intensity of his messages of divine retribution. Moreover, none reiterates as much as Ezekiel the pedagogical purposes of the visitations of the Lord: "that they [Israel and the nations] might know Yahweh." Judgment, then, is not only retributive but redemptive. God's purpose in judgment is not to destroy the peoples He has created but to bring them back into harmony with His creation purposes for them.

The very first word of Ezekiel is one of judgment (4:1-3). By means of play acting the prophet was told to place an iron plate between himself and a drawing of the city of Jerusalem, thus representing the imminent siege of the city by the Babylonians. This is the first stage of judgment. Then he must lie on his left side for 390 days and his right for 40 days to suggest the length of the apostasy of Israel and Judah respectively and to offer hope in himself of an escape from its consequences (4:4-8).[17]

---

17. These numbers have defied solution to the present day. Merely to add 390 and 40 to 592, which appears to be the date of the oracle, or even to 586, the date of Jerusalem's destruction, seems to lead to little result. The two figures 390 and 592 added together would be 982 B.C. and 390 + 586 would be 976, neither of which has significance. The equations 40 + 592 = 632 and 40 + 586 = 626 also lack meaning. Perhaps the answer lies, as Zimmerli implies, in adding 390 to 40 and seeing in the total, 430, an analogy to the 430 years Israel spent in Egyptian sojourn (*Ezekiel*, p. 167). This would still not account for the 390 and 40 year figures, however.

The siege would produce, in the next place, famine and hunger (4:9-17). So severe would be the deprivation that human dung would be used as fuel to bake the bread. With proper abhorrence the prophet objected to this gross departure from the strict requirements of dietary law (4:14; cf. Lev. 11; Acts 10:14). In a gesture of grace the Lord relented and allowed cow's dung to be used instead. This too was unclean but relatively less so. The point is obvious. Judgment was inevitable and would be severe, but even in judgment there was cause for hope in a God who delights in mercy.

The judgment of siege would give way to the judgment of destruction. This took place, as is well known, in 586 B.C. and was attended by fire, sword, and exile. The human agent of the wrath of God was Nebuchadnezzar, king of Babylonia, who led his conquering armies west time after time until he, in the person of his commander Nebu-zaradan, finally captured Jerusalem and razed it. The description of this in Ezekiel is the subject of chapter 21. There the Lord speaks specifically of the king of Babylonia as His "sword" (Ezek. 21:3; cf. vv. 9-11, 19), the instrument that He controlled to such an extent that all nations must acknowledge it (v. 5). The people of Judah might try to disregard the sword (v. 13) but to no avail, for it would accomplish its destructive purposes. Only then would it be withdrawn from slaughter and returned to its sheath (vv. 17, 30).

The sword of conquest also appears in the dramatization in which Ezekiel cut off his hair, burned one third of it, put one third to the sword, scattered one third to the winds, and saved a remnant that itself was burned (5:1-4). The meaning is clear: "A third of your people will die of the plague or perish by famine inside you; a third will fall by the sword outside your walls; and a third I will scatter to the winds and pursue with drawn sword" (v. 12). All this is done so that "they will know that I the Lord have spoken in my zeal" (v. 13).

Judgment of fire, described in this passage, is echoed in greater detail in Ezekiel 15. Elsewhere Israel appears in the Old Testament under the metaphor of the vine (Ps. 80; Isa. 5:1-7; Jer. 2:21; Hos. 10:1), so it is singularly appropriate to speak of her destruction as that of a worthless scrap of wood. Broken and devastated as the wood already was because of Assyrian and Babylonian depredations in recent history, it was of little or no usefulness. How much less suitable would it be once it had been consumed in the fiery wrath of divine judgment (Ezek. 15:5). This parable of Jerusalem made clear the worthlessness of its disobedient citizens. They would perish in the flames of retribution, but even so some good would emerge, for "you will know that I am the Lord" (v. 7).

A similar metaphor appears in 20:45-49. There Judah ("the South") is likened to a forest in which every living tree would be devoured in unquenchable fire. Once more the ultimate truth would ring clear: it is Yahweh who had brought such judgment and not mighty Babylon. In death as well as in life He demonstrates His sovereignty over all.

The most devastating consequences by far of Judah's covenant failure was her depopulation by exile. Virtually all the political and religious leadership of the nation was uprooted and forced to go into ignominious captivity along with the cultural, physical, and material resources it controlled. As long as there was even a remnant of a kingdom with any descendant of David on its throne there was hope. Now Jerusalem, the very heart of the theocratic focus, lay in ashes and its weakling ruler Jehoiachin languished in Babylonian incarceration. Exile had effectively attested to the finality of covenant rupture, for how could the promise have meaning outside the land of promise?

The scene in which Ezekiel prophesied of exile by cutting off his hair (5:12) is fleshed out in other passages where devastation and deportation go hand in hand. Ezekiel 11:1-12 depicts, in graphic terms, the city of Jerusalem as a cooking pot and its inhabitants as meat (v. 3). The pot indeed would be heated but the people would not all remain there to be "cooked." Rather, they would escape the city only to encounter punishment by sword. Not all would die, of course, for some, including Zedekiah the king, would end up in Babylon (12:11-13; cf. Jer. 39:4-7). Others would be dispersed beyond Babylon to the ends of the earth (Ezek. 12:14). Only a remnant would survive to declare to the nations that Yahweh is God (v. 16).

Once more employing the figure of the vine, Ezekiel likens Israel to a plant rooted in fertile ground and abundant in produce (19:10-14). Among other fruit it yielded royal sceptres, kings and princes of power and renown. Violently uprooted because of its sin, that vine now struggled for survival in the dry and barren soil of exile. No longer could it produce a royal branch to rule the people of the Lord (v. 14).

The message of judgment is summarized by Ezekiel in the strongly apocalyptic language of "the day of the Lord."[18] Though not developed here as fully as in the writings of other prophets, the idea of that day as a day of cataclysmic intervention by the Lord is nonetheless unmistakable. The theme finds most lengthy expression in chapter 7.

First, Ezekiel, speaking of the imminent Babylonian conquest of Jerusalem, calls it "the end" (7:2-3, 5-6). To the covenant nation this shattering word must have suggested not only the end of the present political existence of the land but also the end of God's gracious redemptive relationship with her. Even Ezekiel seems to have shared this pessimistic view, for when Pelatiah, a prince of Judah, died, the prophet asked, "Will you completely destroy the remnant of Israel?" (11:12). The dismay of this awful word was not alleviated by its elaboration in the following verses. The end would be a day of doom (7:7), a time when God would pour out His wrath without pity (v. 9).

The city already was under siege, so the Day of the Lord was already present. It was too late for ordinary life to go on as usual. Indeed, it was a foregone conclusion that the routines of the Jerusalemites' existence would be dramatically reversed and that not one individual would remain unaffected. Even as the prophet spoke, the siege was underway and famine and plague were beginning to take their toll. All the

---

18. For a theological definition of the "day of Yahweh," see Gerhard von Rad, *Old Testament Theology,* 2 vols. (New York: Harper & Row, 1965), 2:119-25.

peoples' wealth was to no avail. They could not eat their precious metals and when the day of wrath had reached its climax they would in any case lose all they had to their captors. Worst of all, the Babylonian plunderers would invade the holy precincts of the Temple itself, desecrating and pillaging it (vv. 21-22).

The result would be dispossession of the peoples' land, profanation of their sanctuaries, silence from their prophets, priests, and elders, and the humiliation of their royal house. Only after this terrible Day of the Lord had come and gone would His people know that He is the Lord (v. 27).

Though the nation as a whole was guilty of covenant violation and thus suffered judgment as a collective entity, the prophet's message was addressed especially to those elements of the population which, as individuals, were particularly culpable. In other words, Ezekiel began to articulate for the first time in such unmistakable terms the principle that the individual is responsible for his own sin and must therefore bear its consequences on his own.[19]

Ezekiel launches his teaching on this important truth by quoting an ancient proverb: "The fathers eat sour grapes, and the children's teeth are set on edge" (18:2). This saying, the prophet adds, would no longer be quoted in the day of God's judgment for "the soul who sins is the one who will die" (v. 4; cf. Rom. 6:23). Then Ezekiel illustrates his point by declaring that the man who faithfully observes the covenant statutes of the Lord, thereby demonstrating his righteousness, will live (Ezek. 18:5-9). In line with New Testament soteriological theology, such a one "lives by faith" (Rom. 1:17; cf. Hab. 2:4).

If such a man had a wicked, unbelieving son, however, that son, despite his kinship with a godly father, would perish for his disregard of the mandates of a holy God (Ezek. 18:10-13). If the reverse was true—that an evil father had a religious son—that godly offspring could not be condemned because of his father's waywardness (vv. 14-18).

This principle, though clear from the beginning of Old Testament revelation,[20] had become smothered in the perversion of the concept of covenant solidarity. Israel did indeed enter into covenant relationship collectively and in a collective way was to serve the Lord as a vassal people. But, as Ezekiel (here and in 33:10-20) made so plain, the collective consists of the particulars. The nation is innocent or guilty to the extent that its citizens are. The wicked man who turns to righteousness will live (18:21), but the righteous man who turns to wickedness will die (v. 24). Therefore in that day of wrath the righteous individual will be vindicated before the Lord.

Especially singled out for condemnation are the idolators, whose dead bodies would be scattered round about their idols and altars (6:1-7, 11-14). These would be recognized as individuals and would, as individuals, answer for themselves

19. Joseph Blenkinsopp, *A History of Prophecy in Israel* (Philadelphia: Westminster, 1983), p. 199.
20. Th. C. Vriezen, *An Outline of Old Testament Theology* (Oxford: Basil Blackwell, 1958), pp. 320-25.

and their apostasy. Those whom Ezekiel had seen in vision in the Jerusalem Temple and throughout the city and who participated in the abominable practices he described (8:6-17) would suffer God's merciless retribution, from the elders on down (9:5-6). Those, however, who had refused to participate and who lamented the transgressions of their fellow citizens would receive a mark on their foreheads identifying them as righteous individuals (9:4, 6).

Israel's leaders, both religious and political authorities, carried a particularly heavy responsibility, for by their initiatives and example they set the course for the life of the nation. The judgment message, then, was focused on them in a sharper way than it was on the ordinary individual. For example, when one turned to idolatry and then sought prophetic support or endorsement for his aberrant worship, the prophet who collaborated was as guilty as he who sought his services, and both must suffer the consequences (14:7-11).

The wicked priests also had to expect divine displeasure. They did "not distinguish between the holy and the common," the Lord said (22:26), and they closed their eyes at the corruption of the covenant faith. Equally guilty were the "shepherds of Israel," that is, the kings and other political leaders. They had left off caring for the flock and were concerned only with their own well-being (34:2). They had not rescued the weak and straying but rather had brutalized them. The sheep therefore were scattered and had become defenseless against the wild beasts of the fields and mountains (34:5-6). The worthless shepherds would not go unpunished, however. They would be held accountable for failing to care for God's flock and would lose their privilege as His undershepherds (34:9-10).

Judgment then is clearly a major component of the theology of Ezekiel. God's people had sinned against the omnipotent sovereign to whom they pledged everlasting covenant fidelity. They violated the covenant terms by their idolatrous and apostate attitudes and by their repudiation of its claims on them. They must therefore expect the curses that accompany such egregious covenant defection. But the righteous individual—he who loved and served his God despite the drift of the nation as a whole—would find salvation in the Day of the Lord.

Could judgment, however, be the end of the matter? Were not God's promises unconditional and eternal? Indeed they were, so the prophet Ezekiel turned to the message of redemption, the word that there was glorious hope of restoration in the midst of calamity and exile.

The Message of the Remnant. That not all Judah would suffer destruction was a guarantee of restoration. A remnant would survive and would become the nucleus around which the covenant promises of Yahweh would continue.

The teaching concerning a remnant did not originate with Ezekiel, but the prophet of the Exile certainly added his own contribution to it. In 6:8-10 he points out that the Lord would spare some of His people in the day of His wrath and that in their captivity far from home they would remember Him. They would at last realize that the judgment which had come on them was because of their apostate idolatry, and having realized it they would deeply repent. They would understand that their predicament had been long before threatened and was calculated to bring them to the point that they might "know that I am the Lord" (v. 10).

The same sentiment is expressed in 14:21-23. After Yahweh had brought sword, famine, wild beasts, and plague on Jerusalem—thus decimating its population —some would survive to provide testimony to the prophet that there is hope in the midst of despair. The remnant that survived would become the catalyst around which the promise of restoration and future glory would find reality.[21]

The Message of Restoration. The greatest act of redemption in all Israel's long history was the Exodus. In that mighty event God had delivered the descendants of the patriarchs from bondage to a hostile sovereign in Egypt and had brought them to Sinai where they were constituted as a covenant nation, "a kingdom of priests" (Ex. 19:6), whose allegiance must now be to Him exclusively.

As the watershed of Israel's national life, this complex of salvation became the paradigm of God's continuing and future salvific grace on their behalf. As the need for deliverance rose from time to time the prophets harked back to the Exodus as the reference point on which all future deliverance could be based. In fact, the integrative theme of Isaiah 40-66 is the second Exodus that Yahweh would effect in order to rescue His people from Babylonia—the "second Egypt"—and bring them back to the land of promise.[22]

Ezekiel too utilized this motif extensively, nowhere more pointedly than in 20:33-44. In a reversal of imagery the Lord says He will lead His people into the desert of Egyptian bondage (here the desert of the nations, v. 35) where He will judge them for their sins.[23] Those who yield to His disciplinary grace He will bring into covenant with Himself as He had done at Sinai. Those who rebel, however, will be unable to enter the land of promise. When this second Exodus is completed and the people of the new Israel are in the land, they will confess before all the world that He is the Lord (v. 42) and will offer themselves and their gifts to Him as expressions of worship and praise.

By another metaphor, that of the shepherd and the sheep, Yahweh likens the regathering and restoration of Israel to the shepherd who goes far and wide in search of his scattered flock (34:11-16). No matter where they go the Lord will find them and will bring them back to the fold, that is, to the land of promise. There they will graze in bountiful pasturage under the beneficent watchcare of the Lord Himself. Lost, wounded, and sick as they might be, He will minister to them in justice.

The themes of regathering as sheep and of covenant merge in Ezekiel 34:25-31. The Lord promises to make a covenant of peace with His regathered sheep.

---

21. The authoritative study of the doctrine of the remnant is still that of Gerhard Hasel, *The Remnant* (Berrien Springs,Mich.: Andrews U., 1972).
22. See, for example, Bernhard W. Anderson, "Exodus Typology in Second Isaiah," in *Israel's Prophetic Heritage: Essays in Honor of James Muilenburg,* ed. Bernhard W. Anderson and Walter Harrelson (New York: Harper & Row, 1962), pp. 177-95.
23. Eichrodt, *Ezekiel,* pp. 279-80.

This is not the covenant that makes them His people but the solemn pledge to preserve and bless them as His people.[24] Thus they never need fear the wild beasts, and they can depend on the Lord to provide the showers of blessing (v. 26). The trees and ground will produce an abundance, hostile powers will never threaten, and never again will they have cause to be afraid. They will be the sheep of the great and good shepherd. They will be His people and He will be their God (v. 31).

Increase in the population of God's people will accompany increase in the prosperity of the land (36:10-11). Addressing the mountains of Israel, the Lord promises to cover them once more with men and animals and to make them the inheritance of Israel forevermore. The land, which seemed to her neighboring nations to be a devourer of its inhabitants, will no longer do so, and the people, once restored, will never again be uprooted from it (30:14-15).

The redeemed community will, in fact, rebuild the devastated towns and replant the abandoned fields (36:33-34). Like a new creation Israel will resemble the Garden of Eden. When all this comes to pass, the nations all around will marvel and will know beyond doubt that Yahweh, the God of Israel, has done these things by His own power (v. 36). This too will be the confession of Israel, His redeemed people (v. 38).

The restoration therefore will become the occasion for a demonstration of the sovereign might and faithfulness of Israel's God. It will occur not only for the benefit of His people but preeminently as a means of educating the nations as to who Yahweh is and what He demands of them. The regathering of Israel will cause the Lord to be enshrined among His people in such a way as to attract the nations (28:25) and also to preserve them when He brings these refractory neighbors to account (v. 26).

More important even than new habitations and new prosperity will be the new heart and new spirit that will follow the making of the New Covenant between Yahweh and reconstituted Israel. This concept is indeed central to Ezekiel's understanding of restoration, forming the bridge between its expression in historical, postexilic times and the times of the New Covenant in Christ, both now and in the eschaton. Restoration in the physical and material sense under Cyrus was important, but it was only typical of the fullness of restoration to be accomplished by the redemptive work of the Spirit who would restore the elect people by a totally new regeneration.[25] The ancient promises would remain intact as would the covenant requirements of the servant people. The differences now would be that the people would have a new heart and a new power that would enable them to carry out their covenant-keeping responsibility without fail.

Evidence for all this emerges from a variety of passages in Ezekiel. It is best to look first at the promise of the New Covenant and then to see how that covenant

---

24. Walter C. Kaiser, Jr., *Toward an Old Testament Theology* (Grand Rapids: Zondervan, 1978), p. 241.

25. William J. Dumbrell, *The End of the Beginning* (Homebush West, Australia: Lancer, 1985), pp. 95-96.

manifests itself in a new heart and a new spirit. Then it will be instructive to see how the redeemed and recreated community will live out its existence historically and eschatologically in time to come.

That the New Testament is integrally related to and flows out from the Old (i.e., the covenant at Sinai) is clear from Ezekiel 16:60-63. Here, speaking to Judah as the promiscuous and unfaithful daughter, Yahweh says, "I will remember the covenant I made with you in the days of your youth, and I will establish an everlasting covenant with you" (16:60). As the central recipient of this covenant of grace, Judah will be in a position to mediate salvation to her wayward sisters, Sodom and Samaria (v. 61; cf. vv. 53-54). Yahweh will take the initiative in this everlasting covenant, for He alone makes atonement for His people so that they can forever be free of the shamefulness of their sin (v. 63; cf. Jer. 31:31-34).

The reason for this remarkable transformation lies in the nature of the covenant and its benefits. It will be made with a people who, despite their degrading His holy name, will be redeemed by the Lord from their captivity for His own name's sake and not theirs (Ezek. 36:22). From all nations of the earth (not just Babylonia and thus not just in Old Testament times) they will come to their own land. There they will be cleansed from all impurity, will be given a new heart, and will receive the very spirit of God who will enable them to keep the covenant perfectly (vv. 24-27). Again the Lord reminds them, "I want you to know that I am not doing this for your own sake" (v. 32). Rather, it is for His own glory and for the sake of His own reputation that the Lord will fulfill this ancient pledge to His people to make covenant with them forever.

The new heart of flesh would prevent the regathered people from ever succumbing to idolatry again (11:18). They will come back to the land and remove from it every vestige of pagan worship for they will have undivided loyalty to their God (v. 19).

The New Covenant involves a new heart and a new spirit, to be sure, but it is deeply rooted in history and land.[26] The promise to Abraham was unconditional and included in its benefits a geographical inheritance—indeed, not just any territory but specifically the land of Canaan (Gen. 12:1, 7; 13:15-17; 15:18-19; 17:8). It is that land that is in view throughout Ezekiel's historical and eschatological purview, for unless that land is the focus of God's covenant fulfillment the ancient promises lose their intended significance.

The coalescence of the New Covenant and the renewed land is nowhere in the Old Testament better explicated than in Ezekiel 37. Here the prophet tells of seeing in vision a valley full of dry bones, the dry bones of long-dead people. He was instructed to inform these bones that the Spirit of God will enter them and energize them back to life again. To Ezekiel's amazement it comes to pass and in an instant the skeleton is joined to flesh and fiber and a living being—in fact an army of them—rises to its feet.

---

26. Elmer A. Martens, *God's Design* (Grand Rapids: Baker, 1981), pp. 242-47.

The interpretation follows: These bones are Israel, dead in sin and exile. The revivification is the gracious act of God in making His people alive again and restoring them to the land.[27] Moreover, this is one people, both Israel and Judah, and not just Judah brought back from Babylonian exile (vv. 15-17). That is, this is eschatological Israel, the nation gathered from the ends of the earth in the last times (v. 21). The people will become one in the land and will have only one king, the scion of David (v. 24). Never again will they fall into idolatrous disobedience for they are a cleansed people who will forever remain that way.

Both the apocalyptic language of these "restoration texts" and history itself teach that the regathering and reconstituting of Israel will occur in eschatological times. Though in a certain sense the dry-bones metaphor was fulfilled in the return of the Jews from Babylonian exile, attention to the full context of Ezekiel 37, including chapters 38 and 39, makes clear that at no time in history have all the conditions been met to give the prophecy full accomplishment.

On the other hand, the continuing presence of the evil nations with their unremitting hostility to the Lord and to His people precludes these passages from any reference to the eternal state, that day of God's unrivaled dominion. It is therefore necessary, in line with sound historical-grammatical exegesis as well as Old and New Testament contextuality, to locate these texts within the Millennium, that transition time in which all God's promises to Israel will be fulfilled and the eternal kingdom ushered in.[28]

One basis for grounding the restoration of Israel in the period of the Millennium is, as suggested, the clearly eschatological message of Ezekiel 38-39. Here the prophet describes an invasion of Israel, "a land of unwalled villages" (38:11), by a coalition of hostile powers led by "Gog, of the land of Magog, the chief prince of Meshech and Tubal" (v. 1).[29] This fearsome commander will come from the "far north" (39:2) with a vast army, but he will come not entirely of his own volition but as the instrument of the sovereign God of Israel (38:4). The purpose then is obvious: the Lord will use the nations of men to achieve His own self-glorification (38:16, 23; 39:7, 21, 27-28).

As Gog approaches the holy land, he will be joined by Persia, Cush, Put, Gomer, and Beth Togarmah. Together they will surround the defenseless peoples of Israel who have returned from all the nations of their diaspora to live in peace and safety in the land of promise. The intent of the attacking nations will be to plunder the land, to despoil it of all the wealth its citizens have accumulated in their exile and return.

27. F. C. Fensham makes a convincing case that the dry bones suggest a body left exposed as a result of a curse and that the resuscitation is a reversal of the curse (that is, a blessing). Israel had suffered the curse of covenant violation but will enjoy the blessing of covenant renewal ("The Curse of the Dry Bones in Ezekiel 37:1-14 Changed to a Blessing of Resurrection," *Journal of Northwest Semitic Languages* 13 [1987]: 59-60).

28. Walter C. Kaiser, Jr., "Kingdom Promises as Spiritual and National," in *Continuity and Discontinuity,* ed. John S. Feinberg (Westchester, Ill.: Crossway, 1988), pp. 300-303.

29. The identification of Gog and most of these other personal and place names has been debated to no successful conclusion. For various views, see Alexander, "Ezekiel," pp. 929-30.

None of this will surprise the Lord for He has long ago prophesied that this very thing would happen (38:17; cf. Isa. 5:26-30: 34:1-7; 63:1-6; 66:15-16; Joel 3:9-14). He also predicted that the vicious maraudings of Gog would fail. With cataclysmic judgment the Lord will shake His entire creation and all people on earth will tremble in fear. With direct intervention, in the mode of holy war, the divine warrior will pour out wrath from heaven and overwhelm those who seek to harm His own elect nation (Ezek. 38:22).

As the carcasses of Gog and his allies lie on the hills and plains of the Holy Land, the peoples of the earth will see in their annihilation the awesome power and glory of Yahweh—"they will know that I am the Lord" (39:6). In a dramatic reversal of events, the preserved of Israel will use the very weapons of their enemies for fuel (vv. 9-10). So vast will be the carnage that the people of the land will need seven months to bury the dead. The birds and animals of prey will be enlisted to help in the task of cleansing the land of the decaying flesh of the fallen. Like an enormous sacrifice the corpses will provide sustenance for these carrion-eating creatures until they are more than satisfied.

Again the purpose for all this is clear. Israel had gone into exile because of her sin (vv. 23-24) but had been brought back and delivered from destruction because of God's compassion. This mighty act of redemption will result in a spiritual metamorphosis, a change in heart that will cause Israel to forget her past unfaithfulness and to understand profoundly that He is the Lord their God (v. 28). That this far transcends the return from Babylonian exile or any other of history is clear from the pledge of the Lord that "I will no longer hide my face from them, for I will pour out my Spirit on the house of Israel" (v. 28).

This pouring out of the Spirit cannot be separated from the similar phrasing of 36:26-27, where Yahweh asserts, "I will give you a new heart and put a new spirit in you . . . and I will put my Spirit in you and move you to follow my decrees and be careful to keep my laws." Chapters 36 and 39 both describe this regenerating work of the Spirit in the context of the restoration of the dispersed of Israel to their land, a restoration couched in the language of the cosmic and eschatological intervention of God Himself (36:29-30, 34-36; 39:3, 21-24).[30] This is not a description of any of the returns to the land of historical record, including those under Zerubbabel and Ezra. It is a restoration of such a radical and final nature that it can be located only in the Day of the Lord, the final day of the establishment of His kingdom sovereignty.

The Message of Kingship. This finds support in Ezekiel 17:22-24 where Yahweh says He will take a cutting from a regal cedar and plant it on a high mountain. The diminutive shoot will itself become a giant tree, so impressive that all other trees will marvel at the God who can make so much out of so little. In this parable lies the truth that the remnant of Israel will be planted in the land and will become so mighty that it will outstrip the nation from which it sprang. This can refer only to eschatological Israel.

---

30. So Russell, *The Method and the Message of Jewish Apocalyptic,* pp. 190-91.

Further evidence is available in texts that speak of the renewal of Davidic king-ship in the last days. In a bitter denunciation of Zedekiah (Ezek. 21:24-27) the prophet cried out that his day had come, the day in which he must step aside and sur-render the throne. In his place will be a lowly man who will be exalted, a priest-king to whom the kingdom rightly belongs. This last phrase (21:27) is reminiscent of the blessing of Jacob to Judah: "The scepter will not depart from Judah, nor the ruler's staff from between his feet, until he comes to whom it belongs" (Gen. 49:10). That this messianic text refers to David and the Davidic dynasty is nearly universally main-tained.[31]

In a section describing the restoration of Israel in terms of the gathering of sheep (Ezek. 34), the prophet says in the words of Yahweh, "I will place over them one shepherd, my servant David, and he will tend them; he will tend them and be their shepherd. I the Lord will be their God, and my servant David will be prince among them" (vv. 23-24). In a sense Jesus, the Good Shepherd and the Son of David, is in view here, but the eschatological orientation of the whole passage removes the setting from the period of His earthly ministry in the first century to that of His second advent when He will come to sit on the throne of David.[32] In other words, the prophet looked to the millennial kingdom, whose full elaboration becomes apparent in the New Testament apocalypse (Rev. 20:4-6).

An even more striking case for the eschatological dimension of the kingdom is that of Ezekiel 37:24-28. Continuing the imagery of shepherding, the prophet speaks of David as the king, of full compliance with the covenant decrees of the Lord, and of everlasting occupation of the Promised Land. Most interesting is the promise of the Lord that "I will put my sanctuary among them forever. My dwelling place will be with them; I will be their God, and they will be my people. Then the nations will know that I the Lord make Israel holy, when my sanctuary is among them for-ever" (vv. 26b-27).

The emphasis on the sanctuary as the dwelling place of God among His peo-ple leads naturally to a brief consideration of Ezekiel 40-48, for here the prophet recounts in great detail the Temple that will be constructed in the last days. The sanc-tuary (i.e., the Temple) has already been identified as the sign of God's presence among His people (37:26-27). Now Ezekiel, who witnessed in vision the pattern and construction of the Temple to come, observes that it "is the place of [God's] throne and the place for the soles of [his] feet" (43:7). The Lord promised, "This is where I will live among the Israelites forever" (v. 7).

The Temple as the dwelling place of Yahweh will be the source of blessing for the whole world. From it, waters of healing refreshment will flow so that "where the river flows everything will live" (47:9). This is a picture of millennial blessing,

---

31. For a survey of the exegesis, see Zimmerli, *Ezekiel*, 1:447-48. Von Rad concedes that "the gen-erally accepted view is that the verses [Gen. 49:8-12] constitute a prophetic oracle referring to the kingship of David," though he equivocates on the matter (*Old Testament Theology,* 2:12).

32. Kaiser, *Toward an Old Testament Theology*, p. 241.

when the deserts will blossom like the rose and springs will erupt in the dry and thirsty land. Surrounding the Temple will be the land apportionments of the tribes. The old boundaries of promise will come into effect (47:15-20), and within them the tribes will take their places (48:1-29). The Temple will stand in the midst of the city, which in turn is between the allotments of Judah and Benjamin. Thus the Davidic Covenant promises will be fulfilled in the Prince who will spring from David to rule over God's people forever. No wonder the name of the city from that time on will be *Yahweh shammah*, "the Lord is there" (v. 35).

Proclamation concerning the nations. The second half of Ezekiel begins in chapter 25 with a series of oracles addressed to the nations surrounding Israel. In line with those of the other Major Prophets (and many of the Minor Prophets as well), these messages reveal the concern of the Lord not only for His own covenant people but also for the whole world. The God of Israel is also the God of the nations. In fact, the selection of Israel was for the express purpose of providing through it a servant people who would mediate the salvation of the Lord to all mankind.

The first oracle in the series concerns Ammon, the nation just east of central Palestine (25:1-7). Ammon, with Moab, traced its lineage back to Lot and his daughters, with whom he was involved incestuously (Gen. 19:38). This relationship by blood to Israel, descendant of Lot's uncle Abraham, made Ammon's rejoicing in the desecration of Yahweh's Temple all the more odious than it would have been otherwise.[33] In order, then, for Ammon to recognize the kingship of the Lord and His special favor toward Israel, Ammon will fall to the hordes of the east, presumably the Babylonians (Ezek. 25:4).[34]

Moab, brother of Ammon, falls next under the prophet's indictment (vv. 8-11). Along with Ammon, Moab will be overcome by eastern invaders this time because Moab disparaged God's chosen ones by likening them to all the other nations. This harks back to the judgment of the Abrahamic Covenant: "whoever curses you I will curse" (Gen. 12:3).

Next Ezekiel turns his attention to Edom, the land south of Moab and east of the Dead Sea (Ezek. 25:12-14). The same nation is addressed at the end of the series in a much longer passage (35:1-15) and for essentially the same reason— Edom's long-standing and bitter hostility toward Israel, her sister nation.

The particular occasion for God's judgment on Edom in Ezekiel 25 is the fact that "Edom took revenge on the house of Judah" (v. 12). This same act of hostility may be reflected in Amos 1:11 and Obadiah 10-16, but the historical event in view cannot be determined with certainty.[35] Nor is it necessary to do so, for the

---

33. Though this oracle (and the next three) are undated, the reference to the desecration of the Temple presupposes a date after 586 B.C.

34. This may be documented in Jeremiah 52:30 (as 582 B.C.) in an undated inscription of Nebuchadnezzar. See John Bright, *A History of Israel,* 3d ed. (Philadelphia: Westminster, 1981), p. 352.

35 For possibilities, see Eugene H. Merrill, *Kingdom of Priests: A History of Old Testament Israel* (Grand Rapids: Baker, 1988), p. 382.

theological message in this case is little affected by the specific historical point of reference.

The same circumstance is presumably in view in Ezekiel 35. There the judgment is forthcoming, says Yahweh, "because you harbored an ancient hostility and delivered the Israelites over to the sword at the time of their calamity" (v. 5). To this is added the information that it was Edom's intention to take possession of Israel and Judah "even though I the Lord was there" (v. 10). Edom's hatred of Israel was no less than hatred against God. The desolation of Israel will therefore embrace Edom as well (v. 15). This will cause Edom to "know that I am the Lord" (v. 15).

The prophet turns next to the southwest and addresses the Philistines (25:15-17). Like the Edomites they had taken revenge "with malice in their hearts, and with ancient hostility sought to destroy Judah" (v. 15). Again the historical referent is not clear, but the reason for judgment is: whoever offends the people of God can expect swift and sure retribution.

In a continuing clockwise direction, Ezekiel looks to the northwest and brings the Phoenician city-state Tyre within his purview. His oracle now divides into two sections, one addressed to the political entity itself (chaps. 26-27) and the other to the prince of Tyre (28:1-19). These should be considered separately.

The prophecy against Tyre is dated by Ezekiel "in the eleventh year" (26:1), that is, 586 B.C. That was the year Jerusalem fell to Babylonia, and Tyre's gleeful reaction to that tragedy elicited Yahweh's wrath against her (v. 2). Nebuchadnezzar, who had just devastated Jerusalem, would now march against Tyre and do the same there. After this proud and impregnable city fell, her neighboring states would compose a lament bewailing her unexpected and total collapse (vv. 17-18). Then the prophet himself sings a dirge over Tyre (27:3b-36) in which he rehearses that magnificent city's wealth and commercial success (vv. 3b-26a) but then proclaims the day of her destruction (vv. 26b-36).

He turns then to the ruler of Tyre, and in a poetic prophecy he first points out the boasting arrogance of the king (28:2b-5) and then his violent overthrow and death (vv. 6-10). He concludes with another song of lamentation (vv. 12b-19), which once more consists of a review of the past glories of the king (vv. 12b-15a), his temptation and fall (vv. 15b-16a), and his eventual dethronement and demise (vv. 16b-19). The language of this dirge is filled with reference to primordial themes, such as "Eden, the garden of God" (v. 13), the "guardian cherub" (v. 14), and expulsion from "the mount of God" (v. 16), so much so that one can hardly fail to see the fall of mankind underlying the fall of the ruler of Tyre.[36] This is likely the intent of the oracle, for all wickedness, whether in a ruler or a common man, finds its source ultimately in Adam, the "anointed cherub" who fell through pride. The oracle against the prince of Tyre becomes a theological state-

---

36. Though many scholars see the fall of Satan here, this is unlikely because the expulsion is from the Garden of Eden and not heaven. For arguments supporting this dirge as a reflex of Adam's fall, see J. Barton Payne, *The Theology of the Older Testament* (Grand Rapids: Zondervan, 1962), pp. 294-95.

ment about the origin of all rebellion and insubordination.

Just north of Tyre lay Sidon, the subject of the next word of the prophet (vv. 20-23). No explicit reason for the judgment is given, but since Sidon was a neighbor kingdom she is included in the summation of verses 24-26. With reference to Sidon, as well as the other contiguous nations, Yahweh said, "No longer will the people of Israel have malicious neighbors who are painful briers and sharp thorns. Then they will now that I am the sovereign Lord" (v. 24).

The purpose of the judgment of the nations is therefore most apparent: They have maligned God's own chosen people, thus cursing them (cf. Gen. 12:3), and in line with God's own covenant promise to the patriarchs these nations too must be cursed.

The prophet, however, has one more message to deliver, that to Egypt (Ezek. 29-32). Ambivalent in its relationship to the chosen people from the beginning—now a benefactor and then an oppressor—Egypt typified the world at large.

The first message dates to the tenth year (587 B.C.), the year just before Jerusalem fell (29:1-16). It is directed specifically to the pharaoh, who at that time was Hophra. During the last couple decades of Judah's history before her final fall, her kings had sought to lean on Egypt for deliverance, but Egypt had proved to be an unreliable ally, a broken reed (vv. 6-7; cf. Isa. 36:6). Because Egypt had wounded God's people instead of supporting them and because she boasted in her self-sufficiency, she like Judah would fall to invaders and be scattered across the earth (Ezek. 29:12; cf. 30:20-26). Even after her return she would never again be a mighty nation.

In the twenty-seventh year (570 B.C.) the Lord revealed to Ezekiel that Nebuchadnezzar, who had failed to conquer Tyre, would vent his frustration and rage on Egypt (29:17-20). Because the Babylonian was serving Yahweh (by fulfilling the prophecy of 29:1-16), he would achieve success and would appropriate the treasures of Egypt for his own use.[37] The sovereignty of Israel's God over all nations and rulers is thus attested once more.

In more apocalyptic language, Ezekiel again addresses Egypt with a word of judgment (30:1-19). The day of Yahweh is coming, a day of doom for Egypt and her allies. Nebuchadnezzar and his hosts are about to come down to destroy and disperse the peoples of the south. In the process they will rid the conquered lands of idolatry, burn the great cities to the ground, and once and for all reduce mighty Egypt to weakness. All this will be done so that "they will know that I am the Lord" (30:19).

Turning to the imagery of parable, Ezekile compares first Assyria and then Egypt to a towering cedar tree (31:1-18). Nourished by refreshing streams, the tree had grown so large that all the birds of the sky could nest in its branches and the beasts of earth could rest in its shade. No tree could rival it, not even those in the Garden of Eden. Alas, this giant plant, standing far above all others, became proud and so was delivered over to the feller who chopped it down. Never again would a

---

37. For historical details, see Bright, *A History of Israel*, p. 352.

386   Biblical Theology of the Old Testament

tree grow to such a height and breadth, for such a pride must never again assert itself.

This narrative of the rise and fall of mighty Assyria is intended, says the Lord, to show Egypt that she too, though then towering above the nations, would come crashing to the ground (v. 18). Once more the universal dominion of the Lord will be there for all to see.

In a lament oracle (32:1-16) dated to the twelfth year (585 B.C.) Ezekiel describes Egypt as already in its death-throes. Like a great sea monster she has been ensnared in the nets of Yahweh and will be drawn up on the shore. There her rotting carcass will be carrion for the birds and beasts and the cause of great consternation among all peoples of the earth. This net the Lord identified as Babylon (v. 11), His agent of wrath and destruction.

In one last message against Egypt (vv. 17-32), also in the twelfth year, the unrelenting theme of judgment and desolation continues. Ezekiel was told to wail for Egypt and her hordes, for she shortly would join the other great nations in the pit (vv. 18, 21). Assyria, Elam, Meshech, Tubal, Edom, the Sidonians, and many others were already there because of their arrogant use of terror. Egypt now was about to follow, for she was no better than the others (vv. 19, 28). She too has sinned against God by living autonomously and by refusing to recognize that He is Lord.

CONCLUSION

Fundamentally the theology of Ezekiel revolves around the bipolar themes of judgment and restoration. Judgment, to the prophet, was already a foregone conclusion, for he himself was living among the Jewish exiles in Babylonia and was reminded constantly that the state of affairs was a direct result of God's judgment on His wayward people. All that the earlier prophets had foreseen concerning Judah's defection and deportation had come to pass. All that remained now was for God to remember His timeless and unconditional promises and to restore His repentant remnant to their homeland and covenant task.

The ability to do this depended directly on the kind of God Israel confessed. Was He the God of Israel alone or of all the nations? Was His power limited to His disavowal of His people and His willingness to let them fall to Babylonia, or did it also include dominion over Babylonia and a deliverance of Judah from Babylonian control? To answer these questions, Yahweh revealed Himself to Ezekiel in theophanic splendor and glory almost unrivaled in the Old Testament. The picture of God that emerges from these stupendous self-disclosures is sufficient to demonstrate that He is the Creator, the omnipotent One, who can and will alter the whole course of events to effect the redemption of His own chosen ones.

This God has not acted capriciously in punishing His people with exile and death, for they have broken His covenant by their apostate and idolatrous behavior. All that has happened they richly deserve. But God also will not be capricious in salvation, for He has made an everlasting covenant with the people of Israel and for His own name's sake must create within them a regenerated heart and disposition to know and love Him. Once this comes to pass, they as a restored community can resume the covenant responsibilities to which they were originally called.

Restoration will take two forms or will occur in two phases, however. It will come to pass in history under the beneficent policy of Cyrus the Persian, but that is only a type, a foretaste, of complete renewal and reconstitution that must await the eschaton. Spiritual renovation, indeed, resurrection life, will be part and parcel of that day of grace. Israel, triumphantly recreated, will be the focus of Yahweh's dominion on the earth. Through her king, the Messiah of David, she will at last be a holy nation and kingdom of priests fit in every way to administer saving blessing to all the peoples of the earth. Those nations that now exist in rebellion against the Lord will be visited with awesome judgment until that day comes when they too will know that He is God.

A THEOLOGY OF DANIEL

The fall of Jerusalem, the destruction of the Temple of Solomon, and the deportation of the leadership and upper classes of Judah in 586 B.C. was the most devastating historical and theological event in all of Israel's and Judah's long history. And it evoked a most profound question: Who, indeed, is sovereign—Nebuchadnezzar and his Babylonian and Persian successors, who had brought the catastrophic judgment to pass, or the God of Israel who had either allowed it to happen or was powerless to prevent it?[38]

It fell to Daniel, a young deportee of the first phase of Babylonian conquest in 605, to address that question. After a lifetime of service in the Babylonian and Persian royal courts (from about 605 to 530 B.C.), he took pen in hand and as a ready scribe for the Spirit of God composed the treatise that bears his name, a theological reflection on Israel's (or Judah's) exile, the central theme of which is the very issue of sovereignty.[39]

One may analyze Daniel's approach under the rubrics of (1) the sovereignty of God, (2) the sovereignty of (fallen) man, and (3) the restoration of God's universal dominion. It is immediately apparent that the scope of Daniel's interests far transcends that of merely the covenant relationship between Yahweh and His chosen people, as important as that theme is in biblical theology generally and even in Daniel. Rather, the viewpoint is universal and cosmic. God is the Creator of all things, including mankind and the nations, and as sovereign over them He will someday overcome their rebellion and fallenness and bring them back under His gracious dominion. Israel, the people He elected to achieve this purpose historically, will indeed be restored to pursue it in the future, but not for her own sake. It is Yahweh

---

38. For this assessment of things, see Ralph W. Klein, *Israel in Exile: A Theological Interpretation* (Philadelphia: Fortress, 1979), pp. 1-8.

39. In support of this, see Eugene H. Merrill, "Daniel as a Contribution to Kingdom Theology," in *Essays in Honor of J. Dwight Pentecost,* ed. Stanley D. Toussaint and Charles H. Dyer (Chicago: Moody, 1986), pp. 211-25.

who will be exalted, and all the nations will be judged and then reclaimed as His worshiping subject.

THE SOVEREIGNTY OF GOD

The collapse and fall of both Israel and Judah notwithstanding, the book of Daniel makes crystal clear that the Lord God remains absolutely sovereign over human affairs. This is apparent in the present, despite political and religious conditions that might suggest otherwise, and in the future, when there would be no doubt in anyone's mind.

In the dramatic language of apocalyptic, language used even more extensively in Ezekiel, Daniel's fellow prophet of exile, Daniel first recounts the appearance of Yahweh in theophany (Dan. 10:5-9). This vision of the unspeakable glory of God established, to Daniel's satisfaction at least, that the God who claimed dominion had every right to do so, for His ineffable splendor alone was sufficient to attest to His reality and to His incomparability. Though many scholars identify this "man" clothed in linen as an angel,[40] perhaps Gabriel or Michael, the extravagance of the description and the comparison with other texts, particularly in the New Testament (cf. Rev. 1:13-16; 2:18), make certain that this Being is none other than divine.[41] The brilliance of His countenance and the thunder of His voice brought Daniel to his knees, to a position where he could hear and respond to the awesome revelation that accompanied and indeed was the occasion for the theophany.

This demonstration of God's sovereignty took place in the third year of Cyrus (i.e., 536 B.C.), but Daniel had already come to understand that fact through the long years since his uprooting from Jerusalem and arrival in Babylon. Thus he affirmed that the submission of Jehoiakim, king of Judah, to Nebuchadnezzar as early as 605 B.C. was something that was possible because "the Lord delivered Jehoiakim king of Judah into [Nebuchadnezzar's] hand" (Dan. 1:2). Nebuchadnezzar might (and no doubt did) attribute his success to his own great military prowess and to the power of his gods, but Daniel understood that it was Yahweh who was using mighty Nebuchadnezzar as His own instrument of judgment.

This conviction finds support in a positive way as well, for the God who delivered His people into Nebuchadnezzar's hand was well able to preserve and protect them there. He "caused the [Babylonian] official to show favor and sympathy to Daniel" (1:9); He gave to Daniel and his three young friends "knowledge and understanding of all kinds of literature and learning" (v. 17); and He revealed Himself and His purposes to Daniel in vision (2:19, 28), something even Nebuchadnezzar recognized (4:9, 19), as did the mother of Belshazzar (5:11-12) and Belshazzar himself (vv. 14, 16). At no time was Daniel more conscious of the

---

40. So, for example, Gleason L. Archer, Jr., "Daniel," in *The Expositor's Bible Commentary,* 7:123.

41. Robert D. Rowe, "Is Daniel's `Son of Man' Messianic?" in *Christ the Lord,* ed. Harold H. Rowdon (Leicester: InterVarsity, 1982), pp. 90-91.

sovereign protection of Yahweh than when he was delivered unharmed from the den of lions. Boldly he would proclaim to Darius the Mede, "My God sent his angel, and he shut the mouths of the lions" (6:22).

Perhaps the greatest evidence of Yahweh's lordship in Daniel's own experience lay, however, in his unswerving conviction that his God was the one who appointed and deposed the monarchs of human kingdoms. Because these kings and their subjects thought they were called to their office and given its privileges and responsibilities by their own gods,[42] Daniel's assertion that the God of Israel was in fact the originator and grantor of human authority was a tacit denial of any perceived role for the gods of the nations.

After Nebuchadnezzar told Daniel he had had a dream and then commanded Daniel to interpret it, the young prophet, in earnest prayer, first confessed that God "changes times and seasons; he sets up kings and deposes them" (2:21). He then revealed to the king that the import of his dream was: "You, O king, are the king of kings. The God of heaven has given you dominion and power and might and glory; in your hands he has placed mankind and the beasts of the field and the birds of the air. Wherever they live, he has made you ruler over them all" (vv. 37-38).

This delegation of dominion has striking parallels to the creation mandate in which God assigned to man the blessing and task to rule over all things as His own image or representative.[43] God has said to man and woman, "Be fruitful and increase in number; fill the earth and subdue it. Rule over the fish of the sea and the birds of the air and over every living creature that moves on the ground" (Gen. 1:28). Clearly, Nebuchadnezzar, even as a fallen and unbelieving pagan king, could enjoy the grace of God who allowed him to participate in the dominion mandate. He may have been the golden head of an image of human design (Dan. 2:38), but the image of human government is nonetheless suggestive of mankind created to be the image of God and to rule for Him on the earth.

The kingdoms of human creation will not last forever, Daniel points out, for the day will come when "the God of heaven will set up a kingdom that will never be destroyed, nor will it be left to another people. It will crush all those kingdoms and bring them to an end, but it will itself endure forever" (2:44). That eternal kingdom of God, associated with the restoration of all things, will be discussed later in this chapter.

In a second dream Nebuchadnezzar saw himself as a mighty tree that was cut to the ground and from the stump of which he proceeded as a brute beast grazing in the fields. In his dream he learned its purpose: that he might know that "the most High is sovereign over the kingdoms of men and gives them to anyone he wishes and sets over them the lowliest of men" (4:17).

---

42. For many examples, see Bertil Albrektson, *History and the Gods* (Lund, Sweden: CWK Gleerup, 1967), pp. 42-52.

43. Eugene H. Merrill, "Covenant and the Kingdom: Genesis 1-3 as Foundation for Biblical Theology," *Criswell Theological Review* 1 (1987): 295-308.

Obviously distressed, Nebuchadnezzar turned to Daniel for the full meaning of the dream and learned from the man of God that his kingdom would be taken from him but would be restored "when you acknowledge that heaven rules" (v. 26). A human monarch might rule and indeed may do so in line with the purposes of God, but he must recognize the source and limitations of his authority. The sovereignty of kings is a sovereignty derived from the King of kings.

Belshazzar, the son (i.e., successor) of Nebuchadnezzar, also learned that the true basis for the kingship of his illustrious predecessor lay in the disposition of Israel's God. Having been summoned by Belshazzar to decipher and interpret the mysterious message on the palace wall, Daniel pointed out to him that "the Most High God gave your father Nebuchadnezzar sovereignty and greatness and glory and splendor" (5:18) but that he had been deposed and stripped of his glory when "his heart became arrogant and hardened with pride" (v. 20). Kings rise and kings fall, all according to the dictates of the one true God of all men.

This truth—that Yahweh is Lord over all—was not merely a matter of theological assertion by Daniel, it also finds response in the confession of believers and unbelievers alike. In the former case an example is the confident affirmation of the three young Jewish men who were about to be cast into the burning furnace: "If we are thrown into the blazing furnace, the God we serve is able to save us from it, and he will rescue us from your hand, O king" (3:17). Even more striking are the testimonies of the pagan kings of Babylonia and Persia, for they epitomize, in their role as human rulers, the antithesis between the sovereignty of the God of creation and that of His fallen creatures who oppose His dominion over them. Thus, following the interpretation of his dream, Nebuchadnezzar cried out to Daniel, "Surely your God is the God of gods and the Lord of kings" (2:47). The power of Yahweh to save prompted this same king to confess, on the deliverance of the youths from the fire, "no other god can save in this way" (3:29).

Later, when he recounted his dream about the tree, Nebuchadnezzar publicly proclaimed concerning the Most High God: "How great are his signs, how mighty his wonders! His kingdom is an eternal kingdom; his dominion endures from generation to generation" (4:3). The purpose of the dream, of course, was to persuade Nebuchadnezzar that the Lord indeed is sovereign (v. 25), a purpose that came to pass as the Babylonian king himself attested. Of Yahweh he said, "His dominion is an eternal dominion" (v. 34) and "everything he does is right and all his ways are just" (v. 37).

Darius the Mede, king of Persia, also extolled the sovereignty of the God of Daniel in a remarkable decree published after Daniel emerged unscathed from the den of lions. "In every part of my kingdom," he commanded, "people must fear and reverence the God of Daniel," for "he is the living God and he endures forever; his kingdom will not be destroyed, his dominion will never end" (6:26).

These confessions by both Nebuchadnezzar and Darius should not, of course, lead one to conclude that these kings had become "converted" to Yahwism and had abandoned their respective polytheistic religious systems. For this there is no historical evidence. However, there is likewise no reason to doubt the credibility of Daniel's witness to their confessions, for it was in the very nature of their syncretistic faith to embrace any and all gods who gave evidence of worthiness.[44] It is clear from the inscriptions of Cyrus that he included many gods in his pantheon, though he was most likely a devotee of Ahura Mazda in particular. Ezra's record of the proclamation of Cyrus (Ezra 1:2-4), which permitted the Jewish return to Jerusalem, is clearly compatible with this ecumenical spirit of Cyrus documented in his own inscriptions.[45]

The sovereignty of God is not only a fact of history, it is also a central theme of eschatology. In fact, His dominion in the here and now is little seen and appreciated by the world at large. It is essential, therefore, that the day come when His sovereignty, now largely secret, will become apparent to all people.

THE SOVEREIGNTY OF (FALLEN) MAN

A central theme of biblical theology is that God created man as His image to have dominion and to rule over all things (Gen. 1:26-28). The Fall of man has impaired that purpose and rendered it temporarily incapable of perfect attainment, but the purpose has never been nullified. In the day of God's ultimate triumph man will reign with and for Him forevermore. Meanwhile, the dominion mandate continues to be in effect in history, human government being its expression. Unfortunately the sinful pride of the human race has blinded mankind to the true function of political institutions—that they should be self-consciously the instruments of God's just rule on the earth. Despite this, their rule is sanctioned by the Lord even if not approved by Him in its particular manifestations.

This tension between heavenly and earthly dominion is of great concern to the theology of Daniel. In fact, it is the fulcrum on which his fundamental argument turns. Thus the prophet concerns himself with both the sovereignty of God—addressed in the previous section—and that of human kings and human kingdoms.

Nebuchadnezzar received the first and greatest attention, for he was responsible for Jerusalem's fall and for Daniel's deportation. That deportation, ironically enough, occurred in the first year of Nebuchadnezzar, and for the forty-three years of the Babylonian's reign (605-562 B.C.) Daniel served him in some capacity or other, thereby coming to understand as could no other biblical prophet how this matter of human sovereignty comported with the kingship of the sovereign God.

Daniel first testifies to Nebuchadnezzar's authority over him by recounting his deportation and then his selection to be a choice servant of the king (Dan. 1:3-6). Particularly reflective of Daniel's subservience is his renaming by the king—he was no longer Daniel but Belteshazzar (1:7).

44. Joyce Baldwin, *Daniel: An Introduction and Commentary* (Leicester: InterVarsity, 1978), p. 95.
45. Joseph Blenkinsopp, *Ezra-Nehemiah: A Commentary* (Philadelphia: Westminster, 1988), p. 75.

More directly affirmative of Nebuchadnezzar's position as monarch are Daniel's interpretations of dreams and visions that specifically identify him as king, with divine sanction. The prophet declared that Nebuchadnezzar was the head of gold of the great statue (Dan. 2:38), a fact that suggests he was the "king of kings" (v. 36). Nebuchadnezzar's identification as the enormous tree in the middle of the land (4:10) lends support to his awesome majesty. Daniel confessed without equivocation and as the spokesman of God that this identification led to the conclusion that "you have become great and strong; your greatness has grown until it reaches the sky, and your dominion extends to distant parts of the earth" (v. 22).

Recognition of Nebuchadnezzar's universal rule and justification of its moral and spiritual underpinnings are, of course, two different matters. The creation and maintenance of human government under God must not lead to an uncritical endorsement of the policies and practices of that government, no matter what political form it might take. For government by the ungodly is inevitably government that is ideologically and theologically hostile to the righteous purposes of God. This explains the paradox of God's simultaneous election of and antipathy toward all human institutions that fail to recognize His sovereignty while carrying out the cultural mandate to which they have been called. This is also how Daniel can both confess the legitimate kingship of Nebuchadnezzar and condemn it for its hubris and antitheocratic spirit (Dan. 4: 30, 32).

Belshazzar too reflected insensitivity concerning his accountability to the God of heaven. In an act of incredible blasphemy he hosted a drunken orgy in which the sacred vessels of the Temple of Yahweh were used as table service (5:2-4). All the while Belshazzar toasted the gods of his own vile imagination. Daniel correctly saw this as an unconscionable abuse of power and an abysmal misinterpretation of its true source. Like his predecessor Nebuchadnezzar, Belshazzar (according to Daniel) had not humbled himself but rather had set himself up "against the Lord of heaven" (v. 22). He had praised his lifeless gods of gold and silver but "did not honor the God who holds in his hand your life and all your ways" (v. 23). Again, the issue is not the legitimacy of human sovereignty but its recognition of a higher Lord to whom it is accountable.

This arrogance and self-sufficiency of earthly rulers reached its climax historically and eschatologically in the king of Daniel 11:36-45. Universally identified as Antiochus IV Epiphanes (175-164 B.C.),[46] ninth ruler of the Seleucid dynasty of Syria, he also has come to be understood by many Christian scholars as the Antichrist who will rise in the time of the Great Tribulation to lead one last assault by human sovereignty on that of the Lord God and His saints (2 Thess. 2:4; Rev. 13:5-6).[47]

The rebellion of the creation against its Creator, epitomized perhaps in the self-

---

46. Alexander A. DiLella, *The Book of Daniel: Introduction and Commentary on Chapters 10-12,* The Anchor Bible, pp. 294-303.

47. J. Dwight Penetecost, *Things to Come* (Findlay, Ohio: Dunham, 1958), pp. 321-23; Donald K. Campbell, *Daniel: Decoder of Dreams* (Wheaton, Ill.: Victor, 1977), pp. 131-35.

sufficient posture of mortal kings, finds expression also in the political structures and national entities over which these monarchs reign. Thus rulers and their subjects alike stand condemned as lawless anarchists who refuse to acknowledge and capitulate to the sovereignty of God. This is most particularly apparent in three passages in Daniel (7:3-8, 17; 8:3-8, 20-22; and 11:2-35).

In Daniel's vision in Belshazzar's first year (7:1) he saw four great beasts emerging from the sea: a lion, a bear, a leopard, and an indescribable creature with iron teeth and ten horns. Though none of these is identified to Daniel, it is clear that they represent four successive kingdoms (v. 12) with their respective kings (v. 17). The traditional conservative view is that these kingdoms are Babylon, Medo-Persia, Greece, and Rome.[48] The nondescript fourth beast, Rome, is not further clarified precisely because Daniel himself preceded the time when Rome had become a mighty international power.

As for the ten horns that sprang from the head of the fourth beast, Daniel understood that they were kings and that from them in turn will spring yet another horn, a king who will replace three of the ten and who will "speak against the Most High and oppress his saints" (7:25). This, it becomes clear later (11:36; Rev. 13:6), is none other than the eschatological Antichrist, that ultimate human symbol of creaturely rebellion. Rising from ten nations that themselves are heirs of the Roman political and cultural legacy, the Antichrist will challenge God and His people in a final test of sovereignty.

The vision of Daniel in the third year of Belshazzar (Dan. 8:1) confirms the identity of the kingdoms just listed. Here he saw a ram with two horns (vv. 3-4), interpreted as Medo-Persia (v. 20), waging war with a goat (v. 5), specified as Greece (v. 21). The goat had a single horn between its eyes, a ruler commonly understood to be Alexander the Great. The horn, broken off, is replaced by four others—the Diadochi who split up Alexander's realm among themselves (vv. 8, 22).[49] Finally there emerges a "little horn" (v. 9) that seeks unsuccessfully to wage war against the representatives of the Lord (v. 25). This horn cannot be the horn that had sprung from the ten horns of the fourth beast in the previous vision (7:24), for this one originates in the third beast. He therefore must be understood as Antiochus Epiphanes, who himself is a prototype of the Antichrist.[50]

Further detail was given to the prophet in 11:2-35. There he learned that four Persian kings were yet to come, followed by a great monarch from Greece. He in turn would be succeeded by four kings, two of whom would engage each other in incessant warfare until finally the "king of the north" (vv. 6, 7, 13, 15) would prevail. He would then give way to a "contemptible person" (v. 21) whose rule over the land would be marked by violence and blasphemy. The view that this figure is

48. Robert D. Culver, *Daniel and the Latter Days*. Chicago: Moody, 1954, pp. 125-28.
49. For the historical background, see H. Jagersma, *A History of Israel from Alexander the Great to Bar Kochba* (Philadelphia: Fortress, 1985), pp. 16-17.
50. So Archer, *Daniel*, p. 99.

Antiochus IV Epiphanes is hardly debated and that he typifies the Antichrist of end times is also a matter of virtual consensus, at least in premillennial circles.

There is no question then that the revelation given to Daniel concerning the sovereignty of fallen man identifies it in terms of kings and kingdoms contemporary with and subsequent to his own times. All three major passages, though approaching the theme in different symbols and imagery, agree that the course of human history, itself a record of insubordination of the creature to his Creator, will culminate in a powerful ruler—the Antichrist—who will make one mighty, though futile, effort to resist the sovereign claims of the Lord God. Daniel, therefore, gave attention to the manner in which this threat would be addressed and overcome in the day of God's triumph.

THE RESTORATION OF GOD'S UNIVERSAL SOVEREIGNTY

Since God's relationships with man from the very beginning were articulated in the metaphor of covenant, it is not surprising that Daniel should understand the plight of his nation Israel as resulting from covenant violation and any hope of restoration as God's gracious act of covenant renewal. What Daniel asserts with reference to the resumption of Yahweh's sovereignty over Israel can certainly be applied to God's ultimate dominion over all creation. What is at stake, in any case, is repentance and dependence on God to remember His covenant promises and reactivate them in a great display of His kingship.

Daniel focuses on covenant renewal as the basis for national (and by extension, universal) restoration.[51] In his great prayer of 9:4-19 he addresses Yahweh as the God of covenant (v. 4) against whose covenant principles His people had sinned (v. 5-6). Their dispersion among all nations attests to their infidelity (vv. 7-12). Despite their sorry lot they had not repented (v. 13), a sign they deserved all the calamity that had befallen them (v. 14). Appealing to the mighty redemptive event of the Exodus (v. 15), Daniel prays that Yahweh would remember His commitments to His elect people and for His own name's sake forgive them and restore them to the place of covenant blessing (vv. 16-19).

For this restoration to be achieved—whether on a national or universal level—the antitheocratic elements of the world that oppose the sovereignty of Yahweh must be overcome and destroyed. As suggested already, these take the form of godless kings and kingdoms epitomized at last by the archenemy of Yahweh's dominion, the Antichrist. He is the horn who puts down three other horns (Dan. 7:24), who blasphemes the Most High, and who will run roughshod over God's people for three and one-half years (7:25). His triumph will not last, however, for he will be overthrown and will perish (7:26; cf. Rev. 17:14; 19:20).

A similar picture emerges in Daniel 8, where the prophet, speaking of Antiochus Epiphanes as a type of the Antichrist, describes him as the little horn (Dan. 8:9) who becomes great and, with particular malice toward the Temple and its holiness, lays the sanctuary desolate for more than six years (vv. 13-14). But he will

---

51. Peter R. Ackroyd, *Exile and Restoration* (Philadelphia: Westminster, 1968), pp. 89-90.

not prevail and like his eschatological counterpart, the Antichrist, he will be destroyed by the hand of the Lord Himself (vv. 14, 23-25).

The Antichrist's character and objectives are presented in greatest detail in Daniel 11:36-45. The prophet says that the Antichrist, described here as a king (v. 36), will exalt himself as a virtual deity, enforcing his evil designs on all God's creation (vv. 37-39). His rule will not go uncontested, however, even by earthly kings (vv. 40-43). But, though he will subdue them one by one, he will at last be called to account in the holy land itself. Having exercised a temporary dominion there, "he will come to his end, and no one will help him" (v. 45; cf. Rev. 19:19-21).

The agent of God who accomplishes these mighty acts of conquest and restoration is the "Son of Man," the Messiah figure who appears several times in Daniel's prophecy. Possibly in view in Daniel 10:16-21 ("one who looked like a man"),[52] he clearly is the figure in 7:13-14 ("one like a son of man") who comes with the clouds of heaven, a description used elsewhere of the Messiah, Jesus Christ (Rev. 1:7).[53] Daniel saw Him in His bold access to the Ancient of Days (that is, God the Father) from whose hand the Messiah will receive eternal dominion (Dan. 7: 14; cf. v. 27; 1 Cor. 15:27; Eph. 1:20-22; Phil. 2:9-11; Rev. 19:15-16; 20:4-6). The historical kingdoms of this world and that of the Antichrist in the end of this era will give way to that glorious kingdom of God ushered in and ruled over by the Son of Man and the saints of the Most High.

The reference to the "saints, the people of the Most High" (Dan. 7:27), if it is to be comprehensive and universal, presupposes resurrection, for only renewal of life will allow the people of God of all the ages to participate in the glorious privileges of sovereignty for which they were created. This contingency finds expression in 12:1-3 where the man of God declares that the multitudes who sleep in the dust of the earth will awake, some to experience postresurrection destruction but others everlasting life.[54] God's people, those whose names are "written in the book" (v. 1), will live again to participate in the dominion that was of the very essence of the mandate man received from the beginning (Gen. 1:26-28; cf. Rev. 20:6; 22:5).

The central theological theme of Daniel—that the arrogant, God-denying sovereignty of man will be overturned so that God might reign—finds unequivocal fulfillment in the eternal dominion of His saints who, despite all apparent evidence to the contrary, will eventually prevail. Following in the train of the Ancient of Days (Dan. 7:9-12), the saints "will receive the kingdom and will possess it forever" (v. 8). All the sovereignty of all the kingdoms will then be handed over to them, and at last they will achieve His purposes for them: that they be "crowned with glory and honor" with all creation placed under their feet (v. 27; cf. Ps. 8:5-6).

52. Most scholars correctly identify this figure as an angel. So, for example, Archer, *Daniel*, p. 126.
53. Walther Eichrodt, *Theology of the Old Testament* (Philadelphia: Westminster, 1961), 1:487-90.
54. For the hope of resurrection in the Old Testament, see William Dyrness, *Themes in Old Testament Theology* (Downers Grove, Ill.: InterVarsity, 1979), pp. 239-42.

11

A THEOLOGY OF THE MINOR PROPHETS

ROBERT B. CHISHOLM, JR.

The Minor Prophets are so-called because of their relative brevity in comparison to Isaiah, Jeremiah, and Ezekiel, not because they are less important theologically. The twelve books that make up the Minor Prophets range in date from the eighth to the fifth centuries B.C.:

8th	7th	6th-5th	Uncertain
Hosea	Nahum	Joel	Jonah
Amos	Habakkuk	Obadiah	
Micah	Zephaniah	Haggai	
		Zechariah	
		Malachi	

Though the events recorded in Jonah occurred in the eighth century, the date of book's authorship is uncertain. Some date Joel and Obadiah earlier, but the internal evidence of both books seems to favor a date in the sixth or fifth century. Joel 3:2-3 refers to the Exile as a past event, whereas Obadiah 10-14 denounces Edom's involvement in the fall of Jerusalem (586 B.C.)[1]

---

1. For a more thorough discussion of the dates of these books, see Leslie C. Allen, *The Books of Joel, Obadiah, Jonah and Micah,* New International Commentary on the Old Testament (Grand Rapids: Eerdmans, 1976), pp. 19-25, 129-33; and C. Hassell Bullock, *An Introduction to the Old Testament Prophetic Books* (Chicago: Moody, 1986), pp. 260, 328-30.

Several theological themes overlap many of these prophets, especially within the chronological periods outlined above. So the prophets will be discussed in chronological blocks rather than individually. At the same time the distinctives of each prophet will be noted and discussed. Because of its uncertain date and formal differences, Jonah will be treated separately. Unlike the other eleven books, which are primarily collections of prophetic *messages*, Jonah is a *biographical account* of a prophet's experience.

The prophets did not speak about God in abstract philosophical or theological terms. They portrayed Him as actively involved in the world He created and as intimately concerned with His covenant people. To reflect this relational element each of the following sections (with the exception of Jonah) is organized under the main headings "God and His People" and "God and the Nations."

THE EIGHTH-CENTURY PROPHETS (HOSEA, AMOS, MICAH)

INTRODUCTION

The Lord's covenantal relationship with His people Israel is central to the messages of the eighth-century prophets Hosea, Amos, and Micah. Each of these prophets accused God's people of violating the obligations of the Mosaic Covenant and warned that judgment was impending. Despite painting such a bleak picture of the immediate future, these prophets also saw a bright light at the end of the dark tunnel of punishment and exile. Each anticipated a time when the Lord, on the basis of His eternal covenantal promises to Abraham and David, would restore Israel to a position of favor and blessing. In fact, the coming judgment would purify God's people and thus prepare the way for a glorious new era in Israel's history.

Although the broad outlines of their theological messages are in harmony, each prophet also displays distinct emphases. Hosea, whose target group was the Northern Kingdom, focused on the people's idolatrous unfaithfulness to their covenant Lord, which he likened to adultery. Hosea's vivid imagery gives the reader a glimpse of God's intense emotional love for His wayward people. The heartache experienced by Hosea in his own marriage undoubtedly contributed to his profound insight into the character of God. Amos, who also addressed the Northern Kingdom, concentrated on a different aspect of the people's failure—social injustice. The Lord's relationship to the nations, only a minor theme in Hosea, finds greater prominence in Amos as well. Micah differs from Hosea and Amos in that his primary focus was the Southern Kingdom of Judah. The future role of the Davidic dynasty and its capital city Jerusalem receive greater attention in his prophecy.

GOD AND HIS PEOPLE

Divine initiative: God establishes a covenant people. The eighth-century minor prophets were well aware of the history of God's covenantal relationship with Israel. Their consistent testimony was that the Lord initiated this covenant. Hosea referred to the Lord as Israel's "Maker" (Hos. 8:14). As the mighty God of creation He was responsible for His people's very existence. Of all the nations of the earth the Lord had chosen Israel to have a special relationship with Him. In Amos 3:2 the Lord declares, "You only have I chosen [lit. *known*] of all the families of the earth." The verb translated "chosen" (*yāda'*) is here a covenantal term. In ancient Near Eastern treaties the idiom "to know," when used of a superior party "knowing" an inferior one, meant that the former recognized his subject as having a special relationship to him.[2] One finds a similar use of "to know" in two important Old Testament passages dealing with covenant relationships (Gen. 18:19; 2 Sam. 7:20). In these verses the term refers to the divine initiative in establishing a covenant and is best translated "choose." Likewise in Amos 3:2 this verb refers to God's special recognition of Israel as His people, resulting from His sovereign initiative and choice.

All three prophets referred to major events in Israel's salvation history. The Lord delivered His people from slavery in Egypt (Hos. 11:1; 12:9; 13:4; Amos 2:10; 3:1; 9:7; Mic. 6:4; 7:15), led them safely through the wilderness (Hos. 13:5-6; Amos 2:10), gave them leaders (Amos 2:11; Mic. 6:4), brought them into the Promised Land (Mic. 6:5), and defeated their powerful enemies (Amos 2:9-10).

Thematic and verbal allusions to specific details of Israel's salvation history reveal an intimate familiarity with antecedent Scripture. For example, in Hosea, as in the heading to the Ten Commandments, the Lord's affirmation of covenant relationship is associated with the Exodus (cf. Hos. 12:9 and 13:4 with Ex. 20:2 and Deut. 5:6). Amos spoke of the Lord's "bringing" His people "up out of Egypt," a typical way of referring to the Exodus in earlier literature (cf. Amos 2:10 with Ex. 29:2; Lev. 11:45; Deut. 20:1; Josh. 24:17). The reference in Micah 6:4 to the Lord's "redeeming" Israel "from the land [lit. *house*] of slavery" recalls the language of Deuteronomy 7:8 and 13:5. Historical details to which the prophets refer include the miraculous deeds performed by the Lord in Egypt (Mic. 7:15; cf. Ex. 3:20), the time span (forty years) of the wilderness wanderings (Amos 2:10; cf. Deut. 8:2), the role of Aaron and Miriam as leaders (Mic. 6:4), the identification of Shittim and Gilgal as Israelite campsites immediately before and after the Jordan crossing, respectively (Mic. 6:5; cf. Josh. 3:1; 4:19), and the gigantic size of some of the Canaanites (Amos 2:9; cf. Num. 13:22-23).

The book of Hosea employs vivid imagery in speaking of the Lord's relationship to His people. The Lord likened His love for Israel to that of a father, who affectionately and patiently teaches his young son to walk (Hos. 11:1-3). The father-son imagery and emphasis on "love" reflect Pentateuchal, especially Deuteronomic, motifs (Ex. 4:22-23; Deut. 1:31; 7:8; 23:5; 32:6). The Lord took special delight in His covenant people (Hos. 9:10; 10:1) and bestowed agricultural blessings on them (2:8). He compares His kindness to a man lifting the yoke from his ox's neck and feeding it (11:4).

---

2. Herbert B. Huffmon, "The Treaty Background of Hebrew *YĀDA'*," *Bulletin of the American Schools of Oriental Research* 181 (1966): 31-37.

Israel's response: God's people reject their covenant Lord. How did Israel respond to God's elective love and salvific deeds on her behalf? The Lord Himself provides the shocking answer to that question: "When I fed them, they were satisfied; when they were satisfied, they became proud; then they forgot me" (Hos. 13:6). Instead of responding to God's love with gratitude and faithful obedience, Israel rebelled against the Lord's authority, turning to other gods and rejecting the principles given by God to govern covenant life. Very early in her national life Israel disobeyed and set the pattern for her entire rebellious history (Hos. 9:9-10; 10:9). The more the Lord called to His people, the further they retreated from Him (11:2). They rejected their God-given leaders (Amos 2:12) and attributed the Lord's blessings to Baal, the Canaanite fertility and storm god (Hos. 2:8). Greedy individuals mistreated their fellow Israelites. Despite prophetic warnings (e.g., Hos. 4:15), the cancer of the Northern Kingdom spread to the south (Hos. 11:12; Mic. 1:5-9, 13; 6:16).

First and foremost the eighth-century minor prophets viewed Israel's sin as breach of covenant. The book of Hosea in particular states this in a variety of ways. The Lord declares that Israel had "broken" the covenant (Hos. 6:7; 8:1). They had "ignored" (4:6; lit. forgotten) and "rebelled against" (8:1) His law, regarding its stipulations as "something alien" (8:12). By rejecting the covenant, Israel rebelled against the Lord Himself (7:13). This rebellion is described as "straying off" and "turning away" from the Lord (7:13-14).

In bringing a formal covenant lawsuit against Israel, the Lord observed that there was "no acknowledgement of God in the land" (4:1). The word translated "acknowledgement" refers here to a recognition of God's authority expressed in a tangible way by obedience to His commandments. The idiom "to know," when used in ancient Near Eastern treaties of an inferior party's attitude toward his superior, referred to the subject's recognition of his lord's authority as binding on him. An interesting biblical use of this idiom occurs in Jeremiah 22:15-16, where the Lord says of Josiah, "He did what was right and just, so all went well with him. He defended the cause of the poor and needy, and so all went well. Is that not what it means to know me?" In this passage Josiah's concern for social justice is equated with "knowing" the Lord. This may seem strange to the modern Western mind, which tends to think of knowing God in intellectual terms. However, Josiah "knew" God in the sense that he recognized the Lord's authority and submitted to His sovereign demands, in this case those pertaining to socioeconomic matters. Israel in Hosea's time possessed no such knowledge.

The book of Hosea also illustrates Israel's breach of covenant in several effective ways. Repeatedly Israel's lack of loyalty is likened to adultery (Hos. 1:2; 2:2-13, 4:15, 5:4, 7; 6:10; 9:1). As an object lesson of Israel's unfaithfulness to her divine "husband" the Lord instructed Hosea to marry a woman who would be unfaithful to the prophet (Hos. 1:2-3). In Hosea 6:4 the Lord compared Israel's "love" (or "faithfulness") to "morning mist" and "early dew" which disappear quickly. Any devotion on Israel's part was shortlived at best. Israel was like a "stubborn heifer," intent on pursuing idolatry (4:16).

Micah and Amos also viewed the essence of Israel's sin as breach of covenant. In Micah 6:1-8 the Lord confronted sinful Judah in the form of a covenant lawsuit (cf. Hos. 4:1). In Amos 2:4 He specifically states that Judah had "rejected" His law and failed to keep His "decrees." In Amos 2:4, 6 the Hebrew word used for Judah's and Israel's "sins" (*peša'*) refers to rebellion. The related verb appears in political contexts, being used of a subject state's rebellion and breach of treaty arrangements (cf. 2 Kings 1:1; 3:5, 7).

All three prophets presented ample evidence of Israel's breach of covenant by pointing out specific sins, many of which were in direct violation of Pentateuchal legislation.[3] Hosea accused the Northern Kingdom of breaking the first and second commandments of the Decalogue. Like an adulterous wife, Israel turned to another lover, the god Baal (Hos. 2:2-13). In worshiping this false deity the Israelites engaged in ritual prostitution (designed to ensure fertility; cf. 4:10-19), pagan mourning rites (cf. 7:14, NIV margin), and idolatry (8:4-6; 10:1-2, 5-6, 8; 11:2; 13:1-2). The book of Amos, though not emphasizing this aspect of Israel's rebellion, does mention the worship of false gods in at least two passages (Amos 5:26; 8:14).[4] Micah, like Hosea, compared the Northern Kingdom's idolatry to adultery (Mic. 1:6-7) and criticized Judah for following the example of the north (Mic. 1:5; 5:12-14).

Hosea's covenant lawsuit (Hos. 4:2) mentions violations of five commandments of the Decalogue: false oaths, false legal testimony, murder (cf. 6:8-9), theft (cf. 7:1-2), and adultery. To this list Micah adds disrespect for parents, a violation of the fifth commandment (Mic. 7:6). The Israelites apparently observed the fourth commandment, that dealing with the Sabbath (Hos. 2:11). However, their desire for the holy day to end so they could carry out their covetous schemes made their observance of the Sabbath hollow (cf. Amos 8:5). Certainly their adherence to the letter of the Sabbath regulation was negated by their violation of the tenth commandment, which prohibited covetousness. The Sabbath commemorated Israel's deliverance from oppression in Egypt and was to be a reminder of their social obligations (Deut. 5:12-15). To spend the day planning and anticipating oppressive measures was a complete perversion of the spirit of the Sabbath law.

The clearest manifestation of covetousness came in the form of social injustice, which involved dishonest economic and legal practices. Whereas Hosea only briefly mentioned this sin (cf. Hos. 12:6-7), Amos in the north and Micah in the south made it central to their accusations against the people. Specific reference is made to sale of the poor (Amos 2:6; 8:6), theft of property (Amos 2:8; Mic. 2:1-2, 8), rigged weights and measures (Amos 8:5; Mic. 6:10-11; cf. Lev. 19:35-36 and Deut. 25:13-15), denial or perversion of legal justice due the poor (Amos 2:7; 5:7, 10; 6:12;

---

3. For a convenient list of examples from Micah and Amos, among others, see Richard V. Bergren, *The Prophets and the Law*, Monographs of the Hebrew Union College, no. 4 (Cincinnati: Hebrew Union College—Jewish Institute of Religion, 1974), pp. 182-83.

4. Cf. Hans M. Barstad, *The Religious Polemics of Amos*, Vetus Testamentum Supplement. 34 (Leiden: Brill, 1984).

Mic. 3:1-3; cf. Lev. 19:15), including acceptance of bribes (Amos 5:12; Mic. 3:9-11; 7:3; cf. Ex. 23:8 and Deut. 16:19), and luxurious living at the expense of the poor (Amos 3:15; 4:1; 5:11; 6:4-6).

For the rich to accumulate property in complete disregard of the rights and needs of their covenant brothers was a blatant practical denial of the Lord's ownership of the land. It also disregarded the covenantal principles of equal access to the land God had given and responsibility for the well-being of one's neighbor. The law taught that the land belonged to God, not the people, who, as God's servants (Lev. 25:55), were mere "aliens" and "tenants" on it (Lev. 25:23). God gave the land to Israel so that she might prosper and enjoy its abundance (Lev. 25:2, 38; Deut. 26:9). He allotted a portion of the land to each tribe. Permanent land sales were prohibited (Lev. 25:23-24) and legal provision was made for the continuance of the original ideal. Ideally obedience to the law would preclude poverty in society (Deut. 15:4-5). Though the Lord realistically anticipated the presence of some poor individuals in the land (15:11), He insisted that they be treated with kindness and generosity (15:7-11). Adherence to these and the other principles of the covenant would make Israel a model of socioeconomic justice among the nations (4:5-8).

Rather than being an example to the nations, Israel's crimes exceeded those of the Gentiles. Amos made clear that the Northern Kingdom, though proud of its history and recent successes under Jeroboam II, was more offensive in the sight of God than any of its neighbors. In Amos 1:3–2:5 the Lord denounced in succession the crimes of the seven nations surrounding the Northern Kingdom. In each case He used the introductory formula "For three sins of . . ., even for four, I will not turn back my wrath." Curiously, however, no more than two specific crimes are outlined in any of the seven oracles. Much to the surprise and chagrin of his northern audience, which must have listened with relish to the prophet's announcement of doom on its enemies, Amos concluded his message with a lengthy judgment speech against the north. Only here does the expected list of four crimes follow the introductory, stereotypical formula. The purpose of the earlier series of incomplete lists becomes clear. The Lord sought to highlight the Northern Kingdom's sins and to emphasize its relative guilt. If one were to compile lists of nations' crimes, he would be able to fill Samaria's list before all others.

Despite Israel's breach of covenant, both the north and the south maintained a semblance of religion and worship. In the north worshipers regularly attended cult sites such as Gilgal and Bethel, celebrating feasts, offering sacrifices, and uttering pious affirmations of loyalty (cf. Hos. 4:15; 5:6; 8:2, 11, 13; Amos 4:4-5; 5:21-25). In Judah as well emphasis was placed on sacrificial ritual as the basis for access to God (Mic. 6:6-7).

The Lord declared this outward formalism to be completely ineffective and hypocritical. In addition to being contaminated by syncretism with Canaanite practices, this religion was invalidated by the widespread social injustice mentioned above. Sacrifices could only be a meaningful element in Israel's relationship to God if offered within the framework of genuine loyalty to God (Hos. 6:6) and love for one's brothers (12:6). In Amos 5:4 the Lord commanded, "Seek me and live; do not seek Bethel, do not go to Gilgal, do not journey to Beersheba." A few verses later the prophet elaborated on the meaning of this command: "Seek good, not evil, that you may live. Then the Lord God Almighty will be with you, just as you say he is. Hate evil, love good; maintain justice in the courts" (vv. 14-15*a*). To seek the Lord meant to promote justice and reject the cultic hypocrisy found at Bethel and other centers of worship. Micah informed the people of Judah, "He has showed you, O man, what is good. And what does the Lord require of you? To act justly and to love mercy and to walk humbly with your God" (Mic. 6:8). Before any sacrifice, no matter how costly (cf. Mic. 6:6-7), the Lord required that one "walk humbly" before Him by promoting justice and mercy.

In rejecting hypocritical formalism and stressing the importance of faithfulness in one's relationships to both God and man, the prophets articulate a theological principle that permeates the entire Bible: No vital relationship with God is possible if one is unfaithful to the responsibilities arising out of his God-given relationships with his fellow men. All kinds of God-directed religious and devotional exercises, including sacrifice and prayer, are futile apart from this relational foundation. It is no surprise, then, that James made concern for "orphans and widows" one of his twin pillars of true religion (James 1:27). Jesus reminded the Pharisees that justice was more important than tithes (Matt. 23:23) and taught that reconciliation with a brother took priority over a religious offering (5:23-24). He warned that one's willingness to forgive others was foundational to experiencing God's forgiveness (6:14-15). Peter reminded husbands that improper treatment of their wives could hinder their prayers (1 Pet. 3:7). John explained that one's response to the material and physical needs of a fellow Christian reveals whether or not his professed faith is genuine (1 John 3:16-20).

In addition to idolatry and social injustice, another clear sign of Israel's rebellion against its covenant Lord was the nation's rejection of His word as given through the prophets. In addressing the north, the Lord noted that the people "commanded the prophets not to prophesy" (Amos 2:12). Amos, who was chosen by the Lord (7:14-15), experienced such rejection. Amaziah, the priest of Bethel, the royal sanctuary, specifically told him, "Do not prophesy against Israel, and stop preaching against the house of Isaac" (7:16). According to Hosea, the Lord's prophets were considered raving fools and were treated with hostility (Hos. 9:8-9). In the south matters were no better. People ordered the prophets to be silent (Mic. 2:6) and listened only to those who forecast prosperity (2:11). The prophetic office itself had become corrupt, being filled with mercenaries (3:5).

According to Hosea, the Northern Kingdom had rejected the Lord's guidance in both domestic and international affairs. Intrigue and violence surrounded the throne (Hos. 7:3-7). No attempt was made to acquire the Lord's consent in the choice of rulers (8:4). The North's foreign policy was based on alliances with other nations rather than on trust in the Lord's ability to protect and deliver (5:13; 7:8-11; 8:9-10; 12:1).

All three prophets denounced Israel for its arrogant, self-sufficient attitude. In the north self-confidence was based on the nation's military successes (Amos 6:13), military might (Hos. 10:13), strong fortresses (Hos. 8:14; Amos 6:8), and wealth (Hos. 12:8). In the south as well a false dependence on military might and fortifications prevailed (Mic. 5:10-11).

To summarize, Israel had broken her covenant relationship with God. Idolatry and social injustice were widespread, making hypocritical attempts to worship the Lord through formal, ritualistic means unacceptable to Him. Rather than listening to the Lord's word through His prophets and relying on His guidance and protection, Israel rejected the prophets and trusted in her own schemes and strength.

Divine response: God judges His disobedient covenant people. In response to Israel's blatant and persistent violation of His covenant demands, the Lord announced through His prophets that judgment would fall on His disobedient people. The prophets viewed the Lord's judgment on Israel as the implementation of the curses or threats contained in the covenant, the fullest lists of which are found in Leviticus 26:14-39 and Deuteronomy 28:15-68. Moses specifically warned that these curses would follow breach of covenant (Lev. 26:14-16; Deut. 28:15). Most of the curses fall into these categories: (1) drought, pestilence, and resultant famine (Lev. 26:18-20; Deut. 28:16-24, 38-42), (2) disease (Lev. 26:16; Deut. 28:21-22, 27, 35, 59-61), (3) military invasion and defeat (Lev. 26:17; Deut. 28:25, 49-51), (4) slaughter and carnage (Deut. 28:26), (5) destruction of cities and false worship sites (Lev. 26:30-31; Deut. 28:52), and (6) exile to a foreign land (Lev. 26:33-39; Deut. 28:36-37, 42, 63-68).

Most of these motifs can be found in the announcements of judgment made by Hosea, Amos, and Micah. Hosea in particular emphasized the loss of fertility that would sweep over the Northern Kingdom. The Lord would remove the agricultural blessings He had bestowed on the people because they had mistakenly attributed these gifts to the Canaanite storm and fertility god Baal (Hos. 2:2-13). Drought would sweep over the land (Hos. 4:3; 13:15). Amos portrayed the Lord as one who, with a mighty roar, can cause even the most fertile regions to wither up (Amos 1:2).

Because the inhabitants of the North had also sought to promote human fertility by worshiping Baal, the Lord announced through Hosea that many women would be barren. Those who did bear children would see them destroyed by invading forces (Hos. 9:11-17). Throughout this judgment speech the Northern Kingdom is referred to ironically as "Ephraim," the name of one of Joseph's sons, who was promised numerous offspring (Gen. 48:15-20). This promise would now be reversed. All three prophets described in graphic, horrifying detail the military defeat (Hos. 5:8; 11:6; Amos 2:13-16; 5:1-3; 6:8; Mic. 1:8-16; 5:10), slaughter (Hos. 10:14; 11:6; Amos 6:9-10; 7:17), and destruction (Hos. 5:9; 10:14; Amos 3:11, 14-15; 6:11; 7:9; Mic. 1:6-7; 3:12) both Samaria and Judah would experience.

Each prophet also announced the exile of God's people (Hos. 8:13; 9:3, 6, 15, 17; 10:6; 11:5; 12:9; Amos 4:1-3; 5:27; 6:7; 7:17; 9-9; Mic. 4:10). Whereas Amos only vaguely designated the place of exile as being "beyond Damascus" (Amos 5:27; cf. 4:3), Hosea was more specific, pinpointing Assyria as the location (Hos. 10:6; 11:5). Hosea also mentioned a return to Egypt (8:13; 9:3, 6). This was probably intended to be more symbolic than literal, the point being that Israel's salvation history would be reversed. Micah, while viewing Assyria as an enemy (Mic. 5:5-6) and as a place of exile (7:12), specifically named Babylon as the destination of Judah's exiles (4:10). This distinction between Assyria and Babylon, whether entirely clear to Micah or not (during his time Assyria ruled Babylon), anticipated actual historical events. Whereas the Northern Kingdom was defeated by the Assyrians in 722 B.C., Judah survived until 586 B.C., when the Babylonians sacked Jerusalem and carried many into exile.

Although the judgment announced by the prophets was severe, it was also perfectly appropriate and just. Hosea clearly stated the principle that the punishment would correspond to the crime: "The Lord has a charge to bring against Judah; he will punish Jacob according to his ways and repay him according to his deeds" (Hos. 12:2).

Throughout their writings the prophets emphasized this characteristic of divine judgment through a combination of word pictures and wordplays. For example, those who insisted on seeking fertility through Baal worship would, appropriately, be deprived of fertility. Those who sought to maintain national security through foreign alliances would be destroyed by those very "allies." Corrupt prophets, whose sole motive had become financial success, would receive no more divine revelation and be forced to cover their mouths in shameful silence (Mic. 3:5-7). The rich who had filled their storehouses with dishonest gain would watch foreigners plunder those same buildings (Amos 3:9-11). These same wealthy individuals, who at the expense of the poor had erected fine mansions and planted lush vineyards, would not live in these houses or drink the wine from the vineyards (Amos 5:11). Inasmuch as the rich had stolen fields from the poor, they would watch helplessly as foreigners took those fields from them (Mic. 2:1-5). The "notable men of the foremost [*rē'šît*] nation," who used nothing but the "finest [*rē'šît*] lotions" to anoint themselves, would, appropriately, be the "first [*rō'š*] to go into exile (Amos 6:1, 6-7). Those who had "strayed" (*nādad*) from the Lord would become "wanderers [*nādad* again] among the nations" (cf. Hos. 7:13 with Hos. 9:17). The nation whose faithfulness to the Lord was as transient as the "morning mist" and "early dew" would itself disappear into exile like the mist and dew disappear before the sunlight and its heat (cf. Hos. 6:4 with Hos. 13:3).

The coming judgment would reverse Israel's salvation history. As already noted, Hosea spoke figuratively of a return to Egypt, which would be tantamount to a reversal of the mighty Exodus deliverance (cf. Deut. 28:68). Through Amos, the Lord warned that the Northern Kingdom would be oppressed by its enemies "all the way from Lebo Hamath to the valley of the Arabah" (Amos 6:14). The word translated "oppress" was used of the Egyptian oppression (cf. Ex. 3:9; Deut. 26:7). The geographical boundaries mentioned correspond to those given by the Lord to Israel

during the time of Jeroboam II (cf. 2 Kings 14:25-27). The author of Kings specifically called Jeroboam's conquest of this area an act of divine salvation (cf. 2 Kings
14:27). All this would now be reversed. Israel would again be oppressed by a foreign power and the land won in battle would be taken away. According to Amos 5:5,
Gilgal, Israel's first campsite after crossing the Jordan and a symbol of her possession
of the Promised Land (cf. Josh. 4:19-5; 12), would go into exile. Micah 2:4-5
speaks of a reversal of the original land allotment made by Joshua. Because the
rich had stolen land from the poor, they would watch helplessly as that land was
assigned to invading forces. The word translated "assigns" (*ḥālaq*) was used of
Joshua's distribution of the land to the Israelites (Josh. 13:7; 18:10).

According to Amos this coming reversal of salvation history was the opposite of what the Northern Kingdom anticipated. Apparently many in the north
looked forward to a soon-to-arrive "day of the Lord," in which the Lord would
intervene against the nation's enemies and lead it to greater glory (Amos 5:18).
This expectation was undoubtedly based on the recent successes of Jeroboam II,
referred to earlier. However, Amos declared in no uncertain terms that the Northern
Kingdom's view of the Day of the Lord was inaccurate. The Lord would indeed intervene in power, but Israel, not her enemies, would be the primary object of His
angry judgment. The Day of the Lord would be characterized by darkness (symbolizing judgment), rather than light (symbolizing salvation). It would be a time of
inescapable judgment (5:19) culminating in exile (5:27).

It is apparent that the concept of the Day of the Lord, which became so
prominent in the writings of later prophets, was not viewed by Amos in long-range
or universal terms. Rather, it referred to a specific event in the immediate future,
namely, the approaching destruction of the Northern Kingdom, which occurred in
722 B.C., approximately forty years after Amos prophesied.

The coming judgment of the Lord's day would place Israel in the role of her
traditional enemies. In Amos 5:17 the Lord stated that He would "pass through" the
"midst" of the Northern Kingdom. The language used is reminiscent of Exodus
12:12, where the Lord warned, "On that same night I will pass through Egypt and
strike down every firstborn." The Lord's words in Amos 5:17 represent an ironic
twist in His relationship to His people. He would now treat them in the same way
He had treated the Egyptians in the days of Moses. Micah and Hosea applied language traditionally associated with Israel's conquest of the land to the approaching
judgment of God's people. In Micah 1:7 the Lord announced that Samaria's idols
would "be broken to pieces" and "burned with fire." This is precisely what Moses
did to the golden calf (Deut. 9:21) and what Israel was to have done to Canaanite
idols (Deut. 7:5, 25; 12:3). Ironically God was now forced to do to Israel what
Israel should have done to her enemies. In Hosea 9:15 the Lord warned that He
would "drive out" Israel from His "house" (i.e., the land; Hos. 8:1; 9:8). The word
translated "drive out" is often used of the Lord's driving out the Canaanites from
before Israel (Ex. 23:29-30; 33:2; Deut. 33:27; Josh. 24:18; Judg. 6:9). Because
God's people had assimilated Canaanite practices, the Lord would now treat them

as Canaanites, expelling them from the land. Having become like the Gentiles, they would now be forced to wander among them (Hos. 9:17).

However, even in the midst of the prophets' severe judgment pronouncements, God's concern for His people is prominent. According to Amos 4:6-11, the Lord's prior punishment of the Northern Kingdom had been designed to bring the people to repentance. Even in the context of their seemingly unconditional announcements of judgment, Hosea and Amos issued calls to repentance (cf. Hos. 12:6; 14:1-3; Amos 5:4-6, 14-15, 24). Both teach that genuine repentance entails actively promoting social justice. Though Micah included no such appeals in his message to Judah, his apparently uncompromising prophecy of doom had an implied conditionality, as a comparison of Micah 3:12 with Jeremiah 26:17-19 demonstrates. In Jeremiah's day the elders of the land recalled that Hezekiah's repentant response to Micah's warning had postponed Judah's demise.

The Lord's purpose in judgment was to purify and restore His people. In Hosea 2 He made clear that the Exile, likened to a return to the wilderness, would provide an opportunity for renewal as Israel came to realize that the Lord, not Baal, had been responsible for the nation's past blessings. According to Amos 9:9-10, the coming judgment would destroy "the sinners" among the Lord's people. Micah portrayed the judgment as a time of purification, when Judah's false sources of confidence and objects of worship would be eliminated (Mic. 5:10-14).

Though angry with His disobedient people, the Lord declared that He could never totally annihilate them. Though the covenant curses warned that disobedience would bring destruction so terrible it would rival that of Sodom and Gomorrah (cf. Deut. 29:23), the Lord affirmed He could never go to such extremes. The Lord's compassion was stirred, preventing Him from wiping His people from the face of the earth (Hos. 11:8-9). This emotional change from rage to compassion is highlighted by a wordplay involving the Hebrew term *hāpak*, "turn over" (translated "changed" in Hos. 11:8). This is the same word used to describe God's overthrow (lit. "turning over") of Sodom and Gomorrah (cf. Gen. 19:24-25; Deut. 29:23). However, in Hosea 11:8 it is God's compassion, not His people, that is "turned over" (or "changed").

Divine faithfulness: God restores His covenant people. The messages of the eighth-century minor prophets do not end with judgment. All three envisioned a time of restoration for Israel. The very structure of their messages reflects this positive emphasis. The book of Hosea is arranged in five cycles, or panels, each moving from judgment to salvation:

Cycle/Panel	Judgment	Salvation
1	1:2-9	1:10–2:1
2	2:2-13	2:14–3:5
3	4:1–5:14	5:15–6:3
4	6:4–11:7	11:8-11
5	11:12–13:16	14:1-9

For eight and one-half chapters Amos's message is one of doom, but suddenly he promises restored glory and blessing for Israel (Amos 9:11-15). The book of Micah contains three judgment-salvation cycles:

Cycle/Panel	Judgment	Salvation
1	1:2–2:11	2:12-13
2	3:1-12	chaps. 4-5
3	6:1–7:7	7:8-20

Though some scholars question the authenticity of the salvation sections, the movement from judgment to restoration comes as no surprise. Long before the prophets, the Lord revealed to Moses that Israel would disobey and go into exile (cf. Deut. 31:19–32:43). Moses, however, promised that repentance would bring return from exile, restoration of divine blessings, and transformation of the people's character (Deut. 30:1-10). The prophets' view of Israel's ultimate salvation is consistent with that of Moses.

Hosea and Micah looked forward to a day when God's people would repent, thus making it possible for their restoration to take place (cf. Deut. 30:2-3). According to Hosea 5:15, the Lord anticipated a time when Israel, having suffered punishment (cf. Hos. 5:14), would "admit their guilt" and "earnestly seek" Him. At that time God's people would encourage one another to return to the Lord (Hos. 6:1) and acknowledge His lordship (6:3). Defeated and exiled Israel is pictured in Micah 7 as acknowledging its sin (v. 9) and trusting God for restoration (vv. 9, 18-20).

Of course the efficacy of repentance is based on the Lord's compassionate and merciful character, mentioned by both Hosea and Micah. In Hosea 14:2-3 the prophet urged the people to seek forgiveness from the God who shows compassion to the helpless. In Micah 7:18-20 repentant Israel praised God for His forgiveness: "Who is a God like you, who pardons sin and forgives the transgression of the remnant of his inheritance? You do not stay angry forever but delight to show mercy. You will again have compassion on us; you will tread our sins underfoot and hurl all our iniquities into the depths of the sea. You will be true to Jacob, and show mercy to Abraham, as you pledged on oath to our fathers in days long ago." These verses indicate that God's forgiveness was actually a manifestation of His covenantal faithfulness to Abraham, Isaac, and Jacob (cf. Gen. 22:16; 26:3; 50:24).

The eighth-century minor prophets anticipated the fulfillment of God's promise to Abraham. The essential elements in this promise included numerous offspring (Gen. 22:17), victory over enemies (22:17), possession of the Promised Land (12:7; 15:18-21; 17:8), and universal blessing through Abraham's offspring (22:18). Each of these elements appears in the prophetic visions of Israel's glorious future. First, Hosea and Micah referred to the numerical strength of eschatological Israel. Hosea, alluding to Genesis 22:17, prophesied that the restored Israelites would be like "the sand on the seashore, which cannot be measured or counted" (Hos. 1:10). In Micah 4:7 the Lord, alluding to Genesis 18:18, predicted He would form the remnant into a "strong nation." Second, Amos and Micah looked forward to Israel's military ascendancy over her enemies. In the eschaton Israel will "possess the remnant of Edom and all the nations" (Amos 9:12). The theme of Israel's eschatological superiority to her foes permeates Micah (Mic. 4:12-13; 5:5-9; 7:10, 16-17). Third, all three prophets mention Israel's repossession of the land. In particular Amos 9:15 stresses the permanency of this restoration. There the Lord promised, "I will plant Israel in their own land, never again to be uprooted from the land I have given them." Fourth, Micah 4:14 describes the extension of God's blessings to all nations through Israel.

For the eighth-century minor prophets, Israel's future restoration would reverse God's judgment and its negative effects. This is perhaps most clearly seen in the opening chapters of Hosea, in which the Lord instructed the prophet to give his children names symbolizing His rejection of the Northern Kingdom. The name "Jezreel" pointed to the nation's coming military defeat. Lo-Ruhamah, "not loved," symbolized that the Northern Kingdom would no longer be shown divine compassion, while Lo-Ammi, "not my people," pointed to a cessation of the covenant relationship (Hos. 1:2-9). However, in the immediately following message of salvation (1:10–2:1) the Lord affirmed that a time would come when He would again show compassion to Israel and again call them "my people" (see also 2:23*b* and cf. 9:15 with 14:4). The name "Jezreel," meaning literally "God plants," also takes on a positive significance, symbolizing the Lord's "planting" His people in their land (cf. 1:11 and 2:23).

Hosea personally illustrated this reversal in Israel's relationship to the Lord by recovering his adulterous wife, Gomer (Hos. 3:1-5). In the same way the Lord would again make Israel His bride, alluring her with all the vigor of a romantic young man (2:14) and then betrothing her to Himself (2:19-20). The unfaithful wife (2:2-5) would be transformed into a new bride. All traces of past unfaithfulness would be removed (2:16-17). The broken relationship would not simply be patched up; it would be completely transformed and renewed.

Hosea also emphasizes this reversal in the Lord's relationship to Israel through wordplay. In Hosea 13:7 the Lord pictured Himself as a leopard, lurking by the path ready to pounce on His sinful people in judgment. In 14:8, which envisions the time of Israel's restoration, the Lord promised that He would care for His people, protecting them and blessing them. "Lurk" (in 13:7) and "care for" (in 14:8) translate the same Hebrew verb ($\check{s}\hat{u}r$). The repetition of this word, albeit in a different sense, draws one's attention to the reversal in the Lord's attitude. The ferocious predator of 13:7 would become Israel's beneficent, watchful protector.

Exile, the most terrible effect of judgment, would be reversed. In Hosea 11:10-11 God promised: "They will follow the Lord; he will roar like a lion. When he roars, his children will come trembling from the west. They will come trembling like birds from Egypt, like doves from Assyria. I will settle them in their homes."

Several details in this passage point to a reversal of judgment. The Israelites would return to their homeland from Egypt and Assyria, mentioned frequently by Hosea as the destination of the exiles (Hos. 8:13; 9:3, 6; 10:6; 11:5). The lion and dove motifs, used elsewhere in the book in contexts of judgment, are used here in a positive way. Elsewhere the Lord compares Himself to a vicious lion who violently attacks its prey (5:14; 13:7-8). Here, however, He is more like C. S. Lewis's Aslan, His powerful roar beckoning His children to return from exile. In 7:11-12, the Lord, comparing Himself to a fowler, stated He would capture the silly "dove" Israel with His net. In 11:11, however, the dove imagery is used to describe the swiftness of Israel's return to its home.

The book of Amos, which prophesies the exile of the Northern Kingdom in no uncertain terms (Amos 4:1-3; 5:27; 6:7; 7:17; 9:9), also envisions a return from exile. In Amos 9:14-15 the Lord promised to restore His people's fortunes and plant them once more on their land, never to be removed again.

Micah too anticipated a time when God's people would return from exile in Mesopotamia and Egypt (Mic. 4:10; 7:12). In Micah the exiles are referred to as a "remnant," which is described as lame and injured (in 4:6 "injured" is a better translation than "brought to grief"). However, the Lord would gather this remnant like a flock of sheep and lead them out from their captivity (2:12-13). In an obvious allusion to the Exodus from Egypt, Micah predicted, "You will go to Babylon; there you will be rescued. There the Lord will redeem you out of the land of your enemies" (4:10*b*).

In the coming golden age the nation's political independence and military strength would also be restored. Judgment brought destruction and humiliation for the kings and armies of both the north and the south (Hos. 10:3, 7, 15; 13:10-11; Amos 7:9; Mic. 4:9; 5:1). However, in the eschaton the twelve tribes of Israel would be reunited (Hos. 1:11; Amos 9:11-15; Mic. 5:3) under the rulership of a new David (Hos. 3:5; Amos 9:11; Mic. 5:2-6). Rejuvenated Israel would conquer her enemies (symbolized by her traditional foes Edom and Assyria; Amos 9:12; Mic. 4:11-13; 5:3-9; 7:10, 16-17).

Whereas Hosea and Amos only briefly alluded to the restoration of Davidic rule over all Israel, Micah, whose prophecy was directed primarily to Judah, understandably devoted more attention to this theme. Like Amos he anticipated the humiliation of the Davidic dynasty (Mic. 5:1; cf. Amos 9:11). Ironically the Davidic "ruler" (*šōpēṭ*) would be struck on the cheek with a "rod" (*šēbeṭ*), a symbol of kingship and authority. However, despite this setback the Davidic throne would be restored to its former glory as God fulfilled His covenant promises to David (cf. 2 Sam. 7:8-16).

Like Hosea (Hos. 3:5) Micah envisioned a second coming of David (cf. Jer. 30:9; Ezek. 34:23-24; 37:24-25). This seems to be the point of the famous prophecy recorded in Micah 5:2: "But you, Bethlehem Ephrathah, though you are small among the clans of Judah, out of you will come for me one who will be ruler over Israel, whose origins are from of old, from ancient times." The association of the coming ruler with Bethlehem and the reference to his origins being in antiquity suggest that the reappearance of David himself is in view.[5] Of course this is actually a messianic prediction. Other prophets (e.g., Isaiah in 9:6-7; 11:1, 10) and subsequent biblical revelation make clear that these references to David are fulfilled in the Messiah, who as the Son of David will rule in the spirit and power of His illustrious ancestor.

In Micah 5:2 attention is drawn to the relative insignificance of Bethlehem among the clans of Judah. Ironically, however, the Lord's chosen king would arise from this small town. This pattern of God's elevating the small and insignificant appears elsewhere in the Old Testament (Gen. 25:23; 48:14; Judg. 6:15; 1 Sam. 9:21).

This ruler, who arises from such humble origins, will protect His people like a shepherd (the same was said of David; 2 Sam. 5:2; Ps. 78:71-72). Ruling through the power of the Lord, His fame will reach universal proportions (Mic. 5:4). He and His vice-regents will prevent even the most powerful of Israel's enemies (symbolized here by Israel's traditional enemy Assyria) from invading the land (Mic. 5:5-6).

In conjunction with the restoration of Davidic rule Micah also prophesied a reversal in Jerusalem's fortunes. Micah warned that this city, chosen by David as his capital and the site of the Lord's Temple, would be subjected to siege (Mic. 5:1) and reduced to rubble (3:12). He personified the city in its humiliation as a woman in labor, writhing in agony as she seeks to give birth (4:9-10). From the perspective of the Exile, personified Jerusalem acknowledges the justice of God's punishment and anticipates a day of vindication and restoration (7:8-12). Drawing on the imagery of Micah 4:9-10, the prophet compared the return of Zion's exiled people to giving birth (5:3). In the future the Lord would deliver Jerusalem from its attackers (4:11-13).

The restoration of human and agricultural fertility would also accompany Israel's salvation, again reversing one of the effects of past judgment. Though invading armies had reduced the nation to a mere remnant (cf. Amos 3:12; 5:3; 6:9-10; Mic. 4:7), someday the reunited people of the Northern and Southern Kingdoms would be as innumerable as the sand on the seashore (Hos. 1:10-11) and constitute a "strong nation" (Mic. 4:7). Though divinely appointed pestilence and armies had deprived the nation of its agricultural abundance, that too would be restored in the age to come (Hos. 2:21-22). Amos described the agricultural fertility of the eschaton as follows: "The days are coming . . . when the reaper will be overtaken by the plowman and the planter by the one treading grapes. New wine will drip from the mountains and flow from the hills. I will bring back my exiled people Israel; they will rebuild the ruined cities and live in them. They will plant vine

5. The Hebrew phrases translated in NIV "from of old" and "from ancient times" are frequently used elsewhere of the early periods of Israel's history, including David's time (Neh. 12:46; Pss. 74:12; 77:12; Isa. 63:9, 11; Mal. 3:4). The phrase "ancient times" is even used later in Micah in this way (Mic. 7:14). Amos, in prophesying the restoration of the Davidic throne, used this phrase to refer to the time of David's reign (Amos 9:11).

yards and drink their wine; they will make gardens and eat their fruit" (Amos 9:13-14). The promise that the people would drink the wine from the vineyards they plant (9:14) is a direct reversal of the judgment described in Amos 5:11.

Just as the prophets presented God's judgment as a reversal of earlier divine saving acts, so they described Israel's coming restoration as a repetition of her salvation history. For example Hosea and Micah referred to Israel's return from exile in terms of a new Exodus. The Lord would call the people of Israel out of their various places of exile just as He had summoned them from Egypt through Moses (Hos. 11:1). Again the Lord would display mighty "wonders" (Mic. 7:15; cf. Ex. 3:20; Pss. 78:12-13; 106:22) in redeeming His people (Mic. 4:10; cf. Ex. 6:6; 15:13; Ps. 74:2).

Hosea and Micah also alluded to other events in the nation's salvation history. When released from exile, Israel would tremble again before the Lord's thunderous roar (Hos. 11:10-11) as she did at Sinai (cf. Ex. 19:16). The Lord would again lead His people into the land through the valley of Achor (Hos. 2:15), the site of Achan's sin, which jeopardized the success of the conquest (Josh. 7:1-26). However, in the eschaton Achor would be a symbol of hope, not of disobedience and near failure. When the Israelites reoccupied the land, they would be called sons of "the living God" (Hos. 1:10). This rare divine title (*'ēl ḥay*) was used in conjunction with the original conquest under Joshua (Josh. 3:10). According to Micah 4:13, the Lord would give Israel victory over her enemies. In response Israel would "devote" (*ḥāram*, a verb used frequently in relation to the original conquest) the booty of the land to "the Lord of all the earth." This rare title, like "the living God," was used in the context of the original conquest (Josh. 3:11, 13). As she prospers in her God-given land, Israel would once again be like a fruitful vine (cf. Hos. 10:1 with 14:7) and would respond favorably to the Lord, "as in the day she came out of Egypt" (2:15).

Moving further along in Israel's salvation history, the prophets predicted a return of the glory of the Davidic empire. As noted earlier, Hosea and Micah envisioned the second coming of David (Hos. 3:5; Mic. 5:2), whereas Amos and Micah anticipated a repetition of the Davidic conquests and a revival of Davidic suzerainty over the surrounding nations (Amos 9:11-12; Mic. 5:4-9).

GOD AND THE NATIONS

The nations do not play a prominent role in Hosea, appearing only as an object of Israel's misplaced trust and ironically as instruments of God's judgment on His people. The Lord's ability to deliver His people from exile testifies to His sovereignty over the nations.

Amos and Micah have much more to say concerning the nations' relationship to Israel and to her God. From the outset both books make clear that the Lord's sovereignty is not limited to Israel but extends over all the nations. Amos begins with a series of judgment speeches against the nations surrounding Israel (Amos 1:3–2:3). Micah opens with a vivid portrayal of the Lord's theophanic descent to judge the nations (Mic. 1:2-4). For these prophets Israel's God is "the Lord of all the earth" (cf. Mic. 4:13), who controls the history and destinies of nations (Amos 9:7). According to Amos 9:12, the nations "bear" the Lord's "name." The expression points to the Lord's ownership of and authority over the nations as its use elsewhere makes clear (cf. 2 Sam. 12:28; Isa. 4:1).

The word used in the oracles of Amos 1-2 to characterize the nations' sins refers to an act of rebellion against sovereign authority. The term is used elsewhere of one nation rebelling against the authority of another (cf. 2 Kings 1:1; 2 Kings 3:5, 7). Judah (Amos 2:4-5) and Israel (Amos 2:6-16) had broken the Mosaic Covenant. However, by what arrangement were the foreign nations responsible to God? The crimes listed, which include wartime atrocities, slave trade, breach of treaty agreements, and desecration of a tomb, may all be regarded, at least in principle, as violations of God's mandate to Noah to be fruitful and multiply and to show proper respect for one's fellow man as a divine image bearer (cf. Gen. 9:1-7). Amos may have viewed this Noahic mandate against the background of a suzerain-vassal treaty, the mandate itself being comparable to the treaty demands or stipulations. In a similar way Isaiah interpreted the nations' crime of bloodshed (Isa. 26:21) as a violation of the "everlasting covenant" (Isa. 24:5; cf. Gen. 9:16) that would bring a curse on the entire earth (Isa. 24:6-13). Drought, a common motif in biblical and ancient Near Eastern curse lists, is a prominent element in this worldwide curse (cf. Isa. 24:4, 7-9). In the heading to his series of judgment oracles Amos likewise portrayed the Lord's judgment as bringing drought (Amos 1:2). Drought would seem to epitomize the curses that fall on the nations for their rebellion against their Suzerain.

Micah also referred to the nations' alienation from God (Mic. 4:5). The Lord would judge the nations for their disobedience and sinful deeds (5:15; 7:13). The nations who mocked God's people (7:10) would crawl in fear before the Lord (7:16-17). This subjugation of the nations would usher in the Lord's universal reign over all the earth from His throne in Jerusalem (4:1-4). This golden age would be characterized by the cessation of war and universal worship of the God of Israel.

THE SEVENTH-CENTURY PROPHETS
(NAHUM, HABAAKKUK, ZEPHANIAH)

INTRODUCTION

The seventh-century minor prophets focused on the justice of God as exhibited in powerful judgment on an international scale. Nahum announced Assyria's well-deserved judgment, which in turn would bring relief to God's people and to all who suffered at the hands of this ruthless oppressor. The dialogue between Habakkuk and the Lord focused on the issue of justice. Much to the prophet's chagrin, God's solution to the problem of injustice in Judahite society was to summon the Babylonians as His instrument of punishment. However, He assured Habakkuk that He would also eventually judge Babylon for its crimes and protect and ultimately vindicate His faithful followers. Zephaniah foresaw the judgment of Judah and the surrounding nations as part of a worldwide cataclysm akin to Noah's flood. However, through this purifying judgment, God would reestablish justice in Jerusalem and make the nations His willing servants.

GOD AND HIS PEOPLE

Judgment. Nahum had little to say about God's judgment of Israel. He spoke of it as something that had already occurred (Nah. 1:12). By contrast Habakkuk and Zephaniah prophesied the judgment of God's disobedient people. In both books injustice in Judahite society is a primary reason for this judgment (Hab. 1:2-3; Zeph. 1:9; 3:1-7). Zephaniah also denounced Judah's pagan practices (Zeph. 1:4-6), her wealth (1:11, 13) and her complacent, arrogant attitude (1:12; 3:11).

God's judgment would be severe and violent (cf. Zeph. 1:2-18) yet appropriate (Hab. 1:5-11; Zeph. 1:13). Using the cruel Babylonians as His instrument (Hab. 1:6), the Lord would descend like a warrior on Judah (Zeph. 1:14-16). Zephaniah likened the resulting carnage to an animal sacrifice (1:7, 17). Those who had ignored God's law and treated their countrymen unjustly and violently (Hab. 1:2-3) would, appropriately, experience the violence of the lawless Babylonians (1:7, 9).

Protection and salvation. As He prepared to unleash His angry judgment, God took note of the faithful few among His people. He reminded an anxious Habakkuk that the "righteous" would "live by his faith" (Hab. 2:4). In this context the "righteous" are those who suffer oppression because of their devotion to the Lord (cf. 1:4). The verb "live" refers here to physical preservation through the coming invasion (cf. 1:12; 3:17-19). "Faith" is better translated "faithfulness" in accord with Old Testament usage. Elsewhere the word refers to reliable, honest conduct that conforms to the Lord's moral and ethical standards. By the conclusion of the book, Habakkuk accepts the Lord's assurance, affirming his confidence that the Lord would sustain him through the coming crisis (3:16-19).

Zephaniah also encouraged the Lord's obedient servants, exhorting them to continue in righteousness and faith (Zeph. 2:3; 3:8). He spoke of a remnant that would form the basis of a restored covenant community. This righteous remnant would escape from exile (3:19-20) and populate purified Jerusalem (3:12-13).

The theme of God's relationship to Zion is prominent in Zephaniah. Because of its corrupt practices and leadership the city would be the focal point of God's judgment (Zeph. 1:4-13; 3:1-7). This judgment would eliminate the city's evildoers (3:11). In their place the Lord would populate the city with the aforementioned remnant (3:12-13). The Lord would then restore His protection to the city and never again allow its enemies to enter its gates (3:13*b*-17).

For all three prophets Israel's deliverance and restoration would come in conjunction with God's judgment on the Gentile nations. According to Nahum, whose eschatological vision is the least far-reaching, the destruction of Assyria would release God's people from bondage (Nah. 1:13) and result in celebration, peace, and renewed prosperity (1:15; 2:2). For Zephaniah God's judgment of the nations would bring the remnant of His people release from exile and lead to their elevation to a position of worldwide prominence (Zeph. 3:20) from which they would exercise sovereignty over their traditional enemies (2:6-7, 9). According to Habakkuk, God's destruction of His people's oppressors would be nothing less than salvation history repeated. Several elements in Habakkuk's theophanic portrayal of the Lord's future judgment (Hab. 3:2-15) recall events in Israel's early experience, including God's defeat of the Egyptians at the Red Sea, His self-revelation at Sinai and the victories accomplished through Joshua, Deborah, and David (cf. 3:3-15 with Ex. 15:1-18; 19:16-19; Deut. 33:2; Josh. 10:12-14; Judg. 5:4-5; Pss. 18:7-15; 77:16-19). By describing the future in the language of the past, Habakkuk affirmed that the God of Israel is an everlasting God (cf. Hab. 1:12) who is ever active in history (3:6) and always capable of intervening for His people.

In reflecting on God's future intervention for Israel the seventh-century minor prophets characterized Him as a protector or savior. Nahum affirmed, "The Lord is good, a refuge in times of trouble. He cares for those who trust in him" (Nah. 1:7). Habakkuk addressed God as his "Savior" (Hab. 3:18). Zephaniah, addressing a salvation oracle to personified Zion, declared, "The Lord your God is with you, he is mighty to save" (Zeph. 3:17).

GOD AND THE NATIONS

The seventh-century prophets depicted the Lord as the sovereign ruler over the nations. God raises up nations as instruments of judgment (Hab. 1:6), suppresses their challenges to His rule (Nah. 1:9-12), and destroys even the more powerful among them. None can escape His wrath (Zeph. 3:8).

The primary basis for the nations' judgment was their arrogance. Assyria took pride in her wealth and military strength (Nah. 2:9; 3:8-13) and self-confidently declared, "I am, and there is none besides me" (Zeph. 2:15). Likewise Babylon worshiped her own military might and considered herself invincible (Hab. 1:6-11, 16; 2:4-5). Even lightweight nations such as Moab and Ammon displayed an arrogant attitude (Zeph. 2:10).

The nations expressed this pride in various ways. Assyria and Babylon exploited other nations economically, their greed for material wealth leading them to implement violent imperialistic policies (Nah. 2:11-13; 3:1, 4; Hab. 1:13-17; 2:5-17). In this regard Nahum compared Assyria to a ravaging lion (Nah. 2:11-13) and a seductive prostitute (3:4). Habakkuk likened greedy Babylon to a successful fisherman (Hab. 1:15-16), a drunkard (2:5), death (2:5), and an unscrupulous loan shark (2:6).

The proud nations even had the audacity to oppress God's people. Though the Lord used them as instruments to chastise His wayward people, He did not approve of the attitude the nations displayed. Nahum regarded Assyria's treatment of Israel as a wicked plot against the Lord (Nah. 1:9-11). Habakkuk described the Babylonians as greedily desiring to devour God's people (Hab. 3:14). Zephaniah singled out

Moab and Ammon for their taunts and insults against Judah (Zeph. 2:8, 10).

All three prophets depict the Lord as an angry, vengeful warrior who violently punishes the nations for their arrogance. Each applied to Him the title "Lord of Hosts" (or "Lord of Armies"; Nah. 2:13; 3:5; Hab. 2:13; Zeph. 2:9) and referred specifically to His anger or vengeance (Nah. 1:2, 6; Hab. 3:8, 12; Zeph. 1:15, 18, 3:8).

Theophanies highlight Nahum's and Habakkuk's descriptions of the divine warrior. In Nahum 1:2-8 the Lord comes in a mighty windstorm, His powerful battle cry causing all nature to tremble in fear. He pursues His enemies into "darkness," a symbol here of death and destruction. In Habakkuk's theophany the Lord marches from the south in radiant splendor (Hab. 3:3). As He approaches in the storm (3:4-5) the cosmos shakes in fear (3:6-7).[6] Leading His chariots into battle, He unleashes His weapons against the enemies of His people with devastating effects (3:8-15).

Zephaniah's Day of the Lord theme draws attention to God's role as warrior. As noted earlier, this theme corresponds to the sovereign's day of conquest, a notion found in ancient Near Eastern literature (see pp. 309-10). Zephaniah's characterization of the day is consistent with this: "The great day of the Lord is near — near and coming quickly. Listen! The cry on the day of the Lord will be bitter, the shouting of the warrior there. That day will be a day of wrath, a day of distress and anguish, a day of trouble and ruin, a day of darkness and gloom, a day of clouds and blackness, a day of trumpet and battle cry against the fortified cities and against the corner towers" (Zeph. 1:14-16).

Zephaniah also emphasized the thorough nature of God's judgment on the nations. In Zephaniah 1:2-3 the Lord likens the coming universal judgment to the Noahic flood, by which He wiped out all creatures (cf. Gen. 6:7; 7:4, 23). Zephaniah's oracles against specific nations focus on the totality of the destruction about to come on God's enemies (Zeph. 2:5, 9, 13-15). Alluding once more to Genesis, the Lord announced that Moab and Ammon would become like Sodom and Gomorrah (2:9).

The Lord's judgment on the nations would also be appropriate. According to Nahum, the Lord would treat Assyria as it had treated others. Nahum's descriptions of Assyria's demise contains several parallels to battle accounts in the Assyrian annals. Just as Assyrian armies had besieged, plundered, and destroyed cities, so Nineveh would be surrounded and invaded (Nah. 2:3-10). Assyrian kings, comparing themselves to destructive floods, described in vivid detail their enemies' fear, bloody defeat, and humiliation. In the same way the Lord, using a flood (1:8; 2:6), would terrorize, slaughter, and humiliate the Assyrians (2:10; 3:3, 5-6, 11, 18-19). Assyria would experience several of the treaty curses with which it had threatened

6. Habbakkuk 3:4-5 may be better translated "His splendor was like lightning; lightning bolts flashed from His hand, where His power was hidden. Plague went before Him; a destructive fire-bolt followed His steps."

its subjects, including the destruction of offspring (1:14), the heaping up of corpses (3:3), the loss of courage among its soldiers (3:13), and an "incurable wound" (3:19; probably a figure here for the final demise of the empire).

Habakkuk's woe oracles against Babylon also stress the fitting nature of God's judgment. Babylon would be plundered, just as it had plundered other nations (Hab. 2:6-8). Babylon's physical splendor, made possible by its exploitation of others, testified of its crimes (2:9-11). This glorious empire would fall, experiencing the same humiliation to which it had subjected the surrounding nations (2:15-17).

The Lord's judgment on the nations would have important universal effects. The Lord's superiority to the nations' idol-gods would become apparent to all (Nah. 1:14; Hab. 2:18-20; Zeph. 2:11). By worshiping these supposed deities the nations had rejected the Lord's sovereignty. However, His judgment of the nations would demonstrate how foolish such worship is. Idol-gods are nothing but the products of man's craftsmanship. They have no life and are incapable of providing guidance (Hab. 2:18-19). By contrast, the Lord is set apart from all that is human and rules over the whole earth (2:20).

According to Zephaniah, all nations would eventually worship the Lord (Zeph. 2:11). This restoration of the nations would reverse the judgment at Babel, recorded in Genesis 11. Because of mankind's arrogant attempt at unification and self-exaltation (cf. Gen. 11:4), God confused their language and dispersed them throughout the world (11:5-9). However, according to Zephaniah 3:9, the Lord would "purify [*bārar*] the lips" ("language" in Gen. 11:6-9 and "lips" in Zeph. 3:9 translate the same Hebrew word) He "confused" (*bālal*, which sounds, ironically, like *bārar*, "to purify") at Babel. In contrast to Babel, where proud men united in their effort to invade God's abode, the nations would someday unite in genuine service to God. Those "scattered" throughout the earth (Zeph. 3:10; the Hebrew translated "scattered" in this verse is also employed in Gen. 11:4, 8-9) would come to worship God and offer Him tribute.[7]

Excursus on the Day of the Lord in Zephaniah. The Day of the Lord theme, introduced by the eighth-century prophet Amos, is a central motif in Zephaniah's message. In Amos the concept was rather limited in scope, referring to Israel's impending judgment at the hands of Assyria (cf. Amos 5:18-20). In Zephaniah the Lord's day is more universal and far-reaching.

Zephaniah spoke of the nearness and swift approach of this day of judgment (Zeph. 1:7, 14). Various nations of his day would participate in it,

---

7. Some take verse 10 as referring to Israel's return from exile, but in the context of verse 9 the referent should not be limited so. The group in view may include Israelite exiles (Zeph. 3:19-20), but the literary parallels between Genesis 11 and this text suggest that Gentiles are included as well. The notion of Cushites, who are objects of God's judgment in Zepahniah 2:12, returning to God is consistent with the pattern of reversal seen elsewhere in the book (cf. Zeph. 2:11; 3:8-9).

including Judah, Philistia, Moab, Ammon, Cush, and Assyria. One must conclude then that this Day of the Lord was initially realized in conjunction with the Babylonian conquest of the Near East shortly after Zephaniah's prophecy.

However, this day also has a cosmic and universal dimension that transcends anything that happened in Zephaniah's day. The Lord's day would bring a cataclysmic judgment that would rival the Noahic flood in magnitude (Zeph. 1:2-3, 18; 3:8). In the aftermath of this day God would restore His covenant people to a purified Zion and establish His universal rule over the previously rebellious nations. These developments remain unfulfilled, awaiting realization in the eschaton.

Zephaniah's presentation of the Lord's day thus illustrates the principle of telescoping, so common in the prophetic literature.[8] The prophets often merged near and far-off events, presenting one unified picture of the future in which the chronological gaps made apparent by later revelation and historical developments are not visible. In the case of Zephaniah, one could say the Babylonian conquest, which was nearly universal given the limited geographical proportions of the prophet's worldview, foreshadowed a greater eschatological judgment to come. Zephaniah's vision of universal restoration will be realized after this latter phase of judgment.

THE SIXTH- AND FIFTH-CENTURY PROPHETS
(JOEL, OBADIAH, HAGGAI, ZECHARIAH, MALACHI)

INTRODUCTION

As foreseen by earlier prophets, the Babylonians destroyed Jerusalem in 586 B.C. and carried many off into exile. However, God did not abandon His people. In 538 B.C. He moved Cyrus the Persian, conqueror of Babylon, to allow a group of exiles to return to Judah and begin rebuilding the Jerusalem Temple, a project completed in 516 B.C.

The sixth- and fifth-centuries minor prophets addressed concerns and issues arising out of the experiences of exile and return to the land. Was God really sovereign over the affairs of men and nations? Would the nations be repaid for their mistreatment of God's people? Had God severed His covenant relationship with Israel? Would the promises to the fathers, which formed the basis of the visions of earlier prophets, really be fulfilled?

Sometime after Jerusalem's fall Obadiah warned that God would repay Judah's oppressors, in particular Edom, for their cruelty and mistreatment of His people. Obadiah also looked forward to the restoration of the exiles to their land.

Joel, Haggai, Zechariah, and Malachi addressed the postexilic community. Each made clear that this community was the successor of the preexilic nation.

8. See Gordon D. Fee and Douglas Stuart, *How to Read the Bible for All It's Worth* (Grand Rapids: Zondervan, 1982), pp. 163-64.

Like the fathers the postexilic community was responsible to obey God's covenant demands. As taught by Moses and illustrated throughout Israel's history, obedience would bring blessing, whereas disobedience would result in discipline.

Rather than dwelling on earlier failures, these prophets emphasized the responsibilities of the present, as well as the glorious future God had planned for His people. The return of the exiles to the land marked the beginning of a new era in Israel's history. God would eventually fulfill His earlier promises and accomplish His original purpose for the nation. He would reestablish Jerusalem, restore the Davidic throne, purify the priesthood, and reinstitute worship at the Temple. Ultimately all nations would recognize His universal sovereignty.

The realization of this ideal would not be automatic, however. Only loyal, faithful followers of the Lord would see its fulfillment. Zechariah and Malachi even anticipated a future judgment of the postexilic community, which would purify it of evildoers. The remaining remnant, composed of the Lord's genuine devotees, would then populate the land and experience God's richest blessings.

GOD AND HIS PEOPLE

God's former dealings with His people. The sixth- and fifth-centuries minor prophets said relatively little about the reason for the Exile. Malachi, who never mentioned the Exile specifically, did refer in general to Israel's sinful history (Mal. 3:7). Zechariah recalled how the nation's refusal to heed the prophets led to judgment (Zech. 1:4-5; 8:13-14). More specifically, the people's obstinate rejection of God's covenant demands concerning social justice led to their being scattered among the nations (Zech. 7:9-14).

Through wordplay Zechariah indicated that Israel's sin had been self-destructive and her punishment appropriate. By making "their hearts as hard as flint" (Zech. 7:12), the people eventually "made the pleasant land desolate" (7:14). Repetition of the verb "made" draws attention to the self-destructive nature of their sinful actions. Because they acted "stubbornly" (7:11) the Lord "scattered" them (7:14). The Hebrew word translated "stubbornly" (*sōrāret*) sounds like the verb translated "scattered" (*sā'ar*), suggesting that God's punitive action was an appropriate response to Israel's rebellious attitude. In this regard it is also significant that the words translated "stopped up" (7:11), "would not listen" (7:12; both translate *miššᵉmôa'*), and "flint" (7:12; *šāmîr*), all descriptive of their sin, sound like the word translated "desolate" (7:13; *šāmam*), descriptive of their punishment.

God's relationship to His people. Through the sixth- and fifth-centuries prophets God clarified His relationship to His people. Like their fathers the people were to obey God's law. In turn God was committed to them just as He had been to the preexilic nation.

Malachi made this especially apparent. The book begins with an affirmation of God's elective love for Jacob (Mal. 1:2) and ends with an exhortation to obey the ancient law given through Moses (4:4). In between the Lord denounced the postexilic community for specific violations of covenant laws and principles. The priests had offered defiled sacrifices to God (1:6-14; cf. Lev. 22:17-25; Deut. 15:21), while the people had neglected bringing the tithes and offerings needed to sustain the Levites (Mal. 3:7-10; cf. Num. 18:8, 11, 19, 21-24). To make matters worse, many had divorced their wives or married foreign women, completely disregarding the basic covenantal principle of loyalty to God and to one's fellow Israelites (Mal. 2:10-16). The Lord explained that only His unwavering devotion to the covenant relationship had preserved the community (3:6).

Earlier Haggai and Zechariah had also drawn attention to God's continuing love for His people and to their responsibilities. Haggai criticized the community for neglecting the rebuilding of the Temple, which was the symbol of God's presence among His people (Hag. 1:2-11). The Lord encouraged the people to complete the project, promising them His enabling presence (1:13). Once the project was resumed, He reaffirmed His presence, specifically associating the postexilic community with the very first generation of Israelites (2:4-5). In Zechariah 2:7-11 the Lord urged those exiles still in Babylon to return home to Jerusalem where He would live among them. The Lord regarded His people as the "apple (i.e., pupil) of his eye," a prized and irreplaceable possession to be guarded at all costs (Zech. 2:8). In contrast to their fathers (cf. 7:9-14), they were to promote social justice and ethical behavior within the covenant community (8:16-17).

Joel, using an ancient covenant formula, exhorted his contemporaries, "Return to the Lord your God, for he is gracious and compassionate, slow to anger and abounding in love, and he relents from sending calamity" (Joel 2:13; cf. Ex. 34:6; Num. 14:18). The same mercy experienced by Moses' rebellious generation was also available to Joel's generation.

The covenant principles of reward and punishment, whereby obedience brings divine blessing and disobedience judgment, were still operative in the postexilic community as well. Haggai and Zechariah pointed out that the people's negligence had brought drought, plagues, poor harvests, and civil unrest (Hag. 1:5, 9-11; 2:15-19; Zech. 8:9-10). However, the resumption of the Temple project would result in agricultural prosperity (Hag. 2:19; Zech. 8:11-12). Even foreigners would recognize the nation's blessings (Zech. 8:13). In the past they had regarded God's people as a prime example of an accursed nation and had employed the names "Judah" and "Israel" in their curse formulas (for an example of a curse formula, see Jer. 29:22). However, now they would use the names in their prayers of blessing because God's people would be a paradigm of blessing among the nations (for examples of prayers of blessing using individual names, see Gen. 48:20 and Ruth 4:11). The phrase "you will be a blessing" appears to allude to God's promise that Abraham and his descendants would become a prime example (and ultimately a channel) of divine blessing for the nations (cf. Gen. 12:2).

Because of disobedience Malachi's generation was already under the disciplinary "curse" of God (Mal. 2:2; 3:9), which would eventually culminate in severe judgment (2:3; 4:6). However, if the people repented (3:7), they would experience agricultural blessings (3:10-12).

Because of their sins Joel's generation experienced the horrors of a locust invasion, the magnitude of which was unprecedented (Joel 1:2-20). This was a mere harbinger of the Day of the Lord that would fall on the community in full force if it did not repent (1:15; 2:1-17). When the people responded positively, God took pity on them and promised to restore their agricultural prosperity (2:18-27; the verbs translated "will be jealous" and "will reply" in Joel 2:18-19*a* are better rendered in the past tense as in the NIV margin).

God's future program for His people. Even in the aftermath of Jerusalem's defeat and the nation's exile God's prophets looked ahead. Obadiah concluded his brief message of judgment against the nations with a word of hope for the exiles (Obad. 17-21). The exiles would again occupy their land and emerge supreme over their enemies. Jerusalem would be purified and become the center of God's rule on earth.

The postexilic prophets assured those who had returned from exile that God had great plans for the nation. Haggai focused the people's attention on the Temple. Work on the Temple had been interrupted due to apathy and opposition. Even when the project was resumed many considered the structure to be nothing in comparison to the glorious Solomonic Temple of preexilic times (cf. Hag. 2:3; Zech. 4:10). Nevertheless Haggai boldly predicted that the wealth of nations would eventually flow into the Temple and that its glory would surpass that of the Solomonic Temple (Hag. 2:7-9).

Two major interpretive problems arise in relation to Haggai 2:7-9. The first concerns the referent of "the desired of all nations" (v. 7). Though some interpret this as a messianic title, the immediate context (v. 8) as well as parallel texts (cf. Isa. 60:5-9; Zech. 14:14) strongly suggest that reference is made to the nations' tribute payments. The verb "will come" is plural in Hebrew, suggesting that "desired" (*ḥemdat* [singular]) be repointed as a plural (*ḥămudōt*), "desirable things."

The second problem concerns the fulfillment of Haggai 2:9. Some see this prophecy fulfilled in Herod's expansion of the Temple or in Jesus' physical presence in the Temple while on earth during His first advent. However, the context links the glorification of the Temple with the subjugation of the Gentiles, an event that never occurred before the destruction of the second Temple in A.D. 70. It would seem then that this prophecy will be fulfilled in conjunction with a future Temple. How then is one to explain Haggai's statement "The glory of *this present house* will be greater . . ."? The key to answering this question may be in 2:3, where the second Temple is identified with Solomon's Temple (cf. "this house in its former glory"). In the same way, verse 9 may associate the future millennial Temple with the second Temple. From the divine perspective there is but one Temple, despite its many historical forms. By associating the future glory of the Temple with the structure built in Haggai's day, God assured His people that their efforts, though perhaps insignificant in their sight, would eventually be rewarded. God would again dwell among His people and the splendor of His dwelling place would exceed anything Israel had yet experienced. An era even more grand than Solomon's was just around the corner.

Haggai also envisioned a future restoration of the Davidic dynasty. Though God's people were under the rule of a foreign power and David's royal descendant Zerubbabel was a mere governor, political structures could and would change. God would overthrow the kings of the earth (Hag. 2:21-22) and elevate the Davidic throne to prominence (2:23). By calling Zerubbabel His "servant" and "chosen" one God gave him the same status David had enjoyed (cf. 2 Sam. 3:18; 6:21; 7:5, 8, 26; 1 Kings 8:16). The comparison to a "signet ring" indicates a position of authority and reverses the judgment pronounced on Zerubbabel's grandfather Jehoiachin (cf. Jer. 22:24-30).

The words of Haggai 2:21-23, though spoken directly to Zerubbabel, were not fulfilled in his day. How is one to explain this apparent failure of Haggai's prophecy? Zerubbabel, a descendant of David and governor of Judah, was the official representative of the Davidic dynasty in the postexilic community at that time. As such the prophecy of the future exaltation of the Davidic throne was attached to his person. As with the Temple (cf. Hag. 2:6-9), Haggai related an eschatological reality to a tangible historical entity to assure his contemporaries that God had great plans for His people. Zerubbabel was, as it were, the visible guarantee of a glorious future for the house of David. In Haggai's day some may have actually entertained messianic hopes for Zerubbabel. However, in the progress of revelation and history Jesus Christ fulfills Haggai's prophecy.

The book of Joel also anticipates great things for God's people. Joel's vision concerns both the immediate future and subsequent events associated with the Day of the Lord. After assuring Joel's generation that judgment had been averted (Joel 2:20), the Lord promised that He would restore the crops destroyed by the locusts (vv. 19, 21-26). These acts of divine intervention are classified as "wonders" (v. 26), placing them on the same level with God's mighty deeds in Israel's salvation history (cf. Ex. 3:20; 15:11, 34:10; Josh. 3:5; Judg. 6:13; Ps. 77:14). Like those great acts this new display of divine power would reveal God's presence among His people and demonstrate His superiority to all other supposed deities (Joel 2:27).

The Day of the Lord is a prominent theme in the book of Joel. In the first half of the book this day is strictly one of judgment against God's people (1:15; 2:1-11). However, following the people's repentance (implied in 2:18; see NIV margin), this day is transformed into one of vindication and blessing for God's people as the nations become the object of His judgment.

In the Day of the Lord Israel will experience an unprecedented outpouring of God's Spirit (Joel 2:28-29). Though the phrase "all people" (2:28*a*) has a universal ring, verses 28*b*-29 limit the referent to all *classes* of people *within Judah*, regardless of gender, age, or social status (note the threefold repetition of "your," which points back to verses 18-27, where God's people are addressed). The recipients of the Spirit will exhibit prophetic gifts, fulfilling Moses' desire that "all the Lord's people" would prophesy by His Spirit (cf. Num. 11:29).

The Lord will also supernaturally intervene to protect His people from hostile nations (Joel 2:32; 3:16). At that time the Zion ideal, expressed so clearly in Psalms (esp. Pss. 46 and 48) and in Isaiah, will be realized as the Lord appears in theophanic splendor to protect His dwelling place in Jerusalem from those who seek to profane it (Joel 3:15-17).

The Lord's presence in Jerusalem will assure the nation's agricultural prosperity (Joel 3:18). Vineyards and flocks will be so plentiful and fruitful that the hills will seemingly flow with wine and milk. Even the seasonal wadis will be transformed into perennial streams. As a symbol of fruitfulness and a reminder of the Lord's fructifying presence, Joel envisioned a fountain flowing out of the Temple and running through the land (cf. Ezek. 47:1-12; Zech. 14:8).

Zechariah gave a much more detailed and complete eschatological vision than the other sixth- and fifth-centuries minor prophets. The book is divided into two sections: chapters 1-8, which contain several dated messages; and chapters 9-14, which include two undated "oracles" (cf. Zech. 9:1; 12:1). Chapters 1-8 present a generally positive view of the nation's future, which focuses on the restoration of Jerusalem and the reestablishment of the Davidic throne and the priesthood. This section only briefly hints that the land would require further purification (3:9; 5:1-4). Chapters 9-14 develop several themes from chapters 1-8. Though the overall tone remains optimistic, the prophet foresaw a rejection of the Lord's leadership, which would necessitate purifying judgment. However, the Lord will eventually intervene for His people in a culminating battle. This will lead to their repentance and the bestowal of divine blessings.

The restoration of Jerusalem is central to chapters 1-8. Declaring His intense emotional attachment to the city, the Lord promises to restore its prosperity (Zech. 1:14-17; 8:1-5). He will once again take up residence in Zion (2:10-11; 8:3) and supernaturally protect it (2:5). The focal point of the restored city will be God's dwelling place, the rebuilt Temple (1:17). Those residents of the city still in exile will return to it in vast numbers (2:4, 6-7; 8:7-8). Signs of divine blessing will be seen on the city's streets, where those living to a "ripe old age" will watch young children playing contentedly (8:4-5). Though many might marvel at this reversal in Zion's condition, the Lord Almighty will not share their amazement, for nothing is beyond His power (8:6).

Through the literary device of allusion, this eschatological portrayal of heavily populated Jerusalem is linked to the narrative of Isaac's birth, recorded in Genesis 18:1-15 and 21:1-7. According to Genesis 18:12, barren Sarah laughed skeptically when the Lord announced she would bear a son. The Lord reprimanded her, emphasizing that nothing is too difficult for Him to accomplish (18:14). When the promised child was born (21:2) Abraham named him Isaac (*yiṣḥāq*, from the verb *ṣāḥaq*, "to laugh"), meaning "he laughs." Sarah, whose skeptical laughter had been turned to joyous laughter, explained the name's significance, "God has brought me laughter, and everyone who hears about this will laugh with me" (21:6).

Like the Genesis narrative Zechariah 8:5-6 draws attention to God's supernatural ability to produce offspring against seemingly insurmountable odds (cf. Zech. 7:14). Verse 5 uses the key word from the Isaac narrative to describe the children's "playing" (lit. "laughing," from *śāḥaq*, an alternate form of *ṣāḥaq*) in the streets, and verse 6, like Genesis 18:14, indicates that the Lord can accomplish anything ("marvelous" in Zech. 8:6 translates the same Hebrew word as "hard" does in Gen. 18:14). Through these allusions the future fertility of Jerusalem's populace is related to God's seed promise to Abraham (cf. Gen. 15), which was set in motion by Isaac's birth. Just as Sarah's joyous laughter testified to God's ability to overcome even barrenness in fulfilling His promise to give Abraham a son, so the laughing children of revived Jerusalem would demonstrate God's power to overcome all obstacles (even exile) in making the ancient Abrahamic promise of numerous offspring a reality.

Zechariah 1-8 also focuses on the leadership of restored Jerusalem. Both priest and king play prominent roles in these chapters. In Zechariah's fourth night vision (3:1-10) he witnessed the cleansing of Joshua, the high priest in the postexilic community at that time. Joshua's "filthy clothes," symbolic of sin, were replaced with "rich garments" and a clean turban was placed on his head (3:3-5). The Lord then charged Joshua to obey His commandments and promised to reward his obedience by giving him authority over the Temple service and access to God's council (3:6-7). Of course the message applies to the entire nation because Joshua, as high priest, represented the people. His cleansing symbolized the reinstatement of the nation as a whole and, more particularly, of the priests who mediated between God and the people.

Joshua's cleansing was opposed by Satan (Zech. 3:1-2). The Hebrew word translated "Satan," which means "adversary," often refers elsewhere to human enemies. However, when used with the article (as here and in Job 1-2), a particular angelic being hostile to God's servants is in view. His character, which is not fully developed in the Old Testament, comes into sharper focus in the New Testament, where his Old Testament title becomes a proper name.

The Lord also promised to restore the Davidic throne. In Zechariah 3:8 God told Joshua and his associates that He would raise up "the Branch" for the community. This title was employed earlier by Jeremiah (cf. Jer. 23:5; 33:15) in referring to the ideal Davidic ruler of the eschaton. This "Branch" would rebuild the Temple and rule over the nation (Zech. 6:12-13). Since Zechariah 4:9 assigns the rebuilding of the Temple to Judah's governor, Zerubbabel (a contemporary of Joshua), it is likely that messianic hopes were attached to his person. However, as in Haggai 2:23, Zerubbabel has a representative role here. Though partially fulfilled in Zerubbabel, the ideal expressed in Zechariah 6:12-13 will be realized completely and finally in Jesus Christ.

The relationship between king and priest is an important theme in Zechariah's eschatology. In the prophet's fifth night vision (Zech. 4:1-14) he saw a golden lampstand (probably symbolizing the Temple)[9] with a bowl and seven lamps (rep-

---

9. With only one exception, the word translated "lampstand" in verses 2 and 11 is used of the Tabernacle's golden lampstand or the golden lampstands of the Solomonic Temple.

resenting God's protective presence, cf. v. 10). On either side of the lampstand stood an olive tree (v. 3). The reality behind the trees is never specifically identified (cf. v. 11). However, in verse 12 the picture is expanded to include two olive branches, which provide oil for the bowl. These two branches are identified in verse 14 as "the two who are anointed to serve the Lord of all the earth." In this context these two individuals must be Joshua, the high priest (cf. chap. 3), and Zerubbabel, the governor (4:6-10). The imagery pictures these two as sustaining the Temple. Just as oil was necessary for a lamp to burn, so Joshua and Zerubbabel would be vital to the functioning of the Temple. Zerubbabel would build the Temple (vv. 7-10), and Joshua would supervise its operation (3:7).

Some object to this interpretation because it implies God Himself (symbolized by the lamps) would be dependent on the community leaders. In response one must note that Zechariah 4:6 makes clear that God's energizing power is fundamental to the restoration of the Temple. Verses 12-14 simply emphasize the important role God's appointed leaders would have in maintaining proper worship and assuring God's continued presence among His people.

Zechariah 6:9-15 also closely relates Joshua and Zerubbabel. Here Joshua is crowned (vv. 9-11), a prophecy is delivered (vv. 12-13), and instructions are given to have the symbolic crown deposited in the rebuilt Temple (v. 14). The relationship of the prophecy to the symbolic action is difficult to interpret. According to some, Joshua is here identified with the messianic "Branch," who will rebuild the Temple and rule as a king-priest. This interpretation takes the statement "And there will be harmony between the two" (6:13) as indicating a fusing of the priestly and kingly offices in the person of the Messiah. Others prefer to see two distinct individuals here. Joshua's crowning (vv. 9-11, 14) emphasizes the important role of the priest in the community's future (cf. 3:7; 4:11-14). The prophecy refers to a royal figure, distinct from Joshua, whose task is to rebuild the Temple. Zechariah 4:9 favors this interpretation for it associates the rebuilding of the Temple with Zerubbabel, not Joshua. According to this interpretation, verse 13 anticipates harmony between king and priest. In this view the Davidic ruler, though not a priest as such, will enjoy the full support of the priesthood.

The context, which consistently distinguishes between the king (represented by Zerubbabel) and the priesthood (represented by Joshua), strongly suggests that Zechariah's contemporaries would have interpreted the symbolic action and prophecy along the lines of this latter view. Great hopes were probably even attached to the persons of Zerubbabel and Joshua. Nevertheless, in the progress of revelation, Jesus will fulfill the ideals symbolized by these historical characters. In Him a merger of the royal and priestly offices occurs. Jesus, the "Branch" whom Zerubbabel merely foreshadowed, will rule over Israel. At the same time Jesus assumes a priestly function, for He has become the true Mediator between God and His people.

As noted earlier, Zechariah 9-14 expands in many ways the eschatological vision of chapters 1-8. In particular the generally optimistic view of the earlier chapters is tempered to some degree as the purification motif, introduced briefly in 3:9 and 5:1-4, is developed more fully.

The prophet anticipated a crisis in the postexilic community precipitated by the people's rejection of God's leadership. Through a lengthy allegory Zechariah portrayed this rejection and its negative consequences (11:4-17). First, the Lord commissioned the prophet to be a shepherd over His flock Israel. The prophet took two staffs, symbolizing God's favor to the nation (in the form of peaceful relations with the surrounding peoples; cf. v. 10) and the reuniting of the Northern and Southern Kingdoms (v. 14). Despite his best efforts (vv. 7-8*a*) the misguided people (cf. 10:2-3*a*) rejected him (11:8*b*). The shepherd-prophet renounced his commission and broke his two staffs, indicating that the nation would not experience the peace and unity God offered them (vv. 9-14). The Lord then told Zechariah to play the role of a foolish shepherd, interested only in exploiting the flock for personal gain (vv. 15-17).

This allegory raises several questions, the chief of which concerns the identity of the good shepherd. Since God is viewed as the nation's shepherd in the preceding context (Zech. 9:16; 10:3), it is most natural to see Him behind the shepherd figure here. However, in 9:9-10 God's rule is accomplished through a human instrument. In 13:7-8 this vice-regent is called God's "shepherd" and his rejection is depicted. Thus one may interpret the "good shepherd" as a figure for God's authority as embodied in a human ruler. In an indirect sense, then, the "good shepherd" is a messianic figure. In light of this, it comes as no surprise that Jesus applied Zechariah's shepherd imagery to Himself (cf. Matt. 26:31 with Zech. 13:7).

Because of her rejection of God's authority, the nation will experience oppression and intense suffering (Zech. 11:6, 9). Two-thirds of the nation's population will perish (13:8) as foreigners invade the land. These hostile armies will even invade and humiliate Jerusalem (12:2*b*-3*a*; 14:2). At the last minute the Lord will intervene for His people. He will energize the armies of Judah, enabling them to rout their enemies (9:13, 15; 10:3-5, 7; 12:6). The Lord Himself will burst forth in theophanic splendor (9:14; 14:3), accompanied by lightning, a trumpet blast, and the windstorms of the south (lit. Teman), all symbolic of His military might. The imagery recalls God's self-revelation at Sinai (cf. Ex. 19:16, 19), as well as Habakkuk's theophanic portrayal (Hab. 3:3, 11). The Lord will descend on the Mount of Olives, causing the mountain to split in two and allowing Jerusalem's besieged populace to escape the beleaguered city (Zech. 14:4-5). In typical apocalyptic fashion this day of divine intervention is characterized by unique cosmic disturbances (vv. 6-7) as the Lord will supernaturally annihilate His enemies with terror and plagues (12:4; 14:12-13, 15).

This mighty act of deliverance will prompt the entire nation to repent (Zech. 12:10-14). Led by the royal and priestly families the people will mourn bitterly over the one they have "pierced" (12:10). The phrase "the one they have pierced" identifies more specifically the speaker of the preceding words. Because God is speaking throughout this chapter (vv. 2-4, 6, 9-10), both the phrase "the one they have pierced" and the preceding pronoun "me" most naturally refer to God as the object of the people's past rejection. (The following pronoun [in the phrase, "they will mourn for *him*"] also refers to God, its antecedent being the preceding relative pronoun [translated "the one"]). "Pierced" anthropomorphically compares this rejection to a severe physical wound. Because this rejection is expressed in part through their opposition to God's "shepherd" (11:8; 13:7), this text may also be taken as indirectly messianic. This in turn explains how it can be applied to Jesus' being literally pierced by a spear while on the cross (John 19:37). In rejecting Jesus, God's chosen "shepherd," and allowing Him to be pierced, the nation was "piercing" (i.e., rejecting the authority of) God Himself.

This whole sequence of judgment and repentance will purify the royal family and all Jerusalem's citizens (Zech. 13:1). Idols and false prophets will disappear (13:2-5). Having cleansed the land, the Lord will renew His covenant relationship with the people (13:9), who will become as precious to Him as jewels in a crown (9:16*b*). As their shepherd the Lord will reestablish His protection over Judah and Jerusalem (9:8, 15-16; 14:11). The Lord's presence will make even horses' bells and cooking utensils holy (14:20-21). Such common items will be inscribed with the words "Holy to the Lord," a designation formerly reserved only for the most sacred objects (cf. Ex. 28:36; 39:30). The ancient ideal of a holy nation will finally be realized (Ex. 19:6).

This day of deliverance will also be accompanied by a mass return of God's exiled people. Though many were and are scattered among the nations (Zech. 10:9) and "imprisoned" in exile (9:11-12), the Lord will redeem them (10:8) and restore them to the Promised Land (10:10). Like earlier prophets, Zechariah compared this deliverance to the Exodus. As He did at the Red Sea, the Lord will remove all obstacles to His people's escape. More specifically, He will destroy those nations, represented here by Egypt and Assyria and symbolized by the surging sea, who attempt to oppose Him (10:10-11).

According to Zechariah 9:11, which is addressed to personified Jerusalem, the basis for this redemption of the exiles will be the "blood" of His "covenant" with the city. The covenant referred to here is not specified. The phrase "blood of the covenant" is used in Exodus 24:8 of the Mosaic Covenant, which was ratified by sacrifice (cf. Ex. 24:5-6). However, how could this covenant form the basis of a promise of Jerusalem's restoration? In this context (Zech. 9:9-10) and elsewhere in the Old Testament, Jerusalem's well-being and future glory are linked to the Davidic dynasty, which was the recipient of unconditional divine promises. Because these promises were related to those made earlier to Abraham, one may view the Davidic Covenant as an extension or vehicle of fulfillment of the earlier Abrahamic Covenant. Through an ideal Davidic ruler God will establish Abraham's descendants in the land promised to their ancestor. Having made this connection between the two covenants, one may view the Abrahamic land promise as directly applicable to Jerusalem, the eventual political and cultic center of the Promised Land under the Davidic rulers. Perhaps, then, reference is made in Zechariah 9:11 to the sacrifice whereby God's covenant with Abraham was ratified (cf. Gen. 15:9-11).

Zechariah's eschatological vision culminates with the establishment of God's rule (Zech. 14:9) from His capital city Jerusalem (14:16). That reign will bring agricultural blessing to the land. Using imagery also found in Ezekiel (47:1-12) and Joel (3:18), the prophet envisioned perennial streams ("living water") flowing out of Jerusalem as a symbol of the land's renewed fertility (Zech. 14:8). The abundance of grain and new wine, as well as the presence of robust young men and women, will be clear signs of God's blessing (9:17).

The Lord's kingship will be mediated through a human ruler, whose reign is portrayed in Zechariah 9:9-10. Though he is not specifically identified as a descendant of David, textual clues point in this direction. This ruler is called Jerusalem's king (v. 9, "your [i.e., Jerusalem's/Zion's] king"), suggesting he is of the Davidic line. The description of the king's universal rule (v. 10) corresponds to the ideal of the Davidic Covenant (cf. Pss. 72:8; 89:25-27).

This messianic king is described as "righteous (or, better, "just") and as having salvation (or better, "victorious" or "delivered"). The king will administer justice and his rule will be established from the outset by God's intervention. He is also characterized as "gentle" (or, better, "humble"). This word is used elsewhere of the Lord's loyal servants who promote His cause even in the face of opposition.

The king is depicted as "riding on a donkey, on a colt, the foal of a donkey." This probably points to his royal status, since elsewhere in the Bible and ancient Near Eastern literature a donkey sometimes appears as the mount of rulers (Judg. 5:10; 10:4; 12:14; 2 Sam. 16:2 are biblical examples). His riding a donkey, rather than a warhorse, also symbolizes the peaceful character of his rule (Zech. 9:10). Implements of war will be unnecessary as the king establishes his reign of peace over the whole earth. According to Matthew (21:1-7) and John (12:14-15), the first part of this prophecy was fulfilled, at least in part, in Jesus' "triumphal entry" into Jerusalem before His crucifixion. However, since the nation as a whole rejected Him at that time, the complete and final fulfillment of the prophecy awaits Christ's second coming.

Like Zechariah, Malachi's eschatological vision included the prospect of purifying judgment for God's people. By Malachi's time serious cultic and social problems had arisen within the postexilic community (Mal. 1:6-14; 2:8-17; 3:6-15; 4:6). Failure to repent would necessitate judgment. The Lord Almighty would come as the sovereign Lord of the nation to enforce His covenant (3:1*b*).

Some equate the "messenger of the covenant," mentioned in Malachi 3:1*b*, with the messenger referred to earlier in the verse ("my messenger"). In this case the messenger in verse 1 accomplishes the purification described in verses 2-4 before the Lord's coming (Mal. 3:5). However, since the "messenger of the covenant" is identified as the "Lord" who comes "to His temple," this interpretation is doubtful. It is more likely that the Lord here refers to Himself. As the "messenger of the covenant" He enforces the covenant by rewarding obedience and punishing rebellion. This may be another reference to the Lord's "angel" (lit. "messenger"), with whom the Lord virtually identifies Himself in His role as Israel's covenant Lord (cf. Ex. 3:2-6; 23:20-23; 32:34; Isa. 63:9).

The Lord's judgment will purify the priests (Mal. 3:2-3), whose relationship to the Lord receives special attention in Malachi. By their cultic improprieties the priests had jeopardized their special covenant relationship to God (2:1-9). The precise origin of this "covenant with Levi" (2:4; cf. Neh. 13:29 and Jer. 33:21) is uncertain. The "covenant of salt" made with the Levites in Aaron's day (Num. 18:19) and the covenant of promise with Phinehas (Num. 25:12-13) were more limited in scope than the covenant referred to by Malachi. The covenant alluded to by Malachi was a bilateral agreement whereby God promised "life and peace" in exchange for the priests' loyalty (Mal. 2:5). The coming judgment will remove the offending priests from office (2:3). The Lord will replace them with men who will lead the people in pure worship (3:3-4), as many priests had done in the past (2:6).

God's judgment will also purify society as a whole (Mal. 3:16–4:3). As a result His justice will become apparent to all. Though some accused Him of overlooking and even rewarding evildoers (2:17; 3:14-15), the Lord affirmed that He was carefully distinguishing the righteous from the wicked (3:16). Only the righteous will be preserved through the coming judgment (3:18–4:3).

This group of loyal servants will become the basis for the New Covenant community, which the Lord called His "treasured possession" (Mal. 3:17). This title was used for the nation in the time of Moses (Ex. 19:5; Deut. 7:6; 14:2; 26:18). Though Israel has never lived up to God's standards (Mal. 3:7), the Lord will make the covenant ideal a reality, thereby demonstrating His love and devotion to His people (1:2; 3:6).

The threatened judgment was not inevitable. The calls to repentance dispersed throughout the book (Mal. 2:1-2, 15-16; 3:7; 4:4) imply that punishment could be averted. The Lord even announced that He would send the prophetic messenger Elijah before judging His people (3:1*a*; 4:5). Elijah's task will be to prepare the way for the Lord's coming (3:1) and to bring restoration to society so that judgment might be averted (4:6). The precise nature of this restoration is debated. The NIV translation understands a healing of family strife within the community. Another possible translation is, "He will turn the hearts of the fathers together with (those of) the children, and the hearts of the children together with (those of) the fathers (to Me)." According to this interpretation, society as a whole (including both older and younger generations) is reconciled to the Lord. In this regard, it is noteworthy that the verb translated "turn" is the same word translated "return" in the general call to repentance in Malachi 3:7.

According to the New Testament, Malachi's prophecy of Elijah's coming was fulfilled, at least in part, by John the Baptist (Matt. 11:10, 14; 17:12-13; Mark 1:2, 4; Luke 1:17, 76; 7:27). Of course John himself denied being Elijah reincarnated (John 1:21), and Jesus hinted that Malachi's prophecy was not entirely exhausted in John (Matt. 17:11). Yet Jesus also made clear that John in effect fulfilled Malachi's prophecy because John came in the spirit and power of Elijah. Because the nation rejected John (Matt. 17:12), the judgment threatened by Malachi fell on them and the restoration promised by the prophet was postponed until a future day.

GOD AND THE NATIONS

The sixth- and fifth-centuries minor prophets announced that God's judgment would fall on the nations. Obadiah prophesied the fall of Edom as part of a larger judgment associated with the Lord's day. Malachi later alluded to the fulfillment, at least in part, of Obadiah's prophecy. Joel and Zechariah also referred to judgment on specific nations as part of the destructive Day of the Lord. Obadiah, Joel, and Zechariah considered the nations' mistreatment of God's people to be the primary reason for His anger with them. Each stressed the thorough and appropriate nature of the coming judgment. However, the message of these prophets is not entirely negative. According to Haggai, Zechariah, and Malachi, the nations will eventually become subjects in God's universal kingdom.

As noted above, specific nations receive attention in the sixth- and fifth-centuries prophets. Obadiah singled out Judah's traditional enemy Edom as a special object of God's angry judgment. The Lord denounced Edom for its arrogant self-confidence. Located in rocky, inaccessible terrain, Edom thought it was invincible (Obad. 3-4). To make matters worse, the Edomites had participated in the looting of Jerusalem and had dealt mercilessly with Judahite refugees (Obad. 10-14). Joel (3:2-6, 19) and Zechariah (9:1-8) accused several nations of mistreating God's people. Among the culprits were Phoenicia (i.e., Tyre and Sidon), Philistia, Syria, Egypt, and Edom. The Pheonicians and Philistines, who lived on the seacoast, had sold God's people as slaves (Joel 3:2-6). The Egyptians and Edomites had shed the blood of innocent people in the land of Judah (3:19).

The coming judgment of these and other nations would be thorough. According to Obadiah, Edom's invaders would rob it of all of its treasures. Even burglars and grape pickers leave something behind, but Edom's conquerors would leave nothing (Obad. 5-6). The Lord would eventually enable His restored people to annihilate Edom (v. 18). Through Malachi, who prophesied a century later, the Lord announced, "Esau I have hated, and I have turned his mountains into a wasteland and left his inheritance to the desert jackals" (Mal. 1:3). Even if Edom attempted to rebuild its ruins, the Lord would "demolish" their efforts, for Edom would "always" be "under the wrath of the Lord" (1:4).

The reference to the Lord's hatred of Edom (Mal. 1:3) puzzles some interpreters. Some explain the love/hate language of verse 1-2 as indicating relative degrees of love. In this interpretation "love" means to "love more," whereas "hate" means to "love less." Though this use of love/hate language is found elsewhere in the Old Testament (in marriage contexts; cf. Gen. 29:31; Deut. 21:15-17), this interpretation fails to do justice to the context of Malachi 1:2-5. There is no evidence here that God loved both Jacob and Esau. Rather, the two are sharply contrasted throughout. God treated the two in opposite ways. He chose (or loved) Jacob; He actively opposed and destroyed (or hated) Esau.

Joel and Zechariah also emphasized the thorough nature of coming divine judgment. Joel foresaw the total destruction of the nations' armies (Joel 3:1-16). The slaughter is compared to harvesting grain with a sickle and to trampling out of grapes in a winepress (the allusion to bloodshed is unmistakable). Edom and Egypt are singled out for special judgment. Both, according to Joel 3:19, would become desolate wastelands. Zechariah's description of this culminating battle is particularly vivid. The Lord will strike the enemies of Jerusalem with a horrible plague, causing "their eyes" to "rot in their sockets, and their tongues . . . in their mouths" (Zech. 14:12-15; cf. 12:1-9).

As always the Lord's judgment would also be perfectly appropriate. He would repay Edom for her evil deeds (Obad. 15). Because the Edomites showed no mercy to Israel's "survivors" (v. 14), they would have no "survivors" of their own (v. 18). Because Edom "cut down" (*kārat*) Israel's fugitives (v. 14) she would be "destroyed" (lit. "cut off," *kārat*) forever (v. 10). The very people Edom attempted to wipe out would take possession of the mountains of Esau (vv. 18-21). The Phoenicians and Philistines, who had sold God's people into distant lands as slaves (Joel 3:6), would also be appropriately repaid (3:5, 7). Eventually God's exiled and enslaved people will return to their land, conquer their ancient enemies, and sell them into slavery to far off lands (3:7-8). In fact all the nations who had plundered Jerusalem would themselves be plundered (Zech. 2:9). Because they had participated in Jerusalem's "day of misfortune/destruction/trouble/disaster/calamity" (Obad. 10-14), the Day of the Lord would fall upon them with full force (vv. 15-16).

Joel and Zechariah described the Day of the Lord in highly cosmic terms. The Lord will appear as a mighty warrior (Joel 3:16; Zech 9:14), accompanied by darkness (Joel 2:31; 3:15), earthquake (Zech. 14:3-5), and other unique physical phenomena (14:6-7). He will swiftly and decisively annihilate the nations in one culminating battle outside the walls of Jerusalem (12:1-5; 14:3-5). Joel identified the battle site as the Valley of Jehoshaphat (Joel 3:2, 12), the precise location of which is unknown. The name need not correspond to a literal valley known to Joel, because it is obviously chosen primarily for its symbolic value (the name means "the Lord judges").

By defeating the nations the Lord will overturn the political structure of the world. Those nations who had long opposed His people (symbolized by "the surging sea" and represented by Assyria and Egypt in Zech. 10:11) will be removed. By one cosmic "earthquake" the Lord will overturn kings and eliminate their armies (Hag. 2:6, 21-22), setting the stage for the establishment of His universal kingdom.

In the aftermath of the Lord's victory over the armies of the nations, His fame will spread throughout the world (Mal. 1:11). The nations will recognize Him as their king (Zech. 2:11) and voluntarily worship Him (Mal. 1:11). The Gentiles will come to Jerusalem, the city of the Great King, to pay tribute (Hag. 2:7-

8) and seek the Lord's favor (Zech. 8:20-23). In particular they will celebrate the Feast of Tabernacles (Zech. 14:16). This festival will celebrate the fruit harvest, as testimony to God's power over the land's fertility (cf. Deut. 16:13-15). Consequently any nations who refuse to acknowledge God's sovereignty in this way will suffer drought and plagues (Zech. 14:17-19).

JONAH

INTRODUCTION

Jonah differs from the other books of the Minor Prophets in that it is a biographical account of a prophet's experiences, not a collection of prophetic messages. The overriding theme of the book is the sovereign God's grace toward sinners, illustrated in His decision to withhold His judgment from the guilty but repentant Ninevites. However, there is also an important theological lesson to be learned from observing Jonah's responses to God. The author's portrayal of Jonah is highly derogatory. Jonah's double standards caused his actions to contradict his pious-sounding creeds. Through his negative example the reader is instructed not to resist God's sovereign will and decisions.

GOD'S SOVEREIGN GRACE

Throughout the book of Jonah God appears as the sovereign, omnipotent ruler of the universe. He stirred up a violent storm (Jonah 1:4) and then caused it to cease (1:15). He determined the outcome of the sailors' lot casting (1:7), commanded a great sea creature to accomplish His will (1:17; 2:10), caused a plant to grow (4:6), made a worm kill the plant (v. 7), and summoned the hot desert wind (v. 8). Even the greatest city of the earth was subject to His sovereign decree (1:2; 3:1-10; 4:11).

God exerted His sovereign power toward a particular goal — the reclamation of sinful men. Even though the Ninevites deserved to be punished for their sinful deeds, God in His grace decided to give them an opportunity to repent. In so doing He demonstrated the truth of Jonah's confession, recorded in Jonah 4:2: "you are a gracious and compassionate God, slow to anger and abounding in love, a God who relents from sending calamity."

JONAH'S RESPONSE TO GOD

The confession recorded in Jonah 4:2 did not originate with the prophet. Almost identical words appear in Exodus 34:6-7, where reference is made to God's mercy to Israel following the golden calf fiasco. An abbreviated form of the creed occurs in Numbers 14:18, where Moses asked the Lord to forgive the people following their refusal to trust the Lord for victory over the Canaanites. Jonah's use of this traditional confession should have reminded him that God had shown mercy to Israel from the very beginning of her history.

Despite his disobedience and presumption Jonah himself had experienced God's merciful deliverance and received a second chance. When commissioned by God to go to Nineveh, Jonah fled in the opposite direction. When thrown into the raging sea and swallowed by a fish, he had the audacity to presume that he had been delivered. Rather than offering a humble penitential cry for deliverance, he thanked the Lord for delivering him (Jonah 2:1-9). Yet God preserved and recommissioned His prophet (2:10–3:2). The book ends with a gracious God still trying to persuade Jonah to think correctly about His mercy (4:9-11).

Though Jonah, like Israel, had been a recipient of God's mercy, the prophet denied the same mercy to the pagan world. Ironically these pagans, whom Jonah loathed for their idolatry (Jonah 2:8), displayed greater spiritual sensitivity than the prophet. Jonah claimed to "worship [lit. "fear"] the Lord, the God of heaven, who made the sea and the land" (1:9). His actions, however, contradicted his creed. Whereas Jonah tried to escape from the Creator of the sea via the sea, the pagans genuinely expressed their fear of the Lord through sacrifice and prayer (v. 16). In contrast to Jonah, who disobeyed God's revealed word and presumed on His mercy, the Ninevites responded immediately and positively to God's word and humbly threw themselves at the feet of the sovereign God (3:4-9). Though God sent Jonah to denounce the "wickedness" (*rāʿāh*) of Nineveh (1:2), the disobedient prophet brought "calamity" (*rāʿāh* again) upon the sailors (v. 7) and ended up "greatly displeased" (*rāʿāh* again) by God's gracious treatment of the Ninevites (4:1). This repetition of the Hebrew word (though in different semantic senses) implies that Jonah had, in a sense, become more like the pagans than he realized. By contrast, the Ninevites had turned from their "evil (*rāʿāh*) ways" (3:10).

The book of Jonah is a vivid reminder to God's people that they must not resist or dispute His sovereign decisions to bestow His grace on whom He wills. When God calls His servants to carry out these decisions and be instruments of His grace to sinful men, they must obey, realizing that they too have experienced His mercy both corporately and individually.

Index of Subjects

Index of Persons

Moody Press, a ministry of Moody Bible Institute,
is designed for education, evangelization, and edification.
If we may assist you in knowing more about Christ and the Christian life,
please write us without obligation:
Moody Press, c/o MLM, Chicago, Illinois 60610.